The Foundations
of Primitive Thought

THE FOUNDATIONS
OF PRIMITIVE
THOUGHT

C. R. HALLPIKE

CLARENDON PRESS
OXFORD
1979

Oxford University Press, Walton Street, Oxford OX2 6DP

OXFORD LONDON GLASGOW
NEW YORK TORONTO MELBOURNE WELLINGTON
KUALA LUMPUR SINGAPORE JAKARTA HONG KONG TOKYO
DELHI BOMBAY CALCUTTA MADRAS KARACHI
NAIROBI DAR ES SALAAM CAPE TOWN

Published in the United States
by Oxford University Press
New York

British Library Cataloguing in Publication Data
Hallpike, Christopher Robert
    The foundations of primitive thought.
    1. Thought and thinking   2. Ethnopsychology
    3. Man, Primitive
    I. Title
    153.4′2   BF455   79–40587

ISBN 0–19–823196–2

*Printed in Great Britain by
Richard Clay (The Chaucer Press) Ltd
Bungay, Suffolk*

PREFACE

The use of the word 'primitive' in the title of this book will doubtless cause offence to those anthropologists who have not reflected upon its true meaning, which is derived from the Latin *primitivus* and means 'Of or belonging to the first age, period, or stage', and as such has no derogatory implications whatsoever. It will be objected by other anthropologists that since all primitive societies, like our own, have a history, it is invalid to regard contemporary primitive societies as comparable to the early stages of social development. Beattie says, for example:

> Though this term is still commonly used, it is really not very appropriate, for in the temporal sense no existing society can be said to be more primitive than any other. Nor, as we shall see later, can we suppose that present-day 'primitive' societies represent, in Sir James Frazer's words, 'the rudimentary phases, the infancy and childhood, of human society', so that, if they were left alone, African bushmen or Australian aborigines would eventually grow up into fully-fledged Europeans or something like them. (Beattie 1964 : 4)

But we are not concerned with merely *temporal* succession, and it is not necessary to suppose that all societies have a tendency to develop into something like those of modern Europe in order to claim that in many respects modern primitive societies *have* retained a number of common features (despite immense variety in details) that are inherently characteristic of the early stages of human society. Small-scale societies precede large-scale societies; hunting and gathering precedes agriculture, which precedes industrialization; human and animal labour precedes machines; hamlets precede towns and cities; acephalous societies precede centralized societies; illiteracy precedes literacy; the division of labour becomes more complex, not less. In all these and many other respects it is perfectly obvious that there are numerous features of human society that pass through developmental stages, and that to this extent those contemporary societies that are small-scale, non-literate, relatively unspecialized in the division of labour, based on the muscle-power of men and animals, with residence in small and impermanent settlements, are indeed representative of what may correctly be called primitive stages of social development. While these societies have a history which is necessarily as long as ours, it seems clear that it is the transition from pre-literate and rural to literate, industrial society, rather than from hunting and gathering to agriculture, for example, that produces the really striking changes in modes of thought.

One suspects, however, that the evident qualms of liberal-minded anthropologists about using the word 'primitive' except in quotation marks, or preceded by 'allegedly', 'so-called', and other disclaimers, derive not so much from semantic or sociological scruples, as from their inner doubts about the nature and value of 'civilization', a concept held in almost the same contempt as 'primitive'.

Nor do the terms 'simple' or 'non-literate' provide adequate substitutes for 'primitive'. The initial stages of all human endeavours are usually marked by idiosyncratic complexity, irregularity, and lack of system, while simplicity (in at least one important sense of so difficult a concept) is the product of art and conscious reflection, in which order and clarity of design are imposed only with great effort and deliberation after prolonged trial and error. In these respects it is primitive society that is complex and industrial society that is simple, always striving to axiomatize its values and institutions more clearly and consistently. And while literacy is a factor of great importance in the development of human thought, it is by no means the only factor: we shall see that man's activities in relation to his natural environment and the types of communication with his fellows that are fostered in society are certainly of equal importance in cognitive development.

For the purposes of this book, I shall therefore take 'primitive' societies to be those that are non-literate, relatively unspecialized, pre-industrial, small-scale, and characterized by 'face-to-face' relations in everyday life, while the full implications of 'primitive' when applied to thought are best left to emerge gradually in the course of my exposition.

The principal object of this book is to elucidate as clearly and rigorously as possible those characteristics that seem to be most distinctive and prevalent in the thought processes of primitive peoples. To this extent I draw extensively, in particular, on the work of Piaget and other developmental psychologists, which hitherto has been almost totally ignored by anthropologists. This indifference to a large and highly important corpus of research on the part of those who claim to be studying thought is indefensible; whether or not anthropologists are convinced by the theory of cognitive development advanced here, it will no longer be justifiable for them, or for that matter for philosophers, to address themselves to problems of primitive thought without any empirically based theory of learning and thinking, and if they disagree with that of Piaget and other psychologists the responsibility for producing a better one will be theirs. I have summarized Piaget's analysis of number and measurement, space, and time, causality, and probability, at some length in the relevant chapters because it is also one of my fundamental contentions that anthropologists have failed to grasp some of the most significant aspects of primitive thought on account of an imperfect understanding of the real nature of *our own* thinking on these aspects of reality.

The influence of Lévi-Strauss in particular has made it essential to base any analysis of primitive thought on firm psychological foundations: primitive thought tends to be idiosyncratic, elusive, unsystematic (at the explicit level), inarticulate, and frequently expressed through the imagery of symbolism and metaphor, but it is precisely these qualities that pervade the work of Lévi-Strauss himself. While he frequently employs such crucial terms as 'logic', 'science', 'rationality', and 'abstraction', nowhere does he define them, and despite frequent allusions to 'the human mind', his assertions about it rest upon philosophical speculation and not upon any empirically established psychological theory. The whole tone of his writings is that of the poet or the prophet rather than the scientist, and his basic contribution to the study of primitive thought has been to take an extremely difficult subject and make it impossible.

Developmental psychology is used throughout much of this book to provide a framework for the classification and analysis of primitive thought more rigorous than the current anthropological theories. Such a project inevitably involves a range of equally fundamental issues—the relation between individual psychology and collective representations; the interaction of language and thought; the extent to which mental processes are determined by, or dependent on, the material circumstances of life; and the relevance of such concepts as 'logic' and 'rationality' in the analysis of primitive thought. This book is intended to make a contribution to our understanding of these central problems of our subject, and should not be interpreted simply as an interdisciplinary venture into the realms of cognitive psychology.

I have not, however, attempted to deal with morality or aesthetics; this is not because I consider these unimportant, or because no work has been done on them by anthropologists and psychologists (Piaget's *The Moral Judgement of the Child* being a notable instance), but because the problems they raise are too difficult to be encompassed within a book primarily devoted to purely cognitive processes.

Although it is not my intention to claim that primitive thought is all of a piece, it is unfortunately inevitable, in the interests of coherency, that one should present a standard model, an ideal type, of primitive thought, from which however the thought of particular societies or individuals may diverge. The reader should therefore always keep in mind that when I talk of 'primitive thought' as being unable to understand a particular way of representing the world, or as typically representing the world in one way rather than another, this is not intended as a generalization of necessarily universal application.

I do not need to be reminded of the vastness of my theme— almost every topic with which I deal could be made the subject of a book in itself. As my researches have proceeded I have become ever more conscious when reading each fresh monograph or paper that it is a gateway to unsuspected depths in the relation between the mind of man and the world about him. That I now offer this book to the public is not a sign that I regard its conclusions as definitively established, but simply that they are now ready to be put to a severer test than I have been able to give them, at the hands of my fellow anthropologists and, I hope, of psychologists, classicists, medieval historians, Sinologists, Egyptologists, scholars of the history of philosophy and science, and indeed all who have any interest in the development of human understanding. One of the problems, however, which has faced me throughout this book is the inadequacy of good data relevant to many of the points under discussion. The growth in recent years of cross-cultural developmental psychology and of interest in cognition among anthropologists has supplied much of my material, but from a fairly small sample of societies, and it is to be hoped that this book will serve a useful purpose in suggesting lines of inquiry to ethnographers which they are well qualified to pursue but which might not otherwise have occurred to them, as, indeed, they did not occur to me when in the field. But anthropologists should be cautioned against attempts to replicate the psychological experiments described here without the collaboration of a developmental psychologist. Many of the 'replications' of Piaget, especially those that claim to have refuted him (such as Margaret Mead's study of animism among Manus children (Mead 1932)), have been vitiated by a failure to understand his theory or follow his techniques of investigation. This *caveat* aside, however, there is ample scope for improving our knowledge of primitive thought at the purely ethnographic level, and I should be most interested to receive any material relevant to the issues discussed in this book, either in support or in refutation; this may be sent to me at the Department of Anthropology, McMaster University, Hamilton, Ontario, Canada.

In conclusion, I should like to express my thanks to the following for reading the typescript and for their most helpful criticisms and suggestions for its improvement: Dr R. H. Barnes, Dr Martin Brett, Professor Rodney Needham, Dr A. G. Shannon, Dr Neil Warren, and the Clarendon Press, and to Mr P. J. Rollings for his earlier advice and encouragement. I am also greatly indebted to my wife for her diligent reading of the proofs.

Diptford,   C. R. H.
South Devon,
August 1978

Contents

1

A Theory of Learning and Thinking

1. THEORIES IN SEARCH OF A MIND

The history of anthropologists' attempts to elucidate the ways in which primitive thought does or does not differ from that of modern literate industrial man, and the reasons for this, has been distinguished by the lack of any clear theory of learning and thinking. Terms like 'mind', 'mentality', '*esprit*', 'logic', 'abstraction', 'rationality', 'common sense', 'practical reasoning', and 'science' are used freely and vaguely, but without much evident awareness that some integrated cognitive theory is necessary to raise these terms above the level of amateurish speculation. Developmental sequences from primitive thought to that of industrial man, such as Frazer's 'Magic–Religion–Science' Tylor's 'Soul–Spirits–Polytheism–Monotheism', or Durkheim's attempt to find the earliest forms of thought in 'Totemism', all depend on such analytically vague categories as 'magic', '*mana*', and 'religion' which, in so far as they can be defined, are found coexisting in the same societies. 'Rationality' and 'science', in particular, have very complex connotations which render them especially unsuitable for cross-cultural comparisons between the modes of thought of industrial and primitive society.

The absence of any theory of thinking or cognitive development has allowed theorists of language (such as Whorf) to argue that different languages produce different modes of thought, or, as Lévi-Strauss maintains, that since there are basic structural resemblances between all languages which reflect the basic neural organization of the brain, there can be no fundamental differences between primitive thought and our own. Assertions that there is a 'primitive mentality' are interpreted by some scholars as racialist, since they suppose that this must imply that primitives have different kinds of brain, and hence lower innate intelligence,[1] than our-

---

[1] Since there is an important heritable component in general intellectual function-

selves; and, as in every human science, the issue of primitive thought has been clouded by political prejudice, from the uncritical condescension of some Victorians to the almost equally uncritical determination of some modern academics to prove that our oppressed brothers of the Third World must be our intellectual equals, or if possible our superiors,[2] even though they lack our scientific knowledge and are concerned with *non-technological problems.

Amid this confusion, however, the prevailing assumptions about the nature of thinking seem to be the empiricist theory that knowledge is a passive reproduction and remembering of sensory impressions which are co-ordinated by associational or stimulus–response mechanisms; that beliefs and especially classificatory categories are encapsulated in the language of each culture; and that reasoning itself is an innate function which is similar in all adult human beings.

A few anthropologists, such as Lévi-Strauss, adopt an innatist theory of the mind. Lévi-Strauss regards the mind not as passively receiving the imprint of socially generated collective representations, but as equipped *ab initio* with a set of innate structures which are not developed in any genetic manner by interaction with the environment, but at most become selected and more specialized in different cultures and impose themselves on representations of reality and on the form of social institutions. Such a static model of the mind is radically opposed, like the empiricist model, to the

---

ing, it is in principle liable to natural selection, and hence may very well vary from one population to another. The denials by some anthropologists of any genetically determined variations of intelligence between human groups seem to rest more obviously on a wish about how they would like the world to be than on any scientific evidence. Such evidence is notoriously hard to establish, and in this book I shall be concerned solely with environmental factors in relation to cognitive development. This does not imply that I believe genetic factors are irrelevant. Whatever variations of a genetic origin may exist in the average intelligence of different groups, however, the contrasts between primitive thought and that of literate industrial man certainly cannot be attributed to genetic rather than to environmental factors, since it is obvious that New Guineans and Africans can be taught our modes of thought by attending school and so on. When one considers the uniformities of thought among primitive peoples of many different races, from all over the globe, and the systematic contrasts between this thought and that which prevails in literate industrial societies it is evident that these differences must be predominantly the result of environment rather than heredity, whatever the local variations in intelligence.

[2] e.g. 'many preliterate ("primitive") communities, far from being subrational, may show the human mind functioning on a higher and more complex plane of rationality than among civilized men' (Whorf 1956: 81).

possibility of mental structures being generated in the process of interaction and equilibration with the environment, especially by the *activity* of the subject. Innatists, like the supporters of the empirical theory, must therefore regard the mind as basically the same in all environments, and as having no truly developmental potential. But I shall pay little attention to Lévi-Strauss's theory of the mind in the rest of this book, not because I regard innatist theories of the mind as unimportant, but because it has proved impossible to determine with any precision exactly what his theory is beyond these very general propositions, apart from certain assertions on the nature of children's thought which are quite clear, and also entirely false (see below, pp. 36–9). (For useful discussions of the differences between the theories of mind of Lévi-Strauss and Piaget see Turner 1973: 370–3; and Piaget 1971: 106–19.)

Anthropologists have assumed, in short, that primitive thought is distinguishable from our own only by its content, and that the actual structure of thought, cognitive processes, are the same in all cultures, e.g. 'The reasoning and thinking processes of different peoples in different cultures do not differ ... just their values, beliefs and ways of classifying things' (quoted in Colby and Cole 1973: 63). In the words of Luria,

Over the course of centuries, classical psychology arrived at the idea that there is a unitary, unchanging structure to human psychological processes. This structure is thought to operate on a series of sharply delimited psychological processes: sensation and perception, attention and memory, association and logical relation, judgement and reasoning. The structure of these processes was said not to depend on social-historical conditions and to remain the same at any particular point in history. (Luria 1971: 259)[3]

And as Needham has said:

... there is a body of assumptions about what constitutes human nature, in particular about the essential capacities of the thinking subject. Social anthropology has in the main been founded on the presumption that these were already known, and that the rational and psychological vocabularies of European languages were well adapted to the comprehension and analysis of alien modes of experience. In an enquiry into received ideas about

---

[3] While the theories of Durkheim and Lévy-Bruhl are apparent exceptions to Luria's generalization, this was because their model of 'mind' focused upon the *content* of mind, and took virtually no account of psychological *processes* at all. In so far as it did, the model conforms in general to that of the empiricists, although Durkheim and Lévy-Bruhl appear to regard 'practical reasoning' as innate in all men.

the supposed capacity for belief (Needham 1972), I have tried to demonstrate that we have no such certainty; and that a distinctive task of
social anthropology should be to determine whether there are to be found
any absolute features of thought and action—in the form of natural resemblances throughout mankind—that are indispensable to an objective
conception of humanity. (Needham 1976c: 85)

The empiricist model is well suited to a social-determinist theory
of the individual mind as passive to the socialization process, in
which language is taken to be the dominant influence, and by
which the traditional knowledge and types of classification and
basic assumptions about reality of every culture are put together in
the mind of the individual rather like the preformed pieces of a
jigsaw puzzle being slotted into place in a process of bit-by-bit
accumulation. Such a theory of learning would lead anthropologists to assume that the practical skills and actions demanded by
technology and ecology could have no connection with the modes
of thought involved in collective representations of time, space,
and causation, since the former are simply 'common sense' or 'practical reasoning', which is supposed to be innate.

The assumption that the individual mind simply accumulates the
ready-made ideas, beliefs, and categories of his society through his
acquisition of its language and participation in its processes and
institutions has also fitted in neatly with the main preoccupations
of social anthropologists. As ethnographers whose work is conducted mainly in non-literate societies, we have been obliged in practice to spend a great deal of our field-work simply in establishing
what are the official and generally accepted beliefs and norms of
the societies we are studying and, in non-literate societies where no
use can be made of written questionnaires, our conclusions about
indigenous representations of reality often rest on interviews with
relatively few informants. The result has been that our field-studies
have tended to possess a static quality largely unrelated to the
mental processes of individuals, such as problem solving, concept
formation, and learning generally. As Greenfield (a developmental
psychologist) says, anthropologists' analyses and generalizations
'. . . are not founded upon the analysis of "mind in action", upon
an analysis of behaviour in concrete situations' (Greenfield
1966: 225).

And as social theorists, heavily influenced by Durkheim, we
have considered it methodologically essential to concern ourselves

solely with the structure of collective representations and their relationship with social organization. We have assumed that, as Evans-Pritchard lucidly puts it,

[The social anthropologist] is not interested in the actors in the drama as individuals but as persons who play certain roles. . . . On the other hand, to the psychologist, who is studying individuals, the feelings, motives, opinions, and so forth, of the actors are of first importance and the [social] procedures and processes of secondary interest. This essential difference between social anthropology and psychology is the *pons asinorum* in the learning of social anthropology. (Evans-Pritchard 1951: 46)

Anthropologists, in short, have written as though the problem of 'primitive thought' lay in the nature of 'primitiveness', as though thought itself was a well-determined faculty on which modern psychology had little of any real importance to say; and even if it had, that individual thought processes were irrelevant to the collective representations of society. I shall show that the reverse is the case: the problem of primitive thought lies in the nature of thought and its development in relation to experience through the *activity* of the subject; the general characteristics of learning and thinking among individuals are highly relevant to the types of collective representations formed in any society; and only when we understand how learning and thinking develop in relation to the total environment can we hope to make useful distinctions between kinds of thought and, in particular, to differentiate between the modes of thought common to primitive societies and those that prevail in literate industrial societies.

2. THE PRINCIPLES OF DEVELOPMENTAL PSYCHOLOGY

I shall therefore devote this chapter to a review of the main conclusions of developmental psychology on how human beings in fact learn in relation to their natural and social environment. Developmental, or cognitive, psychology is the product of research in many countries, especially since the 1920s, associated with the names of Piaget, Vygotsky, Luria, Werner, and Bruner, in particular. For the purposes of anthropologists it is most profitable to concentrate on the work of Piaget since not only has he been the dominant influence on the subject, especially in its cross-cultural aspects, but his researches cover a wider area of human cognitive performance than those of any other psychologist, and he has always been concerned with how organized knowledge as a whole develops, not merely with the cognitive development of children. It is this basic interest in 'genetic epistemology' that distinguishes him from other cognitive psychologists and makes him of special significance to those who are concerned with the developmental characteristics of primitive collective representations.[4]

The work of Piaget, based on researches with a team of collaborators over a period of more than fifty years, and published in numerous monographs and papers, is extraordinarily difficult to summarize, not only because of its scope and detail, but because of Piaget's very involved style of writing and presentation. The reader who finds the following sections in any way obscure will discover that the basic principles set out here are repeatedly referred to in subsequent chapters, where they are clarified by many practical examples which should make the essence of Piaget's theory very much clearer than it is possible to achieve in a general introduction; in addition, a glossary of technical terms is provided on p. 496.

Piaget's theory of cognitive development grew out of his early interests in biology (he is an authority on molluscs) and in epistemology. He regards cognitive growth as a particular aspect of general organic adaptation to environment, in which process neither the hereditary characteristics of the organism nor the structure of the environment are in themselves sufficient to explain the patterns of growth in the organism. Rather, he sees thought as a self-regulating system, which strives to attain equilibrium with its environment by constructing stable representations transcending the variability and fluctuations of that environment. His theory is therefore holistic and dialectical, such that mental functioning is subject to an overall organization which is developed by a process of *accommodation* to reality and *assimilation* of experience to existing cognitive structures. By a crude analogy the digestion of food, for example, requires the organism to accommodate to the different physical characteristics of food by a variable repertoire of behaviours in-

---

[4] Developmental psychology is barely mentioned in the literature of social anthropology. I have been able to discover only the following articles in the major anthropological journals which make any substantial reference to Piaget or developmental psychology in general: Dougall 1932; Mead 1932; Werner and Kaplan 1948; Turner 1973; Levine and Price-Williams 1974; Hallpike 1976.

cluding biting, sucking, chewing, licking, and swallowing according to the nature of the food, but the food is in turn assimilated in various ways, depending on the nature of the organism, to the existing physical structure of that organism.

For Piaget, thought is thus an active and selective process, dominated by a constant interaction between accommodation and assimilation, a process in which the child's physical manipulation of objects plays a fundamental part in his gradual co-ordination of his sensory impressions and construction of reality. Such a theory of cognitive development is radically opposed to empiricist theories which regard learning as the bit-by-bit accumulation of data, such that the child's thought is simply a crude copy of external reality and adult models which slowly adds details to achieve a more refined fit, because it is a theory that stresses the internal organization of knowledge as an essential foundation of stability and growth. Because it is constructivist, it is also radically opposed to innatist theories of cognition, which regard the basic cognitive processes such as causal and logical inference, memory, representations of space and time, or linguistic functioning, as innate and common to all normal human beings, whatever their social and environmental milieu. While some thinkers have supposed that it is innately obvious to all normal adults that $5 = (2 + 3)$ and $(3 + 2)$ or that the shortest distance between two points is a straight line or that if man is mortal, and if Socrates is a man, then Socrates is mortal, we shall see that these truths are not innate, or even obvious, to adults in many primitive societies. What have been supposed to be innately recognizable truths are not innate at all, but have to be constructed in the course of interaction with the social and physical environment.

The child's repertoire of behaviours is limited at birth to a few reflexes, such as sucking, crying, tongue movements, swallowing, and gross bodily movements, which are unmodified by experience and uncoordinated. There is also a set of innate perceptual discriminations, such as figure/ground, moving/stationary, light/shade, which are also initially unmodified and uncoordinated. It is the co-ordination of these different behaviours and perceptual discriminations, their extension to a progressively wider range of objects, and their transformation from reflexes (activated as rigid, unmodified totalities) into modes of behaviour that are accommodated to the different aspects of objects, that occupies the first eighteen months to two years, the 'sensori-motor' period or stage 1.[5]

At birth and for many months, the child has no awareness of permanent objects (that a pencil hidden behind a cushion continues to exist even when it cannot be seen), or that objects have constancy of size and shape; nor can he co-ordinate visual, tactile, and auditory space. The neonatal infant relates all his perceptions to his own body as though it were the centre of the universe, but a centre that is unaware of itself. This indissociation between subject and object at the sensori-motor level is only overcome by the progressive co-ordination of action patterns or 'schemes', which form the basis on the one hand of purposive action in the subject, and the construction of stable spatio-temporal and causal representations of physical reality on the other. By the end of this process, at about eighteen months, the child is aware that he is a physical object among other objects. But we shall find that this 'egocentrism', this subject–object indissociation, reasserts itself at higher levels of thought.

In the reflex there is no differentiation between accommodation and assimilation, but after the first month or so of life the child begins to develop schemata of behaviour in the form of acquired accommodations, as the result of fortuitous actions, such as discovering how to put his thumb in his mouth, which is not a reflex. A schema[6] is a cognitive structure characterized by what is repeatable and generalizable in the original action and which, in the course of development, can be applied to a variety of objects in different situations, and also be combined with other schemata. Schemata are thus based on the repetition of actions, which involves the assimilation of the properties of objects acted upon. There are three aspects of assimilation, all integrally related, which are basic to the formation of the schemata—repetition, generaliza-

[5] According to Flavell (1963: 89), Piaget in recent years has expressed a preference for using the term 'period' for the major developmental epochs, and the term 'stage' for the subdivisions of these periods, but for our purposes here such a distinction seems unnecessary, and I shall use 'period' 'stage', and 'level' interchangeably.

[6] It is important to distinguish between 'scheme' and 'schema': 'A scheme is the structure or organization of actions as they are transferred or generalized by repetition in similar or analogous circumstances' (Piaget and Inhelder 1969a: 4n). A schema, however, is a cognitive structure, rather than a structure of actions; though at the sensori-motor stage the distinction is evidently harder to draw between schema and scheme than in the later stages of development.

tion, and recognition or discrimination. All schemata are applied again and again to any assimilable objects of the environment—so a thing is constantly sucked, rattled, or banged against the side of the cot, and so on (reproductive assimilation). Schemata are also constantly becoming more generalized, that is, extending their field of application to assimilate new and different objects:

Thus, according to chance contacts, the child, from the first two weeks of life, sucks his fingers, the fingers extended to him, his pillow, quilt, bed-clothes, etc.; consequently he assimilates these activities to the activity of the reflex ... the new-born child at once incorporates into the global schema of sucking a number of increasingly varied objects, whence the generalizing aspect of this process of assimilation. (Piaget 1952b: 33–4)

But this generalized assimilation is increasingly complemented by discrimination, a recognition that some objects are more satisfying to suck than others: 'This search and this selectivity seem to us to imply the beginning of differentiation in the global schema of sucking, and consequently a beginning of recognition, a completely practical and motor recognition, needless to say, but sufficient to be called recognitory assimilation' (ibid. 36).

These characteristics of repetition, generalization, and recognition or discrimination, are all integral and fundamental in the generation of the schema, as Flavell says:

Repetition consolidates and stabilizes it, as well as providing the necessary condition for change. Generalization enlarges it by extending its domain of application. And differentiation has the consequence of dividing the originally global schema into several new schemata, each with a sharper, more discriminating focus on reality. But it is characteristic of schemata not only to undergo individual changes of this kind but also to form ever more complex and interlocking relationships with other schemata. Two schemata may undergo separate developments up to a point, e.g., generalization to new objects, differentiation, etc., and then unite to form a single supra-ordinate schema. The principal uniting relationship between two hitherto separate schemata is called *reciprocal assimilation*, that is, each schema assimilates the other. (Flavell 1963: 57)

So visual schemata are very early assimilated with hearing schemata, but take longer to become assimilated with those of sucking, and longer still to become co-ordinated with those of prehension and touching:

These intersensorial co-ordinations, this organization of heterogeneous schemata will give the visual images increasingly rich meanings and make visual assimilation no longer an end in itself but an instrument at the service of vaster assimilations. When the child of seven or eight months old looks at unknown objects for the first time before swinging, rubbing, throwing and catching them, etc., he no longer tries to look for the sake of looking (pure visual assimilation in which the object is a simple aliment for looking), nor even for the sake of seeing (generalizing or recognitory visual assimilation in which the object is incorporated without adding anything to the already elaborated visual schemata), but he looks in order to act, that is to say, in order to assimilate the new object to the schemata of weighing, friction, falling, etc. There is therefore no longer only organization inside the visual schemata but between those and all others. It is this progressive organization which endows the visual images with their meanings and solidifies them in inserting them into a total universe. (Piaget 1952b: 75–6)

The progressive co-ordination of schemata and their increasing generalization and discrimination are the means by which accommodation and assimilation are differentiated into the properties of permanent objects and into the means by which they can be manipulated by the subject. Integral to this process is the growth of deliberate experiment, as opposed to the accidental encounters with objects' behaviour which formed the basis of the child's earliest schemata. Intention thus grows from its early beginnings in the co-ordination of familiar schemata, to the manipulation of objects, the development of intermediary acts for the attainment of goals, and the search for new experiences, and at the end of the sensori-motor level allows the child to imagine the consequence of an act before he actually performs it.

It is essential to note that the foundations of the child's later grasp of logico-mathematical relations are laid by the early co-ordination of his actions—such as combining objects, taking them away, and putting them in correspondence with one another, and by his capacity to generalize relationships on the basis of these actions, relationships which are not properties of objects in the sense that size and weight are. This is achieved without any mediation at all by language, and we shall find that a basic principle of cognitive development is that the organization of behaviour and perception is always prior to the capacity to represent one's actions and the behaviour of objects by means of language.

Piaget sees the child's cognitive growth as stimulated by a struggle for equilibrium between the demands for accommodation to the environment on the one hand, and the internal representations of that reality to which he tries to assimilate it on the other. Development is marked by the successive choices of different strategies in problem solving, the earliest being those that are simplest and require least effort. Each strategy generates contradictions with experience, which are then partially resolved by the use of a new strategy, so that periods of incomplete understanding of reality are followed by periods of greater understanding.[7] In his development the child moves from a state of lesser to a state of greater equilibrium, manifesting greater coherence and stability of representation.

There are three aspects to this process of equilibration—the field of equilibration, its mobility, and its stability. The wider a field of application of a schema the more types of phenomena it can deal with, and the less chance there is that it will be thrown into disorder by encountering some new experience. But the wider the field of application, the more mobile and flexible must be the mental operations to co-ordinate the whole conceptual structure. Stability of a cognitive structure is achieved to the extent that it can assimilate new elements without disturbing the general organization of that structure; stability and mobility are thus not opposed, but mutually necessary qualities, and we shall find that it is the rigid structures of thought, based on the phenomenal appearances of things, that are in fact the least stable precisely because they cannot assimilate new experience in a co-ordinated, mobile way.

These general principles of equilibration apply at all cognitive levels, but we shall see that as the child gradually moves from the level of action, through that of mental imagery, to purely verbal representation and analysis, an equilibrium which is initially satisfactory and relatively stable at one level begins to break down under the pressure of new experience and has then to be reconstructed at a higher cognitive level.

For example, at the end of the sensori-motor period, from eighteen months to two years, the child begins by a process of imitation to interiorize the perceptions of things, in the form of mental, symbolic images, accompanied by the beginnings of language, symbolic gestures, and deferred imitation, which are the means by which the child can internalize his actions without the necessity of actually

[7] Bruner (1966a: 4) states, however, that while disequilibrium is a very important factor in stimulating cognitive growth, it does not always have this effect.

manipulating objects so that hitherto successive actions can now be represented simultaneously. This development of symbolic representations presents the child with new problems and also provides him with immensely more powerful representational ability than that of action alone. This capacity for imaged representation (or 'ikonic' as Bruner terms it) marks the beginning of 'pre-operatory' thought.[8]

(a) Pre-operatory thought

The child's sensori-motor intelligence was inherently confined to the actions of the subject on physical reality, and as such had no genuinely *representational* content; it could therefore only operate sequentially with actual objects and could not co-ordinate the relations between them as simultaneously perceived wholes, whereas the representational capacities of imagery allow the child to construct co-ordinated representations of relations that are not confined to here-and-now manipulations. Thus sensori-motor thought is bound to the present in a way that representational thought can escape into the imagination of future states and the reflection on past states. And whereas representations can be communicated in the form of words, concrete symbolism, and gestures, which can be learned from others, sensori-motor thought is essentially private and cannot of itself be the basis for socialized thought.

But the capacity for symbolic representations also involves the child in radically new difficulties of reality construction, since while action and its co-ordination continues to be of central importance in his cognitive development, he now has to integrate these schemata with mental imagery and to achieve the same explicit dissociation between his own representations and physical reality at the level of imagery as he earlier achieved at the level of action, when he succeeded in grasping that he was an autonomous object in a world of other objects. Just as he conserved the permanency of objects, and the constancy of size and shape in terms of perception and action, he now has to recognize these constancies together with those of quantity, length, weight, volume, and so on at the level of imagery and verbal expression, which takes many years and is

[8] The more usual translations of *opératoire* and *préopératoire* are 'operational' and 'pre-operational', but 'operatory' has the advantage of being closer to the French, and of being a more distinctly technical term than 'operational', some of whose connotations are misleading in a Piagetian context.

achieved only at about seven–eight years in the average European child, the more difficult conservations taking longer.

It should be stressed that 'imagery' in the Piagetian sense is not the retinal imagery involved in perception, although it is largely derived from this, nor is it confined to the purely visual images such as occur in day-dreaming or the recollection of the appearances of objects. For Piaget, the most significant type of imagery is that which results from the imitation of the *actions* of objects. His various experiments show that mental imagery is not simply a 'photographic' reproduction of what the child recalls, but is dependent on his capacity to analyse his perceptions and his actions.

For example, when the pre-operatory child is required to draw the stages by which a curved wire is straightened, he may represent the process as one in which the ends of the wire remain at the same distance, as in Figure 1.

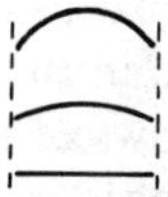

Fig. 1

These drawings do not accurately represent the actual process of straightening a curved wire, since in reality, of course, the ends become further apart; they are expressions of the *image* the child has of the whole process, and in this case they also reflect his inability to analyse a physical process into its component stages.

The child's imagery is initially 'global', such that he cannot analyse a figure into its elements, a perceptual configuration that is static and internally uncoordinated. It is the analysis and re-synthesis of perceptual configurations that is in due course the basis of operatory thought. The rigidity of the child's imagery of the behaviour of objects is the result of the predominance of accommodation, in the form of imitation, over assimilation. The opposite pole is the imagery of play and dream, in which mobility and instability are the result of the predominance of assimilation over accommodation. For a number of years the child's imagery thus fluctuates between the rigid and global representation of objects, and the unstable and affectively dominated imagery of his play and dreams, in which concrete symbolism plays a central part.

The child's representations are also unstable because of his 'centration' on only one dimension or aspect of a figure at a time. It is the co-ordination of dimensional relations and the understanding that they are *systems* of relations—so that, for example, an increase in one dimension is compensated by a decrease in another—that is crucial to operatory thought. So the pre-operatory child cannot conserve length, number, quantity, weight, area, volume, and so on, because he cannot co-ordinate the variations in two dimensions simultaneously. For example, in the case of quantity, when presented with two similar beakers filled to the same level with coloured liquid, the contents of one of the beakers being then poured into another beaker taller and thinner than the first, the child concentrates only on the fact that the *level* in the second is higher than the level in the first, without taking into account that the *diameter* of the second beaker is also less than that of the first. Or, if the contents of one beaker are poured into two smaller ones, and that of the other beaker poured into four smaller ones, the child supposes that there is more liquid in the four beakers than in the two. Or if he is shown two equal rows of beads, in one–one correspondence, and one row is then spaced at greater intervals, he will suppose that the longer row now has more beads, because he cannot correlate the greater length of the row with the lower density of the beads that comprise it.

In all these cases the child is incapable of realizing that an increase in one dimension is compensated by a decrease in another. Conservation is also dependent on a grasp of reversibility, the awareness that the original state can be restored by reversing the actions of the experiment, but while the child is capable of carrying out these actions in practice, he cannot imagine the actual state of affairs and the original state *simultaneously*. He thus remains tied to the phenomenal and concrete appearances of things until he can analyse them into their dimensional attributes and replace static configurations by dynamic transformations that preserve invariant relations, as opposed to static perceptual properties.

The pre-operatory child's classification reflects these problems in representation. The earliest type of classification is the 'heap', in the construction of which the child mistakes his own subjective associations for real relations, and which is consequently thoroughly idiosyncratic and unstable. It is succeeded by various types of complex, a group whose elements are defined by objective factors, such as appearance, use, association, and function; examples would be a bird, a bush, a house, and a car, because the bird sits on the bush and sings, the bush is next to the house because houses have bushes growing beside them, and a car is outside the house because the owner of the house needs one. Unlike logical concepts or 'classes', complexes are based on relations of 'belonging' rather than of 'similarity' of criteria and are thus not composed of elements all of which have at least one criterion in common. (Colour is an exception to this, often found in complexive classification, because colour is a simple perceptual property independent of dimension and other physical attributes.)

It is the prevalence of complexive classification that inhibits the grasp of class-inclusion, at the pre-operatory level. The child can understand part–whole inclusion when it is presented to him with concrete examples, but class-inclusion involves the understanding that an element may be a member of two classes simultaneously, independently of their spatio-temporal relations. If he is shown twelve beads, ten red and two blue, and is asked 'Are there more red beads, or more beads?', he will answer that there are more red beads, partly because he cannot think of them as being simultaneously beads, and also red as opposed to blue, but also because he does not yet grasp the reversible relation that if $A + A^1 = B$, then $A = B - A^1$.

Nor at the pre-operatory stage can the child grasp the principle of *transitivity* of relations, and that if $A > B > C$, then $A > C$, when the problem is put to him in the form 'Mary is fairer than Edith, and Jane is darker than Edith, who is the fairest?', because this involves the grasp of the *relativity* of the colouring of Edith, who is both darker than Mary and fairer than Jane. In the same way, if he sees two rods $A < B$ together, and then the pair $B < C$, he does not conclude that $A < C$ unless he actually sees them all together.

Because the pre-operatory child cannot master, at the *verbal level*, the logic of class inclusion, transitivity, or reversible and compensatory relations and many others, his explicit pattern of reasoning is transductive—i.e. from particular to particular—and not inductive, from particular to general, nor deductive, from general to particular. Transductive reasoning ignores either the whole in favour of the parts (juxtaposition) or the parts in favour of the whole (syncretism) because the child is unable to think simultaneously of the parts as separate things *and* of the relations that unite them into larger wholes. He can see only a succession of unrelated events or a conglomerated whole. Thus the analysis of processual change presents great conceptual difficulty to the child:

Pre-operational thought, then, is static and immobile. It is a kind of thought which can focus impressionalistically and sporadically on this or that momentary, static condition but cannot adequately link a whole set of successive conditions into an integrated totality by taking account of the transformations which unify them and render them logically coherent. And when the child does turn his attention to transformations, he has great difficulty; he usually ends up assimilating them to his own action schemata rather than inserting them into a coherent system of objective causes. (Flavell 1963: 57–8)

The pre-operatory child is also a conceptual realist—that is, he remains unaware of the mediatory function of the mind in the translation of sensory experiences into mental representations, because he cannot think about his own thought processes which are still dominated by imagery, concrete associations, and action. While the child knows that he is a different and distinct physical object from other objects at the level of action, he cannot yet dissociate his own point of view and opinions from those of others and automatically assumes that those around him understand him. It is only by experiencing difficulties in communication and in collaboration that he learns to dissociate himself from others psychically, just as he learns to distinguish his own sensory impressions of objects from their true properties.

Names are attached physically to things; dreams are little material tableaux which you contemplate in your own bedroom; thought is a kind of voice ('the mouth in the back of my head that talks to the mouth in front'). Animism springs from the same lack of differentiation but in the opposite direction; everything that is in movement is alive and conscious, the wind knows that it blows, the sun that it moves, etc. (Piaget and Inhelder 1969a: 110)

The child at this stage thinks of causal properties not as a set of relations between objects, but as the awakening or manifestation of latent and distinct forces which are inherent in the objects. Because of his conceptual realism he derives the notion of force from his own muscular reactions to objects, and does not realize that his own muscular efforts are not the result of the body he moves; so stones, for example, have strength inside themselves. His conceptual realism also leads him to credit objects with volition and consciousness and to explain their existence and behaviour in terms of their significance and utility to man—'Even towards the end of the pre-operatory stage, there still remains a dynamism in objects, forces and purpose that explain their activity' (Piaget 1972). It must be stressed, however, that the child's *actual* manipulation of objects, his behaviour in the real world, is in advance of his analysis and representations of the processes and relations of the world.

Action always precedes linguistic representations. During the pre-operatory stage the child continues, moreover, to derive logico-mathematical structures by 'reflective abstraction' from his own actions:

In order to find out that $3 + 2 = 2 + 3$, he needs to introduce a certain order into the objects he is handling (pebbles, marbles, etc.) putting down first three and then two, or first two and then three. He needs to put these objects together in different ways—2, 3, or 5. What he discovers is that the total remains the same whatever the order; in other words, that the product of the action of bringing together is independent of the action of ordering. If there is in fact (at this level) an experimental discovery it is not relevant to the properties of objects. Here the discovery stems from the subject's actions and manipulations and this is why later, when these actions are interiorized into operations handling becomes superfluous and the subject can combine these operations by means of a purely deductive procedure and he knows that there is no risk of them being proved wrong by contradicting physical experience. (Piaget and Inhelder 1969b: 124)

We have noted that actions and their co-ordination are prior to the representation of reality through imagery and language, and that it is the child's capacity to abstract such features as spatial and temporal order, co-ordination, the nesting of hierarchies of schemes, and causal relations from his actions, that lays the foundation for the later grasp of logico-mathematical relations. In the pre-operatory stage, representation by imagery and language lags behind the child's ability to enact meaning so that children, as Vygotsky points out, can perform the meaning of a picture shown them in action and mime, but at the verbal level can do no more than give a static and uncoordinated list of its component elements in isolation from one another. As Piaget and Inhelder say,

We can divide the cognitive functions into two broad categories according to whether the 'figurative' or 'operative' aspects of knowledge predominate.

The figurative aspects bear on static reality and its observable configurations. Into this category come perception (even when it apprehends a movement from which it then retains the total form or Gestalt), imitation (first direct sensori-motor imitation then delayed imitation of something no longer present, which ensures the advent of the semiotic function), and mental imagery (interiorized imitation).

The operative aspects, by contrast, bear on the transformation of one state into another and therefore include actions and operations, which both aim at the unobservable (since we perceive or 'imagine' the results of transformations and some of their intermediary states, but not the transformation as such which is 'understood' by the intelligence rather than perceived or pictured). (Piaget and Inhelder 1969: 131)

Towards the end of the pre-operatory stage, at about five to six years of age, the child begins to make considerable progress in equilibrating the figurative and the operative aspects of knowledge by what Piaget terms 'articulated intuition', which is the essential foundation of concrete operations, but which is non-quantitative. In problems of conservation, the child now grasps the qualitative identity of substances that change their dimensional form, but still cannot represent this in terms of the mutual compensation of the relevant dimensions. He differentiates between the individual and its class, and can separate a spatial configuration into its elements and distinguish it from them, as opposed to the unanalysed global configurations of the early pre-operatory stage. But he still cannot separate intension and extension for the formation of true logical classes, while 'all' and 'some' are not yet quantified. Thus the child cannot understand the reversible relation that $A < B$ implies $A = B - A'$, and the conservation of the whole class B once the part A is abstracted from its complementary A'. Nor is there a grasp of transitivity, so that if a subject sees two rods $A < B$ together, and then pair $B < C$, he still does not conclude that $A < C$ unless he sees them simultaneously.

The classification of this 'intuitive' substage can transcend the image but not yet attain the true concept. Thinking is still in terms of prototypes or 'pseudo-concepts' (Vygotsky) or 'pre-concepts' (Piaget).

. . . the pre-concept involves the image and is partially determined by it, whereas the concept, precisely because of its generality, breaks away from the image and uses it only as an illustration . . . Since in the case of the pre-concept . . . there is assimilation to a selected object without generalised accommodation to all, accommodation to this specific object is necessarily continued as image when the child's thought is projected on to the others. The image intervenes as essential aid to assimilation, and therefore as privileged signifier, and to some extent as substitute. (Piaget 1962: 229)

The pre-concept however represents a marked progress towards decentration: the child can now establish systematic one–one correspondence between the elements in two rows of objects, for example, but only when they are actually present to him; and there is no lasting equivalence so that when the spatial ordering of the rows is disturbed by the rearrangement of one row, he no longer assumes its equivalence in relation to the other row. He can also construct an ordered series of objects in terms of size of elements, instead of creating small groups of objects unrelated to each other. But these systematic correspondences and orderings do not constitute

... an operational system, but a figure, a figure bound up with accommodation to the action, in contrast to the mobile symbol of a reversible operation capable of use at any time (and in particular after the destruction of the perceived configuration). The only difference between this intuitive figure and the image of the previous stage is that it is a complex structure, a configuration, and not merely a simple individual image. (Piaget 1962: 287)

It is not yet an operational construction, since 'what is still lacking is complete freedom from the image, and accommodation of thought not only to static configurations but to their possible transformations' (Piaget 1962: 287).

(b) Concrete and formal operations

The transition from articulated intuitive, pre-operatory thought leads to the stage of concrete operations. An 'operation' in Piagetian theory is not simply an action, but an interiorized action which is part of a complete system of potential actions. This involves the understanding of reversibility and compensation, which in turn involve the ability to maintain two ideas in the mind simultaneously—the present state of a configuration and a past or future state, for example, between which those relations of reversibility and compensation can be applied. The word 'concrete' emphasizes that the child still reasons only in terms of actual physical objects and events, even though he is able to imagine absent objects and their locations as if they were present, or to project future states of those objects or configurations.

The transition from the pre-operatory level to that of concrete operations is therefore marked by the ability to construct stable systems of relations based on mobile relations of reversibility and compensation, the notion of relative properties as opposed to absolute properties which inhere in things, the avoidance of centration or one-dimensional thought, and the avoidance of the contradictions inherent in image-based modes of representation. We find the progressive objectification of causality, involving the analysis of process and the use of explanations based solely on physical relations between things. This is very different from the psychomorphic causality of conceptual realism, according to which causal relations are represented in terms of volition and vital essences as the inherent, absolute properties of things, awakened rather than produced by interactions. The level of concrete operations also marks the ability to conserve invariant dimensional relations across transformations in the appearances of things—as in the experiment of the different levels of liquid when the contents of one beaker are poured into another of different dimensions. For these reasons operational causality no longer represents processes as sequences of static states, but as integrated systems of transformations. And in the case of classification, the child can now grasp the logical implications of class-inclusion.

While the relations of reversibility and compensation are crucial to operatory thought, it cannot be too strongly emphasized that the most important feature of this kind of thinking is the formation of *integrated systems of relationships*. A good example is provided by a hierarchy of classes (Figure 2).

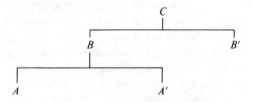

From this can be inferred a whole series of mutually dependent, logically necessary relations which form a closed system that cannot be disturbed by new experience, viz.:

$A < B < C; A < C$

$C > B > A; C > A$

$$B \begin{cases} < C \\ > A \end{cases}$$

$A + A' = B$, therefore $A = B - A'$, $A' = B - A$

All B is some C

Some B is all A

$A + A' + B = B$, or $B + B = B$ (see fn. 9 below)

It is evident that while we may not be fully and explicitly conscious of all these relationships whenever we recognize that the members of a class A are members of a superordinate class B, an operatory grasp of class inclusion certainly involves the implicit awareness of these relations. As Flavell puts it,

One cannot really grasp the concept of [logical] class without understanding what a classification system entails, because the single class is only an abstraction from the total system. This is the central meaning of Piaget's holism in the domain of cognitive operations: the isolated operation can never be the proper unit of analysis, because it gains all its meaning from the system of which it is a part. A given operation, put into concrete effect in the here and now, always presupposes a structured system which includes other, related operations, for the moment latent and inactive but always potentially actualizable themselves and, above all, always a force governing the form and character of the operation which is momentarily on stage. (Flavell 1963: 167)

Concrete operations are not achieved at a stroke, and as Bruner notes, there is a 'tendency of new found structures and strategies to be generalized gradually over an array of related tasks'. Thus conservation problems are solved over a period of time in order of difficulty, so that number and quantity are conserved before area, and volume is the last dimension to be conserved. These 'lags' or 'slippages' (*décalages*) in achieving mastery of what are only different aspects of the same problem are known as 'horizontal *dé-*

---

[9] Logical classes differ from numbers in that whereas numerically $A + A = 2A$, in logical classification $A + A = A$; thus the class of mammals added to the class of mammals equals the class of mammals (the relationship of tautology), and similarly, a subclass added to its superordinate class equals that class, e.g. $A + B = C$ (the property of resorption).

calages'. A 'vertical *décalage*' occurs when a child is able, for example, to solve a problem at the level of action, which defeats him when formulated verbally—that is, a *décalage* between two different levels of thought.

At the level of concrete operations the child is also still bound to the actual relations and properties of physical objects, rather than free to consider potential and quite hypothetical, even counterfactual, hypotheses. In particular, he still does not effectively consider all the possibilities of a situation, the total system of relationships, before he sets out to discover what actually occurs.

It seems that as the child's concrete-operational thinking becomes more practised, precise, and integrated, he begins to encounter incoherencies, gaps, and puzzles which were not apparent while his concrete-operational thinking was in its early stages. In the same way concrete operations were themselves stimulated by the same sort of conceptual inadequacies experienced in the later stages of pre-operatory thought. Because concrete operations are based on integrated systems of necessary relationships of class, relation, and number, they provide the basis by which the child can begin to consider all possible relations before he discovers what is actually the case. (We recall that it was the development of the image, at the transition from sensori-motor to pre-operatory thought which, in the same way, allowed the infant to construct interiorized representations of future states and goals before their realization in reality.) Moreover, the child's increased mastery of language allows him to take the results of concrete operations, cast them into verbal form, and perform further operations on these resulting propositions. Because his thought is now capable of functioning at the purely propositional level, he is liberated from the constraints of concrete reality, and can think in a hypothetico-deductive manner solely on the basis of the logical implications of propositions, which are quite divorced from the constraints of experience. This is the stage of formal operations.

By this stage the child recognizes the conventional status of language and social rules, and can clearly distinguish the word from the thing, the thinker from the thing thought about, the psychical from the physical; all conceptual realism has disappeared. While concrete imagery is still used at the level of formal operations, it is purely for the purpose of illustration. (This does not mean that merely because a person is *capable* of employing formal thought, he always, or even usually, thinks in this way, and I shall shortly deal with the persistence of more elementary modes of thought in the same individual.)

The ability to perform operations on operations, or 'operations to the second power', as Piaget puts it, together with propositional reasoning, are the most important aspects of formal thought, and they allow the child to apply far more powerful logical tools to the problems that confront him—relations of proportion, double systems of reference, and various types of equilibrium and probability, for example, and explicitly logical principles such as implication, disjunction, exclusion, reciprocal implication, and so on. For example, the adolescent can use an exhaustive combinatorial analysis in the solution of scientific experiments of the following kind:

In experiment I, the child is given four similar flasks containing colourless, odourless liquids which are perceptually identical. We number them: (1) diluted sulphuric acid; (2) water; (3) oxygenated water; (4) thiosulphate; we add a bottle (with a dropper) which we will call g; it contains potassium iodide. It is known that oxygenated water oxidizes potassium iodide in an acid medium. Thus mixture $(1 + 3 + g)$ will yield a yellow colour. The water (2) is neutral, so that adding it will not change the colour, whereas the thiosulphate (4) will bleach the mixture $(1 + 3 + g)$. The experimenter presents to the subject two glasses, one containing $1 + 3$, the other containing 2. In front of the subject, he pours several drops of g in each of the two glasses and notes the different reactions. Then the subject is asked simply to reproduce the colour yellow, using flasks 1, 2, 3, 4, and g as he wishes. (Inhelder and Piaget 1958: 108–9)

It is evident that in order to reach a satisfactory solution to the different functions of these flasks, especially 2 and 4, it is necessary for the child to be able to exhaust all the combinatory possibilities of the situation in an orderly and systematic fashion, and to make correct inferences from each trial combination. This type of thinking is essential to any activity that we should call 'scientific'. It is also clear that it is not likely to be found at all in the thinking of those who have not experienced many years of schooling and literacy. And since formal thought also depends on the thorough

---

[10] See Manley *et al.* (1974) for a replication of this experiment with New Guinea schoolchildren using a system of lights and electric switches in place of the chemical flasks.

mastery of concrete operations, it is very hard to see how it could develop in those whose thinking is still largely pre-operatory. I have been able to find no evidence for the existence of formal thought in the collective representations of primitive society, and there are strong grounds for supposing that it will not develop at all even among individuals, since a number of years of schooling and literacy seem essential for it. It is indeed possible that a significant section of the population even in our own society does not advance to the stage of formal thought, which reinforces the probability that it will be even less frequent in non-literate primitive populations. For this reason I shall not consider formal operations any further here, and this book will be concerned mainly with the extent to which collective representations (and, in so far as these can be established, individual thought processes) in primitive societies are concrete operational, or pre-operatory. If we take a particular collective representation from a primitive society, such as a scheme of classification, a spatial representation, or a theory of the nature of shadows, it is possible to ask if it could be understood by a subject at the pre-operatory stage, or if its mastery requires operatory thought at the concrete or formal levels. (I am well aware that there are profound difficulties in trying to assess collective representations in terms of individual psychology, but these will be discussed in detail in the next chapter.)

We shall find that in general the paradigm of the later stage of pre-operatory thought (articulated intuition) is the most appropriate to primitive thought, though in favourable circumstances concrete operations do develop.[11]

One of the distinctive features of Piaget's theory is that while it acknowledges the role of language in focusing, storage, and retrieval, it does not regard language as the foundation of all thought:

... whereas certain philosophical schools, for example the logical positivists, have over-estimated the importance of language for the structuring of

[11] Piaget cautiously suggests that the level of adult thinking in many primitive societies is restricted to that of concrete operations: 'In particular it is quite possible (and it is the impression given by the known ethnographic literature) that in numerous cultures adult thinking does not proceed beyond the level of *concrete operations*, and does not reach that of propositional operations, elaborated between 12 and 15 years of age in our culture' (Piaget 1974: 309). I would go further and assert that in many primitive societies a great deal of thinking is equivalent to that of the pre-operatory stage.

knowledge, it is clear that knowledge, with its logico-mathematical and physical bi-polarities, is formed on the plane of action itself as actions become co-ordinated, and subject and objects begin to differentiate themselves through the progressive refinement of mediating structures. But these structures are still of a physical nature, since they are constituted by actions, and a long process of evolution lies ahead before they can be interiorized in the form of operations. (Piaget 1972: 24)

There are thus three ways of 'knowing'—through actions and their co-ordination, through imagery and concrete symbolism, and through conventional sign systems, of which language is the pre-eminent example. Each of these modes of knowledge has its characteristic features. It is of particular importance to note that the child initially imposes order upon the world (apart from the perceptual discriminations which are present from birth) by the co-ordination of action, and not by linguistic means. Language becomes of increasing importance in cognitive growth, but it cannot be identified with thought itself, of which it is only a particular manifestation. Whether language is an innate faculty of genetically distinct origin from other aspects of thought has not been established, but Piaget and Inhelder draw attention to the parallels between the basic types of action co-ordination achieved in the sensori-motor stage and Chomsky's description of deep structure in language:

At the age of 18 months, before the infant can talk, he can order, temporally and spatially; he can classify in action, that is to say, he can use a category of objects for the same action, or apply different action-patterns to one object; and he can relate objects to objects and actions to actions. The linguistic equivalents of these capacities are concatenation, categorization, and function, where categorization means the major categories (noun phrase, verb phrase etc.) and function the grammatical relation (subject-of, object-of). These are the main operations at the base of the syntactic component which characterizes a highly restricted set of elementary structures from which actual sentences are constructed by transformational rules. These basic rules have, moreover, a particular formal property, namely that they may introduce the initial symbol 'S' (sentence) into a line of derivation, so that phrase-makers can be inserted into other basic phrase-makers. A psychological parallel to this so-called necessary property of the base can be found in the embedding of action-patterns one into the other, which can itself be traced back to the simple circular reactions of a much earlier stage. (Piaget and Inhelder 1969b: 48)

Inhelder makes it clear, however, that Piagetian theory does not imply that the basic linguistic structures are necessarily *derived* from those developed in the sensori-motor stage:

Our hypothesis concerns the existence of parallel *mechanisms*, of parallel constructive *processes* in cognitive development and in the acquisition of syntactic structures . . . the infant has to acquire co-ordinations of sensory-motor schemes, which will later develop into operational structures, rebuilt on a representational level, before he can begin to understand and produce syntactic structures; and the acquisition processes involved in linguistic structuring seem to be parallel to the structuring of action-schemes that has taken place much earlier. (Inhelder 1969: 151–2)

In other words, the child constructs language on the same basic principles by which he co-ordinates action, and does not model his speech on adult syntax, however imperfectly; thus the growth of syntactic structures in the child follows a developmental pattern as it does in the rest of his thought. The question of language and its relation with thought will be pursued in more detail in the next chapter, but it is necessary to emphasize here that, as Bruner points out, the structural organization of the child's grammatical constructions (such as class intersection, modification, hierarchies, and the nesting of categories and predicates) rapidly outstrips his other cognitive activities, because syntactic structures are abstract, whereas perception and action have an immediacy and concreteness that resist organization into the logical structure of syntax for many years. Bruner suggests that it is perhaps the inhibition of motor activity by the capacity for image-based representation that allows the emergence of syntactical structure in language. Whether this is the case or not, it seems that experience must be prepared and organized into non-linguistic form before language can be applied to it, that

. . . there is some need for the preparation of experience and mental operations before language can be used. Once language *is* applied, then it is possible, by using language as an instrument, to scale to higher levels. In essence, once we have coded experience in language, we can (but not necessarily *do*) read surplus meaning into the experience by pursuing the built-in implications of the rules of language.

Until the time this 'surplus meaning' is read off from our linguistic coding of experience, language and experience maintain an important independence from each other. (Bruner 1966b: 51)

And . . . if one is using symbolic [linguistic] representations to guide looking or to guide action, the success of the effort will depend upon the extent to which the sphere of experience or action has been prepared to bring it into some conformance with the requirements of language' (Ibid. 55).

In reviewing the general stages of cognitive development as a whole, it should be stressed that the ages at which these stages or levels are reached are only averages based on normal attainment in European schoolchildren. They are in practice greatly affected by the innate intelligence of each child and by his environmental circumstances. Again, they are not clearly divided from each other, although children may seem to make very rapid progress at intervals: a child may perform, for example, at the level of concrete operations with respect to some cognitive tasks and still be at the pre-operatory level in the case of others (the vertical *décalage*). Thus they are not clear, totally coherent divisions appearing at fixed intervals; the only essential feature is their order of appearance, which may be delayed or totally inhibited by adverse environmental circumstances, but the stages of development cannot be inverted or omitted.

(c) *Factors in cognitive development*

So far I have said relatively little about the factors actually responsible for cognitive growth. The Harvard school supposes that Piaget's theory treats cognitive growth as innate and biologically governed. For example, Greenfield states:

In [Piaget's] view, cognitive maturation is made to appear like a biologically determined and universal sequence. While Piaget admits that environmental influences play a role, the admission is *pro forma*, and inventive experiments remain confined to American and European children, usually middle class children at that. (Greenfield 1966: 226)

Piaget is in fact well aware that cultural and associated environmental factors have great importance in retarding or stimulating cognitive growth, and of the necessity of replicating his experiments cross-culturally in primitive societies (see, e.g. Piaget 1974). His historical studies of the growth of European science are further evidence of his opposition to biological innatism, as well as to a purely environmental determinism. As Inhelder has written,

I feel that Bruner wrongly attributes to Piaget a one-sided genetic explanation which he has never given and which points to a rather serious misunderstanding. While Piaget [1952b] has always shown the inadequacies of the empiricist and Lamarckian explanations, he has just as vehemently and consistently denounced the errors arising from *a priorist* preformism. In his book *Biologie et Connaissance* (1967) he develops a position which goes beyond such a dichotomy and shows the existence of a tertium; the original aspect of this lies in the fact that Piaget seeks to explain the *necessary* character of the products of cognitive development without recourse to predetermination: he tries to show that the concept of a process of construction which is itself the source of new realities (not preformed) can account for this necessary character. In this constructive process it is the continuous equilibrations, i.e. the self-regulations, which play the most important part.

Thus in their final form, the logical structures have a necessary character without being predetermined. Despite his interest in molluscs, Piaget has never believed in permanent structures, even in zoology. The concept of equilibration, and Bruner has not really grasped this, explains the necessity of a form of knowledge without this form being determined in advance.

It is the functioning of the self-regulatory mechanisms and not their programming that is innate in the development of cognitive function. (Inhelder 1969: 183–4)

Piaget, then, clearly recognizes that cognitive development is a dialectical process in which the active manipulation of objects, the demands of communication, argument, and collaboration in tasks, and the reconstruction of knowledge at the different levels of action, imagery, and verbal representation are essential components.

But one must also recognize that Piaget's work has been carried out exclusively with literate European subjects who attend school: the only factors which can be varied in his experiments are age and intelligence, whereas the work of cross-cultural developmental psychologists involves a far wider range of environmental factors, inherent in non-literate societies without formal or specialized schooling, without the products of modern technology, and in which prevailing modes of personal interaction are very different from those of our own society. These psychologists (such as Bruner, Greenfield, Cole, Gay, Dasen, and others) consider themselves to be in significant disagreement with Piaget about the factors responsible for cognitive growth, even though they seem generally to accept his experimental findings on its actual stages. I believe, however, that this apparent disagreement is less profound than the parties themselves seem to imagine, and that the researches of the cross-cultural psychologists complement, rather than conflict with, Piagetian theory. But the reader should bear in mind that this disagreement exists and that especially in the work of Cole, Gay, and others among the Kpelle of Liberia the experiments are mostly not strictly Piagetian in their inspiration. For our broader purposes in this book, however, these disagreements can be treated as of interest primarily to psychologists, and not having any really important bearing on the general theory of cognitive development which will be advanced here.

It is also true to say that Piaget's interests have shifted in the course of his researches from explaining how learning takes place in relation to environmental factors—an issue much discussed in his first books—to the analysis of the logical structure of cognitive processes. There may be some truth in the criticism that at times he seems to give more weight to the demands of logic than to purely psychological processes. As Lunzer has said, 'to deduce from the logical interdependence of certain concepts to their psychological relationship is a dangerous process' (Lunzer 1960: 202).

I only find myself in any substantial disagreement with Piaget in his lack of attention to the role of imagination and creative thinking generally in cognitive growth, a factor he almost completely ignores; in his treatment of symbolism as inherently private, rather than as having considerable potential as a basis of public, social representations; and in his apparent belief that concrete operations are a necessary stage in cognitive development for individuals in all societies. But I shall discuss these questions in more detail in the relevant chapters.

(It will also be necessary, especially in the chapters on symbolism and classification, to draw upon the work of psychologists such as Osgood and Rosch, who are not 'developmentalists' at all, so far as I am aware, but this book is about the foundations of primitive thought, and there is no good reason for narrowly restricting it to developmental psychology when other branches of the discipline are relevant.)

Bruner and his associates also go further than Piaget in regarding language as a prime co-ordinator and integrator of experience. They suggest that the principal factors by which cognitive growth is pushed or retarded are generally those that require translation between the three basic ways of knowing, between action, imagery, and language:

What has become much plainer to us in the course of our work is that there are important institutions and pressures that develop within societies of the technical type, which lead to the demand for confirmation between the three modes of knowing. Whenever learning occurs outside the context [in which] it will be used, outside the range of events that are directly supportive in a perceptual way or indirectly available for pointing, then language enters as a means of conveying the content of experience and of action. Under these circumstances, there is more often than not, a requirement of developing correspondence between what we do, what we see, and what we say. It is this correspondence that is most strikingly involved in reading and writing, in 'school learning', and in other abstract pursuits. There is a greater push towards hierarchical connections in technical cultures than in those that are less technical. The hypothesis is based on the assumption that there are fewer compelling reasons in a less technical society for connecting events to anything beyond their immediate contextual settings such as money value, abstract cause and effect relations, or the intricate uniform timing of work periods (Bruner 1966d: 321–2) . . . It is not that one sees 'better' or represents what one has learned in habit patterns 'better', or even talks or thinks in language 'better'. Rather what seems to be the case is that there is an insistence on mapping each of these systems into another, with a resulting increase of the translatability between each of them. (Ibid. 325)

As we shall see, literacy and schooling are two of the most important experiences leading to cognitive growth, and it is indeed somewhat astonishing that anthropologists, and for that matter philosophers, trying to explain the differences between literate industrial and primitive thought, have not considered the obvious point that people who go to school for a number of years and acquire literacy and numeracy are likely to think in rather different ways from those who have never had this experience.

Apart from literacy, which has special cognitive effects,[12] Bruner suggests that the factors in childhood experience making for difference in cognitive development are the extent to which children are surrounded, as in a modern urban environment, by the work of man; the degree to which they are reared apart from the rest of the community and from which their schooling is in subject-matter a separate world, a factor which itself depends on the degree to which the culture's knowledge transcends the capacity of any one person to master it; and the degree to which children have imparted to them the rules of their society verbally and explicitly by adults instead of learning them implicitly by participating in social life.

[12] See below, Chapter III, pp. 126–32.

While one would not wish to minimize the importance of literacy and schooling in cognitive development, one feels that Bruner and his associates tend to underemphasize the significance of non-verbal interaction with the physical world, especially with respect to the dimensional analysis and quantitative measurement that is essential in a technological environment. Also, in societies where people grow up surrounded only by the organic processes of nature, and never handle mechanical appliances or machines, there will be far less opportunity for developing the later operations of the concrete stage, especially those involving causality. This is partly because in such societies measurement and quantification are poorly developed, but also because the organic processes of nature are irreversible, not easily broken down into component elements, and do not generally lend themselves to the kind of experimental logic that machines do. The organic is also full of concrete symbolic potential and affective significance, especially since one can find there many parallels to the human life process.

I should stress that while this book will be devoted to the environmental characteristics of primitive society and their consequences for modes of thought, I am not, as should by now be obvious, advocating that the mind is passively moulded by its environment. On the contrary, the active role of the mind in reaching an equilibration with its environment should never be forgotten. I shall inevitably be taking these active cognitive processes for granted most of the time after this preliminary exposition, and shall be concentrating on the environmental variables. This may give an impression of 'environmentalism' which is very far from my intention.

These environmental factors and many others will be considered in detail in Chapter III, but at present I am advancing two hypotheses. The first is that since cognitive growth is a product of the interaction of individuals and their environment, and not a process which is purely endogenously generated, inevitable, and spontaneous, it follows that because the milieu of primitive societies is cognitively less demanding than our own, the cognitive development of its members will be correspondingly retarded and will stabilize at a level below that of formal thought. In fact the comprehension of most primitive collective representations of space, time, causality, number, and classification does not seem to require even operatory thought. In short, as Greenfield says,

'. . . traditional non-technical societies demand only the perfection and elaboration of first ways of looking at the world' (Greenfield *et al.* 1966: 318).

I am therefore suggesting that the collective representations of a society must themselves reflect or manifest, in their basic cognitive aspects, the level of cognitive development of the great majority of the adult members of that society (apart from specialized knowledge which is the preserve of an intellectual élite, such as navigational or calendrical skills).

Secondly, apart from this causal hypothesis, it can be claimed that the concepts and general model of learning and thinking provided by developmental psychology are far more precise, theoretically coherent, and soundly based in empirical research than the vague and confused notions hitherto employed by anthropologists and philosophers in their discussions of primitive thought to which I alluded at the beginning of this chapter.

3. BASIC DIFFERENCES OF THOUGHT

The criteria of cognitive development established by Piaget thus may be used to evaluate the representations of space, time, causality, and so on which have been established by ethnographers for a number of primitive societies. There has hitherto been a pronounced tendency, when encountering primitive representations of such basic categories as space and time, to adopt a relativistic stance and evaluate these representations as different from, but equal to, those of educated Europeans: we shall see, for example, that a very obvious characteristic of primitive representations of time is that they conceive it as 'spatialized', in which conventional, recurring sequences of events are in an irreversible and unalterable relationship with one another very like landmarks on a piece of familiar terrain. But we shall also see that this spatialized conception of temporal sequence is not qualitatively different from, nor the cognitive equivalent of, educated representations, but can be clearly related to the developmental paradigm at the pre-operatory stage. Developmental psychology performs an essential methodological part in refuting the hypothesis of wholly distinct modes of thought which cannot be subsumed under a general theory of cognitive processes and which are unrelated to those with which we are familiar.

Developmental psychology also shows that our own literate, industrial modes of thought are not derived from science but from the cognitive demands of our environment, and are also much more complicated than we might suppose. In particular, developmental psychology allows us to escape from stultifying contrasts between 'scientific' and 'primitive' thought. Apart from the problem of defining 'science', it is evident that such cognitive skills as conservation, or the construction of Euclidean and projective space, while they may be necessary to scientific thought, cannot be identified with it, since they are basic to many everyday activities in our industrial society which are common to almost all members of society. Rather than contrasting primitive man with the European scientist and logician, it would be more to the point to contrast him with the garage mechanic, the plumber, and the housewife in her kitchen. In the same way, I shall avoid until the final chapter any use of such concepts as 'rationality' and 'logic'—except in the sense of formal logic—since these, like 'science', provoke as much misunderstanding as they remove.

It should by now have become clear that there is no question of primitive thought being inherently different from that of literate industrial man, since it is an essential postulate of developmental psychology that we can all operate on a number of different mental levels, even if we are capable of formal thought. As we have seen, while cognitive development involves the progressive liberation of thought from the concrete, here-and-now, phenomenal aspects of reality, towards the ability to operate in a purely conceptual manner with no constraints of spatio-temporal particularity, each succeeding level of thought also involves the *reconstruction* of the preceding level with a higher degree of conceptual mobility, generality, and breadth of equilibration, and these earlier levels of thought persist in the subject and may be elicited by unfamiliar problems or displayed in cognitively less demanding situations. There is nothing contradictory in saying that, both cognitively and affectively we, in our society, whatever our educational level, are always liable to regress to more elementary levels of thought in grappling with difficult problems, in creative thought, or when we are emotionally involved in their solution. As Werner says,

Even if such states of consciousness as the dream are disregarded, the normal man does not always function on the same level of mental activity. The same normal individual, depending on inner or outer circumstance, may be characterized by entirely different levels of development. His mentality, genetically considered, is not the same when he is utterly distracted as when he is in a state of perfectly organized concentration. It varies as he moves from some sober scientific or practical work to an emotional surrender to people or things. It may be said that mental life has different strata. At one time man behaves 'primitively' and at another he becomes relatively 'cultured' or 'civilized'. In general, then, developmental psychology attempts to demonstrate that primitive modes of behaviour in the normal adult not only appear under certain extraordinary conditions, but are continually present as the basis of all mental being, and are of vital importance in supporting the highest forms of mentality. (Werner 1948: 4)

This is particularly true of creative and imaginative thought, which is highly autistic at its inception; the philosopher Collingwood, for example, gives the following description of the development of philosophical ideas in his own consciousness:

[As a child] there were no particular questions that I asked myself, there were no special objects upon which I directed my mind; there was only a formless and aimless intellectual disturbance, as if I were wrestling with a fog.

I know now that this is what always happens when I am in the early stages of work on a problem. Until the problem has gone a long way towards being solved, I do not know what it is; all I am conscious of is this vague perturbation of mind, this sense of being worried about I cannot say what. (Collingwood 1939: 4–5)

While the different levels of cognitive development, and the special characteristics of action, imagery, and linguistic representation provide different potentialities for understanding the world, each stage develops out of its predecessor and all thought is based on an interaction of the three modes of representing reality. Formal thought is in some respects different from the thought of concrete operations, which differs again from pre-operatory thought, but equally important are the continuities which result from the fact that each level of thought involves the reconstruction of the representations of an earlier level. In this process the functional invariants of assimilation, accommodation, and equilibration are constant factors and the same struggle to impose permanence on the fluctuations of sensory impressions, to dissociate subject and object, and the need to render action and imagery in verbal form, and to obviate centration, dominate thought at all levels.

I shall argue that the collective representations of primitive society are usually of a type which conforms to the criteria of pre-operatory thought, and that as far as our very limited evidence goes, a substantial percentage of the individuals in these societies also do not seem to attain the level of concrete operations. Yet it will be obvious that even if this is so, it provides no ground for supposing that primitive thought is inherently some strange variant of thinking quite different from our own—rather, primitive thought in its collective aspects represents an elaborate systematization of knowledge with the aid of simpler cognitive processes than are usually employed by literate members of our own society, especially in their official roles. Because these mental processes have become submerged in our society by education, literacy, and technological thinking they now seem strange to us and have to be elucidated by immense intellectual effort, but they are in fact still present in all of us, even if they are now displayed clearly only in children and in the uneducated.

While I wish to emphasize the continuities between primitive thought and our own, this should not be taken to imply that there are not very significant qualitative differences between pre-operatory thought, on the one hand, and concrete and formal operations in particular, on the other. Indeed, it is these very differences which have presented such difficulties in the analysis of primitive thought. The essential point is that primitive thought is not totally alien to our own in its basic characteristics but, in its typical form is more elementary, in developmental terms. Whether this counts as 'difference' in any absolute sense is thus, in the last resort, a terminological issue rather than one of real analytical substance.

The preceding discussion of Piaget's theory has naturally concentrated on *cognitive* growth, but Piaget emphasizes that in practice all thought is inextricably bound up with affective associations and motives, which both empower and distort thinking, and that assimilation itself proceeds by unconscious processes. Thus the attainment of concrete or formal operations is by itself no guarantee that thinking will be correctly carried out, especially since the application or generalization of a strategy to new problems inherently involves the risk of failure. Indeed, since the greater flexibility and analytical power of formal thought is directly dependent on its freedom from concrete imagery and the constraints of the real world, it is by that very fact also given powers of intellectual self-deception denied to those whose thinking remains at the level of pre-operatory or concrete thought, who must be content with the illusions of imaginative fantasy and the deceptions of the phenomenal appearances of things. We shall return in our final chapter to the melancholy theme that theory and formal thought generally can as easily blind as illuminate.

4. THE CHILD AND THE PRIMITIVE

A standard objection raised by anthropologists to the application of the conclusions of developmental psychology to primitive thought (besides the fact that it is psychology) is that its researches are based on the intellectual performances of children. The less perceptive Victorians were in the habit of dismissing primitive peoples as 'childlike' and their thought as in 'the infancy of reason', a gross oversimplification which rightly prompted anthropologists to emphasize the eminent practicality and good sense with which primitives adapt to their environments, the coherence underlying beliefs in witchcraft and magic, and the richness and subtlety of their cosmological systems and categories. Anthropologists also reminded us that many of the supernatural beliefs derided by modern rationalists when encountered in primitive society were adhered to by some of the most learned and intelligent of Europeans until recent times.[13] It is evidently true that there are primitive children and primitive adults, as in our own society, just as there are primitive madmen and educated madmen, and that the white man often appears just as childlike to primitives as they do to the less perceptive members of our society.

Lévi-Strauss goes even further, and claims that there are no cognitive differences between children and adults in any society, and that the only mental differences are in knowledge and experience. According to Lévi-Strauss, the child's mentality differs from the adult's in that it is polymorphic—that is, it contains simultaneously all the possible structures of language and thought of which the human mind is capable—and that the only contribution of the socialization process is to enforce a selection of some forms of structure and the exclusion of others, besides, of course, the acquisition of factual knowledge and practical skills. Since this line of argument is congenial to many anthropologists, even those who are

[13] See also the discussion of paranormal phenomena below, pp. 474–9.

otherwise unconvinced by the theories of Lévi-Strauss, it is worth examining it in more detail.

He says, in the chapter 'The archaic illusion' of *The Elementary Structures of Kinship and Marriage*:

Every newborn child provides in embryonic form the sum total of possibilities, but each culture and period of history will retain and develop only a chosen few of them. Every newborn child comes equipped in the form of adumbrated mental structures, with all the means ever available to mankind to define its relations to the world in general and its relations to others. But these structures are exclusive. Each of them can integrate only certain elements out of all those that are offered. Consequently, each type of social organization represents a choice, which the group imposes and perpetuates. In comparison with adult thought, which has chosen and rejected as the group has required, child thought is a sort of universal substratum the crystallizations of which have not yet occurred, and in which communication is still possible between incompletely solidified forms. (Lévi-Strauss 1969: 93)

This passage might be construed as meaning simply that every child is *potentially* capable of being taught the language, beliefs, and customs of any society into which it might be born. On such an interpretation it is quite unexceptionable and, indeed, trivial. Lévi-Strauss (1969: 91) quotes with approval a passage from the developmental psychologist Basov which appears to support such an interpretation:

In other terms, lower structures from the very beginning serve for the formation of higher ones . . . Yet [this] . . . does not preclude the possibility of such lower structures being formed as such and remaining in this mould without any alteration. If environment did not place the child under conditions which require higher structures, perhaps the lower structures might be the only ones it would be able to produce. (Basov 1929: 288)

This is substantially Piaget's own position, but Lévi-Strauss does not realize this, and greatly confuses the issue by enthusiastically supporting the doctrine of the child psychologist Susan Isaacs that the 'cognitive behaviour of little children, even in these early years, is after all very much like our own' (Isaacs 1930: 57).

Lévi-Strauss asserts that, according to Piaget, 'maturation' is a process of cognitive growth which is independent of experience; that the child's ability to adapt himself to the point of view of others and to acquire knowledge of his own mental processes is the result of an unexplained manifestation of 'social instincts' at seven to eight years of age; that the variability in the actual age at which concepts are acquired invalidates Piaget's paradigm of the basic stages of cognitive growth; and that because Piaget asserts that there are certain resemblances between the seven- to ten-year-old's notions of causality in our society and those of the Pre-Socratics, he is therefore claiming that these philosophers were intellectually the equivalent of seven- to ten-year-old children.

From the preceding exposition of Piaget's research in this chapter it will readily be seen that these criticisms of Piaget are not based on a proper understanding of his work,[14] while no evidence is provided for the alleged 'polymorphic' mentality of children. Lévi-Strauss's failure to understand Piaget seems due to the fact that he bases his opinions not on Piaget's own writings, but on Susan Isaacs's (1930) assessments of Piaget's earliest work alone. He ignores the fact that Isaacs was writing at an early period in the history of developmental psychology, and that her work contains many serious misunderstandings of Piaget—in particular she did not even realize that his references to the ages at which the developmental stages were attained were based on mental, not chronological age. In addition, her research was based on a small group of children in a special school, with an average IQ of 131 (Isaacs 14), many of whose parents were Cambridge dons, whereas Piaget's subjects were ordinary Swiss schoolchildren. It is significant that, although Lévi-Strauss's evaluation of Piaget was wholly incorrect and also obsolete when it was first written, it was allowed to reappear without amendments in the revised edition of 1967, except for four minor changes of wording. The same is true of the English translation of 1969. By this time Piaget's work alone, to

[14] In a slightly later publication Lévi-Strauss (1971: 560–1) claims, confusingly, that he and Piaget are really in agreement on the basic nature of cognitive structures. In referring to Piaget's criticisms of his static, non-genetic conceptions of structure, Lévi-Strauss argues that both he and Piaget agree that while structures can change over time, whether in the case of the mental structures of the child into those of the adult, or of social organizations, the properties of structures are inherent in them and cannot be explained by their content or the nature of their interaction with their environment. Lévi-Strauss thus attempts to present Piaget as an innatist like himself, for whom cognitive structures are necessarily part of the brain itself and unaffected in their essential characteristics by experience even if they can be transformed into other structures and take on particular spacialized forms. This most recent discussion of Piaget's work leaves obscure, however, Lévi-Strauss's opinion of the validity of Piaget's work on children and the extent to which he has changed his earlier wholesale condemnation of it.

say nothing of other developmental psychologists, together with its
cross-cultural replication, had expanded enormously in scope and
volume; that Lévi-Strauss has ignored this great accumulation of
material is the clearest indication of his sense of scholarly responsibility to any point of view that differs from his own.

One of the great mistakes of anthropologists, both in the nineteenth century and today, is to suppose that there is a contradiction
between saying that the cognitive processes of primitive man are
more childlike than those of educated men, and that they can also
attain more complex and profound representations of reality than
those of which children are capable. The root of this mistake is the
failure to distinguish between cognitive processes, on the one hand,
and knowledge and experience on the other. In our own society
cognitive development, such as mastery of logical relationships,
ceases for the average child at about sixteen, though the brighter
child continues to develop longer, and the development of the dull
child ceases before sixteen. We can say that, cognitively speaking,
the adult in our society has the mentality of an adolescent. But
knowledge, skills, and maturity of judgement continue to develop
over an indefinitely long period, and it is these attainments that
distinguish the adult from the child and the adolescent in every
society. In primitive societies, however, because there is less stimulus to cognitive growth from the social and natural environment,
developmental psychology maintains that cognitive growth ceases
earlier, and that formal thought and the more advanced concrete
operations in particular are not developed. For want of a better
terminology, we can refer to cognitive growth of the kind studied
by Piaget as 'vertical' development, and the growth of experience
and judgement as 'horizontal' development. While 'vertical' development will vary according to the milieu, 'horizontal' development, the accumulation of experience and wisdom, will always distinguish the thought of the adult from that of the child, in primitive
societies as well as in our own. And it is surely an extraordinarily
narrow assessment of human beings to say that wisdom, experience, and emotional maturity count for nothing by comparison
with the ability to conserve quantity or to grasp logical inclusion.
One is therefore not implying that adults in primitive society are
intellectually merely the equivalent of children in our society, but
that in primitive societies cognitive skills predominantly of the pre-
operatory type will be developed to a very high degree of skill and

that these will be complemented by the accumulation of experience and wisdom throughout the lifetime of the individual.

Furthermore, collective representations are capable of a rich and complex elaboration which it is quite beyond the capacity of any individual to create. But the rich and complex elaboration of myth, ritual, and cosmology is possible without the attainment of the higher cognitive functions of concrete and formal operations, and there is no contradiction in saying that the collective representations of a society are complex and subtle, but nevertheless based on pre-operatory modes of thought.

Before we can examine the ways in which the primitive milieu affects cognitive growth, it will be necessary to take further account of standard anthropological objections to the use of psychological theory to explain collective representations and to assess in more detail the cognitive functions of language in the development of thought and the extent to which it may be true that differences of language may produce basic differences of thought not accounted for by developmental psychology.

2

Collective Representations and the Thought Processes of Individuals

1. SOCIOLOGICAL VERSUS PSYCHOLOGICAL EXPLANATIONS OF SOCIAL FACTS

It is a truism that while human *capacities* for thought are the product of the genetic endowment of the species, their development in the individual requires him to be a member of a society. He is born into a particular culture, acquires its customs, language, and ways of representing the world, which are enduring and in a sense compulsory in so far as they are basic, below the level of articulate thought, and have no competing alternatives. And for any society to be coherent, for its members to be able to co-operate and make themselves understood by their fellows, it is of course necessary that they should share a common language, common values, and a common set of representations, all of which are developed by social processes.

The Durkheimian tradition goes further and, from the prior existence of culture in relation to any individual, concludes that the individual is passive to the process of socialization. As Gluckman puts it

From infancy, every individual is moulded by the culture of the society into which he is born. All human beings see, but we know, for example, that how they see shapes and colours is to some extent determined by this process of moulding.[1] More than this, their ability to describe their perceptions depends on the categories contained in their respective languages. *A fortiori*, an individual's emotional reactions and his complex ideas for dealing with his fellows and with nature are derived from his culture. (Gluckman 1949–50: 73–4)

[1] See, e.g., Cole and Scribner 1974; 61–97; Postman, Bruner and McGinnies 1948; Bruner and Goodman 1947; Bruner and Postman 1949.

He quotes the case of romantic love in Western culture, and the absence of this ideal in African society as an illustration.

This model of the individual as passive to the values and representations of his culture leads Gluckman, perhaps inevitably, to suppose that they are actually not derived from individual thought processes at all:

Perceptions, emotions, evaluations of right and wrong, ideas of the causes of events—in short, whole systems of thought and feeling—thus exist transcendentally, independently of the individuals in whom they appear. They are what the French sociologists call *collective representations*, which pass from generation to generation, learnt in behaviour, contained in proverb and precept, in technology and convention and ritual, and, with the development of writing, in books. A man's psyche is social, not organic. Therefore a Londoner's baby brought up in an African tribe would be an African and an African baby reared in London by Londoners would be a Londoner. (Ibid. 75)

The model then is that of a culture, on the one hand, with a certain content of ideas and categories embodied in its language, technology, customs, rituals, and so on, which are replicated in the mind of the individual rather like preformed pieces of a jigsaw puzzle being slotted into place. Gluckman evidently does not suppose that the individual does not personally *have* ideas, or *feel* emotions, or *understand* technological processes, but rather, that he does not *invent* them, and that in content and organization they originate solely in society as a result of collective processes, having thus a transcendental life of their own.

Up to a point there is some truth in what Gluckman has been saying. The ability to act as a Lozi or a Londoner is not genetically programmed; one inherits the ability to acquire human culture, not the details of any specific culture. Social processes, moreover, are governed by principles that cannot be reduced to those of psychology—those of economics, for example, or of political alliance formation—and in so far as institutions such as ritual, or magic and witchcraft, or technology, develop according to these principles of social interaction, it is misconceived to attempt to reduce them to pure manifestations of individual psychology. To this extent Durkheim was quite right to reject the psychological theories of primitive thought advanced by anthropologists like Tylor and Frazer (the 'intellectualist school', as Evans-Pritchard (1965) has termed them). They had assumed that the reasoning of prim-

itive man was the same as our own, and that only lack of knowledge and the opportunity for experiment had prevented him from
attaining true scientific knowledge, which (in Frazer's view) had
slowly evolved by a process of trial and error, involving the passage through the earlier stages of magic and religion. Similarly, for
Tylor, primitive man was an active questioner, who over the ages
had built up a comprehensive theory of animism on the basis of his
experience of dreams and hallucinations which provided the basic
notions of soul and ghost. For the 'Intellectualists', then, primitive
man is simply an ineffectual scientist, 'always asking himself questions and giving himself the wrong answers', as Raglan parodied
their position, and for these anthropologists the social manifestations of thought are simply the sum of the ideas of the members of
a society over the generations, an essentially individualistic and
atomistic explanation of social systems of thought.

Two of Durkheim's arguments for the rejection of individualism
are of enduring importance and validity. The first is that different
levels of reality manifest distinctive properties and modes of behaviour, so that we cannot deduce the properties of water from
those of hydrogen or oxygen atoms in isolation from those of the
water molecule, or the properties of living matter from its nonliving components. The second, related, point is that the whole
cannot be explained as the sum of its parts, and that to try to
explain society as the sum of the behaviour of its individual members is as misconceived as trying to explain mental functions in
terms of individual nerve cells: 'We must, then, explain phenomena
that are the product of the whole by the characteristic properties of
the whole, the complex by the complex, social facts by society, vital
and mental facts by the *sui generis* combinations from which they
result' (Durkheim 1953: 29).

As we shall see, these arguments do not apply to the effects of
general characteristics of individuals on the nature of collective
representations, and Durkheim's argument that particular individual characteristics cancel each other out is unsatisfactory, because
we shall be concerned with those characteristics that are common
to all members of a society:

... society does not depend upon the nature of the individual personality.
In the fusion from which it results all the individual characteristics, by
definition divergent, have neutralized each other. Only those more general
properties of human nature survive, and because of their extreme gener-

ality, they cannot account for the specialized and complex forms which characterize collective facts. This is not to say that they count for nothing in the resultant, but they are only its mediate conditions. Without them it could not emerge, but they do not determine it. (Ibid. 26)[2]

Durkheim is here referring to characteristics of personality, but the weakness of the argument is the same whether we are considering *general* features of personality or of cognitive processes: the crux of the matter is the *degree* of that generality, and it is pure assumption on Durkheim's part that the common characteristics of individuals as a whole should be of such *extreme* generality as to have no bearing on the form of specific institutions or collective representations.

But I shall show that the Durkheimian model is based on at least five major fallacies or confusions. The first, already mentioned in the last chapter, is the assumption that learning is passive and that the categories and ideas of a culture can be absorbed ready-made by the individual by a simple process of imitation, without assimilation. The second is that because no single individual's thinking can affect the collective representations of his culture, therefore the thinking of individuals *in general* has no effect on collective representations.

The third fallacy, in considering the interaction between the general cognitive processes of individuals and the collective representations of their society, is the failure to distinguish between short- and long-term effects. Within a single generation the possibility of cognitive changes in the population affecting collective representations is obviously fairly restricted, but this limitation will decrease in significance as the number of generations increases over time.

The fourth is the confusion between the mind considered in terms of its *content* of a certain set of beliefs and ideas, and the

---

[2] Durkheim, like many others of a fertile mind, was not entirely consistent in his theories, and one can find passages such as the following which concede that individual thought processes do influence collective representations: 'Collective representations are the result of an immense co-operation, which stretches out not only into space but into time as well; to make them, a multitude of minds have associated, united and combined their ideas and sentiments; for them, long generations have accumulated their experience and their knowledge' (Durkheim 1947: 16). This cumulative model is not, however, representative of his basic theory of collective representations. I refer to it only to show that Durkheim was aware of the problem of trying to maintain collective representations and the thought processes of individuals in separate theoretical compartments.

mind considered as a system of cognitive *processes*. The fifth is the failure to distinguish between the particular and distinctive forms of collective representations in different societies, such as the various types of divination, and the underlying similarities and common assumptions common to them all, such as notions of fate or luck.

In the first place, the Durkheimian position, by rejecting the possibility of individual thought processes having any effect on collective representations (in *primitive* societies), finds itself in an irresolvable dilemma. If collective representations determine individual thought in the manner suggested by Gluckman, there must be a complete homology between collective representations and that thought, so that it must be possible to deduce the ideas, values, and modes of thought of all the adult members of a society from its collective representations (an inference which also makes any change in collective representations rather difficult to understand). But, on the other hand, if in fact as ethnographers we find that there are sceptics, wise men, and fools, and differences of opinion and variant forms of myths among our informants, how is it possible to maintain that collective representations have the totally transcendental nature claimed for them? Gluckman was too experienced an ethnographer to choose the first solution to this dilemma. After a long discussion of witchcraft beliefs in Africa, he says:

This very brief summary of how beliefs in witchcraft, oracles and magic work, emphasizes that we cannot deduce the mode of thinking of individuals within a primitive society directly from the social beliefs and attitudes of that society. (Ibid. 87)

[and]

... I hope I have shown that the beliefs are not hard and fast rules which can be applied mechanically. They are often, when presented schematically, contradictory. But individuals make use of different beliefs within the system from situation to situation, *for in actual life these beliefs become significant in action, not as ideas in people's minds.* (Ibid. 88) (my emphasis)

One is bound to ask at this point what evidence there is for the existence of 'collective representations' at any transcendental level *except* as the particular manifestations of what particular people do and think in particular situations. Since we never find ourselves in the same situation twice, it is obvious that all members of a society are, at the very least according to Gluckman, called upon actively to interpret their beliefs according to their individual knowledge and ability. Collective representations are thus ideal constructs which are not encountered in their pure form by the ethnographer, who experiences instead a series of concrete and particular variations around a latent theme.

The notion that action can take place without thought, referred to by Gluckman in the passage just quoted, has also been an important device for allowing Durkheimian sociologists to maintain that collective representations can maintain this transcendental existence without any basis in the thought processes of individuals, since actions can be regarded as having an autonomous social organization of their own. As Radcliffe-Brown said,

... it is sometimes held that funeral and mourning rites are the result of a belief in a soul surviving death. If we must talk in terms of cause and effect, I would rather hold the view that the belief in a surviving soul is not the cause but the effect of the rites. Actually the cause–effect analysis is misleading. What really happens is that the rites and the justifying or rationalising beliefs develop together as parts of a coherent whole. But in development it is action or the need of action that controls or determines belief rather than the other way about. The actions themselves are symbolic expressions of sentiments. (Radcliffe-Brown 1952: 155)

In this he follows Robertson Smith's account of ancient religion:

... it is of the first importance to realise clearly from the outset that ritual and practical usage were, strictly speaking, the sum-total of ancient religions. Religion in primitive times was not a system of belief with practical applications; it was a body of fixed traditional practices, to which every member of society conformed as a matter of course. (Robertson Smith 1907: 20)

Mary Douglas writes in similar vein: 'It is misleading to think of ideas such as destiny, witchcraft, mana, magic, as part of philosophies, or as systematically thought out at all. They are not just linked to institutions, as Evans-Pritchard puts it, but they are institutions—every bit as much as Habeas Corpus, or Hallow-e'en' (Douglas 1966: 89). She goes on to argue that these beliefs are the result of the urgent practical concern with the problems of everyday social life:

These insistent demands for explanations [of particular sorrows] are focused on an individual's concern for himself and his community. We now know what Durkheim knew, and what Frazer, Tylor and Marrett did not. These questions are not phrased primarily to satisfy man's curiosity about the seasons and the rest of the natural environment. They are phrased to satisfy a dominant social concern, the problem of how to organize together in society. They can only be answered, it is true, in terms of man's place in nature. But the metaphysic is a by-product, as it were, of the urgent practical concern. (Ibid. 90–1)

This approach to 'religion', 'ritual', witchcraft', 'magic', 'mana', and so on seems to assume that thought consists of conscious, explicit philosophizing and speculation; that if people cannot give a verbal exposition of a custom or practice, or if such explanations as they give are inconsistent or irrelevant, we need look no further for underlying assumptions of a cognitive nature; and that these customs, rites, and beliefs have no cognitive content at all, being simply composed of actions and customary expressions, themselves derived from organized sentiments.

One of the tasks of this book is to show that this rationalistic opposition or gulf between thought and action presupposed by anthropologists such as those just quoted, is mistaken and that merely because ritual is expressed in concrete symbolism which cannot be put into words, or because accounts of witchcraft, magic, and other ideas are incoherent at the verbal level, we have no warrant for assuming that they are simply derived from social behaviour. Non-verbal thought, based on action and imagery, is a fundamental aspect of cognitive processes, and in understanding primitive society the problem is the translation of such non-verbal, image-based thought into verbal form. But nothing could be more false than to suppose that the lack of ability to put thoughts into words signifies the absence of any form of thought, as in the implicit assumptions underlying customary behaviour and concrete symbolism. Indeed, when we come to consider those beliefs that can be put into words, such as notions of witchcraft and magic, it is patently absurd to suppose that these notions can even be transmitted from one person to another without involving some form of thought, even of the kind that Douglas and other Durkheimians would concede to be thought. And to suppose that problem solving, merely because it is 'practical', can take place purely on the basis of action and motivation, without specific cognitive skills and basic (even if implicit) assumptions about the world and man's place in it (just 'chaps on the ground getting along together' in the best traditions of British pragmatism) is a desperate expedient indeed by which to defend a theory of the social determination of thought.

It seems clearly impossible, then, for *particular* collective representations to be maintained in thought-proof compartments immune to the mental processes of the individual members of the society in question. Social action and relations are an integral part of thought. But in the case of the most fundamental categories of thought, of classification, space, time, and causality, it might be argued that because of their pervasiveness, generality, and necessity for all aspects of thinking, they at least can be shown to be the product of purely social factors. As is well known, Durkheim maintained precisely this position:

World space has been primitively constructed on the model of social space, that is to say of the territory occupied by the society and such that the society represents to itself; time expresses the rhythm of collective life; the idea of kind (*genre*) was originally nothing else than another aspect of the idea of a human group; the collective power and its impact on consciousness served as prototypes for the notion of force and of causality. (Durkheim 1913: 36)

This theory of the origin of basic categories was faithfully reproduced in 1973 by Mary Douglas:

Society was not simply a model which classificatory thought followed; it was its own divisions which served as divisions for the system of classification. The first logical categories were social categories; the first classes of things were classes of men into which these things were integrated. It was because men were grouped and thought of themselves in the form of groups that in their ideas they grouped other things. The centre of the first scheme of nature is not the individual: it is society. (Douglas 1973: 12)
(This is in fact a direct quotation from Needham's translation of Durkheim and Mauss (1963), though not indicated as such by Douglas.)

Thus the basic categories of thought in Durkheimian theory are of social-institutional origin and permeate all the thinking of individuals because of their generality, their coherence, and their necessity for all thought—properties which are supposed to be absent from the sensory experience of individuals:

As for those *sui generis* concepts which are called categories, if they are not only social in their origins, but in their contents, this is because they are

pre-eminent concepts: they dominate and envelop all the other concepts
... A time which comprises all particular durations, a space which includes all individual extensions, a total kind (*genre*) which encloses all
known things can be nothing other than time, space, and the entirety of
things which are represented by a subject formed by the totality of particular subjects and which surpass them. (Durkheim 1913: 36–7)

Unfortunately, this theory of the origin of categories (besides
being contrary to what we now know from developmental psychology) is unable to account for the fact that social life could
never have developed at all unless men had had some form of classificatory ability and some representations of space, time, and
cause, of a non-social origin. Durkheim and Douglas are in fact
confused between the mind considered as a set of representations
derived from the culture, and as a system of cognitive processes:

The failure to make this essential distinction was noted nearly fifty years
ago by Gehlke with regard to *Les Formes élémentaires de la Vie religieuse*,
when he observed that Durkheim saw the categories as 'a content of mind
rather than as a capacity of mind', and that this was 'quite consistent with
Durkheim's conception of the mind as a system of representations, rather
than as a functioning whole' [1915: 53]. Some years later, Dennes elaborated
this expository comment into a cogent criticism of Durkheim's work on
religion which applies with equally invalidating effect to Durkheim and
Mauss's main argument [in *Primitive Classification*]. As he writes,
'Durkheim's theory of the origin of the categories depends on his ambiguous
conception of mind' [Dennes 1924: 39]. If the mind is taken to be a system of
cognitive faculties, it is absurd to say that the categories originate in
social organization: the notion of space has first to exist before social groups
can be perceived to exhibit in their disposition any spatial relations
which may then be applied to the universe; the categories of quantity have to
exist in order that an individual mind shall ever recognize the one, the many,
and the totality of the divisions of his society; the notion of class necessarily
precedes the apprehension that social groups, in concordance with which
natural phenomena are classed, are themselves classified. In other words,
the social 'model' must itself be perceived to possess the characteristics which
make it useful in classifying other things, but this cannot be done without
the very categories which Durkheim and Mauss derive from the model.
(Needham 1963: xxvi–xxvii)

Because of this fundamentally confused notion of 'mind', Durkheim had great difficulty in accounting for the existence of cognitive faculties which were evidently displayed by men independently of social institutions, and was obliged to postulate that

human beings had certain innate conceptual powers comprising both practical intelligence and classification:

> ... there is no period in history when men have lived in a chronic confusion and contradiction (Durkheim 1947: 487) And,
>
> It is probable that man has always classified, more or less clearly, the things on which he lived, according to the means he used to get them: for example, animals living in the water, or in the air or on the ground. But at first such groups were not connected with each other or systematized. They were divisions, distinctions of ideas, not schemes of classification. Moreover, it is evident that these distinctions are closely linked to practical concerns, of which they merely express certain aspects. It is for this reason that we have not spoken of them in this work, in which we have tried above all to throw some light on the origins of the logical procedure which is the basis of scientific classification. (Durkheim and Mauss 1963: 81–2n.)

Just why classification by habitat is not a scheme of classification is far from obvious, and such 'practical' classification is, of course, basic to language without which society would be impossible.

Lévy-Bruhl,[3] who followed Durkheim in regarding collective representations as determined entirely by social processes and institutions, was in a similar dilemma over the status of practical intelligence. On the one hand he stated that 'in a man's mental life everything which is not merely the reaction of the organism to the stimuli it receives is necessarily of a social character' (1926: 15), but he was bound to concede that a great deal of thought, and not just reaction to stimuli, is the same in all societies:

> Considered as an individual, the primitive, in so far as he thinks and acts independently of these collective representations where possible, will usually feel, argue and act as we should expect him to do. The inferences he draws will be just those which would seem reasonable to us in like circumstances. If he has brought down two birds, for instance, and only

---

[3] Despite my critical comments on Lévy-Bruhl's theory of language and thought, I consider much of his work on primitive thought to be of great value. Unfortunately he was unaware of the possibilities of cognitive psychology and was thus unable to explain many of the aspects of primitive thought to which he drew attention except by an ineffectual resort to the same sort of sociological explanation as that employed by Durkheim. He did not, however, as various critics have pointed out, ever attempt an analysis of the way in which sociological factors might affect thought. Since this is not a textbook, it would lead us too far from our argument to discuss the merits of Lévy-Bruhl here, but it is worth observing that if we substitute the term 'pre-operatory' for 'pre-logical' in his work, many of his observations on primitive thought have some justification.

picks up one, he will ask himself what has become of the other, and will look for it. If rain overtakes and inconveniences him, he will seek shelter. If he encounters a wild beast, he will strive his utmost to escape, and so forth. But though on occasions of this sort primitives may reason as we do, though they follow a course similar to the one we should take (which in the more simple cases, the most intelligent among the animals would also do), it does not follow that their mental activity is always subject to the same laws as ours. (Ibid. 78–9)

(While Lévy-Bruhl and others have seen this practicality of primitive thought and its 'mystical' aspects as polar opposites, they spring in fact from the same roots—the dominance of sensorimotor and symbolic, image-based schemata over explicit verbal analysis and operatory thought.)

More generally, how can social determinism explain the fact that the form of the categories of space, time, number, causality, and classifications which occur spontaneously in children in modern literate industrial societies are very similar to the categories of primitive peoples, despite the difference in the organization and institutions of industrial society from those of the primitive? How can Durkheim explain the universal similarities between the stages of children's cognitive development in all societies, so that children of the same stage of development in West Africa, Aden, Iran, Hong Kong, and Geneva give almost identical answers to problems set them? How can he explain the fact that children's thought in our society should differ systematically from the models provided by their adult instructors?

We have already seen that the grasp of the inclusion of classes, transitivity, part–whole relations, and logical 'All' and 'Some' are neither innate in all human minds nor received passively from the collective representations of society. They are constructed in the individual consciousness as a result of the active reconstitution of co-ordinated actions and imagery on the verbal level as the result of the child's experience of natural objects and his relations with them. We also noted the difference between complexive and logical classes, and the developmental priority of the complex, with the strong probability that complexes rather than logical classes are the norm in primitive systems of classification. The assumption that social hierarchies of groups are the equivalent of logical hierarchies of classes is arbitrary and, as we shall see, unfounded, since it is possible to conduct social relations in terms of a nested set of groups without conceptualizing these as a set of inclusion relations between classes and subclasses. There are, moreover, as Durkheim realized, inherent discontinuities in nature, as between sea, sky, and earth, which form the natural habitats of a variety of flora and fauna and thus provide a basis for the classification of things in terms of their habitat, morphology, use, and associations quite independently of social organization. Whether natural taxonomies are given symbolic value and related to the groups and institutions of society is contingent and by no means necessary (see e.g., Morris 1976).

Again, while Durkheim perceived the conceptual realism of primitive thought when he referred to the indissociation between words and their referents, and between knower and known, he did not realize that this represents a general stage of cognitive development which cannot be derived from social organization.

We shall also see that primitive representations of space are based on ideas of centre and periphery, laterality and boundaries, which are topological—that is, based on relations of proximity, separation, inclusion, and order—rather than on Euclidean and projective relations. Primitive conceptions of time are static and 'spatialized' and do not involve the co-ordination of duration, succession, and simultaneity, but this aspect of primitive time representation cannot be reduced simply to the *forms* of ritual cycles and calendars. Primitive causality is essentialist, non-probabilistic, and psychomorphic, but these characteristics do not depend on the experience of authority in human relations. In all these cases, underlying the specific features of the collective representations of individual societies are certain basic and universal assumptions and thought processes characteristic of pre-operatory thought.

It is evident, therefore, that the Durkheimian theory not only is incapable of maintaining a thoroughgoing distinction between the thinking of individuals and specific collective representations, but cannot derive the most general and basic conceptual categories from the institutional forms of society, either. By the admission of its supporters, collective representations cannot inhabit a transcendental realm, since they are constantly being applied in daily life by all the individuals who compose society, and there is a great deal of thought which displays universal characteristics independent of the institutions and collective representations of society.

The theory also rests on a bogus contrast between the lone individual—indeed, the lone infant—on the one hand, and the vast resources of the society into which he has been born, on the other. This contrast is then followed by the triumphant exclamation that since anything as pathetic and impotent as a single individual can have no influence on the collective representations of his society, it must follow that individual thought processes as such are irrelevant to the types of collective representations that are developed. The fallacy is compounded by the assumption that learning is a passive process, in which the contents of the collective representations are simply projected on to the minds of individuals, like images on to a screen or photographic film.

We may best illustrate these fallacies by considering the case of the university undergraduate who comes to the study of a new subject—let it be social anthropology. Initially he is in the position of Durkheimian man, the lone individual, intellectually naked, born into a culture—the discipline—which he did not make, and which is vastly greater in scope than any one mind can encompass. But no university lecturer supposes, in the first place, that his students passively absorb the contents of books and lectures like photographic film receiving images. Learning is an active process, to which the individual brings varied abilities, and in accomplishing which he must be able to recast what he is taught so that it becomes a part of his own mode of thinking about anthropological data and theory. No one would regard the parrot-like regurgitation of what a student has been taught as successful learning and, indeed, it is a commonplace among university teachers that the content of the same course of lectures is understood in a wonderful variety of ways by those who attend them.

If a student becomes a professional anthropologist, he is likely to produce some changes in the collective representations of the discipline, for while social anthropology has a body of fundamental theory, it is a matter of historical record that even this has changed as a result of being accommodated to ethnographic experience. So because learning is an active process, constantly confronted by the need to accommodate to experience and to assimilate that experience to existing conceptual structures it cannot be, even in its collective aspects, simply a matter of passive socialization and acceptance of received truths and customs. And because any discipline is composed of real people, it is also fundamentally false to regard the body of data and theory that compose its collective representations as beyond the influence of individual thought processes. Those collective representations, as it might be structural-functionalism, for example, are the product of the accumulated work of a large number of real people, and it is their thought and effort that have made the subject what it is and created those collective representations in the course of their working lives. If this were not so, collective representations could never change, but we know that they have, in the hundred years or so of the history of our discipline, changed out of all recognition.

An academic discipline is not, of course, a society, still less a primitive society; it exists within a larger society, and occupies only a portion of the thought and action of its participants; it is concerned with a narrow aspect of learning—literate, verbal knowledge—and is self-consciously pedagogic and experimental. But while it differs in all these crucial respects from a society, because a discipline is an enduring social process, with basic traditions perpetuated by the social relations of academic life to which new-comers must initially conform, it nevertheless shares with society as a whole some basic properties which illuminate the status of collective thought in relation to the thinking of individuals, albeit greatly speeded up and intensified.

Because Durkheim was so obsessed with the enduring, compulsory, and inescapable quality of collective representations by comparison with the malleability of the individual consciousness, and was also dominated by the empiricist model of the mind as acquiring knowledge by passive absorption and conformity, he could not see that if certain modes of representing reality are brought about in *all* or even a majority of the members of a society as a result of general environmental factors, these modes of thought must be manifested in the basic characteristics, the underlying and implicit assumptions on which specific collective representations are based, even though their detailed form, such as the characteristics of witches, the methods of divination, the occasions and content of ritual, the symbolic associations of spatial locations and orientations, the social role of priest and diviner, are the product of collective, social processes which are of a systemic nature and which cannot, as Durkheim rightly said, be reduced to the thought processes of individuals, as opposed to being influenced by them.

For while the social processes which generate collective representations are often not understood, or even guessed at, by the members of that society, collective representations, unless merely performed by rote, are necessarily based on certain assumptions and mental processes in the minds of individuals, through which they are transmitted from person to person and generation to generation. Because people can transmit ideas only as they understand them, it is inevitable that the cognitive capacities of the average member of society must influence the kind of collective representations that their society develops. In short, to *conform* is also necessarily to *transform*.

For example, we find that in primitive society a shadow is not regarded simply as an area of absence of light, in a projective relation to an object and a light source, but as a kind of thing which emanates from people in particular. This assumption about the nature of shadows is the basis of a wide variety of collective representations concerned with shadow and soul, the magical vulnerability of shadows, their power to pollute food, and so on; however, these various, socially elaborated beliefs about shadows all rest upon the fact that the average member of a primitive society does not think of shadows in the operatory sense, but as a real emanation from a person. And in so far as shadows are understood in this pre-operatory way, no amount of social elaboration can transform the collective representation of shadows into those of a projective type. Collective representations, in short, are themselves rooted in certain basic assumptions about reality which are not specific to the Konso, the Azande, the Tikopia, or the Ancient Egyptians, but which are the result of the way in which human beings think when in the primitive milieu, as a result of interaction with their physical as well as their social environment.

One of the most striking deficiencies of Durkheim's theory is his failure to take account of the thinking involved in man's interaction with his total environment in relation to the rest of human thought. There is an almost complete failure to consider the modes of production and problems of technology, the absence of units of measurement and quantification, the strategies of social intercourse, the cognitive effects of illiteracy and the modes of education, the kinds of discourse and speech forms appropriate to social situations in a primitive milieu. So the list could be prolonged: these are all vital aspects of men's adaptation to, and modes of thinking about, their environment, and it is inevitable that such factors must have a profound effect upon representations of space and time, causality, classification, and the distinction they draw between themselves and nature.

One reason for this omission was that Durkheim was an armchair theorist who had no practical experience of life in a primitive society. Lévy-Bruhl has often been ridiculed for allegedly depicting primitive man as lost in a world of mystical fantasy, but Durkheim's conception of the primitive as submerged in a world of collective thoughts and institutions, except for his innate ability to make perceptual discriminations, is a comparable travesty of the living reality.

A supporter of Durkheim might reply that the various factors crucial to cognitive development, such as schooling and literacy, the freedom of the child to question, the availability of machines and mechanical devices (such as bicycles) for causal analysis, the existence of units of measurements and verbal numbers to facilitate dimensional analysis, the degree of experiment and innovation required by the technology, and so on, are all collective phenomena, and that therefore the findings of developmental psychology really substantiate Durkheim. But this is is not so. In the first place, these factors operate on the cognitive development of *individuals*, whose mental processes Durkheim regards as the consequence of collective representations, and upon which they can have no formative influence, at least at the level of primitive society. Secondly, Durkheim considers that it is social relations and institutions—clan and moiety systems, relations of authority, calendar and ritual cycles, camp layouts, and so on—that are the basis of conceptual categories and collective representations generally. But the environmental factors which developmental psychologists regard as most relevant to cognitive growth are not of this order: a bicycle may be a social phenomenon, but it is certainly not a Durkheimian institution, or a social relation.

Once it is recognized that the social factors influencing the development of individual cognitive processes include the totality of the individual's relations with his fellows and his physical environment, we are no longer in the intellectual world of Durkheim at all, but of Vico and Marx. Like Durkheim, they recognized the reality of collective representations, which are the product not simply of individual thought but of social processes, but they also saw that the *activity* of man exercises a vital and profound influence on the way in which he understands the world. The traditional theory of anthropology, however, presents a model of man with his hands tied behind his back, so to speak, who absorbs his representations of reality by passively looking and listening.

So the incorporation of the findings of developmental psychology into the study of primitive thought does not conflict with sociological analysis, but rather enriches it by allowing us to perceive the relevance of a whole range of factors whose importance for the understanding of primitive thought is incomprehensible on the premises of traditional anthropological theory, since these factors concern the way in which the cognitive development of *individuals* is affected by their general environment.

A critic who accepts that the collective representations of a society are filtered and transmitted through individual minds and assimilated to their existing cognitive structures, may nevertheless raise the objection that even educated members of our own society often use relatively elementary modes of thought in cognitively undemanding situations. May it not be, he will say, that the members of primitive societies are cognitively as developed as we are, but because the demands of their society are so much less than our own, since they are focused on personal relations rather than on technology, or on highly verbalized expression, they do not need to use concrete or formal operations either in their collective representations or in most of their day-to-day problem solving, even if they are capable of these types of thought? For example, in primitive society we do not find our generalized social concepts or the logical analysis of narrative or the construction of formal grammar.

The answer to this question is an empirical one: if we, as ethnographers, had found that members of primitive societies were, for example, quite capable of generalizing to us in abstract terms about the way in which their societies worked and the purposes of their institutions, of distinguishing between logical and narrative order in their myths, of discussing with us logical flaws in argument and analysing the structure of their syntax, even though they were not accustomed to talking in this way among themselves, we should rightly conclude that primitive thought was nothing more than a response to local circumstances and had nothing to do with the cognitive capacities of individuals. But we do not find that primitives can in fact communicate in these ways, and the inference is therefore that primitive thought is not simply a manifestation of particular preoccupations and interests, but of individual capacities as well.

But while the average member, or even the great majority of members, of a primitive society may think at the level of pre-operatory thought, it does not follow that we can deduce from the evidence of a society's collective representations alone that *all* the individual members of that society can function only at the level of those collective representations. The more intelligent persons, or those who have been exposed to more cognitively demanding situations, will very probably be able to transcend some of the collective representations of their society—how many of such people, and by how much, are matters for empirical investigation. Collective representations of a high cognitive level may also be understood by the average member of society at a *lower* level of comprehension. For example, statistical operations are performed by many members of our society by rote, without any real grasp of the underlying mathematical principles. From a given set of collective representations, therefore, we can neither conclude that the cognitive development of *some* members does not go beyond them, or that the cognitive development of others will not be below them. This is as true of ritual as it is of mathematics.

Collective representations, in short, are two-sided phenomena: from one point of view they are, in their most general characteristics, manifestations of the cognitive processes of the average adult member of the society, but from the other point of view they are social phenomena which form an environment with which each individual interacts, an environment which may provide aids to cognitive growth, and which also may retard it.

Cole and Scribner argue that 'it is not possible to make valid inferences about thought processes—that is, about the specific mechanisms producing a particular behaviour or beliefs—solely on the basis of evidence about the beliefs of groups or individuals' (Cole and Scribner 1974: 143). To the extent that it would be extremely rash to make any inference about an individual Bongo-Bongo informant's thought processes *solely* from his account of what 'we, the Bongo-Bongo, say is the cause of thunder', then Cole and Scribner are obviously right, since he might be able to produce reasons for rejecting orthodox opinion. But this is not the end of the matter. In the course of this book we shall examine (*a*) a dialectical, interactionist theory of the development of ways of represent-

ing the world as worked out by Piaget and others, (*b*) the circumstances of primitive life relevant to this theory of cognitive growth,
and (*c*) the *general* characteristics of primitive representations of
space, time, number and measurement, causality, classification,
and so on. Now, to the extent that modes of thought are not
innate, but are developed in relation to the activity of the subject in
relation to his environment (the demands on explicit, verbal thinking, the extent to which imagery and symbolic representation are
sufficient for communication, and so on), it is reasonable to expect
some degree of congruence between the type of representations of
space, time, causality, etc. that are *general* to primitive society, and
the circumstances of primitive life and developmental theory. This
does not imply that gifted individuals or those who have had special cognitive experience such as navigation, land measurement, or
other specific craft skills will not be able to transcend the collective
representations of their society, but to reject the possibility of such
a congruence seems to require an appeal to innatist cognitive structures for which there is little evidence, and which Cole and Scribner
themselves would not support.

The basic hypothesis is as follows. Quite apart from the institutionalized aspects of society, individuals construct representations
of reality by their daily interactions with the physical and social
environment in ways that are not themselves institutionalized, but
are responses to the demands of real situations. Some of these are
universal, since all societies and all natural environments have at
least some features in common. This interaction is the basis of cognitive growth, which is governed by laws general to human beings
in all societies, such that all normal individuals will progress
through a sequence of developmental stages which ends at the
stage of formal operations. However, they may not attain this level
of thought if environmental conditions are insufficiently demanding. In other words, some ways of representing the world are more
elementary than others and consequently will occur before more
advanced representations in the development of every individual.
In societies like our own these elementary forms of representation
are inadequate for accommodation to the socio-physical environment, and so the individual is forced to reconstruct them at a
higher level of mental functioning. But in primitive societies pre-
operatory thinking is perfectly adequate for coping with the demands of everyday life and does not conflict with experienced

reality so as to require pre-operatory thought to be reconstructed at the level of concrete or formal operations.

Thus the collective representations of *non-specialized, unstratified* societies cannot incorporate cognitive processes that are beyond the grasp of even a significant minority of its members and the collective representations of specialized and stratified societies will be understood in different ways by the educated and the uneducated (though just what this percentage might be cannot be predicted without further research). In situations where the natural and cultural environment of a society retards the cognitive growth of its members, so that only a fraction of its members can grasp the solution of certain problems, such as conservation of quantity, the collective representations of that society cannot be conservational.

For example, studies of traditional, non-schooled adults in Papua New Guinea and Australia (Kelly 1971, Dasen 1974) have shown that fewer than 50 per cent can conserve quantity.

Let us assume that in a particular society only 50 per cent of adults can conserve quantity (Figure 3).

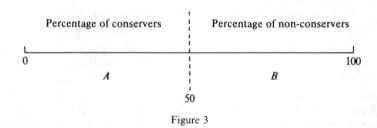

Figure 3

Let us further imagine that in the course of social interactions between two people in which the conservation of quantity is a relevant problem there is an equal probability that they will be either *A* or *B*. Then the frequencies of meetings will be distributed according to the following pattern:

$$
\begin{array}{lll}
(1) & A \longleftrightarrow A & 25 \text{ per cent} \\
(2) & A \longleftrightarrow B & 25 \text{ per cent} \\
(3) & B \longleftrightarrow A & 25 \text{ per cent} \\
(4) & B \longleftrightarrow B & 25 \text{ per cent}
\end{array}
$$

Only in case (1) will the interlocutors understand one another on the problem of conservation (25 per cent of meetings). In cases (2) and (3) there will be misunderstandings or disagreements between interlocutors, and in case (4) they will not even understand that there is a problem. It is therefore evident that mastery of a conceptual problem must be far above the 50-per-cent level in adults if such a notion is to be incorporated into the collective representations of the society.

However, it can be validly argued that if we do not find collective representations incorporating conservation of quantity, this may be because such an operation is unnecessary in the context of that society, and many individual members of that society may therefore have conservational skills that are manifested at the level of private thinking rather than in collective representations. Flavell and Wohlwill (1969) have adopted Chomsky's distinction between competence and performance to account for instances of the rapid learning of cognitive skills such as conservation taking place when members of traditional societies are given instruction. This suggests a latent ability which had not been developed by their culture. Dasen states:

Recurrently, there have been indications that the initial answer a child [or an adult] gives in a Piagetian task may not reflect his 'true' level of reasoning, i.e. the underlying structure or competence. In some cases, with very little 'help' (either further questioning, or additional task situations, or exposure to other operational tasks, or training procedures), they seem to be able to 'actualize' the latent structure. (Dasen 1977: 172)

For example, Bovet's experiments with unschooled adult peasants in Algeria showed in experiments with conservation of weight that in the course of talking with the experimenter they soon moved to a grasp of conservation: 'These adults' reactions seem to replicate in a condensed sequence the developmental trends noted in the children where an initial non-operational conservation finally becomes, at a later stage, an explicit conservation judgement' (Bovet 1974: 325).

It certainly seems that the reason for lack of conservation in *that* culture is that it is irrelevant to practical needs, and that if the needs changed, as, for example, by the introduction of modern technology, the adults would rapidly manifest their latent grasp of conservation of weight. I discuss below the problems in the interpretation of Luria's data on the Uzbeks, in the absence of ethnographic data on the language and culture of the Uzbeks.

But the notion of 'competence' is inherently vague on a crucial issue—just how much 'special training', of the sort the visiting psychologist provides, has to be given? After all, many ideas are obvious when they are pointed out, such as Cartesian co-ordinates, but this does not mean that they can be discovered by all and sundry. It is evident that with sufficient training, perhaps over weeks or months, adolescents or adults in any society could probably be taught conservation. Would we in all such cases conclude that the ability had been latent, and had only needed exposure to the special training situation to 'actualize the latent structure'? And what would 'latency' mean in such a situation?

Again, it seems insufficient to argue that wherever there is a demand for a cognitive skill to become general in a society, that demand will be satisfied. For example, in New Guinea I was surprised that the Tauade had no verbal numbers beyond 'two', despite the fact that their ceremonial distributions of pieces of pork would have been considerably easier if they had had a system of verbal numbers. Indeed one finds that the Tauade are beginning to adopt Pidgin numerals for just this reason. And H. Gladwin (1970) in a study of fish-marketing in Ghana, shows that while the ability to make accurate probabilistic estimates of demand in various markets would be economically highly advantageous to the entrepreneurs, they do not have this ability and proceed by guesswork in a rough-and-ready manner. Merely because a society manages to get by with its existing repertoire of collective cognitive skills it does not demonstrate that these are wholly adequate to its needs, or that cognitive demand will be met by cognitive supply.

The fact that a society does not display a particular cognitive skill in a high proportion of its population is therefore likely to be the result of two factors—that it is not developed in many of them as a result of general environmental factors, and that it is not relevant in that society, though as we have just noted, 'relevance' is not at all easy to define. However, as anthropologists, we are not concerned with whether an ability is latent, if the means for developing it (such as special instruction by visiting psychologists) are not normally present in that society. As Dasen says, the experimental tasks

... measure the spontaneous use of the concepts; the results could be seen as measures of the probability with which these particular concepts would be used in everyday situations, and are thus meaningful. They would not necessarily be measures of the cognitive 'competence' to use the concepts involved, nor to use concrete operations in general. (Dasen 1977: 195–6)

The acceptance of a model of cognition derived from developmental psychology will also require fundamental rethinking of another basic element in Durkheim's theory—the social function of religion in the maintenance of social solidarity.

Faced with what, to him, were the evident absurdities of many primitive beliefs and practices, Durkheim tried to explain how such gross errors had nevertheless managed to flourish and persist into modern society. For this he had two answers. One was based on his linear model of causation, by which the group sentiments of man were facts of nature and in turn produced social groups, which in turn were the basis of collective representations. Thus collective representations are ultimately reflections of natural facts and therefore in a sense 'true'. (Lévi-Strauss puts forward a very similar argument to show that since the brain is a natural phenomenon, and the structure of language is based on the structure of the brain, as well as being the basis of cognitive organization, therefore the structure of thought is a reflection of the structure of nature.) This argument is evidently fallacious since, as Chomsky points out, a computer could easily be programmed to produce an output wholly contradictory to the principles on which the computer itself was built.

A rather more convincing argument for the social function of religion is the following:

... it is an essential postulate of sociology that a human institution cannot rest upon an error and a lie ... If it were not founded in the nature of things, it would have encountered in the facts a resistance over which it could never have triumphed. So when we commence the study of primitive religions, it is with the assurance that they hold to reality and express it ... one must know how to go underneath the symbol to the reality which it represents and which gives it its meaning. The most barbarous and the most fantastic rites and the strangest myths translate some human need, some aspect of life, either individual or social. (Durkheim 1947: 14)

There is, in the first place, no evident relationship between human needs and the facts of life, and it is a matter of common observation that political ideologies and systems of religious beliefs may be emotionally satisfying almost in proportion to the amount of fantasy they contain. Secondly, we do not encounter facts directly: we interpret them according to our existing beliefs and cognitive structures, so that what is to count as a 'resistance' from the facts, especially to primitive religion, is hard to understand. If it can be shown, moreover, that primitive religion is but one aspect of the cognitive processes developed in non-literate societies, if magic, myth, ritual, 'animism', psychomorphic causality, and so on are the spontaneous products of the human mind when it exists in a certain environment, then the whole question of the fundamental social value of religion and magic proposed by Durkheim is raised in quite new terms. For it can now be maintained that while religion and its attendant rituals, with magic and sorcery, may have the *effect* of cementing social bonds, this so-called 'function' will be a mere spin-off from a more basic propensity of the human mind to think in religious and magical terms when in a certain milieu. While these effects may exist, they will have to be empirically demonstrated and not just assumed as an axiom, and in any case will have no explanatory value whatever in telling us why religious and magical beliefs are universal in primitive societies.

(Not only does social solidarity often seem to be a *precondition* of ritual collaboration rather than a consequence, but in the case of magic and sorcery it is hard to see how the belief that many of one's tribulations are the product of human or supernatural malice can do other than *raise* the level of social tension, even if one discharges that tension by magical remedies rather than by violence.)

Rationalist philosophers and sociologists such as Durkheim, Frazer, and Lévy-Bruhl have treated supernatural beliefs not only as peculiarly characteristic of the primitive mind, but as presenting one of our greatest obstacles to understanding it. This last point seems to me to be largely nonsense. Supernatural beliefs are found in all human societies, primitive or not, and are one of the best testimonies to the basic similarity of the human mind; certainly as an ethnographer I have found that native beliefs in God, culture-heroes, ghosts, spirits, and witches have presented far fewer conceptual problems than basic classificatory categories. The real difficulty of primitive thought is that so much of it is expressed in action and concrete symbolism and encapsulated in social institutions and customs—that it is, in short, inarticulate.

As far as the truth and falsity of supernatural beliefs[4] and their

---

[4] Needham (1972) has conclusively shown that there is no faculty of 'belief', and that the concept is indeed one of bewildering complexity. Mindful of these difficul-

conflict with 'facts' are concerned, it is essential to distinguish between what is believed in and the way in which these beliefs are arrived at and justified. Durkheim's emphasis on the *form* of collective representations and his disregard for the manner in which they are understood by individuals (consistently with his view of the mind as a passive receptacle of preformed ideas) made the survival of religion in modern society much harder to account for than if he had recognized that what is outwardly the same belief can be understood at different cognitive levels. Because collective representations are not passively absorbed, but are in a dynamic and constantly changing relationship with the cognitive processes of individuals, it is on this basis, together with environmental and technological changes, that culture evolves, and this is why beliefs which seem to be diagnostic of early cultural stages can survive into more advanced stages—they are no longer the same sort of belief at all. Thus even if it is true that supernatural beliefs and agencies are more widely believed in among primitives, and permeate their customs and institutions more thoroughly than in our society, that is no justification for assuming, for example, as Durkheim grotesquely did, that belief in transubstantiation is a survival of that indissociation between species which he attributed to Australian Aborigines. The Christian beliefs of an Irish peasant and of a Jesuit theologian will evidently have certain essential features in common, but will be understood and justified at quite different cognitive levels in each case.

In Chapter 10 I shall consider the grounds for regarding some supernatural beliefs as founded upon psycho-somatic and paranormal phenomena. Clearly, to the extent that there is empirical confirmation for such beliefs which would convince a member of our own society as readily as a primitive, it is quite mistaken to regard belief in supernatural beings as *in itself* diagnostic of pre-operatory thought.

2. LANGUAGE AND THOUGHT

Language, as both the prime vehicle of thought (at least in its more advanced forms) and as the collective representation which seems

---

ties, I use the term 'belief' sparingly in this book, and where I do it should be construed in the sense of 'received ideas, dogma, orthodoxy, general notions', when collective representations are concerned, and as 'suppose', 'take to be the case' when individual thought processes are referred to (see Needham 1972: 6).

to owe least to the modes of thought of individuals, requires separate and extensive discussion in a chapter devoted to showing how conventional anthropological theories of the relation between collective representations and individual thought processes are mistaken.

In any discussion of the relation of language to thought, it is essential to distinguish between language and speech; language being the totality of syntactical forms and rules, and the lexicon which is associated with them, while speech is the actual use made of language by people in their everyday utterances.

At the level of speech we may expect, and in fact do find, great differences between the usages of the educated and those of the uneducated speakers of the same language, and between primitives and ourselves when we speak their languages—as in the case of missionaries. The kinds of speech characteristics that are relevant to differences in thought patterns are sentence length, use of dependent clauses, hesitation, use of stock phrases, reliance on gestures, facial expression, tone, pitch, and volume, and dependence on the implicit contextual situation rather on explicit verbal ways of conveying meaning. We may expect to find that literacy and schooling, in particular, and types of social relation, e.g. those that encourage individuation as opposed to those that encourage group solidarity, especially of an affective type, will have considerable impact on speech patterns, and that there will be some similarities in this respect between primitive peoples generally and unskilled manual labourers in our own society. Bernstein (1971) for example, on the basis of his studies of the different speech patterns employed by working-class and middle-class adolescents in British society, has described two modes of speech which he calls elaborated and restricted codes, or formal and public speech.

The restricted code (typical of unskilled working-class speech) is distinguished by short, grammatically simple sentences, a preference for the active voice, a simple and repetitive use of conjunctions, frequent short commands and questions, a rigid and limited use of adjectives and adverbs, the infrequent use of impersonal pronouns as subjects, a symbolism with a low order of generality, and the reliance on implicit meanings, as well as a large number of idiosyncratic traditional phrases, and repetitious dialogue which reinforces affective elements in relationships and discourages analysis. The simple verbal structure may limit the possibility of language use in expressing process. Conjunctions are not used as important logical distributors of meaning and sequence, and this results in crude linguistic renderings of logical modifications and stress. The limited and rigid use of adjectives and adverbs severely reduces the individual qualification of objects (nouns) and modifications of processes (verbs).

While some of these characteristics of the restricted code may be culturally specific to the British, they are generally relevant to Konso and Tauade speech patterns as I experienced them, and there is good reason to expect that they will occur widely among primitive peoples generally, though further research will obviously be needed to establish the extent of this generality.

But these differences in speech patterns are superficial in relation to the basic grammar of the language. As Chomsky says,

As participants in a certain culture we are naturally aware of the great differences in ability to use language, in knowledge of vocabulary, and so on that result from differences in native ability and from differences in conditions of acquisition; we naturally pay much less attention to the similarities and to common knowledge, which we take for granted. But if we manage to establish the requisite psychic distance, if we actually compare the generative grammars that must be postulated for different speakers of the same language, we find that the similarities that we take for granted are quite marked and that the divergences are few and marginal. (Chomsky 1972: 79)

So the existence and nature of *language*, as a unique manifestation of the human mind and the principal means by which thoughts are communicated, raises a number of fundamental issues in the discussion of primitive thought. It could be argued that in so far as language is basic to human thought (*if* it is), and the fundamental characteristics of language, such as Chomsky's 'universal grammar', are found among all peoples, this would imply that all minds are fundamentally similar, and therefore the developmental paradigm must be false. If, on the other hand, there are developmental stages of cognitive growth, then these should be manifested in different types of language, and again, if there are different types of language, then these should of themselves produce different types of thought. All these theories make one common assumption—that the cognitive processes employed in problem solving, learning, and in our interaction generally with people and things are linguistic in nature. But as we have seen in the previous chapter, this is a largely false assumption, since language is only one aspect of thought, and may itself be put to different cognitive uses at the different developmental stages.

Jespersen (1922) rejects the commonly held belief of linguists that there is no such thing as a primitive language, and proposes a number of criteria by which the degree of development from the primitive state of language can be assessed. Phonologically, there is a tendency to make pronunciation easier, so as to lessen muscular effort; the gradual disappearance of tone and pitch accent; and diminishing modulation of sentence melody. Grammatically, 'the evolution of language shows a progressive tendency from inseparable irregular conglomerations to freely and regularly combinable short elements' (Jespersen 1922: 429). Increased differentiation between word and sentence is of particular significance:

A characteristic feature of the structure of languages in their early stages is that each form of a word (whether verb or noun) contains in itself several minor modifications which, in the later stages, are expressed separately (if at all), that is, by means of auxiliary verbs or propositions (Ibid. 421)

and he gives the example of the Latin *cantavisset* = (1) 'Sing', (2) Pluperfect, (3) Subjunctive, (4) active, (5) 3rd person, (6) Singular.

This differentiation and specialization is accompanied by the increased regularization of morphology and syntax—'the tendency is more and more to denote the same thing by the same means in every case . . .' (ibid. 425) and by the increasing use of general terms.

If these evolutionary characteristics are valid they are clearly consistent with the paradigm of developmental psychology, and also have many parallels with other areas of thought; but within a language such as Latin, which would be relatively primitive by these criteria, it is still possible for thinking to be expressed at the formal level—after all, Newton first published his *Principia* in Latin. Again, the first growth of Greek philosophy in Ionia was clearly not a reflection of linguistic change, but resulted from social factors such as experience of different philosophies and belief systems (from Scythia, Persia, Babylonia, and Egypt), the socially heterogeneous nature of the communities, the phonetic alphabet which made literacy more easily accessible, and the existence of a legal system not only written in public codes, but arrived at with the consent of the community to serve definite ends.

So while there may be developmental characteristics of language that are consistent with Piaget's theory, the ability of speakers to transcend these limitations and to adapt their language to any level of thought means that the existence of such characteristics tells us nothing definite about the levels of thinking in which its speakers will be proficient.

Lévy-Bruhl is typical of anthropologists in believing that the ideas, categories, and knowledge of a society are encapsulated in its language, and are incorporated ready-made into the mind of the child as he acquires that language:

Relations are expressed by judgments only after the food for thought has first been well digested, and subjected to elaboration, differentiation, and classification. Judgment deals with ideas which have been rigidly defined, and these are themselves the proof and product of previous logical processes. This previous work, in which a large number of successive analyses and syntheses occur and are recorded, is received *ready made* [my emphasis] by each individual in our communities when he first learns to talk, by means of the education inseparably bound up with his natural development; so much so indeed that certain philosophers have believed in the supernatural origin of language. (Lévy-Bruhl 1926: 107)

In this he concurred with Durkheim: 'Now it is unquestionable that language, and consequently the system of concepts which it translates, is the product of a collective elaboration. What it expresses is the manner in which society as a whole represents the facts of experience. The ideas which correspond to the diverse elements of language are thus collective representations' (Durkheim 1947: 482).

Leach has a similar view of the priority of linguistic categories in relation to the thought of individuals:

I postulate that the physical and social environment of a young child is perceived as a continuum.[5] It does not contain any intrinsically separate 'things'. The child, in due course, is taught to impose upon this environment a kind of discriminating grid which serves to distinguish the world as being composed of a large number of separate things, each labelled with a name. This world is a representation of our language categories, not vice

[5] It is all very well for Leach to 'postulate' that the young child perceives the physical world as a continuum, but how does he *know*? The answer is that he does not, but, like so many anthropologists and philosophers, prefers to base his theories on his own home-grown speculations rather than finding out from experimental psychologists what the facts of the matter really are.

versa. Because my mother tongue is English, it seems self-evident that *bushes* and *trees* are different kinds of things. I would not think this unless I had been taught that it was the case.

Now if each individual has to learn to construct his own environment in this way, it is crucially important that the basic discriminations should be clear-cut and unambiguous. There must be absolutely no doubt about the difference between *me* and *it*, or between *we* and *they*. But how can such certainty of discrimination be achieved if our normal perception displays only a continuum? A diagram may help. Our uninhibited (untrained) perception recognizes a continuum (Figure [4]).

Figure 4. The line is a schematic representation of continunity in nature. There are no gaps in the physical world.

We are taught that the world consists of 'things' distinguished by names; therefore we have to train our perception to recognize a discontinuous environment (Figure [5]).

Figure 5. Schematic representation of what in nature is named. Many aspects of the physical world remain unnamed in natural languages.

We achieve this second kind of trained perception by means of a simultaneous use of language and taboo. Language gives us names to distinguish the things; taboo inhibits the recognition of those parts of the continuum which separate the things (Figure [6]).

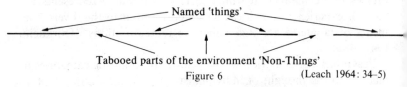

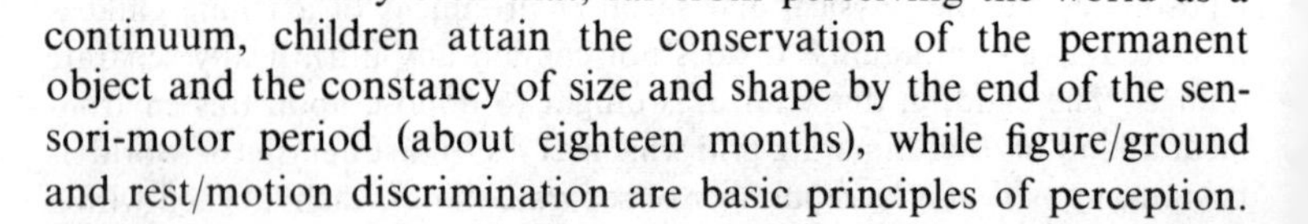

Figure 6   (Leach 1964: 34–5)

We have already seen that, far from perceiving the world as a continuum, children attain the conservation of the permanent object and the constancy of size and shape by the end of the sensori-motor period (about eighteen months), while figure/ground and rest/motion discrimination are basic principles of perception. This capacity to distinguish between objects, to recognize the same object and those resembling it, and to abstract perceptual attributes, is achieved without any linguistic assistance whatsoever. Indeed, in the early stages of language acquisition words have an extremely vague and unstable association with perceived objects. The recognition that the world is full of discontinuities and of stable objects, discrete properties, and discrete types of environment not only is non-linguistic in origin, but is shared by all animals, and is of course basic to their survival.

Moreover, if we learned to discriminate between things only as a result of being taught our mother tongue, it is impossible, on Leach's assumptions, to explain the origins of language at all. While language, like all collective representations, responds more slowly to experience than individual representations do, there can not be the slightest doubt that vocabulary (as distinct from syntax) is ultimately the product of the way in which its speakers interact with each other and with their environment. Thus the English people do not distinguish between 'tree' and 'bush' simply because the English language by some accident happens to have separate words for these kinds of things; the words themselves came to be employed in the way that they are because bushes and trees have a number of distinct properties, such as suitability for firewood, building materials, and quickness of growth, besides such morphological characteristics as the presence or absence of a main stem, which are relevant to the work of farmers, gardeners, and herbalists. The ethnographic literature is replete with examples of elaborate terminological classifications of phenomena, such as Nuer colour terms for cattle, Eskimo categories of snow, or Bedouin categories of horse, which are the linguistic response to the use these peoples make of their physical environment and to the discrete characteristics of that environment, which are sufficiently recurrent and relevant to merit distinctive terms. Leach's theory of reality as a continuum artificially broken up by the culturally generated categories of language is one of the main pillars of cultural relativism, and of the prevailing view of collective representation as transcending and independent of the thought processes of individuals.

Lévi-Strauss goes further, and has argued that the structural principles elucidated in respect of phonology by de Saussure, Jakobson, and Troubetzkoy are general cognitive principles of the mind as a whole, and can be expected to be reflected in a wide variety of social institutions and modes of classification:

... the material out of which language is built is of the same type as the material out of which the whole culture is built: logical relations, oppositions, correlations, and the like. Language, from this point of view, may appear as laying a kind of foundation for the more complex structures

which correspond to the different aspects of culture. (Lévi-Strauss 1963: 68–9)
[and]
. . . there should be some kind of relationship between language and culture, because language has taken thousands of years to develop, and culture has taken thousands of years to develop, and both these processes have been taking place side by side within the same minds. (Ibid. 71)

If this type of correlation is valid,

The road will then be open for a comparative structural analysis of customs, institutions, and accepted patterns of behaviour. We shall be in a position to understand basic similarities between forms of social life, such as language, art, law and religion, that on the surface seem to differ greatly. (Ibid. 65)

But even at the biological level, it seems that the ability to speak is genetically fairly distinct from other manifestations of intelligence. Lenneberg (1964) states '. . . the ability to learn to understand and speak has a low correlation with measured IQ in man' (p. 78). He refers to an unpublished study by Brewer (1963) of the literature on the familial occurrence of language disabilities, and to Brewer's own investigation of an entire family with congenital language disability. This showed that while other areas of intelligence were usually unaffected, the specific genetic trait in question produced a combination of certain defects, including markedly delayed onset of speech, poor articulation persisting into the teens, poorly established hand preference, marked reading difficulties, and either complete inability or marked difficulty in acquisition of second languages. Lenneberg also points out that, in the same way, complete mastery of language can be found in people whose general intellectual functioning is grossly subnormal:

Children whose IQ is 50 at age 12 and about 30 at age 20 are completely in possession of language though their articulation may be poor and an occasional grammatical mistake may occur.

Thus, grossly defective intelligence need not implicate language; nor does the *absence* of language necessarily lower cognitive skills [up to a certain level]. For instance, congenitally deaf children have in many parts of the world virtually no language or speech before they receive instruction in school. When these pre-schoolers are given non-verbal tests of concept formation they score as high as their age peers who hear (Furth 1961; Rosenstein 1960; Oléron 1957). From these examples it appears that language and intelligence are to some extent at least independent traits. (Ibid. 80)

While language is unique to man, thought, in the sense of problem solving and going beyond the information given to new conclusions, is manifested by a wide range of species other than man, and in the case of man himself we find that language is not the only manifestation of thought and that its effective use has no simple correlation with other aspects of intelligence. It is a matter of common experience that a wide variety of human abilities are non-linguistic. As Vygotsky puts it,

Schematically, we may imagine thought and speech as two intersecting circles. In their overlapping parts, thought and speech coincide to produce what is called verbal thought. Verbal thought, however, does not by any means include all forms of thought or all forms of speech—there is a vast area of thought that has no direct relation to speech. The thinking manifested in the use of tools belongs in this area, as does practical intellect in general. (Vygotsky 1962: 47)

If thought and language were not distinct, it is hard to see, for example, how we could ever complete a complicated sentence, since the choice of the early words in the sentence depends to some extent on our knowledge of what the finished sentence will be, and the form of *this* knowledge cannot itself be verbal without involving speakers in an infinite regress. Evidently, we are quite capable of 'seeing' the objection to someone's argument which precedes our verbal formulation of this objection, even to ourselves. And again, we may recognize that two statements utterly unlike each other linguistically nevertheless express 'the same idea'.

Mathematics, like musical composition, while requiring to be taught by the use of words, cannot be comprehended in the same manner as language, and it is a truism that the major function of mathematical notation is to eliminate language as far as possible from mental processes. Similarly, diagrammatic representation, whose mastery is fundamental to many higher cognitive activities, is non-linguistic in nature, while at the more elementary levels of cognitive functioning, as Vygotsky says, we are all familiar with the degree of enlightenment that follows the actual handling of a tool or gadget when previously we have been baffled by the verbal instructions for its use. This last point again illustrates that basic principle of developmental psychology—that the ability to verbalize is subsequent to the ability to understand any aspect of the world in enactive form, or in terms of mental imagery. The use of language is not therefore simply a matter of sticking labels on things, but of learning to reconstruct enactive and image-based representations at the level of verbal thought. We can see, for example, that Piaget's children who succeed in mastering concrete operations are not displaying any greater linguistic skills than they possessed at the pre-operatory stage, in understanding better the use of *words*; their cognitive growth lies in the higher level of conceptual co-ordination.

While speech and the mastery of language are essential to the development of thought, according to Piaget, Vygotsky, and other developmental psychologists they have different roots in development, such that in speech there is a pre-conceptual stage, and in thought a pre-linguistic stage. In the course of a child's development he masters grammar many years before he masters logic of the formal type (if he does at all, depending on his educational experience). Vygotsky points out that there is a correct use of grammatical forms and structures before the child understands the logical operations for which they stand, e.g. the use of 'because', 'if', 'therefore', long before the child grasps causal, conditional, and implicative relations. 'He masters the syntax of speech before the syntax of thought.'

Word meanings are not static, but change developmentally according to experience, as Piaget demonstrated in his first book, *The Language and Thought of the Child*. As Vygotsky says,

The relation of thought to word is not a thing but a process, a continual movement back and forth from thought to word and from word to thought. In that process the relation of thought to word undergoes changes which themselves may be regarded as development in the functional sense. Thought is not merely expressed in words; it comes into existence through them. (Ibid. 125)

Mastery of language, in other words, is a developmental process, involving the individual's total experience, in which accommodation and assimilation are constantly at work, and not the imposition of ready-made categories in linguistic form on the individual mind by his culture. As Bruner says, the task of translating enactive and image-based thought into language is open-ended and never complete. The 'sense' of words is fluid, being the sum of all the psychological events aroused in our consciousness by the word. It is a dynamic, fluid, complex whole; meaning is only the most stable zone of sense, and senses change with context:

As we have said, every thought creates a connection, fulfills a function, solves a problem. The flow of thought is not accompanied by a simultaneous unfolding of speech. The two processes are not identical, and there is no rigid correspondence between the units of thought and speech. This is especially obvious when a thought process misfires—when, as Dostoevski put it, a thought 'will not enter words'. (Ibid. 149)

Vygotsky compares a thought to a cloud shedding a shower of words:

Precisely because thought does not have its automatic counterpart in words, the transition from thought to words leads through meaning. In our speech there is always the hidden thought, the subtext. (Ibid. 150)
[and]
A word devoid of thought is a dead thing, and a thought unembodied in words remains a shadow. The connection between them, however, is not a preformed and constant one. It emerges in the course of development, and itself evolves. To the Biblical 'In the beginning was the word', Goethe makes Faust reply 'In the beginning was the deed'. The intent here is to detract from the value of the word, but we can accept this version if we emphasize it differently: In the *beginning* was the deed. The word was not the beginning—action comes there first; it is the end of development, crowning the deed. (Ibid. 153)

Biology and developmental psychology therefore provide little support for the idea that language is itself the encapsulation of a culture's categories, that it is a transcendental map of thought, or that there is a homology between the structure of a language and other cognitive processes and cultural phenomena (a point to which we shall return in our discussion of Whorf). These contentions are supported by Chomsky in terms of linguistic theory. (I am not qualified, as an anthropologist, to say if Chomsky is right, but as a leading authority in his field his views must be given considerable weight.)

... there seems to be little useful analogy between the theory of grammar that a person has internalized and that provides the basis for his normal, creative use of language, and any other cognitive system that has so far been isolated and described; similarly, there is little useful analogy between the schema of universal grammar that we must, I believe, assign to the

mind as an innate character, and any other known system of mental organization. It is quite possible that the lack of analogy testifies to our ignorance of other aspects of mental function, rather than to the absolute
uniqueness of linguistic structure; but the fact is that we have, for the
moment, no objective reasons for supposing this to be true. (Chomsky
1972: 90)

Chomsky is also unimpressed by Lévi-Strauss's attempts to
apply the principles of phonological linguistics to other areas of
thought and culture;[6] referring to *The Savage Mind*, he says:

. . . I do not see what conclusions can be reached from a study of his
materials beyond the fact that the savage mind attempts to impose some
organisation on the physical world—that humans classify, if they perform
any mental acts at all. Specifically, Lévi-Strauss's well-known critique of
totemism seems to reduce to little more than this conclusion. (Ibid. 74)

The reasons he adduces for discounting the value of applying
structural linguistics to culture in this way are that (a) the phonological principles established by structural linguistics apply to a very
limited range of data, and (b), from the linguist's point of view,
what is truly significant are the generative rules linking meaning,
syntax, and phonetics, and the deep and surface structures of language, not the abstract nature of patterns at one level of language
alone:

For one thing, the structure of a phonological system is of very little
interest as a formal object; there is nothing of significance to be said, from
a formal point of view, about a set of forty-odd elements cross-classified in
terms of eight or ten features. The significance of structuralist phonology
as developed by Troubetzkoy, Jakobson, and others, lies not in the formal
properties of phonemic systems but in the fact that a fairly small number
of features that can be specified in absolute, language-independent terms
appear to provide the basis for the organization of all phonological systems . . . But if we abstract away from the specific universal set of features
and the rule systems in which they function, little of any significance remains. (Ibid. 74–5)

The structural patterns discovered by Jakobson and others,
which Lévi-Strauss regards as fundamental structures of the mind,
are in fact the epiphenomena of yet more fundamental systems of
rules:

[6] For a detailed critique of Lévi-Strauss's theory of the relation between language
and culture, see Moore and Olmsted 1952.

Furthermore, the idea of a mathematical investigation of language structures, to which Lévi-Strauss occasionally alludes, becomes meaningful only when one considers systems of rules with infinite generative capacity. There is nothing to be said about the abstract structure of the various patterns that appear at various stages of derivation. If this is correct, then one cannot expect structuralist phonology, in itself, to provide a useful model for investigation of other cultural and social systems. (Ibid. 75)

One would like to add, as an anthropologist, that even if Lévi-Strauss's programme had been more solidly based in linguistics, its range of application to problems of primitive thought has been extraordinarily narrow, in so far as it deals almost entirely with classification and in particular with the notion of binary oppositions and transformations of these. It has little to say about cognitive processes generating representations of causality, space, time, number, or conceptual realism and tells us nothing about the kinds of environmental factors that we might find related to primitive thought and problem solving and learning generally.

Cognitive structures, let alone collective representations, cannot be reduced to the forms of grammar, and if this were so it would preclude any developmental change in our concepts beyond the level attained by anyone who had mastered the grammar of his language. Concepts can develop in richness and variety, abstraction and generality, and in co-ordination, independently of any purely linguistic growth of skill, even though the more advanced levels of thought become increasingly dependent on verbal expression. Conversely, there is no inconsistency in saying that the syntax of a primitive language may be as complex as a European language, but that the thoughts actually expressed in that language will not rise to the level of formal or even concrete operations. This does not mean that a primitive language is *incapable* of being used for these higher levels of thought, but merely that its speakers may be incapable of so using it. There may be words that we translate as 'therefore', 'because', 'probably', 'some', and so on, but it does not follow that these words have the same implications for the natives as they would have for us as when, for example, we employ them in formal logic.

We shall find that many ideas and assumptions, cosmological categories and principles of classification, are embedded in action, social relations, and institutions in such a way as to render it extremely difficult for the members of these societies to analyse these ideas, categories, and assumptions in an explicit, verbal manner, and that they are thus in many cases below the level of the articulate consciousness of the members of the society. We have seen that operational thought, especially at the formal level, depends on the articulation of thought into words, or the cognitive equivalent of words, such as mathematical expressions and diagrams. In primitive thought, which is diffused in concrete symbolism, institutions, rituals, and customary observances, these conditions of articulability are not met. This does not mean, as anthropologists from Robertson Smith to Radcliffe-Brown and Mary Douglas have supposed, that the rites and customs actually *precede* thought—such a thing is impossible—but that much primitive thought, being encapsulated in action and concrete symbolism, is *non-linguistic* and not derived from the particular forms of the culture's language at all. So basic categories such as purity/impurity, order/disorder, culture/nature, sacred/secular, male/female, and so on have to be elicited by an examination of the total experience of the people, as represented in their institutions, customs, and symbolism. What the people *say* about their beliefs and institutions is therefore often absurd or meaningless or irrelevant, when taken as isolated verbal propositions, even if the linguistic meaning of their utterances is itself plain.

Indeed, the supposition that language of itself is the privileged vehicle of culturally defined concepts and categories can be challenged by the evident fact that in the use of language in social intercourse, the meaning of utterances is never contained by the linguistic content of those utterances alone, but depends on the *total* context of their use. Malinowski puts the essence of the matter thus:

A statement, spoken in real life, is never detached from the situation in which it has been uttered. For each verbal statement by a human being has the aim and function of expressing some thought or feeling actual at that moment and in that situation, and necessary for some reason or other to be made known to another person or persons—in order either to serve purposes of common action, or to establish ties of purely social communion, or else to deliver the speaker of violent feelings or passions. Without some imperative stimulus of the moment, there can be no spoken statement. In each case, therefore, utterance and situation are bound up inextricably with each other and the context of situation is indispensable for the understanding of the words. Exactly as in the reality of spoken or written languages, a word without *linguistic context* is a mere figment and stands for nothing by itself, so in the reality of a spoken living tongue, the utterance has no meaning except in the *context of situation*. (Malinowski 1923: 307)

It is not, therefore, in the context of primitive life that language functions as the encapsulation of thought, but only in the written reflections of scholars, such as philosophers or ethnographers. As Malinowski says:

The manner in which I am using it now, in writing these words, the manner in which the author of a book, or a papyrus or a hewn inscription has to use it, is a very far-fetched and derivative function of language. In this, language becomes a condensed piece of reflection, a record of fact or thought. In its primitive uses, language functions as a link in concerted human activity, as a piece of human behaviour. It is a mode of action and not an instrument of reflection. (Ibid. 312)

To this extent, as we shall discuss in the concluding chapter, the kind of propositional analysis of primitive thought indulged in by philosophers is quite misconceived, though I should not be misconstrued as implying that we can ignore what the natives say, and rely solely on what they do—this would only be replacing one absurdity by another. My point is that we must take account of the fact that language is only one manifestation of thought, that it cannot therefore be taken as a map *par excellence* of thinking, either individually or collectively, and it is the ways in which language is put to use in verbal communication within a culture that will be more significant than any syntactical features it may possess (such as grammatical gender, or distinction between word and sentence). So because in the circumstances of primitive society collective representations and institutions are not exposed to critical analysis and argument, and have not had to be codified, generalized, or discussed, they retain many of the characteristics of pre-operatory thought, such as being incoherent, inconsistent, dogmatically absolutist, governed by no explicit and clear purposes, bound up in concrete imagery, affective in tone, and largely incommunicable to outsiders. They will thus reinforce the pre-operatory thinking of their individual members, and provide yet another inhibition to the development of concrete and formal operations.

We have not so far discussed in detail the implications of

Whorf's[7] theory that the structural forms[8] of language of a particular culture constrain thinking, so that members of that culture are impelled to conceive the world in certain ways and are hindered or prevented from conceiving it in other ways. His theory can best be presented by giving some specific instances of the way in which he applied it to the structure of European languages and thought, on the one hand, and to that of Hopi language and thought, on the other. (The Hopi are North American Indians of the pueblo culture of Arizona.)

One of the basic characteristics of what he calls Standard Average European (SAE), which in practice means English, is that it distinguishes between substantives and verbs, thus creating a polar opposition between things and actions. (While Whorf does not advert to the fact, this distinction is, of course, found in innumerable languages including those spoken by primitive peoples.) But if 'strike', 'turn', 'run' are verbs because they denote temporary or short-lasting events and actions, why is 'fist' a noun? It is also a temporary event. In Hopi 'lightning', 'wave', 'flame', and so on are verbs, since Hopi classify by duration types, and events of necessarily brief duration must always be verbs in their language. More generally, the SAE distinction between substantive and verb is, in his view, basic to subject–predicate logic, notions of actor and

---

[7] Sapir once wrote: 'The "real world" is to a large extent unconsciously built upon the language habits of the group. The worlds in which different societies live are *distinct* worlds, not merely the same world with different labels attached. We see and hear and otherwise experience very largely as we do because the language habits of our community predispose certain choices of interpretation' (Sapir 1929a: 209).

But while it is customary to link Sapir's name with Whorf's and to refer to the Sapir–Whorf hypothesis of linguistic relativity, Bruner suggests (1965b: 51) that this involves a misrepresentation of Sapir's theoretical position, since Sapir also recognized 'the possibility of the growth of speech being in a high degree dependent on the development of thought', and that the relation between speech and thought was one of interaction and mutual refinement, rather than of straightforward linguistic determinism.

[8] Fishman (1974: 74–5) points out that, especially in his earlier work, Whorf concentrated on *lexical* features and their effects on thought, and that 'the emphasis on language *structure* as the critical feature in his linguistic relativity hypothesis is actually a later and more mature level of Whorf's own thinking in this area.' One would not wish to deny that the existence of specialized vocabularies in certain languages makes it much easier to discriminate such phenomena, but this observation has been made by many others besides Whorf and is, by comparison with his theory of the relation of linguistic structures to thought, fairly trivial, and I shall not consider it further here.

action, things and relations between them, objects and their attributes—'the notion became ingrained that one of these classes of entities can exist in its own right, but that the verb cannot exist without an entity of the other class, the "thing" class, as a peg to hang it on' (Whorf 1956: 241).[9] We, SAE speakers, are thus constrained to read into nature fictional acting entities, simply because our verbs must have substantives in front of them, e.g. English 'a light flashed' as opposed to Hopi 'flash [occurred]'.

SAE rules of grammar 'often require us to name a physical thing by a binomial that splits the reference into a formless item plus a form' (141), e.g. 'a cup of coffee'. In Hopi, 'the noun itself implies a suitable type—body or container. One says, not "a glass of water", but "*ka.yi*", "a water" ... The language has neither need for nor analogies on which to build the concept of existence as a duality of formless item and form. It deals with formlessness through other symbols than nouns' (141–2).

Thus the structure of SAE languages leads their speakers to think in terms of substance as formless and distinct from its manifestations in particular shapes. 'So with SAE people the philosophic "substance" and "matter" are also the naive idea; they are instantly acceptable, "common sense"' (141). (Whorf in fact provides no evidence whatever that the ordinary SAE speaker finds the philosophic concepts of 'substance' and 'matter' instantly acceptable.)

The distinctive SAE treatment of substantives and verbs is in his theory basic to an objectification or spatialization of experience, especially significant in the case of our representations of time. In our language and culture

Concepts of time lose contact with the subjective experience of 'becoming later' and are objectified as counted *quantities*, especially as lengths, made up of units as a length that can be visibly marked off into inches. A 'length of time' is envisioned as a row of similar units, like a row of bottles . . .

In Hopi there is a different linguistic situation. Plurals and cardinals are used only for entities that form or can form an objective group. There are no imaginary plurals, but instead ordinals used with singulars. Such an expression as 'ten days' is not used. The equivalent statement is an operational one that reaches one day by a suitable count. 'They stayed ten days' becomes 'They stayed until the eleventh day' or 'They left after the tenth

---

[9] All subsequent references to Whorf are taken from this edition of his papers.

day'. 'Ten days is greater than nine days' becomes 'The tenth day is later than the ninth'. Our 'length of time' is not regarded as a length but as a relation between two events in lateness. Instead of our linguistically promoted objectification of that datum of consciousness we call 'time', the Hopi language has not laid down any pattern that would cloak the subjective 'becoming later' that is the essence of time. (140)

According to Whorf, SAE converts durations into things: we talk of '*at* sunset' or '*in* winter' just as we say '*at* a corner' or '*in* an orchard'. Just as our language provides the basis for formless concepts such as 'substance' and 'matter', so we have a formless item 'time':

We have made it by using 'a time' i.e. an occasion or a phase, in the pattern of a mass noun, just as from 'a summer' we make 'summer' in the pattern of a mass noun. Thus with our binomial formula we can say and think 'a moment of time, a second of time, a year of time'. Let me again point out that the pattern is simply that of 'a bottle of milk' or 'a piece of cheese'. Thus we are assisted to imagine that 'a summer' actually contains or consists of such-and-such a quantity of 'time'.

In Hopi however all phase terms, like 'summer, morning' etc., are not nouns but a kind of adverb, to use the nearest SAE analogy. They are a formal part of speech by themselves, distinct from nouns, verbs, and even other Hopi 'adverbs'. Such a word is not a case form or even a locative pattern, like 'des Abends' or 'in the morning'. It contains no morpheme like one of 'in the house' or 'at the tree'. It means 'when it is morning' or 'while morning phase is occurring'. One does not say 'it's a hot summer', or 'summer is hot'; summer is not hot, summer is only *when* conditions are hot, when heat occurs. There is no objectification, as a region, an extent, a quantity of the subjective duration-feeling. Nothing is suggested about time except the perpetual 'getting later of it'. And so there is no basis here for a formless item answering to our time. (142–3)

[Thus the Hopi have] ... no general notion or intuition of time as a smooth flowing continuum in which everything in the universe proceeds at an equal rate, out of a future, through a present, into a past. (57)

The metaphysics underlying our own language, thinking and modern culture (I speak not of the recent and quite different relativity metaphysics of modern science) imposes upon the universe two *grand cosmic* forms, space and time; static three-dimensional infinite space, and kinetic one dimensional uniformly and perpetually flowing time—two utterly separate and unconnected aspects of reality (according to this familiar way of thinking).

The flowing realm of time is, in turn, the subject of a three-fold division: past, present, and future. (59)

The Hopi universe has two cosmic forms: (1) the manifested or objective, and (2) the potentially manifesting, or subjective.

[The first] includes all that is or has been accessible to the senses, the historical physical universe, in fact, with no attempt to distinguish between present and past, but excluding everything that we call future. The subjective or manifesting comprises all that we call future, *but not merely this*; it includes, equally and indistinguishably, all that we call mental—everything that appears or exists in the mind or, as the Hopi would prefer to say, in the *heart*, not only the heart of man, but the heart of animals, plants, and things, and behind and within all the forms and appearances of nature in the heart of nature, and . . . in the very heart of the cosmos itself. . . . [The Unmanifest] is the realm of expectancy, of desire and purpose, of vitalizing life, of efficient causes, of thought thinking itself out from an inner realm (the Hopian Heart) into manifestation. (59–60)

. . . the Hopi see this burgeoning activity in the growth of plants, the forming of clouds and their condensation in rain, the careful planning out of the communal activities of agriculture and architecture, and in all human hoping, wishing, striving, and taking thought; and as most especially concentrated in prayer . . . (62)

In spatial terms, the subjective or Unmanifest is closely associated with the vertical and inner, the objective or Manifest is associated with the horizontal and exterior. The Manifest is the great cosmic form of extension, and includes all intervals and distance, all seriation and number. Its distance includes what we call time in the sense of the temporal relations between events which have already happened; the element of time is not separated from whatever element of space enters into the operations (62–3).

What happens at a distant village, if actual (objective) and not a conjecture (subjective) can be known 'here' only later. If it does not happen 'at this place', it does not happen 'at this time'; it happens at 'that' place and at 'that' time. (63)

[Thus the Hopi culture] . . . recognises psychological time, which is much like Bergson's 'duration', but this 'time' is quite unlike the mathematical time, T, used by our physicists. Among the peculiar properties of Hopi time are that it varies with each observer, does not permit of simultaneity, and has zero dimensions, i.e. it cannot be given a number greater than one. The Hopi do not say 'I stayed 5 days' but 'I left on the fifth day'. (216)

Hopi verbs do not distinguish between present, past, and future of the event itself, but must always indicate what type of validity the *speaker* intends the statement to have. They can distinguish between momentary, continued, and repeated occurrences, and indicate the actual sequence of reported events. Thus the universe can be described without recourse to a dimensional concept of time. Nor is there any word really equivalent to our 'speedy' or 'rapid'. What translates these terms is usually a word meaning 'intense' or 'very' accompanying any verb of motion. We should have to introduce some term like 'intensity' to render 'speed' or 'rapid' into Hopi.

I have set out Whorf's description of Hopi concepts of time, space, cause, and matter at some length partly to provide the reader with sufficient knowledge of the evidence Whorf thinks relevant to demonstrating the effects of language on a culture's patterns of thought, but also to provide what the reader will come to recognize as a textbook case of pre-operatory thought. Hopi time, for example, is presented as non-universal—its rate varies from place to place, and there is no notion of the potential simultaneity of events at different places; it is not seen as having a uniform rate, since this varies according to the subjective experience of each observer; and it is not homogeneous, since it varies from observer to observer. Whorf mistakenly supposes that 'psychological' time, the individual's subjective impression of duration, is the essence of time, but as we shall see in Chapter VIII, this is only one aspect of time, and the most primitive. The Hopi are concerned with the quality of events—their continuity, repetition, and the sequence of particular events—but they cannot conceptualize velocity and clearly are not interested in comparing and co-ordinating different durations at different velocities or similar velocities over different distances or durations. In all these respects the Hopi concept of time is not strangely different from our Western notions of time, but an excellent example of pre-operatory time.

Again, we find that their conceptions of causation are essentially in the form of desires, purposes, and intentions, rather than of objective interactions, some of which may be random and unwilled, or of mechanistic causation. This, too, is a clear case of psychomorphic causality quite consistent with their pre-operatory understanding of time.

In so far, then, as Hopi thought clearly falls into patterns established by both developmental psychology and comparative ethnography (since these notions of time and causality are typical of primitive thought generally), neither of which takes account of the linguistic structures of the groups of subjects investigated, it is impossible to argue that certain distinctive features of the Hopi language are responsible for these characteristics of their thought, since they can be found in speakers of totally different languages.

Moreover—and this is a crucial test of Whorf's hypothesis—if he were right about the effects of language structure on thought, we should find that children in our own society were capable of what he calls 'scientific' thought about time, causality, quantification, number, process, and understanding the properties of subject–predicate relations and substance–accident relations as soon as they had mastered the elements of English or French grammar. We know that this is not the case. We should also have found that this 'scientific' thinking had been universal throughout the history of the Indo-European speaking peoples, at every cultural level. But we know that these are in fact advanced conceptual processes, only attained historically in auspicious circumstances and, in the case of formal thought, being dependent on many years of schooling and literacy. One of the defects of Whorf's theory is that he confuses 'science' with concrete operations instead of realizing that these modes of thought are only the foundation of science, and had to be established in a section of the population before true science could take root.

More generally, his fallacy is to suppose that any language imposes a rigid set of conceptual restraints on its speakers, whereas the findings of developmental psychology show how children assimilate the language of adults to their own distinctive conceptual structures. Thus meaning can very easily escape from the bonds of syntax and conventional word meanings, as shown by the success of missionary translators of the Bible, for example, and experienced by every ethnographer who has led his informants into discussion of what to them are unfamiliar ideas. As Cohen puts it,

... if any question arises about differences in the potential of different languages it should rather be about the ease or difficulty with which they lend themselves to the expression of different ideas than about the permanent possibilities and impossibilities that Whorf claimed to exist. When Hobbes asks whether in a language in which predication was expressed by the adjunction of subject and predicate rather than by a copula there would be any terms equivalent to 'entity', 'essence', 'essential', or 'essentiality', it is better to answer that in such a language it would be relatively more difficult to develop such a vocabulary than that it would be impossible. (Cohen 1966: 86–7)[10]

And Feuer notes in relation to concepts of time: 'Many languages ... have no future tense, and make use of such devices instead as the use of the present tense to convey futurity. There is no evidence that the people who use these languages have therefore confounded the present with the future in a metaphysical sense' (Feuer 1968: 413). Again, in relation to the ability of philosophers to overcome the apparent syntactical limitations of language:

The Aristotelian metaphysics has not been the exclusive property of the Indo-European languages. It is often overlooked that it was propounded and highly developed by Arabic and Hebrew thinkers even before it was espoused by the medieval Christian philosophers. The syntax of the Semitic language differs markedly from the European tongues, but Semitic syntactical rules proved no insuperable obstacle to the formulation of the Aristotelian ideas. Words were invented to express the novel metaphysical ideas. The Talmudists had been singularly averse to speculative notions, but the medieval Jewish philosophers contrived the necessary forms to convey the foreign concepts. (Ibid. 414)

It is also useless for Whorf to argue that Hopi thought is simply different from Western thought, and that

What we call 'scientific thought' is a specialization of the Indo-European type of language ... (246)

... such languages [as Hopi], which do not paint the separate object picture of the universe to the same degree as English and its sister tongues, point towards possible new types of logic and possible new cosmical structures. (241)

For it is possible to have different types of geometry or of logic only because these are axiomatic abstract systems with no empirical content. We do not find that logicians specializing in Boolean logic are incapable of grasping Aristotelian logic, or that physicists trained in the ideas of Newton could not understand Einstein. As Max Black says,

Yet [despite his relativism] Whorf manages after all to express his philosophy. In describing the 'deeper process of consciousness' upon which lan-

---

[10] There is a useful discussion of the philosophical issues raised by the Whorf hypothesis in Cohen 1966, §8, 'Meanings in a culture', and §9, 'Can a language be a prison?'.

guage is 'a superficial embroidery' (p. 239) he refutes his own claim that 'no individual is free to describe nature with absolute impartiality' (p. 239). Here is the familiar paradox that all general theories of the relativity of truth must brand themselves as biased or erroneous. (Black 1968: 436–7)

When it comes to world-views, to representations of how things actually are, we are entitled to ask of any alternative to our own, 'Is it empirically verifiable?', 'Does it embrace as wide a variety of phenomena as ours?', and 'Is it internally consistent?' It *may* legitimately be claimed that Hopi *thought* takes account of certain paranormal influences at work in the world, which our traditional science has until recently dismissed as superstition; to this extent it is fair to assert that it may be able to correct our view of the nature of things, but even in this respect Hopi thought is not dependent on the distinctive features of the Hopi language, since many other cultures with totally different languages have a similar philosophy. And to the extent that Hopi thought is incapable of analysing physical processes, and of co-ordinating relations of time and space, and has a conceptual realist, psychomorphic attitude to causality, it is evidently conceptually less powerful than our modes of thought.

Whorf hovers uneasily between the modest claim according to which language structures differ, therefore modes of classification differ, and the extreme position that 'language structures differ, therefore modes of reasoning differ, and all are equally valid, and some are more equally valid than others!', e.g.

... in their linguistic systems, though these systems differ widely, yet in the order, harmony, and beauty of the systems, and *in their respective subtleties and penetrating analysis of reality* [my emphasis], all men are equal. This fact is independent of the state of evolution as regards material culture, savagery, civilization, moral or ethical development, etc., a thing most surprising to the cultured European, a thing shocking to him, indeed a bitter pill! (263)

There is a fundamental confusion here in Whorf's notion of language, which conflates the undoubted structural subtleties of all known languages phonologically and syntactically and the kinds of ideas that can be expressed by these different languages. It is his notion of the 'cryptotype' that seems to lie at the heart of this confusion. The cryptotype

is a submerged, subtle, and elusive meaning, corresponding to no actual word, yet shown by linguistic analysis to be functionally important in the grammar. For example, the English particle UP meaning 'completely, to a finish', as in 'break it up, cover it up, eat it up, twist it up, open it up' can be applied to any verb of one or two syllables initially accented, *excepting* verbs belonging to four special cryptotypes. One is the cryptotype of dispersion without a boundary; hence one does not say 'spread it up, waste it up, spend it up, scatter it up, drain it up, or filter it up'. Another is the cryptotype of oscillation without agitation of parts; we don't say 'rock up a cradle, wave up a flag, wiggle up a finger, nod up one's head', etc. The third is the cryptotype of nondurative impact which also includes psychological reaction: kill, fight, etc., hence we don't say 'whack it up, tap it up, stab it up, slam it up, wrestle him up, hate him up'. The fourth is the verbs of directed motion, move, lift, pull, push, put, etc., with which *up* has the directional sense, 'upward', or derived senses, even though this sense may be contradicted by the verb and hence produce an effect of absurdity, as in 'drip it up'. Outside this set of cryptotypes *up* may be freely used with transitives in the completive-intensive use. (70–1)

Whorf applies this notion of cryptotype in the analysis of Hopi ideas, as in the following case where the object is to determine whether they believe that clouds are animate:

Let us suppose that an ethnologist discovers that the Hopi speak about clouds in their rain prayers, etc., as though clouds were alive. He would like to know whether this is some metaphor or special religious or ceremonial figure of speech, or whether it is the ordinary and usual way of thinking about clouds. Here is the sort of problem to which language might be able to give a very meaningful answer, and we immediately turn to it to see if it has a gender system that distinguishes living from nonliving things, and if so, how it classes a cloud. We find that Hopi has no gender at all. The traditional grammar of the pre-Boas period would stop at this point and think it had given an answer. But the correct answer can only be given by a grammar that analyzes covert as well as overt structure and meaning. For Hopi does distinguish an animate class of nouns *as a cryptotype* and only as a cryptotype. The crucial reactance is the way of forming a plural. When members of the Flute Society, e.g., are spoken of as Flutes, this (covertly) inanimate noun is pluralized in the animate way. But the word *?o.mâw* 'cloud', is always pluralized in the animate way; it has no other plural; it definitely belongs to the cryptotype of animateness. And so the question whether the animation of clouds is a figure or formality of speech or whether it stems from some more deep and subtly pervasive undercurrent of thought is answered, or at the least given a flood of new meaning. (79)

The problem is, however, to ascertain that a cryptotype, even if it can be shown to exist in a language, has more than a purely linguistic nature. Whorf does not show how the cryptotypes 'dispersion without a boundary', 'oscillation without agitation of parts', and 'non-durative impact which also includes psychological reaction', have any genuine existence at all other than as linguistic phenomena—with none of these verbs can 'up' be used to signify 'completion' because none of them is a verb compatible with the notion of completing or finishing. We are, however, given no reason to suppose that these cryptotypes are individually distinguished in other areas of thought. As Black says,

The chief difficulty lies in the claim that the cryptotypes *have meaning* for the unsophisticated native speaker. Whorf speaks of 'a sort of habitual consciousness' (p. 69); of 'a submerged, subtle, and elusive meaning' (p. 70); of a 'formless idea' (p. 71); a 'rising toward fuller consciousness . . . of linkage bonds' (p. 69), and so on. But it is hard to believe that the ordinary speaker is aware of a grammatical classification that takes all the virtuosity of a Whorf to discover. I doubt that the ordinary English speaker realises that the particle '*un*' can only be prefixed to transitive verbs of a 'covering, enclosing, and surface attaching meaning' (p. 71) that constitutes a prototype [sic, cryptotype]. Whorf himself must have the concept since he succeeds in expressing it; but the man in the English street simply uses '*un-*' in happy ignorance. Here I think Whorf commits the *linguist's fallacy* of imputing his own sophisticated attitudes to the speakers he is studying. The heuristic value of the notion of a cryptotype is manifested in its capacity to induce verifiable predictions (cf. the discussion of the imaginary verb *to flimmick* at p. 71); the rest is mythical psychology. (Black 1968: 433)

Greenberg addresses himself to this problem of inferring 'beliefs'—which he calls 'ethnosemes'—from linguistic forms—'linguisemes'—in which process of inference a knowledge of non-linguistic behaviour is in fact crucial to success.

The problem, then, is to discover under what circumstances ethnosemes, as opposed to linguisemes, can be defined in linguistic investigation. We cannot a priori decide that situations which in our culture are marked by no common denomination of behaviour might not have one in some other culture. Our evidence then must come from ethnographic observation of the conduct of the speakers to see if such elements can be defined in terms of the behaviour of the speakers.

Let us take as an example the Central Algonquian division of nouns into two classes which we will call, neutrally, I and II. Class I has singular *-a*, plural *-aki* (Bloomfield 1946: 94). Class II has singular *-i*, plural *-ali*, and there are other differences relating to pronominal reference. If we wish to specify the total meaning of the morphemes -*a*, -*aki*, (outside of the ethnosemes of number), we must take the following facts into consideration. Members of Class I include person, animals, spirits and large trees, tobacco, maize, apple, raspberry (but not strawberry), calf of the leg (but not the thigh), stomach, spittle, feather, bird's tail, horn, kettle, pipe for smoking, snowshoe, and a few others. The classification 'animate' covers a large part of this class, but what of the rest? Unless the actual behaviour of Algonquian speakers shows some mode of conduct common to all these instances such that, given this information, we could predict the membership of Class I, we must resort to purely linguistic characterization. If it turned out, for example, that speakers of Algonquian have a shrine to the raspberry and treat it like a spirit, while the strawberry is in the sphere of the profane, and if similar facts could be adduced regarding the other terms, then a definition of Class I affixes would be possible by reference to the non-linguistic behaviour of Algonquian speakers. I do not believe that the ethnographic facts about these peoples will allow of such a definition. Since all persons and animals are in Class I, we have at least one ethnoseme, but most of the other meanings can be defined only by a linguiseme.

Tautologic statements of similarity based on a valid ethnoseme, usually described by a grammatical label, are sometimes made. If, for example, we call I 'animate' and II 'inanimate', then the statement that the Central Algonquians conceive of kettles as animate is merely a tautologic statement of the grammatical fact. (Greenberg 1954: 15–16)

Returning to Whorf's argument that the form of pluralization of 'flutes' shows us that Hopi conceive clouds as animate, because 'flutes' when used to refer to human beings are given a plural form also used of persons and presumably animals, this is insufficient justification for concluding that it is 'animateness' that is the sole and sufficient criterion for the use of the 'animate', plural form. It might be, for example, that all nouns are given the 'animate' plural when used in a metaphorical sense; it is logically inadmissible to assume, as Greenberg has shown, that there is one single and definite criterion for the use of a particular linguistic form. If we wish to know if the Hopi think of clouds as animate—which they may well do (see Whorf, p. 62)—then the ethnographically correct procedure is to examine their beliefs and question them upon these directly. But in so far as we cannot use linguistic structures as definitive tests or indices of cognitive structures, but have to depend on behaviour, including, of course, statements of belief, we have no reason for concluding that linguistic structures stand in a one–one correspondence with thought structures.

Black points out that Whorf's theory of language and thought rests upon a metaphysic of reality as a continuum or flux, which language then dissects in an arbitrary fashion, such that the thought patterns of each linguistically distinct culture are all 'as good as' those of any other:

> Whorf is under the spell of a conception of 'raw experience' (p. 102) that is 'more basic than language' (p. 149), where all is motion and impermanence and even the contrast between past and present has yet to arise: 'If we inspect consciousness we find no past, present, future, but a unity embracing consciousness. EVERYTHING is in consciousness, and everything in consciousness Is, and is together.' (pp. 143–4). And the 'real time' of consciousness is a *becoming*: 'Where real time comes in is that all this in consciousness [the global unity of experience] is "getting later", changing certain relations in an irreversible manner' (p. 144).
>
> Well, it is futile to argue against this picture: insistence upon the continuity and flow of experience is unexceptionable but empty, since nothing imaginable is being denied; but it is a bold leap to the contention that customary reference to time-intervals and temporal relations involves falsification. When Whorf claims that 'if "ten days" be regarded as a group it must be as an "imaginary", mentally constructed group' (p. 139), he must be taking the logic of counting to require the simultaneous existence of the things counted. (Black 1968: 436)

It is this notion of reality as a continuum to which Leach appeals in his theory of language 'cutting up' reality into culturally determined categories. Black notes that this 'butchery' theory of language is also fundamental to Whorf's position:

> [He] speaks of the 'segmentation of nature' (p. 240) and the 'artificial chopping up of the continuous spread and flow of existence' (p. 253); he says 'we dissect nature' (pp. 213, 214) and 'cut' it up (p. 213) when we 'organize it into concepts' (p. 213), and all this 'largely because, through our mother tongue, we are parties to an agreement to do so, not because nature itself is segmented in that way exactly for all to see' (p. 240) ...
>
> The vocabulary of the operating theatre ('cutting', 'chopping', 'dissecting', 'segmenting') is out of place; to speak is not to butcher, *pace* Bergson and other critics of analysis. To dissect a frog is to destroy it, but to talk about the rainbow leaves it unchanged ... He subscribes, consciously or not, to the ancient metaphysical lament that to describe is *necessarily* to falsify. The flat unsatisfying answer is that Whorf, like many others, has

succumbed to the muddled notion that the function of speech is to *re-instate* reality. Well, the best recipe for apple pie can't be eaten but it would be odd to regard that as an inadequacy. (Ibid. 433–4)

Let us briefly summarize our conclusions on the question of language as (*a*) the basic tool of all cognitive processes, (*b*) the means by which reality is given stable conceptual form, and therefore (*c*) a 'transcendental' map of knowledge that is independent of the thinking of individuals, and purely social in nature.

1. From developmental psychology, it appears that language can be used for encoding or describing experience only when that experience has already been organized by non-linguistic means, by the co-ordination of action, and imagery. When the child begins to use language he has already organized his world at the sensorimotor level; deaf children without literacy perform comparably in non-verbal cognitive tasks with normal children at least until the age of about six.

2. Language becomes of progressively greater conceptual importance at the higher levels of thought, such as concrete and formal operations, but even here there are many examples of non-linguistic thinking—mathematics, music, diagrams, and mechanical relations.

3. Mastery of the grammar of a language in itself tells us little about the level at which a person will be able to function cognitively, and while there seem to be developmental characteristics of language, such that Latin may be classified as relatively primitive, it will always be possible for the thinking of individuals to transcend purely linguistic limitations.

4. One does not wish to deny that particular languages, both in syntax and lexicon, are capable of inhibiting the expression of certain ideas and facilitating others. But in the first place, it is a matter of *inhibiting* and *facilitating*, not of *preventing* or *determining*; and secondly, in so far as a limited version of the Whorfian hypothesis is acceptable, it does not apply to the most basic levels of thought, nor is there evidence that the different types of natural language require any reconsideration of the Piagetian levels of development.

5. It is therefore basically fallacious to suppose that there is any significant homology between conceptual and linguistic structures, which latter Chomsky regards as unique to language and incapable of providing a model for other cognitive structures.

6. What is really important for the kind of thinking that will prevail in a society is not whether the language has grammatical gender or a future tense in its verb form, but the extent to which language is used as a means of analysing experience and to which people are explicitly aware of language as a phenomenon distinct from the actual utterances of real people in particular contexts.

3

The Primitive Milieu and Cognitive Development

Having disposed of the major objections to the use of developmental psychology in the analysis of primitive thought, we are now in the position to consider how the particular characteristics of the primitive milieu are likely to affect cognitive development. In considering these factors we shall be looking to see how far they comprise a milieu in which symbolic imagery, rather than explicit verbal analysis and generalization, predominates in thinking; the extent to which the objectification of sensory experience and the dimensional analysis of the kind employed in concrete operations is necessary; the extent to which deliberate experiment and innovation are frequent necessities, with opportunities for encountering significantly different representations of the world; and the extent to which in general mobile, reversible, transformational structures of thought are generated, as opposed to static, context-bound, and action- and image-dominated thinking.

We shall deal first with people's interaction with their physical environment—how they are required to analyse its properties, experiment and quantify, plan their actions in relation to physical tasks—and the consequence for causal analysis of the absence of machines and technological processes generally. The next major topics of inquiry will be the methods of instruction by which children are taught, attitudes to questioning, and the value given to pure intelligence in such societies, the pressure to conformity and the repression of individual attitudes and their expression. Then we shall consider the extent to which primitive institutions are discussed and debated, and directed by clear purposes, and the degree to which members of these societies are exposed to substantially heterogeneous types of experience and belief systems both within their society and by contact with strangers. Finally, we shall examine the conclusions of cross-cultural developmental psychologists on the consequences of schooling and literacy for modes of thought in primitive society, work which sheds valuable new light on the kinds of social factors that stimulate cognitive growth.

1. THOUGHT AND PHYSICAL INTERACTION WITH THE ENVIRONMENT

It requires, for us, a concentrated act of the imagination to think of the world around us without the conceptual structures developed in the course of our education in a literate technological society.

In the primitive milieu, in which the average person spends his life in a very restricted geographical location, the dominant physical features of the environment readily assume absolute and static relations, associated with one another in perceptually familiar but conceptually unanalysed and irreversible configurations. For example, the tribes of the south-west coast of Papua live in an area where the central ranges of Papua New Guinea run roughly north-west to south-east; thus they became accustomed to seeing the sun rise over these mountains and set in the sea. When, during World War II, men from this area worked for the Government as carriers on the Kokoda Trail from Port Moresby to the north coast, they discovered to their amazement that on the far side of the ranges the sun rose in the sea and set over the mountains, a total reversal of what to them had been a fixed association between the natural features of sun, sea, and mountains. As we shall see in our studies of primitive spatial classification, the geographical perspective of the members of any society is tacitly assumed to possess an absolute quality, and certain directions, such as east and west, are given absolute status associated with religious values of birth and death which are totally destroyed by a relativistic model of the earth as a sphere.

Just as the spatial world of the primitive tends to be a static structure of stable concrete and symbolic associations, so his experience of duration is also constructed around a fixed sequence of events and activities, whose mutual relationships are as unquantifiable, qualitatively distinct, and static as those of his spatial representations.

His daily life is bound up with the organic processes of nature which parallel those of his own body and of society itself—the cycles of growth and decay, of new life from old, the similar roles and temperaments of the sexes among both animals and humans, the impregnation of animals and women and the earth with seed, the phases of the moon and the menstrual cycle of women, in short a wealth of resemblances and analogies which provide some evidential basis for the universal belief that the well-being of society and nature are intimately related.

Organic processes, unlike machines, cannot be taken apart; they cannot, without elaborate scientific facilities, be experimentally modified; they cannot be reversed, they were not devised by man, and their operation has generally been far more difficult to analyse scientifically than the working of inanimate nature. They are too, like man himself, open, goal-seeking systems, which seem to display an inner life and an inner purpose. Even if we are not scientists, it is clear that our daily familiarity with such problems as trying to discover why our car will not start or why a radiator in a central-heating system refuses to get hot are typical of thousands of mundane acts of problem solving which our civilization calls upon everyone to undertake. It is in the manipulation and comprehension of man-made objects, machines, and systems that we learn some of the basic principles of conservation of relations and causality, but by a curiosity of history it is these relatively elementary causal systems that have been the last to evolve. Primitive man is faced with understanding the immensely more complicated systems and relations of the biological and social realms which even today continue to daunt the concerted efforts of professional scientists; the primitive's most complex devices are only traps, looms, and sailing vessels. We have the inestimable advantage of growing up in a culture in which we can practise our causal analysis on man-made objects far simpler to understand when we dismantle them or reverse their action. The sciences of mechanics, hydraulics, and geometrical optics, for example, were those in which the greatest progress was first made, together with astronomy, whose objects of study have the regularity and comparative simplicity of machines. It is also notable that Aristotle, who provided the first extensive philosophical analysis of causality, based much of his argument on the nature of artefacts,[1] and technological processes.

[1] See below, pp. 438–9.

But the lack of machinery and other technological devices in primitive society has a more profound effect on modes of thought than on notions of causality alone. For it is by the observation of the ways in which things act on other things that we are able to objectify their characteristics, instead of interpreting them merely by the way in which they affect our own senses and bodies. In our society, for example, we learn to think of 'weight' in terms of objects balanced against one another, as on a pair of scales or a see-saw, or as exerting different forces in relation to the position of a lever and fulcrum, or as expressed in the breaking strains of ropes, beams, and axles. (Even the simple English waggon wheel reveals a complex co-ordination of structural features to accommodate a variety of forces from different directions.) But for primitive man, who usually has no word for weight at all, but only for 'heavy' and 'light', a heavy object is one that makes his back and shoulders ache when he carries it a certain distance, or something a child cannot lift, and a woman only with difficulty. Because weight is sensorily perceived, heaviness will seem to be a property, a thing, possessed in an absolute sense by objects like stones, as opposed to gourds or thatching grass, which are intrinsically light. Primitive man is unfamiliar with the breaking strains of ropes[2] the necessity to distribute weight over a large area, or a host of other instances in which the reaction of things on other *things*, not on a man's body, must be analysed. If wood is hard, this means hard to the blow of an adze, or that it is a good fence post to keep pigs out— there is no conception of hardness in any other terms than of its immediate uses by men and their physical perceptions of it. The sensory manifestations of hot and cold on the human body are quite distinct in their physiological effects (e.g. of shivering and goose-pimples as opposed to sweating and thirst) and thus lend themselves easily to polar opposition rather than to treatment as points along a scalar continuum, and historically, as we know, the thermometer was invented to measure the temperature of non-human phenomena. It would seem as strange to primitive man to suggest that 'hot' and 'cold' had anything in common, such that they were only variations in a single property, as it would be to suggest that 'ferocity' and 'gentleness' were only variable degrees of a common property. The same is true of 'heavy' and 'light' which,

---

[2] It may be that this is a problem for fishing cultures, but I do not know of any ethnographic treatment of this topic.

again, because of their totally different physiological effects seem to be manifestations of opposed and irreconcilable properties. Evidently, the fact that the mid-points, or medium or normal ranges of many scalar properties, are difficult to detect in sensory terms leads to their being ignored and to their representation in terms of polar oppositions.

In his experience of duration, the awareness of primitive man who has been making his way along a track over ridges, across streams, and down the spurs of mountains, is of his own muscular efforts and his state of tiredness; his perceptions of time elapsed will be greatly influenced by these factors and also by the novelty or familiarity of the journey, rather than by any comparison of them with linear distance covered, or still less, with any units of time elapsed. It is this very natural concentration upon his own sensations that makes spells for shortening journeys so plausible; the Fuyughe or Tauade who says a spell to make his destination arrive sooner does not suppose that it will make his feet move quicker or the road suddenly to contract upon itself—this would imply that he was co-ordinating time and distance in an operatory manner. It is precisely because he has no means of objectifying his sensations and actions through the device of miles or hours that he is free to concentrate on his personal feelings and perceptions, which are the more real and compelling to him in such a situation than comparisons of distance covered with distance to be completed, or time/speed calculations.

The same is true of all other dimensions of the physical world. Linear dimensions are commonly based on the human body, as among the Saulteaux Indians:

One man told me, for instance, that in constructing a deadfall for bear, his father made the preliminary measurements in the following manner: after the bedlog of the trap was in place he knelt upon it, bent forward and, keeping his back horizontal with the ground, extended his hands forward as far as they would reach. Where they touched the ground defined the limits of the 'pen'. The fall-log would then be sure to strike the right part of the bear's spine. To judge the height of the notch in the upright post where the outer end of the lever rests, he would elevate a knee. (Hallowell 1942: 67–8)

All estimates of size, or length, or height, or quantity, or duration thus immediately conjure up sensory images or associations of familiar activities and forms of behaviour, of procedures and customary modes of co-ordination, and do not stimulate or require quantitative analysis or dimensional abstraction. The sensations of size, duration, weight, and heat, among many others, are thus necessarily subjectified in primitive experience. Without units of measurement and quantification it is very difficult to separate out particular dimensions and to compare objects in terms of them alone, or to become aware of relations of compensation between different dimensions. Units of measurement, therefore, are not just handy devices for advanced technology which do not happen to be needed in the primitive milieu; they are the cultural crutches or amplifiers for dimensional abstraction, comparison, and compensation.

While cross-cultural tests show that some individuals in primitive societies attain conservation of some dimensions, it is clear that without the development of the culturally standardized unit of measurement, conservation must remain an undeveloped aspect of the thought of the average member of society. In a world of gourds, pots, bamboo tubes, baskets, hollowed-out tree-trunks, string bags, and sewn-up animal skins, which are used for transporting and storing things and not for measuring them, it is extraordinarily difficult accurately to perceive displacements and conservations of quantity or area. Even so simple a problem as finding out how many cups of tea can be obtained from one pot does not present itself in the context of primitive life, since drinking vessels are seldom used.

More generally, we can say that dimensional, quantitative analysis is demanded in situations dominated by scarcities of materials, time, and money and by the need for precision and planning in advance. The problems of house-building illustrate this very well. In our society, our calculations are dominated by the constraints of total cost; by the necessity of obtaining different materials from specialist suppliers and co-ordinating the work of specialist labour; by the artificiality of materials; by the novelty of building plans such that two houses are seldom alike and often embody different techniques of construction, while on the other hand we have the technological power to build almost anything we like, which imposes a correspondingly greater burden of deciding just what we *shall* build.

In a primitive society, a man who wishes to build himself a house can often do the work himself, in his own time—perhaps spread over a month or more when he feels like it—and with materials that are available in unlimited abundance. He does not have to make any explicit calculations to decide whether, within his budget, he would be better off obtaining more materials for walls and less for roofing materials, or vice versa; or whether to employ more men to finish the work sooner, or to use fewer men and take longer. His materials come to him in ready-made sizes and qualities—usually the only modification he will need to make is to the length of timbers—while the use of each type of material—thatching grass or leaves for the roof, canes for the rafters, aerial roots of pandanus trees for binding ties, logs for walls, and bark for floors—is decided for him by the natural properties of the materials themselves. He builds according to well-tried and conventional principles which he does not need to adapt or experiment with. He needs no plan to be drawn before work can begin, nor does he need to calculate breaking strains of lintels or posts or the necessary thickness of beams to support possible loads, as it might be in a granary. The size of openings, the height of verandas from the ground, and the floor area, are decided by the size of the human body and its customary activities, while the limitations of his technology ensure that he will be unable to set himself architectural problems that require more advanced conceptual representations than hitherto. Nor should it need emphasizing that in non-monetary economies there is no opportunity or need for the quantitative analysis that precise costing imposes on the house-builder in our society.

Thus the primitive awareness of the characteristics of physical objects does not rest upon quantitative, dimensional analysis, but is indissociated from subjective experience of the sensory properties of things, bound up with the context of their practical use in the same way that language is only experienced as speech, similarly bound up in practical situations and dialogue between real people, rather than as an objectively describable phenomenon. The general absence of significant relations between objects and other objects, as opposed to interactions between objects and people, in the primitive milieu, inevitably helps to sustain an egocentric, indissociated relationship between man and the physical world as far as any conceptual, operational analysis of their properties is concerned.

Again, while basic devices such as the lever are known, their uses are so diverse that no general principles are readily inferable. Thus levers are used by many peoples in the construction of traps, where they are necessary in triggering mechanisms so that a light pull on the bait may release a heavy weight. The inverse of this principle is also used in the form of digging sticks, when heavy weights such as boulders can be lifted by a relatively light pull. It would be interesting to discover if any general relationship between these two applications of leverage is widely understood by primitive peoples.

Because the range of problem solving in primitive technologies is very narrow compared with ours, and because of the very slow rate of technological change, primitives can make the fullest use of accumulated, *ad hoc* experience of a low order of generality which seldom becomes out of date and is adequate for almost all situations. For example, H. Gladwin (1970) reports that the women of the Cape Coast fish markets of Ghana base their daily rate of payments to the fishermen on so many shillings per hundred fish. In selling fish in the markets in smaller or larger quantities it is necessary to be able to calculate the rate in relation to these different quantities. It appears, however, that these relations are not calculated by each woman but memorized in a form handed down by mother to daughter, which takes account of every price relation. Clearly, someone at some time worked out these calculations, but the basic stability of the market system and the limited range of the problem allowed the solution to be codified and transmitted by memory alone.

This is not to suggest that there is no experimentation in primitive society. All intelligent life involves experiment, from the earliest days of the sensori-motor period, and the technological discoveries of all primitive societies have certainly been the result of experiment. But it seems unlikely to have been the kind of controlled experiment of which we considered an example in Chapter I; moreover, in a technology with a slow rate of change one man's discovery can subsequently be applied by others simply on the basis of observation and imitation.[3]

All the knowledge required by the navigators of Puluwat in the Caroline Islands has been established by the previous experience of generations, and the fact that

... all inputs of information and outputs of decision are so to speak prepackaged or predetermined means that within the navigation system there is little room or need for innovation. Navigation requires the solution of

---

[3] Experiment will be discussed further in Chapter X.

no unprecedented problems. The navigator must be judicious and perceptive, but he is never called upon to have new ideas, to relate things together in new ways. (T. Gladwin 1970: 220)

We frequently find that primitives believe that their knowledge is inborn, or was created ready-made. For example, '. . . the body of knowledge was conceived to be as finite as the cosmic order within which it was contained. It came into the world ready made and ready to use, and could be augmented not by human intellectual experiment but only by further revelation by new or old deities' (Lawrence 1964: 33). But even in New Guinea, where this attitude to innovation and discovery is probably the norm, one occasionally comes across an awareness of the possibilities of learning by experience and trial and error. The following myth from the Yagwoia Kukukuku is unusual in so far as it recounts a discovery (in this case of the means of making stone adzes) by trial and error, which leads to the making of stone clubs:

Once upon a time people had no stone axes to clear their gardens. They did everything with their bare hands. They asked themselves, 'Why do we only do things this way?' A man saw a sharp white stone in a stream; he picked it up and looked for a tree to cut down. He ground it first, then fastened it to a handle. The first time, he fixed it loosely to the handle, and the stone fell to the ground. After this he fastened it with a vine and it held once, and then fell to the ground again. Then he saw a rattan and fastened the stone with rattan to the handle. It held fast there. Everybody cleared their gardens with the stone axe and cut down the whole forest. They said, 'Once, we had no stone axe, now we can work well with it.' And they supplied many stone axes and sent them to all the villages. After this the man made a stone club . . . (Fischer 1967: 377)

More generally we can say that technical problems are an integral part of the total life of society, and not seen as purely intellectual puzzles:

Rice growing is not an analyzed, isolated technical activity in the Kpelle way of life. What Western cultures would compartmentalize into technical science, the Kpelle culture weaves into the whole fabric of existence. The relevant question is not 'How do you grow rice?' but 'How do you live?' (Gay and Cole 1967: 21)

2. SOCIAL RELATIONS AND THE LEARNING SITUATION IN PRIMITIVE SOCIETIES

Carothers (1953: 101) argues that because the African baby has a very close relationship to the mother before weaning, being carried everywhere, and because weaning itself may be delayed until the child is two or three years old, during which time he is prevented from exploring the environment for himself, his environment is cognitively undemanding. By contrast, the European infant is more isolated and freer to explore his environment. He is introduced to balls, building blocks, and a wide variety of mechanical toys, and Carothers suggests that from early infancy the European baby has a cognitively more stimulating environment. In fact, further psychological research casts doubt on this interpretation of the cognitive inhibitions of the traditional African environment on the infant. Studies on Baoulé infants of the Ivory coast by Dasen *et al.* and Bovet *et al.* (see Dasen 1977: 157–66) have shown that the babies of at least one traditional African society in which infants receive the early nurturing described by Carothers display in general the same rate of progress through the substages of the sensori-motor period between six and twenty-four months as French babies in Paris.

The tests included such tasks as pulling a cloth with an object on it so as to draw the object closer; to reach an object by using a toy plastic rake and a ruler; the manipulation of a small mirror and a match-box; a small object was wrapped in a piece of paper and placed in a plastic tube so that it could not be reached by the fingers, and the infants had to use the handle of the plastic rake to push it out; and they were given a small chain of paper clips which had to be passed through the tube.

Dasen concludes:

... the qualitative characteristics of sensori-motor development are quite similar or even identical in French and Baoulé infants, in spite of vast differences in their cultural environment. Not only are the structural properties of the stages, and therefore their order of appearance, identical in both groups, but even the actions and schemes, and the way these are slowly built up into more complex action-patterns which eventually enable the infant to solve rather difficult problems, seem to be identical. (Dasen 1977: 165)

It seems that the traditional infant-rearing practices in this primitive society do not produce the cognitive deprivation that Carothers and others have supposed:

The Baoulé neonate and his mother remain inside the house for the first two weeks after birth; immediately thereafter, the mother returns to normal life, carrying the baby on her back. Compared with an infant lying in a crib for most of the day, the African baby thus receives an enormous amount of proprioceptive, tactile and visual stimulation which enhances its psycho-motor and postural development. The baby may take advantage of this motor precocity to explore his environment, and build up the schemes which lead to the kind of sensori-motor structures of intelligence we have been studying.

Furthermore, the Baoulé infant is breast-fed on demand until weaning occurs at about 18 months. The infant seems to be quite active in this process; he may get immediate satisfaction by crying, but we have also observed many occasions when he actively searched for the breast. Even when he is attached to his mother's back, he wriggles to the side until he can reach for it. This early experience in searching actively for the breast, and in finding that he can build up motor schemes which will lead to satisfaction, may explain at least part of the precocity in object permanency and in the handling of objects which are within easy reach. (Ibid. 162)

It is also extremely interesting to note that the experimental materials used in the tests, which were quite novel to the Baoulé infants, caused them no apparent difficulty. It has been argued that the familiarity or unfamiliarity of test materials has an important effect on test performance (cf. Price-Williams 1962, and Cole and Scribner 1974: 114–18), but this does not seem to be the case at the sensori-motor level.

... the last series in the Casati–Lézine scale (the combination of a tube and a small chain) is, at first sight, a quite impossible task. For one thing, why should the infant wish to combine these two objects? He may just as well look through the tube, roll it on the table, put the chain round his fingers, or throw it at the experimenter. Yet, after stage 5A, almost every infant starts to search for some way of making the chain pass through the tube. When this task is presented to a Baoulé infant, it seems even more ludicrous, since the subject will never have seen a plastic tube or paper clips before. Yet he takes these two strange objects, and combines them exactly as the infants in the day-care centre of Paris did; not only does he get the idea of combining them, but he does this following the same steps, with the same errors, and finding the same successively more and more adapted solutions. (Dasen 1977: 165)

It seems, therefore, that we shall not find any indication of functional differences in the cognitive processes of primitives at the sensori-motor level, and that it is only when we come to higher levels involving imagery and linguistic representation that differences will appear and can be shown to result from specific socio-environmental factors.

However, when we come to these higher levels of mental functioning, which in our society are dependent on verbal instruction of the child by adults, we find that there is good evidence for the hypothesis that the primitive milieu is less encouraging to cognitive growth than our own, since the social relations between children and adults do not encourage articulate verbal questioning and critical learning by children. Fortes's study of the educational process among the Tallensi illustrates this very well.

In this (Ghanaian) society there is very little specialized knowledge, apart from certain crafts and the ritual and ideology of the ancestor cults and the sacred groves. 'As between adults and children, in Tale society, the social sphere is differentiated only in terms of relative capacity' (Fortes 1938: 9). There is no idea of opposition between children's interests and those of adult society or that children should be taught to question the social order. The ideal of life is to acquire 'sense'—*yam*; as when

we refer to a 'sensible man', or 'sound common sense'. As the Tallensi use the term it suggests the quality of 'insight'. Its range of usage is wide. If it is said of someone *u mar yam pam*, 'he has a great deal of sense', the implication is that he is a man of wisdom, or is intelligent, or experienced in affairs, or resourceful. (Ibid. 14)

This attitude towards the proper use of intellect is very general in primitive society. Wober, for example, discussing traditional African concepts of intelligence, writes:

The available literature suggests that ideas about intelligence or human ability do indeed differ in East and South Central Africa from Western models. Barbara Levine (1963) writing of the Gusii in Kenya says 'The good child is the obedient child—smartness or brightness by itself is not a highly valued characteristic and the Nyasongo concept of intelligence includes respect for elders and filial piety as natural ingredients.' Margaret Read (1959) provides a similar picture among the Ngoni of Malawi. She writes, 'Ngoni adults . . . summed up the aims of upbringing of children in one word, "respect". They also wished to inculcate wisdom, which was contrasted with "cleverness" and wisdom included knowledge, good judgement, ability to control people and keep at peace, and skill in using speech.' (Wober 1974: 271)

The Puluwatans do not regard their navigators as displaying special intelligence—'thinking well' for them means, as for Africans, showing good sense and wisdom:

They respect [navigators] because they can navigate, because they can guide a canoe safely from one island to another. There is, it is true, a Puluwat word one can translate as 'intelligent', and in these terms navigators are considered intelligent, but etymologically it refers only to having a good memory. There are furthermore many useful ways to use one's mind in addition to remembering technical information. A Puluwatan who is asked to identify people who think well or use their minds effectively is likely to select those whose decisions are wise, who are moderate and statesmanlike in discussion, not the technicians. (T. Gladwin 1970: 219)

The dominant wish of children, at least among the Tallensi, is therefore to be assimilated into adult life as quickly as possible, and adults offer no resistance to this process:

Increasing skill and maturity, therefore, bring increasing responsibilities but also concomitant rewards—that is, ever closer integration into the system of co-operation and reciprocity which is the basis of Tale domestic economy. The unity of the social sphere, the interest of children in the world of adult activities, and the rapidity with which each advance in educational achievement is socially utilized constitute a ring of incentives which help to explain the eagerness of Tale children to grow up and take their full place in adult life. (Fortes 1938: 33)

There is no reason to suppose that this is an untypical picture of child–adult relations in primitive societies generally (though there seem to be some exceptions, such as the Manus, see Mead 1930), and this being so we can understand why the kind of critical attitudes fostered in Western children to adult institutions do not have the chance to develop in primitive society.

The manual education of Tale children consists in farming, care of livestock, hunting, fishing, building, thatching, cooking, housekeeping, gardening, and specialist technology. Social skills include the knowledge of kinship, ritual, and ceremonial, the knowledge of economically and medicinally useful herbs and roots, law and custom, and buying and selling.

But it is of the greatest importance to note that the learning of these tasks and the acquisition of this knowledge is achieved not by explicit verbal instruction, but by observation in the context of use and by participation in real social activities:

A friend of mine who was a cap maker told me how he had learnt his craft, as a youth, from a Dagban by carefully watching him at work. When he was young, he explained, he had 'very good eyes'. This conception of cleverness is intelligible in a society where learning by looking and copying is the commonest manner of achieving dexterity both in crafts and in the everyday manual activities. (Ibid. 13)

Nor is learning by observation confined to manual skills:

. . . the Tallensi have no technique of isolating a skill or observance from the total reality and training a child in it according to a syllabus, as, for instance, we train children in dancing, the multiplication table, or the catechism. Tale educational method does not include drill as a fundamental technique. It works through the situation, which is a bit of the social reality shared by adult and child alike. (Ibid. 27)

As Gay and Cole observed among the Kpelle,

Gradually the child is inducted into the full life of an adult. He is almost never told what to do in an explicit, verbal, or abstract manner. He is expected to watch, learning by imitation and repetition. Education is concrete and nonverbal, concerned with practical activity, not abstract generalization. There are never lectures on farming, house-building, or weaving. The child spends all his days watching until at some point he is told to join in the activity. If he makes a mistake, he is simply told to try again. (Gay and Cole 1967: 16)

As normal behaviour is always expected, no one hesitates to correct a child or adult who behaves inappropriately through ignorance, and the correction is generally accepted with alacrity and ease. If children are allowed to be present at the activities of adults, they are assumed to be interested and to understand what is being said and done. No one would inhibit his conversation or actions because children are present, or withhold information upon which adequate social adjustment depends from a child because it is thought to be too young. (Fortes 1938: 27)

In consequence of these forms of education, children seldom ask direct questions of adults, as they do in our society, where children's 'Why?' questions are regarded as the norm by developmental psychologists:

The natives say that small children frequently ask questions about people and things they see around them. However, listening to children's talk for 'why' questions, I was surprised to note how rarely they occurred; and the few instances I recorded referred to objects or persons foreign to the normal outline of Tale life. It would seem that Tale children rarely have to ask 'why' in regard to the people and things of their normal environment because so much of their learning occurs in real situations. (Ibid. 30)

Indeed, asking 'Why?' may be treated in some societies as a positive challenge to authority and tradition, as among the Kpelle:

The child must never question those older than himself. If he is told to do a chore in a certain way, he must do it in that way, and no other. If he asks 'Why?' or acts in a manner unsanctioned by tradition, he is likely to be beaten. Moreover, he must know what is expected of him without explicit instruction. A violation of unstated rules is as bad as a violation of explicit commands. (Gay and Cole 1967: 16)

While there is likely to be much cultural variation in the degree to which children's 'Why?' questions are regarded as a positive challenge to authority it is likely that the resentment and disapproval of children's questions reported by these researchers is a general phenomenon among uneducated folk. In the classic trilogy *Lark Rise to Candleford*, the English authoress Flora Thompson records a similar attitude among Oxfordshire villagers in the 1880s. She and her brother were highly intelligent children with a somewhat better educational background than the children of the neighbouring labourers:

As they grew, the two elder children [the authoress and her brother] would ask questions of anybody and everybody willing or unwilling to answer them. Who planted the buttercups? Why did God let the wheat get blighted? Who lived in this house before we did, and what were their children's names? What's the sea like? Is it bigger than Cottesloe pond? *Why* can't we go to Heaven in the donkey cart? Is it farther than Banbury? . . .

This asking of questions teased their mother and made them unpopular with the neighbours. 'Little children should be seen and not heard,' they were told at home. Out of doors it would more often be 'Ask no questions and you'll be told no lies.' One old woman once handed the little girl a leaf from a pot-plant of her window-sill. 'What's it called?' was the inevitable question. ''Tis called mind your own business,' was the reply; 'an' I think I'd better give a slip of it to your mother to plant in a pot for you.' (Thompson 1948: 18–19)

While in many primitive societies children are given specific instruction before initiation in the customs of their society, this kind of instruction is quite unlike the schooling of Western children—in its brevity, among other things. Among the Kpelle, for example, the children are sexually segregated for months in the bush, and spend most of their time in practical occupations such as farming and building huts:

Nothing special except some sex education is taught until the very end of the school, when the secrets are revealed. The secrets are apparently few:

the nature of the 'forest thing' or masked spirit, the type of music that accompanies the appearance of the 'forest thing', the ritual behaviour by which members [of the secret society] identify each other, the threat of death if the secrets are revealed, the techniques of scarification, and the knowledge of special medicines and charms. (Gay and Cole 1967: 17)

We can summarize education in primitive society as conducted in a context of real life, by example and observation, and without much verbal instruction or any specialist training situations. The object of education is not 'cleverness' or the ability to question or experiment or to think for oneself, but good sense, wisdom, and the ability to perform as a good citizen in work and social relations. The child is highly motivated to conform, and his basic learning commitment is not to things or ideas, but to people, especially those closest to him socially.

The upbringing of a Western child promotes very different mental skills. In our type of society an essential aspect of socialization is 'individualization', the growing awareness of the uniqueness of one's own experience, and the use of speech to express this.[4] The use of personal initiative, self-help, and competition, and the cultivation of private sensations through publicly provided facilities, are aspects of a society based on the assumption that maturation necessitates the development and mutual accommodation of different points of view.

But while in many primitive societies there may be a high degree of individual competitiveness, one does not find that isolation of the individual that is typical of our society, in which the child has to discover his own rules for success in life largely unaided by the guidance of adults or to choose between discordant codes of conduct and belief. The child in primitive society is inducted into approved patterns of behaviour by example and the pressure of day-

---

[4] Radin also draws our attention to the often overlooked distinction between the intellectual and the ordinary man in primitive thought: 'No notion of primitive man's concept of the external world, his analysis of himself, of the nature of the godhead, etc. is possible unless it be recognized that, as among us, there exist, roughly speaking, two general types of temperament: the man of action and the thinker, the type which lives fairly exclusively on what might be called a motor level and the type that demands explanations and derives pleasure from some form of speculative thinking' (1957: 229–30). In particular, Radin characterizes the intellectual as concerned with the character of his own thought and with the analysis of process, both of which are crucial aspects of higher developmental levels of thinking. Unfortunately, the extent to which men of exceptional intellect can transcend the limitations of their culture has remained unexplored both by anthropologists and by psychologists.

to-day social relations which do not need to be expressed at the explicitly verbal level. It is therefore possible to have socialization at a much lower conceptual level than Piaget takes as his norm and very much less dependent on language than is the case with European children. While it is clear that primitives are well aware of one another as individuals, that individuality is very much less pronounced at the cognitive level than in our own society. As a result the accommodation to different points of view can take place at the level of action and shared experience, and be expressed in concrete symbolism, in a way that is impossible in our type of society. One can say that in many ways the circumstances of primitive life create in reality that concordance of points of view that the European pre-operatory child tacitly *assumes*, falsely, to be the case.[5]

From the learning situation we can now pass on to consider the cognitive skills most in demand in adult society. In the first place, it is evident that in small, face-to-face societies where everyone knows everyone else and in which experience is largely shared by all, the most important and fundamental rules and categories of experience will not, for the most part, need to be given explicit expression, except on the moral level. The general experience of ethnographers is that members of such societies, while expert in the practical skills and details necessary to operate their institutions, are usually unable to view and describe their operations as a whole, to formulate the general principles of their operation, or, for example in story-telling, to distinguish between logical and narrative order, and so on. Such cognitive skills are only necessary to cater for the rare cases of uninformed but unusually inquisitive outsiders such as anthropologists. Correspondingly, in our type of 'open' society, a vast amount of our very generalized and/or abstract forms of communication is necessitated by the lack of shared experience between communicators, such as farmers, policemen, airline pilots, and coal-miners. Following from this fact of shared experience within a restricted and stable physical environment and the comprehensive mutual knowledge between group members, communication in primitive societies can make much more use than we can of allegory, imagery, allusion, and concrete symbolism, which depend on intimate, specific knowledge of the context

---

[5] The extent of self-awareness in relation to primitive conceptions of the mind is discussed at length in Chapter IX.

of utterance. These techniques of communication are highly effective for social purposes, but generally opaque to outsiders.

I shall take some examples of proverbs and speeches to illustrate this. The following proverbs are from Samoa:

It is only the people of Neiafu who disparage the *to-elau* (the N.E. trade wind)

The explanation is as follows: It is said that two cripples in Neiafu grumbled continually against the northeast trade winds because they did not cause the coconuts to drop immaturely from the trees, as they were not able to climb them. They preferred the west wind which caused the nuts to fall even though they were not ripe. This proverb is used to describe those who despise the good and prefer the bad or who prefer to have a worthless article like an immature coconut rather than have the trouble of getting a good one. (Radin 1957: 161–2)

'The feather blowing of Lavea'
Lavea was the head of a family at Safotu. Their family god was supposed to be present in the fowl and so they were, of course, prohibited from eating or injuring that bird. When Lavea and his family became professing Christians these customs were not observed and as a proof of the sincerity of his conversion, Lavea was asked to kill and eat a fowl and this he consented to do. He was, however, still very much afraid of the family deity and as a compromise he blew away the feathers as an offering to the god and ate the fowl.
    This proverb is used to illustrate the folly of trying to be right with all sides; of a merely pretended allegiance; and that of retaining the best, and offering that which is of no value.

'The body of Galue was bruised in vain'
Galue was a man who was very desirous of getting the best fine mat at a division of the property. He was so anxious for this that in order to show his good will and his respect for the family beforehand, he threw himself down on the stones and was much bruised. After all this, however, the mat in question was given to another man. (Ibid. 163)

This kind of proverbial wisdom is highly effective in primitive environments which place a low demand on generalization and the capacity for co-ordinated conceptual structures which can easily adapt to very novel experience. Because proverbs are so well adapted to particular, recurring types of situation in which a moral or practical point about conduct is to be made they are correspondingly resistant to combination in co-ordinated, wider-ranging commentary on social affairs. By this I mean that there is no way in which the meanings of 'The feather blowing of Lavea', 'The body of Galue was bruised in vain', and 'It is only the people of Neiafu who disparage the *to-elau*' can be combined in a form that is itself proverbial. One has to move to a much higher order of analysis and generalization and talk of discontented persons who defeat their own ends by desiring what is worthless or attempting to reconcile conflicting commitments, and so on.

While a few highly intelligent informants in primitive societies are capable of providing explanations and arguments at this level, it is, I think, a distinctly uncommon skill for the development of which schooling and literacy are likely to be of great importance. As we shall see, Cole and his associates found that while the Kpelle of Liberia were well aware of their reasons for rejecting the cultivation of wet rice in the lowlands in favour of their traditional farming of dry rice in the hills, they were unable to frame these objections as a coherent argument. The point is that while the use of proverbs is not in itself evidence for a lack of ability to express the meaning of those proverbs at a higher level of generality, their very specific concrete references inherently isolate each proverb into an atomistic element of 'truth' which is very difficult to link up with others in a generalized and coherent argument. Thus, the Konso have a large number of riddles (which are very close to proverbs), and while my informants could tell me what the individual words meant, they were quite unable to explain their meaning in more general terms. Similarly, if we examine a series of speeches made at a ceremonial occasion among the Konso we find this same stringing together of concrete, proverb-style, allusions which do not form a coherent or generalized argument. The Konso have a rigorously ordered social system, rich in symbolic categories, with a clearly expressed system of values, yet while the occasion of their speeches was to reinforce these values and traditional standards of behaviour at a very general level, they were expressed in very particular and concrete terms, only comprehensible to the Konso themselves.

The following speech was delivered, with other speeches of a very similar nature, during a ceremony known as *Ĥora Dehamda*, 'Fining and Discussion', held at the Konso town of Būso. These ceremonies are held periodically to review the social shortcomings and bad behaviour of the town, and those who have been particularly troublesome are called upon to pay a public fine by the elders. Because the Konso believe that too much quarrelling is

punished by drought, there is a strong ritual and religious component in this ceremony, including the ritual purification of the men.
The speeches themselves for this reason also include some formal
blessings. At the conclusion of the ceremony, the men are gathered
in one of the public places and addressed by leading warriors and
elders. The warriors are members of Ĥrela generation-grade, whose
traditional function was the punishment of criminals on the orders
of the elders, as well as the military defence of their town. The
elders are members of Kada and Orshada grades and are traditionally responsible for political decision making and for blessing.
Sauwe Ĥambiro, a councillor and elder, addresses the men:

May God bless [?] you with milk gourds. Listen, why do your Ĥrela, your
elders, fine you? It is like this, so that you may be truthful, for this reason
they fine you, so that you may till the soil, therefore they punish you. And
wherefore, consider this, that this person spills blood in the land, that one
is full of drink and cannot sleep on his mat, so that his strength is taken
from him, and by day he hides [?]. Ĥrela have seen this. Listen, wherefore
[you are punished] consider this that after this [assembly] here, with Gar-
fura [the river valley with many fields below Buso] it is well [lit. 'sleeps'].
So that we may suck the breasts of the seven priests; when you suck them
you prosper. [These are the seven most important priestly families, whose
blessings are essential for the well-being of the town.] This grass [for thatch-
ing] has grown tall for building housing, [yet] people are selling it at
Bakaule, at Bakaule, and fathers sell it for drink [?], and tomorrow you
will suffer, and the elders will punish you, and the warriors will punish
you. [This is a reference to the pernicious practice of selling thatching
grass, and also *mida*, a succulent tree foliage eaten with millet, and even
their fields, on all of which their traditional life depends, at Bakaule, the
Government town, where many Amhara live.] The wives have gone away
there [to Bakaule] taking thongs [to help carry the bundles of *mida*] and
after going they buy salt, and the *mida* of the children [?] they give away.
Now there is no sucking the breasts of the seven families [but] within them
you will prosper. Take the hooks and hook down the *mida*, watch, like this
[gesturing as though hooking down *mida*] and Ĥrela watch me doing this
[?] Wherefore because of these [faults] you are punished, and the father on
his mat at night lacks sleep, and Ĥrela lack sleep. Let all this be far from
me, and Ĥrela have observed me. (adapted from Hallpike 1972: 84-5)

The basic principles underlying this speech are, besides the
necessity of preserving peace within the town, the Konso people's
basic antipathy to trade, regarded as destructive of social harmony
which is ideally maintained by co-operation with neighbours and

kinsmen. The speech also conveys hostility towards the Amhara, who are regarded as exploiters of the Konso, in this case by purchasing what should be kept for the well-being of their own children. These attitudes and values are so familiar to the Konso as to be taken for granted; what is effective are references to specific kinds of behaviour, expressed in language which is not only concrete but which, to be understood, relies on knowledge of many local facts, as my numerous comments illustrate. There is a marked use of allegory and symbolism unintelligible to those who do not share the Konso way of life. A later speaker, for example, to make the point that one should not cause dissension by damaging people's property by reckless behaviour, says: 'A boy says "chehe" with his goats in front, and after driving them in this way they do not eat the crops in other people's fields. [But if] the boy throws stones, he is just a fool for throwing stones', i.e. driving goats by throwing stones frightens them and makes them scatter.

The style is highly compressed, and the points made are in no logical order, nor does one find that a general theme is stated and then elaborated. There is, in fact, a tendency to ramble, and to repeat the same point several times. The other speeches (ibid. 84–6) reveal no logical connection; they are highly repetitious, each man following his own train of thought wherever it leads him. None of the speakers, for example, refers back to what any of the others has said.

One finds this same inability to co-ordinate thought at the level of explicit verbal exposition in the incapacity of primitive peoples to distinguish between logical and narrative order. While the older men may know many stories, they are always, at least in my experience both in Ethiopia and New Guinea, quite unable to discuss the themes of the stories and the relations between them apart from the actual sequence of events in the narrative. Piaget notes that this is one of the characteristics of pre-operatory children:

When an adult narrates, he is accustomed to respect two kinds of order: the natural order given by the facts themselves, and the logical or pedagogic order. Now it is to a great extent because of our concern with clarity and our desire to avoid misunderstanding in others that we adults present our material in a given logical order, which may or may not correspond with the natural order of things. The child, therefore, who, when he explains his thoughts, believes himself to be immediately understood by his hearer, will take no trouble to arrange his propositions in one order rather than another. The natural order is assumed to be known by the hearer, the logical order is assumed to be useless. (Piaget 1959: 108)

This analysis of the narrative style of pre-operatory children does not apply to that of primitives in one crucial respect—primitive narrative is highly conscious of chronological order, 'the natural order given by the facts themselves', but one finds that, while one's informants may be able to answer questions on why a certain character in a story did a certain thing, there is little or no ability to ignore the chronological sequence of events and substitute for these an analysis of events in terms of logical order. For example, if we are giving someone an account of a sequence of events of a type with which he is unfamiliar, we may preface our account with an analysis of the salient features of the events which ignores the actual sequence of events in favour of a logical order, e.g. 'This is an example of how tragic consequences are produced by the protagonists' ignorance of their own motives, and their inability to profit by experience.' I have never encountered any such analysis of a myth or other narrative by an informant which replaces chronological order by logical order.

One would not wish to assert, however, that primitives are incapable of separating out individual details from myths and stories generally. For example, Bateson says of the Iatmül:

One detail of the culture is worth mentioning as likely to promote the higher processes rather than rote memory. This concerns the technique of debating. In a typical debate a name or series of names is claimed as totemic property by two conflicting clans. The right to the name can only be demonstrated by knowledge of the esoteric mythology to which the name refers. But if the myth is exposed and becomes publicly known, its value as a means of proving the clan's right to the name will be destroyed. Therefore there ensues a struggle between the two clans, each stating that they themselves know the myth and each trying to find out how much their opponents really know. In this context the myth is handled by the speakers not as a continuous narrative, but as a series of small details. A speaker will hint at one detail at a time—to prove his own knowledge of the myth—or he will challenge the opposition to produce some one detail. In this way there is, I think, induced a tendency to think of a story, not as a chronological sequence of events, but as a set of details with varying degrees of secrecy surrounding each—an analytic attitude which is almost certainly directly opposed to rote remembering. (Bateson 1958: 224)

But while the Iatmül are obviously capable of breaking up myths into discrete elements, this does not amount in itself to the ability to construct a *logical* order independent of narrative order, which would consist of a *rearrangement* of elements into a different pattern or structure from that of the myth itself.

The problem of the logical analysis of narrative leads us naturally to the question of how far the capacity for logical argument in general is developed in primitive society. Cole *et al.* (1971) noted the inability of the Kpelle to put their arguments against growing wet rice in the lowlands instead of their traditional cultivation of dry rice in the hills. The advantages of wet rice are that it gives a better yield, with less labour after the first year; the same ground can be re-used indefinitely, unlike that for dry rice, which is cultivated by slash-and-burn methods; and fish can be raised with the wet rice to provide protein. The disadvantages of wet rice for the Kpelle are that they consider its taste inferior; they cannot grow a number of other cash and food crops with it, as they do with dry rice; the clearing of the bush, the planting and harvesting of hill rice are enjoyable communal activities, with working parties and sing-songs, when the men display strength and endurance as they work. Swamp labour, on the other hand, is considered dirty and uncoordinated, essentially woman's work, and by making farms in the swamps men are liable to lose their claim on ancestral land in the hills. All these are sensible and convincing reasons for refusing to grow wet rice, but the traditional men were incapable of expressing them in a *coherent* manner, and they had to be elicited by a series of questions.

The same inability to communicate what they *knew* on the part of traditional non-literate adults was found in an experiment derived from Piaget. For the performance of the task, a table is set up with two piles, each of ten sticks of different shapes and species of wood identically matched, each pile at one end of the table, separated by a screen. The two subjects sit at opposite ends of the table, so that they can see only their own pile of sticks. The experimenter picks up each stick in turn, and the object is for one subject to describe the stick the experimenter picks up so that the other subject can match it with the corresponding stick from his own pile, relying solely on the verbal description. The sticks chosen are, of course, those with which the subjects are thoroughly familiar in their daily lives.

The results, of which a sample is given in Table I, show that the average non-literate Kpelle is very poor at communicating in a situation where his listener does not share his field of vision.

TABLE I

| English description | Kpelle description | |
	first trial	second trial
thickest straight wood	one of the sticks	one of the sticks
medium straight wood	not a large one	one of the sticks
hook	one of the sticks	stick with a fork
forked stick	one of the sticks	one of the sticks
thin curved bamboo	piece of bamboo	curved bamboo
thin curved wood	one stick	one of the sticks
thin straight bamboo	one piece of bamboo	small bamboo
long fat bamboo	one of the bamboo	large bamboo
short thorny	one of the thorny sticks	has a thorn
long thorny	one of the thorny sticks	has a thorn

(from Cole and Scribner 1974: 179)

These poor results are not the inevitable consequence of some deficiency in the Kpelle language, or of the subjects' misunderstanding of what they were supposed to do. This was shown by an experiment in which a college-educated Kpelle acted as speaker. On this occasion, the other subject made few mistakes in picking the correct stick and also showed that the kind of perceptual distinctions made in the English descriptions are meaningful to a Kpelle. While the Kpelle are adequate communicators in such situations as court cases, they are unable to use their language in situations normally governed by action alone, so that they cannot easily translate knowledge of a sensori-motor or image-based nature into words.

We also find an inability to accept, in the case of problems of verbal logic, that such problems can be solved without going outside the boundaries of the actual words used in the problem. The Russian developmental psychologist Luria, a pupil of Vygotsky, found in experiments among the illiterate peasant Uzbeks of Central Asia,[6] that they refused to treat logical problems purely as

[6] A serious deficiency of Luria's published work is an almost complete lack of information on the cultural background of the people. We are not dealing with a completely non-literate culture but with a facet of Islamic civilization, in which traditionally a section of the population has been literate, e.g. 'The ancient high culture of Uzbekistan is still preserved in the magnificent architecture at Samarkand, Bukhara, and Khorezm. Also noteworthy were the outstanding scientific and

hypothetical, as opposed to problems that could be solved only on the basis of the actual experience of the subject. Luria presented the following problem in deductive inference to an illiterate Kashgar man, thirty-seven years of age, from a remote village (the experimenter's comments have been omitted from all Luria's protocols):

Q. In the Far North, where there is snow, all bears are white. Novaya Zemlya is in the Far North and there is always snow there. What colour are the bears there?
A. There are different sorts of bears.

---

poetic achievements associated with such figures as Ulug-Bek, a mathematician and astronomer who left behind a remarkable observatory near Samarkand, the philosopher Al-Biruni, the physician Ali-ibn-Sinna (Avicenna), the poets Saadi, Nizami, and others' (Luria 1976: 14). In principle, therefore, there is a strong possibility that while the peasantry would not have been directly influenced by these scholars, the culture has cognitive resources in both the language and the system of thought that permit a more rapid acquisition of operational modes of thought than would be possible in a truly primitive society. Luria tends to dismiss the traditional culture in a derogatory and simplistic manner, e.g. '. . . for centuries [Islam] had held back the development of individual thought through subjecting people to religious dogma and rigid behavioural standards' (14), which is an estimate hard to reconcile with the achievements of Ulug-Bek, Al-Biruni, and Avicenna, and the ancient high culture of Uzbekistan. His reference to 'the completely unregulated individualistic economy centered on agriculture' is also hardly consistent with the stereotype of socially imposed dogmatism and rigid behavioural standards. (Indeed, dogmatism and rigid behavioural standards would seem to be just as likely products of Marxism and collectivized agriculture as of Islam.)

The changes from pre-operatory to operatory modes of thought in Uzbek peasants after only two or three years of schooling and some experience of collective farms is remarkably rapid by the standards observed by cross-cultural researchers in Africa, Papua New Guinea, and Australia, for example. Cole, the editor of the English translation of Luria's book, remarks: 'Luria's data are unique in showing very sharp changes among adults exposed to different work contexts and to minimal levels of education . . .' (xv), and he concludes: 'My own interpretation of such data is somewhat different, since I am sceptical of the usefulness of applying developmental theories cross-culturally. Thus, what Luria interprets as the acquisition of new modes of thought, I am inclined to interpret as changes in the application of previously available modes to the particular problems and contexts of discourse represented by the experimental setting' (xv).

We have already noted (above, p. 61) that while a mode of thought may be *latent*, its actual employment in problem solving is none the less novel when it appears. Rather than accepting Cole's sceptical view of the general inapplicability of the developmental paradigm in cross-cultural studies, one should be sceptical about the application of developmental theory in a context where the ethnographic background is ignored. But despite these reservations, Luria's material clearly shows the prevalence of complexive classification in a traditional, non-literate, face-to-face society and the inability to dissociate language from its context of daily use in personal interaction. For this reason I have quoted extensively from it here.

Q. [The syllogism is repeated]
A. I don't know; I've seen a black bear, I've never seen any others. Each locality has its own animals; if it's white, they will all be white; if it's yellow they will be yellow.
Q. But what kinds of bears are there in Novaya Zemlya?
A. We always speak only of what we see; we don't talk of what we haven't seen.
Q. But what do my words imply? [The syllogism is repeated]
A. Well, it's like this: our tsar isn't like yours, and yours isn't like ours. Your words can be answered only by someone who was here, and if a person wasn't there he can't say anything on the basis of your words.
Q. But on the basis of my words—in the North, where there is always snow, the bears are white, can you gather what kind of bears there are in Novaya Zemlya?
A. If a man was sixty or eighty and had seen a white bear and had told about it, he could be believed, but I've never seen one and hence I can't say. That's my last word. Those who saw can tell, and those who didn't see can't say anything. (At this point a young Uzbek volunteered, 'From your words it means that the bears there are white.')
Q. Well, which of you is right?
A. What the cock knows how to do, he does. What I know, I say, and nothing beyond that. (Luria 1976: 108–9)

The lack of grasp of the *interrelation* of major and minor premisses in the syllogism are well displayed in the following protocol (the subject is an illiterate peasant man of twenty-seven years):

Q. The following syllogism is presented: There are no camels in Germany. The city of B. is in Germany. Are there camels there or not?
A. Subject repeats syllogism exactly.
Q. So, are there camels in Germany?
A. I don't know, I've never seen German villages.
Q. The syllogism is repeated.
A. Probably there are camels there.
Q. Repeat what I said.
A. There are no camels in Germany, are there camels in B. or not? So probably there are. If it's a large city, there should be camels there.
Q. But what do my words suggest?
A. Probably there are. Since there are large cities, then there should be camels.
Q. But if there aren't any in all of Germany?
A. If it's a large city, there will be Kazakhs or Kirghiz there.
Q. But I'm saying that there are no camels in Germany, and this city is in Germany.

A. If this village is in a large city, there is probably no room for camels. (Ibid. 112)

This sort of problem provoked similar responses from the Kpelle:

Q. If Flumo or Yakpalo drinks cane juice, the Town Chief gets vexed. Flumo is not drinking cane juice. Yakpalo is drinking cane juice. Is the Town Chief vexed?
A. People do not get vexed with two persons.
Q. Repeats the problem.
A. The Town Chief was not vexed on that day.
Q. The Town Chief was not vexed? What is the reason?
A. The reason is that he doesn't love Flumo.
Q. He doesn't love Flumo? Go on with the reason.
A. The reason is that Flumo's drinking is a hard time. That is why when he drinks cane juice, the Town Chief gets vexed. But sometimes when Yakpalo drinks cane juice, he will not give a hard time to people. He goes to lie down to sleep. At that rate people do not get vexed with him. But people who drink and go about fighting—the Town Chief cannot love them in the town. (Cole and Scribner 1974: 163)

While anthropologists may feel that the Kpelle subject has rather got the better of the psychologist here, he has done so by evading the point of the problem. The subject converts a logical exercise into a practical commentary on actual social behaviour, by treating Flumo and Yakpalo as real people whom he knows. With the further premises (a) that people do not get vexed with two persons at the same time (why not?) but which is irrelevant to the argument, that Yakpalo's drinking is amiable, and (b) that people only get angry with aggressive drinkers, he concludes that since Flumo, the aggressive drinker, is not drinking, the Town Chief has no reason to be angry. There is evidently no inability to draw an inference from an imaginary situation specified by the experimenter, but the inference is based solely on the subject's experience of actual social relations. In the same way, Luria's subjects refused to draw any inferences about the colour of the bears in Novaya Zemlya or the existence of camels in the German city of B. because they had never been there. Thus there is no suggestion of primitives being unable or unwilling to think in terms of hypothetical propositions based on reality. For example, the ethnographer can perfectly well ask such a question as 'If a woman does not prepare her husband's meal when he comes back from the fields, what will he do?' Answer: 'He beats her'; and natives themselves use conditional statements such as 'If your pig breaks into my garden again, I shall shoot it.' What they are not prepared to do is to reason on the basis of propositions which assume knowledge that they do not possess or that is counter to their experience. If, as in the Kpelle case, the problem is one involving a familiar situation, they will add details from their own experience to allow them to draw an inference which is valid in terms of experience and not purely in terms of logic. Secondly, there is an evident inability to consider statements purely as statements, dissociated from the context of utterance and the status of the interlocutors. Thirdly, there is an inability to grasp the syllogism as *a system of interrelated propositions*, such that the relation of major and minor premisses is crucial, rather than as a simple sequence of descriptive statements which might be made in any order. This point is obviously relevant to the inability to distinguish between logical and narrative order. Finally, there is no conception of logical quantifiers, of 'some', 'all', and 'none', so that the Uzbek subjects do not appreciate the logical implication of 'all' in 'In the Far North ... *all* bears are white', or 'none' in 'There are *no* camels in Germany'.

Similar tests were also given to the Kpelle based on the contexts of folk tales, where the characters had to solve logical problems. The results for the traditional, non-literate subjects were the same as for the hypothetical problems: '. . . subjects tended to reject the restricted set of possible solutions if the outcome violated some standard of social truth' (Cole and Scribner 1974: 168). Gay and Cole also report that formal techniques of logical inference are not employed by the Kpelle in their legal disputes:

The primary technique for winning a court case seems to be to produce an argument demonstrating conformity to tradition that the other party cannot answer. A person is admired for his ability to outsmart the other fellow in such an argument. It is not necessary that the point be supported by evidence or that it be logically sound. The important thing is that the statement be one that the other party can reply [to] with, at best, a lame and unsatisfactory answer. It is more nearly a test of wits and understanding of the Kpelle tradition than it is a test of truth and justice. The winning party must be able to convince the majority that he is wiser than those who oppose him. (Gay and Cole 1967: 24–5)

(Evidently, very much more remains to be said about techniques of argument in primitive society beyond the brief review of the matter given here, but the whole subject really requires a separate book for adequate treatment.)

Problems of grammar and syntax present difficulties to non-literates when considered in isolation from actual discourse. In my own experience of the Konso, they found the conjugation of verbs out of context very difficult to achieve without lapsing into practical speech. For example, having successfully negotiated the present tense of 'to go', after lengthy explanations that neither I nor anyone else was really going anywhere, but that I was only making sure that I was speaking correctly, I started on 'I will go'. 'Where will you go?' was the puzzled response. But while non-literate Konso, who had hardly ever seen paper and writing before, were easily capable of speaking to me at dictation speed after a little practice, and repeating, on request, exactly what they had just said, the Tauade, even the most intelligent, were quite incapable of this, even after months of experience. As a result, taking tests from dictation was impossible because they always spoke too fast, and when asked to repeat what they had just said, always altered it. Apparently they could not grasp that my problem was not what they had said, but my inability to represent it in written form. The Konso were also in the habit of giving etymologies of words, so it seems likely that the ability of non-literate peoples to distinguish between the form of an utterance and its use in actual speech is culturally variable. It is likely that folk etymologies and puns display an elementary awareness of language as a phenomenon distinct from speech. But in general it seems fair to say that the ability to give explicit verbal explanations of customary behaviour, to co-ordinate a set of reasons for a course of conduct or an attitude, and to treat logical and linguistic problems apart from their social and practical context are cognitive skills which are undeveloped among non-literates and are greatly affected by schooling.[7]

Primitive man lives in a society whose basic institutions are often inexplicable in the rationalist, causal, utilitarian terms appropriate in accounting for our own institutions such as banks, insurance companies, factories and their location, trade unions, universities, hospitals, and so on. When I was living among the Konso, who have nine patrilineal, exogamous clans, they asked me how many clans there were in England. 'We have no clans in my country.' 'What! Then how do you know whom you can marry?' For them,

[7] See below, pp. 126–32.

the clans have no clear origin, beyond vague traditions of the different points of origin of their forebears. They are basic institutions which cannot be questioned, and without which Konso society as they know it could not continue. Again, they live in walled towns whose populations average about 1,500 persons, and which in all probability, date back for many centuries. This is an extremely unusual form of settlement pattern in East Africa, but there is no evident reason why it should have been adopted. The Konso claim that they came together in towns because there had been too much fighting when they lived in scattered settlements, but this is a vague and most unlikely explanation; if anything, the congregation of the people into these large, traditionally autonomous towns made warfare harder to prevent and produced heavier casualties than would have been likely if they had lived in scattered settlements. The Konso propensity for living in large settlements is evidently an integral part of their ideal pattern of social life, and has no necessary relationship with defence and warfare. The same dense settlements are found in other parts of Konsoland where no defensive walls exist and the Burji, who are culturally related to the Konso, also have similar settlements. And many miles to the north, on a mountainside between Lakes Shamo and Margherita, live the Otschollo, in a single town among the Dorse, who inhabit the scattered homesteads typical of Ethiopia. An ethnographer working among the Dorse informs me that the Otschollo claim to be descended from the Konso.

Konso towns are divided into two named divisions; a man who is born in one division can never live in the other, though he may marry a woman from either division, or from another town. The people could give no explanation for these divisions, beyond saying that the first people to live in them came from different places; but this is no explanation for their persistence or for the rule of residence attached to them.

The Konso, like the Galla and a number of other East Cushitic language speakers, stratify their society by a generation-grading system in which, unlike the ordinary age-grading systems found in many primitive societies, a boy's grade is a fixed number of grades behind that of his father, irrespective of his actual age, so that a number of brothers and cousins will be in the same grade even though they are of widely differing ages. These grading systems regulate the age of marriage, such that a man may in extreme cases be thirty-five years old before he may take a wife, and there is only a rough correspondence between the ages of grade members and their theoretical status in society—boy, warrior, elder. The systems are very complicated to operate and are actually less efficient than ordinary age-grading systems as far as the regulation of social relations between elders and warriors is concerned, or for the coordination of town populations for military purposes. The purpose of the systems is ritual and moral, and the Konso say that without them the crops would not grow. There is, however, no evident practical reason why their ancestors should have established them, and the people can give no further explanation for their existence. Like the clans, the grading systems are an unquestionable and integral part of their society without which social life as they know it could not continue.

These examples could be paralleled among all primitive societies, and the existence of social institutions for which there is no obvious utilitarian purpose has led functionalist anthropologists to invent their own explanations and foist them on the natives. My purpose here is not to expose functionalism to further ridicule, but to emphasize that to be born into a society whose basic institutions are simply accepted without question as the only proper ones, since they often rest on word and symbolic foundations, is a powerful disincentive to the development of the critical, analytical, and generalizing faculty in very extensive areas of social life. One has only to reflect on the continuing debate on forms of government which have been a feature of Western European civilization since the last Tarquin was expelled from Rome, and the political and constitutional theorizing of the Greeks, to appreciate the force of this distinction. While there may be rebellions in tribal society, there are no revolutions (as Gluckman has said), for rebellion accepts basic institutions without question and seeks only to change their personnel.

One would not claim that all primitive institutions are of this type. The Konso, for example, have ward and town councils, town criers, organized working parties, and markets, which have practical, utilitarian purposes obvious to the people themselves. In all primitive societies, however, the basic institutions and social categories have a moral and cosmological significance which cannot be made verbally explicit and phrased in terms of general principles, rules, and purposes by the members of these societies, since, as we shall see in more detail in the following chapters, the classification and symbolism of primitive societies embodies a concrete, non-verbal, sub-linguistic element of associations derived from shared sensory experience and common activities.

The lack of explicit purpose in many primitive institutions is closely associated with the lack of differentiation between what we distinguish as legal, political, economic, and religious institutions, with idiosyncratic features of organization, inconsistencies, and the pervasion of institutions by symbolism and moral values. It is evident that, because primitive technology and ecology are so simple, they can be operated in a wide variety of ways all of which are compatible with survival, but an industrial society has by its very nature to meet stringent requirements of organizational efficiency which are incompatible with an organization in terms of moral values and symbolism:

Given the primary requirement of efficiency, none of the components of a business corporation has any absolute value, beyond its contribution to the success of the whole organization. But one frequently finds that groups and categories in traditional societies do have some absolute moral or symbolic value, irrespective of any putative contribution they may make to the efficiency of the whole society. Craftsmen in many societies of Ethiopia are despised, for example, in spite of their necessity for their host societies. This lack of absolute value by groups and categories is closely linked with another property of industrial organization, which is the substitutability of personnel, in accordance with the changing demands placed upon that organization. It would be impossible to run a large business efficiently if jobs were restricted to members of particular castes, descent groups, age-grades, or one sex or class. As a consequence of this, tasks within the organization and categories of persons from whom the organization recruits its members must be entirely stripped of absolute value and symbolic or moral significance ... (Hallpike 1977: 283)

In other words, societies that are ordered by status and not by contract are permeated with concrete symbolism and moral values, which in turn make it extremely difficult to generalize in explicit verbal terms about the purposes of institutions, and to detect and explain inconsistencies.

Horton correctly draws attention to the fact that in a primitive society, whose representations are homogeneous and whose members have little genuine awareness of significantly different ways of thought and representations of the world, this lack of comparative opportunity is a very important inhibition to more generalized and analytical modes of thought:

> ... the traditional thinker, because he is unable to imagine possible alternatives to his established theories and classifications, can never start to formulate generalized norms of reasoning and knowing. For only where there are alternatives can there be choice, and only where there is choice can there be norms governing it. (Horton 1967: 162)

While members of primitive societies often encounter members of other societies, this is often for specific and limited purposes, such as trade, of which Horton says,

> ... culturally contrasted trading partners remained basically rooted in different communities, from which they set out before trade, and to which they returned after it. Under these limitations, confrontation with alien world views remained very partial. The trader encountered the thought of his alien partners at the level of common-sense but not usually at the level of theory. Since common-sense worlds, in general, differ very little in comparison with theoretical worlds, such encounters did not suffice to stimulate a strong sense of alternatives. (Ibid. 182)

There are thus many reasons why the primitive milieu should foster thinking that is context-bound, concrete, non-specialized, affective, ethnocentric, and dogmatic, as opposed to the generalizable, specialized, abstract, impersonal, objective, and relativist. But one of the most important factors in maintaining these broad characteristics of primitive thought is the absence of schooling and literacy. We must now consider what effects these experiences have on thinking.

3. THE EFFECTS OF SCHOOLING AND LITERACY
ON COGNITIVE DEVELOPMENT

As we have seen, in primitive society most of the children's learning takes place by observation and participation in real life situations. But in a literate society, as Bruner points out, the situation is very different:

> ... there is knowledge and skill in the culture far in excess of what any one individual knows. And so, increasingly, there develops an economical technique of instructing the young based heavily on *telling* out of context rather than *showing* in context. ... For the school is a sharp departure from indigenous practice. It takes learning ... out of the context of im-

mediate action just by dint of putting it into a school. This very extirpation makes learning become an art in itself, freed from the immediate ends of action, preparing the learner for the chain of reckoning remote from payoff that is needed for the formulation of complex ideas. (Bruner 1965: 1009)

With specific reference to the importance and impact of literacy on the child, the conventional attitude of anthropologists is that literacy is simply an aid to the mechanism of communication. Goody, for example, says:

In 1970 I spent a short time revisiting the Lo Dagaa of Northern Ghana, whose main contact with literacy began with the opening of a primary school in Birifu in 1949. In investigating their mathematical operations I found that while non-school boys were expert in counting a large number of cowries (shell money), a task they so often performed more quickly and more accurately than I, they had little skill at multiplication. The concept of multiplication was not entirely lacking; they did think of four times five piles of cowrie shells as equalling twenty. But they had no ready-made table in their minds (the 'table' being essentially a written aid to 'oral' arithmetic) by which they could calculate more complex sums. The contrast was even more true of subtraction and division; the former could be worked by oral means (though literates would certainly take to pencil and paper for the more complex sums), the latter is basically a literate technique. *The difference is not so much one of thought or mind as one of the mechanics of communicative acts.* (Goody 1973: 7, my emphasis)

Besides ignoring the fact that tables are often taught by oral means in Western schools and that some mathematical tasks are harder than others because they involve understanding of more advanced logical concepts,[8] Goody misses the essential point that it is the cognitive demands of writing that are themselves very different from those of oral communication, because in written speech there is no interlocutor, and this is a new situation for the child.[9] In oral speech,

[8] See Chapter VI, pp. 248–52 below.
[9] In more recent publications Goody (1977) and Goody, Cole, and Scribner, (1977) has taken somewhat greater account of the fundamental changes in cognitive processes resulting from literacy, as elucidated by developmental psychology, but even in his recent book (1977) on the consequences of literacy for cognitive processes, he still talks of 'cognitive processes' without reference to any psychological theory of cognitive development and learning. Goody (1977) has made a useful contribution to our understanding of the way in which literacy, in the form of the compilation of lists, can transform classification from the complexive and unsystematic to the taxonomic, hierarchically organized, and exhaustive, and this particular aspect of liter-

. . . every sentence is prompted by a motive. Desire or need lead to request, question to answer, bewilderment to explanation. The changing motives of the interlocutors determine at every moment the turn oral speech will take. It does not have to be consciously directed—the dynamic situation takes care of that. The motives for writing are more abstract, more intellectualized, further removed from immediate needs. In written speech, we are obliged to create the situation, to represent it to ourselves.

Writing also requires deliberate analytical action on the part of the child. In speaking, he is hardly conscious of the sounds he pronounces and quite unconscious of the mental operations he performs. In writing, he must take cognizance of the sound structure of each word, dissect it, and reproduce it in alphabetical symbols, which he must have studied and memorized before. In the same deliberate way, he must put words in a certain sequence to form a sentence. (Vygotsky 1962: 99)

These points are developed by Greenfield and Bruner as follows:

The written language, as Vygotsky (1962) points out, virtually forces remoteness of reference on the language user. Consequently, he cannot use pointing as an aid, nor can he count on simple labelling that depends upon the present context to make clear what one's label refers to. Writing, then, is training in the use of linguistic contexts as independent of immediate reference. Thus, the imbedding of a label in a sentence structure indicates that it is less tied to its situational context and more related to its linguistic context. The implications of this fact for manipulability are great; linguistic contexts can be turned upside down more easily than real ones; this linguistic independence of context produced by certain grammatical modes may favour the development of the more context-independent superordinate structures manifested by the school children. (Greenfield and Bruner 1966: 104)

The studies by Cole et al. (1971) of the effects of schooling and literacy on the Kpelle of Liberia are the most detailed so far conducted by developmental psychologists. They find that children who have been to school and acquired literacy are clearly superior to those who have remained traditionally illiterate, in their ability to explain verbally their reasons for making particular choices in test situations. One finds that illiterates, including adults, even if they are able to make correct judgements, either cannot justify them verbally, or if they make the attempt, give manifestly absurd

---

acy will be considered in more detail in Chapter V, on Classification. But one is bound to add that he treats literacy as *the* factor responsible for cognitive development, and ignores the many other factors (even schooling) which can be shown to be of great importance.

reasons, or reasons of the type 'I did it because I felt like it.' It was found in classification experiments that the more general the class of objects, the harder it was to verbalize about them. For example, illiterate subjects were able to describe the basis of solution only 10 per cent of the time for the two most general classes, but succeeded 25 per cent of the time in the case of specific classes.

A second prominent characteristic of the kind of thinking produced by literacy and schooling is the use of taxonomic categories, e.g. 'tool', 'container', 'agricultural implement', etc., or what Piaget would term 'logical classes', as opposed to perceptual, associational, and functional categories in classificatory tasks. Perceptual properties are those of colour, size, and shape, etc.; associational properties are those of the common contexts in which things are found; while functional properties are the kinds of things that something can do or the uses to which it is commonly put. The non-literate subjects, and those with only a short period of schooling, predominantly classified by 'functional entailment'.

A pair of objects was selected so that the first went with, or operated upon, the second. For example, a potato and a knife were put together because 'you take the knife and cut the potato'. Very rarely was a large group formed, and we virtually never had a classification justified in terms of the way things look or their common membership in a taxonomic category. (Cole *et al.* 1971: 79)

Taxonomic classification is based on generalizable features of a class which are common to all its members and distinguish them from those of other classes. While non-literates can employ taxonomic classification, it seems that they do so with much less facility, and in more restricted circumstances, than people who have been to school.[10]

The experience of schooling and literacy also seems to develop the search for rules for the solution of problems and the awareness of one's own mental operations:

... attendance at school apparently encourages an approach to classification tasks that incorporates a search for a rule—for a principle that can generate the answers. At the same time, schooling seems to promote an awareness of the fact that alternative rules are possible—one might call this a formal approach to the task in which the individual searches for and selects from the several possibilities a rule of solution. Finally, the one

[10] See further below, Chapter V, p. 187–94.

unambiguous finding in the studies to date is that schooling (and only schooling) contributes to the way in which people describe and explain their own mental operation. (Cole and Scribner 1974: 122)

Literacy and schooling can therefore be said to have the following general effects on those who experience them, the comparison with the non-literate, traditional folk who do not experience them. Literacy encourages children to treat language as a thing in itself, as separable from its context of use in everyday life, and to be analysed and played with independently of its practical connotations. This allows verbal problems, especially logical ones of the type we considered earlier, to be solved on their own terms, according to the demands of the particular problem, without recourse to actual experience. In the same way, hypothetical and conditional statements can be evaluated and followed up without reference to considerations of their actual probability or familiarity.

With literacy and schooling goes an increased ability to adopt general, taxonomic modes of classification and to specify articulately what these are when engaged in classification. There is also increased ability to apply these taxonomic criteria over a much wider range of unfamiliar phenomena than the non-literates are capable of, and to reclassify the same phenomena or objects according to different criteria. Associated with this is the search for rules for solving a range of related problems and the ability explicitly to choose between a variety of possible and alternative rules.

Literates have a greater capacity to analyse what they perceive into component elements at the verbal level. This is a probable reason for their greater propensity to classify objects by form rather than by colour, though the experience of written characters, identifiable only by form and not by colours, is likely to be of great importance here also. Literates also tend to be able to draw what they see rather than what they know—this, too, is a facet of the ability to analyse perceptions and to distinguish between different perspectives and points of view of an object, characteristic of concrete operations.

Awareness of language as a thing in itself, ability to explain and communicate efficiently about aspects of experience that are not customarily put into words, and the capacity to escape from the limited perspective of one's own particular experience into the world of the hypothetical and the deductive, are distinctive characteristics of the literate mind which are generally lacking in non-literates. In all these respects schooling is evidently the basis of the formal operations discussed in Chapter I.

But Cole *et al.* warn against the simplistic view that the non-literate member of a primitive society is incapable of conceptual thinking:

It is *not* the case that the non-educated African is incapable of concept-based thinking or that he never combines subinstances to obtain a general solution to a problem. Instead, we have to conclude that the situations in which he applies general, concept-based modes of solution are different and perhaps more restricted than the situations in which his educated age mate will apply such solutions. (Cole *et al.* 1971: 225)

Nor does literacy itself provide some magic talisman by which pre-operatory thought can be transcended. It depends on the use to which literacy is put. If those who acquire it are obliged to use it merely in memorizing sacred texts, such as the Koran, or the Ge'ez scriptures in Ethiopia, without in many cases even understanding the meaning of what they read, it is evident that no cognitive development of any significance may be expected. Or if, as in many underdeveloped countries, 'literacy' merely means the ability to write one's own name and spell out the headlines in a newspaper, which is more commonly used for rolling cigarettes than for reading, then again little benefit will be derived. Written characters in such contexts may be assimilated to the status of other concrete symbols, as when passages from sacred texts are used as amulets or written on paper which is burned and then drunk with water. In its true sense, 'literacy' means the habitual use of writing as a means of expressing ideas.

In short, we find that while educated subjects are capable of applying taxonomic classification to a wide variety of subjects, of reclassifying them, of solving verbal problems that do not relate to their own experience, and of generally searching for rules by which a whole set of problems can be solved and by which sub-problems can be treated as related in terms of a single larger problem, this is not true of non-literate traditional subjects. While they *can* employ taxonomic classification and can reclassify, in some situations, they are far more limited by their own experience and find it difficult to generalize in terms of rules of wide applicability. The educated possess a cognitive strategy which allows them to solve problems in a far wider range of circumstances than that with which traditional non-literates are familiar.

4. CONCLUSIONS

The burden of this chapter is that the verbal analysis of experience, of social behaviour and custom, will be given a low priority in societies where experience is roughly the same for everyone, where behaviour is largely dominated by custom, and where institutions are part of a social structure that is not the subject of debate. Only when we have verbally to translate our experience and way of life for the benefit of strangers do we have to fall back upon verbal analysis and generalization, and in primitive society there are no strangers, or at least no intellectually inquisitive ones.

Generalization is required for instruction out of context, for comparison and analysis, for reconciling felt contradictions between different aspects of life or different representative modes (as when we engage in musical or art criticism for example), and for planning and deliberate experiment. As we have seen, the circumstances of primitive life do not generally present problems requiring generalization. Language in these societies is not a tool of conceptual analysis, but the basic vehicle of social interaction, of conveying information, of persuading, of concerting action, and there is no awareness of 'propositions' dissociated from the context of utterance or of 'language' as a phenomenon distinct from 'speech'.

Generalization is also inhibited in primitive society because their institutions and customs are rooted in behaviour and affect, embedded in a context of action, expressed in a perceptually dominated concrete symbolism, in great measure non-purposive, idiosyncratic, undifferentiated, and unchanging.

In summary we may say that the specific features of primitive society reviewed in this chapter, which seem to be of particular relevance in inhibiting the development of concrete and formal operations, are as follows:

1. There is a rigid association of features of the natural environment into 'global' associations.

2. There is an association between natural and human cycles and life processes generally.

3. Natural and social processes are resistant to causal analysis of a mechanistic type, especially since there are no machines or mechanical devices by which to learn this type of analysis.

4. The natural world is experienced only in so far as it affects

man, not other objects, and hence its properties remain subjectivized and tied to sensory attributes.

5. There is little explicit planning, experiment, or measurement needed for the majority of tasks.

6. Technologically, the range of problems is narrow, and they can be solved by traditional means.

7. The technology is integrated with the rest of social relations, so that it is very hard to think of a technological problem *purely* as a problem.

8. Education is by participation, within the context of real tasks, rather than by verbal instruction out of context.

9. Questioning and non-conformity are repressed.

10. The individualization of experience is poorly developed and there is general homogeneity of points of view.

11. The problems of daily life are chiefly those of personal interaction, in which pre-operatory thought is quite adequate.

12. Shared experience and mutual knowledge permit wide use of concrete and specific symbolism, proverbs, allusions, etc., and inhibit generalization.

13. Proverbial wisdom in particular is refractory to generalization.

14. Argumentation is unformalized and incoherent; there is no idea of purely formal, logical inference; there is a rejection of reasoning on the basis of assumptions that are not within the experience of the individual.

15. Many institutions have no clear purpose, are based on 'status' rather than 'contract', and are permeated with symbolic and moral values, which are opposed to efficiency and planning.

16. There is no detailed experience of alternative belief systems or modes of social organization.

17. The absence of literacy makes an analysis of the forms of language outside the context of utterance, as a distinct phenomenon with its own laws, impossible.

18. Schooling promotes classificatory thinking of the generalizing, taxonomic type; the search for rules that generate answers to a wide range of problems; the awareness of the possibility of different rules; the ability to verbalize the reasons for judgements and to reason hypothetically irrespective of the way things actually are; and an awareness of one's own mental processes.

19. There are no conflicts in modes of representation—such as

the ethnographer perceives, for example, between symbolic meaning and the verbal exposition of that meaning.

20. There are few opportunities for men of high intelligence and intellectual interests to meet and discuss together.

It is of special significance that the great majority of these socio-environmental factors affecting individual cognitive growth are quite irrelevant to thought from the point of Durkheimian theory, which places the fundamental emphasis on institutional forms such as the specialization of labour and bureaucratic regulation in the evolution of thought (Douglas, for example, refers to 'forms to fill in triplicate ... licences and passports and radio-police cars' (1966: 92)). This is because the factors listed here are primarily effective through their influence on individuals, whose thought processes, as we have seen, are dismissed by Durkheimian sociology as irrelevant to the formation of collective representations. But the application of developmental psychology has shown that a rich and varied set of socio-environmental characteristics have important effects in retarding conceptual thinking at the verbal level in primitive society. So by distinguishing between the general characteristics of pre-operatory thought, on the one hand, and the specific elaborations of that thought by purely social processes into the cosmologies, symbolic structures, and official beliefs of particular societies, on the other, we can in fact deepen our understanding of the relationship between society and collective representations. Durkheimian sociology, by refusing to consider the nature of learning and thinking at the individual level, has thus blinded itself to the importance of a wide variety of socio-environmental factors in the formation of collective representations.

4

Symbolism

In previous chapters we have seen that language functions in primitive society as an integral element of social relations rather than as a tool of conceptual analysis or a self-sufficient encapsulation of the categories of the society. Most primitive societies are distinguished from our own by the greater prominence of non-linguistic symbolic representations based on imagery and the shared associations of everyday objects derived from co-operative action, as opposed to linguistic representations. The purpose of this chapter is to examine the extent to which symbolism can both be the vehicle for socially defined meaning and at the same time derive some of its meaning from men's interactions with their physical environment rather than from purely culturally determined origins, and the extent to which symbolism can be the basis of non-linguistic categories of social organization and cosmology. In order to do this it will be necessary to draw upon the researches not only of Piaget but also of psychologists such as Asch and Osgood who have not approached symbolism from a developmental point of view.

But before pursuing the distinction between language and symbolism, it is necessary first to distinguish between 'private' and 'social' signifiers and further, between the index, the symbol, and the sign.[1] The *index*, of which a good example is the footprint of a man which we discover in the mud of a path, or a high body temperature in the presence of fever, signifies its referent by some causal, physical relationship with it. The *symbol*, however, cannot be related in any causally inferential manner to its referent since, while there is some physical or perceptual association between the

[1] The definitions of these terms given here differ markedly from those of other authorities e.g. Leach 1976. There is no standard or authoritative set of definitions, and it is most convenient to follow those of Piaget 1962.

symbol and what it stands for and, as we shall see, usually an affective one as well, the association has an arbitrary element of variability which prevents the identification of symbol and referent by inductive inference alone. Thus stone may be the symbol of permanence, or of power and strength, or of lifelessness, and just which of these associations is intended when stone is used symbolically in a social context cannot be known with certainty merely from the fact that it is stone that is being used. Moreover, symbols are 'motivated' in a way that words are not; that is, they have an inherent relation to the signified which words do not. Words are *signs*—that is, unmotivated signifiers related to the signified purely by convention, and to this extent they are entirely social devices for the representations of meaning unlike the symbol, which as we shall see derives much of its meaning from non-social experience. This is not to say that words may not also have symbolic value, especially at the phonological level,[2] and that the *utterance* of a word or words in a real situation may not also be an index, e.g. of rage, pain, etc. The interpretation of indices is, of course, well within the power of all animals, and is indeed the basic means of their survival but, apart from some very limited use among the higher primates, the employment of symbols and signs is a distinctive manifestation of human thought.

1. SYMBOLISM AND PRE-OPERATORY THOUGHT

Symbolism makes its appearance at the end of the sensori-motor period, when the child has developed his grasp of the permanent object and can form images of things and events not physically present to him, the image being an interiorized imitation, a kind of schema or summary of the permanent object. The image functions as a symbol when it is used to evoke absent realities. It thus represents a continuation of accommodation to the physical world, but is inherently accompanied, in the Piagetian scheme of things, by assimilation, whose tendency is to incorporate the perceptions of external objects and events into its existing schemata. Until the stage of concrete operations, the child's representations vacillate between a predominance of accommodation, in the form of imitation, and the predominance of assimilation, in the form of play and dreams.

---

[2] On the symbolism of words see Ch. 9, pp. 410–13.

The image is not the product of pure perception, but of imitative accommodation, which itself bears witness to the existence of an activity which is above perception and action but below reflective thought. (1962: 75) ... [There are two distinct levels in the mechanism of perception, those which produce, for example,] the geometric illusions which are common to all ages and many animals, and the 'perceptive' activity consisting of comparisons, analyses and anticipation etc. which is the source of corrections and regulation and which grows regularly with age. (Piaget 1962: 76)

[When we form a mental image of a visual scene perceived earlier] We analyse, compare and transform, using an activity which starts in perceptive regulation and comparison, but is integrated in a system of concepts enabling us to give meanings to the elements and relationships thus analysed. Now it is this perceptive activity and not perception as such which produces the image, which is a kind of schema or summary of the perceived object ... (Ibid. 77)

—and the image so produced is immediately integrated into conceptual intelligence as a 'signifier'.

Imitation between the ages of two and seven years involves a perceptive activity which tends to be incapable of analysis and comparison, of anticipation and transposition, such that the child is cognitively passive to what he perceives and his imagery is undetailed and rigid. At about seven to eight, when he starts to become capable of imitating detail, with analysis and reconstruction of the model, he begins to dissociate what he is imitating from his own ego (to abandon conceptual realism) and to discriminate. Imitation becomes deliberate and reflective, controlled by intelligence as a whole, whereas before this, conceptual realism can result in unconscious imitation.

Piaget regards imitation of people as the consolidating factor of social life, even though it is never anything more than a vehicle, and is not a motive, of inter-individual relations:

To our mind, the dynamic link is to be found either in compulsion, authority, and unilateral respect, which give rise to imitation of the superior by the subordinate, or in mutual respect and intellectual and moral equality, which are the origin of imitation between equals. (Ibid. 73)

In play and dreams, however, we have the predominance of assimilation over accommodation:

Unlike objective thought, which seeks to adapt itself to the requirements of external reality, imaginative play is a symbolic transposition which subjects things to the child's activity without rules or limitations. It is therefore almost pure assimilation, i.e., thought polarized by preoccupation with individual satisfaction. Since it is a mere expansion of tendencies it freely assimilates things to one another and everything to the ego. While therefore in the initial stages of representation the aspect of copy which is inherent in the symbol as 'signifier' is a continuation of imitation, what the symbol signifies i.e. the 'signified' may vary between the adequate adaptation characteristic of intelligence (assimilation and accommodation in equilibrium) and free satisfaction (assimilation subordinating accommodation). Finally, with the socialisation of the child, play acquires rules or gradually adapts symbolic imagination to reality in the form of constructions which are still spontaneous but which imitate reality. (Ibid. 87)

So some symbols are mere egocentric assimilation, while at the opposite pole other symbols, because of the accommodatory character of their representation, converge on the conceptual sign, though without being identified with it, and can thus be the basis of socialized communication and culturally determined meanings. An example of the latter would be the symbolism of heraldry, which is public and rule-governed, while the symbolism of egocentric assimilation is inherently private and cannot be made the basis of socialized communication.

While the mental image is derived from perception, as interiorized imitation, what the image is used to signify is not based on imitation, but on assimilation, and this is true for exteriorizations of images, as in the case of symbolic gestures and the selection of concrete objects to symbolize others. Because the image is derived from perception and is therefore 'motivated', it is inherently appropriate as the signifier of feelings and concrete experiences, as opposed to language which, being arbitrary and collective in origin, is the necessary vehicle of general and impersonal ideas. Symbolism is prior to, and independent of, language, which itself initially functions as symbol, not as sign.

Although the basis of the symbolic function is in individual mental processes and the assimilatory aspects of individual symbolism are inherently private and unstable, it is possible for Piaget's theory to comprehend the use of symbolism as a means of social communication. While the sign, i.e. the word, is always social, 'there is in all verbal and conceptual thought a stratum of imaged representation which enables the individual to assimilate for himself the general idea common to all' (ibid. 164). Again, there are many symbolic representations common to children and to primitives, such as the notion of water and wind as the origins of life which, while they have their origins in private perceptual images, are so common in experience that they can become the basis of collective representations. In other cases, the collective symbolic representations of a primitive society derive from common experience of a particular range of physical phenomena, such that there is a convergence of private imagery which allows private symbolism to be co-ordinated and used as a basis of communication.

There are thus a number of functional equivalents between social symbolism and private symbolism. The first general similarity is derived from the fact that private symbolic thought is not accommodated to reality, and therefore cannot be given conscious, purposive verbal formulation. In the case of general symbols, this is because the process of their assimilation is below the conscious level of individual thought, and in the case of social symbolism, because individuals are unaware of how particular symbolic conventions have come to be established in their society.

Secondly, symbolism is independent of language, and, indeed, the symbolic object, being a real substitute for what it represents, makes it actually present in a way that the verbal sign can never achieve. Moreover, affective schemata, which are an inherent aspect of symbolism, do not achieve the same degree of generalization and abstraction as logical schemata (except in the one case where they are regulated by reversible operations of reciprocity and thereby become moral schemata).

Thirdly, symbolic thought is but one facet of pre-operatory thought, whose representations are in the form of concrete images (as opposed to those of operational thought) and lack logical classes which are replaced by complexes represented by the image not merely as illustration but as prototype. The pre-concepts represented by concrete symbols are half general, half individual schemata, for which words or other collective signs are still inadequate. The image of the pre-concept signifies it because the image constitutes a partial substitute for the thing signified through a kind of 'adherence to the sign', typical of all primitive symbols. As we shall see in the case of primitive representations of space and time, articulated intuition is based

on perceptual configurations, in which a set of elements is linked into a single total form, but which is still basically an image. It is, therefore, no longer the image of an object, but of a schema, an image which in intuitive thought is as essential to the existence of the schema as the image of the prototypical individual is to the existence of the pre-concept. Thus in intuitive seriation and inclusions, in the various cardinal and ordinal forms of intuitive correspondences, either the perception or the image of the configuration is indispensable to the thought. Only at the operational level do we have accommodations that are the same for all possible situations, and the operation is independent of any particular figure of the chosen system, while concrete imagery assists thought only in the capacity of illustration. (Ibid. 243–4)

Symbolic reasoning is closely associated with transductive inference, which lacks a reversible nesting of a hierarchy of classes and relations. Transductive inference may look superficially like logical reasoning, with integration of particular cases in general classes or propositions, but really the generalizations are in no sense operational, because they are still centred and irreversible, even though this method of inference can give correct conclusions in some cases.

It should be noted, however, that 'condensation' and 'displacement' of symbolism are the functional equivalents of the generalization and abstraction found in operational thought. 'Condensation' involves giving a common meaning to a number of distinct objects, and 'displacement' in the realm of images and affective assimilation corresponds to abstraction.

While Piaget does not, therefore, rule out the possibility of symbolism as the vehicle of culturally defined meaning, he regards 'socialized thought' as basically the product of linguistic communication. No doubt, since his subjects have been the children of industrialized society, in which socially defined symbolism has little place by comparison with primitive society, Piaget had considerable empirical justification for regarding symbolism as inherently a private aspect of cognition rather than a public aspect. Indeed, he seems to discount the possibility of stable socialized systems of representation below the level of concrete operations, regarding accommodation to the thought of others as on a par with accommodation to physical reality through operational thinking at least at the concrete level:

The essential condition for objectivity of thought is that assimilation of reality to the system of adapted notions shall be in permanent equilibrium with accommodation of these same notions to things and to the thought of others. It is obvious that it is only by the constitution of systems of logical operations (reversibility of transformations of thought), of moral operations (preservation of values), and spatio-temporal operations (reversible organisation of elementary physical notions), that such an equilibrium can be achieved, for it is only through operational reversibility that thought becomes capable of preserving its notions despite the fluctuations of reality and incessant contact with the unexpected. (Piaget 1962: 166)

I argue, however, that while this may be true in literate and industrial societies, it is not necessarily true of the primitive milieu, where experience both of other people and of things is very much more stable and has very much less of the unexpected than Piaget takes to be the norm. To this extent, modes of cognition—pre-eminently symbolism—which Piaget regards as egocentric may indeed be adequate for accommodation to social and natural reality both for individual and collective representations, and Piaget does not take account of the fact that in primitive society the demands for accommodation to physical reality in particular are very much less than they are in our type of technological society.

To illustrate this perhaps controversial point we may consider a myth of the Yagwoia Kukukuku, who say that the sun is a man and the moon a woman, wife of the sun. The dew is the moon's urine and the sun is red in the morning because he is embarrassed by his wife's urination, which he quickly dries up by his heat (Fischer 1968: 384). This 'explanation' of dew and the redness of the sun is evidently a symbolic assimilation no different in kind from ludic and dream symbolism generally, since it is not based on systematic observation of dew and the sun's redness and fails to accommodate to the evidently non-human characteristics of the sun and moon, which are far more numerous than the 'resemblances' of which the myth does take account. Because this account of sun and moon is evidently based on the predominance of assimilation, it is immune to refutation by experience, since the 'experience' of the Kukukuku does not extend to a systematic observation and co-ordination of the incidence of dew and of the redness of the sun in the morning, e.g. the occasions when there is no dew, but the sun is red, or when there is dew, and the sun is not red. In the milieu of the Kukukuku, dew and the redness of the sun are of no relevance whatever to survival, hence the Kukukuku are free to elaborate whatever fantasies they please about the nature of these heavenly bodies and dew, which would be impossible for meteorologists or astronauts.

A further deficiency of Piaget's theory of symbolism from the anthropological point of view derives from a general characteristic of his developmental theory—he takes no account of imaginative, non-logical processes beyond saying that the process of assimilation, unlike accommodation, takes place below the level of consciousness. But we noted earlier (pp. 33–4) that non-logical, autistic thought processes are evidently a component of the highest levels of thought. Piaget's lack of attention to the accommodatory aspects of fantasy and imagination has been common to most psychologists until recently (cf. Vernon 1970) and does not diminish the value of his positive achievements, but it does mean that Piaget's theory cannot take proper account of those aspects of primitive thought such as mythology and cosmogony which, while they certainly have elements of fantasy, are also worthy of being considered as creative and imaginative representations of the relations between man and the world about him, in the same manner as a perceptive novel.

For these reasons Piaget's theory has relatively little to tell the anthropologist about the cultural potentialities of symbolism. More importantly, he does not consider the ways in which universal factors of perception common to all human beings, not only through their physiology but because they all inhabit the same physical world, may produce certain very general symbolic associations, especially those trans-sensory conjunctions such as colour/mood or sound/form associations known as 'synesthesia'.

But before we consider the ways in which men's physiology and interaction with the physical world may produce symbolic meanings that are largely independent of particular cultures, we must consider the main difference between language and symbolism, and the cognitive limitations in the articulation of mental processes.

2. LINGUISTIC AND SYMBOLIC MEANING

The essential characteristic of language as distinct from symbolism is that it has two levels—the phonological and the semantic. At the phonological level language has structure, but no meaning, nor even symbolic associations (with certain exceptions to be discussed in Chapter 9). The structuring of sound patterns is arbitrary and hence has enormously rich combinatorial possibilities, analogous to the combinatorial potential of written signs. Because language is thus liberated from concrete and affective associations, it is able to express a whole range of states and relationships that have no counterpart in the physical world—assertions of truth and falsity, hypothetical and conditional statements, statements of existence and non-existence, references to time, mood, and quality of action in the aspect of verbs. The use of language allows us to indicate the reliability of utterances, to make distinctions between speaker and hearer by means of the inclusive and exclusive pronouns. Most important of all, linguistic statements can be the referents of other linguistic statements.

Symbols, however, have an inherent appropriateness to the things or events with which they are associated, even though these associations will be multiplex so that one will seldom be able to predict with certainty which association hair cutting or red will have in any given culture, or even in any given symbolic context within that culture. Because symbolic 'statements' are not propositions, they cannot be paraphrased, and do not possess analyticity (as Sperber (1975) has reminded us); symbols have homology, not paraphrase; correspondence, not tautology; opposition, not contradiction; and their motivations are absolutely ungeneralizable. Symbolic relations are not syntactic but based on those between material objects—contiguity, resemblance, sensible, intelligible, near or far, synchronic, diachronic, static, and dynamic. They are means of *organizing* experience, not of assessing, commenting on, explaining, or reducing it to conceptual principles and general laws—the Ndembu call symbols '*chijkijilu*', 'land-marks'.

While symbols do not have meaning but rather associations, and are instead motivated by their concrete associations in everyday life and experience, they have 'significance'; by this I mean that when used in a particular context by certain people in certain circumstances, one or some of their associations will thereby be selected as relevant, and others ignored. Significance, in this sense, is also, of course, a property of *utterances*, since these are spoken at a definite time in a definite place by a particular person, and can then, like physical objects and events, take on symbolic properties.

It is the combinatorial properties of symbols that, together with their motivation, give them the power of representing the categories of the society in a structured manner, to a degree which surpasses that of language in respect of emotional impact, concision, and immunity to refutation or contradiction, though one must remember that language can also be the vehicle of symbolic statements—in magic, ritual, myth, and dream narratives. To put a thought into words is often to render it affectively impotent; by stating something explicitly one lays it open to dispute and misunderstanding; a concrete symbol has a power that is quite lacking from the evanescent word.

It is in the expression of the basic social and cosmological categories that symbolism has a range and significance in primitive society which it has lost in our own. Our symbols are isolated from each other because our society has articulated its official categories —by which I mean legal, constitutional, political and economic— by purposive debate. Our way of life has largely excluded manifestations of the natural world from official consciousness, with the result that symbols function for us as metaphors and illustrations, not as potent entities in their own right which are parts of a total representative system. Primitive symbolism is collective, conventional in its associations, and systematic, and is in these respects unlike the ludic symbolism of children; but like ludic symbolism it clearly serves purposes that language cannot. It is made possible by the shared experience of a homogeneous, small-scale society living close to nature, so that individual imagery will converge far more closely than is the case for members of our own society. It is thus possible to construct a collective symbolism on the basis of co-operation and common experience to an extent that has considerable independence from language.

Since symbolism is integrally related to modes of classification, we can expect to find it predominant in societies where non-taxonomic classification based on complexes is the norm. It will become apparent that symbolic thought is basically static and rigid in imagery, and depends on prototypical images and perceptual configurations, that it is irreversible and uncoordinated in an operatory manner, without analysis of elements or comparison, unlike the mobile and generalizable transformations of operatory thought, and that it represents the predominance of assimilation over accommodation.

Because these symbolic collective representations preserve some of the basic characteristics of all symbolism—e.g. they are assimilative, motivated, and prototypical images and configurations— and because they represent the frequently implicit categories of the society, they cannot be challenged, analysed, or shown to be self-contradictory. To this extent they will not be accommodated to reality; they may achieve stability, but not equilibration between accommodation and assimilation, as we saw in the case of the Kukukuku myth of the sun and the moon; Kluckhohn has referred to myths as the collective dreams of the society.

Primitive symbolic systems achieve coherence and order, at the sub-linguistic level, but this has very limited explanatory application, and cannot be challenged empirically. These symbolic systems can become ever richer and more complex, but because they do not accommodate to reality and are inherently pre-conceptual, they can never develop in the way that operatory representations of reality do.

Symbolism in primitive society is not, however, simply a collectivization of individual imagery—if a society is poor in its social and cosmological categories it will have an impoverished social symbolism. A good example of this is provided by the Tauade, whose primary concern is with individuals and the particular relationships between them. Tauade society is extremely amorphous and atomistic, and while some symbolism exists, it is principally confined to representations of power—images of height and weight—and permanence—stones. It would be quite misleading to suppose that because symbolism is particularly characteristic of pre-operatory thought, it will therefore necessarily emerge and flourish prolifically in all primitive societies. For this to happen, the intermediary agencies of social and cosmological categories are necessary.

Because symbolism is inherently sub-linguistic, the ethnographer can never be completely sure that he has properly understood the meaning of a piece of symbolism, and in many cases he can only hope to make educated guesses. In so far as it is symbolic, primitive thought is therefore intellectually inaccessible to the European investigator, but this is not because of some innate difference between primitive thought and our own, but simply because it is in the nature of symbolism to be verbally untranslatable, at least in any complete or certain way.

Because beliefs and cosmological categories can be expressed non-verbally, in concrete symbolism, many of the most important social categories may be innominate, and the evidence for their existence may be scattered through a wide range of observances and particular concrete observances.

A good example of these points is provided by tree symbolism among the Umeda of the Sepik River, New Guinea, as described by Gell (1975). The Umeda cosmology is concerned with three types of tree: the coconut palm, the areca palm, and the Caryota or wild sago palm. The areca palm is *pul*, which also means 'fence', and forms the basis of the name of the culture hero Pul-Tod, 'areca-nut man', or 'human being'.

Areca palms are planted around the outer fringes of the hamlet and other inhabited sites. The inner hamlet is defined by the ring of houses and the shade-giving coconut palms; a vague outer circle is made up of plantations of Areca . . . In terms of spatial layout, . . . the Areca palms, planted in the ill-defined region between the hamlet proper and the surrounding secondary bush, stand in the same relation to the hamlet as the fence stands in relation to the garden, i.e. demarcating the boundary. (Gell 1975: 125)

Umeda village is divided into two moieties, *edtodna* and *agwatodna*, which are symbolically asymmetrical. *edtodna* is male, associated with the 'original' ancestors of the Umeda, the 'insiders', based on the ridge where the hamlets lie, and with the culture hero Toag-tod and the coconut, which is a symbol of culture; *agwatodna* moiety is female: its ancestors provided the first wives of the original Umeda, associated with the bush man, Naimo-tod, and the Caryota palm (wild sago), and with wild nature in general.

In Umeda mythology, the original man, Toag-tod (coconut man) the ancestor of the *edtodna*, had a younger brother, Pul-tod (areca-nut man), who later became Toag-tod's adopted son. Thus

$$\left. \begin{array}{c} \text{Toag-tod} \\ \\ \text{Coconut} \end{array} \right\} : \left\{ \begin{array}{c} \text{Pul-tod} \\ \\ \text{Areca} \end{array} \right. :: \left\{ \begin{array}{c} \text{eB} \\ \\ \text{F} \end{array} \right. : \left\{ \begin{array}{c} \text{yB} \\ \\ \text{S} \end{array} \right.$$

When compared with the coconut palm, the areca can be seen as a juvenile version of it:

Coconuts are characterized relative to most other palms by their greater height, and slow growth. Their long life-cycle corresponds roughly to that of a man. When old they acquire a gnarled, immemorial appearance. Areca palms are in this everything that coconut palms are not; slender, flexible, rapidly springing up, green-stemmed and swiftly maturing. A mature areca palm is about two-thirds the height of a mature coconut palm, slim and straight, with a mop of quite succulent green fronds bunched on top. A similar relationship obtains between the fruits of the two palms; the areca nut is, so to speak, a miniature, succulent, shell-less coconut; very like, in fact, an immature fruit from the larger palm. (Ibid. 125)

But there is a further spatial association between the areca palm, youth, and marginality. The older men congregate during the day in the centre of the hamlet in daily life, where their infant sons play with them. As they become older, the young boys are ejected from the centre of the hamlet to its periphery, to form the small boys' peer group.

Given the formula yB = Son = Areca, it is possible now to appreciate the strict parallelism between the spatial arrangement of the two species of palm (coconut = central/areca-nut = peripheral) and the similar spatial or field-relationship between the social groups of whom the palms are symbols (adult men = central/small boys (younger brothers and sons) = peripheral). And these relationships conform to the schema ... whereby *pul* in its dual meaning 'fence' and 'areca' corresponds to the idea of 'marginality'. (Ibid. 127)

Pul-tod, areca-nut man, is himself a marginal figure in the myths—he kills his father and marries his mother, is symbolically castrated, and 'wanders around in the bush, avoiding society (particularly feminine) and, as an informant put it, "he is not a real man"' (ibid. 128).

The Caryota palm is *naimo*, closely associated with the bush, and with women and the female moiety, *agwatodna*.

[It] is a wild palm species, called, in pidgin 'wild sago' (*wailsaksak*), though actually not a true sago species (*metroxylon*) at all. *Naimo* can be pounded up for its starch content, though Umedas would not do this except in the most dire emergency. Mostly, *naimo* is exploited as a source of edible grubs (*namos*), being specially felled so that the grubs may hatch in the trunk ... it was from a *naimo* palm that Naimo-tod, the ancestor of the *agwatodna* moiety emerged, together with his two daughters, who were the spouses of the *edtodna* ancestor. (Ibid. 128)

Why does it have this special place in the symbolism of the two moieties? Semantically, *naimo* is composed of two elements, *nai* and *mo*.

In isolation, *nai* has the meaning 'skirt', while *mo* has the meaning 'gullet' (also, by extension, 'word', 'speech'), *mo* also means 'larynx', 'Adam's apple'. Now while the latter element (*mo*) remains, at first sight, rather a puzzle, an immediate clue is afforded by *nai*: skirt. It is not simply that *nai* is a symbol of femininity, and matrilateral relations in general—matrikin being called *naina* 'of the skirt' (as we say, 'on the distaff side') as opposed to patrikin who are *pedana* 'of the penis-sheath'. *Nai* goes a long way towards explaining why it is Caryota, and not some other wild palm, which is seen as the origin of the 'feminine half' of the society. (Ibid. 129)

The argument here depends on the visual characteristics of the Caryota palm and its fruit. There is 'a striking similarity between the dangling fruit stems which are particularly characteristic of Caryota (and not, e.g. sago etc) and the fibre skirts worn by Umeda women. The fruit stems (*agwoi*) and fruit (*mov*), that is, the reproductive part of the trees, are in fact seen as intrinsically feminine' . . . (ibid. 129), and Gell concludes that it is likely, in view of this resemblance, that the *nai* in *naimo* is related to *nai* meaning 'skirt'. But there is also a physical and a semantic relationship between 'skirt' and 'sago':

Women's skirts (*nai*) are made from the fibrous immature leaf-material of the sago palm (*na*); being made of sago-fibre, skirts and sago are intrinsically linked together. Hence I am inclined to see the close relation between the segments *na* and *nai'* as no chance phenomenon. Nor is it difficult to perceive the nexus between both of these and *na*: mother's brother; we have seen that matrikin are *naina*: 'of the skirt', and matrikin are simply the class of mother's brothers and their descendants. At this point a consistent set of relationships can be seen to emerge: the *nai-* in *naimo* being motivated on several planes simultaneously, i.e. both in terms of the actual palm with its skirt-like fruit-stems, and also in terms of the mythological role of the palm as the supposed origin of the female half of the society. For in mythological terms the relation of the moieties, the male 'village' *edtodna* moiety, and the female 'bush' *agwatodna* moiety, is a hypostatization of the basic schema of marriage alliance, whereby the individual exogamous hamlets receive their wives from, and form matrilateral alliances with groups other than their own, which seen from the standpoint of a male ego are 'lateral' or peripheral groups 'in the bush'. It is this structural opposition between the axis of ego and his agnates, coinciding with the permanent hamlet site, *versus* the peripheral field, the bush, the sago stands, the foreign hamlets from whom ego's group has obtained women, and with whom he stands in a relation of affinity and matrilateral alliance, which explains the lexical identity of sago, on the one hand, and the mother's brother on the other. Caryota, which is seen as a variety of sago (*na*), shares with it this association with maternal and matrilateral relationships. Thus, it is not only the skirt-like fruit-stems which correspond to *nai* in *naimo*, but also its characteristic habitat (bush as opposed to hamlet) and its association with sago, which is, in turn, the botanical analogue of the mother's brother. (Ibid. 131–2)

A similar analytical procedure allows us to relate the element *-mo* in *naimo* to the basic themes of fruit and femininity:

mo	gullet, Adam's apple
mo-tod	daughter, female child
mol	girl, daughter
mol	vulva
mov	fruit (*movwi*)
mov	vulva (polite) also *amoi*, small girl, daughter, vulva
amov	termites (cf. *namos*, grubs)

What is apparent in the list of *mo* words is a series of analogies which seem to be implicit in Umeda vocabulary, between parts of the body (gullet, vulva), parts of tree and plant structure (fruit, in this instance), and a social role (daughter, girl) . . . the *naimo* palm is mythologically the origin of daughters (*mo-tod*), i.e. marriageable girls. Girls (*mol*) are to be identified with fruit (*mov*) and . . . *naimo* is characterized by a truly incalculable number of individual fruit (*movwi*)—a feature which distinguishes *naimo* sharply from the local sago cultigens which are almost all infertile, producing no fruit at all. (Ibid. 132–3)

3. UNIVERSAL ASPECTS OF SYMBOLISM AND THEIR NON-CULTURAL ROOTS

Leach claims that: 'The indices [symbols] in non-verbal communication systems, like the sound elements in spoken language, do not have meaning as isolates but only as members of sets. A sign or symbol only acquires meaning when it is discriminated from some other contrary sign or symbol' (Leach 1976: 49).

As we have seen in the case of Umeda tree symbolism, the *contrasts* between the three types of trees, in their physical characteristics, locations, and the associations of these with social categories, focus attention on the distinctive characteristics of each type of tree and emphasize them, but it goes too far to claim that the areca palm can be thought of as having the associations of 'marginality' only by contrast with the coconut. Undoubtedly, the opposed characteristics of the coconut palm make those of the areca more evident, but it would still be possible for the Umeda to use the areca as a symbol of marginality even if they had no coconut palms and if there were no other specific symbol for 'centrality' or 'insiders'. It is the specific physical characteristics of each symbol, not its relation with other symbols, that are fundamental; as we have seen, symbols are distinguished from signs precisely because they are *motivated*, and do not derive their significance from relations akin to the syntactic structures of language. Moreover, if Leach were right, it is hard to understand how we find so many examples of cross-cultural symbolic equivalences, such as white = pure, good; black = impure, bad; or stone = power, permanence, and so on. Leach's argument would confine symbols to a complete culturally determined relativism, whereas it can easily be shown that the generality of symbolic associations derives from man's physical relations with his environment and from the metaphorical appropriateness of some of these associations to social relations and cultural values. This is not to say, however, that the physical associations of symbols necessarily tend to uniformity of interpretation, even within the same culture. Within any culture, however, they can be expected to be ambiguous: Turner's data on colour symbolism among the Ndembu of Northern Rhodesia provide a good example.

For the Ndembu whiteness has both auspicious and inauspicious aspects. Auspiciously, it is associated with breast milk, semen, and cassava meal, and so stands for life, health, fertility, the continuity of the matrilineage, strength, and eating; it is associated with light generally, and with the sun and moon, 'Whiteness as light streaming forth from the divinity has, in the sense we are considering here, a quality of trustworthiness and veracity, for Ndembu believe that what is clearly seen can be accepted as a valid ground of knowledge'[3] (Turner 1967: 76). It is associated with cleanness and purity; while the Ndembu are Negroes they still distinguish between skin coloration in terms of the black/white opposition, and blackness is associated with dirt. Whiteness is associated with grey hair, and hence with maturity and wisdom; and with the whiteness of the teeth, as when one laughs and displays one's teeth, thus being a sign of openness and honesty. Turner sums up the auspicious connotations of whiteness as follows: 'Behind the symbolism of whiteness, then, lie the notions of harmony, continuity, purity, the manifest, the public, the appropriate, and the legitimate' (ibid. 77). But there is another side to whiteness, and here I shall quote an extended passage from Turner's exposition, in which he refers to the symbolic value of whiteness in Melville's *Moby Dick*:

The Ndembu, like Melville, have an ambivalent attitude towards whiteness. For example, in their herbal therapy for leprosy, the white-spotted bark of a certain tree is used as a sympathetic cure for the white spots made by that dreaded disease. The white gum of the *kapumbwa* tree and certain white roots represent the pus produced by venereal infections.

[3] The Ommura of New Guinea have a similar notion: see below, pp. 394-5.

Whiteness also represents the destructiveness of lightning. In hunting rituals, too, whiteness has terrifying and lethal associations. *Mundeli*, for example, is said to be a mode of spirit affliction which appears in dreams in the form of a European. It was formerly believed that Europeans lived under the South Atlantic, and that their skin got its corpse-like bleach from long immersion in the salt water. Another spirit, believed to persecute hunters, Mukala, is represented in the ritual of that name by such white symbols as white clay and white beads, because it takes the form of marsh lights (described as 'white') which lead hunters to their destruction in morasses. As lightning, and as will-o-the-wisp, light has its malevolent manifestations. Here another affinity with 'Moby Dick' should be noted, cf. Chapter CXVIII, the candles where the ominous corpusants burn on the lightning rods of the *Pequod*: 'Three tapering white flowers; God's burning finger laid on the ship', 'the white flame but lights the way to the white whale'. It is significant, too, that only *Chihamba* [the White Spirit] and *Mukala*, among modes of spirit manifestation, are believed to have the power of causing death, and not merely misfortune. It should be noted that such 'white' beings as chiefs and ancestor spirits have the power to punish those who disobey them. They are feared by their juniors and inferiors. No less than Ishmael do the Ndembu find white things 'appalling'. (Turner 1962: 90)

Whiteness, then, is also associated with destruction, bleaching, absence of life, punishment, and sickness. Turner's central point about the ambivalence of whiteness and of Kavula, God, of whom it is the principle symbol, is that the Ndembu perceive Him as embodying both destruction and restoration, punishment and healing:

Like all primitive and peasant communities they have a sensitive awareness of cyclicality, of successive phases of drought and rain, of heat and cold, of hunger and plenty. It is because they trust in the supersession of phases inimical to human prosperity, that they can in ritual feel emboldened to represent in symbols the humiliation, poverty, and death of their ritual subjects. And precisely through plumbing the depths they expect to regain the heights. In one sense Kavula represents simultaneously, in a lightning flash, so to speak, the whole cycle. That is why his attributes are so ambivalent. (Turner 1962: 94)

So while whiteness has many symbolic facets among the Ndembu, and while the auspicious aspects are more in evidence in some contexts than others, where the inauspicious aspects are emphasized, it is untrue to say that the 'meaning' of whiteness simply depends on the context. The context selects from a range of meanings, but this range is not decided by context, but by the stable discrete characteristics of the physical world as they are ordered by

Ndembu cosmology. To this extent the meaning of whiteness, its range and ramifications of association, are context-independent. Indeed, it is the stable characteristics of things that permit their use in symbolic communication in the first place; thus it would be impossible to have a symbolic system (as opposed to a language) in which the symbols had no primary associations and in which their meaning was entirely relative and context-dependent, like phonemes.

A good example of the cross-cultural generality of symbolic significance is provided by the symbolic theme of hair and its cutting in ritual contexts (see Hallpike 1969 for a full discussion).

Vegetation and hair in their natural states grow into a tangled mass, unless checked by other natural forces; but cutting is an activity and manifestation of human culture, like the cooking of food. It is thus appropriate that the ritual cutting of hair should be symbolic of socialization, that long hair should be symbolic of standing in some way outside society, and that short hair should symbolize the restraints imposed by society. Again, animals are hairy while man, relatively, is not, and this opposition provides a complementary theme which reinforces the first. Hair also has great manipulative potential, since it can be cut off painlessly or dressed in various ways; and it can act as a *pars pro toto* extension of the body for magical purposes or for self-mutilation.

Thus we find that monks, soldiers, and convicts, who live under the discipline of institutional life, are marked in many societies by having their hair cut short. The Bible provides a series of equations between hairiness = outside society (morally, spiritually, or physically), and hair cutting = social control, incorporation into society:

hairiness	= hunter (Esau)
,,	= wild beasts (Nebuchadnezzar)
,,	= physical strength (Samson)
,,	= rebellion (Absalom)
,,	= asceticism (Elijah, John the Baptist)
growing long hair	= separation from society to God (Nazarites)
shaving hair	= rejoining society, or submission (Nazarites; when lepers are cured; when female prisoners of war are incorporated into society by marriage)
covering hair	= discipline (woman's acceptance of husband's authority)

It is clear that the long hair/short hair opposition incorporates a number of different ideas: one can be outside society as a saint, a beast, or a madman, and one can be incorporated into society or an institution as a prisoner, a volunteer, or because it is conventional to join it.

But the theme of 'hairiness = animality' is very widespread cross-culturally. For example, Gibbon says of the religion ascetics of Egypt,

The monks were divided into two classes; the *Coenobites*, who lived under a common and regular discipline; and the *Anachorets*, who indulged their unsocial, independent fanaticism. The most devout, or the most ambitious of the spiritual brethren, renounced the convent, as they had renounced the world ... All superfluous incumbrance of dress they contemptuously cast away, and some savage saints of both sexes have been admired, whose naked bodies were only covered by their long hair. They aspired to reduce themselves to the rude and miserable state in which the human brute is scarcely distinguished above his kindred animals; and the numerous sect of Anachorets derived their name from their humble practice of grazing in the fields of Mesopotamia with the common herd. They often usurped the den of some wild beast whom they affected to resemble ... (Gibbon 1960: 516)

Most primitive societies give animals an important place in their cosmologies, in which they often symbolize the chaos of untamed nature before the process of socialization. The culture-hero Dribidu of the Lugbara as described by Middleton is a good example of this association:

They [the two culture heroes] were not human as men are now: Dribidu means 'the hairy one', since he was covered with long hair over most of his body. He is also known as Banyale ('eater of men'), since he ate his children until he was discovered and driven out of his earlier home on the east bank of the Nile ... (Middleton 1960: 231) ... In our own terms, the significant difference between the periods before and after the heroes is that in the latter the personages were ordinary human beings, who behaved as people behave now, and who were members of clans and so of society, whereas in the former they behaved in a contrary manner and lived in isolation, in a world in which there were no clans. (Ibid. 233)

'Hairiness = animality, non-social life' is also the basic theme of the following Kukukuku myth from New Guinea, in which hairiness is associated with a state of primeval ignorance in which men were covered with hair and cooked their food on the women's genitals. The demonstration by a culture-hero of the proper method of cooking food, by fire, allows the hair to fall off their bodies:

Once upon a time the women cooked the food on their genitals, and everybody ate it. The men ate sweet potatoes raw. They smeared the sap from the stem of a plant (*himaluwje*) on branches and thus caught birds, which they dismembered and laid out in the sun. The sun dried them, and they ate them in this way. When it got dark they all went into the men's house to sleep [instead of sitting round the fire as now]. The bird *tabadewje* sawed fire on the branch of a tree. He said: 'I am no bird, I am a man.' The man who had smeared bird lime on the tree wanted to take the fire, but the bird nevertheless put it out quickly. The man asked: 'What do I do now, then?' Then the bird took a piece of split wood and a bamboo strip and tinder and threw them on the ground. The man sawed with the bamboo strip on the piece of wood and smoke appeared. The bamboo strip broke and he had fire. He roasted a bird and tried eating it. It tasted very good. He took pieces of wood and bamboo strips and dried them on the fire. Then he doused the fire and went to the bachelor house to sleep. The next morning they gave him sweet potatoes that had been cooked on the women's genitals. He said: 'I don't like that; give me raw sweet potatoes!' They gave him raw sweet potatoes; he ate half and put the other half in his string bag. Then he went and cooked it on the fire and ate it, whereupon all the hair of his skin fell off. At that time all men were hairy, because they cooked their food on the women's genitals. The man went back to the men's house and the other men asked him: 'What have you done to make all your hair fall off?' He said: 'I shaved it off with a bamboo knife'.

[But eventually he shows them the secret of fire-making, and they, too, lose all their hair, and so to this day men have no hair on their bodies.] (Fischer 1968: 395–6)

There is, however, a further association of hair and that is, obviously enough, with the head; there are numerous instances of the various features of the head being given sexual significance and of the genital area symbolically performing functions normally reserved for the face. This is because these are the only two regions of the body with orifices, which also have radically opposed functions, that of the face being the communication of words and non-verbal information by facial expressions, thus making it the basis of social intercourse and the essence of personal identity to one's fellows. The genito-anal region, on the other hand, is concerned with excretion, the totally non-social, and with copulation, the most dangerous intrusion of the physical into the social. The nose and tongue are analogues of the penis, as the mouth and ear are of the vagina or anus. It is not surprising, therefore, that because the natural, physical realm confronts the social-intellectual so blatantly in these two regions, an interchange between them should sometimes be appropriate in humour, magico-religious contexts, and popular sexual lore. It is clear from Onians's account of Ancient Greek and Roman beliefs about the body that the head was believed to be the source of semen, in the form of cerebro-spinal fluid (Onians 1954: 109–10), and that hair was an indication of sexual vigour (ibid. 232). Hershman (1974) shows that there is an explicit association between the head and semen in Punjabi thought—'It is well known to Punjabis that true ascetics are able to store up their semen and concentrate it in the form of spiritual power at the top of their heads' (Hershman 288).

A striking picture, usually in the form of a printed calendar which stands in most Hindu Punjabi houses is that of Shiva . . . The whole shape of the head is distinctly phallic and his matted locks are snake-like and piled upon his head in conical shape. From the top of the cone of matted hair there is always depicted a thin jet of white liquid. This liquid is the Ganges river and in its flow semen and spiritual power are symbolically equated. (Ibid. 287–8)

If hair is considered as that which grows naturally and as a distinguishing characteristic of animality, it will have one range of associations, whereas considered in relation to the head, it may take on some of the head's associations with the genito-anal region, which itself has close associations with animality, as we have seen.

Hershman contends that it is the subconscious association of head and genitals that gives hair symbolism its affective power among Punjabis, even though their hair symbolism has many different meanings, depending on the context—

. . . a message becomes empowered by the subconscious associations of the symbols in whose terms it is expressed, but . . . its communication content remains something entirely different. So it is my hypothesis that in its symbolic usage hair gains its power through its equivalence with the genital organs in the individual Punjabi subconscious but that it is then culturally employed in ritual, in co-ordination with other symbols, as a means of communicating certain essential values of Punjabi society. (Ibid. 274)

While we may accept that for some cultures, such as the Punjabi, there is an association between the head and hair on the one hand, and genitals and semen on the other, these ethnographic facts do not require the support or explanation of Freudian theory, or such concepts as castration and repression. In many cases the association between head and genitals is not subconscious at all. Both Hershman in the case of the Punjabis and Onians in that of the Ancient Greeks show that these associations are quite conscious, and derived from the observation of animal and human physiology, even though the Punjabis evidently regard it as indelicate to make such an association explicit. It is true that, normally, we regard these two regions as basically separate; indeed, it is the gulf between them in our everyday thought that makes the sort of interchange between them to which I have referred effective at all, and this association need not necessarily be conscious. But does it follow that even when awareness of a relationship is unconscious, it is therefore *repressed*, and derives affective power from this?

It has been made clear that the evolution of symbolic systems is inherently non-verbal, and that their structure cannot, in most cases, be expressed in words. In fact, given the essential economy and evocative power of symbols, they are the more effective because their meanings cannot be articulated with any precision by members of the culture in question. But these considerations also apply to body symbolism which even the most ardent Freudian would not claim to be related to sex, such as the symbolic function of the right and left hands, or the head/feet opposition in relation to superiority/inferiority relations, or the symbolic function of the body as a microcosm.

The fact that members of a particular society do not recognize the true meanings of a symbol does not entitle us to deduce that they are *repressing* this awareness, rather than that they are unable to put it into words because of their lack of skill in translating imagery into linguistic form. The claim that when we are unaware of the sexual aspects of symbolism this is always because we are repressing the knowledge, but that in the case of other sorts of symbolism, unconnected with sex, the knowledge is simply latent, merely assumes what it is trying to prove. The inarticulate is not the same as the subconscious, and what is subconscious is not necessarily repressed.

Notions of 'repression' are inadequate to explain the unconscious motivation of symbols, since the field of unconscious symbolism is far wider than those symbols included in Freudian theory. Not only is much unconscious anatomical symbolism (e.g. 'left' and 'right') not the product of repression, but in general, all assimilation which does not become equilibrated with accommodation and does not result in purposive generalization takes place unconsciously, both in the affective, and in the intellectual field as well. This is particularly true of dream symbolism, in which the subject loses all consciousness of the ego and is in some ways reduced to the extreme conceptual realism of the infant. In adults, wishes may be translated into external imagery because their complexity does not allow them to be verbalized in the dream. More generally, while repression of desires and wishes undoubtedly occurs, the repression of a tendency is the refusal to accommodate it to reality, and so it inevitably has a disguised appearance and is dissociated from the conscious ego. Dreams are not understood by the subject because repression is a spontaneous regulation resulting from the interaction of affective schemata whose roots elude consciousness, a process paralleled in intuitive intelligence generally; there is certainly no reason for affective schemata to be more conscious than intellectual schemata.

A more relevant factor, which leads primitives to assume that there is a force in their symbols, is not Freudian notions of repression but conceptual realism. One of the most striking aspects of primitive notions of causality is the evident assumption that what we would regard as purely symbolic associations are more than this, that they are physically effective relations between symbol and symbolized. When we talk of 'symbolic meaning', we have the resources of a model of 'mind', in terms of which we can make a clear distinction between 'signifier' and 'signified', but this explanation of symbolic representations is not available to primitives, who are conceptual realists and have no notion of the mind as mediating and encoding experience in conceptual structures. Referring to Konso beliefs in the practical efficacy of their symbols to change the world I wrote:

It would be hard to demonstrate any belief in 'vital force', or any other immanent supernatural power to explain their belief in the efficacy of their symbolism. For it would be difficult enough to explain how such a force could be present in physical objects like *hallashas* [phallic head ornaments] or soot, and be absent on mundane occasions, and even harder to show how a number or a colour could even be the vehicle of such a force.

Moreover, there is no reason to suppose that the Konso believe in such a force, as it is never referred to. So it has no use as a hypothesis. But they do not regard their symbolism, as the outsider would do, purely as symbolism; for them it is also efficacious in changing the real world. Just as dreams and hallucinations are mental experiences which, by their clarity and force, are believed to possess objective reality, so their symbols, in ritual contexts, also possess a clarity and force in the expression of Life and Death which for them is objectively real. They clearly consider their experience of the signification of symbols to be a real force. What they suppose to be the power of symbolism is in fact a projection of the impact these symbols make upon their minds, into the real world. These considerations would also apply both to ritual medicines and magic.

Thus there is no 'inner mystical nature' of the objects used which is thought to be released in magic or during rituals. In ordinary circumstances the [sacrificial] bullock is just a bullock, the *ĥalala* which garlands it is just a plant, and the milk aspersed over Ĥrela [warrior grade] will be simply milk ... The components of Konso rituals—the plants, the sacrificial animals, and the colours and numbers, for example—only have these auspicious properties within the context of the ritual, because they are all assembled in one place, for one purpose, in accordance with anciently prescribed rules, which all serve to separate them from their mundane aspects. On these occasions, within the precincts of the *mora* [sacred place], their symbolic, not their physical, properties are the important ones, and take on a life and potency of their own. (Hallpike 1972: 284–5)

Thus symbols are effective for the Konso because, like dreams and hallucinations, they regard the emotive and conceptual power of symbols as inhering in the symbols, as being 'out there', and not as subjective reactions of their own minds. (Ibid. 286)

Symbolism, in turn, fosters conceptual realism; unlike the word, the symbol really does participate in what it signifies and recreates it in the mind of the symbolizer by the concrete and affective associations it conjures up. Thus a drawing of a man participates in that man, because it produces some of the same reactions one feels when seeing the real man of whom it was made. So it is far harder to dissociate representations from what they represent, thought from the object of thought, or the thinker from the thing thought about, in the case of symbolism than in the manipulation of words. We shall pursue the implications of symbolism for conceptual realism in Chapter 9.

Leach supposes that there is some 'logic' by which we are able to translate the impressions of one sense into those of another:

The basic argument is that the messages we receive in different modes (through our various senses of touch, sight, hearing, smell, taste, etc.) are readily transformed into other modes. Thus we can visualise what we hear in words; we can convert written texts into speech; a musician can transform the visual patterns of a musical score into movements of the arms, mouth and fingers. Evidently, at some deeply abstract level, all our different senses are coded in the same way. There *must* be some kind of 'logical' mechanism which allows us to transform sight messages into sound messages or touch messages or smell messages, and vice versa. (Leach 1976: 11)

Like Lévi-Strauss, Leach does not base these assertions on any theory of cognitive processes, while his use of the word 'logical' in inverted commas implies that he does not mean 'logic' in the accepted sense, but some other, which remains obscure. We shall see in our discussion of synesthesia that there is a variety of perceived associations between colours, sounds, tastes, shapes, and so on, but Leach confuses the issue by making linguistic translation or written codes the apparent basis of these cross-sensory associations. It therefore begs the question to say that 'we can visualize what we hear in words', or that a musician can translate a score into physical movements, since words and musical scores are structurally independent of the senses, so that words, for example, can be transmitted by written signs, by physical gestures as in deaf-and-dumb language, by touch as in Braille, by sound as in speech or in the Morse code, and so on. Leach has not been exploring the means by which we translate the impressions of one sense into another, but has merely been illustrating the fact that *codes* may be expressed in a variety of physical media, a thoroughly trivial conclusion which has nothing to do with the basis of those cross-sensory associations known as synesthesia. Here again, Leach seems to suppose that because we can use *language* to translate one sensory mode into another there must be a basic homology between linguistic structure and that of reality, another example of the fallacy that language somehow reconstitutes or recreates reality.

There is, however, a type of communication between the different senses which is an essential basis for symbolism and known to psychologists as 'synesthesia', in which the mediating factor is not some kind of 'logic' but our experience of the physical world. In our culture we associate 'up' or 'high' with happiness, and 'down' or 'low' with sadness; and 'high' and 'low' are so closely associated with musical pitch that we have no other words for differentiating the two extremes of the scale. Again, if we were to ask members of our society what sensory attributes they associated with dirt and purity, it is very likely that they would construct a series of oppositions of this sort:

TABLE II

Dirt[4]	Purity
dark	light
wet	dry
soft	hard
viscous	non-viscous
low	high

Synesthesia has been studied by a number of psychologists who are not, as far as I know, developmentalists, and whose findings we may now consider in some detail.

Asch (1958) conducted an experiment to determine the extent to which there are cross-culturally general links between sets of psychological and physical properties. The languages chosen were Old Testament Hebrew (Semitic), Homeric Greek (Indo-European), Chinese (Sino-Tibetan), Malayan (Dravidian), Thai (Sino-Tibetan), Hausa (Sudanese), and Burmese (Sino-Tibetan). Sets of terms such as warm, cold, hot; right, left; straight, twisted, crooked; sweet, bitter; rough, smooth; high, low; etc. were selected, and an informant or scholar proficient in each of these languages first

---

[4] It will be clear from this that I do not accept Douglas's assertion that 'dirt is matter out of place', for the simple reason that many objects considered dirty have become so as a result of use—baths with a ring of scum round them, soiled handkerchiefs, doormats on which feet have been frequently wiped, and so on—which are examples of matter very much *in place*. A bathroom in a broom-closet would certainly be out of place, but only a neurotic would regard it as dirt; the rest of us would merely consider it confusion. While there is no doubt that ideas of dirt, purity, and contamination are easily and appropriately incorporated, by metaphorical association, into systems of social classification (the classic case being, of course, the caste system of Hindu society), I believe it can be shown that notions of dirt and systems of social classification are inherently distinct, and that ideas of dirt rest on synesthetic prototypes of the kind I suggest in Table II—indeed, the prototypical image of dirt may well be that of faeces; Meigs (1978) also advances the plausible argument that dirt is frequently associated with processes of decay. (On the question of dirt being matter out of place it is also worth bearing in mind Bulmer's cautionary observation: '... the trouble is that things can be out of place in so many different ways, in terms of so many different, even if linked, dimensions' (Bulmer 1967: 22).)

selected the native term that most clearly translated the respective English words.

He was then invited to give a few instances of phrases or sentences in which the morpheme referred to physical properties; these were transcribed, and the literal translation into English of each morpheme was obtained, followed by the English equivalent of the entire expression. This first step had the purpose of establishing the distribution of the term in physical contexts, and of permitting us to decide whether it corresponded to the English equivalent. Thereupon, the informant was asked whether the same morpheme referred also to psychological properties. If it did, he illustrated the usage with phrases or sentences; these were first translated literally and then idiomatically. (Asch 1958: 88)

All the languages considered had terms which simultaneously describe both physical and psychological properties. Asch's examples are the terms *sweet, bitter, sour.*

Sweet

Hebrew: sweet to the soul (said of pleasant words) (Prov 16: 24)

Greek: sweet laughter, voice (etymologically linked with the verb of 'please')

Chinese: a sweet smile (colloquial); sweet, honeyed words = specious words

Thai: to be sweet is to faint; to be bitter is medicine = beware of people with whom you have relations

Hausa: I don't feel sweetness = I don't feel well

Burmese: face sweet = pleasant-faced; voice sweet = pleasant voice; speech sweet = pleasant speech

Bitter

Hebrew: I will complain in the bitterness of my soul (Job 7: 11)

Greek: bitter pain, bitter tears

Chinese: bitter fate = hard lot in life (literary and colloquial)

Thai: as in English

Hausa: bitterness of character = an unpleasant disposition; he felt (or perceived) the bitterness of this talk = he was very upset by this talk

Burmese: to speak bitterly = to speak in an unfriendly manner

Sour

Hebrew: for my heart was soured (Psalm 73: 21)

Chinese: sour man = a misanthrope; sour hear = sick at heart, grieved

Burmese: I am very sour toward that person = I detest that person (Ibid. 88–9)

It might seem that these terms referred only to very general psychological dispositions, but this does not appear to be the case:

Sweet does not stand for just any positive psychological quality; it is not employed, for example, to describe courage or honesty. It seems appropriate to conclude that it describes, in the main, those psychological characteristics that we may call soothing. Similarly, *bitter* and *sour* are not synonymous with any negative quality. Our records do not contain reference to bitter or sour fear. (Ibid. 89)

Languages often have terms that refer only to physical properties: 'If, for example, the category of intelligence is not of outstanding importance, we will not find terms such as *penetrating* or *bright* to qualify it' (ibid. 329). And languages may develop their own range of meanings which seem to be culturally specific: *sweet* as 'specious' in Chinese, for example, and *sharp lips*, which both in Chinese and Hausa stand for fluency or glibness. Some terms, 'such as *straight* and *crooked*, develop a remarkably uniform psychological meaning, in contrast with others, such as *hot* and *cold*' (ibid. 92).

Early work was carried out by psychologists into colour and form associations of music, and tests by Odbert *et al.* (1942) on American subjects to determine what, if any, associations were made between musical mood and colours suggested clear associations between pieces of music agreed as being of different emotional moods and various colours (Table III).

TABLE III

Colour		Mood
Red	1. exciting	2. vigorous
Yellow	1. playful	2. gay
Green	1. leisurely	2. tender
Blue	1. leisurely	2. tender
Black	1. sad	2. solemn

Wexner (1954) criticized these experiments as insufficiently rigorous, but nevertheless found a generally similar range of associations:

Red is more often associated with exciting–stimulating, blue with secure–comfortable, orange with distressed–disturbed–upset, blue with tender–soothing, purple with dignified–stately, yellow with cheerful–jovial–joyful, and black with powerful–strong–masterful [and with melancholy]. (Wexner 1954: 434)

Thus while there is some disagreement among experimenters (the literature is too extensive to review here), and Wexner also draws attention to the importance of shade as well as hue in the affective associations of colours, there is also considerable convergence of results, which is found cross-culturally.

Karwoski *et al.* (1942) conducted experiments into visual responses to music which showed the following associations:

Volume: loud = large, near, angular, thick, heavy
soft = small, far, rounded, thin, light
Rhythm: fast = light, thin, moving, small, distinct
slow = dark, thick, stationary, large, blurred
Pitch: treble = light, up, small, thin, distinct, angular
bass = dark, down, large, thick, blurred, rounded

Further experiments were conducted (Osgood 1960) with American ('Anglo'), Japanese, Navajo, and Mexican-Spanish subjects, in which they were asked to associate a set of thirteen pairs of pictures, illustrating such perceptual attributes as thick/thin, rounded/angular, vertical/horizontal, with a set of twenty-eight concepts such as heavy, fast, good, etc. The 'Anglos', Navajo, and Japanese (the Mexican-Spanish were not given the full lists of concepts and pictures) were agreed on the associations shown in Table IV, among others.

Tests with colour chips on Navajo and 'Anglo' subjects yielded the following agreements:

Brightness { White: good, happy, pretty, sweet, clean
Black: bad, sad, ugly, sour, dirty

White tends to be more active and feminine, black more potent and masculine.[5]

Saturation { Low (yellow and green): weak, soft, light, small, thin
High (red, blue, purple, brown): strong, hard, heavy, large, thick.

Hue { red: active
blue-purple: passive

[5] It is interesting to note that in European and American advertising material females are in a very large proportion of cases contrasted with males as fair/dark.

TABLE IV

Heavy	down, thick dark	thin, bright		Light
Good	homogeneous, bright	heterogeneous, colourless, thick, dark, crooked		Bad
Fast	thin, bright, diffuse	down, horizontal, blunt		Slow
Happy	colourful, bright	colourless		Sad
Energetic	colourful			
Excitement	colourful			
Woman	colourful, thin, bright			
		thin, bright		Weak

Colourful	Bright	Thin
happy	happy	woman
energetic	woman	weak
excitement	good	fast
woman	weak	

Colourless	Dark	Thick
bad	bad	bad
sad	heavy	heavy

(Osgood 1960: 153, Table 3)

Other results are too variable for concise summary.

From these and other tests carried out on American, Japanese, Chinese, Navajo, Mexican-Spanish, Hindus, Kannada speakers, Afghans, Iranians, Lebanese, Yugoslavs, Poles, Finns, Dutch, Flemings, and French, Osgood concludes that there are three dominant factors or dimensions of synesthetic judgement: *evaluation* (good/bad, pleasant/unpleasant, positive/negative); *potency* (strong/weak, heavy/light, hard/soft); and *activity* (fast/slow, active/passive, excitable/calm). He notes (1963) that there is a resemblance between these factors and Wundt's tri-dimensional theory of feeling—pleasantness, strain, and excitement; and experiments on facial expression have shown that pleasantness, control, and activation are the three factors that pretty well exhaust the semantic space of facial communication. This Evaluation/Potency/Activity system is remarkably constant across those cultures that have been tested (admittedly, with the exception of the Navajo, these are confined so far to literate societies), and Osgood suggests that

the highly generalized nature of the affective reaction system—the fact that it is independent of any particular sensory modality and yet participates in all of them—is at once the reason why Evaluation, Potency, and Activity appear as dominant factors *and* the psychological basis for metaphor and synesthesia. (1963: 246–7)

In these studies of synesthesia we seem to be approaching some sort of explanation of trans-sensory association and significance, and one which is very much more soundly based in empirical research than Leach's hypothetical 'logic' referred to earlier. It is thus in the affective qualities of our interactions with things that their properties take on associations that are to a considerable extent independent of the particular culture, because all men have the same basic sensory equipment and inhabit essentially the same physical world. And it is man's *activities* that play a crucial part in the associations he ascribes to things and physical properties; as Asch says,

What are we trying to say when we call a thing, say the surface of a table, *hard*? We mean that it resists change when pushed or pressed, that it supports other things placed upon it without changing its own form. Hardness is resistance to change imposed by external forces; it describes a mode of interaction. Correspondingly, what is soft takes on the form of things acting upon it, as does the table-cloth that follows the contours of a surface. What now is the sense of *hard* when it refers to a person? It describes an interaction that is formally similar. We see a man refusing the appeal of another. This interaction we experience as a force proceeding from one person, having as its aim the production of a change in the other, which, however, fails to *move* him, or which produces *resistance*. The hardness of a table and of a person concerns events radically different in content and complexity, but the schema of interaction is experienced as dynamically similar, having to do with the application of force and of resulting action in line with or contrary to it. What holds in the preceding instance applies to the other terms in the same category. *Warm*, aside from thermal qualities, stands for bringing closer, or for drawing into a union, while *cold* excludes or isolates. *Colourful* designates not only the possession of colour but also the presence of diversity capable of eliciting interest. (Asch 1958: 92)

Osgood points out that this type of non-verbal interaction and communication is extremely primitive and independent of the higher cognitive functions:

Yet further testimony to the primitiveness of the affective meaning system and its cross-modality pervasiveness is to be found in studies of non-verbal (gesturing, postural, facial) communication among humans. In one study of hand gesturing, for example, Gitin (1970) had subjects rate photographs of just hands in various postures against 40 SD [semantic differential] scales; her first three factors were clearly A (*active, interesting, exciting,* etc.), E (*pleasant, good, friendly,* etc.) and P (*dominant, strong, certain,* etc.), and in this order of magnitude. In summarizing many studies reported in a recent book on non-verbal communication, Mehrabian (1972) proposes three primary referential dimensions—positiveness of interpersonal relationships (our E), relative status (our P), and responsiveness interpersonally (our A). Why? 'Our answer is based on the premise that non-verbal behaviour is a developmentally earlier and more primitive form of primitive communication which man shares with animals' (p. 14). (Osgood 1975: 398)

What is important to us now, as it was back in the age of Neanderthal man, about the sign of a thing is, first, does it refer to something *good* for me or *bad* for me (is it an antelope or a saber-toothed tiger)? Second, does it refer to something which is *strong* or *weak* with respect to me (is it a bad saber-toothed tiger or a bad mosquito)? And third, does it refer to something that is *active* or *passive* with respect to me (is it a bad, strong saber-toothed tiger or a bad, strong pool of quicksand which I can simply walk around)? Survival, then and now, depends upon the answers. (Osgood 1975: 395)

In another paper he emphasizes the affective basis of synesthetic judgement and its independence of verbally mediated higher cognitive functions:

... this affective meaning system is intimately related to the nonspecific projection mechanisms from the hypothalamic, reticular, or limbic systems and their cortical connection, in the frontal lobes. Both are gross, nondiscriminative, but highly generalized systems, and both are associated with the emotional purposive and motivational dynamics of the organism. As yet, only some incidental and entirely inadequate evidence on aphasics supports this last speculation. In a study of a small sample of aphasiac patients, it was found that despite gross disturbances in labelling, sequencing, and other denotative and grammatical tasks, these patients seemed to have no impairment in appropriate affect and made synesthetic judgements essentially like normals on a pictorial (nonverbal) form of the semantic differential. (Osgood 1964: 199)

The data from synesthesia research also provide further refutation of the linguistic determination of thought. For example, it appears that the most important evaluative concepts across the twenty-five cultures so far studied are always close synonyms of 'good' or 'big'. Experiments with bilinguals in Finnish/English, Kannada/English, Japanese/English, and Korean/English showed that there was no strong evidence for any variation in the responses to SD (semantic differential) tests according to the language which the particular bilingual was using (Osgood *et al.* 1975: 65, 392).

Again, when three cultures were studied in which social milieu and language family varied independently of one another, it was found that it was culture rather than language that determined the responses to the SD tests:

In one tri-community analysis (Delhi Hindi, Calcutta Bengali, and Mysore Kannada) one might have expected the similarity pattern to be DH + CB (both Indo-European) vs. MK (Dravidian), but nothing of this sort appears. In the other tri-community analysis (Iranian Farsi, Afghan Dari, and Afghan Pashtu) one might have expected the two variants of Persian (IF and AD) to be more similar than either with the more remote Pashtu (AP) if linguistic determinism were operating, but it was clearly AD + AP vs. IF (the much more urban site) in the data. (Ibid. 392)

4. CONCLUSIONS

From the examples of symbolic classification in primitive society that we have studied, it has become clear that these are stable and integrated at the non-verbal level with the cosmological and social categories of the society. The reasons for this stability of symbolic, static, irreversible, and complexive images of the world are two. The first is that the regular associations and properties of physical objects at the level of phenomenal experience provide a restricted set of motivated signifiers, as we saw in our study of synesthesia, and it is thus possible to express basic social and cosmological categories non-verbally by the use of concrete symbolism whose range of significance is defined and restricted by culturally generated rules. The second is that in the world of society and nature there are many constantly recurring regularities which can be represented at the phenomenal, concrete level of perception by articulated intuition; the proportion of these familiar, constantly recurring associations of events and objects is much higher in relation to unexpected and unfamiliar associations of events and objects in the closed world of primitive society than it is in our world. It is only in our world that the thought of the child is not in equilibrium with its environment until he understands natural processes by concrete operations.

The vast range of concrete symbolism briefly considered in this chapter is an apposite expression of constantly recurring relations between men—creation and destruction, alliance, power, old age and virility, the relation of mother and child, agnates and affines, insiders and outsiders, the cycle of birth and death, and so on. At the root of all societies lie certain assumptions about the nature of man and the differences that separate nature from culture, the wild from the tame, and which make the issues of cannibalism, bestiality, buggery, and incest as vital in our society as they are in the world of primitives.

The world-view of symbolic classification, unlike the mobile, transformational, reversible, and generalized schemes of operatory thought, is static and uncoordinated at the level of explicit, verbal thought, but it also manifests the imposition of a cognitive order on the world of experience, by selecting a limited number of symbolic possibilities from the indefinitely large range of potential symbolic associations and by giving these significance in relation to the cosmological categories of the society.

It can therefore be said that, like a novel or a painting, symbolic systems express a point of view. They do not explain, argue, or justify their position against criticism. They merely assert, and the point of view they assert is often a meaningful comment on the predicament of man. The elaboration of symbolism, moreover, seems to be one of those areas of human cognitive performance which are largely independent of any particular developmental stage.

But while symbolism has its roots in man's interactions with the physical world, it also depends on systems of classification if it is to be generalized into more than a range of associations. It is therefore to primitive modes of classification that we must now turn.

5

Classification

My purpose in this chapter is to show how the properties of symbolic association are intimately bound up with the characteristics of primitive classification through the latter's dependence on prototypical images and the concrete, phenomenal associations of objects. Primitive classification is concerned to impose conceptual order on aspects of experience that are practically or ritually significant for the particular society; it is not concerned with logical inference, or with constructing consistent and exhaustive classificatory systems, such as scientific taxonomies or our type of legal system, which is designed to take account of all possible eventualities and instances by precise definition of categories. Because pre-operatory thought is static and tied to the phenomenal properties of things, rather than transcending appearances by conserving the invariant relations underlying those appearances, primitive classification is inherently bound up with phenomenal reality in a way that operatory classification escapes. In this chapter, we shall first examine the extent to which primitive thought is 'abstract'. This term has been used in a confusing variety of ways by anthropologists and psychologists and we shall see that it is not in fact a unitary faculty at all, which people either possess or do not possess. We shall then examine the difference between the complex and the logical class, and show that primitive classification, rather than depending on the elucidation of taxonomic criteria, is dominated by concrete associations, in the ordering of which prototypical imagery is of special significance.

As we saw in Chapter 2, Durkheim and his followers have supposed that hierarchies of social groups—moieties, phratries, clans, sub-clans, lineages, for example—are the prototypes of all classificatory systems. This will be shown to be false. There is frequently no clear association between social groupings and other taxonomies; it does not follow that hierarchies of social groupings are understood as 'logical classes' at all by the members of the society in question, and we shall see that in any case hierarchical classification is not of particular relevance to many aspects of classification.

Lévi-Strauss supposes that dualistic classification is the primary human mode of classification. While we shall not minimize the importance of 'opposition' in primitive classification, it will be shown that oppositions are of various different types, which are not mutually reducible, and that binary classification in general is as much a reflection of certain structural features of the world as it is of the human mind. It will be shown that, in any case, binary classification itself has little diagnostic value in the analysis of the distinctive features of primitive classifications and may be employed both at the pre-operatory and the operatory levels of thought.

1. ABSTRACTION AND GENERALIZATION

The extent to which primitive thought is, or is not, abstract, has occasioned great debate among anthropologists and philosophers. The root of this confusion is that 'abstraction' is often used interchangeably with 'generality', e.g. by Lévi-Strauss in Chapter I of *The Savage Mind*, who concludes from the evident fact that primitives use some *general* words like 'tree' and 'person' that they therefore possess *abstract* thought. Indeed, Lévi-Strauss even supposes (1966: 1) that the linguistic device for converting an adjective into a substantive, e.g. 'poor'—'poverty', is a case of abstraction. As we shall see, 'abstract' and 'general' are not the same, while abstraction itself may occur at different cognitive levels.

Psychologists, too, have not clearly defined their use of 'abstract':

Abstract and *concrete* have been used in a rather loose manner to designate a number of different operations, which do not always co-vary: the particular attribute the individual selects as the basis for grouping; whether he uses this attribute consistently to form all groups in an experimental task; whether he switches from one basis of classification to another; and how he describes and explains the classes he makes.[1] With these many meanings of the term in mind, it is clear that experimental findings do not allow the conclusion that in general the thinking of any group of people is, or is not, abstract. (Cole and Scribner 1974: 121)

[1] And cf. Price-Williams 1962, who regards the ability to form alternative classifications of the same array of objects as *the* criterion of abstract thought.

It is therefore necessary to do some preliminary semantic ground-work before we can usefully discuss the extent to which primitive thought is or is not abstract. The basic sense of 'abstraction' is the mental isolation of some particular attribute of a thing from the rest of its attributes—the consideration of the colour or size of an object irrespective of its other properties—and it is this activity that is the basis of generalization, namely the recognition that other things possess this attribute as well. The properties of a class constitute its 'intension' or 'connotation', while its members, defined in terms of those properties, are its 'extension' or 'denotation'. Thus abstraction is the basis of intension and generalization is the basis of extension; but it is important to note that one can have abstraction with a low order of generality and, conversely, generality with a low order of abstraction, e.g. 'People have feelings'. The importance of distinguishing between 'general' and 'abstract' is therefore that while the opposite of 'general' is 'particular', the opposite of 'abstract' is 'concrete'. But some general terms have *concrete* referents, such as 'man', 'tree', etc., yet in two senses of 'abstraction' (which we shall discuss shortly) abstract words do not have concrete referents. Thus the second aspect of 'abstraction' involves the formation of concepts whose referents have no immediate counterpart in physical reality.

If we consider for the moment the first aspect of abstraction, the consideration of one property of a thing in isolation from the rest of its properties, it is certainly not a distinctive or unitary faculty of thought. As Werner says,

Such a definition usually implies that abstraction is a unitary function which comes into being at a certain stage of mental development and increases gradually with age. If we hold, however, that the term 'abstraction' does not mean a unitary function, but rather a process that may be effected by different functions on quite different levels, then any such question as determining the age at which the faculty of abstraction appears becomes meaningless. (Werner 1948: 234)

Abstraction and generalization are to be found at the sensori-motor level, not only in man but in animals; thus the abstraction of properties is a basic phenomenon at the sensori-motor level, with a close association between the perceptual apprehension of physical properties and concrete perceptual grouping:

This perceptual grouping is dependent on a basic tendency in perceptual organization to bring elements together which exhibit any kind of perceptual similarities. For example, our desk is in great disorder. Papers lie scattered round, strewn amid books, inkwell, pencils, pens and knife. Observe how, when we cast a critical eye over the surface of the desk, the white papers unite in a sort of group. Other objects also tend to come together. Hard objects such as the penwiper, ash tray, and inkwell seem to attract each other. Long objects such as pencils, penholder, knife and scissors group themselves together. And so, of a sudden, a harmonious organization arises out of disorder. It is characteristic of this grouping that it may be completed in the purely perceptual sphere with hardly any conceptual-abstract support. It operates according to the laws of configuration. (Werner 1948: 223)

These perceptual *Gestalts* are the most basic form of abstraction, in which things with similar qualities tend to come to perceptual attention in the form of a unit in which the apprehension of the equality of one property is dependent on a simultaneous awareness of contrast. So we find that even the lower vertebrates can form an abstraction of perceptual relationships, as in the case of chickens which can be trained to peck grain from the lighter of any two backgrounds. Conditioned to peck the grain from a grey background and not to peck it from a black background, when they are presented with grain on white and grey backgrounds, they peck it from the white background, thus maintaining the constancy of their response by choosing the relatively brighter area. Relative size is understood by chimpanzees and by children still at the sensorimotor stage. 'The child [at this stage of mental development] understands and is able to transpose diverse opposites: outline vs. solid, symmetrical vs. asymmetrical, thick vs. thin, small vs. large, round vs. angular etc.' (ibid. 219).

So far, we have been considering the abstraction of the perceptual *properties* of things, but an equally important aspect of abstraction is the abstraction of *relationships*, including relationships of actions. At the level of concrete experience it is possible to abstract and to generalize actions in the form of verbs and spatiotemporal relations in the form of adverbs and prepositions—above, below, with, from, etc.—but these differ from the properties of objects in that they cannot actually be perceived. So while we often find object concepts of a relatively high level of generality, such as 'tree' or 'animal', in primitive cultures concepts of actions and relations are not so highly generalized, except for concepts of social behaviour such as 'crime' or 'gift'. There is a large number of general relational concepts necessary for concrete and formal operations which do not exist in primitive thought—'alternation', 'succession' (as opposed to 'next'), 'relation', 'position' (as opposed to 'place'), 'reversal', and so on. We shall see in the chapter on number and quantification that primitive languages do not have words for weight, area, volume, length, heat, and other dimensional concepts. This is for the evident reason that, in the first place, these words do not denote things or the properties of things, but rather the procedure by which these concepts are attained. That is, one cannot point to weight or area, but has to explain how these concepts are *constructed* (cf. *SOED* 'Weight': '*measurement* of quantity by means of *weighing*; quantity as *determined* in this way'). Secondly, concepts such as weight, length, height, etc., are necessitated by the differentiations and combinations we make between them; we talk of 'weight' to distinguish it from, and relate it to, volume or density. In other words, dimensional concepts derive their meaning from co-ordinations between them, which, as we have seen, are characteristic of operatory thought. It is in the construction of systems of relations and transformations between invariant properties that we are able to transcend the variable features of the phenomenal world. (Significantly, many of our 'abstract' words in this second sense end in '-ion' and are derived from Latin *verbs* rather than from nouns or adjectives.) Now we have seen that subjects become aware of relations through their actions, and it is by the process of abstraction and generalization performed on his actions that the child builds up logical structures. This is the basis of the second aspect of abstraction we have been considering, the abstraction of action, and hence of relations, which is one of Piaget's most important contributions to cognitive psychology and which must be clearly distinguished from perceptual abstraction, even though this is indispensable to it.

As an example, consider a child who counts ten pebbles and finds they always make ten. In this case he is really not experimenting with pebbles, but with his own activities of arranging and enumerating, varying the order at will and observing that no matter what combination of activities he employs, whether he numbers from left to right or from right to left, he always arrives at the same result. (Mays 1972: 4)

So it is because many operatory concepts are the products of generalized co-ordination of actions, and hence of relations, that they are beyond the grasp of pre-operatory thought and also have no direct and ostensible denotation in the perceptible world.

Finally, there is verbal, propositional abstraction, which provides a further means of transcending the sensory world, when propositions in either words or other conceptual equivalents such as mathematical expression are themselves the subject of operations which may be logical, grammatical, mathematical, and so on. Grammatical and logical concepts, such as 'noun', 'verb', 'meaning', 'proposition', 'inference', are of this type, and do not seem to occur in primitive thought.

'Abstraction', in its primary sense of 'isolation of the properties of things' is in effect 'analysis' whose necessary complement in the formation of concepts is 'synthesis', that is, the combination of the criteria of a class to form the intension of that class. We shall see that the way in which the synthesis of intension is performed is one of the crucial distinguishing marks between operatory and pre-operatory classification. The intension of a 'complex' pre-operatory grouping may vary from item to item; the intension of different complexes may overlap; and intension may be dominated by use, function, and association rather than by taxonomic criteria.

There is, then, no such mental function as 'abstraction' which primitives, or anyone else, either have or do not have. Abstraction occurs at every level of cognitive functioning and is of three different types—of perceptual properties, of relations, and of propositions. Classes or complexes are also constituted by the synthesis of that which is abstracted. Rather than talking in terms of 'abstraction', we should ask to what extent collective or individual representations of reality conform to the criteria of operatory thought, both in spatio-temporal systems and in taxonomic systems.

2.   LOGICAL CLASS AND THE COMPLEX

While it may be the case that, *sub specie aeternitatis*, all is flux, Bulmer rightly observes that

. . . from the vantage point of the *particular human community*, living in a restricted geographical area, and over a restricted period of time, there are very evident discontinuities in nature, that is, in living flora and fauna; and perception of these is vital to human survival, as indeed it is to the survival of other forms of animal life. And these discontinuities occur most frequently and relevantly between forms which zoologists and botanists regard as species, and which for the most part would always have regarded as species since zoology and botany became sciences, regardless of the theoretical rationales applied. (Bulmer 1970: 1083)[2]

It is evident that some types of phenomena come to us ready packaged, as it were, by the natural order of things, such as the species of flora and fauna, and their association with particular habitats. The stable and discrete properties of these natural categories are also possessed by many aspects of the man-made world, especially in the circumstances of primitive society. Thus the kinds of classification that claim the attention of ethnographers are folk taxonomies, whose investigation is designed to show how the world of the native informant is cognitively structured both in terms of specific taxa and of more general categories, such as 'things of the bush', 'of the village', 'of the sea', etc. While these taxonomic structures are certainly an aspect of classification, it has frequently escaped the attention of anthropologists and psychologists that such classification is primarily concerned with the *intension* of classes, with their defining properties and how these are shared and differentiated between different groupings of phenomena. The *extension*, the logical quantification of class membership, is largely ignored, so that informants are not asked questions designed to reveal their understanding of 'all', 'some', 'none', 'more than', 'less than', or 'equal to', or problems of class inclusion. Because *some* hierarchical structuring is displayed in all primitive taxonomies, it is therefore assumed that primitive classification is essentially like our own scientific, taxonomic classification.

There is, then, another aspect of classification which is largely ignored in this ethnographic type of analysis—the classification of arbitrary arrays of elements that are not 'given' by the environment. It is this type of problem that dominates psychological studies of classification: it involves giving subjects an array of objects differing in colour, shape, and size, for example, and asking them to sort together all those things that are similar in one respect, to select one element that is incompatible with the others or to re-classify the objects according to different criteria, with the requirement to give explicit justifications for such choices (though many

---

[2] Cf. Lévi-Strauss: '. . . the diversity of species furnishes man with the most intuitive picture at his disposal and constitutes the most direct manifestation he can perceive of the ultimate discontinuity of reality. It is the sensible expression of an objective coding' (1966: 137).

such studies do not include questions involving 'some' and 'all' and concentrate on the extent to which subjects classify taxonomically, and are able to re-sort the array according to multiple criteria). The crucial difference between inquiries into taxonomy and sorting tasks is that to ask whether a bat is a bird or an animal only involves problems of intension, of the relative importance of properties (in this example, of morphology and habitat), whereas the problem involved in sorting arrays of things may also involve extension and its co-ordination with intension.

An operatory grasp of logical class involves the ability to differentiate and co-ordinate intensive and extensive properties. Intensive properties are (a) those that are common to the members of the class and to the members of other classes to which it belongs, and (b) those that are specific to the members of the class and that differentiate them from members of other classes. Extensive properties are part–whole relations of class membership and inclusion, conveyed by the quantifiers 'all', 'some', and 'none'. More formally, logical class has the following criteria:[3]

1. There are no isolated elements, i.e. elements not belonging to a class. This amounts to saying that all the elements must be classified and that, if an element (x) is the only one of its kind, it must give rise to its own specific (but singular) class.

2. There are no isolated classes: i.e. every specific class A characterized by the property a implies its complement A' (characterized by not-a) within the closest genus B $(A + A' = B)$. Thus a might be the property of having a particular father and b the property of having a particular grandfather; first cousins would all share the negative property not-a to distinguish them from brothers, who are also b.

3. A class A includes all the individuals having the property a.

4. A class A includes only individuals having the property a.

5. All classes of the same rank are disjoint (non-overlapping): $A \times A' = 0$.

6. A complementary class A' has its own characteristics which are not possessed by its complement A.

7. A class A (or A') is included in every higher-ranking class which contains all its elements, starting with the closest, B: $A = B - A'$ (or $A' = B - A$) and $A \times B = A$, which amounts to saying that 'all' A are 'some' B.

[3] Adapted from Inhelder and Piaget 1964: 48.

8. Extensional simplicity: the inclusions in (7) are reduced to the *minimum* compatible with the intensional properties.

9. Intensional simplicity: similar criteria (e.g. colours) distinguish classes of the same *rank*.

10. Symmetrical subdivision: if a class B_1 is subdivided into A_1 and A'_1 and the same criterion is applicable to B_2, then B_2 must likewise be subdivided into A_2 and A'_2.

Logical class is not itself a perceptual property of things, in the way that similarity and difference are; when we see an orange and say 'this is an orange', we assimilate the orange we see to a perceptual and sensori-motor schema which is an 'empirical *Gestalt*'. The particular configuration of properties distinctive of the orange has acquired its stability as the result of previous sensory experience of colour, taste, and smell, and is closely linked to habitual actions involved in eating it, such as cutting and peeling, chewing, squeezing the juice, and so on. So while the logical classification of 'orange' is based on perceptual and motor schemata of this kind, the sensory recognition of objects (schematic assimilation) merely involves intension, without consideration of extension.

Again, we may grasp that a particular type of thing, such as a nose or a leaf, is part of a larger configuration, such as 'face' or 'tree', but this 'partitive membership' is only spatial ('infra-logical'), and hence extensive; no explicit enumeration of the properties of noses or leaves is necessary to recognize their inclusion in faces or trees. Thus part–whole relations can be understood at the pre-operatory level without the necessity of having to understand the principles of the logical inclusion of classes and subclasses, and familiar objects can be defined purely in terms of their properties without consideration of their membership of other classes. Indeed, we shall see that classification at the 'folk' level is often based on images which are not usually analysed into their distinct features at all.

Unlike spatio-temporal systems, *logical* classification is independent of space and time, since the members of a class need have no contiguity in space and may exist at different times. Although we habitually employ diagrams, such as taxonomic trees or Euler's circles, to facilitate our thinking about class membership, Piaget emphasizes that at the operatory level of thought these spatial representations are merely symbolic and are not a necessary, constituent aspect of our classification. But for the pre-operatory child spatial relations are an inherent aspect of his classification, so that when the child is asked to 'put together the things which are alike' he initially groups objects to form lines and, later, other more complex shapes and patterns. The child thus treats classification as the construction of a complex concrete object which only exists when its parts or elements are in physical relationship with the whole. For this reason Piaget refers to these early groupings as 'graphic collections', the distinctive feature of a collection being that 'it exists by virtue of the union of its elements in space, and ceases to exist when its sub-collections are dissociated'.

The child groups objects not only in accordance with spatial and figurative criteria, but in accordance with the associations of everyday life. In one test children were given toys comprising four animals, four human figures, four kitchen utensils, and four articles of furniture, and asked to classify these objects in open boxes with the instruction 'Put together whatever goes together best.' The younger children constructed heterogeneous collections ('heaps') in each box, while children of four to five used the boxes to distinguish between collections. These were based not on generic, taxonomic similarity—such as 'furniture', 'kitchen utensils', etc.—but on associations of everyday life in terms of which the things were felt to *belong* together, e.g.:

Pie (5; 0) Box A: (Baby + chair + chair)
Q. Why? (He puts the baby on one of the chairs, adds a man, and says):
A. The man is sitting with the baby.
   (He adds a pig)
   The baby is playing with the pig.
   (Then a pot)
   It's for the pig to eat out of.
   (Another man)
   The man is looking after the pig.

Box B: (Man + monkey)
A. The man is looking at the monkey.
   (A bird)
   The bird and the monkey are playing.
   (Later)
   The bird is drinking out of the pot; the man is sitting on a chair:
   (A fish)
   Then he catches a fish . . . (Inhelder and Piaget 1964: 41)

The differentiation between 'similarity', the basis of taxonomic classification, and 'belonging', derived from a variety of concrete associations on which complexive classification is based, is a crucial feature of logical classification. Piaget's 'graphic collections' are essentially what other psychologists such as Bruner and Vygotsky term 'complexes'. Unlike the 'heap', which is a congeries of images linked only by fluctuating and arbitrary subjective experiential associations, without any organizing principle, 'in a complex, individual objects are united in the child's mind not only by his subjective impressions but also by *bonds actually existing between these objects*' (Vygotsky 1962: 61). These bonds, however, are concrete and factual, based on the experiences and associations of everyday life, rather than generalized abstractions, and the elements of the complex have a functional and concrete unity, rather than a logical coherence. 'Any factually present connection may lead to the inclusion of a given element into a complex.' While a concept groups objects according to their possession of at least one common attribute, 'the bonds relating the elements of a complex to the whole and to one another may be as diverse as the contacts and relationships are in reality' (ibid. 62). Vygotsky compares complexes to 'families', in which any one of a multiplicity of diverse relationships is sufficient for the child to give an element the 'family' name. This is the most elementary type of complex, the associative, but there are also complexes based on functional complementarities between objects such as cups, saucers, and spoons, or sets of clothes, on the basis of their participation in some practical operation. In associative and functional complexes there is a nucleus of prototypical elements, but in chain complexes the decisive criterion keeps changing during the process of selection, so that there is no nucleus, and relations exist only between individual members.

Vygotsky sums up the distinctive characteristics of complexes as follows:

A complex does not arise above its elements as does a concept; it merges with the concrete objects that compose it. This fusion of the general and the particular, of the complex and its elements, this psychic amalgam, as Werner called it, is the distinctive characteristic of all complex thinking and of the chain complex in particular. (Ibid. 65)

Piaget finds that even when the child is no longer bound by spatial and associational imagery and can form 'non-graphic col-

lections', he is still unable to grasp the relationship of class inclus-
ion, that is, if $A + A' = B$, then $A = B - A'$, $A' = B - A$, $B \times A = B$, or 'Some B is all A', even though he can form hierarchical
classificatory systems at this stage—that is, form large collections
and subdivide them.

If, for instance, we give a subject a set of twelve wooden beads,
ten blue and two red, he will be well aware that they are all
wooden, and that some are wooden and blue, while others are
wooden and red. But if he is asked 'Are there more wooden beads,
or more blue beads?', he will reply that there are more blue beads
than wooden beads, if he has not yet attained operatory classification.[4] In other words, it is possible to grasp the
hierarchical relationship that the red and the blue beads are all
wooden, just as roses and daisies are all flowers, or men and
women are all people, but still to lack a true grasp of class inclusion. Class inclusion, that if $A + A' = B$, then $A = B - A'$ etc.,
involves the grasp of the quantifiers 'all', 'some', 'none', and the
relations 'more than', 'less than', and 'equal to'.

What seems to be necessary for the grasp of class inclusion is
that the subject shall be able to classify according to a plan before
he starts, or very soon after:

... what is more the plan enables them to pass freely from whole to part
and vice versa. In other words their behaviour has the mobility to combine
an upward process (uniting) and a downward process (sub-dividing) ...
We may therefore state as our hypothesis ... that the inclusion of classes
depends on an anticipatory schema (the same schema as that which under-
lies the transition from the direct operation $B = A + A'$ to its inverse $A = B - A'$, so that the latter ceases to be a contingent result of hindsight
and becomes a necessary inverse operation). We believe that such a
schema is essential, not only for reversibility, but also for the use of 'all'
and 'some', and for the understanding of quantitative relations of the form
$B > A$. (Inhelder and Piaget 1964: 55-6)

We here encounter yet again the basic characteristic of operatory
thought—the capacity to co-ordinate a set of reversible relationships *simultaneously* into a total system of invariant relationships

---

[4] The reader may suppose that this question is so elementary that no normal
adult in any society could fail to answer it correctly. Allen *et al.* in a survey of
mathematical skills at Goroka Teachers' College, Papua New Guinea, among recently graduated mathematics teachers, set exactly this question to this subjects: 30
per cent of them failed to answer it correctly (Allen *et al.* 1975: 6–7).

which has a necessary quality and transcends the variability and rigidity of concrete experience.

'Some' and 'all' are thus fundamental notions of logic and basic to propositions of inclusion which relate parts to wholes. 'All' denotes the totality of a set A, while 'some' denotes '$A - x$' (where x is greater than 0). In primitive usage, however, it is possible that while words are used that ethnographers translate as 'some' and 'all', 'all' does not denote 'all possible members of set A', but 'all those in our experience' or simply 'a lot'. In so far as primitive thought is not usually concerned with working out the theoretically maximum number of items in a set, it will tend to use 'all' in the sense of 'very many'; while if all possible members of a set are physically present, the primitive may indeed say 'all', but in the sense of 'full' or 'complete', which is derived from a spatial conception, as of a container that has been filled up.

In the case of 'some', whereas in logic it is always used in relation to a totality, in pre-operatory thought 'some' retains an absolute meaning bound up with the actual number of elements present, e.g. 'a few' instead of being grasped as a part–whole relation. It is the notion of a theoretical totality, with anything less than this as standing in a part–whole relation to the totality, that is so alien to primitive thought. If one examines the way in which words we translate as 'some' are actually used in primitive society they seem to mean not the logical 'some', but 'few', 'a certain amount', or the disjunction of 'some men beat their wives, others don't'.

Dr Neil Warren, for example, tells me (private communication) that the Kamano of the New Guinea Highlands use their word for 'many' to do duty for what we would translate as 'all'; he also reminds me that the Pidgin *olgeta* has the connotation of 'many' rather than 'all'. In the same way, among the Tauade I found that the word that I was initially inclined to translate as 'all', *kuparima*, was more accurately rendered as 'many'. *kupariai* is the word for 'two' or 'pair', *-ai* being the dual suffix, and *-ma* is one of the plural suffixes; thus *kuparima* seems to have the literal meaning of 'pairs', i.e. 'many', and is certainly so used in conversation. It should also be noted that *kuparima* is not an adjective, but a noun, and refers to a state of affairs, 'multiplicity', rather than being a property of a class. The same is true of *mui*, which is more accurately translated as 'nothing' than as 'no' or 'none'. When these terms are combined with classes of thing, as in *vale kuparima*, 'all men', 'everybody', 'many men', *vale mui*, 'nobody', it seems that the relation is one of apposition rather than one of qualification. Again, in the Konso language, there is a word *alega* which means 'many'. This word has the standard adjectival form: initial *a* and terminal *a*, with the assertative form initial *i* and terminal *i*: thus 'there are many' would be *ilegi*. But the word one would translate as 'all', *pisa*, does not have this adjectival form—one cannot say *ipisi*, 'it is all'; so it seems that, even while the Konso do distinguish between 'many' and 'all', their notion of 'all', as in the case of the Tauade, is not a property, but a state of affairs, a notion of concrete completeness, as when we say, after counting a finite set of objects, 'That's the *lot*.' Similarly, the Konso word *we'en* should not be translated as 'no', 'none', but as 'nothing', since, like *pisa*, it does not have adjectival form and can be used in isolation from other nouns, like our 'nothing' or 'the lot'. Like *pisa*, *we'en* seems to denote not a property of things but a state of affairs, in this case that of 'emptiness', as when we look inside a box and say that there is 'nothing' in it. Nor is it possible, either in the Konso or the Tauade languages, to express the sense of 'No *A* is *B*', or 'All *A* is some *B*', since we also find that in both these languages the words for 'some' are indistinguishable in meaning from 'few'.[5]

Thus, simply because primitive societies may use words that ethnographers translate as 'some' and 'all', it does not follow that their indigenous users grasp the *logical*, as opposed to the concrete, implications of these terms.

Operatory logical classification also involves the grasp of seriation: if classes $A + A' = B$, $B + B' = C$, then $A < B < C$, and operatory seriation, as we saw in Chapter I, also involves the grasp of transitivity, that $A < C$, and reversibility: if $C = A + B$, then $A = C - B$ etc. The subject must also be able to give an explicit verbal definition of the intension of a class in terms of a more general class, and in terms of one or more specific differences between the class in question and another class. This inherently involves the coordinated use of comparatives which, as we shall see, is apparently rare in primitive society.

The logical class or true concept is thus based on taxonomic

[5] Professor Needham informs me that while the language of the Penan of Borneo has distinct terms for 'all' and 'many', it has no evident equivalent for 'some' as the expression of a part–whole relationship, though the Penan may, like us, use an equivalent of 'some' in the more elementary sense of 'a bit', 'a certain amount'.

principles, which require a differentiation between 'similarity' and 'belonging', thereby transcending spatial and concrete associations of everyday life, and is unambiguously definable. Vygotsky summarizes the essential differences between collections or complexes, on the one hand, and logical classes or true concepts, on the other. To form a true concept,

> it is also necessary *to abstract, to single out* elements, and to view the abstracted elements apart from the totality of the concrete experience in which they are embedded. In genuine concept formation, it is equally important to unite and to separate: synthesis must be combined with analysis. Complex thinking cannot do both. Its very essence is overabundance, overproduction of connections, and weakness in abstraction. (Vygotsky 1962: 76)

But mere abstraction of a single attribute is found at the perceptual level among animals, and associative complexes presuppose the abstraction of one trait common to the different elements. But as long as complexive thinking predominates, the abstracted trait is unstable, and easily surrenders its temporary dominance to other traits. Only when the abstracted criteria or traits are resynthesized do genuine concepts emerge. Even at this stage in concept formation, we find adolescents able to use concepts but unable to give verbal definitions of them, and obliged to revert to the more primitive level of giving concrete examples of concepts. The greatest difficulty of all is in applying concepts to new concrete situations.

It is necessary to point out here that the traditional definition of logical class, all of whose members have at least one property in common, and which Piaget takes as the norm, is not necessarily the most advantageous even in scientific thought, especially in fields such as botany and zoology, where it may not be clear which properties will prove to be the most significant.

Needham (1975) has pointed out that it is an accepted practice in natural-science taxonomies to employ 'polythetic' classes; quoting Sokal and Sneath (1963: 13): 'A polythetic arrangement . . . places together organisms that have the greatest number of shared features, and no single feature is either essential to group membership or is sufficient to make an organism a member of the group.'

Such modes of classification may, as Needham points out, be advantageous in the exploratory stages of scientific investigation, but while they may be hierarchically organized, they will evidently have an ambiguous denotation and cannot therefore be used for logical inference. But the crucial difference between this type of polythetic class and the complex is that the polythetic class is quite explicitly based on clearly defined properties that have been selected according to general principles of biology or botany, whereas the complex is based essentially on global configurations which have a perceptual, imaged unity not dependent on analysis into discrete properties. Logical classes and the polythetic classes of scientific classification are therefore linked to explicit verbal formulations of their properties—an important aspect of concept formation being that the understanding of logical class is derived from conscious reflection on our mental processes, e.g. on our classification among other things, and this consciousness is stimulated by puzzlement and an awareness of logical failure. Concept formation is an aim-directed process and for it to begin a problem must arise that cannot be solved except by the formation of new concepts.

Having established the basic characteristics of operatory, logical classification, we are now in the position to assess the extent to which primitive classification is most aptly characterized as complexive. We should also note that complexive classification is also inherently linked with concrete imagery, and hence we may expect to find that categories of things are conceived very much in terms of prototypical models.

A good example of a complexive category is that of *ăgo* among the Tauade, whose range of meanings covers our notions of 'ancestor', 'prototype', 'wild form', 'non-human', 'source of fertility', and 'immortal'. The principle of *ago* are the *agotevaun* (*ago* + *tev(e)* (person or thing) + *-aun* (plural suffix) comprising culture heroes and the prototypes of all species of plants, trees, and animals; and we find that there is a close association between the *agotevaun* and stones. There are legends recounting how various culture heroes turned into rocks which are now familiar landmarks, and they are supposed to have been responsible for the carved stone pestles and mortars that have often been dug up in the area. The first ancestors of the Tauade—who were distinct from the culture heroes—are also said to have emerged from a large rock, while there are many pairs of animal *agotevaun* which live underground in stones and maintain the particular species of animal of which they are the originals. While the modern word for stone is *evite*, the word for heavy is *agotu*, while in the case of *toneago*, 'fightstones', and *poruago*, 'pigstone', both used magically, the ending -*ago* is said to mean 'stone'. There is thus some linguistic evidence to support the other associations between the *agotevaun* and stones, such that stones are prototypical images, and it is also clear that stones are seen as potentially active, the sources, or at least repositories, of power and fertility. We noted earlier that for the primitive mind stone, through being heavy, is perceived as possessing power through its effect on the muscles of those who lift it, which is why symbolically it is appropriate for stone to be represented as active rather than passive. Additionally, for the Tauade in their Neolithic culture, stone was used for adze heads, for clubs, and bark cloth beaters, all of which must have reinforced their awareness of its power, while their experience of it in the making of earth ovens, when stones were heated in fires and used to cook the meat and vegetables, would show how impervious is stone to the destructive influence of fire.

Thus the natural characteristics of stone form the complex of 'repository of power', 'immortal', and 'unchanging', which are prominent aspects of the various *agotevaun*, although, as we shall see, the characteristics of the *agotevaun* are even more various.

The *agotevaun* as culture heroes are represented as non-human beings with long hair and tusks, of great physical power, who originated the killing of pigs and the associated ceremonies together with burial rites and initiation, and who carved out river valleys, could fly through the air or burrow the earth, and killed and humiliated the ancestors of the Tauade. When killed, they could put themselves back together again, and are said to have either turned into rocks or gone to live on the tops of mountains. Chiefs and white men are explicitly likened to the culture heroes.

The animal and plant *agotevaun* are also immortal and the source of fertility as the originals of their respective species, while the plant *agotevaun* illustrate a further aspect of the central notion of *ago*, that of 'wild form', since almost every plant, including the domesticated varieties, is supposed to have an archetype which is said to be found in the wild, usually in the forest. The *agotevaun* of trees and plants are known and named individually: some of these *ago* trees seem to be larger and thicker than the normal specimens (as in the case of ginger, vines, and creepers), but in other cases they are actually more spindly and more 'primitive' or 'archetypal' in appearance. No *ago* tree is ever planted by man, and otherwise ordinary-looking trees will be referred to as *ago* if they have seeded

TABLE V

agotevaun	original form	wild	*ago* criteria source of power	source of fertility	immortal	unchanging	self-determined; independent of men
culture heroes			+		+		+
animals	+	+		+	+	+	+
plants	+	+		+	+	+	+
first artefacts	+		?				
first riches	+		?				
rain and wind					+	+	+
heavenly bodies			+		+	+	+
corners of houses					+	+	

themselves. Here we find a further aspect of the *ago* complex—self-determination, and lack of dependency on men.

In other cases it is the first or original of any class of things that is considered an *agoteve*. For example, Ila Otauruma was the archetypal string bag (*ilata* = string bag), made by a famous female *agoteve*. But the string bag in question is not now an *agoteve* in so far as it no longer exists; it was simply the archetype of all subsequent string bags. Similarly, the first riches—shells, dogs' teeth, nose-bones, armlets, and other bodily decorations which first came to a tribal area—are named, and referred to as *agotevaun*, as are the first drums of a tribe, whose individual names have been retained by later drums.

The theme of immortality is expressed in another kind of *agoteve*—the types of rain and wind that come regularly from particular directions, as Continental Europeans refer to the *mistral* and the *Föhn*, and the sun, moon, morning star, and evening star. Most insubstantial of the *agotevaun* are the corners of houses. One can see that as constructional forms they are changeless and undying elements necessarily manifested in any rectangular type of structure.

So while the basic image of the *agoteve* seems to be that of stone, we find that the examples of *agotevaun* spread beyond the notions of immortality, strength, and permanence, to include those of arche-type, wild-form, and self-determined. If we consider any particu-lar example of *agoteve*, such as a named type of wind or rain, moon, first drum or string bag, culture hero, plant or animal *ago-teve*, or house corner, we shall find some of these characteristics of the *ego* complex, but never all of them. There is no single char-acteristic common to all, although immortality comes closest to this.

Luria's research among illiterate Uzbek peasants in the early 1930s demonstrates very well the propensity of uneducated adults to classify things in terms of complexes based on the practical, situational relations between them, rather than by concepts based on the taxonomic properties of the elements.

In the first type of problem a subject was given drawings of four common objects, one of the four being taxonomically inapprop-riate. The subject in this case is an illiterate male peasant aged thirty-nine, who is shown pictures of a hammer, saw, log, and hat-chet:

Q. Which of these things could you call by one word?
A. How's that? If you call all three of them a 'hammer', that won't be right either.
Q. But one fellow picked three things—the hammer, saw, and hatchet—and said they were alike.
A. A saw, a hammer and a hatchet all have to work together. But the log has to be there too!
Q. Why do you think he picked these three things and not the log?
A. Probably he's got a lot of firewood, but if we'll be left without fire-wood, we won't be able to do anything.
Q. True, but a hammer, a saw, and a hatchet are all tools.
A. Yes, but even if we have tools, we still need wood—otherwise we can't build anything. (Luria 1976: 56)

This type of response to a suggested taxonomic classification—in this case 'tool'—is typical of all other responses to such possible classifications as 'weapons', 'cooking vessel', 'garment', 'animal', 'flower', and so on. Although words for these categories exist in the Uzbek language, the illiterate subjects invariably rejected them as irrelevant or silly for classificatory purposes, and grouped objects from different taxonomic categories either according to their mutual necessity in some practical task, or according to their suitability for inclusion in some graphic situation of real life, as when a subject grouped a house, a bird, and a rosebush together because 'a rose bush should be near a house, while a bird can sit on the bush and sing'. Luria also points out, following Binet, that the ability to detect differences between objects appears developmentally long before the ability to establish a basis for their similarity (as opposed to 'belonging'). It is the recognition of similarity that is the foundation of classification, as we have seen. Thus the more general the class, the harder it is to express it, and when given the task of finding similarities between two objects as the basis of assigning them to a general category, the illiterate peasants

. . . merely described each of the objects, insisting that the two had nothing in common. They would provide a detailed account of the purposes they served, the situations in which they were usually encountered, or try to establish some closer connection between them by imagining a concrete instance in which the two interacted. In some instances they tried to think of a situation in which both objects performed identical operations, thereby assuming they could establish a functional basis of similarity. Another approach—one wholly irrelevant to the job of categorization—was to determine some physical resemblance between the two objects. (Ibid. 81)

For example (the subject is a thirty-eight-year-old illiterate man):

Q. What do a chicken and a dog have in common?
A. They're not alike. A chicken has two legs, a dog has four. A chicken has wings but a dog doesn't. A dog has big ears and a chicken's are small.
Q. You've told me what is different about them. How are they alike?
A. They're not alike at all.
Q. Is there one word you could use for them both?
A. No, of course not.
Q. What word fits both a chicken and a dog?
A. I don't know.
Q. Would the word 'animal' fit?
A. Yes. (Ibid. 81–2)

Despite this subject's agreement here, it might be objected that in Uzbek culture the word 'animal' is perhaps not customarily used to include both birds, even flightless birds, and terrestrial creatures. Such an objection would have even more force when subjects are asked to find a common generic term for 'fish' and 'crow'. More generally, it might be argued that while these peasants rejected generic concepts in classification tasks, it must nevertheless be the case that since their language has words for generic concepts like animal, weapon, tool, and so on, the subjects were therefore not so much incapable of using generic concepts as indifferent to them, since there was no cognitive demand for them in the circumstances of their daily life. Luria's investigations suggest, however, that while there are generic terms in the Uzbek language, the illiterate subjects do not understand these words taxonomically, but as complexes. The following protocols illustrate this clearly. In the first, there are three illiterate male subjects, I aged twenty-five, II aged thirty-two, III aged twenty-six. All were shown drawings of saw–axe–hammer:

Q. Would you say these things are tools?
A. All three subjects 'Yes'.
Q. What about a log?
A. I It also belongs with these. We make all sorts of things out of logs—handles, doors, and the handles of tools.
A. II We say a log is a tool because it works with tools to make things. The pieces of logs go into making tools.
Q. But one man said a log isn't a tool since it can't saw or chop.
A. III Some crazy fellow must have told you that! After all, you need a log for tools ... together with iron it can cut ...
Q. Name all the tools you can.
A. III An axe, a mosque [light carriage on springs], and also the tree we tether a horse to if there's no pole around. Look, if we didn't have this board here, we wouldn't be able to keep the water in this irrigation ditch. So that's also a tool, and so is the wood that goes to make a blackboard. (Ibid.: 93–4)

In another protocol, the subject is a barely literate peasant man of fifty-seven years of age. He groups together a hammer, saw, log, and hatchet and calls them *asbob*.

Q. What other things do you call tools?
A. An axe, a hatchet, a saw, two men with a saw—they're all tools.
Q. Can you really call people tools?
A. No, but all life comes down to one thing: people join together to work.
Q. Can you call a log a tool?
A. Yes. All these things belong here. If you use the axe to chop the log, it will split.
Q. But if I split the log with hands, could I call my hands a tool?

A. Yes, of course! They've got power, and it's with this power that we split wood.

Q. What else can you call a tool?

A. A tractor, bulls with an axe [?], grain—we can nourish ourselves with it. Everything that goes into our stomachs is a tool. First a man uses his strength to plant a seed, then it grows, and then we eat the grain that ripens. (Ibid.: 94–5)

Among the Kpelle of Liberia, in an extended investigation of classification by Cole *et al.* (1971), subjects were asked to classify a variety of objects non-verbally by sorting.

In order to test subjects' responses to the request to classify objects and to work out instructions, we gathered together a set of items that were potentially classifiable in a variety of ways—according to function, semantic class, length, size, colour, and so forth. These objects were laid out on the floor in front of the subject, who was asked to sort them into piles that made sense to him.

The dominant mode of classification in this pilot work was what we have called 'functional entailment'. A pair of objects was selected so that the first went with, or operated on, the second. For example, a potato and a knife were put together because 'you take the knife and cut the potato'. Very rarely was a large group formed, and we virtually never had a classification justified in terms of the way things look or their common membership in a taxonomic category. (Cole *et al.* 1971)

One clear exception to this occurs, however, in the sorting of leaves: 'The Kpelle play a game in which twenty to thirty leaves are tied to a rope. The object of the game is to name and describe the function of each leaf without hesitation—a long pause or an error and the player is "out"' (ibid. 88). A selection of twelve leaves, six from vines and six from trees, was made by a Kpelle college student; the twelve leaves were presented to ten non-literate Kpelle adult farmers and ten American adults working at Cuttington College in the area. The leaves were spread out on a table in front of the subject, who was told, 'I have some leaves here, I want you to sort them into two piles according to which ones you think go together. There should be six leaves in each pile.' The Kpelle scores were roughly twice those of the Americans, not surprisingly, but in this case, the Kpelle used taxonomic principles.

Cole *et al.* conclude that

Semantic [taxonomic] classes can serve as a means of organizing verbal behaviour, but the extent to which this happens in naturally occurring contexts is very much open to question ... in conducting interviews prior to begin the work that generated the seŋ[6] chart, John Kellemu tried out a number of informal procedures designed to elicit ideas of category membership. The first few of these procedures produced interesting results, but not a taxonomic classification system. In one, the men were given an example of a general class and asked to group all the examples they had named into subgroups. This technique elicited what Kellemu called 'informal classification'; the men organized the objects according to *function* and *use* rather than according to a formal semantic system of classes.

Three other techniques also resulted in functional schemes of classification. In one, persons were asked to name all the things they had seen in a given day and then to group these things. A second technique was to have the men name all the things visible in a given scene and then to group them. The third asked them to name all the things similar to a given thing. In each case the subject drew on immediate experience.

The use of alternative classification principles emerges from our studies of the way in which objects are sorted. In pilot work using a large array of objects bearing no salient relations to each other, functional pairing was a dominant means of classification. But when objects bore a class relation to each other, and when only two classes were permissible, semantic class relations were strongly expressed. Finally, where taxonomic relationships are habitually used as a basis for classification (such as was the case for the leaves that we asked our subjects to sort), the recognized taxonomic class was the dominant basis for classification. (Ibid. 90)

The ability to remember is closely associated with the ability to classify—good recall depends to a significant degree on the efficiency with which material can be sorted into groups of items that 'go together', and for this reason many of the cross-cultural tests of classification have focused on the way in which subjects performed memorizing tasks. Tests conducted among the Kpelle and the Wolof of Senegal showed that the ordering of data by semantic (taxonomic) categories was a function predominantly of schooling and literacy, and to some extent of age:

With respect to the various Kpelle groups studied, it appears from the evidence of our free-recall studies that semantic control (as manifested in clustering) became general in people with more than four to six years of schooling. How much more schooling we are not sure. Such control was not an inevitable consequence of maturation, because our adult populations differed little from younger groups.

The evidence from our American work shows really sizeable amounts of clustering beginning to appear around the sixth grade, and it is possible

[6] seŋ = 'thing'; see below, p. 207.

that a similar finding could be obtained with the proper observation in
Liberia. From Liberia we have the following pieces of evidence:
(1) Comparisons of educated and nonliterate groups when the grades involved were second through fourth produced minimal clustering and slight
differences in recall.
(2) Comparison of high school students with non-literate groups indicated
rapid learning and significant clustering in the former.

Thus, it would appear that some time in the fifth- to eighth-grade range
in Liberia, there is a change to a general use of semantic categories to
control learning. (Ibid. 140)

And so, it should be noted, simply going to school for three or four
years does not immediately produce a marked change in cognitive
skills, probably, among other reasons, because school is so different from the traditional environment and because teaching in Libe-
rian schools is based on rote learning and also seems highly in-
efficient. Cole *et al.* conclude:

The high school student does not require specially structured situations in
order to 'have it occur to him' to use the semantic characteristics of the
material to organize his recall—he produces that structure for himself. The
non-literate (and the same applies to those with little schooling) has not
learned to spontaneously produce such structures under as wide a set of
circumstances. He naturally uses them in some situations (when remembering stories) and can use them in a large variety of specially contrived
situations (such as those provided by certain of our experiments). (Ibid.
141)

Consistently with this, the more general the class, the more difficult it proved to learn, and the more difficult to describe. Subjects
were able to describe their solution of classificatory problems involving the two most general classes (town things and bush things)
in only 10 per cent of cases, but succeeded in 25 per cent of cases in
describing specific classes when these were the solutions of classificatory problems.

It should be noted that it is *taxonomic* classification that increases with education, not simply grouping or classification in
itself. Studies of the Wolof by Greenfield suggest that even in the
absence of schooling there will be a steady tendency for the systematic classification of objects to increase with age. Ten familiar
objects are laid on a table in front of a child (non-literates were
used) who is then asked to 'pick those that belong together'. 'The
set contained four articles of clothing, four round objects, and four

red objects (one of which was an article of clothing and one a round object), permitting the child to form groups according to function, form, or colour' (Cole and Scribner 1974: 102). By the age of fifteen, almost every Wolof child is able to make a systematic classification, but this is based, in the majority of instances, on colour—that is, a perceptual feature which is not the basis of genuine taxonomic classification.

It has been found in almost all tests that there is a very clear correlation between literacy, with a tendency to classify by form, and a developmental tendency whereby young and/or non-literate children classify by colour and only later, as a result of acquiring literacy, switch to classification by form.

Further tests on classification among Wolof non-literate, traditional children and adults, schoolchildren all from the same town, and schoolchildren from the capital, Dakar, with the use of coloured pictures, gave additional evidence for this:

Children who had attended school, whether from the small bush village or the city, performed very much as American children did; preference for colour decreased sharply with grade, while form and function preferences increased. Furthermore, an increasing proportion of the older children justified their classification in terms of a superordinate category ('it's the round ones'). The children who had not attended school and lived in the bush responded quite differently. Such children showed *greater* preference for colour with increasing age and rarely justified their responses by noting the category to which the pictures belonged. (Cole and Scribner 1974:103–4)

(Suchman (1966) among the Yoruba, and Serpell (1969) in Zambia came to similar conclusions on the developmental priority of colour classification.) As Greenfield, Reich, and Olver say,

... this perceptual development is basically a conceptual one ... By conceptual we mean that school is teaching European habits of perceptual *analysis*. An analysis into parts is ... plainly crucial to concepts based on the multidimensional attribute of form, whereas unitary global perception could suffice for colour grouping. (Greenfield, Reich, and Olver 1966: 316)

One of the most noticeable features of these tests is that, as we might expect from Piaget's work, wherever subjects, especially non-literate, traditional people, are given assistance in classification or memory tasks by concrete, contextual cues, their level of performance increases, as it does when they are familiar with the objects being used in the tests, e.g. in tests of recall,

... asking the subject to place the items in a bucket, or to sort the items into cups, had a large effect on the number recalled and greatly increased the amount of semantic clustering. In the latter study, we seem to have hit upon a mechanism for making the recall performance of the nonliterate Kpelle approximate the kind of recall we have observed in literate groups. The most likely candidate for the cause of the improved recall was the fact that subjects manipulated the items that were said to 'go with the cups'. (Cole *et al.* 1971: 131)

It is fairly clear that taxonomic classification, with clearly bounded categories, exhaustive and unambiguous, hierarchically organized from the general to the particular, is a characteristic of operatory thought, not usually to be found at the pre-operatory level; and there is good reason to suppose that literacy in particular will have important consequences for classification. We have already examined some of the consequences of literacy for classification in Chapter 3, but Goody (1977) has also drawn our attention to the special importance of the effects of written lists on classificatory processes, taking many of his examples from Ancient Mesopotamia and Egypt. The list is an ordering of discontinuous, discrete elements taken out of the context of daily speech and life; especially when arranged in rows as well as columns they can be read from left to right or right to left, and from top to bottom, as well as from bottom to top. Lists are bounded both at the beginning and the end, thus helping to clarify categories; this tendency to produce bounded categories also tends to promote an exhaustive enumeration of members of categories. Lists also encourage a hierarchical ordering of categories, from general to particular; most significantly, the act of listing elements involves the explicit choice of criteria by which those elements are to be selected, and hence the awareness of alternative criteria of selection. While Piaget's material shows that one can attain operatory classification without any emphasis on the writing of lists, and Goody pays no attention to purely cognitive processes, it is undoubtedly the case that the demands of preparing lists is one factor in promoting operatory classification. We may consider one of his examples in more detail:

[In the case of the Onomasticon of Amenope] The scribe entitles his manuscript ... 'Beginning of the teaching for clearing the mind, for instruction of the ignorant and for learning all things that exist: what Ptah created, what Thoth copied down, heaven with its affairs, earth and what is in it, what the mountains belch forth, what is watered by the flood, all things upon which Rē' has shone, all that is grown on the back of the earth, excogitated by the scribe of the sacred books in the House of Life, Amenopĕ, son of Amenopĕ, He said:

There follow some 600 entries, though this was only part of the original (possibly 2000). In presenting this list, the author was not simply enumerating but also classifying, with rubrics often marking the beginning of a fresh category, though the cohesion of the categories is sometimes questionable. The whole composition is divided by Gardiner into the following sections:

I   Introductory heading
II   Sky, water, earth (Nos. 1–62)
III   Persons, court offices, occupations (Nos. 63–229)
IV   Classes, tribes, and types of human beings (Nos. 230–312)
V   The towns of Egypt (Nos. 313–419)
VI   Buildings, their parts, and types of land (Nos. 420–73)
VII Agricultural land, cereals and their products (Nos. 474–555)
VIII Beverages (Nos. 556–78)
IX   Parts of an ox and kinds of meat (Nos. 579–610)

The degree of order in the Onomasticon of Amenope can be exaggerated, but when Maspero edited this work, he gave it the title of *Un manuel de hiérarchie égyptienne*, thus recognising the fact that the scribe deliberately, intentionally, starts 'from the top with deities, demigods and the king, and follows mankind through his various ranks and callings, down to the humblest of free occupations, that of the herdsman' (Gardiner 1947: i, 38) Thus the author aimed at some sort of 'rational classification', an arrangement from the highest to the lowest (II, III), and from the general to particular. (Goody 1977: 100–1)

Goody elaborates on some features of this list as follows:

We can see here the dialectical effect of writing upon classification. On the one hand it sharpens the outlines of the categories; one has to make a decision as to whether rain or dew is of the heavens or of the earth; furthermore it encourages the hierarchisation of the classificatory system. (Ibid. 102)
[and]
... the beginning and end of clusters can be indicated by spatial separation, by insetting, by diacritical marks and in numerous other ways. And as the items within a list are set in an implicit hierarchy by the order of listing (an order that may be indicated by numbers), so too the first level clusters may be grouped in a similar way, either by further levels of clustering (as in the kind of tree diagram that forms the stock in trade of many scientists) or in a simple linear hierarchy, which gives some overall order to the clusters and their constituent items. (Ibid. 104)

3. PROTOTYPES AND NATURAL CATEGORIES

We have noted that the complex is based on imagery, rather than on explicit taxonomic criteria which are characteristic of the logical class. So before we consider the extent to which hierarchical systems of classification occur in primitive society, we must consider the extent to which classification is dominated by prototypes.

In an important paper on 'Human categorization', Eleanor Rosch (1977) points out that, despite the long-standing awareness of complexive classification among developmental psychologists: 'Categories [classes] have tended to be treated in philosophy, psychology, linguistics, and anthropology as "Aristotelian" and digital, that is, as logical, bounded entities, membership in which is defined by an item's possession of a simple set of criterial features' (op. cit. 18)

Rosch's original and important contribution to the study of classification consists in showing that much classification of natural categories in ordinary life does not rest on a 'digital' enumeration of discrete properties as the basis of ascribing membership of a class to a thing, but rather, on an 'analogue' procedure which rests on assimilation to a prototypical image of the ideal 'thing'—be it bird, colour, facial expression, or whatever. We shall see that the notion of 'prototypical' classification as developed by Rosch is particularly compatible with that of complexive classification and with the prevalence of symbolism in thinking.

Rosch's research began with a study of Brown and Lenneberg's (1954) finding, in relation to Whorf's theory of linguistic determinism, that colours named with a single word could be more easily recognized and recalled than colours designated by a phrase. In other words, colours for which the language provides greater ease of codability are more readily distinguished than colours with less codability and, as is well known, different cultures use their colour terms to denote different ranges of colours. This Brown and Lenneberg study has therefore been taken as a partial validation of the Whorf hypothesis. But Brown and Lenneberg also noted that red, orange, yellow, green, blue, purple, pink, and brown are the eight commonest chromatic colour terms in English, and that their subjects were able to select a particular colour chip from the Munsell series as the 'best' example of each colour with a high level of agreement (Brown and Lenneberg 1954: 458).

Later work by Berlin and Kay (1969) showed that there is a maximum of eleven basic colour names (the eight chromatic colours previously mentioned, plus black, white, and grey) in any language, 'basic' here implying a name which is only a single linguistic unit of meaning, referring only to colour. Basic colour terms, so defined, emerge in a clearly defined evolutionary sequence, so that many cultures have only a few of these, while some cultures, especially in New Guinea and Australia, are restricted to black and white as basic terms. Significantly, Berlin and Kay discovered that while the boundaries of colour classes are very variable cross-culturally, the 'best' examples of each colour are remarkably constant from culture to culture. Heider[7] (1972b) confirmed in a test given to speakers of twenty-three diverse languages representing seven of the major linguistic families, that 'focal' colours are given shorter names and are named more rapidly than non-focal colours. On the hypothesis that, despite variation on the boundaries, there are cross-culturally invariant focal-points in the spectrum, Rosch then conducted experiments in New Guinea to see if, despite the paucity of basic colour terms there, focal colours are learned more readily than non-focal. The Dani, of West Irian, have no basic terms for colours other than black and white, but it was found that they could remember the focal colour chips four times as successfully as the non-focal, in a situation where linguistic codability could have played no part.

When taught to name three types of colour—focal, non-focal, and colours intermediate between these—the Dani found it easiest to learn names for focal colours and hardest to name non-focal colours. Rosch also showed that children learn and remember the perceptually salient colours most readily, so that when the names are learned they tend to become attached first to the salient stimuli and are only later generalized to other similar instances. There appears to be a neurological basis for some of the focal colours, such that one element of the nervous system is sensitive to red/green, and another to yellow/blue, while the dominant wavelengths of the focal Munsell chips for red, green, yellow, and blue seem to correspond fairly well to the focal hue points. But the essentially prototypical structure of colour classification does not depend on any neurological basis of this type. Rosch was thus able to show that the results of Brown and Lenneberg's work, while apparently

[7] Until 1973 Heider was the married name of Eleanor Rosch.

supporting a Whorfian relativism, in fact lead, when fully examined, in a diametrically opposite direction.

It was found that while the Dani have graphic representations of squares, triangles, and circles in their art (though they have no terms for them), they were able to learn well-formed examples of these shapes quicker than distorted forms, while Ekman (1972) demonstrated the existence of a prototypical structure of the classification of facial expression which possesses cross-cultural generality. On the assumption that there are six basic emotions (happiness, sadness, anger, fear, surprise, disgust) and that these are associated with limited facial expression, he assembled pictures designed as expressions of pure emotions, which were recognizable by American, Japanese, Brazilians, Chileans, and Argentinians. The last three might seem to anthropologists only variants of a common culture, but Ekman and Rosch found that the Fore and Dani could also recognize the intended emotions when shown the pictures, and my own, albeit very unsystematic, observations of the Konso and Tauade certainly confirm that they, too, both use and recognize facial expressions similar to ours in the registration of basic emotions.

So while logical classes (with the exception of polythetic classes used in scientific taxonomies) are clearly bounded, and all elements possessing the qualifying properties of the class have a full and equal degree of membership, so that one instance is as good as another once the rules of class membership have been learned, it does not follow that in the real world people, even in our own society, actually employ this mode of classification when they assign anything to a class. The hypothesis is that prototypical classification is the norm in most areas of primitive classification, except for kinship and a few other specialized categories.

In the case of prototypical categories, as we have seen, some members are better members than others which may be seen as peripheral or ambiguous, and the prototype will be conceived in terms of sensory images rather than in terms of the possession of discrete criterial attributes. (Such a theory of classification is, of course, very damaging to the theories of structural anthropologists such as Leach and Douglas, who regard ambiguity as only pertaining to things that fall between classes, and derive therefrom a ritually dangerous, anomalous status. But if ambiguity is general to all non-prototypical things, it is hard to see why it should be the focus of any ritual attention.)

So far, we have been establishing the existence of prototypical classification in areas of experience such as colour, form, and facial expression, which may in principle be expected to have relatively little culture dependence. But it is clear that many, if not the majority of classes have no obvious physiological basis and are highly culture dependent. Do we find that with this sort of category, too, subjects can make consistent and meaningful judgements about the prototypical status of some members, and that the prototypical structuring of categories affects the degree to which some members are regarded as focal members of the category? We shall find that prototypical classification is effective (a) because the world, as we have seen, is experienced in a 'pre-packaged' way, many attributes of things being interdependent, (b) because some of these attributes are good predictors of the presence of other attributes, and (c) because the prototype can help to maintain the discreteness of categories despite the inherent tendency of prototypical categories to be fuzzy about the edges.

We may now consider these points in more detail. Free sorting tests, of the kind discussed earlier, assume that the elements to be classified are unstructured, thus forcing the subjects to fall back on criteria such as colour and form. But these criteria are too general to be of much use in practical problems—earth, dead leaves, and cows are all brown, but this is not a helpful generalization for a Kpelle farmer.

Because the real world manifests inherent regularities, the problem for the individual who tries to order it is to be able to predict as many properties as possible on the basis of as few criteria as possible. This would lead to a system of many categories with fine distinctions between them, but it is also to the individual's advantage not to make distinctions which are irrelevant to the purpose at hand.

This introduces the notion of 'cue validity', a probabilistic concept according to which the validity of any cue (perceptual attribute) as the predictor of a category is proportional to the frequency of the association between it and other cues. The cue validity of an entire category may be defined as the summation of the cue validities for that category of each of the attributes of that category, so that categories whose criterial attributes have a high frequency of concurrence will be more distinct than categories that have a low cue validity. Because 'in the domain of nature and man-made objects, there occur information-rich bundles of perceptual and functional attributes that form natural discontinuities', we can see that cue validity will be maximized at a particular level of classification, at which more attributes will be common to members of the category than at other levels of classification. It may therefore be more efficient to classify in terms of those basic objects that are at the level of abstraction for which cue validities are maximized. So, for example, 'dog' and 'cat' may be more useful categories than 'animal', or 'table' and 'chair' than 'furniture', since high-level categories such as 'animal' and 'furniture' possess few attributes common to all members of the category, while subordinate categories, such as 'Chippendale chair', or 'Labrador Retriever' involve a specificity which limits their use unduly in too many contexts.

Basic object categories, such as 'dog', 'hammer', 'chair', etc. are given their coherence by image-based prototypes, which are products of the cue validities produced by the structuring of the real world and which maintain the discreteness of the basic categories.

It follows, if this account of practical classification is correct, that hierarchical classification of the form 'Labradors are dogs', 'dogs are mammals', 'mammals are animals', etc., is of relatively little use in the classification of the world for utilitarian purposes. We are likely to find that, rather than employing classificatory hierarchies, we, as well as primitives, classify primarily at 'basic' levels; that superordinate and subordinate classificatory levels are of relatively little significance; and that classificatory systems are much more reflections of real world structuration and much less dependent on language or on arbitrary cultural factors than anthropologists have commonly supposed.

Ethnoscientists have claimed that the 'genus' is the level of classification which most closely corresponds to the basic level, in which organisms possess bundles of correlated features constituting 'obvious' differences from other organisms. Tests showed that for these and other non-biological taxonomies, such as musical instruments, fruit, tools, clothing, furniture, and vehicles,

... very few attributes were listed for the superordinate categories, and a significantly greater number of attributes were listed for the supposed basic level objects. Subordinate level objects did not receive significantly more attributes listed than basic level objects. The few additional attributes listed for subordinate object names tended to be adjective rather than noun or functional attributes. (Rosch 1977: 32)

Again, subjects were told to describe the movements made when using, or interacting with, the objects named in the samples. Each activity was then analysed into the parts of the body used, and how. While there were virtually no movements in common for supposed superordinates, basic objects had large numbers of movements in common, while there were no more in relation to subordinates than to basic objects.

In the case of tests based on two-dimensional outlines of objects, the results showed that the ratio of overlapped to non-overlapped areas, when the outlines of two objects from the same basic level were superimposed, was far greater than when objects from the same superordinate category overlapped. The gain in information obtained from shifting from the basic level to the superordinate was significantly less than the gain from shifting from the superordinate to the basic level.

When outlines of objects were averaged, it was found that when subjects were asked to identify these outlines, the basic objects were the most general and inclusive categories at which the objects depicted could be recognized. Subordinate-level objects were no more identifiable in this form than basic objects.

This result was particularly important because it suggests that the basic level may be the most inclusive level at which it is possible to form a mental image which is isomorphic to an average member of the class and, thus, the most abstract level at which it is possible to have a relatively concrete image. (Ibid. 35)

Rosch suggests that while the prototypes of physiologically based categories appear to be perceptually salient stimuli, which are salient before the formation of the category, in the case of 'artificial' categories such as the 'noun' categories of all cultures, the prototypes appear to develop through the same principles (such as maximization of cue validity) as those governing the formation of the categories themselves. In so far as the attributes of categories are quantifiable, then the prototypes represent the means of those attributes. Items having a mean value are obviously closer to other items in the category than a member with an extreme value, while more highly correlated attributes are probably given greater weight in the formation of the prototype than the same attributes which are not correlated with each other. So if categories form to maximize the information-rich clusters of attributes in the environment, the prototypes of categories appear to form so as to maximize cue validity still farther within categories. Prototypical thinking therefore enables a person to use the structured properties of the environment 'without his being forced to engage in the laborious cognitive process of contingently computing and summing the validities of individual cases'.

Prototypes are clearly dependent on imagery rather than on explicit verbalization, and may be the most inclusive level at which it is possible to form a mental image isomorphic to the appearance of members of the class as a whole. While pre-operatory children accomplish sorting tasks (at the superordinate level) complexively Rosch finds that at the basic level they sort basic objects taxonomically. Colour in particular is useless for sorting unless the objects are unrelated, but we find that in societies without Western schooling, subjects sort unrelated objects in terms of colour because they are unable effectively to use the superordinate levels of classification, even though colour vocabularies are usually poor in these societies.

4. HIERARCHICAL CLASSIFICATORY SYSTEMS AND THEIR RELATION TO GROUP HIERARCHIES

Since primitives base their classification primarily on complexes derived from the functional and associational relations between things experienced in real life rather than on logical class and taxonomic criteria, it is inevitable that while it will be possible to construct hierarchical classificatory systems with large general categories divided into more particular categories, such systems may be based on shifting criteria and may contain overlapping classes and classes that are not united in any superordinate class. (The existence of general and particular terms, such as 'tree' and 'oak', in the lexicon of a natural language, does not necessarily mean that the people themselves actually conceive these terms as denoting classes standing in a relation of class inclusion. Thus Piaget notes that while little children of three or four can understand that a daisy is a flower or that a woman is a person, they do not understand these hierarchical relations in terms of class inclusion.) The importance of prototypes in classification also renders multilevelled hierarchica systems of relatively little use in the circumstances of primitive life, since basic level categories are the most useful for information processing. Rather than employing taxonomic categories, we find that primitives tend to classify their universe into 'realms' such as 'things of the forest', 'things of the village', 'things of the sea', and so on, which are not ordered hierarchically.

Theorists such as Lévi-Strauss have greatly exaggerated the well-ordered nature of taxonomic hierarchies in primitive societies. For example, the taxonomies employed by the Yurok, Karok, and Smith River Indians of south-west California in the classification of their fauna are unsystematic and unco-ordinated.

We nearly exhaust the universe of living things with multilevelled hierarchical classifications such as 'plant, bush, berry bush, gooseberry bush', or 'animal, insect, louse, body louse'. The Indians, by contrast, have relatively few generic terms, and many terms which do not fall into any hierarchy.' (Bright and Bright 1970: 70)

For example:

Yurok: quadruped mammal; fish; snake; bird (especially small bird); fir tree, tree; bush; grass; flower; berry.
Smith River: snake; duck, bird; fir tree, conifer; bush, non-coniferous tree; grass; flower; berry.
Karok: snake; bird; tree; bush; grass; flower; berry.
In this framework, a term like Yurok . . . 'body louse' cannot be subsumed in larger classes 'louse' or 'insect', since none exist; nor is the classification *ho're?mos*, sometimes translated 'animal', conceded to apply to it. The answer to the question . . .' 'What *is* a body louse?' is simply . . . 'It's a body louse'. Furthermore, Yurok informants, asked to identify a plant or animal for which they know no name, often say that it is 'like such-and-such', rather than assigning it to a class; thus several flowering bushes were described as *sahsip segon* 'like wild lilac', although they bore little resemblance to the wild lilac, from a white man's point of view . . . When generic terms exist, they may also refer to a specific member of the class. This parallels the use of English 'man' to refer both to human beings as a class and to adult males as a subdivision of that class; but the phenomenon is commoner in the Indian languages. Thus Yurok *tepo* refers to 'fir tree' or 'tree' in general; Smith River *tšeeyaš* is 'duck' in particular or 'bird' in general. (Ibid. 70–1)

Whereas in a logical hierarchical classificatory system based on class inclusion, because any element of a class either is a member of the class or is not, it is therefore unambiguously also a member of the next higher order of classification, or it is not:

But there is no way of indicating, in a hierarchical tree, the situation where a specific term like Yurok *tepo* 'fir, tree' or Smith River *tš'aamé?* 'fir, conifer' can also be used as a generic term, thus including other trees which resemble the fir by being coniferous. In addition, there is no way of indicating when an item is classified in a certain way because it is 'like' another item which is more central to the focus of the domain in question. (Ibid. 71)

So the native taxonomy can be better represented by a 'sphere of influence' model (Figure 7) than by a hierarchical model.

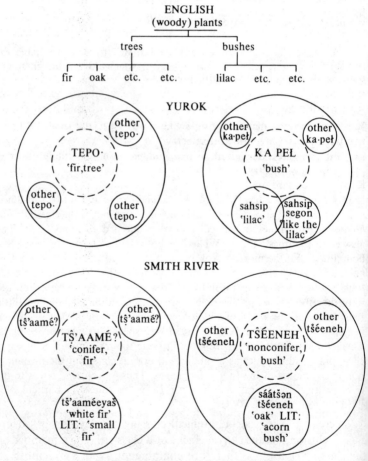

Figure 7 (Bright and Bright 1970: 72)

For Smith River, woody plants are either *tš'aamé?* or *tšéeneh*; there is a choice only of these two generic terms or of specific lexemes. In Yurok, classification does not fall into such strict lines: an item may be included in the *ka.p'el* 'bush' domain if it is merely *like* another member of that class. (Ibid. 74)

The Karam of the New Guinea Highlands also provide an example of faunal classification in which hierarchical classification is applied only in a very restricted way. At the highest level of generality, 'There are no Karam taxa corresponding to "reptile", "lizard", "snake" and so forth' (Bulmer 1967: 6). There are no fewer than ninety-four primary taxa ('primary' denoting the highest level of generality in the taxonomic system) and Bulmer observes that at this upper level of the taxonomic system cultural criteria play a more important part than criteria of morphology or habitat. When we come to intermediate taxa we find that these are usually absent (in eighty-eight out of ninety-four cases, in fact) and that most primary taxa are simply divided into terminal taxa. Apart from the primary taxon of *yakt* (flying birds and bats) which has twenty-three intermediate taxa and 181 terminal taxa, two primary taxa have two intermediate taxa, and three primary taxa have one intermediate taxon, while no less than sixty-six primary taxa are also terminal taxa. With regard to terminal taxa Bulmer writes:

. . . at this level Karam show an enormous, detailed and on the whole highly accurate knowledge of natural history, and . . . though, even with vertebrate animals, their terminal taxa only correspond well in about 60 per cent of cases with the species recognised by the scientific zoologist, they are nevertheless in general well aware of species differences among larger and more familiar creatures. The general consistency with which, in nature, morphological differences are correlated with differences in habitat, feeding habits, call-notes, and other aspects of behaviour is the inevitable starting point for any system of animal classification, at the lowest level. (Bulmer 1967: 6)

The Karam taxonomic system is thus based to a significant degree on the salient natural resemblances and discontinuities of nature at the level of terminal taxa, where the relevant criteria are predominantly morphology, habitat, and behaviour, but at the higher levels also embodying such diverse cultural criteria as relationship with man, purity/impurity, edibility, ideological aspects of forest, open country, gardens, and homesteads, and the symbolic realm generally. Given this variety of criteria, it is not surprising that their taxonomic system is not reducible to any consistent logical principles, or that it has a large number of primary taxa which are also terminal taxa, though these are not deficiencies from the Karam point of view.

A similar lack of hierarchical organization can be observed in the Konso classification of animals and human beings (Table VI), despite the fact that the Konso are highly concerned with categorization.

TABLE VI

Konso Human/Animal Classifications				
nama (person)	(no collective name)	*pinanda* (wild animal)		*hambira*	*muguja*
man, person		animals resembling	other†	birds	fish
dogs	cattle	cattle, sheep and	animals		
monkeys*	sheep	goats			
	goats				[May not
		types of deer	lion		be eaten]
[May not be	[May be	buffalo	leopard		
eaten]	eaten]	zebra	terrapin		
		giraffe	crocodile		
* the monkey is regarded		rhinoceros	snake		
as *pinanda* in many respects,		pig	etc		
however		etc			
			[May not		
		[May be eaten]	be eaten]		

Criteria of category selection	
1. domestic/wild	† because inhabit different
2. appearance	elements,
3. habitat	or carnivorous
4. social relations	or nocturnal
with man	or burrowing
5. edibility	or have human resemblances
6. resemblance to paradigm	
animals or to man	

Classificatory systems are not, of course, confined to those of flora and fauna. The lexicon of a language however is of little use in establishing classificatory systems, and so Cole, Gay, and their associates used a variety of sorting tasks to elucidate the implicit classificatory system of the Kpelle world, on the basis of a tentative system established by an educated Kpelle, John Kellemu, in discussion with a small group of elders (Table VII).

THINGS

	TOWN THINGS						FOREST THINGS								
Playing things	People	Town works	Town animals	Working things	The earth*	The earth*	Traps‡	Animals	Root crops	Water foods	Mush-rooms	Vines	Trees	Shrubs	†Evil Things
dancing equip-ment	children adults	houses sheds	walking animals	vehicles medicines	dirt stone	dirt stone		hoof (two-part)	wild planted	water oil		wild planted	wild planted	wild planted	poro head sande head
dancers	good people	fences	birds	herbs	sand	sand		hoof (four-part)		honey					fearful things
drums	evil people	bench		charms	mud	mud		claw							witches
horns	workmen	loom		societies				dragging snakes							genii
games	status			evil				snails							dwarfs
	appearance			divining				fish							spirits
				western				nonscaly							
				household things				scaly							
				sleeping things				worms							
				beds				crawling							
				cloths				edible							
				mats				nonedible							
				tools				water							
				clothing				burrowing							
				cooking things				tree							
				utensils				leaping							
				foods				edible							
				prepared forest†				nonedible							
				traps‡				flying							
								birds							
								insects							
								edible							
								nonedible							

* The earth is a major subclass of both town and forest things.
† The edible forest things within the dotted lines are also a subclass of town things as indicated.
‡ Traps are a major category of forest things and a subcategory of town things.

(Cole et al. 1971: 64)

In this classificatory system the Earth is a major subclass of both town and forest things; edible fauna and cultivated flora are a subclass of town things. Traps are a major category of forest things and a subcategory of town things:

In many, if not all cases, the ambiguities in classification arose because of the enormous complexity of classifying, sub-classifying, and cross-classifying such a large domain of objects. As a consequence of the diversity of things being classified, the basis of classification often shifted in subtle ways.

The following example may serve to make these difficulties understandable. Suppose that someone asked an American college student for a classification of things. He might answer all things are living or inanimate. How then would he classify such things as a farm, or the earth, or food? Clearly, the choice would depend on ad hoc criteria made up for the purpose. At several points in working out the various subsets of things and their relations, Kellemu encountered the problem of shifting criteria of classification leading to the overlapping categories in Table [VII]. For example, a banana is a *town thing* in so far as it is a kind of food, but a *forest thing* in so far as it grows on a tree in the forest. (Cole *et al.* 1971 : 63)

The problem is therefore that the Seŋ or Thing chart may well be an overformalized and artificial system, imposed to some extent by an educated Kpelle on his informants, which may mask alternative classificatory schemes. Further research showed that the Kpelle classify in different ways when relationships between things are elicited in different ways, such as by sentence substitution, free association, or non-verbal sorting. Thus the very notion that there is a final, 'true', or authoritative classificatory system within a particular culture is highly dubious.

Various methods were used to elucidate these aspects of the Thing chart, the first being that of sentence substitution, in which subjects were given class names from the chart and asked to make up sentences containing each of them. Then they were asked which of the words could sensibly be substituted for other words in these sentences:

The resulting data matrix, reflecting the degree to which words could be used interchangeably in different sentences, was analyzed, using a technique developed by Stefflre (1963), in which the set of words was rearranged so that those that substituted in a similar manner into the various sentences are placed near each other. Our concern was to determine if words classified together on the seŋ chart would appear as groups accord-

ing to this sentence-substitution method. In general, classes defined by the
seŋ chart appeared again in the results of this study. (Ibid. 65)

(Subjects for these studies were traditional Kpelle adults between the ages of eighteen to fifty.) The principal results were as
follows:

The major split between *town* and *forest things* and most of the classes at
the next level of specificity are approximately maintained. However, ambiguities masked by, but present within, the orderly presentation of the seŋ
chart appear. For example, *working things* does not appear as a unitary
category; its ambiguous status in the chart is reflected by its tendency to
divide into clumps that attach to other classes on the chart. *Cooking things*
and *town animals* appear in a group next to *foods*, reflecting what seem to
be natural relations that are suppressed in the search for order in the
dichotomy between *town* and *forest* in the chart. Likewise, *structures*
appear together with *clothing, tools,* and *sleeping things,* all of which are
kept in the houses that compose the village. (Ibid. 66)

It is easy to see that when the Kpelle, or any other people, are
called upon to classify things, while their classification will be relatively unambiguous when confined to the objective resemblances
and discontinuities of natural species, nevertheless, since all their
criteria of class membership are based on habitat, appearance, function, or use, their classification will become increasingly ambiguous
when it has to impose order on the heterogeneous collection of
items comprised in the *seŋ* chart, which are not ordered in the same
neat way as natural species. There are, of course, no 'natural' classes for these items, and so the only logically satisfactory order is
one of an arbitrary, conventional nature, based on taxonomic criteria and governed by theoretical considerations. But the Kpelle,
like other primitive peoples (and ourselves, unless we have given
the matter close attention), attempt the task on the basis of complexive classification, dominated by concrete associations and
'functional entailment'. So their resulting system of classes is inevitably ambiguous and founded on shifting criteria.

A third method of eliciting classifications was that of free association:

For example, a person can be asked 'What do you think of when I say
"cars"?'. Properly analyzed, the free-association technique can provide
evidence on the extent to which the set of stimuli (in our case, words from
the seŋ chart) elicit each other and other words as associations. The
strength of association among a set of stimuli, as well as class membership,

can be evaluated using both common associates (*cat* and *dog* both elicit
the associate *hair*) and direct associations (*cat* and *dog* elicit each other) as
indicators of the relationships among words (Deese 1962) ... Once again
the general result was a replication of the content of classes contained in
the seŋ chart, although as was the case when the sentence-substitution
method was used, the pattern of relationships among classes was often
different, and in some cases class membership was different (for example,
snake is grouped with items that fall in the class of *medicines* rather than
the class of *animals*). (Ibid. 67)

The results of this test of twenty-four words is most conveniently
displayed in Figure 8, representing the hierarchical grouping of the
words according to their similarity scores. 'The greater the similarity between items, the closer to the right-hand side of the figure is

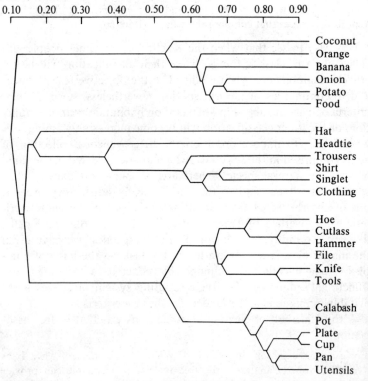

Figure 8   Results of Johnson Hierarchical-Clustering Program Applied to Free-
Associations of Clusterable Stimuli; Kpelle Subjects

(Cole *et al.* 1971: 74)

the point where they are connected by a line. The numbers at the top of the figure represent the degree of overlap represented by items that intersect at that point' (ibid. 73–4).

On the *seŋ* chart (Table VII), however, under the heading 'household things', food and utensils are subclasses of 'cooking things', whereas here utensils are associated more closely with 'tools', and both these are more closely associated with clothing than with food. Examination of the table also shows that the generic terms 'food', 'clothing', 'tools', and 'utensils' have a prototypical relation with onion and potato, shirt and singlet, knife, and pan, respectively, and that other members of these taxonomic clusters are seen as more distantly related to the prototypical members.

I remarked earlier that primitives tend to classify their universe into 'realms', based on physical, spatial, and functional associations between the things in each realm. These realms may often have important cosmological significance. For example, the Konso employ a triadic classification of God, Earth, and the Wild. God, Waga, is associated with the sky, and with rain in particular, so that the Konso believe that He withholds the rain from towns in which there is too much quarrelling. God is not seen as the creator of the Earth but as the source of morality, and therefore the elders are regarded as the corporate representatives of God in carrying out their duties of leadership, wise counselling, peace-making, and blessing. The earth is seen as independent of God and specially associated with women, food, physical fertility, and well-being in general. But women are regarded as outside society in so far as all the principal institutions are male; women do not take part in decision-making and cannot bless, which is an essentially social, male function. The Wild is associated with the jungles of the River Sagan on the border between Konso territory and that of the Borana Galla, and with the bush generally, and therefore with evil spirits, wild animals, and enemies. But the forms of the Wild are ambivalent since priests and mediators and spiritual power are seen as having affinities with the Wild. The most sacred places, including the abandoned homesteads of priests, are overgrown with wild vegetation which must not be cut; and priests, one of whose basic functions is mediating between men, are not supposed to live in the towns, where their presence is mystically dangerous to men, but to make their homesteads out in the fields.

This is not a hierarchical, taxonomic system, but one based on prototypical imagery and concrete associations, whose cognitive function is to impose and generalize an order in which supernatural agencies and forces have an integral part in a dynamic system of relations. We noted similar characteristics in the Umeda system of categories associated with coconut palm, areca palm, and wild sago palm.

In short, there is little evidence that hierarchical systems of classification are typical, well constructed (in a logical sense), or even of much utility in the circumstances of primitive society.

Durkheim, Douglas, and others have maintained that the hierarchies of social organization are the basis for other taxonomic hierarchies. We are now in a position to evaluate this claim, especially bearing in mind the general paucity of hierarchical classification in primitive society.

In one of Piaget's earliest investigations into the growth of logic in the child (Piaget 1928: 119–30), he studied the processes by which part–whole relations came to be understood between the ages of seven and ten. One of the problems involved understanding the relationship between different levels of social grouping. He found that the child initially cannot understand that towns, cantons, and nations are on different hierarchical levels—for the child they are simply different groups. At the second level, the child realizes that one of them can be inside another, as Geneva is inside Switzerland, but this inclusion is purely geographical and involves juxtaposition, not logical inclusion, because the child cannot think of a part as simultaneously distinct from, yet still a component of, a larger whole. For him, a boy is Genevan, not Swiss, or if he says 'Genevans are Swiss', he says that Genevans are also Vaudois (and members of other cantons simultaneously). Only in the final stage does the child realize that it is possible for a person to be simultaneously a member of two groups, one of which is included in the other.

As Piaget points out, one of the child's difficulties is that he has no concrete experience of towns, cantons, and nations, and thinks of countries and other social units in terms of their name rather than as territorial divisions located in real space. But this is not the case in primitive society, whose members have an extensive experience of the spatial distribution of groups, and of their segmentation over time genealogically and politically. It might be supposed, therefore, that, at least in the sphere of social organization, the members of primitive societies must be capable of grasping the logical relation between part and whole. While this may be so, it is not necessarily true, since physical inclusion is not the same as logical inclusion. There is a clear and important difference between being able to distinguish a tree into 'roots', 'trunk', 'branches', and 'leaves'—'partitive membership'—and the ability to grasp the principle of class inclusion. The understanding of descent groups as articulated into clans, subclans, lineages, etc., is possibly closer to the understanding of partitive membership than to that of a logical hierarchy of class inclusions.

Durkheim supposed that the logical hierarchies of classificatory systems were originally provided by the hierarchical structure of group organization: tribe–moiety–phratry–clan–lineage, etc. I shall argue, however, that while there is indeed a similarity between group and logical hierarchies this is superficial and misleading as an indication of the thought processes involved in the conceptualization of these two sorts of hierarchy.

As an ethnographer, quite unfamiliar with most of the individual members of the societies I was studying, and concerned with establishing, among other things, the general organizational form of social groups, I was very much struck by the difference between my conceptualization of social groups from that of the natives. For them, quite naturally, each group was composed of people most of whom they knew, with familiar histories, particular places of residence, and general characteristics of behaviour in common. They evidently had these concrete associations of the sum of each group's membership in mind when they told me which group's members were also members of more inclusive groups.

Among the Tauade, for example, the 'tribe' is an autonomous group of about 200 individuals inhabiting a specific territory bounded by torrents or mountain ridges, and each tribe has its own name. Several tribes comprise one of eight dialect groups, and within the tribe are a number of clans. Membership of a tribe depends on a number of factors:

The bonds which they recognize are those of blood; upbringing in the same family or hamlet; possession of rights of use of land and pandanus trees; co-operation in gardening; common residence and the mutual support in disputes which that implies; the bonds between men created in the men's house; and the inheritance of influence by sons from their fathers. (Hallpike 1977: 84)

Tribes fought with some degree of unity in battle, and tribal membership is expressed in particular by the statement that its members share pandanus trees. Within the tribe are a number of clans, each supposed to be descended from a group of original migrants to the present tribal territory. Membership of a clan is normally inherited through a man's father, but there is no clear jural rule of patrilineality; the clans are associated with particular tracts of land and specific, traditional hamlet sites, and each clan also has a cave in which were deposited the bones of its dead. But the clans have no relevance to the membership composition of the hamlets into which each tribe is also divided, and it is impossible to deduce anything from a man's clan about residence, marriage, or garden co-operation. The effective groups of the tribe are hamlets, whose population is constantly changing, and the family, usually comprising a man and his adult married son or sons, two or more brothers, or sometimes the sons of brothers, between whom are strong bonds of affection.

Thus there is an implicit hierarchical ordering of social groups (see Figure 9). But this is certainly not a logical hierarchy, and the

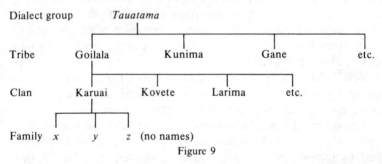

Figure 9

levels in it consist of a series of heterogeneously defined groups, not logical classes. The classificatory basis of the dialect group is not the same as that of the tribe, and differs again from that of the clan, and yet again from that of the family. It might be suggested that one common characteristic of every level is that all the group members come from the same dialect area, but this is not true, in fact, and members of the same tribe may come from different dialect areas. We are not, of course, dealing with a system of classification at all, but of social relationships: each level of grouping is governed by different criteria from the levels above and below it, and while a man of *x* family is included in Karuai clan, of Goilala tribe, these inclusions are not logical, but pragmatic.

A further indication that we are not dealing with a system of logical classification is the absence of generic terms for every level of grouping. There are, in the Tauade language, no words for 'family' ('parents' is a different idea, and expressed by *inatsi*, literally 'mother–father'). Likewise, there is no word for 'clan', 'tribe', or 'dialect area'—only the proper name of each group. It is inconceivable that if this were a system of classification there would be no means of referring to any of its levels by some generic term.

The Tauade are an extreme case of social vagueness, but the absence of generic terms for the levels of what superficially could be taken as classificatory hierarchies, as well as for systems of social organization, is notable in primitive society. For example, among the Nuer, whose society is a classic example of a segmentary lineage system, there are grave difficulties in assimilating the levels of descent groups and territorial divisions into a model of logical hierarchy.

The Nuer lineage system is presented schematically by Evans-Pritchard in the following form (see Figure 10).

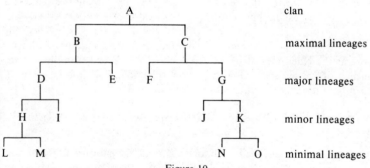

Figure 10
(adapted from Evans-Pritchard 1940: 193)

The descent system is agnatic, and each clan and lineage, of every level, is a distinct group in the following respects:

Clans and lineages have names, possess various ritual symbols, and observe certain reciprocal ceremonial relations. They have spear-names which are shouted out at ceremonies, honorific titles by which people are sometimes addressed, totemic and other mystical affiliations, and ceremonial status towards one another. (Evans-Pritchard 1940: 193)

Thus the Nuer descent system might seem to provide an excellent example of a social hierarchy of classes by which people are categorized, and which is therefore a system of logical classes, in the manner envisaged by Durkheim, Douglas, and others, the more especially since '. . . lineages are distinct groups only in relation to each other . . . There is always fusion of collateral lineages of the same branch in relation to a collateral branch . . .' (ibid. 197). Thus N and O are united in opposition to the lineages of J, lineages J and K unite in opposition to the lineages of F, and so on. This might reinforce the belief that the Nuer see their lineages as a system of classes, but, as we shall see, such an interpretation of their descent system would radically misinterpret the ethnographic facts.

In the first place, there are no Nuer terms for any of the different classificatory levels of the descent system; Evans-Pritchard's nomenclature of clan, maximal lineage, major lineage, minor lineage, and minimal lineage is not a translation of vernacular items into a more convenient analytical terminology, but represents a conceptual classification which has no parallel in native thinking:

> . . . a clan is not to Nuer an abstraction and there is no word in their language that can be translated 'clan' in ours. One may obtain the name of a man's clan by asking him who was his 'ancestor of yore' or his 'first ancestor' (*gwandong*) or what are his 'seeds' (*kwai*), but it is only when one already knows the clans and their lineages and their various ritual symbols, as the Nuer does, that one can easily place a man's clan through his lineage or by his spear-name and honorific salutation, for Nuer speak fluently in terms of lineages. (Ibid. 195)

Nor are there any generic terms for the different levels of the lineage:

> A lineage is *thok mac*, the hearth, or *thok dwiel*, the entrance to the hut, or one may speak of *kar*, a branch. *Thok dwiel* is the commonest expression to denote a line of agnatic descent in those situations when genealogical exactness and precision are relevant, but in normal everyday usage Nuer employ the word *cieng* [meaning 'local community'] . . . (Ibid. 195)

If Nuer were in the habit of using, or even conceptualizing, the descent system as a system of classes, it is hard to imagine how they might do so without any generic terms for the different levels in the hierarchy. Indeed, it is evident that they conceive their descent system as an articulated thing, somewhat like a tree—hence *kar* = branch—rather than as a system of classes, and the points of segmentation are provided by particular ancestors, not by any systematic differences in the criterial attributes of the members of different levels of the hierarchy:

When a Nuer is asked his lineage he gives it by reference to an ancestor, the founder of his minimal lineage, who is from three to six, generally four to five, steps in ascent from the present day . . . It is evident that after five or six generations the names of ancestors become lost. Young men often do not know them, and there is frequent confusion and disagreement among older persons. The founder of the minor lineage must be placed somewhere between the founder of the minimal lineage and the founder of the major lineage; the founder of the major lineage must be placed somewhere between the founder of the minor lineage and the founder of the maximal lineage; and the founder of the maximal lineage must be placed somewhere between the founder of the major lineage and the founder of the clan. The names of these founders of lineage branches must go into the line of ascent somewhere, and in a definite order, because they are *significant points of reference* [my emphasis]. It is immaterial whether other names go in or not, and their order is without significance. Consequently some informants put them in and some leave them out, and some put them in one order and others in a different order. (Ibid. 199)

The Nuer are thus concerned to articulate a sequence of ancestors who are significant because they mark the points of origin of specific groups and their splitting off from, and differentiation from, other groups, but they are interested in the structure of group relations, not in creating any classificatory system as such. 'A Nuer clan, therefore, is a system of lineages, the relationship of each lineage to every other lineage being marked in its structure by a point of reference in ascent' (ibid. 201). But because they are concerned to define a structure, and not to create a system of classification, they are indifferent to the status of those ancestors who do not mark a crucial point of reference in the system, omitting or confusing many.

Not only do links drop out of the direct line of descent, but also collateral lines merge. It is clear from a study of Nuer genealogies that the descendants of one or two brothers become numerous and dominant, that the descendants of others die out, and that the descendants of yet others are relatively few and weak and attach themselves, . . . by participation in local and corporate life, to a stronger and dominant collateral line. They become assimilated to this line in ordinary lineage reference and eventually are grafted on to it by misplacement of their founder, who becomes a son instead of a brother of its founder. (Ibid. 200)

The notion of 'lineage', therefore, is not one that has any precise denotation; *thok dwiel* means 'line of agnatic descent' rather than denoting any clearly definable group:

A lineage is a relative term, since its range of reference depends on the particular person who is selected as the point of departure in tracing descent. Thus, if we were to begin with a father, the *thok dwiel* would include only sons and daughters, but if we were to take a grandfather as our point of departure, it would include all his sons and daughters and the children of his sons. A larger and larger number of agnates would be included the higher up in the line of ascent we were to take the point of departure for counting descendants. (Ibid. 195)

[and]

One cannot say definitely how far up a line of ascent Nuer will go in selecting the apex of a minimal lineage. They may go back only two steps, to the grandfather, making in all three generations of agnates, but a minimal lineage of four or five generations is more usual. (Ibid. 196)

Further evidence that the Nuer descent system is not conceptualized as a hierarchical system of classes, but as a set of concrete relations, is provided by the close association of descent relationships with those of residence.

Political and lineage groups are not identical, but they have a certain correspondence and often bear the same name, for a tribal area and its divisions [which Evans-Pritchard distinguishes as primary, secondary, and tertiary sections, parallel to the segmentation of the clan] are often called after the clans and lineages which are supposed to have first occupied them . . . Thus Gaawar is the name of a tribal area, of the tribesmen who inhabit it, and of the members of a clan which have in that area a socially dominant status. (Ibid. 194)

The ways in which descent and residence relationships intertwine with one another are clearly described as follows:

A Nuer does not normally say that he is a man of such-and-such a *thok dwiel* (lineage) when he denotes his social position, but says that he is a man of a certain local community, *cieng* . . . What he is telling you is that he is a member of a group of people who live together in a village or district or tribal section. In ordinary situations of social life it is irrelevant whether he is, or is not, a member of the lineages from which these local communities derive their names. Moreover, since in ordinary speech a lineage name has a local rather than a strict kinship connotation, those who share community life with the members of the lineage speak of themselves as though they also were members of it, because politically they are identified with it. (Ibid. 204)

It is thus incorrect to suppose that descent, of itself, is the paradigm of everyday social relations, such that a knowledge of a man's actual ancestry will be of much predictive value, or the basis of a system of classification such as segmentary descent systems are alleged to provide.

A *cieng*, in the sense of 'homestead', is called after the man who owns it, e.g. the homestead of Rainen is called '*cieng* Rainen'. When Rainen is dead and his sons and younger brothers and nephews live in his home they may call the hamlet after him, and it will be said that they are all members of *cieng* Rainen. If Rainen was an important man, and proves to have been the begetter of a strong line of descent, the whole village wherein live his agnatic heirs, and strangers who have intermarried with them or in other ways become attached to them, may thus become known as '*cieng* Rainen'. In course of time his descendants multiply and constitute the nucleus of a tribal section which is called '*cieng* Rainen'. Hence it has come about that many tribal sections are called after persons, e.g. *cieng* Minyaal, *cieng* Dumien, *cieng* Wangkac, etc. A lineage thus becomes identified in speech with the territory it occupies; the district occupied by the major lineage of WANGKAC, for example, being known as *cieng* Wangkac. A Nuer then talks about the local community and the lineage which is its political nucleus as interchangeable terms. (Ibid. 204)

I have said that the Nuer think of lineages as splitting off from one another, on the analogy of the branches of trees, and that the position and sequence of particular ancestors is crucial in articulating the structure of any clan. Evans-Pritchard presents a model of various clans in the form of trees, of which an example is given in Figure 11.

But it seems that the basic Nuer conceptualization of their descent system is not in the form of trees,[8] although it would appear

[8] Even if the Nuer do not explicitly base their lineage model on that of 'tree', the matrilineal Maenge of New Britain certainly do: 'All the clans existing in the Maenge country are said to have evolved from one another through a process of repeated scission, the first clan having emerged from a tree stump. Not only is a vegetal origin thereby ascribed to mankind, but the current conceptualization of the differentiation process itself is also based on a vegetal metaphor. Indeed, all the descent groups are seen in their relations to one another as arranged like limbs, branches, and twigs along the bole of a tree. This representation, which is still adhered to by everybody, is of outstanding importance because it gives the Maenge a means of ordering the advents of their different clans and subclans in a fixed series which is agreed upon. Thus, although most people cannot retrace their descent even to the founder of their minimal group, either their local subclan or its local branch, they do know what senior group theirs has arisen from, and conversely who are their juniors' (Panoff 1969: 163). Thus while superficially the Maenge clan system might appear to be a classificatory system employing class inclusion, on closer examination it proves to be a classic case of a graphic image of partitive membership.

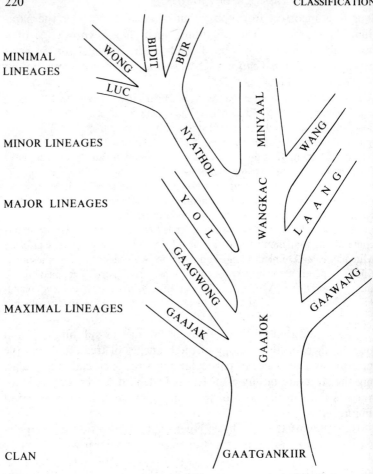

Figure 11
(Evans-Pritchard 1940: 197)

that they do in fact have some such conception, however vague
Evans-Pritchard gives an example (Figure 12) of how the Nuer
represent the structure of the same Gaatgankiir clan illustrated i
Figure 11.

When illustrating on the ground a number of related lineages [the Nuer
do not present them the way we figure them in this chapter as a series o
bifurcations of descent, as a tree of descent, or as a series of triangles o
ascent, but as a number of lines running at angles from a common point

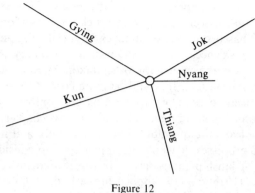

Figure 12
(Evans-Pritchard 1940: 202)

Thus in Western Nuerland a man illustrated some of the GAATGANK-IIR lineages, using the names of their founders, by drawing the figure above on the ground. This representation and Nuer comments on it show several significant facts about the way in which Nuer see the system. They see it primarily as actual relations between groups of kinsmen within local communities, rather than as a tree of descent, for the person after whom the lineages are called do not all proceed from a single individual. Jok, Thiang, and Kun are three sons of Kir and founders of the maximal lineages GAAJOK, GAAJAK, and GAAGWONG of the GAATGANKIIR clan. Thiang and Kun are shown next to each other because jointly they form the lineage framework of the Gaajak tribe. The Gying lineage does not belong to the GAATGANKIIR clan, but it is shown next to Kun because of the proximity of the Reng section, of which it forms part, to the Gaagwong section. Nyang is shown as a short line at the side of Jok because, although the lineage which springs from him belongs to the group of lineages founded by Thiang, they live in the Gaagwang tribe together with a lineage descended from Jok, and the Gaagwang tribe is closely associated with the Gaajok tribe. The Nuer, outside certain ritual associations, evaluate clans and lineages in terms of their local relations. (Evans-Pritchard 1940: 202–3)

It seems, then, that while primitive taxonomies may embody hierarchical relations, these are typically not exhaustive or well ordered; the taxonomic systems that we have considered are dominated by imagery and by relations of 'belonging' rather than of taxonomic class membership and, as Rosch has shown, there are fundamental factors of information processing that render hierarchical taxonomies of limited utilitarian value in ordering the world. Even

when descent systems appear superficially to resemble a logical hierarchy of classes, it seems likely that on closer inspection they will
prove to be based on concrete images of social relations such as
descent and residence. Thus the Durkheimian theory that social
classification was the model for other taxonomies seems to have
little foundation on fact. It would be more correct to say that primitive classification both of men and nature conforms to certain
general criteria which we have elucidated in this chapter.

Before we leave the question of social structure and its relation
to cognitive processes, it would be appropriate to consider briefly
the subject of kinship categories in relation to cognitive development. Piaget (1928: 62–119) applied his early developmental paradigm to the child's understanding of kinship relations. The child
is asked questions about his own family, including how many brothers and sisters he has. The object is to determine, among other
things, how far he is able to understand that the term 'brother' is
not a static, absolute attribute of a person, like 'boy', but a relative
attribute, a relationship which in the case of 'brother' is also symmetrical, so that if X is Y's brother, Y is also X's brother. Such an
understanding also involves the abandonment of egocentricity in
the ability to regard oneself as someone else's brother by considering one's own status from someone else's point of view.

LeVine and Price-Williams (1974) attempted to replicate this
study among the Hausa, but found that in this society, as in many
others, there is no simple term for 'brother' or 'sister'.

... the sibling terms used in the domestic group for both reference and
address are *wa* (elder brother), *ya* (elder sister), *kane* (younger brother),
and *kanwa* (younger sister). These are the terms with which children are
most familiar. Unlike the English and French terms for brother and sister,
they are not symmetrical and therefore cannot be used to indicate the
child's development of the capacity to understand the logical concept of
symmetrical relations. (LeVine and Price-Williams 1974: 27)

Nor is it possible to find a simple equivalent term in Hausa for
our 'family', meaning the unit comprising parents and children.
'There is no straightforward Hausa counterpart of the Western
nuclear family, particularly as an environment for the developing
child, and comparability cannot be achieved by presuming otherwise' (ibid. 28). Despite the problem of any exact replication of
Piaget's tests, it was possible, by the use of the compound as the
reference group, to devise tests embodying the basic cognitive

processes in which Piaget is interested, and it was found, as Piaget predicts, that Hausa children first master kinship concepts from an egocentric perspective and only later from the point of view of another person (ibid. 34). LeVine and Price-Williams also found that:

(1) The abilities to apply kin terms to ego-centred and other-centred relationships, and to define a kin term, increase pronouncedly with age for both sexes in our sample.

(2) Younger children show a fair ability to apply kin terms to ego-centred relationships but very little ability to apply them in other-centred relationships; this discrepancy is greatly diminished among children of seven and older.

(3) The abilities to apply kin terms to ego-centred and other-centred relationships are correlated with each other and with one test of left–right reversibility, holding age constant, in our sample.

(4) The youngest children in the sample tend to identify compound residents in terms of physical presence, location, stature, nick-names, or visible occupation rather than relational concepts and to define kin terms with specific persons and their actions rather than with general properties underlying the relationships. (This is not a quantitative finding.) (Ibid. 41)

Fortes's (1938) study of the Tale child's cognitive growth with respect to kin relationships does not consider the question of ego-centred versus other-centred terms, or the grasp of symmetrical relations, but it does confirm the initial dependence on non-kinship attributes such as those mentioned in (4) above for the classification of those with whom the child interacts in his earliest years. Fortes records that initially the three- to four-year-old child distinguishes kinsfolk from non-kinsfolk, equating the former mainly with people living in close proximity. While he can precisely distinguish his own father and mother he can already extend these terms to others, but he cannot discriminate purely genealogical relations, and depends on the criteria of age and spatial proximity; thus an adult brother may be described as 'Father'. The six-year-old knows the correct terms and appropriate behaviour defining its relations with its own paternal family, and can classify by descent, but still bases his notions of kinship beyond the family on spatial proximity and relative age. The ten- to twelve-year-old can master these extra-familial relations, except for some collateral and affinal kinsmen, the terms for which are known though the relationships cannot be described (ibid. 43–4).

Since virtually no work besides these studies has been carried out in primitive societies on cognitive growth with respect to kinship concepts (the work of 'cognitive anthropologists' such as that in Tyler (ed.), *Cognitive Anthropology* is not developmental), it would be premature to make any definite generalization, but it seems likely that the representation of categories and relationships of descent and alliance may be *the* one area in primitive culture in which cognitive processes of an operatory nature are most likely to exist as the norm rather than the exception among the individual adult members of such societies.

5. BINARY CLASSIFICATION

Lévi-Strauss argues that binary classification is a fundamental property of human mental processes:

... perhaps it must be acknowledged that duality, alternation, opposition and symmetry, whether presented in definite forms or in imprecise forms, are not so much matters to be explained, as basic and immediate data of mental and social reality which should be the starting-point of any attempt at explanation. (Lévi-Strauss 1969: 136)

But he also appears to think that binary classification is derived from the social relations of reciprocity,

... the notions of opposition and correlation basic to the definition of the dualistic principle, which is itself only one modality of the principle of reciprocity. (Ibid. 83)

What are the mental structures to which we have referred and the universality of which we believe can be established? It seems there are three: the exigency of the rule as a rule; the notion of reciprocity regarded as the most immediate form of integrating the opposition between the self and others; and finally, the synthetic nature of the gift. (Ibid. 84)

Exactly what Lévi-Strauss means here is, as usual, thoroughly elusive, but he appears to suppose that all forms of binary classification—such as alternation, opposition, and symmetry—are logically reducible to a common form and are derived from a common origin, and that this is the relation of self to others in the relation of reciprocity.

In fact, it seems that psychologically the most basic binary classification is simple differentiation, which at the perceptual level takes the form of figure–ground discrimination and the awareness of discontinuity. Logically, we express this elementary differentiation

in the form of contradictories, A and not-A, and it is certainly true
that the ability to distinguish, together with the ability to perceive
resemblance, is basic to all cognitive processes. To this extent Lévi-
Strauss is evidently right in supposing that binary classification is
fundamental to thought, even though there is no reason to link it
with reciprocity, which is a social relation with no claim to be a
fundamental *cognitive* structure.

I would argue that the prevalence of binary classification in primitive thought, as in our own, is due in considerable measure to
the fact that 'pairs' of various types are commonplace in the
physical world. We must therefore review the various ways in
which these 'pairs',[9] whether similar or dissimilar, may be generated. I refer to these methods of generating pairs as 'situations' and
note that the members or elements of pairs may be properties,
objects, or classes of objects, relations, or classes of relations.

The first situation is that of differentiation, which may be a cognitive or a perceptive act which simply distinguishes anything from
anything else, let it be figure from ground or one class of thing
from any other. Differentiation may or may not involve the drawing of a boundary, but the drawing of a boundary necessarily involves differentiation.

Differentiation, however, does not of itself create a relationship
between those things that are differentiated, except in the trivial
sense of contradiction, namely, that A and not-A are related as contradictories.

A relationship assumes differentiation, since there can be no relationship between things that are not in some way differentiated,
but there need be no relationship between classes of things merely
because they are differentiated, e.g. between butter and tin-tacks.
So relationships necessarily generate pairs because any relationship
requires at least two elements.

A boundary when drawn necessarily creates two elements, but
there need be no *relationship* beyond the elementary topological
one of separation, as it might be land and sea, or two nations.

A break is similar to a boundary, in that it creates a pair of
elements, at least, but the difference between a break and a boundary lies in the fact that a break produces a relation between whole
and part, whereas no such relation is necessarily produced between

[9] The following discussion of pairs is partly influenced by C. K. Ogden's work on
opposition (Ogden 1967).

elements separated by a boundary, nor are all relations of the part/ whole type.

An axis is a conceptual construct, like a boundary, but, like a boundary, it is derived from the nature of the physical world. It has three basic properties—rotation may take place around it; movement or variation may take place along it in two directions; and it may be orthogonal to other axes. Movement introduces yet another form of pair-reversibility, both circular and linear; and where there is reversibility there is the possibility of end points, between which motion or variation may occur, but beyond which they do not—that is, *scales*.

We can see that differentiation does not of itself generate relationships; that boundaries and breaks produce differentiation, but that differentiation does not produce boundaries or breaks; that whereas boundaries do not imply part/whole relations or indeed relations of any kind, breaks imply that a part/whole relationship exists between the things that are broken apart. An axis is the basis of end points because it has direction, and direction is the logical basis of motion, which may be reversible in a circular or linear form, but not all relationships imply reversibility of motion or variation or end points. An axis is not a boundary or a relationship, though it may be divided by a boundary, and there will be a relationship of some kind between its end points.

Thus there are a number of situations that generate pairs but are not reducible to the conceptual or perceptual act of differentiation. We may say that differentiation, relationship, boundary, break, axis, and reversibility of motion or variation are all mutually irreducible, and are all basic situations producing pairs, whether similar or dissimilar. It is also plain that these situations may exist at the levels of logical classification, imagery, perception, action, in the physical organization of the world, or as a combination of any of these.

We may now consider the various characteristics of the pairs generated by these different situations. The first of these, which is a logical pair, is the contradictory A/not-A. Examples are human/not-human: moving/stationary; edible/inedible; and the characteristic of contradictories is that together they exhaust the domain of the classified elements and do not permit intermediaries. The second type of pair is the contrary: hot/cold; wet/dry; black/white, etc., which are scalar properties and which do not exhaust the domain of the classified elements because there may be entities that are neither hot nor cold, wet nor dry, and so on. Complementaries are inherently of part/whole type and are distinguished by a break rather than by a boundary, and may be related logically or functionally. Logical complementaries are debtor/creditor; husband/ wife (because either term implies the other), while functional complementaries are lock/key, cartridge/gun, and in some respects, therefore, male/female. These complementaries are dissimilar, but both logically and functionally one can have similar complementaries, e.g. logically: enemy/enemy, brother/brother, and functionally, the dual divisions of Konso towns. Associates form another kind of pair whose elements are related because of some kind of empirical conjunction, as sun and moon, hammer and chisel, butter and toast, which is purely contingent and not derived from any logical or functional complementarity or scalar relationship. Correspondingly there are dissociates, such as village/bush, which may be seen merely as different, and not as contraries. Sun and moon may be, according to the classificatory system of the culture, either associates or dissociates.

While 'symmetry' and 'asymmetry' are often applied to what I classify as similar and dissimilar complementaries, it seems analytically more useful and precise to treat these properties as inherently topological, that is, derived from the relationships of order and inclusion so that a symmetrical order is produced by rotation around an axis or by the bisection of a regular figure. It is an evident fact that some aspects of physical structures are symmetrical, as in the bilateral symmetry of many organisms, and others asymmetrical, as in the relation of head and feet.

It is clear from this summary of the basic characteristics of pairs that there is no one–one relationship between differentiation, relation, boundary, break, axis, scale, and reversibility of motion; and contradictories, contraries, complementaries, and so on. Thus boundaries may separate contraries, dissociates, or asymmetric pairs, and relations may exist between complementaries or asymmetric pairs but not between associates; or axes and reversibilities may have no connection with contradictories, complementaries, associates, and so on.

We may therefore map out the relations between situations generating pairs, and the characteristics of such pairs, as in Table VIII.

While there are mental processes that generate pairs—differentiation and comparison—it is also clear that the world itself is organized in such a way that pairs of various types are generated in great profusion. Thus the prevalence of dualistic classification is not principally a manifestation of a binary property of the human mind, imposing itself on a neutral range of phenomena, but rather an accommodation to a dualistic reality. Again, it is undoubtedly true that people at all levels of mental development have a propensity to *reduce* complex situations to binary relations and that comparison in particular seems to be facilitated by the consideration of elements two at a time; but this does not justify the contention that binary *classification* is simply an expression of a dualistic propensity of the human mind.

TABLE VIII

Situation		Characteristics
Differentiation		Contradictories
Relationship		Contraries
Boundary		Complementaries
Break	Pairs, similar and dissimilar	(*a*) logical
Axis		(*b*) functional
Scale		Associates
Reversibility		Dissociates
		Symmetry
		Asymmetry

For the reasons just given, dualistic classification is a fundamental feature of human thought, and we find it in the representations of the educated and literate as well as among primitives. 'Dualism' as such, therefore, is not related to the developmental stages of thought; but what *is* significant in terms of developmental theory is the manner in which dualistic classifications are co-ordinated into total systems. I shall argue that in primitive thought dualism is only one means of ordering among many others used in systems of classification, and does not of itself provide a coherent and integrated logical system in the way that binary classification can be employed at the level of formal operations in our society. A good example of primitive binary classification is provided by Needham's studies of Nyoro symbolism (Needham 1967: 1976b). He sets out to show why, despite the fact that 'left-handed people in Bunyoro are "hated", and nothing may be given with the left hand ... [yet] ... in divination by the casting of cowrie shells, which is by far the commonest technique resorted to whenever Nyoro are in trouble, the diviner holds the shells in his left hand . . .' (Needham 1967: 426).

Goody would have us believe that the problem of left-handed diviners is quite simple: '. . . there is no problem of the diviner as a left-handed man among the Lo Dagaa; for it is in his left hand that he holds the divining stick, leaving the right free for other purposes such as holding a rattle . . .' (Goody 1977: 67). Yet even if this delightfully simple-minded explanation could be applied from the case of the Lo Dagaa to the Nyoro, it would fail entirely to take account of the wealth of ethnographic facts which Needham adduces to show that '. . . in the crucial events of life, and the major institutions of the society, the right is pre-eminent and auspicious while the left is inferior and inauspicious' (Needham 1967: 427). Thus, for example, the afterbirth of a male baby is buried on the right side of the door of the house, and that of a female baby on the left side; at a coronation, the Royal bow is restrung with sinews from the right side of a man who has been kept in a state of ritual purity; in divination for the king, a fowl's throat is cut, and if the blood flows more freely from the right artery, it is auspicious, while if more freely from the left artery, it is an inauspicious omen; women are buried on their left sides, men on their right, and so on. Such elementary considerations of convenience and utility as Goody proposes are wholly inadequate to account for these systematic and consistent associations of right/left in Nyoro symbolism.

But Needham is concerned with more than the range of symbolic associations of left and right in Nyoro society. The significance of the diviner is that he is a man, but is ascribed female status through his association with the left hand, with the number 'three', while at initiation into the diviner cult the novice is given to believe that he must demonstrate his genuine possession by the spirits by *becoming a woman* (ibid. 437). And '. . . Nyoro women are thought especially to possess the "evil eye" . . . and . . . the word *mutende*, which means "handmaid, concubine, king's dairymaid", also means "pupil of *embandwa* [diviner]' (ibid.)

As a biological man who is nevertheless ascribed female status as an integral aspect of his office, the diviner is a symbolic reversal of the princess who, biologically a woman, is ascribed masculine status. Her placenta is buried on the right side of the door, and she is buried on her right side, like a man; she is treated as a boy, herds cattle, and has her teeth extracted in the same way as a prince. She is forbidden to marry although sexual liaisons are allowed and any children that result are normally killed. In all these respects the princess differs from the queen, who alone of the princesses was allowed to marry; she was in practice forbidden to bear children since she was expected always to be at the king's disposal, but there was no law forbidding her to have children (see Needham 1976: 238); and accordingly, while the princesses are buried in the fashion symbolically appropriate to men, with their hands placed under the right side of the head, the queens are buried with the hands under the left side of the head, in the manner of women.

The same theme of symbolic reversal is clearly displayed in the myth of Mpuga Rukidi, the first king of the Bito dynasty but of alien origin, who usurped the throne when the queen fell in love with him and poisoned her husband.

Mpuga Rukidi is a naked hunter ('Rukidi' means 'the naked one') born a twin (highly inauspicious among the Nyoro), who cannot even speak Lunyoro, and does not know what milk is; he wears a sheepskin, worn only by women and young boys among the Nyoro, while the sheep is associated with sacrifice and divination; he has no possessions, apart from some chickens—again, associated with divination—and as his name 'Mpuga' signifies, he is black on his left side and white on his right side.

Goody proposes the traditional functionalist explanation that the myth is '. . . a way of justifying the advent of a new dynasty, an interpretation which a number of authors have made of similar stories of regal origin' (Goody 1977: 65). But as Needham says,

Alien origin, illegitimacy, twin birth, menial status, savage ignorance, usurpation, adultery, misalliance, and accession by treacherous murder at the hand of a woman are hardly the instruments to confer aristocratic prestige or to emphasize the 'distinction and antiquity' of Bito antecedents. These scandalous and sinister origins cannot establish any credentials to govern, for they are worse than spurious; they are, significantly, the very negation of all valid credentials. (Needham 1967: 445–6)

Even this brief summary of Needham's argument will suffice to show that there is a wide range of oppositions associated with right and left in Nyoro symbolism, and that systematic reversal is a conceptual device for defining social prototypes of the kinds we have been considering in the cases of the diviner, the princess, and the savage outsider. But when we examine the full range of oppositions in Nyoro symbolism (Table IX), it becomes evident that opposition by itself is insufficient to provide a classificatory system.

TABLE IX

A	B
right	left
normal, esteemed	hated
boy	girl
brewing	cooking
giving	[sexual intercourse]
(social intercourse)	
king	queen
man	woman
chief	subject
good omen	bad omen
owner of land	hunter
health	sickness
joy	sorrow
fertility	barrenness
wealth	poverty
heaven	earth
white	black
security	danger
life	death
good	evil
purity	impurity
even	odd
hard	soft
princess	diviner
political rank	mystical office
Kitara-Unyoro	Bukidi
legitimacy	illegitimacy
normal birth	twin birth
cattle	chickens, sheep
milking	hunting
clothed	naked
shaven hair	long hair
bark-cloth	animal skins
Nyoro language	alien dialect
civilization	savagery
royal endogamy	misalliance
fidelity	adultery
personal combat	murder
moon (beneficent)	sun (maleficent)
culture	nature
classified	anomalous
order	disorder

(Needham 1967: 447)

It is immediately obvious that Table IX comprises a number of factors or relationships which, while they may be generally characterized as auspicious or inauspicious, and have corresponding associations with left and right, are logically heterogeneous.[10] 'Woman' has no association with 'hunter', 'barrenness', 'death', or 'sun'; 'savagery' has no association with 'cooking', 'soft', 'subject', 'earth', or 'barrenness'; 'divining' has no association with 'cooking', 'subject', 'hunting', 'nakedness', 'savagery', or 'barrenness', and so on. The factors or relationships to which I have alluded comprise, among others, male/female, culture/savagery, life/death, ruler/subject, political authority/mystical power, and order/disorder, but they cannot be treated as strictly analogous to one another. Thus mystical power comprises both blessing and the evil eye, which cannot both be placed on the same side in the table of oppositions, just as in the relation 'ruler/subject', both elements belong to 'order', rather than 'disorder'.

In short, while Nyoro culture is permeated by symbolic opposition, in which colour, number, certain animals, and left/right have a number of constant associations, and while it can be shown that symbolic reversal, as in the status of the diviner and the princess or of Mpuga Rukidi in relation to Nyoro values of kingship, occurs in a constant way, opposition and reversal are insufficient in themselves to constitute a system of classification (especially since the classification involved here is based on imagery and association, not on any taxonomic principles). For in order to interpret Nyoro symbolism and the ordering function of opposition and reversal, it is necessary for us to understand a vast range of facts about Nyoro life—kingship, female status, kinship, class stratification, divination, land tenure, the uses of animals such as cattle, sheep, and chickens, and so on. It is this implicit knowledge, the common

[10] This point, essential for understanding the significance of tables of opposition such as that just quoted, is discussed at length in Needham 1973: xxiii–xxx and also in Needham 1967: 26, discussions which appear to have escaped the notice of Goody, since (1977: 65–7) he imputes to Needham the simple misconception that the elements of one column are opposed as a total homogeneous class to the elements of the other.

The suggestion that such tables of opposition originate in the mind of structuralist ethnographers and are imposed on the data can most easily be refuted by the consideration that if this were so it should be possible to construct such tables with equal facility for any society. In fact this is not so: within my own experience the Konso while having a great propensity to categorize, made little use of binary opposition and the Tauade, whose categories are vague and amorphous, provide even fewer examples of binary opposition.

property of the Nyoro people, that really gives meaning to the symbolic oppositions; the range of oppositions is itself parasitic upon the rest of Nyoro culture and depends on a further range of ideas, both explicit and implicit, which have an essential function in providing conceptual order. It is not the case, therefore, that dualistic opposition functions among the Nyoro as a sufficient device for ordering their total system of categories (as a taxonomic tree orders a domain of elements in a scientific system of classification), since these categories are related by a complex set of associations which are not reducible to dualistic form. Nor must we forget that the list of dualistic oppositions which Needham provides are very much the product of literate thought, as are the examples of dualistic transformation in myth given by Lévi-Strauss; collective representations may have a dualistic structure which is beyond the capacity of the individual members of the culture to employ explicitly in their own reasoning.

We may therefore expect to find pairs of items which are conventionally associated in the collective representations of all cultures, in any of the wide variety of ways already discussed; and it also seems to be the case that differentiation and comparison are fundamental both at the perceptual and the conceptual levels of mental functioning, and the division of, or grouping of, things into pairs is the simplest form of differentiation or comparison.

But it is also clear that a culture may recognize a variety of pairs without any systematic dualistic scheme of classification in terms of which these pairs may be ordered hierarchically on taxonomic principles. Thus Chinese philosophy was markedly dualistic, but dualism here was evidently part of an explicit theory of the nature of change and stability (curiously similar to that of Heraclitus), which transcends the use of opposition in primitive classification. For example,

In its primary meaning yin is 'the cloudy', 'the overcast', and yang means actually 'banners waving in the sun', that is, something 'shone upon', or bright. By transference the two concepts were applied to the light and dark sides of a mountain or of a river. In the case of a mountain the southern is the bright side and the northern the dark side, while in the case of a river seen from above, it is the northern side that is bright (yang), because it reflects the light, and the southern side that is in shadow (yin). Thence the two expressions were carried over into the Book of Changes and applied to the two alternating primal states of being. It should be pointed out, however, that the terms yin and yang do not occur in this derived sense either in the actual text of the book or in the oldest commentaries. Their first occurrence is in the Great Commentary, which already shows Taostic influence in some parts. In the Commentary on the Decision the terms used for the opposites are 'the firm' and 'the yielding', not yang and yin.

However, no matter what names are applied to these forces, it is certain that the world of being arises out of their change and interplay. Thus change is conceived of partly as the continuous transformation of the one force into the other and partly as a cycle of complexes of phenomena, in themselves connected, such as day and night, summer and winter. Change is not meaningless—if it were, there could be no knowledge of it—but subject to the universal law, tao. (Wilhelm 1968: lvi)

We are here in a very different conceptual world from that of the Nyoro. An apparently elementary opposition becomes the basis for a dynamic analysis of change, process, and stability, seen as a general system of relations of universal application.

Again, at the formal level of thought, dualistic principles may be employed in hierarchical taxonomic systems which proceed from the general to the particular and attempt to exhaust all taxonomic possibilities in the process which, as Goody rightly points out, are the characteristics of literate, educated thought, and not to be found in primitive society. This procedure is the basis of such games as 'Twenty Questions', which is an excellent demonstration of the logical efficacy of successive differentiations, but this process of successive differentiation itself depends on taxonomic classification and an overall conceptual strategy to guide the questions, and which is lacking in the variegated pairs of primitive classification.

Dualistic classification may therefore occur at any level of thought and is in any case as much an accommodation to the 'two-ness' of reality as an expression of a binary propensity of the human mind. What *is* developmentally significant is the extent to which binary categories are systematized, either into an integrated explanatory framework such as that of the Chinese or into exhaustive and hierarchically organized, goal-directed, classificatory procedures.

6   CONCLUSIONS

It seems, then, that primitive classification is based on functional, associational relationships derived from concrete properties and everyday associations, and is inherently complexive in type, although in restricted instances primitives are clearly capable of employing taxonomic classes. Such classification is inherently closely associated with prototypical images, and while some hierarchical classification exists in most primitive societies, it is not well formed or of particular utility. More significant are categories based on realms of experience, which need not be hierarchically organized. There is no evidence that social hierarchies are conceptualized as logical hierarchies, and while binary classification is a pervasive theme in many primitive cultures, it is a variable one; it is not so much the result of the imposition of any 'binary structure' of the mind on to a neutral range of phenomena as an accommodation to the 'twoness' of reality. Binary classification itself may be of different developmental levels. The only fundamental binary structures of the mind, if they deserve that description, are differentiation and comparison, which occur at all developmental levels.

6

Number, Measurement, Dimensional Analysis, and Conservation

It has been argued so far in this book that primitive experience is represented in terms of perceptual configurations and qualities, which are not analysed into invariant relationships transcending phenomenal appearances, but into concrete elements and associations. In our study of classification we saw that even if roughly hierarchical schemes of categorization existed, they were not based on logical classes, but on prototypes and complexes. It is therefore necessary to consider apparent exceptions to this generalization, namely number. For if a society has a set of verbal numerals, even if they extend no further than to 5 or 10, it might be argued that the adult members of such a society must therefore understand that '5' is a logical class, whose members all share the property of having 5 members, and that any member of the class '5' is the result of the addition of $2 + 3$, $3 + 2$, $2 + 2 + 1$, $1 + 2 + 2$, etc.

It will be shown that in fact it is possible to have verbal numerals, and to be able to count by using these numerals, without understanding the logical properties of number classes or of the relation between cardination and ordination. Some societies may not grasp that numbers are classes at all, while even if the classificatory aspect of number is understood, there may be no understanding of class inclusion. Primitive concepts of number are not necessarily based on the grasp of logical class, but can be explained in terms of the generalization of the action of adding (of bending one finger after another, for example) and of the construction of concrete groups of objects, such as shells or stones—number, in short, can be constructed at the pre-operatory level. In so far as this is the case, the existence of verbal numerals among primitive peoples does not of itself *prove* that the members of such societies conceive numbers as a system of logical classes. While in some cases the majority of the adult members of a primitive society *may* understand the logical basis of number, this will have to be demonstrated empirically, and cannot be deduced merely from the existence of a series of verbal numbers, even a series extending to 100 or 1,000 or more. Piaget (1952a) considers that the cognitive development of numerical thought is closely associated with the development of the capacity for understanding logical relations, and in particular that the operational construction of number depends upon the ability to conserve a total quantity despite the various possible decompositions and rearrangements of its elements— that is, the ability to grasp fully part–whole relationships and their compensations. This is a point of fundamental importance in Piaget's analysis of the number concept.

The mere ability to count—that is, to repeat the words for numbers in their correct sequence—tells us little or nothing about the numerical understanding of the child, nor does the ability to perform the elementary processes of addition, multiplication, etc., since these can, up to a point, be learned by rote in the form of tables, quite mechanically and without true understanding. Nor does it follow that the ability to construct a series physically— primitive addition—and to name the successive members of that series, will in practice be accompanied by the ability to decompose the series in such a way that it can be seen as the sum of its parts (e.g. $8 = 5 + 3$; $8 - 3 = 5$) that is, the ability to grasp the reversible relation between addition and subtraction; nor will the ability to construct a set by addition necessarily be accompanied by the ability to multiply sets or to divide them. So counting up objects to reach a total, or 'tallying', is a cognitively elementary skill, which does not imply an operatory understanding of number; and a full understanding of the logical relations between addition, subtraction, multiplication, and division is attained, in Piaget's view, only at the operational level. This does not mean that by, say, the physical manipulation of counters, beads, or stones, or other objects, it is not possible for children to multiply and divide before the operatory stage, but merely that they do so mechanically, and without fully understanding what they are really doing. And as we have already noted many times, enactive thought is always in advance of representational thought.

Piaget's primary contention is that the operational understanding of number is based on an understanding of logical relations, and in particular on the synthesis of cardination and ordination, that is, of systems of inclusion (hierarchies of classes) and systems of asymmetrical relations (qualitative seriation) that is, such relations as 'bigger than', 'to the right of' and so on, together with the ability to equalize differences by partition of any class or series into units, and the establishment of one–one correlations between the members of two or more series.

The properties of number are discovered, however, in the course of the counting and measurement of physical objects. We shall therefore make primitive concepts of measurement and dimensional analysis integral aspects of our study of number concepts. In this regard we shall examine the extent to which the conservation of length, weight, quantity, etc. are likely to be attained by the average member of a primitive society, since conservation is closely related to measurement. Before we consider these ideas in more detail, it is necessary to survey the ethnographic evidence on the ways in which number and counting are employed in the average primitive society.

1. PRIMITIVE CONCEPTS OF NUMBER

The study of primitive conceptions of number has been much neglected in this century, after the initial interest in the last part of the nineteenth century and the early twentieth century by Tylor (1871), Conant (1896), Lévy-Bruhl (1912), and others, who collected examples of number systems from hundreds of non-literate societies. This early work concentrated on number terminologies, which were easily accessible to the amateur ethnographers of the day. Most attention was paid to such problems as the highest number for which a term existed in any particular system, the base (quinary, decimal, vigesimal, or whatever), the method of enumeration such as fingers, or fingers and toes, or other objects such as stones and shells, and the etymology of the terms, if any could be found. On the basis of this material Lévy-Bruhl and Conant in particular reached a number of important conclusions—that it is possible to have counting without verbal numerals ('for long ages primitive man counted before he had any numbers' Lévy-Bruhl 1926: 202), that actions were the basis of this 'innumerate' counting, that some societies have number words only up to 'three' or even 'two' although their members can count higher on fingers and toes; that primitives are basically interested in counting as a means of reckoning totals, of tallying in fact, rather than in performing arithmetical operations with the constituent numbers of those totals; and that primitive number concepts are bound to concrete objects and not conceived as logical classes having a necessary relation to one another.

The operational understanding of number, therefore, has to be clearly distinguished from the ability to manipulate sets of objects such as fingers and toes, stones, or cowrie shells and to perform elementary addition and subtraction with them. The essence of primitive counting is tallying, the construction of perceptual series, such as the bending of each of the fingers in turn or the placing of one object, such as a shell or a stone, in conjunction with others in a series of successive actions, a co-seriation such as Piaget describes for pre-operatory stage II.

Thus the Zuni numbers 1–5 are:

1	*töpinte*	taken to start with
2	*kwilli*	put down together with
3	*ha'ī*	the equally dividing finger
4	*awite*	all the fingers all but done with
5	*öpte*	the notched off

(Conant 1896: 48)

Similarly for the numerals of the Montagnais of northern Canada:

1	*inl'are*	the end is bent
2	*nak'e*	another is bent
3	*t'are*	the middle is bent
4	*dinri*	there are no more except this
5	*se-sunla-re*	the row on the hand
6	*elkke-t'are*	three from each side
7	$\begin{cases} \textit{t'a-ye-oyertan} \\ \textit{inl'as-dinri} \end{cases}$	there are still three of them / on one side there are four of them
8	*elkke-dinri*	four on each side
9	*inl'a-ye-oyert'an*	there is still one more
10	*onernan*	finished on each side

(Ibid. 53)

In this way primitive counting

proceeds in a concrete fashion. It has recourse to the representation of the movements which add units to the original whole or else subtract from it . . . It associates a regular series of movements with successive totals in such a way as to recall any of these at need by repeating the series from the beginning. (Lévy-Bruhl 1926: 184)

If it is not the movements involved in tallying, it is the configurations of things constructed as a result of these movements or an essential part of them, such as the hands and feet. So it is that numeral bases are often as follows:

hand	= 5
both hands	= 10
both hands and a foot	= 15
both hands and both feet, or 'man'	= 20

For example, among the Betoya of South America:

teente	hand	= 5
caya ente	two hands	= 10
toazumba-ente	3 hands	= 15
caesea-ente	4 hands	= 20

(Conant 1896: 57)

or among the Galibi of Brazil:

atoneigne oietonaï	one hand	= 5
oia batoue	the other hand	= 10
poupou patoret oupoume	feet and hands	= 20

(Ibid. 138)

Conant cautions us that

More than enough has been said to show how baseless is the claim that all numeral words are derived, either directly or indirectly, from the names of fingers, hands, or feet. (Ibid. 97)

Among almost all savage races one form or another of palpable arithmetic is found, such as counting by seeds, pebbles, shells, notches, or knots; and the derivation of number words from these sources can constitute no ground for surprise. The Marquesan word for 4 is *pona*, knot, from the practice of tying breadfruit in knots of 4. The Maori 10 is *tekau*, bunch, or parcel, from the counting of yams and fish by parcels of 10. (Ibid. 93)

The principle is even clearer in the case of 'round-the-body' counting, often encountered in Melanesia, where the fingers of one hand, say the left, are succeeded in the enumeration by the wrist, elbow, shoulder, left side of neck, left eye, forehead, right eye, right side of neck, and so on down to the fingers of the right hand. Totals of over thirty can be reached by this method, but one frequently finds that the same terms, e.g. 'side of neck', occur twice, showing clearly that we are not dealing here with conceptual classes but with strictly physical points in a fixed and irreversible series, which cannot be broken down into units or subclasses of units, and which cannot therefore be made the basis for any grasp of class inclusion. The Kewa 'round-the-body' system is shown in Table X.

TABLE X

1	little finger	47
2	ring finger	46
3	middle finger	45
4	index finger	44
5	thumb	43
6	heel of thumb	42
7	palm	41
8	wrist	40
9	forearm	39
10	large arm bone	38
11	small arm bone	37
12	above elbow	36
13	lower upper arm	35
14	upper upper arm	34
15	shoulder	33
16	shoulder bone	32
17	neck muscle	31
18	neck	30
19	jaw	29
20	ear	28
21	cheek	27
22	eye	26
23	inside corner of eye	25
	between eyes	
	24	

After the mid-point has been reached, the Kewa qualify the names of the body parts on the other side with the word *mendaa,* 'another of the same'. One Kewa unit, forty-seven, is *paapu,* 'around the body parts'.

In some cases people who employ body-counting systems can point without hesitation to the place where a number higher than the base would normally be indicated. They are able to carry the base in their heads, and count out high numbers by going through several revolutions on a single body. Other people seem to require several bodies to count out numbers larger than the base, as they can carry this only in physical form. They seem to have no expression for multiples of 'one man finished' or the base. (Wolfers 1972: 218–19)[1]

This mode of counting is basically only a conventionalized variant of that employed by the New Guinea woman who tied a knot in a piece of cord for every occasion that her husband beat her, and took it to the Patrol Officer as concrete evidence of her ill-treatment. In both cases a graphic and concrete object is the basis of a series of actions, which are repeated to produce a graphic total. For example,

among the Metlpa, Western Highlands, a small length of bamboo is added to those already hanging horizontally from a man's neck each time he gives a partner eight token *kuia* shells in ceremonial exchange . . . The Parevavo, inland from the Gulf of Papua, tie a knot in a length of twine for each man killed in battle and unravel the knots as each death is avenged. Some Chimbu groups reputedly kept score boards in red pigment on the walls of rock shelters, one mark for each important man who died in battle. The Elema, Gulf of Papua, kept a positive and negative tally of men killed ('ours' on the right, 'theirs' on the left) by sticking pieces of *selo* (the hard outer covering on the stalk or midrib of the frond) into either side of a stripped sago palm frond. They used a similar device, with *selo* pieces variously shaped, to record the different kinds of earthenware pots and quantities of sago that they exchanged with their Motuan partners in the *hiri*. (Ibid. 217)

Indeed, it is not at all clear that primitive enumeration, because it is so closely tied to action and graphic configurations, conceives the natural number series as the product of the successive iteration of the unit 'one', rather than seeing each number as a distinct con-

[1] Wolfers draws attention to the distinction between counting systems that have a 'modulus' and those that have a 'base'. The essential mathematical feature which distinguishes a modulus is that it cannot be carried in the form of multiples, as can a base: 'The hour hand on a clock, for example, can never proceed beyond twelve. It cannot show whether it is morning or night or what day, week, month or year it is. Once it reaches twelve it starts again; it cannot carry or otherwise indicate the total number of times it has passed twelve' (ibid. 219).

'The Huli, Southern Highlands, for example, count in fifteens—but not by indicating body parts—until they reach fifteen fifteens, 225, when they start again. They have no way of expressing multiples of 225, although more than 225 units of a single kind of object may be physically present. The Huli counting system, therefore, has a base of fifteen and a modulus of 225, at least verbally' (ibid. 219).

figuration in its own right, at least in the case of numbers below about ten. Some confirmation of this supposition can be found in the fact that many peoples, especially in New Guinea and Australia, have number words only for one, two, three, and four (and sometimes only for one and two), and beyond this rely on purely physical enumeration on fingers and toes.

A possible explanation for this may be that the 'one', 'two', or 'three' of these very simple number systems may not be understood as a series of integers, each differentiated from its predecessor by the addition of 'one', but as the names of *configurations*, e.g. 'single', 'pair', 'triad', and so on, which are each seen as of special and unique significance. Piaget points out that the numbers up to five can be understood intuitively in terms of their part–whole relationships by children who are a long way from attaining an operatory understanding of number. But this does not explain why number *names* should stop at four or so, unless it is that individuals in such cultures are more interested in the different *types of relationship* between groups of twos, threes, and fours than in the fact that they form a series. Among the Tauade, for example, there is no commonly used word for any number above two, although they use finger and toe counting, but they have a great interest, for social reasons, in pairs, and their language differentiates in the Dual between pairs of males, pairs of females, and pairs of one male and one female. The same interest in the relative properties of groups may therefore characterize those systems with terms up to four or five. In other words, while we may translate these numbers by 'two', 'three', and so on, the natives may see them as designating certain prototypical groupings, which are mutually unrelated in real life; if this is so, we can understand why a triad is *not* the sum of 'pair + 1', in human terms; and equally why, if they are not interested in higher number groupings, they should have no names for them. In such cultures the classificatory function of number is evidently not understood.

It is clear, for example, that the Umeda, who are typical of New Guinea cultures in only having verbal numerals for 'one' and 'two', but who tally on parts of the body to express higher totals, are unaware of the classificatory function of their tallying operations, and think of number in terms of concrete collections and configurations specific to each occasion:

Thus an Umeda does not say 'I have six children' (child number one, number two, number three, etc.). Instead, the set of children is defined by a criterion appropriate to the specific set, i.e. by their names (Harry, Jim, Susan, etc.). Similarly with months, which are not *enumerated*, but are specified by the relevant criterion—'what we are doing during that moon'. Thus Umeda lack an overall number system (one-ness and two-ness excepted) but supply the deficiency by creating *new series* whenever a particular set must be specified. Hence, perhaps the poor performance of the pupils in the catechist's school when it came to maths (the catechist himself came from a culture with only two numerals, which may not have helped). Take a typical Umeda 'sum' series:

$$1 + 1 = 1$$
$$2 + 2 = 2$$
$$3 + 3 = 3 \text{ etc.}$$

For the Umeda pupil, this series of 'sums' was a set of independent formulae: what *we* recognize as numbers, were, for them, objects: they tried to count the numbers—not the (notional) objects that the numbers represented. Quite unaware that numbers were not objects in their own right, but signs for sets of objects the catechist's pupils readily lost themselves in formulaic incantations which bore no resemblance to the elementary maths they were supposed to be learning.

As it happens, I was present during one delirious afternoon when the children finally did catch on to the basic principles of number—the fact that with numbers you can count *anything*. Released from the schoolhouse, the excited children ran hither and thither in little groups, applying their new-found insight: they counted the posts of the houses, the dogs, the trees, fingers and toes, each other—and the numbers worked, every time. (Gell 1975: 162n)

The 'configurational' aspect of number is, of course, dominant in the case of 'mystical numbers', of which Lévy-Bruhl has said,

Every number, therefore, is imagined ... especially for itself, and without comparison with the others. From this standpoint numbers do not constitute a homogeneous series, and they are accordingly quite unsuited to the simplest logic or mathematical operations. The mystic personality contained in each makes them unable to be added, subtracted, multiplied or divided. (Lévy-Bruhl 1926: 206)

Thus from the Konso the mystical numbers are two, three, five, six, and nine. 'Two' represents woman, and seems to be derived from the binary aspect of the female genitals, while 'three' represents man, being equally derived from the 'threeness' of the penis and testicles. 'Five' represents fertility, the product of 2 + 3 in copulation, while 'six', hostile to women, seems to be derived from the addition of man + man, 3 + 3, in homosexual intercourse, and 'nine' represents the period of gestation of the human foetus. This is not to say that the Konso, who have a highly developed number system, are not also quite capable of using these numbers for ordinary computation, at least in addition and subtraction, but rather, it shows that each number has for primitives separate and unique concrete associations bound up with graphic configurations not very far removed in concreteness from hand and body which are the primary vehicles of calculation.

According to Lévy-Bruhl, primitive numeration does not begin with the unit—it imagines, on the contrary, collections of entities or objects which are familiar both by nature and by number, the latter being felt and perceived, though not conceived in the abstract. The primitive mentality

... does not distinctly separate the number from the objects numbered. That which it expresses by speech is not really numbers, but 'number-totals', the units of which it has not previously regarded singly. To be able to imagine the arithmetical series of whole numbers, in their regular order, starting from the unit, it must have separated the number from that which the number totals, and this is precisely what it does not do. (Lévy-Bruhl 1926: 192)

Even where a culture possesses an extensive verbal system of numbers, we are not entitled, from that fact alone, to deduce that the members of that culture have an operational grasp of number. Such a conclusion must rest on empirical evidence of the way in which their numbers are used. But while the existence of verbal number systems is not in itself evidence for an operational grasp of number, there can be no doubt that a verbal system is an essential prerequisite for it, since if one has no terms for distinguishing verbally between groups of objects it would seem impossible for relational judgements of any complexity to be formulated.

Even in the case of societies with verbal number systems, computation seems usually to be limited to the calculation of totals, while multiplication and division rely on the use of objects as counters. Prince, for example, writes of New Guinea societies, '. . . Systems of counting seem to be used almost entirely for counting numbers of concrete objects, such as wives, children, houses, pigs, and in the case of the larger counting systems numbers of shells to make a bride price' (Prince 1969: 31).

Gay and Cole (1967), in their study of Kpelle mathematics, write that when the Kpelle put objects together, take objects away, or share objects among sets of people, they never have occasion to work with pure numerals, nor can they speak of them. All arithmetical activity is tied to concrete situations, so that cardinals are either preceded by the noun they enumerate or by a pronoun—'of it', for example. The statement 'two and three are five' is linguistically impermissible. The Kpelle can perform simple addition and subtraction by the use of stones, in which they are accurate only up to about thirty or forty. Multiplication, as in 'three sets of two chickens are six chickens', is achieved by a repeated addition of sets, where the total is arrived at by counting the objects that result from these additions. There seems to be no such operation as multiplication. 'One person was asked a complex problem, which reduced in our terms to multiplying 6 by 7. He was evidently trying to count, in his head, all the objects, but he got lost on the way.' Division is achieved by the use of stones, shared out into as many piles as the divisor.

'Equality' is expressed qualitatively, rather than quantitatively, by such notions as 'to be of the same strength as', or 'the ability of one to perform or act in the same way as another'. The 'same as' is 'of one type'. The term 'equal to' is restricted to the thing itself and means 'identical' in our terminology, while 'appears to be like' applies to objects only vaguely similar to the first object. For 'similar' they use 'active' or 'smart': 'the tallness of Tokpa is active on Flumo = Tokpa is of similar height to Flumo.' It is possible to express comparisons of magnitude, but only clumsily, as in 'this house in smallness it passes over that one', but usually the greater is compared with the less, rather than vice versa. (We shall return to the question of comparison later.)

Physical numeration therefore is closely bound up with physical objects that are counted, with the actions involved in counting, and with the perceptual configurations, such as hands and feet, the body, or with heaps of objects used in tallying, such as piles of cowrie shells, knotted cords, and so on. Because of this dependence on concrete objects and configurations it seems very probable that primitives do not conceive number as a system of hierarchies of logical classes and simultaneously as a system of asymmetrical relations.

It might be supposed that in societies whose verbal number

system allowed them to express relations of multiplication those who do so must necessarily realize that numbers are systems of inclusions, e.g. if $3 \times 4 = 12$; $2 \times 6 = 12$; then $12 \div 3 = 4$, $12 \div 4 = 3$, $12 \div 6 = 2$, etc. While the matter can be properly decided only by testing in the field, there are some indications that this is not necessarily the case. For example, the Konso can use the distributive suffix -*a* to express multiplication, as in *sagal*[*a*] *sessa,* 'nine times three', to make twenty-seven, but there is no correspondingly simple locution for twenty-seven divided by three. Division, as in the case of many primitive peoples, is accomplished by dividing a set of counters into as many piles as the divisor, but this does not imply that further logical relations will be established between dividend and quotient. The point is that even in societies with verbal number systems, tallying is still highly dependent on manual operations; in particular, since addition is commonly performed by successive increments of ones, it will not *necessarily* be obvious that, even if $1 + 1 + 1 + 1 + 1 + 1 + 1 = 7$, then $7 = 4 + 3$, and $5 + 2$, etc. Similarly, when subtraction is performed by successive crossings out of marks or by untying knots, it will not necessarily be obvious that $7 - 3 = 3 + 1$. Similar considerations apply to manual techniques of multiplication and division, where these exist at all. Thus the dependence of tallying on manual techniques, which often also operate on the basis of the successive addition or subtraction of ones, does not necessarily imply that the practitioners will grasp the logical relations between the totals reached and the numerical subclasses they comprise.

We noted in the previous chapter that the operatory understanding of logical class involved the co-ordination of intension and extension. The operatory grasp of number correspondingly involves the quantification of intension and extension, which we shall now examine in more detail as the prelude to a discussion of measurement.

Even in cultures whose members grasp that numbers are classes, there may be little or no grasp of the class inclusion of number. The addition of classes by inclusion produces hierarchies of classes, in which the subclasses are related to the class as parts to whole. This qualitative or intensive relationship is the basis of an elementary set of quantitative, extensive relationships: 'less than', 'equal to', and 'more than', since parts are less than the whole; the whole is more than any of the parts; some parts may be equal to other parts, and the whole is equal to the sum of the parts. But this qualitative or intensive quantification does not depend on a partition of classes into elements. Class memberships may, of course, intersect, and it is intersection together with inclusion that is the basis for the qualifiers 'some', 'all', and 'none'. But this, like the elementary quantitative relationships 'less', 'more', and 'equal', cannot be the basis for true or 'extensive' quantification based on specific numerical values.

The grasp of extensive quantification involves this grasp of asymmetrical relations and the equating of differences. Differences between *elements* are expressed in asymmetrical relations—'to the right of', 'preceding', 'more than', 'redder than', and so on. Elements in asymmetrical relations may also be qualitatively identical, in which case their only distinguishable feature will be their *position* in the series, which will thus be a 'vicariant ordering', since the elements may be placed in any order, and only the positional relations will be invariant. A series is thus composed of a set of *positions,* and if the elements of a series are otherwise indistinguishable with respect to their qualities, they must still be distinguishable one from another, so that one element can precede or succeed another.

A series based on asymmetrical relations introduces three further logical relationships. We can deduce that if $A < B < C < D$, or $A \rightarrow B \rightarrow C \rightarrow D$, then $A < D$, $A \rightarrow D$, that is, we can apply the principle of transitivity. We are also able to reverse this, and deduce that $D > A$, and also, of course, $D > B$, $D > C$, and that $D \leftarrow A$, and $D \leftarrow B$, $D \leftarrow C$. Thirdly, if we are to grasp seriation operationally, we must be able to understand the relativity of relations, to see that e.g. B is not only $< C$ but simultaneously $B > A$, $C < D$, and $> B$, etc. (In the same way, in a hierarchy of class inclusions, we must also be able to see that if class A is included in class B, and class B is included in class C, then B is simultaneously included by C and includes A, and that A is included in C as well as in B.) The understanding of seriation is in fact the understanding of logical addition.

But a series of asymmetrical relations cannot itself be sufficient for the establishment of extensive quantification, as we have already noted, even in the case of vicariant ordering, since we cannot deduce any *precise* numerical values from 'less' and 'more'. Therefore the differences which are composed[2] cannot be equated because there is no necessary equivalence between them, e.g. $12 < 16 < 47 < 129$, where each succeeding figure is more than its predecessor, but by an unequal amount in each case. Now we can equate differences only if we can partition a series into elements that have the same value (vicariant ordering), e.g. 5, 5, 5, 5, or a series where the *differences* between the elements have the same value, e.g. 1, 2, 3, 4, 5. . . . The basic method of partitioning a series is by establishing a one–one correspondence between its elements and those of a second series. Numerical correspondence differs from qualitative correspondence, since in the latter, elements of a set are differentiated from one another simply by their qualities (such as colour, size, shape, etc.), whereas in numerical (extensive) correspondence each element need not be distinguished qualitatively, but only by its position, from the others. Thus each red counter, for example, in a set can then correspond to one of the blue counters in another set, but to one only. Again, a set of red counters may, by numerical correspondence, be treated simply as '3', as opposed to the class of red counters forming a triangle, and so on. In this numerical correspondence, the elements are distinguished from each other solely by the order in which they appear in the correspondence, an order which is relative and which varies from one operation to another—vicariant order. It is also possible, of course, to have series whose elements differ qualitatively, but where seriation is still possible, as in scales of length. Numerical correspondence thus represents the construction of *units* which are at the same time equal to one another and susceptible of seriation; and this construction takes place through the equating of differences. The understanding of one–one correspondence is basic to the notion of the integer, but not sufficient for it, since, as we noted earlier, it also requires a grasp of the synthesis of systems of class inclusion, or, to put it another way, the co-ordination of ordination (asymmetric seriation) and cardination (hierarchies of classes).

In Figure 13 the Sets A_1 and A_2 are both classes (in this case of 4), and their elements also have position. Even if the actual elements within a series, e.g. A_1, are moved to different positions, the total number of elements in the set and the order of succession of

---

[2] The 'composition' of differences involves the seriation of a set of unequal magnitudes, such that the differences between them necessarily form a series.

the positions remain the same; this is true even if all the elements of the set A_1 are replaced by those of A_2. Moreover, it is now possible to see that the total of the set, its cardinal value, is directly related to

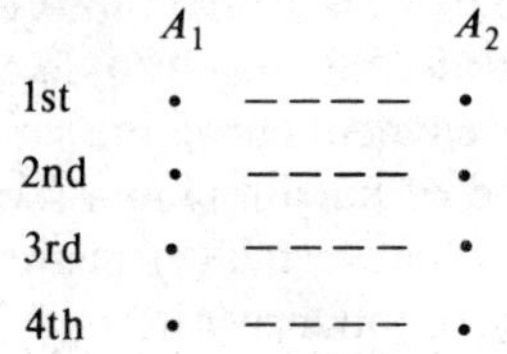

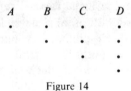

Figure 13

the position of the final element (t), so that it necessarily has ($t - 1$) preceding elements, whose number corresponds to their position, each position and each cardinal number differing from its successor and predecessor by 1. (This is not necessarily so, but is adopted here for the sake of simplicity.) The elements of a set are all quantitatively equal to one another, but all different in respect of their position in the enumeration. Cardination (number) and ordination (position) are thus fundamentally related.

$$
\begin{array}{cccc}
A & B & C & D \\
\bullet & \bullet & \bullet & \bullet \\
 & \bullet & \bullet & \bullet \\
 & & \bullet & \bullet \\
 & & & \bullet
\end{array}
$$

Figure 14

In Figure 14 we see that A, B, C, D are all classes, but that they each also have a seriable position in relation to the other classes, and this set of positions is related in terms of constantly increasing size. The seriable position of each class is expressible in terms of the number of units (here 1) by which each class is greater than its predecessor, units thus forming the basis by which the difference between the classes can be equalized. This illustrates the proposition with which this exposition began, namely, that number is the union in a single operation of class inclusion and asymmetrical relation, together with partition of a set and the equalization of differences by means of units. (Numerical addition differs, however, from logical addition, so that the union of classes $A + A = A$, whereas iteration is basic to numerical addition, so that $A + A = 2A$.)

Equalization of differences is simply another aspect of compensation, the very general operation whereby an increase of so many units in one dimension is compensated by a decrease of an equivalent number of units in another dimension. It is also the basis of the related operation of reversibility.

A further aspect of the equalization of differences is the multiplication of relations, which depends on the grasp of serial correspondence, as opposed to simple seriation.

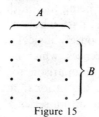

Figure 15

In Figure 15 a serial correspondence of $A(B)$ or $B(A)$ is also an additive composition of $A + A + A + A$, or $B + B + B$. More generally, a number is an additive union of units, and one–one correspondence between two sets (or more) also entails multiplication. $A_1 + A_2 = 2A$ is a multiplication as well as an addition in which set A_1 is coupled with another set A_2 in one–one correspondence. Additive and multiplicative composition, simple seriation, and serial correspondence, whether numerical or qualitative, are therefore correlative, and mastery of one implies mastery of the other. Logical addition precedes logical multiplication, but in Piaget's view there is no basic difference between logical and numerical addition, or between logical and numerical multiplication. What he does claim is that extensive (arithmetical) quantity cannot be entirely derived from intensive (logical) quantity, but requires partition into units and a grasp of one–one correspondence.[3]

A full understanding of number therefore is cognitively much more demanding than the ability to recite the names of numbers in the correct order or the simple ability to add physical elements to a heap. Nor is it even comprised by the processes of addition,

[3] Piaget supposes that logical multiplication develops in an integral manner with logical addition, but the researches of de Lacey (1974) into the classification of Australian Aborigines have shown that it is possible for subjects to have a good grasp of logical addition, but for logical multiplication to be largely absent.

subtraction, multiplication, and division, since these procedures can be carried out by the use of physical counters without any true grasp of the logical foundations of these procedures. An operational grasp of number also extends beyond mere arithmetic and is integrally related to measurement and conservation.

2. PRIMITIVE MEASUREMENT

It will have become clear from this exposition that the unit of number, or integer, is almost identical with the unit of measurement, the only difference being that in the case of measurement we are dealing with concrete, part–whole relations, while integers and numerical seriations are purely logical constructs. Both rest upon the equalization of differences, which is essential for the transition from purely qualitative comparison to the construction of truly numerical compositions. Operational measurement thus involves the partitioning of a thing into a series of iterable units, and as we noted earlier, the basic method of partitioning series is by establishing one–one correspondences between its elements and those of a second series, the units of which are at the same time equal to one another and susceptible of seriation. Operatory measurement is emphatically not merely '. . . the general procedure of assigning numbers to the properties of objects' (Lenzen, V. F., 'Procedures of empirical science', in *International Encyclopaedia of Unified Sciences*, 1(5)(1938), 9).

When discussing 'measurement' in the context of primitive society it is therefore essential to distinguish between simple standardization, as when a conventional length of cloth is sold in a market-place on the basis of an 'armspan', or grain by the cup, etc., and the measurement involved in quantitative analysis, since mere standardization does not involve seriation or dimensional comparison.

While it is possible to measure by the iteration of any *ad hoc* physical element such as a piece of stick, a length of string, a hand-span, or a container, and not necessarily by some culturally defined unit such as feet and inches, operatory measurement is not simply a matter of metric standardization, but involves the partitioning of a thing into a series of elements and the construction of a one–one correspondence between this and a second series; as when children are required to construct a tower of blocks of a height equal to that of a model tower, and finally solve this by using a stick and by counting the number of iterations equivalent to the height of the model tower.

But as soon as one measures the length of one dimension, one has *ipso facto* laid the foundation for the grasp of compensations—that an increase of so much in the width of a piece of land by comparison with another may have been compensated by an equivalent decrease in its length, thus illustrating that conservation and measurement are integrally related. Moreover, the measurement of any dimension, such as height, inherently creates a distinction between *this* dimension and others—length, breadth, and so on—and we shall see that in primitive thought there is a general absence of terms for dimensions such as 'weight' 'length', and so on, which suggests that they have little occasion to abstract particular dimensions and consider them in relation to others.

Primitive systems of measurement, in so far as they exist, tend naturally to be based on bodily 'units' which are often informal and *ad hoc,* and even if culturally defined are usually incommensurable and often confined to particular types of thing, so that they are mutually inconvertible. It must therefore be very difficult to construct any more than very elementary metric relations on such a basis, or to built up any awareness of the various dimensions:

[The Saulteaux] do not even have any common units which are applicable to *all* classes of linear measurement, to say nothing of a graduated scale of such units. This means that such measures as they employ for different kinds of linear distances are not comparable, nor is it possible to convert measures of a lower order into those of a higher order and vice versa. Consequently distance-away, or distance apart, when thought of in terms of places or objects in space is an entirely different thing from the length of a manipulable object of some sort like a canoe or a piece of string. There is no means of bringing linear concepts of all kinds into a single unified category of spatial attributes because the units of measure expressing the distance travelled on a journey, for example, are categorically distinct from those applied to the length of a piece of string. (Hallowell 1942: 65)

Among the Kpelle, each crop is measured in different units, by a variety of tins, buckets, and bags. Length is measured by armspans, or from the centre of the chest to the tip of the middle finger, by handspans or by foot-lengths:

The Kpelle . . . is likely to use 'handspan' to measure a table, 'armspan' for a rug, 'footlength' for a floor, etc. In other words he has separate metrics

for separate situations requiring measurement. There is no standard relation between the metrics in the sense that the Kpelle does not translate
from 'handspan' to 'armspan' in the way that we translate from foot to
yard. (Cole, Gay, and Glick 1974: 168)

Among the Saulteaux the units of length are the right forearm
with the elbow as base, and variable lengths may be marked off on
this arm by using the side of the left hand. Also used are the thumb
and first-finger spread, thumb and middle finger, the width of
three, four, and five fingers, the fist with thumb extended, the breast
bone to finger tips, both arms extended, and the pace (Hallowell
1942: 69).

While it is quite practicable to measure by handspans, or by
pacing, the fact that different situations require different units and
techniques of measurement, and that different types of things often
require different types of unit—as armspans for cloth, paces for
distance, and handspans for tables—inevitably hinders the awareness of general dimensions and their quantitative analysis. In any
case it is probably rare in primitive society for measurement to be
used in a quantitative as opposed to a standardizing fashion, e.g. in
New Guinea:

It is rare for numbers to be associated with units sub-dividing a physical
quantity. A few groups seem to speak of 'two lengths of a garden', or 'two
lengths of a piece of wood'. But the units are not of fixed size and the
number of units so used is apparently limited to the smaller whole numbers. (Prince 1969: 31)

Hallowell notes that among the Saulteaux such quantitative
measurement as 'The wabano pavilion of John Duck at Little
Grand Rapids was said to be fourteen steps long and six steps
wide' was very unusual (Hallowell 1942: 69).

But it is not the *ad hoc,* bodily nature of primitive measurement
that is cognitively significant so much as the lack of dimensional
analysis and quantitative iteration engendered by our forms of
measurement. When there is a need for the precise manufacture of
objects which can be handled, 'manipulable areas', as Hallowell
terms them, then we find that relations of proportion and the construction of co-ordinated spatial relations by straight lines and *ad
hoc* units of measurement are very much more readily generated
than in the case of representations of non-manipulable areas such
as pieces of terrain, or the simple standardizing measurement of

the market-place, though even here intuitive judgements of appearance seems to be essential complements of measurement:

If we now turn to manipulable areas, we find that the Saulteaux deal with them more effectively. But their approach is pragmatic rather than abstract. There are several reasons for this. In the first place, elementary processes of perception are more adequate as a basis for making discriminations in the size of manipulable areas than in the case of those of greater magnitude. And through experience in handling materials and objects of various kinds excellent quantitative judgements can be made. In the second place, the Saulteaux are compelled to deal with simple problems of proportion in order to convert raw materials such as hides and bark into objects of domestic use. In making a bark container, for example, its proportions must be adequately controlled from start to finish. But in these relatively simple manufacturing processes area never has to be handled in a purely quantitative abstract way. The size, shape and proportions of the object being produced are all inseparable. Initially, of course, the question 'is this piece of skin "big enough" to make a pair of moccasins' or 'is this piece of bark "big enough" to make a rogan'[4] does arise. But it can be answered in terms of an estimate based on experience, how it 'looks', without resort to actual measurement. Once the process of manufacture itself is started further judgements become chiefly relevant to the interrelations of size, shape and properties which the finished product will have.

Measurement is not in terms of any standardized unit; the basic unit chosen is some part of the object itself or a series of them. (Hallowell 1942: 73)

Hallowell also refers to measurement practices among Pueblo potters:

Methods of measurement analogous in principle are described by Ruth Bunzel, *The Pueblo Potter* (1929), p. 50. In this case the problem is to adjust the proportions of the designs to be executed to the size of the area to be painted. 'All potters measure the surfaces of their jars in one way or another', although 'there is a considerable individual variation in the amount of measuring that is done'. One customary measure is the distance between the thumb and the tip of the middle finger when spread apart. The procedure of one expert pottery maker is described as follows: 'First she studied carefully for some minutes the undecorated form, turning it around in her hands. Then she measured hastily with her thumb and middle finger the greatest circumference of the jar. Then she drew in the outlines of the first design, which were to be used four times around the jar. After the first element was completed, she measured it and the remain-

[4] The spatial concepts involved in the making of a rogan will be considered below, pp. 314–16.

ing space and drew in the second element. The two together occupied a little more than half the space, so the remaining two had to be slightly crowded, but this was hardly perceptible in the finished product.' One informant commented: 'If I start to paint before it is all measured, then I get nervous that it may not come out right.' (Hallowell 1942: 75n)

So the construction of co-ordinated wholes in which proportion has to be maintained is an important factor in generating the awareness of units of measurement.

Measurement as an autonomous principle divorced from the nature of the body or the nature of the thing being worked upon probably depends upon the development of Euclidean concepts of space and the awareness of the various dimensions as distinct conceptual entities. Thus Thom (1967) has shown that for the megalith builders the yard was rigorously standardized at 2.72 feet, a degree of uniformity necessary because the architects of the stone circles based them on the geometrical properties of the Pythagorean triangle, the equilateral triangle, the circle, and the ellipse. In order to utilize the geometrical properties of these figures it was necessary to use an invariant and constant unit of measurement. In addition those concerned placed a high value on arranging the dimensions of their structures to be in the form of whole numbers:

They concentrated on geometrical figures which had as many dimensions as possible arranged to be integral multiples of their units of length. (Thom 1967: 27) [and, for example], It will be shown that in a significant number of cases the discrepancy [between actual and nominal diameters] is produced by a small adjustment made by the erectors to the diameter, to bring the circumferences nearer to an integer. This desire to have both dimensions integral has a further consequence in that at many sites it affects the integer chosen for the diameter. (Ibid. 44)

(The early British megalith builders provide a fascinating instance of a non-literate people, some of whom at least had advanced to a very high level of cognitive development, but in the absence of any other ethnographic data besides the monuments themselves and the inferences to be drawn from these one is quite unable to do more than speculate about the reasons for the high level of cognitive skills displayed.)

This type of measurement is quite divorced from the concrete attributes of the world and uses metric units for the construction of wholly 'imaginary' entities, in which measurement is here employed for the analysis and co-ordination of a system of geometrical relations.

3. DIMENSIONAL ANALYSIS AND COMPARISON

While the languages of primitive societies have words for 'big' and 'small', 'heavy' and 'light', we often find a lack of specialization in terms for the description of physical qualities:[5]

> ... none of the New Guinea languages being investigated by the Summer Institute of Linguistics appear to contain specific words for length, area, or volume, which would enable speakers to distinguish between the various types of physical size which these words denote. The languages do generally have a word which means 'heavy' or 'weight',[6] and this quantity is distinguished from the more general words denoting 'big' or 'little'. But the latter words have to serve to cover all the various kinds of physical size which must be distinguished if precise measurements and comparisons are to be made. (Prince 1969: 31)

We seldom find, as far as I know, that primitives use terms for dimensions such as 'weight', 'length', 'distance', and so on, as opposed to heavy/light, long/short, near/far, etc., and substantives formed from these adjectives. Evidently, one needs to talk of 'length', as opposed to 'long' only if one is comparing or relating length to some other dimension such as breadth or weight. It is this type of conceptual relation that is the foundation of concrete operations. The Kpelle, for example, can say 'bigness' or 'heaviness', but there is no way of saying 'weight'. They 'do not usually isolate or discuss the aspects or qualities named by adjectives. They do not therefore think of length, weight, or size as independent realities' (Gay and Cole 1967: 60).

Primitive modes of thought tend to regard weight and lightness, for example, like hotness and coldness, as absolute properties opposed to each other rather than as points along a single scale. Our dimensional concepts are scalar and relative, such that A is heavier than B, which is heavier than C; thus we can think of B as simultaneously heavier than C and lighter than A. In primitive thought

---

[5] The hypothesis is not that the absence of certain terms or linguistic forms in itself proves that primitives *cannot* grasp the corresponding concepts (this would be to relapse into Whorfianism), but merely that the absence of such terms, or the clumsiness of the locutions needed in their place, is a likely indication that primitives do not normally, or easily, do so.

[6] While Prince here refers to 'weight', it is clear from the rest of his book that it is meant in the sense of 'heaviness', not in the dimensional sense.

one finds that sets of properties conceived as absolute are associated together, such that weight and size are not clearly distinguished, or thin objects are seen as inherently light, and thick ones as heavy.

As we saw in Piaget's analysis of number, comparison is basic to operational quantification, especially in relation to transitivity, but one finds that in many primitive languages there are no *simple* equivalents for our comparative forms. The locution known as 'intensification' is frequently used, by which, if one wishes to say that *A* is bigger than *B*, one says '*A* is big; *B* is very big' or words to that effect. Intensification may also be achieved by repeating the adjective a number of times in proportion to the number of the entities being compared, or by increasing the volume or pitch of the adjective in proportion to the degree of comparison intended. If the word 'more' exists, it is commonly a synonym for 'again'. Prince discusses New Guinea modes of comparison:

. . . linguistic devices for expressing comparatives are usually very limited. The normal way of saying that A is bigger than B is to say that 'A is big, B is little'. This makes it extremely difficult to say that A is bigger than B and B is bigger than C, without becoming ambiguous. Verbal expressions and no doubt the related modes of thought, stemming from the indigenous culture, persist markedly through several years of English education. Thus Grade 5 or Grade 6 children, who had experienced six and seven years of education in the English medium respectively, and had been taught the use of comparatives at about Grade 3 or Grade 4 level, would commonly answer the question about which of two objects was larger with the statement, 'This one is big, and this one is little'. (Prince 1969: 31–2)

Piaget comments as follows on the different forms of pre-operatory and operatory comparison, referring to work done by H. Sinclair (1967):

The subjects of these two groups [one of older, conserving children, the other of younger, non-conserving children] are asked to describe some objects (e.g. a short and thick pencil, another long and thin; several little marbles, a smaller number of bigger marbles). The language used in the two groups differs as to the comparatives used: whereas the nonconserving subjects make use largely of what the linguist Bull has called *scalaries* (e.g. 'big', 'small', 'a lot', or 'a little), the subjects at the operational level use *vectors* ('more' or 'less', etc.). Furthermore, the structure of the expressions differs: the conservers use binary modes (e.g. 'this one is longer and thinner'), whereas the nonconservers use quaternary modes (e.g. 'this one is thick and the other one is thin; this one is long and the other one is short'). (Piaget 1974: 308)

In so far as comparison seems linguistically clumsy and therefore difficult in so many primitive societies, and there is a general absence of dimensional terms, it seems likely that there will be very little of that analysis of objects into different dimensions and comparison of them, which is an essential aspect of concrete operations.

4. SOME DEVELOPMENTAL EXAMPLES

Having considered the ethnographic evidence relevant to dimensional analysis and comparison in primitive society, we are now in a position to relate this to the various stages in the child's development of understanding in these respects, and especially to his developing grasp of conservation. Such psychological evidence as exists on the extent of conservation in individuals in primitive society will be presented at the end of this section.

In the early pre-operatory stage, the child is only able to make global comparisons between quantities, based on physical appearances. In the case of liquids, for example, Piaget's most famous experiment showed that children cannot understand that if there are initially two beakers, A and B, of identical dimensions, filled with liquid to the same level, and if the contents of A_1 are poured into A_2, which is tall and thin, and the contents of B_1 are poured into B_2, which is flat and wide, the amount of fluid in A_2 and B_2 is still identical—the initial response being that there is more fluid in A_2 because the level of fluid is higher than in B_2. This lack of conservation is attributable to the failure of the child to see that the increased height of A_2 is compensated by its decreased cross-sectional area, the converse being true for B_2. Because the child's thought is dominated by perceptual appearances, and because he is yet unable to think simultaneously of change in *two* dimensions, he is unable to master relationships of compensation. In the same way he is unable to grasp the reciprocal relations of the length and density of a continuous set, let us suppose of counters, laid out in front of him; so a row of five counters, widely spaced, will seem to be equal in quantity to a row of ten counters closely spaced.

The child's initial conception of the quantity of any set, therefore, is not decomposable into the elements of the set, or into the different dimensions which it occupies. Comparison of such global quantities is therefore rigid, because it is not decomposable, but also unstable, because it is perceptually dominated. Thus true quantification is impossible. The only quantitative comparisons of which the child at this stage is capable are those of 'more', 'less', and 'equal'.

It should be noted, however, that in many cases this qualitative or intensive comparison will be sufficient to reach correct conclusions on quantitative change. If, to take an example from continuous (liquid) quantity, there are two containers A_1 and A_2, in the following conditions it will be possible to infer whether the capacity of one is greater than that of the other without the ability to conserve quantity:

height +	diameter +	= greater quantity
height +	diameter =	= greater quantity
height =	diameter +	= greater quantity
height =	diameter =	= equal quantity
height =	diameter −	= less quantity
height −	diameter =	= less quantity
height −	diameter −	= less quantity

In these cases either one dimension alone varies, or both increase or decrease *simultaneously*, and here it is not necessary to be able to co-ordinate the variations of two-dimensional change.

| height + | diameter − | = ? quantity |
| height − | diameter + | = ? quantity |

it is impossible to tell by intensive or qualitative comparison alone whether the total quantity of one vessel is greater, the same, or less than that of the other, unless variations are very gross in one dimension. For this, it is necessary to be able to think of both dimensions simultaneously, to decompose the quantity into units, and to equalize the differences between the two, by imagining a compensation in terms of these units.

The child at this stage is also unable to construct a series using a set of objects of *unequal* size (as opposed, of course, to a series of homogeneous objects), starting with the smallest and continuing to the largest (or vice versa), because this depends on the ability to grasp that if element A, for instance, is the smallest of the series, then *B* is simultaneously both larger than *A* and smaller than its immediate successor, C. There are thus no co-ordinations of the form 'B is preceded by A and succeeded by C'—that is, the concept of *relative* size—and instead the child thinks only in terms of such absolute qualities as 'big' and 'small', rather than in terms of the relationship 'bigger' and 'smaller'. Least of all is he capable of the co-ordination 'both bigger than A and smaller than C'. Nor has the child at this stage any idea of a constant relationship between the elements, such as increasing or decreasing size, in such an asymmetric series.

When two series of objects, A, B, are placed in a spatial one–one correspondence, the child can see that e.g. A_5 corresponds to B_5 if these elements are also adjacent, but as soon as the elements of one of the series are displaced, e.g. by compression, the child chooses, say, B_8 as now corresponding to A_5, if these two elements now happen to be the closest to one another. When a series is disarranged, he cannot reassemble it again, and choses elements at random in his attempts to do so.

A whole is therefore not conceived as an addition of parts, such that $A + A' = B$; $A = B - A'$, etc. The child can think either of the whole or of its parts, but not of parts and whole simultaneously. Thus, if he is given a set of wooden beads B, comprising ten brown As and two white A's, and asked whether there are more beads, or more brown beads, he will invariably reply that there are more brown beads. For him, the set B is simply characterized by two attributes—brown and not-brown. When the brown beads A are considered separately from the whole, B, they form a new set, characterized simply as 'brown'. But if they are so dissociated, then the whole set, B, is regarded as being reduced to A', defined by the attribute 'not-brown'. If, as in this case, A' is smaller than A, the child then says that A is larger than B, which is regarded as identical with A'. This for the early pre-operatory child, a whole divided into parts, even mentally, ceases to exist; qualitatively, the child obviously understands that one bead can be both brown and wooden, but from the point of view of quantitative classification he cannot place the same bead in two sets simultaneously. Or, as we saw in the previous chapter, he cannot co-ordinate intension and extension.

Again, if a child is told that on one day a boy is given four sweets after lunch and four sweets after dinner, and on the next day seven sweets after lunch and one after dinner, he will not

realize that the additions and subtractions necessarily cancel each
other:

$$\left.\begin{array}{l} \text{I } 4(-3) + 4(+3) \\[2mm] \text{II } 7(+3) + 1(-3) \end{array}\right\} = 8$$

On the one hand, the child does not regard the whole II as permanent, in
spite of having himself removed three sweets and changed the structure
4 + 4 into the structure 7 + 1. On the other hand, his comparison of the
structure 7 + 1 with 4 + 4 does not help him to discover this permanence
of the whole. [This is just another manifestation of the failure to conserve.] . . . The reason why he fails is that, once again, he is guided by the
perceptual relationships, which he does not correct by means of operations, and therefore, according as he concentrates on the seven or the one
in set II, thinks that there are more or less in II than in I. And yet he is
perfectly aware that he has to compare the set 7 + 1 with the set 4 + 4.
Gin, for instance, says: 'There's a big lot (seven) and a little lot (one).
There (I) there are four and four.' In spite of this, the only criterion for
these children is perception, and they do attempt to construct the sum
7 + 1 = 8 and compare it with the sum of 4 + 4. (Piaget 1952a:
187–8)

At this stage wholes are not logical classes, but rather, elementary schemata of assimilation or 'synscretic aggregates' in which
the relation between the part and the whole is not yet a quantitative relationship or even 'intensively' quantifiable, i.e. there is
neither part nor inclusion, but merely qualitative participation.

At stage II of the pre-operatory level, the child's thought is still
dominated by global and perceptual qualities, with lack of differentiation between the space occupied by a set and the number of
elements. But the child is now able to construct a correct series by
trial and error and to form a second series whose elements correspond positionally with those of the first. He does not, however,
immediately grasp the whole set of relations necessary for seriation
and proceeds by combining the elements in subsets, one of his
major difficulties at this stage being to make the transition from
the qualities 'big' and 'small' to the relations 'bigger' and 'smaller'.

Because he is better able to decompose sets into their elements,
and to analyse the composition of figures, he is now able, by comparison of parts, to reproduce all the figures whose shape depends
on the number of elements. But while this is a great improvement

on the first stage, it still only enables the child to compare certain static states of the sets—those that give figures of familiar shape. So while there is some dimensional co-ordination, this is only in the construction of the figure, and is not maintained if the figures are broken up.

At this stage there is therefore an intuitive grasp of correspondence, which is entirely based on perceptual or representational images and which is not preserved outside the actual field of perception or clear recollection. The child can now perceive that the succesion of intervals separating elements, and the sum of these, is identical with the total length of the row, a qualitative addition, and that to co-ordinate length and density is simply to decompose length into segments which define density. He can also co-ordinate length and density into two rows and thus consider two relationships simultaneously; but this co-ordination—a qualitative multiplication—does not go beyond the level of perception, for when the density or length of one of the rows is altered, he ceases to believe in the conservation of the number of elements which he has previously asserted to be equal on the basis of one–one correspondence. This is because he cannot understand that the displacements compensate each other and that the differences in length and density (in this instance) can be equalized. This, in turn, can be accomplished only by the use of units (not necessarily culturally defined units such as feet and inches; they may consist of the iteration of any *ad hoc* physical element such as a piece of stick or a length of string or a vessel, anything in fact that can constitute a common measure). We find at this stage a vacillation between length and density, for example, so that in some instances set *A* will be judged to have more elements because it is *longer* than set *B,* but in others the child will change his mind and assert that B has more, because it is denser.

While the child can seriate, he cannot successfully insert extra sticks (in the case of non-vicariant series), because he cannot co-ordinate the relationship of an inserted member *B* being simultaneously bigger than *A* and smaller than *C,* nor can he yet maintain a constant relationship between the elements of a series, such as increasing or decreasing size.

The child's seriation thus produces rigid series into which extra elements cannot be introduced and which cannot be reconstituted once they have been broken up. Nor can he grasp the relations between the total number (since he has still no grasp of number) and the parts. For example, if the child is shown a series of steps A .... T (in the experiment, in fact, a series of sticks of unequal length) up which a doll is supposed to climb, he is unable to see that if the doll is at step N, the number of steps still to be climbed is equal to $T - N$, because he cannot yet co-ordinate the two inverse relations $N > A$, $N < T$, and is therefore, operationally speaking, still incapable of grasping the true meaning of subtraction and of the relation of the remainder to the total. When he is asked to equalize two unequal sets, his manipulation of the two unequal heaps into figures forces the child frequently to compare the two sets and to notice that each transfer of elements between them is at the same time an addition to one set and a subtraction from the other (and we recall the example of the eight sweets given in different combinations referred to above). He still does not yet think of the remainder as the result of a numerical subtraction, but as the result of an empirical transfer of a purely intuitive set of objects. While he can thus empirically add and subtract—that is, physically place any number of extra elements with the existing elements of a set or take away elements from a set one by one—he still does not grasp the logic of part–whole relations.

The child's inability to say, without counting the actual steps, how many remain to be counted, and to rely for this conclusion on the subtraction of the remainder from the total, is also associated with the inability at this stage to combine ordinal and cardinal values.

When, for example, the order of one series is reversed in relation to another series, and the child tries to discover which element now corresponds (say, in rank order of size) to the appropriate element in the other set, he tries to discover this empirically or by counting, but repeatedly confuses the correct position with that of the preceding element. For example, when it is a question of finding the element corresponding to an element n, he counts the preceding $n - 1$ elements in set A, and then goes to set B, where he finds $n - 1$ and then stops, supposing that this $(n - 1)$th element corresponds to the nth element in A. To solve this he must, of course, dissociate the position of n from the number of elements preceding n, but at this stage position, ordinal value, does not yet possess for the child a cardinal value of the same nature as he uses to count the preceding terms. Ordinal position thus presupposes cardinal value, and vice versa, but the child cannot see that each position is itself a number, and that this number is inseparable from the whole aggregate of which it is a part, that the nth element of A corresponds to the nth element of B, nor that it forms a set whose cardinal value is n, and that the nth element must be the last of a series of n elements.

Conversely, for a cardinal value to correspond exactly to a given position, it is necessary that the nth position shall be seen to be permanently after the $(n - 1)$th, and before the $(n + 1)$th, and this presupposes the invariance of the sets $\{n - 1\}$, $\{n\}$, $\{n + 1\}$ . . .

The inability to conserve sets and positions and to understand the reciprocal compensation of addition and subtraction, is partially explicable, as already noted, by the inability to grasp the notion of units. Thus children at this stage fail to see that if flask A completely fills flask B, and if B completely fills flask C, then B is common measure of the capacity of both A and C, and also that $A = B = C$, therefore $A = C$, etc. The operation of transitivity, too, is beyond the grasp of these children, but it is of course essential to an understanding of the equalization of differences.

So while there is progress in seriation and correspondence and in dimensional analysis at this stage, this is only true when sets of objects are actually in front of the child. He can make no deductions of a purely logical nature at this stage when the sets are broken up, reversed, or disarranged, and this thought is still perceptually dominated and irreversible. Such deductions as he makes do not seem logically necessary to the child, but simply true on the basis of his previous experience, which itself may be falsified by future experience.

More generally, in the relation of parts to wholes, as we have seen, the child is incapable of treating, for example, the brown beads as part of the total set of wooden beads, comprising white beads as well as brown beads. So when he is asked whether he can make a longer necklace of the brown beads, or of the wooden beads, he always replies 'the brown beads'. This incapacity for logical multiplication in the synthesis of attributes (in thinking of two attributes simultaneously) also derives from the concrete quality of the child's imagination.

The fact that I have imagined a necklace made of brown beads in no way prevents me from using the same brown beads when I imagine a necklace made of the set of wooden beads. The child, on the contrary, apparently regards his mental experiences as actual, and therefore, when he has constructed one necklace mentally, he cannot mentally make another with the same material. (Piaget 1952a: 178)

At stage III, the child can now completely decompose a series, and understand the relation of the parts to the whole. He does not now have to recombine and reseriate all the steps to find out how many remain to be climbed, and grasps that they are equal to the number of sticks left on the table. In other words $(N \ldots T) = (T - N)$ or $(A \ldots T) - (A \ldots N)$. He also sees that the number of steps behind the doll $= N - 1$, showing that he sees the Nth position corresponding to a cardinal value which is both greater than $A \ldots (N - 1)$ and less that $(N + 1) \ldots T$. Cardination and ordination are co-ordinated, the former having become independent of the parts and being applied to all the terms as equivalent units, and the latter being no longer dependent on the qualitative attributes of the particular elements—their actual size, length, etc. The element n therefore represents both the nth position and the cardinal value n.

Differences can now be equated in terms of units, by the operation of transitivity, which leads to an understanding of relations of proportion.

In seriation, the child constantly considers the set of relations between all the elements since with each new step he looks for the biggest (or smallest) of the remaining elements. At this stage, therefore, he can construct correspondences between the elements of different sets not, as in stages I and II, by first constructing one set in full, then constructing the other set(s), and then finding the corresponding position, but by immediate correspondence, in which he simultaneously selects the first, second, third, etc. elements of each set before the remaining elements of either set have been seriated.

Relations are now reversible; operational seriation is independent of changes in the field of perception, being based on relations that can be composed because they are capable of rigorous inversion; and series can be set out in either direction, based on the co-ordination of inverse relations.

The child can now understand the compensation of addition and subtraction in the equalization of unequal sets, and the compensation between dimensional variations in compensation tasks. This multiplication of relations, or equalization of differences, is also made possible by the understanding of the additive composition and partition of a series, which is the basis for the notion of unit.

The child can now grasp the hierarchical relation of classes that constitutes the cardinal value of a set (as in Figure 16)

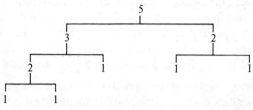

Figure 16

and the integration with class of asymmetrical relation (i.e. position, or ordinal value) and also the nature of the unit, which, too, is necessary for the operational construction of all measurement and quantification, being the essential factor in the equalization of differences.

5. CONSERVATION

One of the best indications of the extent to which operational understanding of quantity, and hence of measurement, is likely to be attained in primitive societies is provided by tests of the ability to conserve quantity, length, weight, area, and volume. These experiments have been carried out in only a handful of traditional, non-literate peoples, but with the exception of Price-Williams's work among the Tiv of Nigeria,[7] they strongly suggest that conservation of these basic dimensions, especially of area and volume, is subject to considerable 'lag'. A number of studies report that it is not attained by a majority of adults, and hence we cannot expect to find that an operational grasp of quantification and number will be a cultural norm in many primitive societies.

Prince, in his tests of New Guinea schoolchildren (primary schools range from Grades 1 to 6, secondary schools from Forms I to III), found that even at the stage of Form III, after about nine years of schooling, only 82 per cent of the pupils solved both simple tests of the conservation of quantity correctly (with plasticine and liquid). In area conservation only 58 per cent of Form III correctly solved all three questions, and the success rate in tests

[7] See below, p. 272, for a discussion of the validity of these findings.

of conservation of volume was about the same. Success rates in the lower forms were very much lower, suggesting that conservation of all the various dimensions scarcely exists in the traditional adult population which has had little or no contact with Europeans or the skills associated with their technology. He found that the order in which dimensions are conserved successfully is length, followed by quantity, weight, and finally area and volume, which is generally similar to the order of acquisition in European children, with the exception of the relative orders of weight and area:

Thus the general pattern of conceptual development in regard to the five physical quantities is not essentially different from that which has been found in a Western culture, except for the delay which is encountered in the non-Western situation. *But the delay is a substantial one, so substantial that the capability of progressing with school science curriculum seems likely to be affected.* (Prince 1969: 60)

Greenfield reaches roughly similar conclusions on the Wolof, though their success rate in conservation, whether in bush or urban schools, was considerably higher than the New Guineans'.

The oldest unschooled bush children (eleven to thirteen year olds) show no significant increase in conservation [of quantity] over the eight- and nine-year olds. Only half of the unschooled bush children attain conservation at this late age. It is possible, of course, that development is simply slower without school, so that an adult group might manifest 100 per cent conservation behaviour. Other results, however, obtained both from these subjects and from subjects in other cultures do not make it seem likely. A study of conceptualizing was done with unschooled adults ... when we found that eleven-to-thirteen-year-old children had responded in essentially the same manner as the eight- and nine-year-old group. No further changes in the pattern of conceptual thought were observed in the adults, save for decrease in the variability of the response from subject to subject. That experiment and this one suggest that, without school, intellectual development, defined as *any* qualitative change, ceases shortly after age nine ... [Goodnow 1962] found no difference between minimally schooled Chinese adolescent boys and a matched group of adults in Hong Kong in the percentage of subjects with conservation. (Greenfield 1966: 233–4)

In fact, she notes that the level of perceptually based, pre-operatory judgements actually increases with age in the case of the unschooled children, as opposed, to the sharply decreasing level of perceptual judgements in children attending school.

P. R. Dasen (1974) has carried out a number of conservation tests among two groups of Australian Aborigines, varying in the extent of their contact with the white man. He included in his group of subjects some non-literate adults, which makes his results of particular interest.

The results of the tests on the adults at Hermannsburg and Areyonga are given in Table XI.

TABLE XI

Performance of adult subjects in conservation tasks		C %	NC %
1. Conservation of quantity (liquid)	H	40	60
	A	30	70
2. Conservation of weight	H	20	80
	A	10	90
3. Conservation of volume	H	30	70
	A	0	100

(Dasen 1974: 395–6)

M. M. de Lemos (1973) carried out similar tests at Elcho Island, a group with relatively low contact with white men, and also at Hermannsburg; he did not, however, test any adults, and his oldest group comprised fifteen-year-olds, whose results on a series of conservation tests are given in Table XII.

TABLE XII

Performance of fifteen-year-old subjects in conservation tasks			C %	NC %
1. Quantity	(n = 12)	H	50	50
	(n = 5)	E	60	40
2. Weight		H	67	33
		E	80	20
3. Volume		H	25	75
		E	40	60
4. Length		H	42	58
		E	40	60
5. Area		H	42	58
		E	40	60
6. Number		H	42	58
		E	60	40

(de Lemos 1973: 77)

Bovet (1974, 1975) studied the conservation of weight among illiterate Algerian adults, ten men and twenty-six women.[8] The results are given in Table XIII.

TABLE XIII

Performance of adult subjects in tasks of weight conservation		%	
Conservation	19	53	
'Pseudo-conservation'; (conservation followed by non-conservation)	4	11	
			47% Non-conservers
Non-conservation	8	22	
No answer	5	14	

(Bovet 1975: 107)

The case of the 'pseudo-conservers' is particularly interesting, since they evidently based their initial 'conserving' responses solely on the fact that 'it was the same as before' and that nothing has been done to change the weight of the clay, ignoring the dimensional changes altogether. When the experimenter drew their attention to these dimensional changes they immediately ceased to conserve, showing that they had 'conserved' only by ignoring altogether the problem of dimensional variation and compensation.

The phenomenon of 'pseudo-conservation' was also encountered among the children in problems of conservation of quantity, both liquid and solid, as well as of weight. Children of seven to eight.

. . . affirmed the conservation of quantity, despite the changes in shape [of the balls of plasticine and the liquids when poured from one container into

[8] 'A number of the [illiterate] adult subjects and the children came from various areas located on the outskirts of Algiers. The inhabitants of these areas were not from the city itself, but had originated from rural areas some 100 to 200 km away, and had emigrated to the capital. The remainder of the population came from two villages, one of which was situated 20 km from Algiers, and the other some 50 km from Orleansville. These villages were each composed of approximately 10 houses' (Bovet 1974: 315).

The women spent their time on housework and seldom left their houses, the market being the province of men. The men were usually away from home, either trading in the outskirts of Algiers, or working on the land.

'The interviews were held in Arabic, and were conducted by psychology students of Algiers University who had been trained to interview the subjects and were perfectly competent to do so' (ibid. 315).

another]. It seemed, however, that the subjects of this age paid surprisingly little attention to the dimensions of the objects; this was particularly clear when we tried to draw their attention to these features with the aim of obtaining a justification of their judgements of invariance (e.g. the compensation of the two dimensions which had been changed). (Bovet 1974: 316)

[and],

The subjects asserted conservation in the form: 'It is the same thing as it was before' (before the modification). This judgement withstood objections from the experimenter, but without justification. Or else, if an argument succeeded in making them abandon their judgements of invariance, this was only temporarily, and these were subsequently reaffirmed spontaneously. A striking characteristic of these responses is the indifference with respect to shape. No active comparison between the distorted dimensions was apparent. (Bovet 1975: 28)

These pseudo-conserving responses were also associated with non-conservation of number and a general inability or unwillingness to express or discuss with the experimenter the reasons for any decision. Because the children were unable to give verbal justifications of their 'conservations', it was ascertained by further experiments that when asked to pour equal quantities of water into pairs of glasses differing in diameter, height, or both, and when asked to predict the level that the liquid in a full glass would reach when poured into a number of glasses of differing dimensions, they were unable to solve these problems, which can be solved by subjects who have a genuine grasp of conservation. As already noted, this same substage of pseudo-conservation was also noted in the adults' responses to problems of weight conservation, whereas all the adults had found no difficulty in the conservation of liquid and solid quantity. To quote an example, after the breaking up of one of the balls of clay into several fragments:

Certain subjects asserted straight away that the weights had remained the same, but expressed a non-conserving judgement as soon as one asked them for a justification while emphasising the different shapes obtained. We have classified these responses as 'Non-conservation', but it is interesting to note this spontaneous invariance which disappeared when one drew attention to the dimensional configurations, because this detail may have some analogy with the non-operatory conservation of type III among the children. (Bovet 1975: 100)

In the course of the dialogue, however, the subjects [not all of them] would return to a conservation judgement, and would be able to relate the various dimensions of the objects by means of a reasoning based on compensation. These adults' reaction seem to replicate in a condensed sequence the developmental trends noted in the children where an initial non-operational conservation finally becomes, at a later stage, an explicit conservation judgement.

For some of the nonconserving subjects, all that was required for them to grasp the notion of conservation was to weigh the two pieces of clay once on a pair of scales in front of them. They then accompanied their judgements by logical justifications and, what is more, generalized their conservation responses to various changes in shape. (Bovet 1974: 325)

The precocious 'conservation' of quantity of the seven- to eight-year-old Algerian children, which is not true conservation at all, may be relevant to the extraordinary results of Price-Williams's (1961) experiments in the conservation of quantity among unschooled Tiv children between seven and eight years old in rural Nigeria, in which he claims that 100 per cent of them attain conservation of quantity. Dasen (1977: 170) provides a comparative chart showing the results of twenty-six cross-cultural experiments in the conservation of quantity, and Price-Williams's Tiv children outperform the European children at Canberra by about two years and are wholly and incomparably superior to *all* other groups of non-schooled subjects. Price-Williams suggests that the Tiv children can conserve because they are familiar with the board game known as the African hole game, and it should be noted that these children were very active, doing the pouring themselves. Despite these special factors, the marked divergence of Price-Williams's results may perhaps be a case of pseudo-conservation of the type discovered by Bovet, especially since he did not apparently verify the genuineness of the conservation by further experiments of the type that Bovet conducted.

Bovet also points out that the concentration of the Algerian subjects on the action of pouring is the same as that of the Wolof subjects of Greenfield and Bruner (1966); in other words, that one can attain a pseudo-conservation by this alone.

Bruner argues that Piaget is mistaken in thinking that conservation is attained first by inversion ('If you pour it back, it will be the same') and then by the grasp of dimensional compensation. According to Bruner, Piaget does not distinguish between identity and equivalence. Children may realize that the water itself has not changed, but think that the *quantity* in the tall thin jar is no longer equivalent to the *quantity* of the original jar, because equivalence of quantity is subject to perceptual illusion. Children of four and five who are non-conservers can still grasp that the water remains the same throughout the sequence of pourings, but

... the four- and five-year-old has plainly *not* differentiated the idea of identity into a form that contains base (what the water *really* is) and a surface (what it *looks* like) or into a metric (amount) and continuity (its perduring sameness). In effect, he is operating ... with one 'moment' or one event at a time, each event constituting the basis of a single sentence. He can say in *this* situation 'Now A is more than B' and in the next say that B is bigger than C, but then fail completely in seeing a relation of A and C ... Since each situation is self-contained, save for the important, undifferentiated identity that characterizes the child's experience, language obviously does not help him 'put things together', nor is it adequate as a medium for communicating to an adult what the child experiences.

In time, when the child develops the sort of hierarchical structures that permit him to organize a series of experiences into variants of a base form, he will easily master the task just as he has already mastered the task of realizing that the object before him is the same object as one that a moment ago was out of view. And as the child proceeds further, he then finds means for verifying and checking and extending his simple conception of identity; through an appeal to reversibility, through compensation, through measure, and so forth. (Bruner 1966c: 205)

In support of their contention, Bruner and Greenfield conducted experiments with Wolof children to remove the perceptual illusions involved in conservation problems, and in particular the children's idea that the experimenter's action of pouring changed the quantity of liquid. These experiments involved screening from the subjects, the actual operation of pouring, and asking them whether there will be the same *amount* of water in the wider glass after pouring. With the six- and seven-year-olds the rate of conservation was nearly doubled, and reasons for conservation were 'It's only the same water' and 'You only poured it'. Reversibility and compensation are given by some children who have not grasped the identity of the water as reasons for *non-conservation*. Bruner argues that reversibility and compensation could not therefore in themselves produce conservation, but are rather justifications which draw their force from a prior intuition of identity.

But in response to Bruner, Piaget writes:

... the qualitative *identity* [my emphasis] of the elements concerned raises no problems: for example, when a liquid is poured from one container into another, the subject will recognize that it is 'the same water': although he will believe that its quantity has increased or diminished with a change in level, thus making an ordinal evaluation according to height alone. J. Bruner sees in this identification the starting point of conservation, and it is, indeed, a necessary preliminary condition. But it is by no means a sufficient condition, for identity only distinguishes from among the observable qualities those which remain unchanged and those which are modified; quantitative conservation presupposes, on the contrary, the construction of new relations, including, among others, the compensation of variations in different dimensions (height and breadth of a column of water, etc.), and thus operational reversibility and the methods of quantification that it entails. (Piaget 1972: 33)

It seems that, especially in the primitive milieu, one can attain a pseudo-conservation by not thinking about dimensional transformations at all, but by thinking in terms of the continuing identity of the permanent object, and of the reversibility of actions which have produced transformations in liquids or solids.

As regards identity, what sets it apart from the concept of conservation is that identity is only qualitative, and can therefore be acquired by the dissociation of a perceptive quantity from other perceptive qualities: e.g., with liquids if a = colour, b = the quality of being a liquid and c = shape, then abc stays 'the same water' for the subject because a and b have not changed and only c is modified. Conservation, however, involves quantities that are not perceptive, but have to be constructed by compensation between different dimensions . . . (Piaget 1967: 533)

(Weight, of course, has the property that it can be conserved by weighing in a balance or in the hands quite independently of the dimensional transformations of objects, a property which would seem to make it particularly liable to pseudo-conservation, just as colour may be used as the basis of a classification that can subsume all possible things, because, like weight, it is a simple perceptual quality of things that may be abstracted from them without consideration of other dimensional properties. But while colour may thus function like a logical class and be used in a system of superordinate categories, it does not follow that those, such as unschooled Africans, who rely on colour increasingly for classification of objects, are really employing superordinate categories or logical classes.)

It should also be emphasized that conservation is not a problem which commonly presents itself in primitive life. As we noted earlier, it is only when one dimension increases and the other decreases that dimensional analysis and an understanding of compensation is called for. But in the great majority of cases when primitives have to transfer liquids, they simply collect, say, water from a spring or from a well in gourds or bamboo tubes, which they bring home and either drink from directly, use as storage vessels, or pour into storage vessels whose capacity in terms of so many loads of water is known to their owners. In the course of four years' field-work, I cannot recall a single instance in which any conservation problem arose, whether a liquid or solid quantity, length, area, weight, or any other property.

Dr R. H. Barnes however has drawn to my attention the Kédang system of measuring, in particular, ivory tusks, in which length is co-ordinated with circumference:

Parts of any public negotiation is the measuring of actual tusks. A tusk is picked up and measured and passed on from man to man among those men particularly involved in the bargaining and to any others who are interested. The body serves as a graded rule for measurement, marked into recognised points of division corresponding to the features of the human anatomy up the arms and across the chest from finger tip to finger tip. One holds the tusk with the base at the finger tips of either hand and the tusk running along the arm and across the chest. The length is then estimated according to where the point lies along the body. The length is then compared with the circumference of the base, measured by placing the index finger and thumb of one hand around the base of the tusk and determining the size of the gap between the top tips [of index finger and thumb] with the fingers of the other hand, much as one measures whiskey in a glass. [Thus a tusk with a one-finger gap is thinner than a tusk with a two-finger gap, and so on.] (Barnes, personal communication)

The point of this system of measurement is that the Kédang use it to ascribe a similar number of units of measure to a tusk that is long and thin and to one that is shorter but fatter, thus displaying an awareness of compensation, e.g.: '*pitun sue* (14 units): (*a*) from the finger tips to the top of the opposite upper-arm muscle, with a gap of five fingers, or (*b*) from the finger tips to the centre of the opposite upper-arm muscle, with a gap of four fingers ... [extracted from a table]' (ibid.).

Barnes remarks 'The Kédang are aware of this interchangeability and make use of it', and it is clear from the account of a particular negotiation supplied by Barnes that the unschooled elders are, when dealing with totals below twenty, '... proficient in the addition, subtraction, multiplication, and comparison of value demanded by a somewhat complex set of negotiations. All calculations were done in the head, without any aid, unfalteringly and swiftly enough to keep up with the pace of bargaining rhetoric' (ibid.).

Such arithmetical competence clearly facilitates the grasp of compensation between dimensions and hence of conservation of quantity. It would be most interesting to know how unschooled Kédang would perform in the problem of conservation of liquid quantity; one suspects that they would be actual or latent conservers.

Some psychologists and anthropologists have argued that the ability to conserve is basic to survival. Margaret Mead, for example, objects that

... The Manus child would be dead if it made the mistakes in real life that some Swiss children make in the experimental situation of Piaget's tests. They don't think that when they change the shape of something they change its weight. If they did they couldn't handle their canoes, and load things from one to another. They have to know *in activity* all these things that they are only able to conceptualize much more slowly. (Mead 1960: 114)

Far from only 'some' of the children making the mistakes to which Mead refers, *all* of them fail to conserve until some stage, but failure to conserve occurs only at the conceptual level and when attention is drawn to the problem. It does not mean that non-conservers are unable to carry out practical activities like loading their canoes properly, since in such situations it will never need to occur to primitives that changing the shape of a package will change its weight.

Greenfield also says,

It is obvious that in order to survive all peoples must somehow come to terms with a few basic laws of the physical world, despite profound differences in 'world view'. Certainly, the conservation of a continuous quantity across transformations of experience is one of these basic facts. (Greenfield 1966: 255–6)

Two other psychologists have observed in similar vein:

One of the most baffling questions is how we are to interpret the finding [in Greenfield and Bruner 1966 of the Wolof] that volume [quantity] conservation is present in only *half* of the 13-year-olds who had no schooling and is, according to Greenfield, absent in non-literate adults. As Greenfield herself points out, all people have to come to understand certain basic laws of the physical world (or at least behave in accordance with these laws) if they are to survive. Can we imagine an adult who would pour water from a small bucket into a larger one and believe that the amount of water has been decreased by this fact? In desert communities where water is a treasured commodity, everyone can be expected to conform to certain laws of conservation. (Cole and Scribner 1974: 151–2)

But with due respect, the question is not baffling at all; the whole point is that, as I have already emphasized, primitive peoples do not, by and large, have small buckets and large buckets, or tea-pots and tea cups, by which they can puzzle themselves about problems of liquid quantity, nor do they engage in other technical activities which involve them in problems of conservation. It has become abundantly clear from the reports of psychologists that in primitive society people have seldom even considered the question of conservation until it has been presented to them in the experimental situation. Indeed, Dasen refers to a practical situation involving primitives in the use of European containers, described by de Lemos (1973):

... in which adult Aboriginal women in central Australia could choose between one measure of sugar poured into a tall and narrow container and two measures poured into a larger one [but which was shorter and fatter]; of 12 women, eight chose the one with less sugar, but where the level was higher. (Dasen 1977: 172)

What is truly surprising is that *any* member of a primitive society such as that of the Australian Aborigines develops conservational abilities in the traditional milieu. The difficulty here is that none of the investigators quoted has had access to truly traditional adults in these societies, who have had no significant contact with Europeans or their technology and way of life. It is possible that the proportion of conservers among such subjects would be very much lower than among those populations investigated by the psychologists referred to.

6. CONCLUSIONS

We have seen that the use of number in primitive societies is devoted to tallying, the calculation of totals of physical objects, and that the mere existence of a verbal number system is no warrant in itself for inferring that the adult members of that culture have an operational grasp of number. Counting can be non-verbal and is initially nothing more than the construction of a series of actions in relation to a perceptual configuration such as the hand, or a pile of pebbles, in a one–one correspondence to the set of things that has to be counted. This does not imply the co-ordination of cardinality and ordinality, the understanding of relations of logical inclusion, or the ability to conceptualize number dissociated from any concrete object whatever.

Measurement, like number, depends on the grasp of the unit by which differences can be equalized, and we saw that there is an important difference between mere standardization, as of the market-place, and measurement which involves seriation and iteration of a unit. It seems that the need for constructing integrated physical systems of relationships, such as bark containers or stone circles, in which constant proportions are maintained, may have important consequences for developing concepts of measurement.

Dimensional analysis is an integral aspect of operatory measurement, and we saw that the concepts of the various dimensions seem generally lacking in primitive thought (as opposed to scalar opposites such as hot and cold). The linguistic modes of expressing comparison, another essential aspect of measurement, also seem poorly developed among primitive cultures. These factors are consistent with existing psychological evidence that the conservation of quantity, length, weight, etc. is not attained by a substantial percentage of primitive adults.

All this confirms, as we suggested in the previous discussion of classification, that primitive representations are essentially pre-operatory and bound up with imagery and concrete associations of things, with the phenomenal characteristics of the world, as opposed to the invariant relationships and relative properties that are constructed at the level of operatory thought. We shall find that these conclusions are substantiated when we examine the collective representations of space and time in primitive society. Equally important, we have seen that it is the mode of interaction with the physical environment, in association with the socially prescribed tasks of the economy, that is the crucial factor in the development of representations of reality. Ideas of number and measurement, like those of space, time, and causality, do not just emerge ready-made from the recesses of the mind, nor are they imposed by the categories of the culture; they depend for their development on the kinds of problems that have to be solved and the means available for their solution.

7

Space

1. PERCEPTUAL AND CONCEPTUAL SPACE

If we are engaged in hammering nails into wood we soon discover that nails that are initially bent when struck by the hammer tend to buckle rather than to penetrate the wood, and we straighten such nails by laying them on a flat surface and hammering the curvature out of them. Primitive man discovers that arrows which are bent will not fly true, and the degree of curvature of an arrow can be found among other ways by rotating it between the palms of the hands. When it ceases to vibrate or to present a blurred image, then it is straight. In both of these cases, the requisite performance of the artefact depends on its approximation to straightness, but since curvature is a perceptible property which has a variety of concrete manifestations, there is no reason to suppose that any abstract awareness of straightness as the shortest distance between two points or the conservation of direction in relation to two points, or that produced by the intersection of two planes, is necessary to the procedure of straightening an arrow or a nail. 'Straightness', in other words, can be apprehended at the perceptual level merely in terms of 'not crooked', or 'not curved'. When the savage looks down his arrow shaft he does not conceptualize the shaft in terms of its deviation from an imaginary straight line projected between point A, the nock, and point B, the tip, but as a total thing of which the ends are indistinguishable parts, with the positive quality of curvature, or the making of vibrations when it is twirled, or by buckling up when struck in the case of a nail, and so on. And when this property of curvature is removed by bending he does not inevitably realize that end-points A and B necessarily become further apart. In the same way we can hammer the curvature out of nails so as to 'make them good', i.e. not the kind that buckle up when hit, without abstracting the geometrical properties of straight lines. 'Straightness', in short, can be conceived simply in concrete perceptual terms and not as a *relation* between points or planes. And just as the straightness of nails and arrows is manifested to the simple observer through other properties than the purely geometrical, so also are the other aspects of space, such as 'middle' or 'boundary', apprehensible at the perceptual level in terms of concrete properties without the necessity for representation through the mediation of projective and Euclidean concepts.

Therefore the first essential distinction to be made is that between perceptual space and conceptual space. It is evident that primitive peoples, like us, and like children and the higher animals and birds for that matter, are perfectly capable of conserving the size and shape of physical objects at the sensori-motor level—that is, of realizing, for example, that people do not really become smaller as they recede from us and larger as they approach, and that a plank of wood does not really become thinner as it is rotated from a plan view to an edge view. These basic conservations of size and shape are the result of sensori-motor co-ordinations of action and perception that are culture-independent. Again, the ability to make detours, that is, to pass directly from point *A* to point *C* and omit a previously experienced mid-point *B* on a route *A–B–C*, is also attained solely by sensori-motor co-ordination. The purely sensory co-ordination of the perception of shape, distance and dimensional movement in relation to sight, touch, and hearing, aided by comparison, transposition, and anticipation, continues its development until adult life, and while it will be modified by the kinds of physical skills required by a particular culture and ecology, it is not basically an ability dependent on symbolic representations—still less on co-ordinations of an operatory type. This is true also of direction-finding, which is a skill possessed sometimes to a high degree by animals as well as by man.

Conceptual space, however, is the ability to analyse dimensional relations and to represent by drawing, modelling, or in verbal form, the topological, metrical, and dimensional transformations and angular relationships of objects in the physical world. While the growth of this ability depends continually on interaction with the physical world, it is *reflection* on these actions, their generalization, and the formation of mental images of them, that provide the basis for the construction of conceptual space. It therefore follows that there is a considerable lag between the generation of the phy-

sical skills for performing adequately in a three-dimensional world
and the capacity for representing that world at a conceptual level.
As Piaget and Inhelder say:

> Thus the child can already perceive things projectively and grasp certain
> metric relationships by perception alone, long before he can deal with per-
> spective in thought, or measure objects through operations. In addition,
> his ability to perceive forms in this way (straight lines, curves, squares,
> circles, etc.) is far in advance of his capacity to reconstruct them at the
> level of mental images or representational thought . . . it is not until after 7–
> 8 years of age that measurement, conceptual co-ordination of perspective,
> understanding of proportion etc., result in the construction of a concep-
> tual space marking a real advance on perceptual space. (Piaget and In-
> helder 1956: 13)

While I shall argue that primitive societies normally represent
only the simpler aspects of Euclidean and projective space at most
(in many cases not even these), and that their collective representations are, indeed, predominantly topological, this is not to deny
that primitives are in some ways even more efficient in practical
skills, such as direction-finding, than we are. But the ability to
follow a determined course over land, or to orient oneself, may be
purely perceptual.

In the course of our examination of the ways in which children
develop their powers for the conceptual representation of space, it
will become clear that they depend not only on interaction with,
and manipulation of, physical objects, but on exposure to a special
set of experiences. The most important of these seems to be the
availability of means of graphic representation, the experience of
regular Euclidean shapes in physical forms that permit study of
their transformations,[1] and the necessity of sighting between two
points. The evident lack of these experiences in many primitive
societies, together with the absence of need for dimensional analysis, noted in the last chapter, will be shown to be crucial in retarding the growth of conceptual representations of space, at the operatory level.

I emphasize the notion of 'operation' here to draw attention to
another widespread misunderstanding about conceptual space—
that it is a static, as well as an intuitive, model. That our familiar
system of three-dimensional co-ordinates and projective relation-

---

[1] See the literature on the 'carpentered world' hypothesis, e.g. Segall *et al.* 1966;
Cole and Scribner 1974: 75–7.

ships is far from being intuitively obvious to all men from sense perception alone will become plain as we examine the great difficulties that children, even in our literate industrial society, have in attaining a grasp of it. But it should also be emphasized that our Euclidean and projective system of spatial co-ordination is not static but mobile, since it is essentially a means of representing all possible *transformations* of viewpoint and all possible *relations* of position. We shall see that while primitive societies have terms for 'above/below', 'right/left', 'in front/behind', etc., these are not at all comparable with the three-dimensional co-ordinate axes of Euclidean and projective space; the primitive terms, even if general, are static, absolute, and uncoordinated or else co-ordinated according to symbolic rather than geometrical criteria, while the Euclidean axes are co-ordinated, relative, and capable of accommodating all possible transformations of viewpoint, relation, and position. It will be suggested, therefore, that the conceptual representations of space in primitive societies are more elementary than our own model of space, a model which, however, we have forgotten how we acquired—indeed we never understood the process of acquisition at the time—and thus mistakenly suppose to be innate in all men. There are those, on the other hand, who deny the innateness of Euclidean concepts of space on the basis of cultural relativism— Whorf being but one example. They would have us believe that primitive representations of space are simply 'different' from our own; it will be shown, however, that while primitive representations of space are topological in the main, the topological representation of space is completely comprehended in the developmental paradigm and is not 'different' but simply elementary.

In Piaget's view, the first spatial relationships that are understood are topological in nature. Topological relationships are those of proximity, separation, order, inclusion, and continuity. Some preliminary discussion of these concepts will be necessary if we are to understand why topological space is easier to understand than Euclidean and projective space.

The basic characteristics of topological space are that its relationships are independent of distances, straight lines, angles, parallels, and co-ordinates, or, in short, of size and shape. Proximity or 'near-byness' is the most elementary spatial relationship, together with its complement, separation—that is, segregation of units or the discrimination of an object from its background. Separation of objects results in their ordering or succession, of which a particularly important case is symmetry (e.g. the order *A B C/C B A*). Ordered sequences also possess the property of enclosure or surrounding ('betweenness'), as when in the sequence *A B C, B* is enclosed by *A* and *C*. The centre of a circle is enclosed by the periphery and in three-dimensional space objects are enclosed within houses or boxes. A variant form of enclosure is 'openness', and we shall see that all closed figures such as squares and circles are initially regarded as identical, as opposed to such open figures as crescents and crosses. Lines and surfaces also possess the property of continuity, in which only the end-points are distinguished, but the mid-points are not. Continuity is therefore a synthesis of the relations of proximity and separation and is the last of the topological relations to be fully grasped at the conceptual level of spatial representation, because of the child's problems with part–whole relations and with understanding how a line, for example, can *simultaneously* be thought of as continuous *and* partitionable into a set of smaller lines or points.

Projective concepts are those of perspective, sections, projections, and plane rotations, while Euclidean concepts are those of the conservation of straight lines, parallels, angles, proportion, and the construction of general co-ordinate systems of reference. Both Euclidean and projective concepts depend on the development of the concept of the straight line.

Having established these essential ideas, we may first consider some of the ethnographic evidence on the spatial representations of primitive peoples, to establish the extent to which they conform to the operatory criteria of mobile systems of transformations of relations and the co-ordination of spatial relations within general co-ordinate systems, or are more aptly characterized as topological, composed of static associations, with a basically symbolic significance, and bound up in concrete imagery. In the course of this survey we shall assess the extent to which primitive space is ordered by general topological concepts and symbolic principles; the conceptualization of relations between natural features of the environment; the way in which cardinal points function as co-ordinate systems; the importance of manipulability in the analysis of shapes; the primitive grasp of the concept of area; and the cognitive demands of navigation and mapping; before considering the stages of cognitive development in the representation of space and the existing evidence from cross-cultural psychology on primitive conceptualizations of spatial properties and relations.

2. PRIMITIVE SPATIAL CONCEPTS

The dominant spatial concepts of primitive society are those of inner/outer; centre–periphery; left/right; high/low; closed/open; symmetrical/asymmetrical order; and boundary. These orderings are basically topological, as opposed to Euclidean or projective, and are associated with concrete physical features of the natural environment such as sky/earth, village/bush, and especially with the prototypical images of the human body and the house, and are closely integrated with moral values and social relations. More generally, we shall see that primitive orderings of space are qualitative and bound up with the physiognomic aspects of the landscape. The characteristics are illustrated by some common associations of left/right, high/low, and centre/periphery/outside (Table XIV).

These concepts not only act as the focus of a number of cosmological and social categories, but their inversion is a common symbol of disorder, as in the case of 'inside out', 'upside down', and

TABLE XIV

Right	Left	High	Low
superior	inferior	superior	inferior
sacred	secular	sacred	secular
male	female	sky	earth
strong	weak	male	female
light	dark	noble	plebeian
life	death	head	feet
sun	moon		buttocks
high	low		
noble	plebeian		

	Centre	Periphery	Outside
	men	women	
	adults	young people	
	hosts	guests	
	agnates	affines	affines
	culture		nature
	village	gardens	bush
	good spirits		evil spirits
	friends		enemies
	sharing, co-operation		gift exchange

'topsy-turvy', so that in some societies 'upside down' is a characterization of incest or of totally alien customs, while reversals of left
and right may be symbolic of abnormal status. It is also obvious
that the body, as a bounded figure in which the axes of head/feet,
front/back, left/right are basic to its structure and which forms the
necessary reference point for the most elementary spatial constructs, will be of special significance in the representation of space.

Boundaries are intrinsic to these schemes of order, as Hertz
(1960) and van Gennep (1960) have so clearly shown us, and the
nature of a figure's boundary defines whether or not it is closed or
open. Thus gates, doors, and bodily orifices are often crucial
aspects of spatial ordering, especially in the context of motion and
forces and their penetration of demarcated spaces:

The room Temne inhabit is accordingly divided into two sorts of space,
closed and not closed. This constitutes one of the most important features
of Temne space. The verb to close is *kanta*, the instrument used to close
off space in this way is *akanta*, and the same noun is used for the area so
closed off. Space not so closed off is never in ordinary speech designated
the opposite, i.e. 'open' (*kanti*) (though Temne assured me it would not
sound foolish to them to do so); closure is effected against a background
of the rest of space. Three sorts of space regularly closed off are those
occupied by farms, houses and the human body. (Littlejohn 1963: 6)

We shall also see that complex systems of spatial ordering can be
built up by the repetition of these basic classificatory notions, often
on the basis of dualistic opposition. A house may be simultaneously divided into upper and lower, right and left, inner and outer,
and this total scheme itself may be opposed to its enclosing yard,
as inner to outer, and so on. But this type of complexity should not
be confused with representations of space at the level of concrete
or formal operations.

Apart from these basic topological principles, primitive space is
ordered in terms of the physiognomic properties of the landscape
and the movements of the heavenly bodies, and the affective and
symbolic properties of these. Littlejohn says of the spatial concepts
of the Temne:

... ordinary Temne space is not the featureless container of things it is for
us, analysed through ideal forms and bearing systems of numerical
measurement; instead it falls round them in meanings read off from the
physiognomy of landscape and the human body combined in images embodying notions of good and evil. (Littlejohn 1963: 14)

Essentially the same, primarily topological, symbolically governed and qualitative space is found in Mesopotamian and Ancient Egyptian cosmology:

The spatial concepts of the primitive are concrete orientations; they refer to localities which have an emotional colour; they may be familiar or alien, hostile or friendly. Beyond the scope of mere individual experience the community is aware of certain cosmic events which invest regions of space with a particular significance. Day and night give to east and west a correlation with life and death. Speculative thought may easily develop in connection with such regions as are outside direct experiences, for instance, the heavens or the nether world. Mesopotamian astrology evolved a very extensive system of correlations between heavenly bodies and events in the sky and earthly localities. Thus mythopoeic thought may succeed no less than modern thought in establishing a co-ordinated spatial system; but the system is determined, not by objective measurements, but by an emotional recognition of values. (Frankfort H. and H. A. 1949: 30)

An example of this is the Egyptian belief that

. . . the creator was said to have emerged from the waters of chaos and to have made a mound of dry land upon which he could stand. This primeval hill, from which the creation took its beginning, was traditionally located in the sun temple at Heliopolis, the sun-god being in Egypt most commonly viewed as the creator. However, the Holy of Holies of each temple was equally sacred; each deity was—by the very fact that he was recognized as divine—a source of creative power. Hence each Holy of Holies throughout the land could be identified with the primeval hill. (Ibid. 30)

The temples of Philae, Memphis, Thebes, and Hermon were each regarded as the location, the hill, where the creator emerged from the waters of chaos, and every entrance into the Holy of Holies from court or hall was raised up by steps or a ramp. Again, the royal tombs were treated as equivalent to the primeval hill, from which they would be reborn in the hereafter, and the shape of the pyramid was a stylization of the primeval hill.

To us this view is entirely unacceptable. In our continuous, homogeneous space the place of each locality is unambiguously fixed. We would insist that there must have been one single place where the first mound of dry land actually emerged from the chaotic waters. But the Egyptian would have considered such objections mere quibbles. Since the temples and the royal tombs were as sacred as the primeval hill and showed architectural forms which resembled the hill, they shared essentials.

And it would be fatuous to argue whether one of these monuments could be called the primeval hill with more justification than the others. (Ibid. 31)

The human body, the house, and the settlement are the focal points of these types of spatial representation in many primitive societies. For example, the Dogon village is a symbol of man:

The village may be square like the first plot of land cultivated by man, or oval with an opening at one end to represent the world egg broken open by the swelling of the germinating cells. Whatever its shape it is a person and must lie in north to south direction; the smithy is the head and certain particular shrines the feet. The huts used by women at their menstrual periods, situated east and west, are the hands; the family homesteads form the chest, and the twin-ness of the whole group is expressed by a foundation shrine in the form of a cone (the male sexual organ) and by a hollowed stone (female organ) on which the fruit of the *Lannea acida* is ground to express the oil.

Not only is the village anthropomorphic but each part or section of it is a complete and separate entity and, so far as possible, must be laid out in the same pattern as the whole. Thus, individual families are fitted into a grouping which is itself a unity. (Griaule and Dieterlen 1954: 96)

This unity and co-ordination is evidently one of graphic resemblance to the body and of symbolic relations between the functions of the various parts of the village and the corresponding parts of the body. It might be argued that the orientation of the village menstrual huts in relation to east and west is a case of the use of a generalized co-ordinate system, but in fact the 'co-ordinates' used here are nothing more than the rising and setting positions of the sun, and the north–south axis of the village as a whole is derived from this, not from any awareness of this axis as orthogonal to that of east–west.[2]

The essentially graphic and topological representation of space employed by the Dogon is most vividly displayed in the plan of the homestead itself:

The big house [of each lineage within the village] comprises the *dembere* or 'room of the belly', that is to say, the central room, around which are placed a kitchen (*obolom*), three store-rooms (*kana*), a stable for goats (*ende*) and the *denna* or big room, flanked by the entrance (*day*) and another stable (*bel de*). On either side of the entrance and at the angles of one of the rooms are four conical towers surmounted by domes (*arsobo*).

[2] It should be noted however that Griaule and Dieterlen do not explicitly state that the Dogon do *not*, in other contexts, use these axes as a genuine system of spatial co-ordinates. See below, p. 299.

The plan of the building is said to represent, on the one hand Nommo [the son of God] in his human form, the towers being his limbs; on the other hand, the kitchen and stable are said to be the heavenly placenta and its earthly counterpart, together representing the head and legs of a man lying on his right side [and copulating], whose other limbs also have their architectural counterparts: the kitchen represents the head, whose eyes are the stones of the hearth; the trunk is symbolized by the *dembere*, the belly by the other room, the arms by the two irregular lines of store-rooms, the breasts by two jars of water placed at the entrance to the central room. Finally, the sex organ is the entry which leads by a narrow passage to the work-room, where the jars of water and the grinding-stones are kept. On these, young fresh ears of new corn are crushed, yielding liquid which is

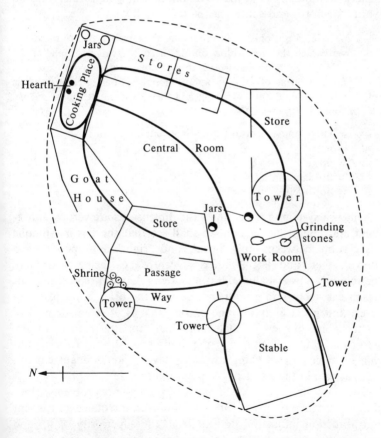

Figure 17   The family homestead and the man. (Griaule and Dieterlen 1954: 98)

associated with the male seminal fluid and is carried to the left-hand end
of the entry and poured out on the shrine of the ancestors [see Fig. 17].
(Ibid. 97)

But while primitive representations of space are largely qualitative and closely related to the physiognomic aspects of landscape, it
would be a mistake to ignore the extent to which complex systems
can be built up on the basis of those general concepts of left/right,
inner/outer, high/low, etc., to which I alluded at the beginning of
this section.

I take an example of such a system from the Kédang, who are
maize farmers living on a mountain on the island of Lembata in
eastern Indonesia. As in many Indonesian languages there are no
words for north and south; east is *timur* and west is *waraq*,

These are related not only to the course of the sun but also to the directions from which the winds blow during the two great monsoons of the
year. . . . However, *timur* and *waraq*, though comparable to our 'east' and
'west', are not terms of primary importance in spatial orientation. This
role is reserved for the following set and their dyadic extensions: *oté/olé,
oli/owé* and *ojo*. (Barnes 1974: 79)

> *ojo* = lateral movement to left or right, but *not* up or down
> *oli* = up
> *owé* = down
> *oté* = up/right
> *olé* = down/left

This is a system in which the basic dimensions are vertical movement and lateral movement; we shall see that there is a symbolic
association between 'up', 'head', and 'right' as superior, and
'down', 'feet', and 'left' as inferior, 'centre' also being superior to
'periphery'. As we shall see, it is a system of spatial representations
which can incorporate both motion and the orientation of structures, and is certainly not egocentric—that is, it is not dependent
on the point of view of each individual, nor is it relative to any
particular concrete feature of the landscape, although the mountain on which the Kédang live does have a predominant circum-
stantial role in their system of spatial representations.

The first three direction indicators present no problems, since
they are unambiguous: *oté* and *olé*, however, introduce an element
into direction indication derived from the superiority of up and
right versus down and left. One may therefore use *oté* to mean in

some contexts 'to the right', as when one is referring to a movement laterally towards the centre point of the village or clockwise around the mountain, or to mean 'up', as when one is referring to a movement up the mountain. In other words, one uses *ojo* when referring to lateral movement of a symbolically insignificant kind, and *oté/olé* when such movement is symbolically significant, but in symbolically significant movement up and right are together contrasted with down and left.

The application of these spatial principles of order can best be appreciated by a more detailed examination of the Kédang physical milieu and the significance of the mountain in particular. Traditionally, and until recent times, the villages were on the slopes of the great volcanic mountain Udjo Lewun, long since dormant, which is about 5 miles in diameter at the base, and reaches a height of over 5,000 feet. The summit of the mountain is believed to have been the origin of the human race (whose ancestors once lived on the summit), and also of all animals. Succeeding generations of Kédang made their villages at successively lower levels on the mountain, and in recent times the Dutch Administration ordered them to live on the beach at the base of the mountain. *Koda* is the term for the mountain summit, but the old part of each village has an offering stone also called *koda* somewhere at the top of each village. *Koda* stands therefore for the connection which each village maintains with the original site of habitation, and consequently with the descendants from that site in other villages.

The villages themselves are clearly bounded entities, and only the interior of a boundary has ceremonial value. The layout of the village is consistent with the viewpoint of someone descending the mountain, facing away from it (see Fig. 18).

But the ethnographer emphasizes that the village itself is *not* conceived as a person or based on the specific image of the human

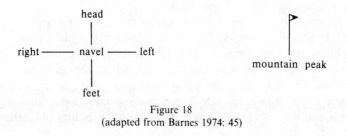

Figure 18
(adapted from Barnes 1974: 45)

body. The centre of the village, the navel or *leu puhe*, is of great symbolic importance, being marked by a flat offering stone, distinct from the *koda* stone previously mentioned. The village of Léuwajang is supposed to have two snakes, male and female, which represent the spirit of the village and are closely associated with the centre or navel of the village. The importance of the centre of the village is also emphasized by the proximity of the temple and by the fact that various prohibitions, such as on the growing of maize, lontar palms, or cloth working, apply at the centre of the village.

The maintenance of the proper relations between upper and lower is of great importance—indeed, confusion of up and down, or high and low, is regarded as the archetypal case of *anomie* and idiomatically associated with incest. This principle of order is of particular importance in house- and boat-building: the house, or rather the granary, which is the ritually superior domestic structure, is *planted*, and it is essential that the posts that support the four corners of the roof maintain the same relation to the tree from which they were cut as they have when planted in the ground—in other words, the root ends of the trees must form the base of the posts. The rafters must also preserve the same relationships *vis-à-vis* the ridge pole, that is, have their bases on the top of the walls and their tips resting on the ridge pole. In a different culture, on the same island, the masts of a boat must have the root ends of the timber at the bottom of the boat, and timbers used for the sides must have their base to the prow and their tip to the stern. Returning to the house, we find that the planks for the walls must always be laid to the right around the house—that is, looking down the slope on which the house is built, the planks of the upper wall point to one's right; while the right hut post—that is, the one on the upper side, to the right, when seen from above—is associated with the ancestors. Women are associated with the inner compartment of the granary, and only they may take grain from there; the men are associated with the outside.

A further highly important aspect of the house or granary is the attention paid to points of transition, these being in fact the lines of intersection of surfaces—the ridge pole, the four corner ridges (since the roof is hipped), and the place where the posts enter the ground. These are all regarded as transition points, or boundaries, where spirits may enter. (Dr Barnes is not certain if the junction of walls and roof is regarded as such a transition point, and believes

that the Kédang may not have clear ideas on this point either.)
'The house is for the Kédang regularly divided into solid portions
and interlinked points of transition, that is articulated and seg-
mented like, for example, bamboo ... this is the characteristic of
all bodies which have form or structure.'

It should also be noted that while the orientation of houses is of
the greatest importance, this is not determined either in relation to
the path of the sun (east or west), or even to the slope of the
mountain itself. Houses are oriented to the slope on which they are
built, the ridge pole running transversely to it, and that side of the
structure facing up the slope is considered the front.

While the basic concepts of up/down, right/left, and centre/peri-
phery are not employed with specific reference to the mountain of
Udjo Lewun, it is nevertheless true that the mountain has a special
place in the Kédang conceptualization of space, for while apparently
east and west are not used in orientation, the mountain is. The use
of a single reference point for orientation presents a conceptual
problem when the Kédang try to represent movement around it:

The practical feasibility of going round the mountain was very clear to
them. What perturbed them was that the mountain always stayed on the
same side ...

Now, in encircling the mountain, one's prime reference point is naturally the mountain itself ... This has the effect that instead of moving
within a fixed field determined by the cardinal points as we comfortably
do, one has the sensation that this field also moves. It swivels, so to speak,
with one; so that only the top of the mountain appears to provide a fixed
point of reference. To show the consequence of this, we may compare
what it is possible to say about going round the mountain in English. If we
set out in Léuwajang, the mountain is to the south of us (actually south-
east). We walk east until the mountain is to the west of us; when we have
completed half of the journey, the mountain is to the north; and so
it goes until we have returned and the mountain is again to the south.
Our terms support a sense of accomplishment. However, in Kédangese
all one can ever say in any stage of the trip is that the mountain
stands *ote*. This is a real conceptual difficulty and one which apparently
only the mountain causes them. (Ibid. 84–5)

It should be noted that going round a tree presents no conceptual
problem for the Kédang, nor does the encirclement of other mountains. The problem is not that the mountain of Udjo Lewun is very
big, but that in this instance it is the single point of reference, and

hence there are no other points to which the course around it can be related.

Thus the Kédang certainly have no effective system of co-ordination for orienting themselves in the horizontal plane. Nor can the axes of vertical and lateral travel be interpreted as a co-ordinate system to which all possible locations or directions of travel can be related. The justification for this assessment is that the two axes are not used *simultaneously* in a multi-dimensional relationship which permits a direction to be specified with respect to its angular properties. The only possibility of characterizing motion in two dimensions simultaneously is provided by the *oté/olé* pair, but in the first place, these are ambiguous, and secondly, they exclude cases of motion up and to the left, or down and to the right. *ojo*, lateral movement, is indefinite with respect to left or right. To this extent, since movement can be specified only in terms of one axis at a time, the 'quadrant' provided by the two axes is not truly comparable to that, say, of the Australian Aborigines who use the north/south and east/west axes simultaneously to characterize the angularity of a large number of possible courses.

So while the Kédang system of spatial representations is indeed based on very general notions which are independent of the point of view of any particular individual, it is not a true system of co-ordinates, and its complexity is one of symbolic associations. In particular, the notions of straight lines and angles appear to have no place in the system of spatial concepts.

On the basis of the Kédang material one can see that the basic spatial concepts typical of primitive society are capable of being employed for a general ordering of space and that even such basically egocentric terms as left and right can be given a conventional significance which allows them to serve as means of objective orientation for all members of society. It is possible to build up systems of great complexity by the dualistic opposition of these basic topological relationships, as in the case of the Atoni house, which is divided into upper and lower, left and right, inner and outer, the house itself being differentiated from its enclosing yard as inner to outer, house and yard being opposed to their environs as inner to outer, and as above to below, all these spatial orderings having social and cosmological symbolic value (see Cunningham 1964).

Even when Euclidean shapes such as quadrilaterals or circles are employed it does not follow that they are understood in terms of co-ordinated and projective systems of spatial representations. Endicott writes that in Malay cosmology the world is conceived as a quadrilateral, with a mythical sheikh in each corner surrounded by ring fences of white iron.

Many lesser demarcations of space are defined as quadrilaterals, sometimes with strong suggestions that the area indicated is a diminished copy of the world. When a likely site for a house is found, some ground is cleared and a rectangle of sticks laid in the centre. Soil is dug up inside the frame and the lords of the spot are addressed as follows:

> Ho, children of Měntri Guru,
> Who dwell in the Four Corners of the World,
> I crave this plot as a boon

If the omens are good, the four corners of the main building are pegged out with dead sticks and the area cleared. Then the ceremony for erecting the central house-post is begun. The shed that forms the Malay theatre is square. The *pawang* [magician] defines the space needed for the performance by moving from within the enclosure 'four paces in each direction of the four corners of the universe' and asks the spirits within that area not to be disturbed. Before rice-seed is sown in a field, a rectangular frame of poles is placed in the middle of the clearing and four small plants (banana tree, lemon grass, sugar cane, and saffron) planted at the corners. The time to plant is divined by watching for omens affecting the frame and the coconut shell full of water that is placed in the centre. Before the rice-soul is cut, knots are tied in rice leaves at each of the four corners of the field and a ceremony performed to confine noxious spirits to the boundaries of the field thus defined. Even the temporary clearing in the jungle made by the pigeon hunter is rectangular; railings are placed round it, and the space contained is called King Solomon's Palace Yard.

Certain basic items of magical equipment are also quadrangular. Altars, offering trays (*anchak*), and the platforms erected in the house of the bride and groom are usually approximately square. (Endicott 1970: 122–3)

The rectangular figure is, of course, a Euclidean shape, but we shall see in subsequent discussion of Piaget's work that the ability to recognize and copy Euclidean shapes develops during the pre-operatory stage. Evidently, for the Malays the rectangle is a concrete symbol for the Universe, and the particular examples of rectangles used in ritual are microcosms, which also have the more basic ritual purpose of demarcating a bounded space—an inherently topological function. But we do not find that rectangles are used for plotting position (as we noted when we considered the orientation of rectangles in relation to the cardinal points). As Endicott says with regard to the topological function of the rectangle, as opposed to the circle:

> The fundamental distinction that is being made with regard to space seems to be between bounded and unbounded space, and the quadrilateral is, for the Malays, the bounded space *par excellence*. Occasionally enclosures are circular as, for example, cock-fighting pits, but usually, I think, circles are contrasted to quadrilaterals as unbounded to bounded space. The contrast between terrestrial and heavenly space is expressed in the legend that the creator made 'the Earth of the width of a tray and the Heavens of the width of an umbrella, which are the universe of the Magician'. Winstedt interprets this to mean that the universe was created in miniature, but I suggest that shape, not size, is the important factor. The circular umbrella of the heavens is unlimited, but the earth was created by being defined as a quadrilateral like an offering tray. (Ibid. 123–4)

3. CARDINAL POINTS, CO-ORDINATE SYSTEMS, MAPPING, AND NAVIGATION

Many primitive societies have terms for east, west, north, and south, and some for zenith and nadir as well. Such a terminology for the cardinal points might suggest that it is normal for primitives to conceptualize space as a system of Euclidean co-ordinates in the same manner as we do, and philosophers such as Kant have indeed supposed that Euclidean geometry only expresses ideas that are innate in all men. Such an interpretation of primitive spatial concepts would be strengthened by the evident fact that the four cardinal points cannot be derived from the phenomenal characteristics of the horizon itself, which appears to be circular in relation to the observer. But closer examination of the facts shows that the cardinal points are indeed derived from the perceptual attributes of nature, and that their conceptualization in various cultures varies from genuine systems of co-ordinates to static associations of purely symbolic and cosmological significance.

East and west are derived from the rising and setting positions of the sun, which in tropical latitudes do not vary greatly in the course of the year. We find that the words for 'sunrise' and 'sunset' are the basis of those for 'east' and 'west' in many societies. But there are no obvious and universal features of the physical world corresponding to north and south, apart from the Pole star, the Southern Cross, and some circumpolar stars, which are not apparently much utilized by primitive peoples, whose use of stars is primarily related not to navigation but to those stars that are useful in computing the agricultural cycle. Even in navigation the polar stars are given little attention, at least in tropical latitudes. North and south in fact do not seem to derive from the external world at all in many cases, but from the left/right axis of the human body, such that if one is facing east, which is the dominant direction in most societies, one's left arm points north, and one's right arm points south. Thus among the Konso the commonest word for 'east' is *birtota*, 'sunrise', and for 'west', *dumateta*, 'sunset'; while 'south' is *akitandesa*, 'from the right', and 'north' is *pititandesa*, 'from the left', though north and south have very little importance for the Konso. The human body may also provide a model of two orthogonal axes when viewed in plan form, with one axis from head to feet and the other from left to right:

'The aspect of the cross,' writes St Jerome (*Com. in Marcum*), 'what is it but the form of the world in its four directions? (*Ipsa species crucis, quid est nisi forma quadrata mundi?*) The east is represented by the top, the north by the right limb (looking *from* the cross), the south by the left, the west by the lower portion. (d'Alviella 1911: 326)

A representation of the four directions is reproduced in the orientation of Christian churches with the nave running east–west, and the transepts north–south.

The cardinal points are in some cases related to prevailing winds, as well as to the body and to the point of sunrise and sunset, in a combined representation, as among the Dakotas who wear it as an ornament:

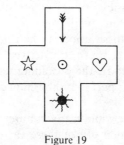

Figure 19

(Mallery 1893: 725)

The 'Greek' cross [as opposed to the Latin cross, which with its extended lower limb represents the mosquito-hawk] represents to the Dakota the four winds which issue from the four caverns in which the souls of men

existed before their incarnation in the human body ... The top of the
cross is the cold all-conquering giant, the North-wind, most powerful of
all. It is worn on the body nearest the head, the seat of intelligence and
conquering devices. The left arm covers the heart; it is the East-wind,
coming from the seat of life and love. The foot is the melting burning
South-wind, indicating, as it is worn, the seat of fiery passion [one assumes that it indicates the genitals or the belly, rather than the feet, which
could hardly be described as 'the seat of fiery passion']. The right arm is the
gentle West-wind, blowing from the spirit land, covering the lungs, from
which the breath at last goes out, gently, but into unknown night. The
centre of the cross is the earth and man, moved by the conflicting influences of the gods and winds. This cross is often illustrated as in Figure
[19]. It is sometimes drawn and depicted on beadwork and also on copper
... (Mallery 1893: 724-5)

In Australia, an informant said: 'A blind man ... would still know
where places are through the memory of all places in his head. He
would know the directions from the wind. Wind from the north
hot; west wind a bit cooler; east colder still, south proper cold' (D.
Lewis 1976: 275-6). Boas says of the Central Eskimo:

So far as I know, all these tribes call true south piningnang, while the
other points are called according to the weather prevailing while the wind
blows from the different quarters. In Cumberland Sound uangnang is west–
northwest; qaningnang (that is, snow wind), east–northeast; nigirn, south-
east; and aqsardnirn, the fohn-like wind blowing from the fjords of the
east coast. (Boas 1888: 235)

It seems that the rising and setting positions of the sun universally
provide two of the basic cardinal points (though not all cultures
have cardinal points; thus while the Tauade had expressions for
'sunrise' and 'sunset' these evidently had no directional connotations), while north and south are derived from the left/right or
head/feet axes of the body; the prevailing seasonal winds also play
an extremely important part in establishing cardinal points in some
cultures.

But we shall see that while many cultures recognize the cardinal
directions, the conceptual use of these varies greatly; among sedentary agriculturalists they are static locations, bound up with concrete associations and values, while among the hunters and gatherers who travel long distances, such as the Australian Aborigines
and the Eskimo, they are genuine systems of co-ordinates in terms
of which orientation is established and courses followed, while

Pacific navigators use a star compass, and seem to give little attention to the cardinal points.

By 'genuine system of co-ordinates' one means not only that *both* axes are used simultaneously as a means of locating a direction which does not lie on either axis, e.g. north-east, south-south-west, etc., but also that the cardinal points are used as axes to co-ordinate a system of movements and reversibilities, that is, to conserve direction and location after displacement. An example of this is provided by the remark of an Australian Aborigine, also quoted below, p. 306: 'If I go south 10 miles, then a little east; to get back home I must go north 10 miles and a little west.' And here, it should be noted, conservation seems to depend on a metrical notion of distance covered. For example, the Dogon who are sedentary agriculturalists of the French Sudan link the cardinal points of their cosmology as follows:

According to their own accounts, the Dogon are all derived from one stock. This they explain by the tradition that the original four pairs of twins gave birth to four tribes, Arou, Dyon, Ono, and Domno, who in theory shared the universe among themselves, and in particular the stellar system. Each tribe originally had its habitation at one of the four cardinal points and was associated with one element. Naturally, also, they divided between them the various social and economic functions. (Griaule and Dieterlen 1954: 89)

Their distribution is shown in Table XV.

TABLE XV

Ancestors	Tribes	Cardinal points	Elements	Functions
Amma Seru	Arou	East	Air	Chieftainship Medicine Divination
Dyongu Seru	Dyon	South	Fire	Agriculture
Binu Seru	Ono	West	Water	Trade and crafts
Lébe Séru	Domno	North	Earth	Trade and crafts

(Griaule and Dieterlen 1954: 89)

In the same way the Temne cardinal points do not have a co-ordinating spatial function, but a static, symbolic meaning:

For us the cardinal points are co-ordinates for establishing location. The Temne never use them in this way, though should the necessity arise they will use one of them to indicate the general direction in which a place lies.

Their cardinal points contain meanings which qualify activities and events in various ways. (Littlejohn 1963: 9)

The qualitative organisation of Temne space is apparent also in regard to the cardinal points. These are not mere co-ordinates for plotting position (the Temne have no maps) but directions of existence. Pre-eminent among them is East. The word for East is *Rotɔron*; ro = place of, tɔri = to disclose tɔrine = to appear. Prayers are uttered to the East, animals' throats must point East before being slit at sacrifice, blood flows towards the East. 'We think of East as rising up, like a hill, of everything going up to the East,' say Temne. Correspondingly the word for West, *ro-pil*, is frequently used for 'down' both in the sense of going down a slope and in the social sense as, for example, 'down town'. As facing East is where orientation is taken from, the word for North is that for 'left hand' and for South that for 'right hand'. (Littlejohn 1967: 334)

[and]

The pre-eminence of East over the other cardinal points arises not just through its being the direction of understanding and revealing but also because the first Temne, that is the ancestors 'came from' there. (Ibid. 336)

Malays recognize the four cardinal directions of north, south, east, and west, but in these latitudes close to the Equator the sun rises within a few degrees of due east, and sets within the same limits due west all the year round, whereas in higher latitudes the fixing of true east and west becomes a much more difficult operation, involving the bisection of the angles between the rising and setting positions of the sun at the summer and winter solstices. While therefore 'the sides of a square altar used for propitiating earth spirits are said to "face accurately towards the four cardinal points"', and 'Graves in Trengganu are oriented on a north–south axis with the corpse's head to the north and the face turned west towards Mecca', these orientations are easily derived from the rising or setting position of the sun. Evidently, once a single side of a rectangle faces the rising or setting position of the sun, all the other sides must correspond to the three remaining cardinal points. Moreover,

despite the frequent recognition of the cardinal directions in siting quadrilaterals, it would be a mistake, I think, to give the directions primacy over the shape. The names for directions vary from place to place and are sometimes connected with concrete facts of geography. For example, in parts of Kelantan the term for north includes the word *hilir*, downstream, and south is called *hulu bani*, 'up-stream people'. This would not apply in other parts of the peninsula where the main rivers run east and west. Furthermore, Rentse implies that only ritual specialists are much concerned with the four directions and what they should be called, and I have been told that people usually use the terms for up-stream and down-stream to orient themselves. (Endicott 1970: 123)

So far, we have been mainly considering the representations of static features of the environment, but travel and orientation produce a different set of problems.

Mere travel, if it is along existing, marked routes, evidently calls for no skills of orientation, as in New Guinea, where established paths traverse many miles of uninhabited mountain and forest. In such a situation the natives can easily become lost if the track peters out and they have to cut across the bush to find another path, as the following passage on the direction-finding abilities of the Upper Watut Kukukuku indicates: 'They know the bush in the neighbourhood of their own village, but have no special ability in finding their way about in strange country—when our patrol party ... went off the track in the Upper Watut country our carriers relied on Mr Noakes, the Government Geologist, to guide them' (Blackwood 1978: 27). Those who can rely on tracks, or who in any case travel only in fairly close proximity to their homes, can orient themselves by the simplest perceptual cues, and we may expect to find that general co-ordinate systems are not developed.

For the Australian Aborigines, movement over considerable distances of scores of miles seems to have been fairly commonplace, and the ability to locate water holes and food resources with great precision was a necessity. As we shall see, the Aborigine did not construct maps that were in any way accurate representations of orientation or scale; and while he would use the sun in totally unfamiliar territory he normally proceeded on the basis of constantly updating a mental image of his location and track in relation to topographical features, which he could recall with great accuracy even after many years. He also used winds, to some extent:

All the Aborigines with whom I travelled demonstrated extraordinary acuity of perception of natural signs and ability to interpret them, and almost total recall of every topographical feature of any country they had ever crossed. A single visit 40 years ago would be sufficient to make an indelible imprint. (D. Lewis 1976: 271)

Because the topographical features of the Australian Outback are permanent, closely studied, and the subject of frequent mention in group discussion and myth, it is evidently possible for the Aborigines to orient themselves and follow courses by reference to terrain in a way that would be very much more difficult for the Eskimo over snow or for navigators at sea. Significantly, in view of this particularity of topographical knowledge, we find that the Aborigines apparently make no use of the stars for navigational purposes:

Practically all the available evidence is against stars having any such role . . .

Maegraith, in a detailed study of the astronomical lore of the Aranda and Loritja tribes . . . states categorically that 'no Central Australian native can find his way by night by reference to the stars, although in the daytime he possesses the utmost skill in respect of location'. (Maegraith 1932: 25, cited in D. Lewis 1976: 273)

The less permanent features and monotonous character of the snowy landscape of the Eskimo requires them to make use of a wider variety of sensory cues, and stars are evidently of some importance, at least among some groups, e.g. the Central Eskimo:

If the weather is clear the Eskimo use the positions of the sun, of the dawn, or of the moon and stars for steering, and find their way pretty well, as they know the direction of their point of destination exactly.

They distinguish quite a number of constellations, the most important of which are the Tuktuqdjung (the deer), our Ursa Major; the Pleiades, Sakietaun; and the belt of Orion, Udleqdjun. (Boas 1888: 235)

Though Carpenter et al. say of the Aivilik Eskimo, 'Stars are sometimes used as guides, but rarely, and stories were told to me of men who had been misled when they used them.' The various winds are of the greatest importance in Eskimo navigation over land:

I cannot overemphasize the role of winds in Aivilik life . . . With such concern, it is understandable how a traveller can orient himself by them, how, almost unconsciously, he can record their slightest variation. Even a good lead dog is apparently indoctrinated with some of this knowledge, or at least possessed of a remarkable ability of spatial orientation. A hunter sits on his sled, usually facing to one side, away from the wind, with his parka hood closed except for the small hole through which he breathes and sees, but at a slight change in the wind, which he notices from the direction the fur on his parka blows, he checks his position and keeps on. (Carpenter et al. 1959)

Apart from the wind, Eskimo clearly deduce their position from the variable *relations* between a range of natural features:

[When travelling by car through a North American city] I begin with the assumption that the streets are laid out in a grid and the knowledge that certain signs mark my route. Apparently the Aivilik have similar, though natural, reference points. By and large these are not actual objects or points, but relationships: relationships between, say, contour, type of snow, wind, salt air, ice crack. (Carpenter *et al.* 1959)

It is in navigation by sea that the construction of courses in terms of straight lines related to celestial objects becomes of the greatest significance by comparison with other natural features, as we find in the navigational techniques of the Pacific islanders.[3]

Again, the ability to orient oneself and to follow a predetermined course over land or sea must be clearly distinguished from the ability to represent one's location and track in graphical form. The first ability is manifested in animals often to a striking extent—as in the case of migrating birds, or of dogs who return to their homes after separations of hundreds of miles over unknown country—and must therefore be regarded as an elementary cognitive process, however striking its manifestations. The researches of Blaut *et al.* (1970) with children from Massachusetts and Puerto Rico of five, six, and seven years of age, either pre-literate or barely literate, seem to show that the ability to recognize concrete spatial relations depicted in aerial photographs and to plot hypothetical courses between particular features on such photographs is developed at the pre-operatory level. Further studies in the West Indies have shown that 'six year olds from a peasant community in which there is no exposure to television and little to pictorial imagery can nevertheless interpret vertical air photos' (Blaut *et al.* 1970: 347).

In principle, the ability to understand spatial relations from an aerial photograph involves the ability to shift one's perspective through 90°, from the horizontal to the vertical; to interpret an overall diminution of scale; and to interpret the symbolic representation of objects when these are presented in photographic form. Blaut *et al.* accept that the problem of perspective discussed by Piaget (in which the child has to represent the way a set of objects

[3] See below, pp. 307–13.

would look from different and imaginary viewpoints in the horizontal or to represent changes in the appearance of a single object, such as a stick when it is tilted from the vertical to the horizontal, and vice versa) is very much more difficult than the simple shift of viewpoint from the horizontal to the vertical and the ability to make *overall* reductions in scale: 'Piaget's findings do not bear on the special case of perceptual recognition through a rotation to the vertical perspective, and the equally special case of an overall reduction in stimulus size' (Blaut *et al.* 1970: 340). They suggest that the pre-operatory child learns to form elementary cognitive maps of the kind involved here by his experience of looking down on displays of objects (p. 347) such as toys and toy-like objects which function as models, whose relations can easily be generalized to represent relations in the larger environment. It should be noted, however, that while most of the subjects in these tests were able to make imaginary journeys between two features on the maps, they were required to do so by following the roads. No problems of orientation, co-ordination of relations, or conservation of direction were involved, since courses were directly related to representations of physical features.

Nevertheless, the findings of these researchers seem to show that the understanding of maps is not in itself a cognitive skill at the level of concrete operations.

We may expect to find that the orientation abilities displayed by primitives will be a complex mixture of the purely perceptual, and the conceptual; D. Lewis suggests that in the case of the Australian Aborigines, who have remarkable powers of orientation,

It would appear then that the essential psychophysical mechanism was some kind of *dynamic image* or *mental 'map'*, which was *continually updated* in terms of time, distance and bearing, and more radically *realigned at each change of direction*, so that the hunters remained *at all times* aware of the precise direction of their *base and/or objective*. (D. Lewis 1976: 262)

In other words, their principle of orientation by this account seems to resemble that of inertial navigation. Lewis's informants said explicitly that they kept the directions 'in their heads' rather than relying on the sun, and as we can see from the map (Fig. 20), which is a very distorted representation of the track followed, they could orient themselves on the ground very accurately although unable to draw their track:

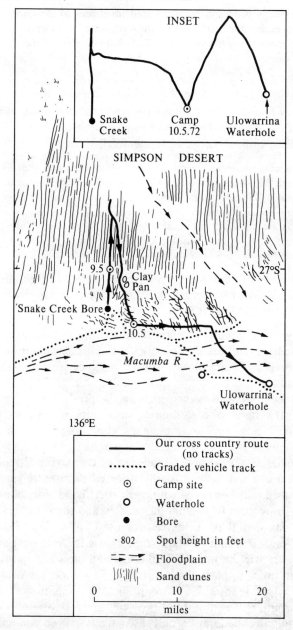

Figure 20 Survey map of route with Wintinna's diagram inset. (D. Lewis 1976: 266)

This diagram is geographically distorted in respect to directions, angles and distances, but the 'map inside Wintinna's head' was clearly attuned to the actual conditions 'on the ground'. For, after 3 days and 75 km. of angled courses off tracks of any sort (but with occasional landmarks) he directed the Landrover straight to the water-hole across the plain. (Ibid. 265)

It seems however that, despite their poor abilities in graphic representation, Aboriginals do have some conceptual understandings of spatial co-ordinates, e.g. at Jupiter Well Jeffrey stated:

'Yayayi is east (*kakarra*) of us, because we went north (*kayili*) round Yunula and Walawala, and for the last part of the way have gone southwest (*yulparira-wilurarra*), and these have evened out, so our direction of travel from Yayayai has averaged west (*wilurarra*).'

This was accurate enough in all conscience. Yayayi actually bears 95° from Jupiter Well, rather than due east (90°). [Yayayi was 600 km. (375 miles) from Jupiter Well.] (Ibid. 264)

And again, Wintinna, another informant, said: 'If I go south 10 miles, then a little east, to get back home I must go north 10 miles and a little west' (ibid. 265).

Evidently, Aboriginals can understand the use of general co-ordinate systems, even though their orientation is basically in terms of mental images of terrain, with some assistance from the sun and from winds.

Nor does it seem to be necessary in the production of maps to use general systems of co-ordinates, since some Eskimo seem capable of producing fairly accurate maps without basing them on the cardinal points but on concrete topographical knowledge. Thus Carpenter *et al.* (1959) note in the case of the Aivilik Eskimo: 'In making these maps, several Aivilik oriented them by having West away from the body and North on the right hand side, but others chose to draw them from still other angles, and there was no agreement.' Boas says that, in the case of the Central Eskimo, 'Their way of drawing is first to mark some points the relative positions of which are well known. They like to stand on a hill and to look around in order to place these correctly. This done, the details are inserted' (Boas 1888: 235–6). According to Boas, map-making was an important skill in the traditional culture, and would evidently have required collaboration and discussion between a number of expert individuals, as among the navigators of the Pacific:

As their knowledge of all the directions is very detailed and they are skilful draftsmen they can draw very good charts. If a man intends to visit a country little known to him, he has a map drawn in the snow by someone well acquainted there and these maps are so good that every point can be recognized. (Ibid. 235)

It seems inevitable, given the necessity for imparting precise topographical information, in a snowy landscape lacking many of the distinctive and permanent features of the Australian Outback, that the Eskimo in their traditional society would have collaborated in the drawing of maps, despite the fact that Mathiassen (1928: 97) says that the Iglulik Eskimo were unfamiliar with maps, and that Rasmussen (1932: 91) describes the Netsilik as having no previous knowledge of paper and pencil. The practice of drawing maps in the snow can scarcely be distinguished from map-making with paper and pencil. Moreover, in view of the greater demands for maps among the Eskimo for conveying precise topographical information in a landscape relatively poor in memorable detail[4] by comparison with Australia, it seems possible that the corporate discussion of maps would have generated greater cartographical skill than we find among the Aborigines.

Despite their considerable accuracy, Eskimo are nevertheless liable to suffer from two major errors:

The two most conspicuous defects of Eskimo maps will be observed at once: distances and directions cannot be relied upon. A stretch of country that has been of importance to the drawer, one that he knows well and where he has lived for a long time, is involuntarily drawn bigger and with more detail than areas which he only knows from fleeting visits. (Mathiassen 1928: 99)

This is evident in the maps from two Aivilik Eskimo, reproduced in Figure 21, in comparison with a modern map. The island illustrated is Southampton Island, of 20,000 square miles, and the peninsula is the Bell Peninsula, a favourite hunting ground, which is greatly exaggerated in size compared with its true values.

Gladwin's study of Puluwat navigation techniques in the Caroline Islands of the Pacific (T. Gladwin 1970) provides excellent evidence for the relationship between navigational skills and operatory representations of space. The island of Puluwat is one of the

---

[4] It is significant that while Eskimo maps name large numbers of topographical features, these are in the great majority of cases on the shoreline, and not in the hinterland.

Caroline Group, comprising a belt of low coral atolls between about 2° and 10° N., and 130° and 165° E., stretching for about 2,000 miles, 200–400 miles broad. Travel between islands has always

Native map

Native map

Modern map

(Carpenter *et al.* 1959)

Figure 21

taken place for trade, marriage, warfare, and other purposes, and the natives of Puluwat in particular are famous for their navigational skill. In the vicinity of Puluwat there are about twenty-six islands to which living navigators have sailed, and about fifty-five commonly made journeys among these islands. Distances sailed vary from two or three score miles to frequent journeys of 100 to 150 miles, but other journeys are made to islands about 300 miles away, and in rare cases they have sailed to Guam and Saipan in the Philippines, 500 and 600 miles away.

While compasses are now used, they are never employed to set a course, but only to maintain one; courses are set by use of the traditional star compass, as shown in Figure 22.

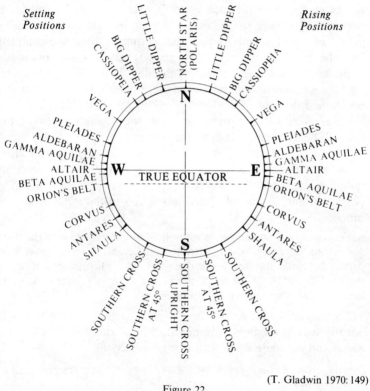

(T. Gladwin 1970: 149)

Figure 22

Stars in this latitude rise and set vertically in relation to the horizon, and it is always possible to use another star 'that travels the same road' if the main sighting star is too high above the horizon for a bearing. In any case the natives usually 'steer by the shape of the sky' and not just in relation to a dot of light. It will be seen from the star compass that the majority of stars cluster on the east–west axis; this is consistent, of course, with the orientation of the majority of sailing journeys made, along the island pattern of the Carolines. It will also be seen that the stars used are convenient for reciprocal courses along the east–west axis; thus the star from Namoluk to Puluwat is the setting of Vega and the star from Namoluk going in the opposite direction from Puluwat is the rising of Antares.

The star compass must of necessity be memorized, together with all the stars used with each possible journey. This knowledge is imparted by master navigators over perhaps a dozen years, using maps[5] of pebbles and sticks. 'The learning job is not complete until the student at his instructor's request can start with any island in the known ocean and rattle off the stars both going and returning between that island and all the others which might conceivably be reached directly from there' (T. Gladwin 1970: 131). It is not, however, purely rote learning, part of a long mnemonic chain, but must all be discretely available for recall.

The sun is also used for navigation in the morning and afternoon, though as its rising and setting are only in one direction, sailing in any other direction than east–west requires an angle to be estimated, and this is calculated in relation to the structure of the canoe.

Remembering the course they want to hold and the position of the rising and setting sun ... they can tell with considerable exactness over what part of the canoe the sun should ride—the end of the outrigger float, off the bow, the centre of the lee platform, and so on—in order to keep the canoe headed where they wish. (Ibid. 179)

The natives keep track of the changing path of the sun throughout the year in relation to standard physical points on their home island and correlate them with star positions:

The sun sets each evening over Allei. Every navigator knows where each of the navigation stars sets on Allei as seen from his own canoe house: Orion's Belt by the old dead tree; Altair over the half-sunken ship; Aldebaran between the two tall breadfruit trees; and so on. He need only glance at the setting sun. Without waiting for stars to appear he at once knows the sun's position. Next day he can set his course by equating the sun with the navigation star which sets at the sun's setting position of the evening before. (Ibid. 180)

    [5] Regrettably, these are not described by Gladwin.

Navigators also set courses from Puluwat by aligning known physical features and taking back-sights upon them, a very necessary procedure, since many journeys often begin at around noon, when the sun is useless for navigators and the stars invisible.

Besides the stars, navigators also steer by the pattern and form of submarine reefs, which are distinctive and well known, and this information must also be committed to memory. There are also three distinct types and directions of wave form which are used for orientation. The 'Big Wave' comes from due east, and is steep and short; the 'North Wave', in fact, usually comes from ENE and is in the form of a long swell. The 'South Wave' comes from ESE, but is much weaker and less regular in occurrence than the other two.

The ocean currents are primary factors in causing deviation from course:

In this part of the Pacific Ocean there is great variability in currents. To the north, the North Equatorial Current runs westward, while to the south the Equatorial Counter-current goes in the opposite direction. The Caroline Islands not only lie along the line of transition between them, but here too a large proportion of the Counter-current is actually generated by a reversal of the North Equatorial Current. Thus there are both vast eddies and abrupt changes in the direction of the currents which occur almost from day to day. (Ibid. 161)

The speed and direction of currents can be judged only at the beginning of a voyage while land is still in sight, and a suitable compensating course must be set and held by the navigator using his practised judgement.

Because of the problem in estimating drift, especially if the canoe is overtaken by a storm, and also in estimating distance covered, courses are designed not as straight lines between two points, but to allow the maximum use of all the physical features that can assist location. They will therefore pass as close as possible to reefs, shoals, and islands. Sea birds are of great use as direction indicators, and the habits of the most reliable species are known in detail, since they fly out from land in the morning and return in the evening, sometimes from distances of 20 to 25 miles. Courses are designed as far as possible to approach from a direction in which more islands lie behind the destination island, to act as a sort of long stop, in case of inaccurate navigation. An error of better than 10 miles on either side is commonly achieved.

We may now consider the conceptualization of changing spatial relationships known as *etak*.

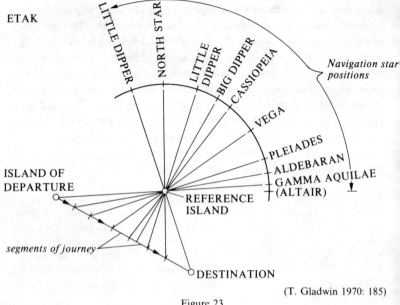

(T. Gladwin 1970: 185)

Figure 23

The navigators employ a representational system known as *etak*, which involves the selection of a reference island about 50 miles from the proposed course and roughly equidistant from the islands of departure and destination, as shown in Figure 23.

The star bearings of the reference island from both the starting and ending points of the trip are known, since on another occasion the reference island may itself become a destination. In between there are other navigation star positions under which the reference island will pass as it 'moves' backward. Its passage under each of these stars marks the end of one etak and the beginning of another. Thus the number of star positions which lie between the bearing of the reference island as seen from the island of origin and its bearing as seen from the island of destination determine the number of etak, which can here be called segments, into which the voyage is conceptually divided. When the navigator envisions in his mind's eye that the reference island is passing under a particular star he notes that a certain number of segments have been completed and a certain proportion of the voyage has therefore been accomplished. (T. Gladwin 1970: 184)

This system adds no *information* to that which the navigator already has; in order to know where the *etak* island lies he will have to recall the maps of the islands depicted with pebbles on the canoe-house floor during his training (unfortunately there are no examples of these maps in Gladwin's monograph), and the star bearing from the point of departure. Again, distance covered has to be computed from 'his skill in judging the speed of his canoe under various conditions of wind, a skill sharpened by long experience, and his attention to the time which has passed as shown by the movement of sun and stars'. In the absence of clocks and nautical logs to estimate distance in terms of units of length, Gladwin compares the navigator's means of gauging distance to '. . . a person walking across a familiar field in the dark. He is not likely to count his paces even if he knows their exact length. Instead he estimates intuitively that he is one-third or perhaps halfway across by knowing subjectively how long and how fast he has been walking' (ibid. 186).

It is clear, then, that the conceptual system of *etak* involves the co-ordination of a set of sightings between the island of departure and the island of destination, and the reference island, which are the means of segmenting a straight-line course into a series of unequal intervals.

The navigational system of Puluwat generally relies on the concept of the straight line—the ability to sight between two points, to take back sights, and to conserve direction—and on the understanding of angles, on a mobile co-ordinate system composed of star bearings and their reciprocals, on notions of distance as a product of speed and time elapsed, and on conceptions of proportion, all of which involve Euclidean and projective concepts. Navigators also have to co-ordinate a wide variety of factors, such as speed, drift, wind and wave direction, star bearings and sun position, etc., in relation to the general coordinate system. All this justifies us in concluding that the navigators have attained an operatory understanding of space and, equally important, we have managed to obtain some understanding of the kinds of problems whose solution is necessary for this level of cognitive development. Unfortunately, Gladwin did not attempt to replicate any of Piaget's experiments on space and time. We are thus at present unable to be more specific about the extent of the navigators' cognitive skills in respect of space and time.

4. PRIMITIVE CONCEPTUALIZATIONS OF AREA

We shall find that this static representation of space becomes more analytic and more capable of transformations and of mobile, reversible relations when primitives are concerned with the manipulation of small objects, as when they are engaged in orientation and navigation.

Hallowell (1942) points out, as we noted in the previous chapter, that we find a higher level of conceptualization of space when subjects handle and make objects—'manipulable area', as he terms it—than when they are trying to conceptualize non-manipulable areas, that is, when they are in the static and passive situations already referred to. His example of manipulable area is that of the manufacture of the rogan, or bark container, whose stages of manufacture illustrate very well that in such cases spatial relations are conceptualized in terms of straight lines, rectangles, and proportions, even though, as we have seen, the units of measurement are derived from the object itself and supplemented by purely qualitative estimation.

Once the process of manufacture itself is started further judgements become chiefly relevant to the interrelations of size, shape and proportions which the finished product will have. Measurement is not in terms of any standardized unit; the basic unit chosen is some part of the object itself or a series of them.

Of course, in the past the flat patterns for such manufactured objects were developed through cutting and fitting directly. Perhaps when a new one was needed, the old one was taken apart and thus the flat pattern shape exposed. With this as guide the outline of a new one could be traced on the material. Today these patterns may mediate the judgements of whether the material is 'enough'. The 'key unit' will be judged against the actual object (for example the length of the foot in the case of a moccasin) and the rest of the pattern adjusted to keep the shape and proportions constant. The manufacture of a bark container, a rogan, may be taken as an example. In this case the bottom is the basic unit, although of course, the total overall size of the finished product is the initial guiding judgement.

1. To begin with a rectangular piece of bark is chosen. Its size is a matter of judgement based on the experience of the woman undertaking the task.

2. The median point (A, B, C, D) on each edge of the rectangle is determined by folding the bark upon itself.

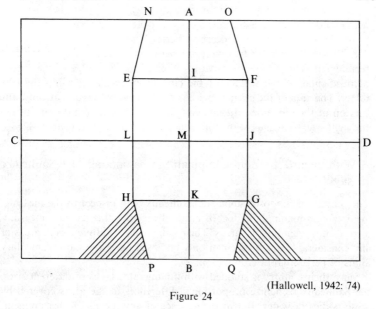

(Hallowell, 1942: 74)

Figure 24

3. The median points on opposite edges of the rectangle are now joined by lines made lightly with a knife.

4. The next step is to measure off the area that will form the bottom of the container (E, F, G, H). This area may be square or rectangular. In the example given it is square. Its size is not measured by any conventional quantitative unit but is arrived at by a process of proportional measurement in the following way:

A small strip of bark, judged to be half the length of the bottom of the rogan is prepared (the worker usually experiments a little first before adopting a length). With this piece of bark the distances from the centre M to points I, J, K, L are measured and marked on the bark; then the distance from L to E, L to H and so on. In this way the corners of the bottom, E, F, G, H, are defined. Small holes are punched in the bark at these points with an awl.

5. The points N, O, P, Q are not determined by measurement; they are a matter of 'shape judgement'. When marked, a line is drawn from the corners of the bottom of the rogan to them.

6. The lines referred to above serve as guides for cutting. This is now done and the pieces left free are folded up along the lines EF and HG.

7. The remainder of the bark sheet is now folded to form the sides of the container in such a way that the shaded parts appear on the outside of the bottom. The corners of these are temporarily tied together with string and

where the other pieces of bark overlap at the sides, they are held together with wooden pins until the sewing is complete. (This step and the treatment of the rim need not concern us here.)

8. The lid is made of two pieces of bark, one circular, the other a long rectangular strip. These are sewn together so that the edge of the strip is perpendicular to the surface of the circular piece and fits into the container. The area of the circular piece is determined by direct matching with the top of the container after its completion: it is cut round more or less the right size, tried against the top, and trimmed to fit. (Hallowell 1942: 73–5)

With regard to non-manipulable area among the Saulteaux, he says:

The limitations imposed upon the Saulteaux with respect to the measurement of non-manipulable length naturally restrict the accurate measurement of non-manipulable areas. Their judgments of differences in areas of any considerable magnitude can only be based upon the most elementary kinds of perceptual discrimination.

Since their country is studded with innumerable lakes of different sizes, the Saulteaux recognize proportional differences in the areas covered by these bodies of water. But in the absence of any means of measurement, area, as an abstract spatial attribute, cannot be mentally manipulated in an accurate fashion. Instead of being abstracted, area to the Saulteaux mind is only comprehended as a concept that remains closely linked with 'region' or 'place'. It retains all the character of a particular locality. If a region has natural boundaries like a lake, that set it off from the surrounding country, it is easily comprehended in semi-abstract areal terms, and belongs more to the category of 'thing' or 'object' having shape and size and perceptible surface extensity. Otherwise it may never even be thought of in this way at all. (Ibid. 70)

In short, Saulteaux conceptualizations of area are restricted to purely intuitive, perceptually based images which remain unanalysed. Referring to maps of hunting territory drawn by the Saulteaux (or delineated on existing, Western-type, maps) for the benefit of ethnographers, Hallowell says:

I believe that the reason why the Saulteaux do not make areal abstractions and comparisons of their hunting territories is not due simply to the lack of any accurate measures; it is, rather, explained by the absence of cultural values that would motivate such an abstraction on their part. If we consider for a moment how deeply the concrete details of the terrain over which they hunt must be embedded in their personal experience and their lack of knowledge of other districts than their own, it is difficult to see

why judgments in abstract spatial terms should occur without an extremely forceful motivation as a leverage. And it is just this sort of motivation that we search for in vain. (Ibid. 71)

And he cites Kroeber's observations on the spatial conceptualizations of the Californian Indians to substantiate his very reasonable claim that in the circumstances of indigenous life the natives
did not represent their territorial areas in metric or projective fashion:

The native did not think, like modern civilized man, of his people owning
an area circumscribed by a definite line, in which there might happen to be
one or many water courses. This would have been viewing the land
through a map, whether drawn or mental; and such an attitude was
foreign to his habit. What he did know was that the little town at which he
was born and where he expected to die lay on a certain river or branch of
a river; and that this stream, or a certain stretch of it, and all the creeks
flowing into it, and all the land on or between these creeks, belong to his
people; whereas below, or above, or across certain hills, were other
streams and tributaries, where other people lived, with whom he might be
on visiting terms or intermarried, but who had proprietary rights of their
own. (Kroeber 1925: 160–1)

The Saulteaux, as hunters and gatherers, are not interested in the
area of their land for its own sake, but for the value of its usufruct,
nor is there any direct correlation between the size of the winter
hunting group and the area of the hunting ground they occupy:

This is to be explained, perhaps, by the sectional variability in the incidence of the fur-bearing animals, differences in hunting skill and maybe
other variables. Finally, what is even more important is the fact that a
smaller hunting territory may afford a living equal to, or even better than,
a larger one. Consequently, it is impossible for the Saulteaux to measure
areas in units of productivity (e.g. skins of animals trapped), as we find to
be the case among some agricultural peoples (e.g. how much barley or rice
can be grown). (Hallowell 1942: 72)[6]

[6] Hallowell appends the following note: 'I was informed of another method of
areal measurement by Ann Fuller (private communication): Among the peasants in
Palestine the measure is "enough land to plant 200 vines." This is a more accurate
measure than produce since it actually involves *spacing*. A very ancient method of
measuring land in the Old World which survived into modern times was based upon
the *quantity* of grain required to plant it. These are the so-called "seed-measures."
See Edward Nicholson, *Men and Measures: A History of Weights and Measures
Ancient and Modern* (London, 1912), pp. 65–66, 90–92, 256–258. Hallock and Wade,
Outlines of the Evolution of Weights and Measures and of the Metric System (1906),
observe, p. 15, that: ". . . Babylonians, in common with other Asiatic nations, also

Prince's researches among New Guinea schoolchildren confirm that in the case of non-manipulable area primitive peoples have great difficulty in conceptualizing spatial relations in terms of Euclidean and projective relations involving awareness of straight lines, rectangles, metric relations, and proportions, unless the circumstances of their material existence demand such conceptualizations. The following tests were given to investigate the subjects' understanding of area (from Prince 1969: 134f.):

1. Show to subjects two equal area gardens and equal area houses. (The word for area was 'room', and it was previously established that sweet potatoes etc. could not be grown within houses, a practice unknown in New Guinea.)

Which garden has more ground outside the house, or do they have the same?

(a) A < B ⎫
(b) A > B ⎬ Possible responses
(c) A = B ⎭

2. Insert second house as shown, in B. Same question.

employed for measuring land the amount of seed required to sow a field and statements based on this idea are found in many old Assyrian documents." And, p. 20, "For the measurement of area the Hebrews employed generally the amount of seed required to sow the land, or the amount of ground that could be ploughed by a yoke of oxen, the latter unit being the zemed, which in the *Old Testament* is translated by Acre (1 *Samuel* XIV, 14; *Isaiah* V, 10).""

3. Insert second house in A, as shown. Same question.

A

B

4. Show two cardboard rectangles, A, B, and that they are of same size, but B is diagonally bisected:

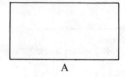

A

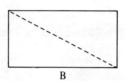

B

Rearrange B thus:

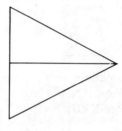

Which piece of cardboard, A or B, is bigger, or are they both the same size?

(a)   A < B ⎫
(b)   A > B ⎬ Possible responses
(c)   A = B ⎭

Fairly naturally, it was found that question 2 was easier for the subjects than question 1, since they could see without further analysis that two houses, wherever located in the garden, would leave less room than only one. But with regard to question 1,

The great majority of incorrect responders were influenced by the large open space left by putting the house in the corner. For instance, a Form II boy said, 'The right hand garden has more ground left because one house is in the corner and the other house is in the middle. The house in the corner gives a lot of space!' When the second house was added [question 2] this same boy selected the garden with one house as having more ground, and when the second house was added to this one he then decided that the two were the same. From then on he gave conserving responses, and he appeared to have been on the threshold of conserving. He only needed the experience of being asked questions for a short while to become a consistent conserver. (Ibid. 55)

Question 4 was more difficult than 2 and 3, but easier than 1, showing that while conservation may be achieved with some configurations it may not be readily generalizable to others.

The results of the four questions in terms of the percentage of correct answers for the different school forms and grades are given as in Table XVI.

TABLE XVI

| Question | Percentage of correct answers | | | | | | |
| | Primary grade | | | | Secondary grade | | |
	3	4	5	6	I	II	III
1	21	24	42	55	65	76	77
2	47	57	61	76	82	85	85
3	32	44	58	62	70	76	82
4	30	33	49	60	71	75	83

Comparable results from European children in their own schools in Papua New Guinea for the same tests were greatly superior (Table XVII).

TABLE XVII

| Question | Percentage of correct answers | | | | | | |
| | Primary grade | | | | Secondary form | | |
	3	4	5	6	I	II	III
1	76	72	89	84	93	92	100
2	87	88	93	86	94	91	98
3	83	82	91	85	90	92	96
4	78	82	87	90	95	96	93

(Prince 1969: 53)

Having surveyed some of the ethnographic evidence on the representation of space in a range of primitive societies, we may conclude that topological relations, concrete associations, and imagery predominate when space is apprehended in a static and perceptual manner (Hallowell's 'non-manipulable area'), but that the construction of artefacts, in relation to 'manipulable area', and the problems of navigation and, it should be emphasized, *com-*

municating with others about these problems and conveying information generally, in relation to non-manipulable area, will generate Euclidean and projective concepts, in which the notions of straight lines, angles, metric relations, proportions, and general co-ordinate systems are understood.

5. THE STAGES OF DEVELOPMENT IN THE UNDERSTANDING OF SPACE

The priority of topological relations can be seen at the sensori-motor stage, when an infant, initially incapable of conserving size and shape is nevertheless able to recognize a face because, while its size and shape will appear to alter, its component parts will retain the same relationships of proximity, separation, order, and so on. Thus the mouth is next to the nose, but separated from it, and there is a constant symmetrical order of ear–eye–nose–eye–ear, etc. The special characteristic of topological relationships is that they remain constant despite changes in size and shape of figure.

Topological shapes are the first to be grasped perceptually because the abstraction of shape, whether topological or Euclidean, is by touch and the co-ordination of actions. It is

... by virtue of the *actions* which the subject performs on it, such as following its contour step by step, surrounding it, traversing it, separating it and so on [that] these relationships of proximity and separation (from which openness and closure derive) and interlacement take on a far greater importance, from the point of view of perception, than even the simplest euclidean relationships. (Piaget and Inhelder 1956: 27–8)

The ability to deal with problems of topological space at the level of imagery progresses during the pre-operatory and concrete-operational levels. Initially, there is no awareness of linear order, and children of about three years can only copy *types* of objects presented to them in a linear array, but cannot reproduce the actual order of these objects. Then single elements of the model order can be copied, but there is no co-ordination between these pairs; the next stage is the ability to form a complete correspondence between the order of objects in the model, but only when the copy is directly adjacent to the model. The ability to reproduce an order when the model is at some distance from the copy, the transposition of linear to circular order, and the reversal of orders are finally achieved with certainty at the beginning of concrete operations. The notion of order is abstracted, not directly from the objects themselves, but through the increasing co-ordination of *actions*, such as transposing elements of an order both physically and mentally, and replacing them step by step and piece by piece.

The understanding of the relationship of 'surrounding' ('betweenness') is also impossible until the child has learnt to reverse a series, since only then does the invariant quality of 'betweenness' become apparent, e.g. A *B* C, C *B* A.

The notion of continuity is also essential to the ability to represent topological space, but it presents particular difficulties to the child, since initially he cannot understand how, if a line or surface is broken up into a series, the original continuity can be maintained, or how the original line or surface can be reconstituted. In other words, the points into which the line or surface is decomposed are seen as being qualitatively distinct from the original. Nor does the child find it easy to subdivide a line or surface into a large number of elements. Until the stage of concrete operations, the child believes that the elements must be isomorphic with the original whole, and can only make a very limited number of subdivisions. Only at the stage of concrete operations can he make a large number of these and recombine them into the original linear surface. The child has to attain the capacity for formal operations before he realizes that lines or surfaces are *infinitely* divisible into points that have no shape or size. Until this final stage, while the child can perform reversible or combinatory operations of subdivided lines and surfaces, he is still tied to the concrete and physically perceivable, and because he has no understanding of an infinite number of points, he is still puzzled by the synthesis of what appear to be the contradictory relations of proximity and separation. (The child's problems over continuity are closely related, of course, to his problems in conserving length, already discussed above, p. 14.)

One of the most important characteristics of topological space is that it is concerned with the *internal* arrangements of the parts of a whole, rather than with the co-ordination of the relationships between objects, which depends on the ability to construct more general systems of spatial co-ordination and reference. In this respect, topological relationships are unco-ordinated, static, concrete, and absolute. Thus the ability to recognize and to represent topological relations is the first to appear in the representation of conceptual space—the child initially treats all closed figures, such as circles, squares, triangles, etc., as similar in shape, and only distinguishes them from open figures such as crosses or intertwined figures, whereas angular and curved shapes are not clearly distinguished from one another. Moreover, the perceptual recognition of Euclidean shapes precedes the ability to reproduce them either by drawing or by the manipulation of sticks or other material simulacra. Piaget's observations, quoted earlier, on the abstraction of topological shapes can profitably be repeated in relation to the abstraction of Euclidean shapes:

. . . the 'abstraction of shapes' is not carried out solely on the basis of objects perceived as such, but is based to a far greater extent on the actions which enable objects to be built up in terms of their spatial structure. This is why the first shapes to be abstracted are topological rather than euclidean in character, since topological relationships express the simplest possible co-ordination of the dissociated elements of the basic motor rhythms, as against the more complex regulatory processes required for co-ordination of euclidean figures. (Ibid. 68)

Euclidean shapes—squares, triangles, circles, and so on— begin to be drawn between the ages of four to seven. Piaget suggests that the abstraction of these geometrical shapes is derived from tactile recognition and from drawing:

It is not the straight line itself which the child contrasts with round shapes, but rather that conjunction of straight lines which go to form an angle. [The experience of 'pointedness', in other words. Nor is the representation of angles a simple case of direct abstraction from the physical characteristics of objects.] (Ibid. 30)

To consider the angle as two intersecting straight lines . . . and especially to incorporate it in a closed figure, the child has to be able to reconstruct it, and this necessarily implies that abstraction comes from the action rather than direct from the object itself. In this respect the angle is the outcome of a pair of movements (of eye and hand) which conjoin. (Ibid. 31)

Drawing is an extremely important vehicle for the development of spatial representation (which is largely absent in primitive society): '. . . the drawing, like the mental image, is not simply an extension of ordinary perception, but is rather the combination of the movements, anticipations, reconstructions, comparisons and so on, that accompany perception and which we have called perceptual activity' (ibid. 33). Referring to children's drawings at the stage of pre-operatory thought, in which the child, as an intellectual realist, portrays what he *knows* to be the properties of objects rather than what he can actually observe (e.g. a profile of a face which nevertheless has two eyes),

... it is obvious that intellectual realism marks the appearance of straight lines, angles, circles, squares and other simple geometrical figures, though naturally without any exact measurements or proportions.[7] But at this stage, their construction cannot in any way result in a comprehensive, euclidean organization of space. On the contrary, the distinctive features of intellectual realism are as remote from such a structure as they are from the coordination of perspective viewpoints ...

Thus intellectual realism in children's drawings be defined in geometrical terms by saying that while this particular structure derives its elements from concepts which are just becoming projective and euclidean, nevertheless its relationships are expressive of a representational space belonging to a level of understanding which is mainly topological and consists primarily of relationships of proximity, separation, order, surrounding and continuity. (Ibid. 51)

Thus, before the child can successfully co-ordinate Euclidean shapes (as opposed simply to their isolated representation), he has to grasp the geometrical properties of the straight line, and in order to connect a given straight line with others at certain angles he has to

... take into account their inclinations, parallelity, number of lines, points of conjunction and their distances. It can therefore be easily understood that the organisation of this whole complex is vastly more complicated than the simple topological relations found [at the conclusion of the sensori-motor level] or the angles taken as a whole. ... (Ibid. 71)

The ability to understand the geometrical nature of the straight line is basic to the representation of projective and Euclidean space, and we must devote some attention to it here. The initial inability of the child to draw or to form a straight line on paper or with objects is one of motor co-ordination, but even when, at four to seven years, the child can form or draw straight lines and distinguish them from curves, he is at first able to draw straight lines

[7] Thus we often find that Euclidean figures are employed in primitive art and decoration, but they are not co-ordinated in a Euclidean or projective way.

in the absence of straight edges as models when he realizes that straight lines are formed by taking aim or sighting between two points. But the child does not grasp the significance of sighting between two points until he realizes that his own viewpoint is unique at any one place and that other viewpoints differ from his. The geometrical straight line is not only the product of sighting between two points, representing the conservation of a constant direction, but is also the product of the intersection of two planes and is therefore the basis not only of projective but of Euclidean representations of space. These two types of conceptual space are very closely linked both conceptually and developmentally.

One of Piaget's most important experiments relating to the development of the grasp of perspective is the use of a model of three mountains, differently coloured and shaped, on a table; a doll is placed in different positions in relation to the mountains and the child is asked to reconstruct inferentially the apparent changes in what the doll will see from these different positions. He is given three shaped pieces of cardboard and asked to reconstruct the kind of photograph which could be taken from each position of the doll. Secondly, a set of pictures of the mountains taken from different points of view is produced, and the child is asked to select the one which is appropriate to the view seen by the doll in particular positions. Finally, the child chooses a picture and then tries to find the position which the doll would have to occupy in order to see the mountains in the relationship portrayed in the picture.

The initial reactions of the child in the pre-operatory stage are egocentric; that is, his models of what the doll will see from different points of view all turn out to be same—they represent only what he can see from his own point of view. There are a number of reasons for this, a basic one being his unawareness in the early pre-operatory stage of any viewpoint but his own. Secondly, his spatial imagination tends to remain centred on a position corresponding to his present viewpoint, and it is this lack of decentration, found so frequently in the cognitive development of children, that inhibits the representation of views of the physical world as sets of transformations. Thirdly, as a result of these factors, spatial relations between objects are initially regarded as fixed, and children tend to cling to ideal representations of 'the object itself', whose spatial configuration is basically unchanging from whatever angle it is seen—hence the familiar phenomenon, already referred to, of the conceptual realism of children's drawings, in which they draw what they *know* to be the case, rather than what they *see*, as in the case of the profile of a face which nevertheless has two eyes. It is worth emphasizing yet again at this point that children *perceive* the world as we do; it is their *conceptual* representation of it that differs:

> Thus, in contrast to perception, representation of perspective implies operational, or at least conscious, co-ordination between object and subject; or in other words, a recognition of the fact that they both occupy the same projective space extending beyond the object and including the observer himself. . . . [One can therefore have perceptual awareness of perspective, and representational ignorance of it.] (Ibid. 178)

But before the child can fully co-ordinate the changing perspectives of groups of objects he has to understand the perspective transformations of single objects; initially he cannot, for example, represent in drawing the changing appearance of an upright stick that is lowered from the vertical to the horizontal position away from him, and will argue that it is impossible to draw the stick lying in an end-on view, since this would mean 'going through the paper'. Adequate representation of this requires an understanding of 'sectioning'—that is, the masking of the more distant by the nearer, as well as the grasp of representation from a single point of view—and the ability to represent continuous variation as opposed to a simple set of key positions—upright, tilted, and horizontal. Eventually the child realizes that a vertical stick, or a line projected on to a screen, decreases in length as it is tilted backwards, because relative to his own viewpoint what it *loses* in height it *gains* in depth, a continuous process whereby the whole of the height is transposed into depth. (In the same way, of course, the child has to understand in problems of the conservation of liquid quantity that the height of the container is similarly transposable into cross-sectional area or diameter.) He thus learns to co-ordinate a continuous set of transformations from one dimension into another and most importantly, discovers that these transformations are governed by *invariant relations*. In the same way, children who draw converging railway lines as moving closer together in a series of irregular and sudden changes of direction eventually learn to represent them as continuously converging, and also grasp the invariant relation that 'the sleepers between the rails are always a little closer together'. They are thus able to search for *general rules* governing all possible transformations of a similar type, though this occurs only in the later stages of concrete operational thought. This understanding of spatial relations by the grasp of invariant relations is in contrast to the child's earlier thinking in terms of absolute shapes and fixed, ideal relations between groups, and distinctive of concrete operational thinking.

(It may be noted, however, that the child's understanding of perspective develops most rapidly when he is dealing with objects or scenes close at hand, in relation to which he can most easily change his position. While children even of four are able to conserve *representationally* the shape of small, familiar objects, they find it much harder to do this with large objects such as mountains and seem to suppose when encountering changes of perspective here that the mountain has really changed its shape. For this reason before/behind relationships are reversible sooner than left/right relations since there is a greater perceptual difference between a background beyond reach and a foreground directly subject to it, than there is between the rotation of perspective from left to right through 180°. As the co-ordination of perspective develops, however, all the relations of up/down, left/right, before/behind, become relative, co-ordinated, and mutually transformable. We shall find that as far as our very limited evidence takes us, perspective concepts are very poorly developed among primitives.)

While projective space conserves straight lines and co-ordinates viewpoints, Euclidean space conserves parallels, angles, and distances, and is also referred to as metric space. Both Euclidean and projective space have in common the conservation of the straight line, as we have already noted. The idea of the parallel appears at the same time as that of the angle, since a pair of straight lines intersect to form an angle whenever they are not parallel. Like other geometrical concepts, that of parallelity is conceptual rather than perceptual, and is derived from the notion of 'taking aim' and of the common orientation of a number of lines. Following parallelity, angles and finally distances (displacements) are also conserved.

The relation of proportion is developed fully in the cases of speed, movement, and probability only at the level of formal operations, but it is easier to understand in geometrical terms, where the invariance of dimensional ratios can be understood at the level of concrete operations.

Initially, when a child is shown a rectangle of size $h_1 \times l_1$, and told to construct a similar figure of dimensions $h_2 \times l_2$, he concentrates only on one dimension, e.g. l_2, which he increases out of all proportion. At the concrete-operational stage he then discovers a constant difference of the form $D(hl) = l_1 - h_1$, which is at first conceived as absolute and then is discovered to be a ratio

$$D(hl) = \frac{h_1,}{l_1,}$$

and can understand simple ratios such as $1:2$. This is as far as the child can go at the concrete level, but at the level of formal operations he can understand more complex, continuous ratios of the form

$$\frac{h_1}{l_1} = \frac{h_2}{l_2}$$

and apply this to all cases. The development in the child's understanding of proportion is one of the best examples of the increasingly important role of the discovery of invariant relations in cognitive growth.

This lengthy exposition of the stages of cognitive growth in the representation of conceptual space has been leading up to what, for the purposes of the anthropologist, is the most important aspect— the construction of systems of reference. Piaget describes systems of reference thus:

... a reference frame is not simply a network composed of relations of order between the various objects themselves. It applies equally to positions within the network as to objects occupying any of these positions and enables the relations between them to be maintained invariant, independent of potential displacement of the objects. Thus the frame of reference constitutes a euclidean space after the fashion of a *container*, relatively independent of the mobile objects *contained* within it, just as projective co-ordination of the totality of potential viewpoints includes each viewpoint actually envisaged. (Ibid. 376)

[and]

... the essential character of a reference frame does not reside in the choice of stationary reference objects, but in the possibility of co-ordinating positions and intervals without limit, through constantly enlarging the original system. (Ibid. 377)

[and]

... the grouping of displacements leads to the gradual replacement of positional relations between objects by relations of order and distance between the positions themselves. (Ibid. 377)

As we saw, topological space is concerned with the relations between parts and whole, internal to an object or pattern of objects. It is for this reason that children are initially incapable of relating changes of position to any overall system of co-ordination. A good example of this is their inability to represent the changes in the position of the level of water in a square bottle as it is tilted from the vertical to the horizontal. They cannot at first accept the evidence of their senses that, no matter what angle the bottle assumes the surface of the water remains horizontal, and depict it in their drawings as parallel to the bottom of the bottle even when the bottle is lying on its side. They also fail to note the successive transformations of relationship of water surface to the configuration of the bottle, and a preliminary attempt to achieve this results in the water surface being drawn between the top and bottom corners of the bottle when lying on its side. While eventually they can draw the surface parallel to the side of the bottle when it lies on its side, it requires a great deal of time before they can represent the water surface in its proper position when the bottle is inverted.

The reason for this is that the child has no general system of spatial co-ordinates by which to orientate the different relations of water surface and bottle angle. The spatial relations of the water surface are initially confined within the bottle itself and are not transferred to an external point of reference such as the table top. Spatial relations and orientations are thus broken up into a series of local relationships, tied to a variety of concrete reference points. For this reason one finds that in the early drawings of children, houses, for example, are always drawn perpendicular to the slope of a hill, rather than truly vertical.

Initially, therefore, the child cannot isolate lines and planes at all, conceptually speaking. When he can, he is still unable to make use of reference points of a general nature, outside the object or configuration of things he is considering. It is only in the later stages of concrete operations that he can construct more extended systems of reference, with co-ordinate axes embracing the entire conceptual field.

Finally, at the beginning of formal operations, we find that

... their system of co-ordinates has become virtually conventional or hypothetico-deductive. 'I say that the base is horizontal' 'tis decrees, 'and I draw the water in relation to the base', after which he proceeds to arrange the whole affair according to a set of parallels and perpendiculars, whether the paper lies straight or askew. Physical horizontals and verticals have thus become no more than an occasion for making a finished drawing in terms of orthogonal co-ordinates. (Ibid. 411)

Relatively little work on primitive spatial concepts relevant to Piaget's theories has been done by psychologists, but the following observations by Cole and Gay on the spatial concepts of the Kpelle are worthy of note. Referring to the paucity of terms for Euclidean shapes, and the vagueness of such terms as are used, they say:

It is tempting to say that they represent topological concepts rather than Euclidean concepts. That is, it is not so much the precise figure that matters, but the way in which space is divided. Thus the term *pere*, 'path', can refer to a straight line. However, it can be applied equally well to a curved or jagged line. These distinctions, which we require in English, are unimportant to the Kpelle. The important thing about that which they term *pere* is that it extends from one place to another place without crossing itself. It is therefore much closer to our topological concept of a path dividing a surface into two parts than it is to our Euclidean straight line. (Gay and Cole 1967: 53)

Similarly *kere-kere*, 'circle', is also used to describe the shape of pots, pans, frogs, sledge-hammers, tortoises, water-turtles, and rice fanners. 'It is, therefore, closer to our topological concept of a single closed path, although some slight measure of circularity is required for the term to be used' (ibid. 54).

Again, the word for 'triangle', *kpeilaa*, is applied to tortoise shell, arrow head, monkey's elbow, drum (like an hour-glass), bird's nest, and bow. The term is not restricted to figures formed of three-line segments, but includes similar shapes.

By contrast [to that for 'triangle'], the term for quadrilateral refers directly to the fact that the figure has four sides. It is called *bela-naán*, 'four parts'. Informants told us that a rectangular house, a plank, a doorway, a chair, and a table are all of this shape. All of these items have assumed a rectangular form only in modern times and it is possible that the form *bela-naán* has recently been coined by the Kpelle people. (Ibid. 54)

The cone is called *soo*, and appears as the roof of a round house, *ton-pére*. It is the shape of a spear head, the inside of a mortar, and one type of drum. The cylinder is called *torontoron*, and is the shape of many common objects. Informants applied it to a tree trunk, a bottle, a mortar, a bucket, the pestle for a mortar, a round house, and a tin can. The sphere is called *kpuma*, the shape of an orange, a tomato, and a papaya (which is far from spherical, from our point of view). Also, the objects which can be called *kpuma* include things we would identify as cubes. So, there are *kpuma* which are called *kere-kere*, 'round', and *kpuma* which are called *lebe-lebe*, implying that they have sides. The bouillon cube (an essential item in any store) is called *kpuma*, and so is the kola nut, which has curved sides. It is this sort of observation which leads us to think it is the topological and not the Euclidean shape that this term defines. The Euclidean rectangular solid also has a name, *kálan*, which is probably a somewhat later addition to the language, because such solids are not older than the encroachment of western civilization. (Ibid. 54)

And Littlejohn says of Temne concepts of geometrical figures: '... they distinguish straight line from "bent", *foh-conah* [four-corner?] serves for square, rectangle and cube, and *kél-kél* is the term for circle' (1963: 4). Thus while both the Kpelle and the Temne have terms which *may* be used to describe Euclidean shapes, it seems that the Euclidean shapes do not provide the 'ideal' image of these terms, since subjects found difficulty in applying the Kpelle words to the geometrical figures given them in tests. 'The circle was described variously by others as like a wheel, a pot, a bell, and a pan. The triangle was described as branched, straight, having three senses, the butt of a gun, a checkerboard, and a musical instrument.' Out of nineteen subjects, three could not verbalize geometrical concepts at all, only four named the circle as round, and two named the triangle, using Kpelle terms.

Piaget's theories about the prior development of topological space and the growth of Euclidean and projective representations of space from the level of pre-operatory thought to that of concrete and formal operations have been tested by, among others, de Lemos (1974) among Zulu and white schoolchildren in South Africa, and rather more extensively by Dasen (1974) among groups of Australian Aborigines of varying degrees of education and acculturation to the literate, European way of life.

De Lemos's results, which we shall consider first, were not based on data from non-literate children or adults in their traditional society, but on schoolchildren from five to twelve years of age in a Zulu township on the outskirts of Pietermaritzburg. Their parents were mainly from the higher wage-earning group, though it appears that the language of instruction in school was Zulu, and their environmental and home circumstances were largely those of the traditional society. The value of these results is twofold: they provide, in the outcome, a confirmation of the applicability of the general Piagetian theory of the development of spatial concepts outside the confines of European culture, and secondly, they show that even among non-Western schoolchildren there is a consistent failure to develop the more advanced spatial concepts. This is a strong indication that the development of the higher levels of Euclidean and projective space is likely to be even more retarded in those populations totally without schooling and literacy, and in purely rural, traditional societies.

1. Topological space

> Subtest 1: Copying of geometrical figures.
> Subtest 2: Haptic perception–identification; this involved the handling of a set of cardboard geometrical shapes, Euclidean and topological, behind a screen, so that they could not be seen, and their identification with a duplicate set of cardboard shapes that could be seen.
> Subtest 3: As above, except that the shapes handled were identified by drawing instead by the use of the duplicate set of shapes.

In these tests, it was found that in Subtest 1 the first identifications made were between open and closed forms; then followed the distinction between curved and straight-sided figures. The children only gradually mastered the copying of Euclidean shapes. Piaget predicts that only at the stage of concrete operations are children able to copy all the figures correctly, and this stage was reached at about six years by the majority of white children and at about nine years by the majority of Zulu children. 'Our results confirmed the stages of development described by Piaget, and the age of achievement for the white children, but the development of the Zulu children lagged some three years behind that of the white children, although following the same pattern of development.'

2. Projective space

> Subtest 1: The construction of a straight line, parallel and oblique to the edge of the table.
> Subtest 2: The drawing of perspective views of a pencil and a penny (a) from the child's own viewpoint, and (b from that of an observer sitting at right angles to the child.

Subtests 4 and 5: As above, but in this case the child was asked
to identify the correct perspective views from a set of drawings
including correct and incorrect perspectives.

Subtests 6–8: The child was asked to identify the correct perspective view of a model of three different coloured mountains seen
from different positions. In Subtest 6 the child had to construct
the correct perspectives using duplicate cardboard cut-outs. In
Subtest 7 he chose the correct perspectives by choosing from
different pictures, and in Subtest 8 he was shown the pictures
and asked to place a doll in the corresponding position around
the model from which it would see the particular view represented. The reader will, of course, recognize these tests from our
earlier discussion of Piaget's researches.

In Subtest 1 the Zulu children displayed a similar time lag of
about three years, the majority of white children mastering the task
at about six years. Interestingly, there was no evidence for the pre-
operatory substage described by Piaget in which the child cannot
construct straight lines obliquely to the table's edge, and to this
extent his prediction was not confirmed.

With Subtests 2–5 de Lemos reports that

There were marked differences between the Zulu and white children in
their ability to represent and to recognize perspective views. The majority
of the Zulu children up to 9 years were unable to recognize changes in
shape with changes in perspective. From 10 to 12 years most of the children were able to recognize or to represent some change in shape with
changes in perspective, but only a few children were able to distinguish
between their own point of view and that of an observer, and so to reach
the criterion for Piaget's stage of concrete operations.

The white children, on the other hand, were able to recognize that changes in shape occur with changes in perspective from 5 years, and to distinguish between their own view and that of an observer at 7 years, thus
achieving Piaget's Stage III at the same age as Swiss children.

Thus the recognition of perspective changes develops much later in Zulu
children than in white children, and few of the Zulu children even up to 12
years were able to represent perspective changes correctly. (Ibid. 374)

He also notes, however, that the problem for all the children was
not so much a *belief* that theirs was the only correct view of the
mountains, but 'they appeared to be aware of changes in perspective, and were sometimes able to state what the correct perspective

would be, although they were unable to construct or select the correct representations' (ibid. 378).[8]

Subtests 6–8. Piaget found, as we recall, that the comprehensive co-ordination of viewpoints is not achieved until about nine to ten years (Stage IIIb):

The correct co-ordination of perspectives was found in the white children from about 10 years. However, very few of the Zulu children succeeded in this task. From 7 or 8 years the children usually showed some awareness of perspective, recognizing that the view of the mountain seen from different positions would change. However, they were generally unable to construct the correct view of the mountains from different positions, or to relate the views to the pictures representing them.

These results therefore confirm those of the previous subtests, indicating a failure on the part of the Zulu children to deal operationally with problems of perspective. (Ibid. 374–5)

3. Euclidean space

Subtests 1–4: The similarity of rhombi and triangles, by reference to the parallelism of sides, and the direct comparison of angles by superimposition. Piaget found that Swiss children achieved this at seven and a half to nine years, and that an understanding of dimensional proportion (at the concrete level) was achieved at nine to ten, Stage IIIb, 'Very few of the Zulu children and relatively few of the white children achieved the Stage III level.'

The results were inconsistent, however, and it seems that the way in which these tests (and those of the similarity of rectangles, subtests 5–7) were presented confused the children. So this aspect of the testing programme cannot be regarded as conclusive, though it does seem that recognition of the similarity of figures and of proportion was noticeably poorer in the Zulu group compared with the white. De Lemos concludes:

It is clear that there are marked differences between the white and Zulu groups in the development of spatial concepts. Topological, projective, and Euclidean relationships emerge at a later age level in the Zulu than

---

[8] The problem is complicated, however, by the fact that the representation of perspective involves the use of pictorial conventions which, as the history of Western art demonstrates, are by no means obvious (see Cole and Scribner 1974: 64–71). But the representation of perspective in art cannot be merely conventional, as they imply, since these same 'conventions' are reproduced in the perspectives of photographs.

they do in the white children, and in the Zulu group relatively few children appear to understand the representation and co-ordination of perspectives or the principles of geometrical similarity and proportion. (Ibid. 379)

Doubtless the levels of teaching and instructional aids are much poorer in the Zulu schools than they are in the white schools, but the very admission of this is itself the recognition that the development of the conceptual representation of projective and Euclidean space is not a spontaneous cognitive skill that emerges in all cultures (even if it is not utilized in collective representations), but a highly specific skill closely related to schooling and literacy and to the cognitive demands imposed by the environment.

The second detailed attempt to test Piaget's theories of the development of spatial representations is Dasen's work (1974) among the Australian Aborigines at Areyonga and Hermannsburg, already referred to in Chapter 6. Dasen was interested in testing the hypothesis 'that people with a hunting economy should develop the concepts of space [Piaget's] in preference to concepts in other cognitive areas on which there are no or fewer cognitive demands' (1974: 385), and in particular, the hypothesis that they will develop spatial concepts more readily than logico-mathematical concepts. He also wished to test the hypothesis that the stages of cognitive growth are the same in Aborigines as in Europeans, but that the rate of development is slower, and that this retardation is greater for the low-contact group (Areyonga) than the medium-contact group (Hermannsburg).

The tests which concern us here are those of Order (Test 6), Rotation (Test 7), and Horizontality (Test 8).

Test 6: Order. This was in three parts: of linear order, when the subject was asked to copy a linear display of nine miniature clothes (of cardboard hung on a string); of reverse order, when the subject was asked to choose the same 'clothes' as in the model but to reverse the order; and circular order—'The experimenter put nine items into a circle on the table and asked the subject to copy the display in the same order, but in a straight line' (p. 392).

Test 7: Rotation. This test involved two identical model landscapes, adapted to the Central Australian landscape but incorporating the same spatial features used by Piaget and Inhelder (1956: 421). These were 'placed side by side on a desk, in the same orientation'. When the child had been shown their exact correspondence,

The experimenter then placed a toy sheep in several locations on one of the models, asking the child to place his toy sheep in exactly the same positions (checking the location and the direction 'into which it looked'). After the child understood the problem, one of the models was turned around by 180°, and the same check items were repeated. Finally a screen was placed between the two models to prevent the possibility of a purely perceptual solution. For the test items, the sheep were placed successively in seven standard positions on one of the models, the child being asked to find the same position and direction on the rotated model. The child was not asked to verbalize his reasoning. (Dasen 1974: 392)

Test 8: Horizontality.

[A cylindrical bottle] half filled with blue coloured water, was placed in the vertical position on a stand. The subject was presented with a corresponding outline drawing, and was asked to draw the water in the bottle. The bottle was then hidden in a bag, so that the shape was still apparent but the water no longer visible, and a second check-item in the vertical position was performed. (Ibid.)

In part 1 of the test,

The bottle, still hidden in the bag, was placed successively in five different positions (from the subject's point of view: 1, tilted to the right; 2, on its side, cork to the right; 3, upside down; 4, tilted so that the cork touched the stand on the right; 5, tilted to the left). Each time the child was given the corresponding outline drawing, the record sheet being folded so that only one picture was visible at any one time. The subject was asked where the water was, and to draw it. (Ibid. 392–3)

In part 2, when the child failed correctly to reproduce the water level on any position, the bag was removed and the same procedure was repeated. In part 3, for positions on which the child's performance in part 2 had improved on part 1, the bottle was again hidden in the bag.

Adults were tested for horizontality only, not for rotation or order. The order problem was presented to the following age groups: five to eight in Canberra, six to ten in Hermannsburg, and six to eleven in Areyonga.

Dasen found no difficulty in correlating the responses and explanations of the Aboriginal children with Piaget's stages, and goes so far as to say:

A detailed qualitative analysis of the results revealed an exact correspondence between the answers and explanations given by the Aboriginal children and by European children in Canberra. The Aboriginal child may use
only a word or two, or a gesture, instead of a long verbal explanation, but
the reasoning he expresses is precisely the same. (Ibid. 394–5)

The only major qualification to this (if it is a qualification), is his
observation that by about ten the European children start making
more complex statements using formal concepts which may not be
fully understood, and, more significantly:

They also tend to formulate their explanations into general laws (for example, 'It is always the same weight, whatever you do to it, unless you add
some or you take some off').
   No such generalizations or complex explanations were given by Aboriginal subjects. This may be due partly to the lack of verbal fluency in
English. However, even the older subjects and the adults who had acquired a very good command of the English language did not make any of
these involved statements. The formal properties of thought, which are
evidenced by some of the formulations the European children use, are
absent from the explanations the Aborigines give. (Ibid. 395)

Dasen's conclusions on the inability of the Aborigines to give explicitly verbalized justifications for their judgements conform closely
to the findings of other cross-cultural developmental psychologists
which we noted in Chapter 3.
   Table XVIII shows the levels of cognitive development reached
by the different groups of subjects in the problems of order, rotation, and horizontality. It will be seen that, while on the test for
order, all the children reached the stage of concrete operations, this
was not so in the rotation and horizontality tests. In the case of
rotation, while all the Canberra children were at Stage III by age
twelve, only 80 per cent of the Hermannsburg children were, and
this had not improved among the fifteen- to sixteen-year-olds. The
achievement of the Areyonga group was even less. The horizontality problem presented even greater difficulties, and the performance of the adults is not much better than the fifteen- to sixteen-
year-olds. While it was found that the Aborigines acquired the set
of spatial operations tested before they acquired the logico-mathematical operations (of conservation and seriation), the more
acculturated Aborigines of Hermannsburg scored higher in the
spatial operations than did the less acculturated. This suggests that

these spatial concepts are more relevant, or at least easier to develop, in European culture than they are appropriate to the ecological needs of Aboriginal life.

TABLE XVIII

ORDER (Stage III)

	5	6	7	8	9	10	11	
				Years of age				
Canberra	20	80	80	100	100	—	—	Percentage
Hermannsburg	—	50	79	80	100	100	—	of correct
Areyonga		0	40	100	88	100		responses

ROTATION (Stage III)

	5	6	7	8	9	10	11	12	13	14	15	16	
					Years of age								
Canberra	0	10	0	30	70	100	80	100					Percentage
Hermannsburg		0	10	0	20	40	50	30	80		80		of correct
Areyonga		0		25		0		36		37·5			responses

HORIZONTALITY (Part 1 Stage IIIb)

	5	6	7	8	9	10	11	12	13	14	15	16	Ad	
							Years of age							
Canberra	0	0	0	30	10	20	70	50						Percentage
Hermannsburg	0	0	20	0	20	10	0		30		30		40	of correct
Areyonga		0		17		0		7		30			20	responses

(Dasen 1974: 398 ff.)

6. CONCLUSIONS

As in other areas of cognition, we find that primitive representations of space are highly dependent on the phenomenal appearance and contextual associations of the physical world which are experienced in everyday life, such that representations tend to be static and heavily loaded with symbolism. Boundaries, centre and periphery, above and below, left and right, and other topological relations abound, and while many cultures recognize the four cardinal points these are often conceived in a static manner, based on the rising and setting positions of the sun and the axes of the human body, and are not used as co-ordinate systems for orientation. Navigation indeed is perfectly capable of doing without the cardinal points altogether. The human body is also frequently employed as a microcosm according to which houses and villages are laid out on the ground. In many primitive societies the geometric notion of the straight line as the product of the intersection of planes, or a segment which is the shortest distance between two points, may not be developed in the absence of problems that do not demand, for example, sighting between two points. Again, while many primitive societies depict some Euclidean shapes in art, they may not use them in the construction of co-ordinated systems (as for example the megalith builders did to a very high degree) or in the organization of experience.

The absence of measurement and quantification, especially in relation to land measurement and surveying, is clearly a major factor in the general lack of Euclidean and projective spatial representation, together with the lack of representative drawing and mapping, which seem to occur in relatively few primitive societies. Only in societies where navigation is an important cognitive problem do we find that some projective and Euclidean concepts are developed. Even here it is possible for much orientation to be achieved at the perceptual level rather than by explicit conceptual representations—we recall that Aboriginal maps are metrically and projectively greatly inferior to those of the Eskimo, but the Aborigines nevertheless seem able to orient themselves very successfully by the constantly updated image-based map.

The tests of cognitive performance by primitives conducted by psychologists, despite the paucity of such studies, largely confirms Piaget's theory of the development of spatial concepts and strongly suggests, apart from the ethnographic evidence, that the average member of a primitive society which lacks navigation or the need for maps in the conveying of information will represent space in a predominantly pre-operatory fashion. The available evidence suggests therefore that primitive concepts of space are not of a type distinct from those of literate industrial man, but that they are simply more elementary than those that our type of society requires as the norm for its average citizen.

8
Time

1. TIME AND PROCESS

Anthropologists, in attempting an analysis of the basic characteristics of primitive thought, have generally lacked a clear comprehension of the modes of thought prevailing among the average
members of our own society. This is especially true of their treatment of notions of time. In particular, anthropologists often write
as though our Western concepts of time were based on scientific
theory, e.g. 'Peoples without writing do not have any units of time
based on the concepts of mathematical physics' (Vansina
1973: 100), and the passages from Whorf previously quoted. In
fact, the formal concepts of mathematical physics are necessarily
based on a prior grasp of concrete-operational time, without which
they could not have evolved. But a concrete-operational concept of
time is not peculiar to science, being employed by the average citizen in the course of his daily life in our society.

Time, more than space, number, causality, or perhaps even than
probability, is a particularly difficult and elusive concept. Therefore if we are properly to appreciate the different ways in which it
may be understood by primitives and by ourselves, it is essential to
grasp the logic of time as it is in fact used in our society, not
among scientists, but in our everyday life.

Time is part of the structure of the universe, which comprises the
four great categories of object, space, causality, and time. There is
no object without space and vice versa; the interaction of objects
defines causality, and time is the co-ordination of these interactions
or motions. As we saw in our analysis of operatory concepts of
space, it is not a static representation, a mere container, but a
system of operations by which all possible positions of objects and
their transformations can be co-ordinated. In the same way, time is
not, at the operational level, a static dimension, fixed in the past

and future in relation to the present, like a succession of annual dates in a calendar, but a system of co-ordinations of *successive* spatial states, that is, of motion.

More precisely, space suffices for the co-ordination of simultaneous positions, but as soon as displacements are introduced, they bring in their train distinct, and therefore successive, spatial states whose co-ordination is nothing other than time itself. Space is a still of time, while time is space in motion—the two taken together constitute the totality of the ordered relationships characterizing objects and their displacement.

But though, in the case of space, we can ignore time to construct geometrical relationships (to do so we need merely postulate a fictitious simultaneity and describe motions as pure displacements at infinite velocity or as displacements independent of their velocity), when it comes to time, we cannot abstract the spatial and kinetic relationships, i.e. we cannot ignore velocity. It is only once it has already been constructed, that time can be conceived as an independent system, and even then, only when small velocities are involved. In the course of its construction, time remains a simple dimension inseparable from space and part and parcel of the total co-ordination which enables us to correlate the kinetic transformations of the universe.

If this is the case, the study of the genesis of the concept of time must prove highly instructive. If time is really the co-ordination of motions in the sense that space is the logic of objects, we must expect to discover the existence of *operational time*, involving relations of succession and duration based on analogous operations in logic. Operational time will be distinct from *intuitive* time, which is limited to successions and durations given by direct perception. Operational time itself may be *qualitative* or *quantitative*, depending on whether the operations involved are analogous to those involved in classes and logical relations, or whether a numerical unit comes into play. (Piaget 1970: 2)

Thus there are three basic aspects of time—duration, succession, and simultaneity; duration and succession are basic characteristics of all processes, while the co-ordination of two or more processes involves the notion of simultaneity. Points of time are involved at the transition from one period to the next and in the establishment of simultaneities. If for the time being we leave on one side the problem of the co-ordination of duration and succession, we can see that in so far as processes have duration, they have extension, and in so far as one process or one stage of a process succeeds another, processes may have boundaries, and to this extent sequences of events have a spatial quality. Indeed, the

English word 'time' is derived from the Old Teutonic *tîmon*, composed of the root *ti-*, to stretch or extend, + the abstract suffix *-mon*, *-man* (SOED, 'time').[1]

I shall argue, with Piaget, that awareness and representation of duration and succession are elementary cognitive skills, inherent in the experience of process, including the subjective processes of our own bodies, and that such representations of 'time' are structurally indistinguishable from representations of space, except that while motion in space is reversible, motion in time is not. Thus calendrical systems are composed of activities and events with duration and of points of transition, all of which are associated together in the same fixed manner as the features of a landscape; even if the durations between points is variable, the order of succession remains the same. For this reason we commonly find that spatial and temporal vocabularies are interchangeable, at the commonsense level, both in primitive society and in our own. To go beyond this elementary conception of time and to be able to represent it in its most general sense as a dimension by which two or more processes can be co-ordinated in respect of duration, succession, and simultaneity requires the co-ordination of relative velocity, and this is a cognitive skill which is not developed in primitive society, being characteristic of concrete operations. Thus a subject who has attained an operatory understanding of time would be able to solve the following type of problem:

Two cars, 1 and 2, start from two points A_1 and A_2 simultaneously and travel on two parallel tracks towards B_1, B_2. Car 1 travels faster than car 2, and when the cars stop simultaneously car 1 has travelled further than 2, e.g.:

A_1 — B_1

A_2 — — — — — — — — — — — — B_2

A subject at the pre-operatory level will suppose, however, that the

---

[1] The same primitive conception of time as extension seems to have existed among the early Chinese, among whom the word for 'space' was *yü*, and 'time', *chou*: 'The original meaning of both these two ancient words was 'roof', of house, cart or boat, so that the semantic significance is that of something stretching over an expanse to cover it. So indeed we still in English say that such and such an exposition 'covers' ten or fifteen centuries. The word for duration (*chiu*) is explained by the Han lexicographers as derived from the character *jen*, man, a man stretching his legs and walking 'a stretch', just as a roof stretches across a space, and time stretches from one event to another' (J. Needham 1965: 1).

cars did not stop simultaneously, and that 1 travelled for a longer period than 2, because such a person cannot dissociate time elapsed from distance covered or work done.[2] As a consequence, it is impossible properly to co-ordinate duration, succession, and simultaneity. (We shall examine a number of variations on this theme later in the chapter.)

The primitive grasp of time, however, as I have stressed, is confined to the awareness of duration and succession as these are embodied in natural and social processes. Now it is evident that all processes in the real world are inherently temporal as well as spatial, but it is methodologically essential to distinguish time from process. As we have seen, time is a system of co-ordinations of successive spatial states, but these successive spatial states or processes have other structural aspects which are distinct from time. For example, some processes are non-recurring or linear, such as the history of a particular society; repeating or cyclical, such as the succession of the seasons; in others the stages are reversible, such as the ebb and flow of the tide; in others there is alternation, as in a sequence of gift exchanges between two parties; in others there is a slow build-up to a peak or climax, as in the stages leading up to a pig feast in New Guinea, after which the sequence begins again; in others there is what may be called undulations, peaks and troughs of high and low intensity of activity; in some processes one stage leads to another by imperceptible degrees, while in others the transitions are clearly marked, even catastrophic. But while process is an integral part of all nature, all life, and all society, it is sheer confusion of thought to maintain that representations of linear process are one kind of time, representations of alternations a second, representations of cycles a third, and so on. There is only one time, but there are many types of process. In the same way, there are curved sticks, crooked sticks, and straight sticks, but it makes no sense to talk of curved or crooked or straight *length*, and when we bend a stick we are not bending length, but a piece of wood.

Thus Leach argues, on the basis of our subjective awareness of duration and of such phenomena as the phases of plant growth,

---

[2] Thus, in the same way, if two people, *A* and *B*, are piling up bricks, and *A* is working faster than *B* and so piles up more bricks, and both start and stop simultaneously, the pre-operatory subject will conclude, as in the case of the cars, that *A* has been working longer than *B*.

that our modern European conception of time as regular and continuous is culturally relative and imposed on reality:

> ... the regularity of time is not an intrinsic part of nature; it is a man
> made notion which we have projected into our environment for our par-
> ticular purposes ...
>
> But if there is nothing in the principle of the thing, or in the nature of
> our experience, to suggest that time must necessarily flow past at constant
> speed, we are not required to think of time as a constant flow at all. Why
> shouldn't time slow down and stop occasionally, or even go into reverse?
> (Leach 1961: 133)
>
> Repetitive and non-repetitive events are not, after all, logically the same.
> We treat them both as aspects of 'one thing', *time*, not because it is
> rational to do so, but because of religious prejudice. The idea of Time, like
> the idea of God, is one of those categories which we find necessary because
> we are social animals rather than because of anything empirical in our
> objective experience of the world ... (Ibid. 125)

But fairly evidently, neither our representations of time nor
those of primitives are directly derived from the physical world in a
purely perceptual manner, in the same way as colour, for example,
but are constructed in the process of interaction with it, like representations of space, number, causality, and so on. It is therefore
fallacious to demand, as Leach does, that sensory impressions of
duration or experience of such phenomena as the phases of plant
growth, should be treated as some kind of privileged data, by
comparison with which any conceptual representations may be
adjudged as impositions on a neutral reality, and therefore in a
sense fictitious and culturally relative. (Leach's argument on the
nature of time is, of course, just another facet of the philosophy
that posits a continuous reality upon which distinctions are imposed arbitrarily and artificially by each culture.)

J. A. Barnes says of Lévi-Strauss's theories of time:

> He frequently contrasts synchrony with diachrony, the axis of simultaneity
> with the axis of successiveness, and discontinuity with continuity. In his
> work on kinship and elsewhere, he contrasts reversible with irreversible
> time, and there are also straight, circular, progressive, empty, non-cum-
> ulative, statistical, psychological, visceral and other kinds of time as well
> as micro-time and macro-time. Strictly speaking, these contrasts might be
> better described as between different kinds of temporal process rather than
> between different kinds of time, but the nomenclature is now too well
> established to change. (J. A. Barnes 1971: 541)

Barnes may well be right in assuming that the usage 'time-reckoning' is now too firmly established to be changed, but we shall nevertheless reach a far better understanding of primitive 'time-reckoning' if we recognize that rather than being '*time*-reckoning' it is really 'process-classification' and 'process-marking'. But, as Piaget points out, awareness of process does not in itself provide us with an operatory understanding of time:

We must guard against the belief that time can be discovered from the outside, all ready-made in some physical process or another: physical processes do not have any bearing on the development of the time sense unless they become incorporated into an overall operational structure . . . (Piaget 1970: 70)

I would therefore argue that in the typical primitive society there is no more awareness of 'time' as distinct from 'process' than there is of 'area' as distinct from sensorily perceived expanses of land which have different implications for crop yields or amounts of labour necessary for tilling.

There are indeed primitive societies that have words that the ethnographer may properly translate as 'time' in a limited sense. For example, the Tauade have a word, *lova*, which might be translated as 'time'; *oilova* = 'this time, now'; *telova?* = 'what time, when?'; *opolovan*, 'olden time', etc. Significantly, however, apart from the use of *lariata*, 'daylight', for 'day', they have no other 'time-reckoning' terms. *One*, 'moon', is not used as the basis of a lunar calendar, nor do they have any word for 'year', nor do they divide the year into seasons such as wet or dry, nor do they divide the various stages of the human life-cycle into any named categories beyond those of girl/woman, boy/man, or baby/young person/old person. In view of the almost complete absence even of 'process-classification' in their culture, it would be highly implausible to suppose that the Tauade have nevertheless arrived at some intuitive operatory grasp of time merely because they have a word such as *lova*. It is much more likely that what they mean by *lova* is 'sequence of events' or 'period'. Thus *oilova* would more accurately be translated as 'this sequence of events', i.e. the sequence of events in which the speaker and his interlocutor are presently involved; and *telova?* would mean 'what sequence of events?' e.g. '*telova* will you go to Port Moresby?', 'In what sequence of events will you go to Port Moresby?', 'After the aeroplane has brought my mail to the Mission'.

Similar considerations seem to apply to the Kaguru, of whom Beidelman writes:

> The Kaguru have two terms for the abstract 'time': *ugele* (or *ngele, gele*) and *daha*. The term *ugele* appears to refer to a span of time longer than a day. Thus, when a storyteller refers to a period in which certain conditions such as famine or warfare prevailed, he says *ugele uya*, 'that time'; or when a Kaguru wishes to stipulate a long span of time, he may say *kwa gele wa minyaka*, 'for a time of years'. The term *daha* appears to refer to a relatively short time, usually less than a day. Thus, if a boy is sent on an errand and has loitered, returning late, a Kaguru may ask where the boy has been 'all that time', *idaha dyose*. Or if a Kaguru wishes to express the idea of quickness, that it 'took no time at all', he may say *ng'halonda idaha*. This may also be expressed in the negative: 'no time', *siludaha*, sometimes best translated into English as 'soon'. Refinement of the meaning of *daha* may be made by adding the prefix *i-*, which indicates large size (see examples above), or the diminutive prefix *chi-* (*chidaha chidodogi*, 'a little time'). Kaguru are imprecise in not always limiting *ugele* to periods of over a day and *daha* to shorter periods, but, in general, this definition holds. (Beidelman 1963: 11)

It is evident that what Beidelman is here translating as the abstract concept of 'time' can more precisely be rendered as 'period' or 'sequence of events'; that is, Kaguru time concepts are concerned simply with the succession of events and their duration and the relation of these successions of events with the present; and this is not evidence of an abstract awareness of time as a dimension in relation to which several processes can be co-ordinated.

But the lack of an operatory conception of time has more profound consequences than the inability to co-ordinate duration, succession, and simultaneity. For to the extent that primitive time is spatialized and bound up with particular processes, particular concrete sequences of events in the natural and social worlds, it will lack what Piaget concludes are the three fundamental attributes of operational time—homogeneity, continuity, and uniformity. Homogeneous time is common to the whole universe, and not localized or subjective. In continuous time the present is only a single moment in a single process in which there are no gaps, while uniform time flows at the same rate. We have already noted however (in Whorf's description of Hopi time, for example) that primitive representations of time may not treat it as the same in different places, such that 'now' is relative to each location. Calendrical systems often have gaps in which time ceases to be reckoned according to any generally agreed criteria, while both at the individual and social levels duration is conceived as having different rates in different situations.

The fundamental distinction between primitive, pre-operatory conceptions of time and those of concrete and formal operations which we employ in many areas of our thinking, is therefore that primitive time is based on sequences of qualitatively different events, such as those of the seasons or daily activities. In such cases it is evident that these qualitative sequences are peculiar to each community, so that it becomes impossible to co-ordinate duration, simultaneity, and succession from place to place, while the flow of time will appear to proceed at different rates depending on the nature of the activities, thus making different sequences of events incommensurable. And to the extent that the sequence of those custom-events used for time-reckoning is cyclical in nature, it is also unvarying, which adds to its irreversible and static quality, static in the sense that each event is uniquely linked with its predecessor and successor. Such a sequence of events is closely comparable to a landscape, with each land-mark in a fixed relationship with every other, and relations of time can therefore be comprehended by spatial concepts such as near, far, beyond, behind, and so on. The spatialization of time, its incorporation in process and the lack of homogeneity, continuity, and uniformity are the principal characteristics of primitive time.

At the level of concrete operations, however, the decentration of thought and the resulting reversibility of temporal concepts—that is, the comparison of later with earlier durations—allows time to be conceived as a continuum, but the continuity of time also depends upon systems of qualitative colligations, which lead to the partition of durations, and upon quantitative operations, which play an important part in making time not only continuous, but homogeneous and uniform. Temporal uniformity, indeed, rests on the construction of quantitative time and upon the ability to grasp the homogeneity and continuity of time.

Pre-operatory time therefore involves an intuitive awareness of duration and succession, characterized by the now familiar features of irreversibility, perceptual domination, lack of co-ordination between simultaneity, succession, and duration (which is closely related to irreversibility), lack of compensation, and lack of conservation of velocity and duration; and is as yet not dissociated from distance covered, work done, and velocity.

2. PRIMITIVE REPRESENTATION OF TIME

Nilsson (1920) in his classic work on primitive time-reckoning draws our attention to the fact that 'time indications', such as 'sun rise' or 'full moon', precede time-reckoning in terms of periods, and that these time indications are not durative, but aoristic or indefinite. The counting of time is thus based on sequences of qualitatively defined time points, such as 'sleep' for 24-hour period, 'harvest' or 'winter' for year, which represent what we should think of as the units of day or year on a *pars pro toto* basis. Because time-reckoning is based on these concrete indications, whether celestial or derived from social activities such as the domestic or agricultural cycles, it is based on phenomena which are durationally incommensurable and qualitatively unique, fluctuating, or with gaps between the end of one period and the beginning of the next, and so cannot be quantitatively seriated and colligated. In addition, the lunar and sidereal cycles and the diurnal rotation of the earth are mutually unrelated and incommensurable, which poses additional problems to the construction of a unified system of time-reckoning based on celestial phenomena.

We shall also see that because time is frequently reckoned in terms of activities, such as a journey or cooking a meal, it is inherently very difficult to isolate duration and to correlate it with succession and simultaneity, which is essential for an operational conception of time. While primitives frequently refer to things as fast or slow, they do so not in relation to duration or distance, but on the basis of the vigour of that which is faster or of one man overtaking another on a journey. And because durative intervals are large (such as 'day') or of varying length, there is no means of comparing velocities of objects except by observations of activity or overtaking. The lack of a stable, seriable system of units makes an awareness of duration which is not tied to spatial displacement or activity even harder to grasp than the dimensions of length quantity, or weight. Correspondingly we find no words in primitive languages for 'time' as such (except, as we have seen, in the sense of 'sequence of events'), any more than we do for the dimensions of length, weight, and so on. Thus we shall find that time is no abstracted from spatial displacement or activity in most primitive societies, the only exceptions being the correlations between lunar and sidereal calendars in a very few societies.

It will be suggested that the calendrical systems of primitive peoples do not usually require an operational grasp of time by the ordinary member of society, and that in general the collective representations of time among primitive peoples are characteristic of pre-operatory thought. We cannot deduce from this, of course, that at least some individuals in these societies, especially those such as calendrical experts, do not in fact develop an operational grasp of time, but the very small amount of psychological evidence we possess at present strongly suggests that such persons will be in a tiny minority. Theoretically, moreover, the fact that an operational grasp of time depends on the ability to dissociate it from distance and velocity and work done renders it the more likely that it cannot be operationalized independently of space, velocity, and number. The operational representation of time is greatly assisted by some means of replicating uniform and partitionable motion, especially (but not necessarily) by the use of some form of clock, such as an hour-glass or water-clock, which are not found in primitive societies.

I shall seek to show, therefore, that the *collective representations* of time in primitive society are pre-operatory, and do not depend on a co-ordination of succession, simultaneity, and duration, and that primitive time is not uniform, continuous, or homogeneous, being indissociated from spatial concepts, action, and the structure of social relations.

We may usefully begin our analysis with an examination of the kinds of seriation and colligation of durations involved in calendars. In the first place, primitives are primarily concerned with weather, with the qualities of seasonal variations and their prediction, rather than with time-reckoning as such:

For the Homeric Greeks time was not homogeneous; it had quality; it differed at large for the whole world within the horizon. There are all the changes of the day from dawn to the end of night, all the changes of the year from the beginning of spring on through summer, autumn, and winter. For the Romans time was weather, weather time, *tempus, tempestas*; and the thought survives in the modern French idiom: *il fait mauvais temps*, etc. (Onians 1954: 411)
[and]

The early Greeks [e.g. Hesiod] felt that different portions of time had different quality and brought this change or that, favoured this activity or that, ὧραι [such that the different portions of time, the months and days, each had their unique quality, favourable or unfavourable for this activity or that.] Thus the fortunes or activities of human beings on a day were attributed to that day. It was spoken of as if it were alive, a personal spirit, δαίμων (cf. ὧραι) (ibid. 413)

Onians continues:

Hesiod defines the qualities of recurring seasons and days for whole classes of beings. Homer is concerned with individual men and individual times, recognising that time differs for different persons or collections of persons, even though they may be near together in space, e.g. victor and vanquished; for each it is coloured with this or that, is experienced as this or that fate. The particular phase of fortune had duration, was time experienced. The most natural unit is the day. Homer identifies the 'day' with the fate experienced, speaks of the fate as the ἦμαρ, αἴσιμον ἦμαρ (cf. μόρσιμον ἦμαρ, ὀλέθριον ἦμαρ) means not the date, but the fate of death, visualised, conceived as concrete, put in a balance and weighed. In such phrases ἦμαρ is the fate experienced by the individual, not the daylight universally shared, and it does not last just a day but is a phase of fortune of greater or lesser duration. (Ibid. 413–14)

It is perfectly possible to manage an agricultural system without any calendar at all, as we find, for example, in New Guinea (although it should be noted that tuber agriculture, especially in a climate such as that of New Guinea, is seasonally less differentiated than cereal or grain agriculture). Girard says of the Buang of New Guinea:

The impossibility of conceptualizing the future unfolding of the different phases of a season phenomenon displays itself in a particularly surprising way when we try to discover from a group of men how, in the course of the agricultural year, they will carry out the necessary work in the cultivation of yams, to which they devote the major part of their efforts. On this particular evening it was impossible for us to obtain any information on the order of the tasks with which they would occupy themselves in the weeks and months to come for the successful cultivation of this plant. This failure could not be attributed to any ill-will; a few days later, two of our informants did not hesitate to make a detour of several hours' journey to come and inform us that they had just seen the passage of a certain migratory bird which indicated that the time had come for beginning a particular task in the gardens. They do not represent to themselves, in their totality, the agricultural tasks to be carried out in the course of the year;

the appropriate moment for beginning each of them is not determined by the counting of time; it is the appearance of a seasonal phenomenon of similar periodicity which is taken as the reference point. It is for this reason that the garden magician (*prêtre agricole*), on whom falls the responsibility of ensuring the prosperity of the yams of the group, who chooses the plots to cultivate from the fallow land, and who decides the appropriate moment for undertaking the different tasks, does not rely on the counting of years, months or days: he derives his knowledge from an acute and attentive observation of the different signs which nature affords him. (Girard 1968–9: 173–4)

In the same way, with regard to the duration of pregnancy, '... although the women make the connection between the cessation of the menses and pregnancy, they do not calculate the period of gestation. To know if their delivery is close, they do not depend on the reckoning of time but on the position taken by the child' (ibid. 173).

For the practical purposes of primitive life, therefore, it is possible to depend on empirical correlations of regularly recurring events in nature, such as seasonal fluctuations in winds and rain, the appearance and disappearance of stars and constellations, bird migrations, the order of flowering of certain species of plants, and so on. It is interesting, however, that the Buang were apparently incapable even of listing the sequence of these natural events, despite the absence of a lunar calendar.

Indeed, in the correlation of human activities with natural phenomena, the natural phenomena need not be given priority as an empirical yardstick with which to estimate the duration of the human activity. Gell writes of the Umeda,

... when walking between villages with a youth, I remarked to him on the rather leisurely pace we were keeping, suggesting that we might not arrive before dark. He (knowing perfectly well that there was no danger of this, as it proved) assured me that if we were to walk fast, then the sun would go down correspondingly quickly, whereas if we stuck to our leisurely pace, then the sun would do likewise. In short, lunar or other astronomical indices of time were not considered to be more rigidly or accurately determinate than any other events, a yardstick against which they could be measured, but simply on a par with human activities, the seasonal cycle, biological processes, the weather etc., all of which hang together in an unanalysed way, but none of which was seen as the prime mover of all the rest. (Gell 1975: 163)

Because activities are basic to primitive experience of duration, they produce an incommensurable set of time divisions as among the Tiv:

For Tiv, time is divided by natural and social events into different sorts of periods, but since the events often belong to different logical series, there is little attempt to correlate the different sorts of division of time. Tiv make no attempt to correlate moons with markets or either with agricultural activities, or seasons. If one asks how many 'moons' there are in a year, the answer varies between ten and eighteen; if one asks the number of markets in a moon, the answer varies between three and eight; if the number of days in a moon, between ten and fifty. (Bohannan 1967: 323)

Nor are the subdivisions of days capable of quantitative seriation. For example, a typical subdivision of the day is that of the Konsò:

first light	*parāë*
just before sunrise	*janjamīda*
sunrise	*birtota*
sunrise until 9 a.m.	*tēganda*
9 a.m.–11 a.m.	*gudāda*
11 a.m.–2 p.m.	*guiada'guta*, or *tagalida*
2 p.m.–4 p.m.	*kalagalla*
4 p.m.–5 p.m.	*harsheda akalagalla*
5 p.m.–6 p.m.	*kakalseema* (when the cattle
sunset	return home)
6 p.m.–7 p.m.	*dumateta*
7 p.m.–8 p.m.	*shisheeba* (twilight and sunset)
	shisheeba'guta (when it becomes
8 p.m. and for a time	quite dark)
after	*edowa* (suppertime)
night	*halgeta*

(the use of hours here is only approximate)

Evidently, it is impossible by this system to say that three *shisheebas* are one *gudada*, or that from *teganda* to *guiada'guta* is the same as from *kalagalla* to *edowa*, not only because the units are vaguely defined in boundary and duration, but because they overlap with others and are not in fact quantified at all. The same may be true of divisions of the year, even if they are expressed as months. For example, among the Nuer,

It is true that the year is divided into twelve lunar units, but Nuer do not reckon in them as fractions of a unit. They may be able to state in what month an event occurred, but it is with great difficulty that they reckon the relation between events in abstract numerical symbols. They think much more easily in terms of activities and of successions of activities and in terms of social structure and of structural differences than in pure units of time. (Evans-Pritchard 1940: 103–4)

And of the Tiv Bohannan says:

Although there are various named periods during the day and various named seasons during the year, there is no word which means a sub-division of a day, and there is no word for 'season'. There is no notion of periods of the day which can be counted; nothing of which you can say that there are four or five between dawn and dusk. Likewise, it is impossible to say that there are four or five 'seasons' or 'sub-seasons' during the wet season, for there is no generalized thing in the Tiv idea which can be counted. (Bohannan 1967: 323)

There is clear evidence that for many primitive peoples there is no such entity as a 'year' with a definite beginning and ending and of which the months are seen a sub-units and the days sub-units of months. As Nilsson pointed out, primitive time tends to be punctiform rather than based on units of definite duration. That is, when reckoning the number of days or months or years between two events, one point in a recurring series is chosen as representing the whole, e.g.

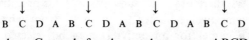

(where C stands for the total sequence ABCD)

Usually we find that 24-hour periods are reckoned in 'nights' or 'sleeps', 365-day years in winters, and months in new moons. It might be argued that 'sleeps' and 'winters' are not points of time, like, e.g., the edge of the sun's disc at the moment when it rises above the horizon. But the significance of the reliance on qualitatively distinct events in a recurring sequence is that it is not necessary to ascribe any fixed duration to a sleep or a winter, or to conceptualize the *total* sequence at all. Time periods conceived in such a way need not therefore be assigned any definite beginning or end, and so the chosen event ('sleep' or 'winter') will not be related to that totality as part to whole. Intuitive recollection is sufficient to ensure, given the regularity of cyclical change in nature, that we can calculate the passing of time by choosing a single element of the series as standing in place of the whole series, and so it is that for many primitive peoples the year has no month which is convention-ally accepted as being the first of the year.

Even when the successive moons are counted and named through the annual seasonal cycle, they do not necessarily form an independent system of units dissociated from the activities of daily life, as Evans-Pritchard notes of the Nuer, who have a year of twelve lunar months:

I do not think that they ever experience the same feeling of fighting against time or having to co-ordinate activities with an abstract passage of time, because their points of reference are mainly the activities themselves, which are generally of a leisurely character. Events follow a logical order, but they are not controlled by an abstract system, there being no autono-mous points of reference to which activities have to conform with pre-cision. (Evans-Pritchard 1940: 103)

Indeed, because the periods of the earth's rotation on its axis, its revolution about the sun, and the moon's rotation about the earth, are causally independent, they are not exactly commensurable, and because the seasonal sequence is also liable to considerable fluctua-tions, it is very difficult to build up any unified calendrical system, and in particular to base a year on a sequence of twelve lunar months if the year is also to remain in a stable relationship with the seasons—a problem which produces the necessity for inter-calation.[3] We therefore find many examples of primitive calendars with well over twelve names for months, from which the most appropriate name (for an activity) may be selected to suit the prevailing climatic conditions or agricultural activities.

Thus the Masai have twelve months, but they can repeat one of them if necessary:

The great rains cease with *loo-'n-gokwa*, which is named from the evening setting of the Pleiades. Should the rains still continue at the beginning of the following month, the Masai say: 'We have forgotten, this is *loo-'n-gokwa*'. Should the hot season not be over at the beginning of the month following *ol-oiborare*, they say: 'We have forgotten, this is *ol-oiborare*'. (Hollis 1905: 334, adapted by Nilsson, 1920)

Goodenough (1951) in a paper on the navigational and calendrical system of the Central Caroline Islands gives valuable data on the synchronization of lunar and sidereal calendars on Ngulu Island,

[3] See below, pp. 355–6.

which seems to require an operatory understanding of time by those responsible for devising the system and maintaining it.

As we saw in the earlier chapter on space, the navigators in this area use a star compass for plotting courses, based on the rising and setting positions of various stars. The navigators of most of the Central Carolines use a calendar composed of twelve star months (months in which a particular first rises), which are of necessity of varying durations:

Each month begins with the first appearance at dawn in the east of the star for which it is named. The sidereal year begins with the heliacal rising of either the Pleiades or Antares. Some calendars, therefore, name a month for the Pleiades. The solar year in the southwestern islands begins when the sun rises in the compass position marked by Altair. (Goodenough 1951: 109) [See Figure 25]

In Ngulu, however, the navigators

... divide the year into twelve lunar months, with a thirteenth for leap years, but arbitrarily name them for constellations following the sidereal calendar

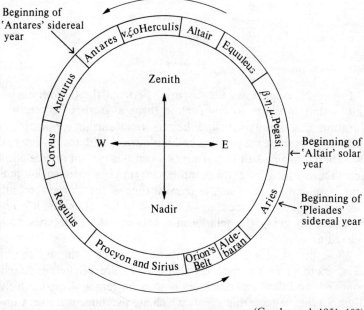

(Goodenough 1951: 109)

Figure 25

of their neighbours. Keeping the sidereal calendar as well, they have learned how the lunar and sidereal months of similar name change their relationship to one another and use the extra lunar month to bring the two calendars back in phase in leap years. (Ibid. 109)

In other words, they are aware of the different durations of two series of time units, the lunar and sidereal series of months, and are capable of bringing them back into the original relationship by a coseriation involving the interposition of an additional element. (This relationship between the lunar and sidereal series is essentially similar to that of the two flasks experiment which will be discussed later in this chapter.) Thus in order to co-ordinate the two sequences, it is necessary to conceptualize them.

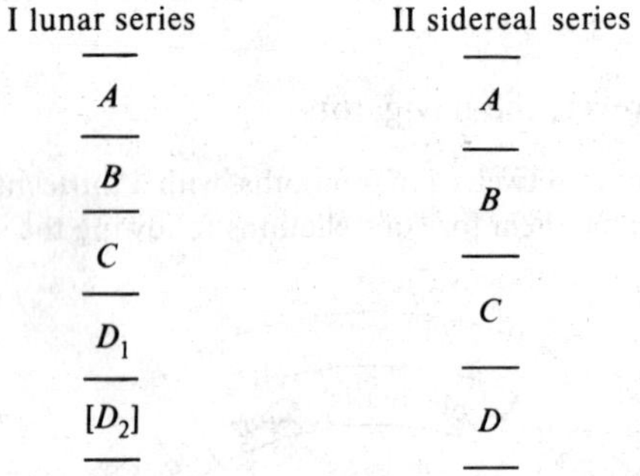

I lunar series	II sidereal series
A	A
B	B
C	
	C
D_1	
$[D_2]$	D

Figure 26

Figure 26 exaggerates the disparity between the two series, but shows that in order to co-ordinate them a grasp of succession, duration, and simultaneity and their interrelationship is essential, in order to appreciate the position and timing of the intercalary interval D_2. There is an evident difference between this type of intercalation and that in which the extra month(s) are simply dependent on putting in an extra month, e.g. at harvest time, if the 'harvest' month has already passed at the time of harvest. In the latter case it is not necessary to grasp the relationship between the two series considered as *wholes*.

While primitive societies may therefore employ the notions of days, months, and sometimes years, these are often not clearly bounded, and time-reckoning tends to be in terms of qualitatively distinct types of recurring events which are incommensurable. Consequently it is difficult to find any means of representing time as a uniform flow which occurs at the same rate in different places simultaneously,[4] and at the same rate at different dates in the past, present, and future. So the co-ordination of events rests entirely upon the memory of chains of events, and the structure of social relations.

Tiv are capable of direct correlation of two events in the past, or the life cycle of the individual, e.g.

'That market hadn't yet moved when my eldest son was born, for I bought camwood there to rub on him' is made specific by the fact that one can see the son and so get some idea of the time involved. 'The Europeans came after I had been circumcized, but before I married' is a typical expression of time indication over such a longer period of time. (Bohannan 1967: 324)
[and]
Tiv, by and large, do not even correlate events over a period of time beyond a generation or two. There is only a dim 'long ago' (ngise) which can be increased by saying 'long long ago' (ngise ngise)—the more times you say the word, the longer ago or further removed it was.

It is interesting that the Konso who, in the Garati region, reckon years by a fixed and necessary sequence of eighteen sacred-drum holders, do not use this device when it comes to making quantitative estimates of duration. I was given a text by a well-informed and intelligent old man, which correlated the arrival of the Amhara in Konsoland, in 1897, with this drum-holder sequence. His method was to state that the Amhara came when X family held the sacred drum, and then to enumerate the successive holders in each cycle down to the latest holder, but he did not conclude from this that so many years, or even so many cycles, had elapsed during this period—his conception of this duration was entirely qualitative and structural.

Hallowell records of the Saulteaux Indians, 'just as they will reply to the query: How many children have you? by naming them, a direct request for the number of "moons" will result in the naming of them one after another' (Hallowell 1937: 669). The generational sequence of a descent group, or of a succession of age-sets, 'structural time', as Evans-Pritchard terms it, does provide a basis of time-reckoning but one which is no different in kind from other

---

[4] Whorf 1956: 63 notes that the Hopi do not regard time as synchronous in different places, and Prince (1969) found the same idea among New Guinea University students.

types of primitive time-reckoning. It is evident that in the case of a lineal-descent group, the social relations between the generations, and between collateral relatives of the same generation, are products of elapsed time. The same is evidently true of a sequence of age-sets, but Evans-Pritchard points out:

We have remarked that the movement of structural time is, in a sense, an illusion, for the structure remains fairly constant and the perception of time is no more than the movement of persons, often as groups, through the structure. Thus age-sets succeed one another for ever, but there are never more than six in existence and the relative positions occupied by these six sets at any time are fixed structural points through which actual sets of persons pass in endless succession ... the Nuer system of lineages may be considered a fixed system, there being a constant number of steps between living persons and the founder of their clan and the lineages having a constant position relative to one another. (Evans-Pritchard 1940: 107)
[and]
Beyond the annual cycle, time reckoning is a conceptualization of the social structure, and the points of reference are a projection into the past of actual relations between groups of persons. It is less a means of co-ordinating events than of co-ordinating relationships, and is therefore mainly a looking-backwards, since relationships may be explained in terms of the past. (Ibid. 108)

Lineage and age-set 'time' is thus purely qualitative, and 'simultaneity' can be translated as 'of same generational level' or as 'initiated in the same ceremony'; and 'succession' as 'inheritance'; while 'duration' is a qualitatively perceived interval between the birth of one generation and the next.

In the Cushitic generation-grading or *gada* systems, the duration of the interval between one initiation ceremony and the next rests upon a fixed number of years, but it does not appear that this number is made the basis of any further quantitative reasoning. It is true to say, however, that in the generation-grading system we seem to come very close to an institution whose understanding requires an operatory concept of time, as can be seen from the way in which these systems can conserve a quantitative relationship between the grading of successive generations and correlate these with the annual cycles.

(Generation-grading systems differ from age-grading systems in that one's position in a generation-grading system depends not on one's actual age but upon that of one's father, and a son must be a fixed number of grades behind him.) An example of one of the Konso systems, from Turo region, will clarify this.

There are four grades, Raga, Pulada, Dalda, and Farida, a person remaining in each grade for only five years, with the exception of Raga, in which a man remains for the rest of his life. Each man is also a member of a named set in which he remains permanently, every set being simultaneously promoted every five years into a senior grade, except that in Raga no promotion is possible, and the sets in it are differentiated by mutual seniority alone. What is distinctive, cognitively speaking, about this system by comparison with ordinary age-grading systems is the linking between the sets of fathers and sons and successive generations, so that eldest sons occupy the set immediately senior to younger sons, and a fixed interval separates these categories of sons from similar categories of *their* sons, e.g. as in Table XIX.

TABLE XIX

Fathers		Sons	
eS	$\longleftrightarrow$	eS	6 sets
eS	$\longleftrightarrow$	yS	7 sets
yS	$\longleftrightarrow$	eS	5 sets
yS	$\longleftrightarrow$	yS	6 sets

This relationship can be seen more clearly in Figure 27.

In Figure 27 we have a homogeneous series of units, each of which has acquired its name five years before the previous unit on reaching Pulada grade and being allowed to marry. Each unit of fathers is separated generationally by a determinate number of units from that of the sons, the same principle applying to eldest sons and younger sons. There is then a partitioned series of units, in which the units are in a fixed relationship of units to other units, and the whole series corresponds to a quantified reckoning of time based on five-year intervals. Now it is very likely that those mainly responsible for co-ordinating this and the other Konso generation-grading systems were able to envisage the working of the systems as wholes. However, this is not the case even with intelligent informants with whom I discussed the systems during field-work. They are quite unable to state the relationships between the sets of the two categories, of fathers and sons, in quantitative terms of the

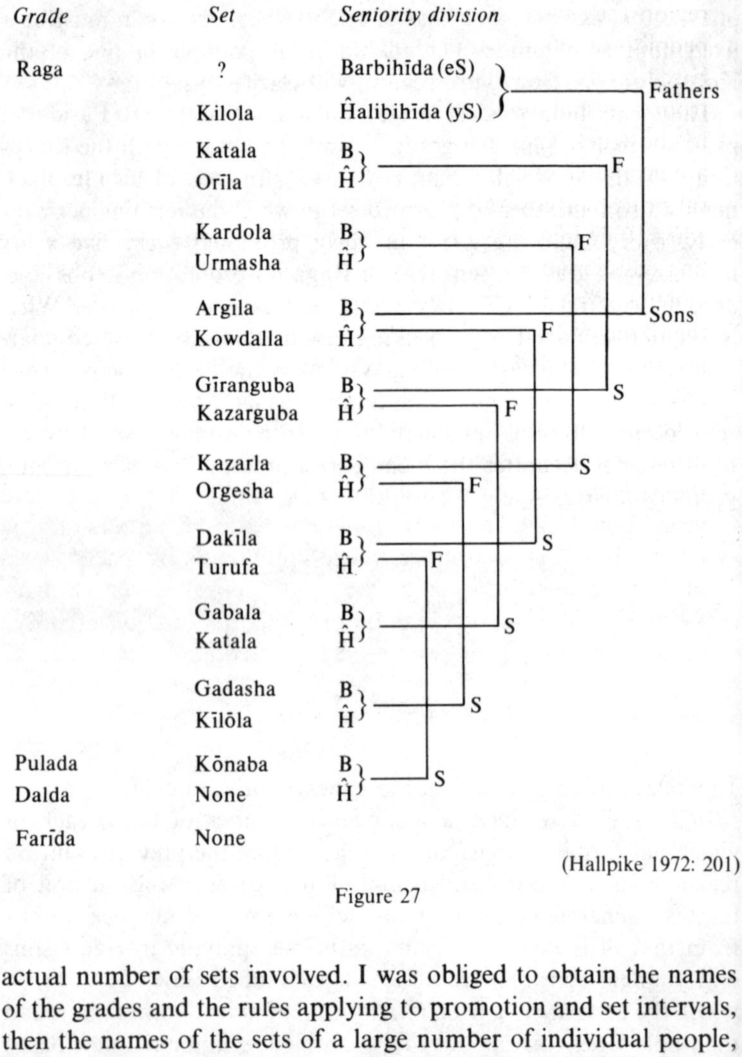

Grade	Set	Seniority division
Raga	?	Barbihīda (eS)
	Kilola	Ĥalibihīda (yS)
	Katala	B
	Orīla	Ĥ
	Kardola	B
	Urmasha	Ĥ
	Argīla	B
	Kowdalla	Ĥ
	Gīranguba	B
	Kazarguba	Ĥ
	Kazarla	B
	Orgesha	Ĥ
	Dakīla	B
	Turufa	Ĥ
	Gabala	B
	Katala	Ĥ
	Gadasha	B
	Kīlōla	Ĥ
Pulada	Kōnaba	B
Dalda	None	Ĥ
Farīda	None	

(Hallpike 1972: 201)

Figure 27

actual number of sets involved. I was obliged to obtain the names
of the grades and the rules applying to promotion and set intervals,
then the names of the sets of a large number of individual people,
together with the sets of their fathers and sons, and to find out if
these were eldest or younger sons, and then finally to obtain a list
of all the sets in order of seniority. On the basis of this I was then
able to reconstruct the relations between the sets as shown in
Figure 27.

One finds that the people themselves perceive these systems in
terms of large numbers of persons known to them. In the Takadi

region they were able to tell me correctly the grades of fifty-two people out of fifty-four. Clearly, their mastery of the system is based on a wide knowledge of particular facts and does not derive from a formal model of the type that the anthropologist is obliged to construct. They are aware of the rules governing the system, but are incapable of expressing them verbally or of discussing the general principles governing the systems and the varying distortions to which they may be subject, as a result, for example, of men begetting children at an unusually late age. This inability to analyse the systems explicitly, despite their rigorous rules, but only to live them, seems clear evidence that the vast majority of the Konso do not understand them and their temporal aspects at an operational level.

On structural grounds, the Tiv believe that their genealogies prove that they are more numerous now than they were in the past; the parents' generation must always be smaller than their children's generation. 'That Tiv say they increase with the passage of generations is primarily a cosmographical notion, and its spatial aspect is of vastly greater importance than its temporal aspect' (Bohannan 1967: 326). They also believe that the amount of their territory has always increased from generation to generation.

In primitive society, then, temporal concepts are inherently socio-spatial concepts. Pocock rightly points out that the wider the co-ordination, the greater the unification and systematization that will be imposed on time-reckoning:

It does not need to be argued at length that the more diverse are the activities of a number of people or groups, the more abstract and systematic must be the time-reckoning if any form of co-ordination is desired or effected. The larger co-ordination subsumes the less. This is true of political activity as much as of economic activity. Two men who go out separately to fish in the morning can arrange to meet again when the fish are no longer rising. This event will bring them together at roughly the same time. If one has gone to hunt and another to fish, some other indication than their activities must be found, such as the position of the sun. In political organization the activity ... of a political group overrules the activities of the smaller groups. (Pocock 1967:307)

But while primitive time-reckoning may have, in its structural aspects, greater or lesser degrees of generality, it is still qualitative and an integral part of social relations and activities, not dissociated from them:

Tiv have not elicited the time element implicit in their lineage and political structure any more than they have elicited 'time' from the course of a human life, the recurrence of the phases of the moon or of five-day markets. Time is implicit in Tiv thought and speech, but it is not a category of it. (Bohannan 1967: 328)

Structural time is in fact indistinguishable, formally speaking, from spatial time, in so far as the points of reference—generations, descent groups, and age groups—are in fixed, irreversible relations to each other and to the individual who passes through the social system. (The only difference is that the individual cannot even displace himself in the case of structural time, whereas he can move about in space.) Among the Tiv, 'the word *cha* means "far" and is used of space, of time, and of kinship. However, such words are not dependent on time indication or reckoning for their primary meanings' (Bohannan 1967: 315). In so far as primitive time does not involve the correlation of different velocities and has no grasp of the compensatory relationship between distance and velocity, or of quantifiable and reversible seriations of temporal units, it is therefore basically spatial and events can be referred to as 'far', or 'near', 'distant', 'behind' or 'in front', 'after' and 'before', and so on. (We, of course, use precisely this spatial conception of time in many of our ordinary time-reckonings, but in addition we also have operational time concepts available to us.)

It is particularly noteworthy that many Konsiña words for time and movement can be used for space and movement. *Ħata isegi* means 'Long ago, it is far'. *Porra isegi* means 'the path is far'. In the same way *idehi*, 'it is near', can be used of a place or an event, or a month, or a day. Words of movement can also be used in spatial and temporal contexts, e.g. *loalla ideni*, 'the cattle are coming', and *Sambatta ideni*, 'Sunday is coming'. *Mackina paleda itarbe*, 'the car has passed the town', and *Pardubota itarbe*, 'Pardubota (month of) has passed'. *Kodasede ibiramde*, 'this work has been finished', and *parama ibiramde*, 'this year is ended' . . .

I think they do conceive the sequence of years, months, and days as analogous to points on a journey, landmarks on a path along which they are going . . . The word for future, *turoba*, is a good illustration of this, as it can also be used in the sense of 'beyond', spatially—*irõda turoba*, 'beyond the hill'. (Hallpike 1972: 175)

A further illuminating account of the spatialization of time is given by Middleton in his account of the Lugbara cosmology:

Lugbara apply one conceptual scheme (which we can express only in the separate categories of time and space) to both of two situations: to the mythical and genealogical past and to the contemporary social environment. In mythical and genealogical distance any actual or comparative time-scale is irrelevant. In the myths of origin and that of the coming of the Europeans the same thematic pattern emerges. Similarly any actual or comparative scale of topographical distance is irrelevant to the spatial categories. The same thematic pattern is found in the socio-spatial categories of any group anywhere in Lugbara. It does not matter that for one group the beings with superhuman powers or inverted attributes live ten miles away and for another group they live twenty or fifty miles away ... In both schemes the essential distinction is between the close people— members of one's own field of social relations, validated by genealogical tradition—and the distant inverted people, who are outside the field of social relations and outside genealogical tradition. (Middleton 1960: 237)

Thus social distance is expressed in spatial terms, which among the Lugbara are not differentiated from the temporal, both dimensions also being united in terms of social behaviour.

There are clearly degrees of inversion, corresponding to degrees of social distance. In general inverted beings are asocial and their behaviour is amoral, outside the system of authority, but the degrees of asociability and

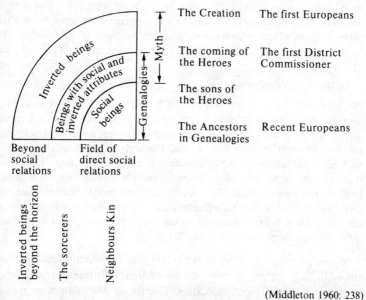

(Middleton 1960: 238)

Figure 28   Lugbara categories of social space and time

amorality vary in different circumstances: the incestuous cannibals are more inverted than are the sorcerers, and are socially far more remote, being in fact beyond contact altogether. The more remote the being, the more its behaviour is conceived as being the utter negation of that to do with kinship: for an ordinary man to eat his own children is for Lugbara beyond comprehension, whereas to ensorcell someone is not. (Ibid. 237–8)

While the tenses of verbs necessarily have a temporal relevance, we find that in the languages of primitive societies, as in those of literate civilizations, their verbs express *aspect* rather than tense. Lyons (1977) distinguishes between 'tense' and 'aspect' by treating tense as inherently involving an explicit or implicit reference to the time of utterance, whereas aspect is concerned simply with the quality of the actions or events referred to—whether they are complete/incomplete, continuous/discontinuous, durative/instantaneous, isolated or taking place as part of a sequence of events, and so on—and not with locating the point in time of the utterance with relation to some other point in time past, present, or future. Lyons also remarks that

Aspect is, in fact, far more commonly to be found throughout the languages of the world than tense is: there are many languages that do not have tense, but very few, if any, that do not have aspect. Furthermore, it has been argued recently that aspect is ontogenetically more basic than tense, in that children whose native language has both, come to master the former more quickly than they do the latter (cf. Ferreiro, 1971). (Lyons 1977: 705)

In the case of New Guinea languages, for example,

Workers with the Summer Institute of Linguistics report that in at least some of the Melanesian languages there is no time marking system in the verb at all, and that in some of these languages there are also very limited numbers of other time marking words. The verb tense or aspect will relate to reality and unreality, or to completion and incompletion. These two pairs of aspects, both in a somewhat different way, may be used to give a kind of time indication. But it is a very different time indication from our own. The root ideas behind completion and incompletion are very different from those behind past and future, and the concepts of reality are quite different again. (Prince 1969: 72)

While primitive peoples make references to velocity and distance they do not normally need to co-ordinate different trajectories or motions at different velocities. Durations are dealt with by referring to activities that are intuitively familiar to all, e.g. the cooking of rice, the burning of a torch, the time to traverse a standard distance, and so on. But these durational models provided by such familiar activities and processes cannot be compared and colligated by means of unitary measurement into a scale or series: 'The Saulteaux are confined to gross time estimates and relatively simple qualitative judgements about speed based upon the observation and comparison of objects in their immediate environment. It would be impossible for them to measure the rate of moving objects at all' (Hallowell 1937: 669).

Thus a really significant aspect of primitive time-reckoning is the absence of any units of time for small durations, equivalent to our 'minute' and 'hour', which can be used in the co-ordination of the velocities of objects. Whereas the day (from sunrise to sunset, or from sunset to sunrise), the lunar month, and the sidereal 365-day year are natural phenomena, smaller divisions of time require man himself to be able to produce an arbitrary and regular motion which can be divided into units, and this has historically only arisen with sand-glasses and water-clocks. To appreciate the significance and utility of these clocks requires, of course, an operational concept of time—it would be quite wrong to suggest that clocks *lead* to operational time concepts; they merely facilitate their acquisition, but may still be understood in a pre-operatory manner:

Those Tiv who are acquainted with the idea of 'hours' from Europeans seem to have changed the idea somewhat: Tiv servants and clerks use the word *ahwa* for 'hour'. Besides its obvious similarity to the English word, this is a plural form of *ihwa*, which means 'mark' or 'tally'. One o'clock is 'one mark' and six o'clock means 'six marks'. They are, in fact, counting the marks on a watch, I believe quite unaware that the watch is merely a device for counting standardized symbols for artificial units of time. (Bohannan 1967: 328)

Primitive time, like primitive space, is therefore not a dynamic system of reversible correlations and transformations of units, but a static, 'spatialized', series of irreversible relationships between fixed points and intervals of varying and overlapping duration which are differentiated from one another not as part to whole or in quantitative terms, but on the basis of their qualitative features, and cannot therefore provide the basis for the conception of a homogeneous, universal, and uniform notion of time.

3. PIAGET'S EXPERIMENTS ON THE UNDERSTANDING OF TIME

Piaget's work on time relies in particular on the results of an experiment whose design is basic to his analysis of time and to his elucidation of children's developing grasp of it. I shall describe this experiment before considering his analysis of the logic of an operatory grasp of its implications.

We present the child with two flasks or jars, one on top of the other. The upper flask (I) is in the shape of an inverted pear. It is filled through a hole at the top, and emptied by means of a glass tap communicating with the lower flask (II). The latter is perfectly cylindrical, fairly slender, and of the same capacity as (I). [(II) is of course empty at the beginning of the experiment.] (I) is filled with water coloured with fluorescein. At regular intervals, fixed quantities of liquid from I are allowed to run into (II) until (II) is full and (I) is empty. The quantities run out from I correspond to graduated increases in the level of (II).

The subject is supplied with a series of cyclostyled drawings, showing the two empty flasks with a space between them. From the beginning of the experiment, when (I) is full and (II) empty, and thereafter at each change of level, including the last, the child is asked to indicate the respective levels in the two flasks by drawing a horizontal line on the paper in green pencil [the same colour as the liquid]. For each new level a new sheet is handed out and the experimenter must make sure that the levels of both (I) and (II) are drawn in clearly enough for the child to distinguish them afterwards. When all the liquid has been transferred, the sheets (6–8) are shuffled and the child is asked to put them in order ... (Piaget 1970: 7)

If the child can achieve this, the sheets are then cut in two horizontally, so as to separate the drawings of I from II, and shuffled together, and the child is asked to reorder them. 'Naturally this task is more difficult ... because (I) has to be arranged in descending order and (II) in ascending order of levels, and the two have to be put into one–one correspondence' (ibid. 8).

This experiment has the following analytical characteristics:

1. There are two simultaneous motions, which can be observed together, but which are spatially distinct. (The minute time difference between opening the tap, and the jet of water landing in II does not affect the experiment, nor does the slight change of pressure in the upper flask as it empties.)

2. The motions are in opposite directions and of different

velocities, owing to the variable dimensions of I and the constant dimensions of II. Thus water appears initially to rise more quickly in II than it falls in I, but towards the end of the experiment this relationship is reversed, and the water appears to rise more slowly in II than it falls in I.

3. There is a causal link between the two flasks, supplied by the tap which controls the flow of water.

4. The sequence is divided into a set of clear stages, and is not a continuous process.

5. The velocity of the flow, the lengths of the intervals, and the graduated increases of level in II are uniform.

The problems to be mastered are therefore those of seriation (of the successive levels in I and II separately); the co-seriation and colligation of the successive levels in I and II considered together; the comparative estimation of the duration of each interval in I and II considered separately; the estimation of the simultaneities of each interval; and most important, the distinction between the factors of velocity and distance as observed in the rates at which the levels in the two flasks change. The child is not required to co-ordinate a continuous variation because a set of stages is built into the experiment, nor is he required to solve a problem of variable velocities—as we have already seen, the velocity of water flow from the tap is constant.

It will be immediately apparent that this experiment demands the child's ability to conserve quantity, since until he can grasp that at the end of the experiment flask II now contains exactly the same amount of water as was originally in flask I, he will be in no position to appreciate the causal, and temporal, significance of the tap between the two flasks, as the effective causal 'guarantor' of simultaneity.

Piaget has worked out the logical structure of an operatory awareness of the relationships between simultaneity, succession, and duration. I shall now present this, before considering the successive stages in the development of children's understanding of them as revealed in Piaget's experiments.

If the water in I moves through the stages I_1; I_2; I_3; ... this defines a direction or succession of spatial states which may be written symbolically as $I_1 \xrightarrow{a} I_2 \xrightarrow{a'} I_3$, where $\rightarrow$ denotes 'precedes', and 'a', 'a'' are labels for the duration of the intervals between successive states.

So if I_1 precedes I_2, and I_2 precedes I_3, then I_1 precedes I_3, an additive grouping of asymmetrical relations, or qualitative seriation; 'qualitative' because for the present no use of units of measurement is involved, which is the criterion of quantitative seriation.

But all cases of real motion must involve time as well as space. Yet if we consider only cases of *single* relations of motion, it is not necessary, or even analytically possible, to distinguish time sequences from spatial sequences. Space is a system of positions (placements) and changes of position (displacements); time, however, is a system of co-positions (co-placements) and co-displacements.

Figure 29.   A spatial sequence

The principal characteristic of a spatial sequence of displacements is that they are analysable in terms, for example, of difference in angular relationship without taking velocity into account. Thus A, B, and C in Figure 29 are interchangeable. Consider, however, the time sequence shown in Figure 30.

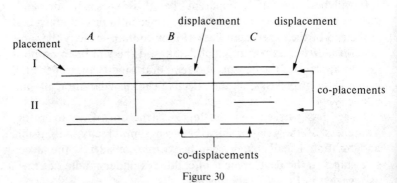

Figure 30

In Figure 30 it is the relative velocities of the objects in boxes *A, B, C* that determine in which box any spatial state is represented. If, for example, the object in II were to have moved faster, it would have produced the situation shown in Figure 31.

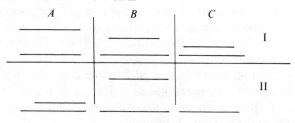

Figure 31

Thus it can be said that each co-placement defines a simultaneity; each co-seriation of distinct co-placements defines a time sequence; and each co-displacement defines duration and velocity.

Returning to the experiment of the flasks, we can say then that when we introduce, by means of II, a second motion with a different trajectory and velocity from I, we have

(1) $II_1 \xrightarrow{a} II_2$; $II_2 \xrightarrow{a'} II_3$ ... and it follows:

$II_1 \xrightarrow{\cdot b} II_3$; $II_1 \xrightarrow{c} II_4$ ...

When these stages are correlated with those of I, it produces a new system of relations between I_1 and II_1, I_2 and II_2 ...; in the first place, *simultaneity*, or null succession, which can be represented as:

(2) $I_1 \xleftrightarrow{0} II_1$; $I_2 \xleftrightarrow{0} II_2$; ...

Secondly, on the basis of the simultaneity of stages $I_1 \longleftrightarrow II_1$; $I_2 \longleftrightarrow II_2$; ... we can give 'before' and 'after' a temporal as distinct from a purely spatial significance; we can, in fact, form a *succession* of co-displacements, by combining (1) and (2) as follows:

(3)
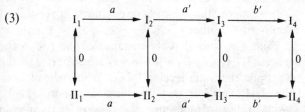

This is a multiplicative, as opposed to an additive, grouping of relations, or 'co-seriation', since we are here thinking of *two* series, instead of the elements of one only. From this representation we are able to deduce temporal as well as spatial relations, such as 'I_1 comes before II_2', or 'I_3 comes after II_1'. These relations have, of course, no spatial meaning.

They are also, as we have seen, asymmetrical (that is, $I_1 \rightarrow I_2$ but $I_2 \nrightarrow I_1$) and transitive ($I_1 \rightarrow I_2 \rightarrow I_3 \therefore I_1 \rightarrow I_3$), and being coseriative form a temporal order which co-ordinates the various positions of a system of co-displacements.

But this system of relations is also isomorphic with the system on which the colligation of durations is based, e.g. If I_1 comes before I_2 or $I_2 II_2$ before $I_3 II_3$, then we need have made no quantitative measurements of the distances or times involved to be able to deduce that the interval between I_1 and I_3, or II_3, is longer than the interval between I_1 and I_2 or II_2. The *interval* between spatial states $I_1 II_1$ and $I_2 II_2$ or $I_3 II_3$ is itself *duration* (assuming, of course, constant water flow), and there will be a symmetrical relationship between these intervals.

(4) $I_1 II_1 \xleftrightarrow{a} | I_2 II_2; I_2 II_2 \xleftrightarrow{a'} | I_3 II_3; I_3 II_3 \xleftrightarrow{b'} | I_4 II_4$, where $a = a' = b'$. If we define relations of the $\longleftrightarrow$ type as the set of all relations defined by inclusions in one and the same interval between all the possible levels, we can add them:

(4a) $(I_1 II_1 \xleftrightarrow{a} | I_2 II_2) + (I_2 II_2 \xleftrightarrow{a'} | I_3 II_3) = (I_1 II_1 \xleftrightarrow{b} | I_3 II_3)$
so $a + a' = b$.

There is, however, a further obstacle before the nature of duration as analysed here can be understood. This is the correlation between distance and velocity, and the comprehension that neither of these factors considered separately can give a correct estimate of duration. (As we shall see, children initially consider distance and velocity separately, and also suppose that time is a direct function of either of them independently of the other.)

So when the child discovers that the distance of the rise in the water level between $II_1 II_2$ (s_2) (s = distance) is greater than the distance of the drop in the water level in $I_1 I_2$ (s_1), and when he has also grasped that $I_1 II_1$ and $I_2 II_2$ are simultaneous, he will, at the operatory stage, be able to deduce that the *velocity* of the rise in level between $II_1 II_2$ (v_2) is greater than the *velocity* of the drop in level between $I_1 I_2$ (v_1). If he now also succeeds in equalizing the *durations* I_1I_2 and II_1II_2, this is because he realizes that, in relation to these durations, the greater *distance* covered by the level in II than in I $(s_2 - s_1 = s'_1)$ is also compensated by the increase in the *velocity* with which the level in II rises $(v_2 - v_1 = v'_1)$. To express the relationship in more general, and more familiar, terms, the duration of a motion of lower velocity over less distance may be equalized with the duration of a motion of greater velocity over a greater distance. (Of course, this equality only holds true in circumstances such as this experiment, where the flow of water between the two flasks is at a constant rate.)

If this common duration is called a, then

(5) $\quad a_{s_1v_1} = a_{s_2v_2}$ because $(s'_1) \times (-v'_1) = 0$

It is the realization of this relationship, that, in formal terms, $t = s/v$, enables the child in practice to equalize synchronous durations and to see that $I_1I_2 = II_1II_2$; $I_2I_3 = II_2II_3$.

Now if all intervals can be treated as distances covered at a given velocity (or as work done at a given rate) then duration becomes a whole whose parts can be colligated:

(6) $\quad a + a' = \beta$; $\beta + \beta' = \gamma$; ... where a, a', β are defined as in 4(a).

But the colligation of durations is still at the level of qualitative time, that is, it is limited to the comparison of partial and total durations. For the attainment of quantitative time, it is necessary for the child to have the mental reversibility to compare a given duration with an earlier or later one and, in this experiment, the realization that the successive amounts of water run out during each opening and closing of the tap are equal. He has the additional assistance of knowing that, causally speaking, the difference in levels $II_1II_2 = II_2II_3$ ... must also be the durational equivalents of the differences in levels $I_1I_2 = I_2I_3$ ...

This provides him with a system of units of the form

$$(I_1II_1 \xrightarrow{a} I_2II_2) = (I_2II_2 \xrightarrow{a'} I_3II_3) = (I_3II_3 \xrightarrow{\beta'} I_4II_4) \ldots \text{ from which}$$
he concludes that $\beta = a + a' = 2a$; ...

Quantitative time, involving the comparison, as opposed to the simple colligation, of successive durations, thus requires the carrying forward of a unit a from the equalization $a = a' = \beta'$, which provides us with a means of counting the units involved in every total duration $\beta = 2a$; $\gamma = 3a$ . . . The *equalization* of successive durations therefore leads to the transformation of (6) into a system of quantitative colligations:

(7) $a + a' = 2a(=\beta)$
$2a(=\beta) + a = 3a(=\gamma)$ . . .
where a, a', γ stand for:

$$I_1II_1 \xrightarrow{a} I_2II_2$$

$$I_2II_2 \xrightarrow{a'} I_3II_3$$

$$I_1II_1 \xrightarrow{\gamma} I_4II_4$$

But the equalization of two successive durations $a = a'$ calls for more than (5) $a_{s_1v_1} = a_{s_2v_2}$ because, as has been stressed throughout this exposition, although the child realizes the compensation between s and v here, he is only able to do so because in this particular experiment, the two motions begin and end simultaneously. So in practical situations other than this experiment, the equalization of two successive durations a, a' depends on a person's ability to measure *actual* velocities and distances, so that

1. If durations a and a' can be associated with a given distance and velocity (by (5) and (6)) they will be equalizable only if measurement can establish that the distances and velocities are equal too:

(8) $a_{sv} = a'_{s'v'}$, if and only if, $s = s'$, $v = v'$.

Or,

2. Durations a and a' will generally be equal if the work is done at a constant rate r,

(8a) $a_r = a'_r$, if and only if, $r = r'$.

This applies whenever the child does not simply measure time by the distance between two successive levels, but by the quantity of water displaced at a given velocity.

But the establishment of conditions 1 and 2 involves measurements not called for in operations (1) to (6), that is, the quantification of the distance traversed ($s = s'$) or of work done (or the quantity of water displaced, $r = r'$) and, above all, the quantification of the velocity as a result of which the conservation of velocity can be treated as a particular case of uniform motion. As Piaget summarizes these cognitive requirements,

In short, much more even than qualitative time, quantitative time involves a system of geometry, a system of dynamics, and a system of mechanics, all at once, since over and above the relation between the work and the rate at which it is done, it also introduces the constancy of the velocities under consideration (uniform rectilinear motion or regular periodicity). (Piaget 1970: 79)

As I emphasized at the beginning of this chapter, time is only part of the structure of the universe, being intimately associated with space and causality. It is therefore unlikely, to say the least, that we shall find collective representations of time among primitive peoples that are at the operatory level if their spatial and causal representations are pre-operatory and if there is in general an absence of operatory co-ordination of dimensional abstractions. But it will assist our analysis of primitive representations of time if we first consider the practical problems experienced by children in understanding time.

We may begin by considering the main stages in the understanding of succession and simultaneity, bearing in mind that stages I and II are pre-operatory, and stage III is that of concrete operations.

In stage I, the children are unable straight away to arrange the shuffled, uncut drawings from the flasks experiment in the correct order, without continual correction—nor can they seriate spatially at this stage either, as we saw in earlier chapters. Thus they cannot even grasp the order of succession of the water levels at all. At stage II, the child can correctly seriate each sequence of stages in flasks I and II, but cannot co-ordinate them. So while they have now acquired a coherent intuition of the physical processes of flow in each flask, they cannot master relations of co-displacement, nor, therefore, the operational relations of simultaneity and succession. Finally, at III, they are able to establish the correct serial correspondence of the two series, and therefore the mastery of succession and simultaneity. But, as we have already seen, the grasp of duration depends on the mastery of relations of succession as well as of simultaneity:

'... a child cannot be said to have grasped the simultaneity of, say, I_1 and

II_1; I_2 and II_2, etc. simply because he explains that they happened 'at the same time' or 'together'—he must also have realized that *duration* [my emphasis] I_1I_2 is equal to the *duration* II_1II_2. Similarly, the child cannot be said to have grasped the fact that I_2 precedes I_3 simply because he explains that it 'came first' or even that 'it contained more water', etc.; he must also grasp that the duration I_1I_2 or II_1II_2 is shorter than the duration I_1I_3 or II_1II_3 ... succession and simultaneity are not grasped operationally unless they lead to the construction of a system of colligated durations, much as durations are not grasped operationally until they can be placed in one to one correspondence with a system of successions and simultaneities. (Ibid. 35)

At stage I, the child supposes that duration is directly related to velocity—greater velocity = greater time and vice versa—and to distance covered or work done. Thus when he sees the level rising in flask II_1II_2 more rapidly than it falls in I_1I_2, he has no capacity to equalize those durations I_1I_2, II_1II_2. According to Piaget, the child's understanding of duration at this stage is that of 'direct intuition', as opposed to 'articulated intuition'. In direct intuition, perceptual relations are reproduced without operational or semi-operational co-ordination, though in some cases direct intuition may lead to empirically correct conclusions. For example, it leads to the correct appreciation of *fairly large displacements* in which two bodies start from virtually the same place and travel in the same direction along parallel straight lines, but not of bodies starting from points differently aligned and following diverging trajectories. In the same way with velocity, if one of the two bodies overtakes the other, it will be judged the faster, but if two bodies stop moving at the same point, whether they started from the same or from different points, their velocities are judged equal. In particular, when the two bodies pass each other out of the observer's view, but are seen to start and stop simultaneously, their velocities will generally be judged equal. Velocity, then, is not initially grasped as a ratio or relationship.

Again, with duration, direct intuition leads to the correct conclusion only when two bodies have the same velocity and start from the same point at the same moment, but do not stop simultaneously. In this case it will be correctly concluded that the motion of the one that stops first is shorter than the motion of the one that stops after it, but this is simply because it has covered a shorter *distance*.

In all these cases, direct intuition does not rely on co-ordination, compensation, or the grasp of ratios, but infers on the basis of comparisons of a single dimension—greater speed, greater distance—or of the direct comparison of similar trajectories.

In the same way, the direct intuition of inner duration leads to the correct conclusion when one of two tasks performed with equal speed is discontinued first—'It took a shorter time.' But here, too, as in the case of the two bodies moving with equal velocity, one of which stops before the other and covers less distance, shorter duration will be inferred from the fact that less *work* was done in the task that stopped first. As soon as velocities of bodies or the rate of work differ, direct intuition can no longer lead to correct conclusions, since duration has become distinct from space traversed or work done and must now be constructed from the co-ordination of the motions themselves.

Again, direct intuition is insufficient to allow the determination of simultaneities, except in the special cases when the moving bodies come to rest at the same point in space or in two distinct points after travelling with equal velocity. And the direct intuition of succession is limited to the serial position of a single body or of two bodies moving with equal velocity.

At this stage, then, apart from these special cases, duration and the order of events are not co-ordinated, nor are succession, duration, and simultaneity.

But it should also be noted that in these special cases direct intuition can lead to correct judgements of duration, simultaneity, and succession. For this reason we find children capable of using such expressions as 'before/after', 'longer/shorter', and 'at the same time as', quite correctly in many cases. Similarly, we noted that direct intuition can produce correct estimates of quantitative change, except where the dimensions of a vessel vary inversely from those of the original vessel.

At stage II, the child appreciates that duration and velocity are inversely related, and begins to understand that time intervals may be divorced from velocity or distance, but is still unable to co-ordinate these intervals. Thus he continues to assert that the duration I_1I_2 is longer than the duration II_1II_2 because the water level drops more slowly in I than it rises in II. He still cannot, therefore, correlate duration with the order of events and fit different moments of time into a unified system. Nor can he colligate partial durations and see that $I_1I_2 < I_1I_3$. This ability to seriate is what Piaget means by 'articulated intuition', 'that phase in the development of temporal concepts in which the child can reconstruct the phases of a single motion, but is not yet able to relate them to phases in the motion of other bodies' (ibid. 19).

At this stage, the child is still capable only of the seriation of two distinct displacements (by articulated intuition) and not of the co-ordination of displacements. This is because the child's thought is still centred on his subjective impressions of each of the motions in turn, instead of making an operational, reversible co-ordination of two motions simultaneously. Consequently, his notion of time is still spatialized, since while he can compare the partial to the total duration of a single activity and see, for example, as we have already noted, that $I_1 \rightarrow I_2 \rightarrow I_3$,

When it comes to the comparison of the partial duration of one process (for instance the flow II_1II_4) to the total duration of a different process, (e.g. the flow I_1I_5) it is no longer possible to fit the part into the whole by spatial perception alone. Simultaneities and successions have also to be taken into account: I_1II_1 are simultaneous, but II_4 precedes I_5, therefore I_1I_5 is of longer duration than II_1II_4. Now this kind of colligation, which is based on co-displacements and is therefore specific to time, is quite beyond children at stage II. (Ibid. 56)

Again, not only is the colligation of partial durations of separate motions beyond children at this stage (qualitative time) but they are unable to construct quantitative time because of their inability to conserve velocity. As we saw earlier, the ability to construct time units of the type

$$(I_1II_1 \xrightarrow{a} I_2II_2) = (I_2II_2 \xrightarrow{a'} I_3II_3): \beta = a + a'$$
$$\beta = 2a$$

depends on his ability to see that the water is flowing at the same rate between the two flasks, and during successive intervals, which in turn is the basis for the equalization of durations, on which the concepts of a unit rests.

Again, it requires reversibility of thought

To grasp that the duration a ($= II_1II_2$) is shorter than the duration b ($I_1I_3 = II_1II_3$), once the water has reached II_3 ($=I_3$), the child must, in effect, go back in thought to II_1 ($=I_1$) and hence be able to traverse the intervals II_1II_2, and II_1II_3 in either direction. But in that case, it is thought alone which becomes displaced: the child moves a mental clock in such a way that an hour in the past is always equal to an hour in the present or an hour in the future. In other words, before it can grasp a $(=II_1II_2)$ and a' $(=II_2II_3)$ and pose that b $(II_1II_3) = 2a$, the child must first be able to 'mobilize' the time m of the watch $(=$ the flow of the water at a certain velocity over a given distance $II_1II_2 = II_2II_3 = II_3II_4 =$ etc.) so as to apply it equally well to liquid that has flowed in the past, to liquid that is still flowing, and to liquid that will flow in the future. (Ibid. 58)

Unlike spatial measurement, time measurement cannot utilize direct displacement. It requires the reproduction of motion; the children's clock in this experiment is simply the flow of water. But the conservation of velocity is not the result of direct intuition; it involves a complex elaboration of compensation and co-ordination of co-displacements—the capacity for qualitative time grouping. And so a grasp of the conservation of velocity alone cannot be a sufficient explanation of the operatory construction of time.

At stage III the child can co-ordinate co-displacements, equalize durations, and construct quantitative as well as qualitative time.

The essential difference between stage III and stages I and II is bound up with the operatory reversibility of thought—children at II clearly appreciate the equality of the quantities of water represented by each level, but do not draw any quantitative conclusions as to the equality of the corresponding durations—for them the latter remain heterogeneous. (Ibid. 69)

4. CROSS-CULTURAL PSYCHOLOGICAL EXPERIMENTS ON THE UNDERSTANDING OF TIME AMONG PRIMITIVES

Experimental investigation of the extent to which members of primitive societies attain an operational concept of time is very difficult, and consequently has rarely been attempted. Cole, Gay, and Glick (1974) state: 'Despite the abundance of both disciplined and casual observations, almost no experimental research has been done on time measurement among non-Western peoples' (p. 174), and this assessment remains substantially true at the time of writing. Their own experiments, designed to investigate the relative accuracy of the Kpelle and American subjects in estimating explicit time intervals, are not relevant to our interests. Prince also notes that 'most published work appears to analyse the understanding of our Western terms and dating systems rather than dealing with time conceptualization in a more fundamental sense' (1969: 69), and suggests that the lack of work on time conservation 'is probably due to the extreme difficulty of experimental work in time concepts, especially if, as seems possible, conservation of time is an underlying problem' (ibid. 69). Prince himself conducted the following experiment in time-conservation in New Guinea:

Over one hundred 1968 University Preliminary Year[5] students were given a demonstration test involving time, distance and velocity in the third week of their course. Two simple pendula of identical period and amplitude were first allowed to swing in phase and questions were asked about whether they were released simultaneously, had the same period, covered the same distance and travelled at the same speed. The configuration was then altered in various ways to vary phase, amplitude and period. When the two amplitudes differed only half the students appreciated that the periods were the same, even though the pendula were in phase with each other. When two pendula of different periods were swung with the same amplitude 15% of the students thought the periods were the same and a further 30% selected the wrong one as having the longer period. (Ibid. 74)

Considering that this experiment was conducted with university students, it is quite astonishing that such a substantial proportion of subjects was unable to attain conservation. Prince notes that 'it is also not fully understood by all Preliminary Year students that the time interval which is passing here in Port Moresby is synchronously passed in Goroka, London and New York' (ibid. 74).

Time is something within the lifetime of the individual, and possibly his father's time. Beyond this, time relationships do not seem to be grasped. *The concept of time as an infinite line, along which a vast succession of events can be located, does not exist.* Hence the *temporal inter-relation of events* is not appreciated. (Ibid. 70)

M. C. Bovet's work among illiterate Algerian adult peasants, to which we alluded in Chapter 6, provides substantial evidence for the lack of an operational concept of time in primitive society. As we have seen, an operatory grasp of time requires an operatory grasp of length and speed as necessary foundations, and so in the case of Bovet's experiments it will be necessary briefly to dwell on the results of the adults' performance with problems of length and

---

[5] This year is a matriculation year, and the students are not therefore undergraduates in the usual sense.

speed before considering their responses to the problem involving time.[6]

The length problems were of the form:

to construct a straight line *B* beginning under the left extremity of *A*, of the same length as *A*. This test was conducted with six men and eighteen women, and only the six men and two of the women produced correct solutions (33 per cent of the total). After further presentations of the problem, and with much trial and error and questioning by the examiner, ten more subjects were successful. In so far as so many subjects had difficulty in understanding this problem of length, it is to be expected that they would have even greater difficulty in the conservation of speed.

Two problems of speed were presented to twenty subjects, seven men and thirteen women, thirteen of which subjects had taken part in the experiment with length.

Problem I involved two concentric paths, drawn on paper (Figure 32).

Figure 32

Subjects were all well aware that path *B* was longer than path *A*. A model car was placed at the beginning of each path, and both were started simultaneously, moved around the paths together, and stopped simultaneously. Since the cars do not pass each other, this problem tends to elicit the incorrect judgement that the speeds of *A* and *B* cars are equal.

In Problem II (Figure 33), car *A* starts first, and after a delay car *B* starts, gradually catching up with *A*, to finish simultaneously with it. This problem tends to elicit the correct judgement of relative speeds.

Seven subjects had great difficulties with both problems, five vacillated, and eight succeeded in giving operatory responses after trial and error and questions by the experimenter. Six of the eight

[6] For the following section and diagrams see Bovet 1975: 114ff.

Figure 33

were men. The chief errors were: in I considering the speeds of *A*
and *B* as equal; and in II, with the delayed departure of *B*, the
relative speeds were judged equal because both *A* and *B* stopped
simultaneously, and side by side, or else the speed of the inner
vehicle was considered greater because of its earlier departure.
These errors were similar to those observed at Geneva: side by side
= in same time = same speed; points and moments of arrival
simultaneous = equal speeds; when moments of departure delayed, first to leave = sooner = faster. A woman of thirty years
judged the speeds as equal in problem I despite being able to evaluate correctly the greater distance of *B*. After further work with
the experimenter she could judge that the speed of *B* was the greater, but could not explain why, except for saying that car *B* worked
better. When the problem was restated in terms of straight and
zigzag lines (Figure 34), the subject could tell that path *B* was
longer, but in the case of synchronous displacement she first said
that the speeds were equal, and then said that *A* was quicker, be-

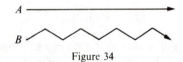

Figure 34

cause *B* was delayed by the zigzags.

Of the five subjects who gave correct answers to the length problem only two gave correct judgements on speed, and these were
those who had most easily mastered the conservation of length.

We are now in a position to consider the subjects' performances
in problems of conservation of time. It was apparently necessary to
do a great deal of preparatory work with the subjects (the same
twenty as those who took part in the speed problem), since they
had great difficulty in dissociating the idea of time from work
accomplished (activity or distance) and the speed with which this
was done. Lamps were used which lit in succession, one for a shorter time than the other; or which lit synchronously, with simultane-

ous or delayed extinction. To assist understanding, practical examples were given, such as preparing a meal, in the case of the female subjects; and cultivating a field by comparison with briefer activities, in the case of the men, together with examples based on journeys by horse and foot between near and distant villages, with simultaneous departures and arrivals. For the activities, the correct relations of durations were easily grasped, because duration is proportional to the amount of work done, but for the journeys, estimates of time were spontaneously linked to the distance covered, despite the experimenter's insistence on the simultaneity of departure and arrivals. After this preparatory work, three problems were presented, as follows:

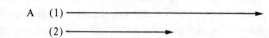

These trajectories were drawn on a sheet of paper and then followed by two toy cars, which started and stopped simultaneously. Subjects were then asked such questions as 'Which journey took longer?' 'Did one car travel for a longer time than the other or did they take the same time?' 'How did they leave, together or one before the other? How did they arrive, together or one before the other?'

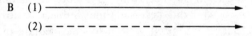

In this case trajectories were of equal length, but the departure of (2) was delayed, and it then caught up (1), so that they arrived simultaneously. The same type of questions were put as in problem A.

C   (1) ——————————————————→
     (2) —————————— — — — →

In this problem the trajectories were the same as in problem A. 1 and 2 started together but in this case (2) arrived *after* (1), thus suggesting that (2) took less time than (1), because of the shorter trajectory of (2).

The results showed that of the twenty subjects, seven could not really understand the problems at all; ten made some correct responses, but also persisted in wrong answers, while only three managed to give entirely correct answers to all the problems. Even these could only do so after trial and error, and corrections. The errors consisted, in the case of duration, in basing judgements on the distance covered, so that longer distance = longer time. In the case of A, it was said that (1) took longer; in B that they both took the same time; and in C, that (2) took less time. Duration was seldom judged in relation to speed, but often answers relating to speed alone were given instead of judgements of time. In the case of temporal sequences of departures and arrivals, there was frequent confusion with spatial order, but on the whole these were found to be the easiest questions.

A woman of fifty years, in problem A, said that journey (1) had lasted longer than (2), and that (2) had stopped before (1), thus basing her judgement on spatial order alone. In problem B, she judged the durations of the journeys as equal, and thought that the departures as well as the arrivals were simultaneous. After further demonstrations she saw that (2) had stopped after (1), but could give no judgement of the relative duration. In problem C, she said that (1) took longer than (2), her judgement being tied to the greater length of trajectory (1) or its greater speed. While correct in saying that (1) passes (2), she was mistaken in thinking that they arrived together. This subject had given poor responses in the experiments on length.

Among the eight subjects who gave correct answers on speed were the three who did best on time. Subjects who were at the intermediate level on speed were also intermediate or inferior on time, while subjects who had serious difficulties with speed failed in time, or could not grasp the problem at all. Even when experiment C of the time problem was eliminated, since it is harder than its equivalent C in the speed problem, time still remained conspicuously harder than speed. While the men performed better than the women in problems of length and speed, the time problems were equally difficult for both sexes. Bovet suggests that men performed better than women in length and speed problems because these were less relevant to the daily activities of women, whose life is spent in domestic tasks, whereas problems of time are equally irrelevant to both sexes.

Bovet substantiates Piaget's theory that pre-operatory time is spatialized:

Yet we have noted that the general error consists in judging duration according to the length of the tracks in the experimental situations, and not according to the speed of the displacements. In the same way, in the

accounts of journeys used as an introduction [to the tests], a longer duration was always ascribed to the person who had covered the longer distance. This dominance of length seems to show that, in the interrelationship
of factors at work there—temporal and spatial orders, speed, length, and
duration—the spatial dimension is the best structured aspect and accordingly the most easily differentiated. Even the temporal order reveals itself
as still closely attached to the spatial order, as we have observed. As for
speed, we have seen to what extent it is only apprehended with difficulty
other than in situations of perceptible overtaking. Without doubt, the fact
that it is not invoked with respect to duration is due to its very labile
status. (Bovet 1975:121–2)

Thus the fundamental distinction between primitive, pre-operatory conceptions of time and those of concrete and formal operations, which we employ in many areas of our thinking, is that primitive time is based on sequences of qualitatively different events,
such as those of the seasons or of daily activities. In such cases it is
evident that these qualitative sequences may be peculiar to each
community, giving rise to an identification of 'this time' with 'this
place', so that it becomes impossible to co-ordinate duration, simultaneity, and succession from place to place, while the flow of
time will appear to proceed at different rates depending on the
nature of the activities. This mode of time-reckoning inherently
involves incommensurable periods, and because the sequence of
those customary and concrete events used for time-reckoning is
usually cyclical in nature, it is also unvarying, which adds to its
irreversible and static quality, static in the sense that each event is
uniquely linked with its predecessor and successor. Such a sequence
of events is thus closely comparable to a landscape, with each land-
mark in a fixed relationship with every other. Relations of time can
therefore be comprehended by spatial concepts such as near, far,
beyond, behind, and so on. In addition, as Bovet points out, the
fact that spatial representations may be better structured than those
of time will be further reason for the 'spatialization' of time.

Primitive 'time-reckoning' is thus essentially devoted to the ordering of the experience of duration and change, and of natural and
social processes in general, rather than with the apprehension of
time in an operatory sense as a co-ordination of velocities.

9

Conceptual Realism

The human body occupies a unique position as the location of the brain, within which mental functioning takes place, as the means by which we obtain sensory information about the world, including information about other people through speech, and also as the means by which we convey information about our inner states to other people. It is therefore not surprising that the disentangling of mental from bodily functions, of thought from speech, and the subjective, sensory impressions of things from their objective properties, should present such great difficulties, of which ample evidence is provided both by developmental psychology and by the history of philosophy and science.

Awareness that one is a separate individual from other individuals in a physical sense is apparently attained at the end of the sensori-motor period, but as Piaget and others have shown, for some years afterwards the child implicitly continues to suppose that his own perspective, comprehension, attitudes, and feelings are shared by those around him. For the pre-operatory child, his own view of the world is immediate, subjective, and absolute. In particular, he remains quite unaware of the existence of 'thought' as a distinct phenomenon, and although he discovers by about the age of three years that reality is not always in accord with his desires and assertions, and so uses words like 'appear' and 'believe', or 'brain' and 'mind', it does not follow that he fully grasps the adult implication of these words, namely that there is a reality which is perceived, and also a thinking process which mediates these perceptions and a language process in which thought is encoded. He is therefore unable to distinguish names and words from their referents and believes initially that they are inherent in the objects they denote; for the child, at this stage thinking is a physical process, identified with the mouth or with speech, and he supposes that dreams occur outside himself. While he is aware of his own thoughts and feelings, he sees nothing incongruous in crediting the physical world also with will and purpose and emotions. Even at the level of physical perception, the child may suppose that his eye emits a beam when it perceives things, and wonders why people's 'eye-beams' do not collide when they meet, or supposes that the force exerted in lifting a stone is a force that is being actively exerted by the stone.

He is thus cognitively incapable of distinguishing clearly between subjective and objective, of recognizing the constant operation of his own mental processes, not only in interpreting the world, but also in creating illusions of sensory perception, language, and point of view. He lacks objectivity of judgement, and Piaget terms his implicit confusion of subjective and objective 'conceptual realism'. While he may use a word like 'think', he does not grasp its *cognitive* implications, and for him it means 'concentrating', 'making a mental effort', e.g. when trying to remember something. Piaget considers that three effective tests for the mastery of the notion of 'thought' and the elimination of conceptual realism are the understanding, (a) that thought is a process in the head which is invisible and immaterial, (b) that names and words are quite distinct from their referents and are conventional in origin, and (c) that dreams are located in the head. Though none of these is by itself a conclusive test, the understanding of all three is alone sufficient to show that realism has been eliminated. In view of the enormous difficulty of grasping the cognitive function of 'mind' (which the history of Western philosophy demonstrates again and again), it is not surprising that realism persists to a late stage in children's cognitive development—about eleven years on average—and only seems finally to disappear with the beginning of formal operations. We find ample evidence of conceptual realism even among the Pre-Socratic philosophers, and it should therefore come as no surprise that non-literate peoples are even less capable of forming any clear representations of the distinction between subjective and objective, of linguistic meaning, and of the cognitive aspects of thought.

Having outlined the basic characteristics of conceptual realism, it may be helpful to consider the stages in the elimination in rather more detail. At the first stage, when the child can even understand the meaning of the question (at about six), he supposes that we think with the mouth when we speak, and by association also identifies thoughts with breath, air, and smoke, or else equates thinking with hearing, and hence regards it as something we do with our ears. Words (including names, a concept which the child finds easier to understand than 'word') are regarded as a part of the things they denote, and the function of the ears and mouth is therefore limited to collaborating with things—receiving words and sending them out. Words themselves therefore have strength, or weight, or swiftness, or any other physical quality possessed by their referents. And no distinction is, of course, made between a statement and what is affirmed or denied by such a statement. At the first stage, therefore, there are two related confusions—between thinking and the body, and between the sign and the thing signified. There is certainly no understanding of the notion of 'idea'— the idea of something *is* that thing.

The development of the understanding of names is particularly revealing, for 'name' is a much clearer concept for the child than 'word'. At the first stage, when a child learns the name of something, he supposes that he is thereby reaching to the essence of that thing and discovering some real kind of explanation. Things did not exist before they had names, or, if there is a name there must be something to which it corresponds. Because names are properties of things, they are discoverable, and we come to know the names of things just by looking at them.

At the second stage, names are supposed to have been given to things by their makers, God, or the first men, but may still be thought in a sense to be 'in the things' or else as being 'everywhere and nowhere'. Even if we cannot recognize a thing's name when we see it, the child still supposes that there is an inherent 'rightness' about names—the word 'sun' involves 'shining, round, etc.' The child can now understand that there is a problem about the relation between words and things, but still fails to solve it.

Only at the third stage does he come to realize that names are purely signs, conventionally bestowed and then handed down by tradition. They are progressively understood to be located in the voice, in the head, and then in thought itself, which has by now come to be located in the head, as an unobservable and immaterial process.

The child's inability to grasp the distinction between subjective and objective and the internal nature of thought naturally causes him particular difficulty when he has to explain the most vivid, yet the most subjective, of phenomena—dreams. The development of their understanding parallels that in other areas of the progression from realism to objectivity.

At the first stage, the dream is regarded as coming from outside, and remains an external event. The belief in the external nature of these images is extremely insistent: 'It is I that am in my dream, it is not in my head.' 'It isn't in me, or I should not see it.' Dreams at this stage are supposed to be where their content is located, or, if this is rejected by the child as impossible, then he believes that the dream is in the bedroom. But it is not the innate absurdities of dreams, such as flying through the air, and so on, that assist children to grasp the true nature of dreams, but the contradiction between the dream's content and the facts of waking reality, and opposition to the views of others. Even when the child can distinguish the dream from reality, and especially from memories, with which dreams are easily confused, and accepts that dreams are deceptive, he still regards them as occurring outside himself in 'real' space, and deriving their content from the objects that figure in them. Even a child who knows that dreams are unreal and that only he can see them, thinks that he himself participates in his own dreams or that whatever is dreamed of is partly the cause of the dream. This is another example of participation, between dream object and real thing, resembling that between names and the thing named.

At the second stage, the child admits that the origin of the dream is in himself but still refuses to admit that the image itself is internal. He is still unable to distinguish the image from what it represents and to regard it as detached from physical reality and connected solely with speech, sight, and thought. At this stage, the dream is like a shadow or an image in a mirror.

Finally, the dream is recognized not only to be of internal origin, but to take place wholly within the body. Just as thought comes to be conceived as 'a voice in the head', so dreams are 'in the eyes'. 'Being' and 'seeming' are finally distinguished.

But there is a further aspect of conceptual realism, the child's inability to accommodate to the rules of a social system, which must clearly be overcome by adults in any society if it is to survive at all. Piaget treats this social realism as an integral aspect of conceptual realism as a whole, but we shall see that in so far as primitives are perfectly well aware of objective social rules to which they must conform, this is an important aspect of Piaget's work on children which must be adapted when applied to primitives, just as we had to adapt his theory of symbols from the private to the public domain.

1. PRIMITIVE AWARENESS OF 'INNER STATES' IN RELATION TO CONCEPTUAL REALISM

The consciousness of 'inner states' occurs at an early age in children and certainly appears to be universal in human societies. When one says that primitives are unaware of the cognitive aspects of the mind one therefore means something very much more specific and restricted than awareness of inner states such as feelings, dispositions, knowledge, memory, intention, deceit, and so on. Awareness of the *cognitive* aspects of the mind involves an awareness of processes of reasoning; of the distinction between appearance and reality, between image and object, between the subjective and the objective; and between statement and meaning; of the possibility that our representations of things are mistaken because of distorting processes inherent in our own understanding of those things and that we may impose a conceptual order on things that is not inherent in them.

Needham (1972: 25–8) points out on the basis of Kiggen's Nuer–English dictionary that the Nuer, for example, have a wide range of terms designating inner states, e.g. we can say of an individual that he is:

inattentive	irritable
selfish	unafraid
complacent	bewildered
timid	absent-minded
sincere	discouraged
slightly angry	remorseful
thoughtful	perplexed
jealous	upset
shy	disappointed
benevolent	satisfied
bored	nervous

hypocritical	lustful
lovesick	sorry
thoughtless	worried
kindly disposed	repentant
prejudiced	happy
broken hearted	embarrassed
	sick at heart

and that the individual feels:
  sorrow
  disgust
  surprise
  fear
  suspicion
  rancour
  doubt
  pity
  shame
  compassion

It is fairly evident, however, that while these terms refer to combinations of feelings and cognitive activities, the analysis of such inner states is not a prerequisite for using or understanding such terms. Thus a selfish man is one who hides his food when visitors appear or who disappears into the bush when his neighbour needs help with house-building; a bored man yawns, drums his fingers on his knees, or lets his eyes wander aimlessly; doubt is expressed by verbal statements of disbelief or by lack of enthusiasm when there is apparent agreement; shame is obvious in blushing, downcast looks, or by a rapid change of subject in conversation. All these are characteristics of behaviour in any of its multifarious forms, and while all concerned are no doubt aware that these outward manifestations are *accompanied* by particular inward sensations and dispositions, it is not these that are primarily being assessed when we use such terms as shame, boredom, selfishness, doubt, and so on. While I regard his theory of mind as untenable, Gilbert Ryle is certainly correct in his claim (in *The Concept of Mind*) that at the commonsense level our assessments of mental processes are in fact assessments of behaviour.

But Needham also lists translations of some other Nuer words and expressions which seem to refer more unambiguously and explicitly to inner states of a cognitive type, e.g. think, know, remember, forget, think back, change his mind, believe, imagine, etc. One would certainly concede that primitives are aware of some manifestations of cognitive processes and may have words for 'know', 'think', 'remember', 'forget', 'clever', 'stupid', 'understand', and so on. But the point is that all these aspects of cognition have behavioural manifestations, too, so that a man who 'knows' something is able to answer questions on that topic or to carry out the necessary actions of a craft. To 'remember' a genealogy is to be able to repeat it; to 'understand', which in many primitive languages is translated by the same word as to 'hear', may be to act in accordance with instructions or to correct a mistake when making something, and so on.

In short, it is the external manifestations of inner states in which primitives are interested, and in these external manifestations the body has a crucial role. For example, in an analysis of ancient Israelite conceptions of the person, Johnson (1964) draws attention to the wide variety of inner states which can be typified by reference to behaviour, bodily movements, and facial expressions. He shows that in ancient Israelite thought there is no clear distinction between what we should distinguish as mental and physical functioning (a point we shall consider in detail below, pp. 404–7).

With reference to the mouth Johnson says:

Thus it is said of the mouth,[1] not merely that it speaks in and of itself, but that in a given case it may speak wisely or foolishly, and offer praise or blame; and, what is more, it is also associated in a corresponding way with ethical terms, being linked for the most part with crookedness and falsity. Much the same holds good occasionally of the palate, which is said in certain cases not only to taste but also as an organ of speech to pronounce moral judgements, speak the truth, or commit sin. Similarly the tongue is said not merely to speak or sing, but also to plan or be contentious; and accordingly in certain circumstances it may be referred to on the one hand as speaking constructively, e.g. with justice and knowledge, or on the other hand as being responsible for boastfulness, slander, deceit, and the like. The lips again, besides being referred to as speaking or exulting or even as betraying fear by their quivering, are said in various contexts to preserve knowledge, bestow praise, or be involved in dispute; and they too may be described in ethical terms as capable of truthfulness

---

[1] The Hebrew equivalents for this and other terms given by Johnson have been omitted throughout.

or charm, and as being correspondingly helpful, or again as the instruments of deceitfulness, and indeed mischief in general.

What is true of the mouth, with its palate, tongue, and lips, is equally true of the eye, which is frequently referred to as itself seeing whatever may be the particular object of vision; and, what is more, it may be said not merely to see or watch, but to watch carefully. Indeed to refer to the eye or the eyes as turned towards or fixed upon an object is a frequent method of indicating the concentration of one's attention, just as wandering eyes betray inattention and, therefore, may be regarded by a teacher as the mark of a fool ... Indeed the behaviour of the eye is found to be related to a wide range of psychical activity, i.e. pride or humility, favour or disfavour, desire and hope, or disappointment; and in view of the ease with which the eye may be affected by distress of any kind it is not surprising that it should be found capable of pity. (Johnson 1964: 45–8)

Even when we encounter among primitives a word we are disposed to translate as 'think', it commonly has the basic meaning of 'obvious mental effort', as it does among Piaget's pre-operatory subjects (cf. the Tangu word *gnek'gneki*, 'to think, ponder, cogitate, rack one's brains' (Burridge 1969: 176)). We have already encountered similar problems in the translation of other terms in the languages of primitives, such as 'some/all', 'straight', 'number' and 'time', and, as we shall see, the word 'probable'. Thus, in a primitive culture, 'some' may not mean 'any number less than the theoretically possible total', but 'few'; 'straight' commonly means 'without curvature', not 'shortest distance between two points'; 'number' means, if the word is present at all, 'things for counting', not the mathematical concept of 'number' as an asymmetrical ordering of classes; while 'time' means in the primitive context 'duration' or 'sequence of events', not the operatory conception of time as the co-ordination of duration, succession, and simultaneity. In the same way, when we are considering words that relate to cognitive processes, such as 'think', it would be prudent to remember that this word, together with those for 'know', 'remember', 'clever', 'stupid', and 'understand', can bear simpler interpretations than the purely cognitive, and that it is possible for primitives and the uneducated generally to use them in relation to behaviour, facial expressions, bodily movements, and speech, while leaving out of account their distinctively cognitive aspects. We would not expect to find discussions in primitive society about the difference between knowing and believing, for example, or appearance and reality.

We shall recall, moreover, from earlier chapters, that the awareness of cognitive processes is highly dependent on literacy, and on
schooling in particular. We become aware of the cognitive functions of language and the distinction between meaning and statement when we write statements out of the context of real-life situations, transpose the order of words and sentences to express our
meaning more clearly, solve problems out of context, become
aware of the possibilities of hypothetical reasoning independent of
actual day-to-day realities, and become capable of deductive inference. Again, at the stage of concrete operations we become aware
of our own cognitive processes when we correct our sensory impressions, as in the case of the two beakers of water, when we
realize that the tall thin beaker contains as much as the short fat
beaker and that the *appearance* of more fluid in the tall thin beaker
is only an illusion. In the absence of all these sorts of experience,
which have been discussed throughout this book, it is extremely
difficult to see how primitive peoples *could* reach any clear understanding of the cognitive functions of the mind. While, as individuals, they are necessarily directly aware of their own knowledge,
memories, purposes, and feelings, they evaluate these inner states
in others on a behavioural basis. In so far as primitives are concerned with distinctions between inner states and their outward
physical or social manifestations, they are not so much displaying an
awareness of the distinction between subjective and objective as of
the distinction between private and public, which is a very different
matter, as we shall see in our discussion of the Ommura.

Indeed, the realm of purely private experience and motives, as
distinct from the evaluation of actual behaviour, is given little attention in many primitive societies, as anyone can see who studies
published examples of oral literature and court cases or texts from
informants provided in ethnographers' monographs. Neither the
Konso nor the Tauade, for example, ever spontaneously referred
to private experience when discussing behaviour beyond using such
vague generalities as 'he was afraid', 'he was angry', 'he was sorry
for', etc. The Tauade, in particular, while regarding an individual's
behaviour as motivated by his passions and intentions, never
attempted to analyse these. In answer to an inquiry as to why X
had done something, they would say, 'omei omene kimuv a', 'he
did [it according to] his insides', or, slightly more expansively, in
the case of a man who acted aggressively, 'his insides were like
fire', or in the case of someone who was by nature peaceful, 'his

insides are like water [cool].' The only exception to these generalizations in my own experience was a highly intelligent informant
among the Tauade, who had worked for many years with the
Fathers of the Catholic Mission and assisted them in the selection of
Tauade words for Bible translation, although he spoke no English.
His texts were remarkable for several references to what the protagonists were thinking as an explanation of their actions.

The claim that the realm of purely private experience receives
very little elaboration or analysis at the level of public discourse
can be clarified by an example of how a novelist in our culture is
able to describe the private states of thought and feeling of one of his
characters:

[Margaret's] evening was pleasant. The sense of flux which had haunted
her all the year disappeared for a time. She forgot the luggage and the
motor-cars, and the hurrying men who know so much and connect so
little. She recaptured the sense of space, which is the basis of all earthly
beauty, and, starting from Howards End, she attempted to realize England.
She failed—visions do not come when we try, though they may come
through trying. But an unexpected love of the island awoke in her, connecting on this side with the joys of the flesh, on that with the inconceivable. Helen and her father had known this love, poor Leonard Bast was
groping after it, but it had been hidden from Margaret till this afternoon.
It had certainly come through the house and old Miss Avery. Through
them: the notion of 'through' persisted; her mind trembled towards a
conclusion which only the unwise have put into words. Then, veering back
into warmth, it dwelt on ruddy bricks, flowering plum trees, and all the
tangible joys of spring. (E. M. Forster, *Howards End*)

It is significant that in this passage Forster uses no words, with
the possible exceptions of 'sense' and 'mind', with any specialized
cognitive or psychological connotation, and even these two words
could have been avoided. This illustrates yet again that it is not the
lexical or syntactical resources of the language so much as the
ability to use it in certain ways that distinguishes the more developed
cognitive processes from the more elementary.

This inability to analyse private experience, as opposed to social
behaviour, the paradigm of the knowable, is well illustrated by
ethnographic evidence from the Ommura, of the Eastern Highlands Province of Papua New Guinea.[2] Like many primitive peoples

[2] I am most grateful to Miss J. R. Mayer for supplying me with this information,
for corresponding with me about it, and for allowing me to use it here. It constitutes
part of her Ph.D. thesis currently being prepared at the University of Sussex.

in New Guinea and elsewhere, the Ommura use the same verb
(*iero*) for 'understanding' or 'comprehending', and the 'hearing' of
a sound etc. *dapi* corresponds fairly closely to 'clear', 'distinct', as
opposed to 'obscure' or 'confused', and thus the expression *dapi
iena* means 'that sound which we can hear clearly' and also, when
used in the sense of understanding, the notion of 'hearing' implied
in such contexts relates to the sound of the name, *nrutu,* of the
object being spoken. (The equation of 'understanding' with hearing
is very common in primitive society and is, of course, quite consistent with the statements of Piaget's subjects that 'we think with our
ears'.)

I think it would be correct to say that in terms of Ommura conscious
models, the sphere of that which is represented as being amenable to clear
verbal representation is more or less co-extensive with that which is represented as falling within the realm of ordinary comprehension and control.
Those areas of expression which Ommura claim 'not to understand' or
'not to hear the name' are those which are represented in most contexts as
falling outside the realm of ordinary Ommura comprehension and social
control. (Mayer, personal communication)

Areas of experience which fall into this last category are spirits
and ghosts, and when the Ommura speak about these 'They almost
invariably emphasize that what they are saying is "only a personal
impression" (*ni nrato tina*, "my ear says") as it were and that they
"do not understand, have not heard clearly in verbal terms", what
goes on in these spheres.' The manners and customs of other cultures, especially those of Europeans, are categorized in the same
way, as are the 'inner states' of other people.

There is a general absence of terms to describe inner states, despite the fact that the Ommura are well aware that people *have*
sensations, intentions, motives, and so on. The point is that these
are inaccessible to others, and so one can never be 'clear' about
such things, especially in a culture like that of the Ommura, where
it is considered that people often intentionally misrepresent matters. 'Generally speaking, what we would describe as "inner states"
etc. tend to be treated in most contexts as dangerous, unpredictable, and "asocial" and to be closely associated with sorcery
activities.' (Ibid.)

The Ommura, in fact, are concerned to distinguish, not between
the cognitively subjective and objective, but 'what makes sense because it can be seen to conform to known rules, and discussed' and

what does not. This contrast is expressed in the distinction between 'only what my ear says'—personal impressions, unreliable and inaccurate, and those experiences that are amenable to clear and accurate representations in terms of the Ommura language:

From an Ommura perspective, dreams, states of possession etc. that we would tend to regard as being in large part 'internally generated', may be represented either as 'clear', 'accurate', and 'externally generated', or as 'only what his ear says', and therefore unreliable, depending on such factors as the position of the dreamer or dream interpreter in the status quo, the content of the dream, etc. (Ibid.)

But significantly, there seems to be no notion that, even if some dreams or states of possession have vague or indeterminable meanings, they are therefore, in our sense, 'subjective', that is, products of purely mental activity.

While, therefore, the Ommura regard language, or more exactly, speech, as an essential basis for clear, social representation, they still treat utterances as integrally related to their contexts of use.

To be able to comprehend something involves, for the Ommura, finding the words for it, to 'hear' the correct *nrutu* or name of the phenomenon, and for the Ommura naming something simultaneously involves its control, or potential control. *nrutu* most commonly means 'personal name', and when one refers to the *nrutu* of an object or relation one does so

only in contexts in which the process of 'naming/controlling' them is consciously reflected on, as in contexts in which there is an attempt to clarify one's perception of something or exert control over it through the medium of its *nrutu*. In most contexts, one would not ask 'What is the *nrutu* of this?', but simply 'What is this?', and the usual kind of answer would be 'This is a sweet potato'. (Ibid.)

The term *nrutu* is also used to refer to any words when they perform a 'proper' or 'accurate' descriptive or referential function. Thus the garbled words of babies or imbeciles are said not to perform this function; one may express one's doubts as to the 'genuine' nature and hence efficaciousness of somebody's spells by saying that the words used 'are not real *nrutu'*, in much the same way as we might say that something was 'merely hocus pocus' or 'mumbo jumbo', but with the additional implication that it was therefore incapable of exerting control. In its verbal form *nrutu* may be used in approximately the sense of 'to call for', or 'to invoke'.

This essential quality of 'control' as an attribute of naming is found in Ommura attitudes to speakers of different languages. 'People whose language one cannot hear' ('does not understand') are, in many contexts, those with whom relations are unpredictable and outside one's immediate sphere of potential control. And it should be noted that actual linguistic differences may be secondary:

When Ommura wish to assert 'sameness' or solidarity with a particular group they often use the idiom of 'same language' [cf. Pidgin 'wantok' (one-talk) = 'same language person', for a member of one's own social group] even though the dialect differences between the two groups may, objectively speaking, be considerable. On the other hand, when difference is being stressed it is often said of the other group, 'We cannot "hear" (understand) their language', even though, objectively speaking, the dialect differences may be almost nonexistent. (Ibid.)

Thus a great deal of ritual activity is also based on the principle of 'finding and speaking the *nrutu*':

The harmful effects of a sorcerer's secret activities may, for example, be nullified by speaking his name out loud and perhaps describing his harmful actions verbally. The sorcerer's identity and the nature of his actions are first manifested, usually in non-visual form, in the outcome of various kinds of divination procedure. But only by means of describing them aloud in verbal form may they be brought under control. (Ibid.)

Again, many things have secret names, knowledge of which enables those who are initiated to control them. These secret initiation names are *mbo-nrutu*, literally, 'other name'.

It is quite clear that, in the Ommura case, at least, the power associated with using the *mbo-nrutu* of something derives from the fact that the *mbo-nrutu* is represented as being the *nrutu* of the *mara-uha* aspect of something and thus as a potential means of controlling/understanding that aspect. '*Mara-uha*' may be roughly translated in this context as 'that sphere of efficacy in terms of which relations are possible that transcend the ordinary restrictions of time and space (as delineated in Ommura culture) or are outside the realm of ordinary everyday perceptions'.

In keeping with the general Ommura association between social and linguistic distance, the sphere of the '*mara-uha*' which is distinct from the sphere of everyday efficacy, is represented as having a 'different language'. The *nrutu* which relate to the 'ordinary' aspects of something cannot thus bring its '*mara-uha*' aspect within the realm of comprehension and control.

One finds in Ommura culture, as well as many other Melanesian cultures, a particularly strong emphasis on the use in magical verbal formulae of words which are represented as being 'foreign', 'archaic', or otherwise 'unintelligible', on certain levels at least. The use of these terms suggests that much Ommura magical activity involves an attempt to find *nrutu* for such phenomena in the language represented as being that of their place or origin. Thus, for example, the secret male and female initiation songs which are couched in terminology that is represented as being archaic ('The language of the ancestors') may be seen as means of gaining some kind of access to powers originating from the ancestors. (Ibid.)

Similarly, most Ommura agricultural rituals at present involve the singing of songs represented as coming from many different language and dialect groups. The explicit reason given for this is that 'We sing songs in the Gadsup language so that the sweet potatoes from Gadsup will come to our village. We then sing songs from " Australia" so that the sweet potatoes from Australia will come to our village, etc.' Pidgin is seen as a means of potential control in matters to do with Europeans and the Administration, and the practice of mimicking the sounds of animals when hunting is another manifestation of the same principle.

Thus for the Ommura, language is an integral part of social relations, being in many respects closely associated with control as well as merely with comprehension, with the public domain, in fact, the external outer world of common experience, while the interior world of the private individual is hidden and unpredictable. But one finds here no sense of language as something that can be analysed independently of its context, or the systematic comparison of different languages, and certainly no notion of mental activity as an essential aspect of all communication. Quite the opposite—in so far as the Ommura are aware of private mental states or acts, they are vague and incommunicable, and have no mediating influence on communication and perception.

Yet even if the Ommura display no awareness of the function of mind in the mediation of experience, it might be argued that their representations seem to be the very reverse of those of the child. Far from regarding their own individual perspectives as immediate, objective, and absolute, they appear to discount them as wholly unreliable, and to regard only mutually comprehensible and verifiable statements as valid. But in order to establish something clearly and accurately by mutual discussion it is necessary for all participants to be able to evaluate the perspectives and to discount the biases intrinsic to one another's personal points of view. In my personal experience of arguments among the Konso and Tauade, however, while there were of course differences of opinion, no one ever attempted to undermine any one else's opinion by using the kind of argument so familiar to us: 'You only say that because you have a limited experience of . . .' or 'because you are just being loyal to one of your own clan' and so on. The only attempts to refute statements on the basis of personal attitudes or perspectives are those based on the *social* incapacities of the opponent—'He is too young to know that' or 'Women have no skill in such matters' or 'He is a liar and likes to cheat you' or 'He is a fool.' There is no attempt here to assess the particular motives or biases of an opponent as an individual; still less the possible causes of such biases or motives.

Referring to the experiments on Kpelle difficulties in communication (see above, pp. 116–17), Cole and Scribner (1974: 180–5) discuss the suggestion that primitives resemble children by being egocentric in the Piagetian sense that 'they have failed to develop the capacity to take a listener's point of view'. They draw attention to various contexts, such as deliberately ambiguous language whose effect depends on taking the interlocutor's point of view into account, and the playing of rule-governed games in primitive society, which depend on the general ability to adopt an objective point of view of one's own behaviour in relation to a publicly recognized body of rules. They rightly conclude, as I have done in the case of the Ommura, that is these and other respects, such as co-operative work in farming and housebuilding, law-suits, etc., 'Kpelle adults seem to represent the antithesis of a Piagetian child.'

But, as I have already emphasized, it is of the greatest importance to distinguish between the ability to take account of another person's point of view in so far as that depends on his social role, age, sex, and the history of his personal relationships as they are known in the local community, and the ability to consider what another person might be thinking as an *individual,* which is a very different matter. For it is fairly clear that in primitive society (and among the uneducated working class in our own society, as Bernstein points out), the development of the awareness of, and the capacity to express, private experience, remains largely undeveloped, as Evans-Pritchard reports the Azande saying: 'One cannot know what is going on inside a man. That is the meaning of one of their most quoted proverbs: *i ni ngere ti boro wai i ni ngere ti baga?* 'can one look into a person as one looks into an open-wove basket?' (Evans-Pritchard 1962: 228).

The use of *sanza,* calculated ambiguity of language, has been carried to a high level of skill by the Azande: the following example clearly illustrates their awareness of the other person's publicly observable 'point of view', and indeed the necessity for this awareness if such devices as *sanza* are to be possible at all.

A man wants his blood-brother to allow him to have pleasure of his daughter. Though some blood-brothers might permit this if the girl were unmarried, many would refuse such a request and it is not an obligation of blood-brotherhood to grant it; so the man proceeds warily, making his suggestion in *sanza* saying 'does one not know what a man is longing for, my blood-brother, sir?'. His blood-brother replies 'what are you talking about?' The man says 'eh, sir! Those women in this home, sir, how shall I say it? What shall I put in the mouth of the dog, sir?'. His mention of women gives a hint of what he really wants, then he goes off at a tangent, asking how shall he say what he wants, and ends by remarking that as a dog eats everything how should one know what it wants. By his allusion to women he tells his blood-brother what he wants but then goes undercover, as it were. The father of the girl laughs 'aha ha ha, aha ha ha, my blood-brother, then those thoughts inside you, sir, with which you have come to my home here, why do you hide them from me, sir?'. He knows what his friend wants but is not going to say so directly, and his friend knows that he knows but is also not going to say so directly. He replies 'master, I was frightened of you; master, I was frightened of you, my lord'. Then they both laugh together, for this is *wene sanza,* good *sanza,* which, though it conceals a purpose, is good humoured, as it should be between blood-blothers. (Ibid. 216)

For this exchange to be effective, or even possible, it is necessary for both participants to understand the general characteristics of adult male behaviour in their society and the rules and customs associated both with it and with particular male roles, such as those of blood-brothers, fathers, and suitors. It is in relation to this public, objective knowledge that individual behaviour is assessed in this case. Thus while it may be true that 'he [the father] knows what his friend wants but is not going to say so directly, and his friend knows that he knows but is also not going to say so directly', such mutual knowledge is concerned purely with the social situation and does not involve either party in any attempt to evaluate the particular and unique feelings, ideas, and so on in the mind of the other—they deal with one another purely in terms of social status and observable behaviour.

Thus while adult behaviour in primitive society is in one way the antithesis of the egocentricism of Piaget's children, it is also to be distinguished from that of educated adults in our own society, since we spend a great deal of time learning to analyse our own inner states of mind and to understand those of other people. There is, among ourselves, a constant interaction between the expression of private points of view and those of the group or of society as a whole, which is largely missing in primitive society. Primitives are aware that individuals *have* these private points of view (their comments on the very impenetrability of private experience attest to this awareness), but because private experience goes unexpressed there is no means of developing any awareness of the ways in which it differs from, or misrepresents, or for that matter corrects, public representations. It is precisely this awareness of the distinction between private and public representations, explored in particular by novelists, that is of such importance among us generating an awareness of the mind. Only when we are aware both of the actions of characters in the public arena and the social significance of what they, and also of their differing private representations of these public events, is our attention focused on the ways in which publicly observable events are privately interpreted—that is, on the mind as the agency which mediates private and public experience.

Communication and co-operation thus occur in primitive society on the level of public interaction, and it is because of the essential homogeneity of this experience that different individual points of view are assessed in terms of observable, publicly verifiable standards, leaving the truly private aspects of experience in darkness. We may treat the resulting social interaction as a kind of corporate egocentrism in which people learn to co-operate through action and participation in the same kinds of experience, which allows what we should term the subjective aspects of experience to be ignored. (In this connection the reader will recall from Chapter 3 our discussion of learning in primitive society as based on instruction in context, by participation, and not on the exposition of rules out of context.) Thus there is no real equilibration between private and public representations at all, since representations of private experience are overwhelmed by the social consensus. Our conclusions therefore suggest that co-operation, argument, and so on do not as such necessarily have the consequence of producing an accommodation to other people's private points of view that Piaget suggests will occur. The crucial factor is the *nature* of that interaction: if it is largely based on action, in the form of common tasks and a shared, homogeneous experience for the acquisition of which participation is of far greater importance than explicit verbal analysis and explication, then there need be no accommodation to private points of view, but rather the development of a social consensus in terms of which private representations are ignored. This, which seems to be the norm in primitive society, is evidently not the same thing as our own clear awareness of the interaction between public events, the public arena, as it were, and the variety of private representations of it, since in our own society learning and interaction with one's fellows depends on the analytical use of language in contexts removed from real-life situations (as in Western-type schools which engender skills in the expression of private representations), quite apart from the assessment of the public roles and behaviour of individuals attained by primitives.

2. PRIMITIVE REPRESENTATIONS OF THE MIND

Lienhardt, from his researches among the Dinka, has provided us with a striking confirmation of the absence of a concept of 'mind' among this people:

The Dinka have no conception which at all closely corresponds to our popular modern conception of the 'mind', as mediating and, as it were, storing up the experiences of the self. There is for them no such entity to appear, on reflection, to stand between the experiencing self at any given moment and what is or has been an exterior influence upon the self. So it seems that what we should call in some cases the 'memories' of experiences, and regard therefore as in some way intrinsic and interior to the remembering person and modified in their effect upon him by that interiority, appear to the Dinka as exteriorly acting upon him, as were the sources from which they derived. Hence it would be impossible to suggest to Dinka that a powerful dream was 'only' a dream, and might for that reason be dismissed as relatively unimportant in the light of day, or that a state of possession was grounded 'merely' in the psychology of the person possessed. They do not make the kind of distinction between the psyche and the world which would make such interpretations significant for them. (Lienhardt 1961: 149)

There is a great deal of evidence, both in Lienhardt's book, and from other ethnographic sources, that mental states and feelings are often regarded by primitive peoples as external to the person, and as entities whose existence is independent of their being thought or felt (and correspondingly, they may emphasize the psychomorphic and volitional behaviour of what we would regard as purely natural phenomena). Lienhardt gives the following examples:

A man who has lived for a time in a place very foreign to him may think that that place (we should say, its 'influence') follows him (*bwoth cok*), as divinities are said to 'follow' those with whom they have formed a relationship. A man who had been imprisoned in Khartoum called one of his children 'Khartoum' in memory of the place, but also to turn aside any possible influence of that place upon him in later life. The act is an act of exorcism, but the exorcism of what, to us, would be memories of experiences. (Ibid. 149)

Even in the usual expressions of the Dinka for the action of features of their world upon them, we often find a reversal of European expressions which assume the human self, or mind, as subject in relation to what happens to it; in English, for example, it is often said that a man 'catches a disease', but in Dinka the disease, or Power, always 'seizes' the man. (Ibid. 150)

The fetish, or medicine bundle Mathiang Gok, used to intimidate debtors by mystical means, relies on a similar reification of what to us would be subjective processes:

This fetish, according to Dinka accounts, works analogously to what, for Europeans, would be the prompting of a guilty conscience. The European emphasis there is upon an integrally interior subject of activity, the conscience. For the Dinka, MATHIANG GOK is a presence acting upon the self from without, and employed by someone to do so. The image (as we have called it) of the experience of guilty indebtedness (to take the usual situation in which MATHIANG GOK is thought to operate) is extrapolated from the experiencing self. It comes (as memories often do) unwilled by the debtor, and is interpreted as a Power directed by the creditor. (Ibid. 150)

Another example of this imaging of experience is seen in the relationships which Dinka think themselves to have formed with objects, or more usually illness, which have affected them individually, and which are akin to 'individual totemism' or 'nagualism'. The clan-divinities are such items passed on as species from the founder of a clan to his descendants as a group. When a man has formed an individual relationship, he will *thek*, respect, the emblem of the thing which has affected him, and count it among his divinities. Here again he seems to see in that which has affected him the self-determining subject of activity, and himself the object of it. People do not choose their divinities, they are chosen by them. (Ibid. 151)

In his book *The Greeks and the Irrational*, Dodds produces a significant parallel to these African assumptions about the external origins of some mental phenomena. In Homer, unwise and unacceptable conduct is attributed to *ate*:

Always, or practically always, *ate* is a state of mind a temporary clouding or bewildering of the normal consciousness. It is in fact a partial and temporary insanity; and like all insanity, it is ascribed, not to physiological or psychological causes, but to an external 'daemonic' agency. (Dodds 1951: 5)

A word next about the agencies to which *ate* is ascribed. Agamemnon cities, not one such agency, but three: Zeus and *moira* and the Erinys who walks in darkness ... Of these, Zeus is the mythological agent whom the poet conceives as the prime mover in the affair: 'the plan of Zeus was fulfilled'. It is perhaps significant that ... Zeus is the only individual Olympian who is credited with causing *ate* in the Iliad (hence *ate* is allegorically described as his eldest daughter). *Moira*, I think, is brought in because people spoke of any unaccountable personal disaster as part of their 'portion' or 'lot', meaning simply that they cannot understand why it happened, but since it has happened, evidently 'it had to be'. People still speak in that way, more especially of death, for which μίρα has in fact become a symonym in modern Greek, like μόρος in classical Greek. . . . (By) treating his 'portion' as an agent—by making it *do* something—Agamemnon is taking a first step towards personification. Again, by blaming his *moira* Agamemnon no more declares himself a systematic determinist than does the modern Greek peasant when he uses similar language. To ask whether Homer's people are determinists or libertarians is a fantastic anachronism; the question has never occurred to them, and if it were put to them it would be very difficult to make them understand what it meant. What they do recognise is the distinction between normal actions and actions performed in a state of *ate*. Actions of the latter sort they can trace indifferently to their *moira*, or to the will of a god, according as they look at the matter from a subjective or an objective point of view. In the same way Patroclus attributes his death directly to the immediate agent, the man Euphorbus, and indirectly to Apollo, but from a subjective standpoint to his bad *moira*. (Ibid. 6–7)

We have noted that primitives (like us at a commonsense level) judge the 'inner states' of others by outward, behavioural manifestations. We might therefore expect that our distinction between the mind in its cognitive aspects (and, indeed, the feelings) on the one hand, and the body considered as a purely physical system on the other, would not be drawn nearly as distinctly in primitive culture as in our own and that, correspondingly, there would be a fusion between the psychical and the physical. According to Johnson, for example,

... in Israelite thought man is conceived, not so much in dual fashion as 'body' and 'soul', but synthetically as a unit of vital power or (in current terminology) a psycho-physical organism. That is to say, the various members and secretions of the body, such as the bones, the heart, the bowels, and the kidneys, as well as the flesh and the blood, can all be thought of as revealing psychic properties. (Johnson 1964: 87)

A very similar fusion of psychic and physical functions is reported of the Gahuku-Gama of New Guinea:

The biological, physiological and psychic aspects of [man's] nature cannot be clearly separated. They exist in the closest inter-dependence, being, as it were, fused together to form the human personality. To an extent to which it is perhaps difficult for us to appreciate or understand, the various parts of the body, limbs, eyes, nose, hair, the internal organs and bodily excretions are essential constituents of the human personality, incorporating and expressing the whole in each of their several functions. It follows that an injury to any part of the body is also comparable to damage to the personality of the individual sustaining the injury. Similarly, the loss of any of the bodily substances through excretion is, in a rather obscure sense, the loss of something that is an essential part or element of the whole, a loss to the personality itself. (Read 1955: 265)

This fusion may be expected to apply to the cognitive aspects of psychical functioning as well as to the emotional. Thus according to Onians,[3] the identification of thought with breath is a characteristic of early Greek thought: 'How do Homeric notions of the main processes of consciousness differ from our own? A good deal is explicit. Thinking is described as "speaking" and is located sometimes in the heart but usually in the $\phi\rho\dot\eta\nu$ or $\phi\rho\acute\epsilon\nu\epsilon\varsigma$, traditionally interpreted as the 'midriff' or 'diaphragm' (Onians 1954: 13). Onians claims (p. 24) that the correct translation of $\phi\rho\acute\epsilon\nu\epsilon\varsigma$ is in fact 'lungs',

---

[3] See also Snell 1960, chapter I.

and that in the same way the Latin *praecordia* also meant both 'lungs' and the seat of consciousness.

$\theta\upsilon\mu\acute{o}s$ is 'breath',

But it is clear that $\theta\upsilon\mu\acute{o}s$ expressed a much richer concept for the Homeric Greeks than our 'breath' or mere outer air received and expelled. (Ibid. 46).

This $\theta\upsilon\mu\acute{o}s$ is not the blood-soul as opposed to the breath-soul nor indeed mere breath but breath related to blood, not mere air but something vaporous within, blending and interacting with the air without, some thing which diminishes if the body is ill-nourished, but is increased when the body is well nourished. (Ibid. 47–8)

They [the speeches of a man] come forth with the breath that is intelligence in them, they are parts of it, and the listener puts them, takes them, into his $\theta\upsilon\mu\acute{o}s$, thus adding to his store, his knowledge. They pass from lung to lung, mind to mind. Penelope 'put the $\mu\tilde{\upsilon}\theta\acute{o}s$ $\pi\epsilon\pi\nu\upsilon\mu\acute{e}\nu os$ [breathing word?] of her son in her $\theta\upsilon\mu\acute{o}s$' and words are continually said to be 'put in the $\phi\rho\acute{e}\nu\epsilon s$' [lungs]. Not only the evident connection between breathing and emotion already urged, but also the belief that thoughts are words and words are breath—$\acute{e}\pi\epsilon\alpha$ $\acute{a}\acute{e}\rho\iota\alpha$ as Sappho seems to have called them—would lead to the belief that the organs of breath, the lungs, are the organs of mind. (Ibid. 67–8)

[and]

Returning to Homer, we may wonder whether, though words and thoughts might naturally be believed to come *from* the lungs, they could be thought to go *to* them, be perceived, received by them, when the ears and eyes in the head must inevitably be recognised as sense organs. That they were so thought there can be no doubt. There are the many statements that the words of a speaker are 'put into the $\phi\rho\acute{e}\nu\epsilon s$' of the hearer and the less conclusive descriptions of people whose '$\phi\rho\acute{\eta}\nu$ is delighted as they hear' singing or themselves play the lyre. . . . The sound, the breath, of which the words consist passes through the ears not to the brain but to the lungs. This, though it may seem foolish to us, is in fact a natural interpretation of the anatomy of the head, which shows an air passage direct from the outer air through the ear to the pharynx and so to the lungs. (Ibid. 69)

Malinowski refers to the association of thought and speech among the Trobrianders:

The mind, *nanola*, by which term intelligence, power of discrimination, capacity for learning magical formulae and all forms of non-manual skill are described, as well as moral qualities, resides somewhere in the larynx. The natives will always point to the organs of speech, where the *nanola* resides. The man who cannot speak through any defect of his organs, is identified in name (*tonagowa*) and in treatment with all those mentally deficient. The memory, however, the store of formulae and traditions learned by heart, resides deeper, in the belly.

A man will be said to have a good *nanola*, when he can acquire many formulae, but though they enter through the larynx, naturally, as he learns them, repeating word for word, he has to stow them away in a bigger and more commodious receptacle; they sink down right to the bottom of his abdomen. (Malinowski 1922: 408–9)

And referring to a particularly accurate and knowledgeable informant, Malinowski continues: 'I paid him well for the few formulae he gave me, and inquired at the end of our first session, whether he had any more magic to produce. With pride, he struck his belly several times, and answered: "Plenty more lies there!"' (ibid. 409).

Again,

The Gahuku-Gama [of New Guinea] do not ascribe any importance to the brain, nor have they any conception of its function. Cognitive processes are associated with the organ of hearing. To 'know' or to 'think' is to 'hear' (*gelenove*); 'I don't know' or 'I don't understand' is 'I do not hear' or 'I have not heard' (*gelemuve*). (Read 1955: 265n)

Not only is understanding commonly associated with speech, hearing, the mouth, the larynx, and the breath, but a wider range of psychological processes is commonly located in physical organs, e.g.

The Elema have a simple physical psychology by which they allocate all emotion, desire, and thought to the liver, *iki*. [n. Thus the terms *iki vere*, desire; *iki heaha*, bad temper; *iki beveke*, good temper; *iki haroe*, compassion; *iki ore*, knowledge; *iki kekere*, thought, belief etc.] Of the two sides of this organ the right (*mai-ore*) is the seat of kindliness, sociability; the left (*mai-keva*) of the angry passions, strong talk, unsociability. Not being cannibals the Elema had to base their knowledge of internal anatomy largely on the analogy of the pig, and there is some confusion in their ideas, even some uncertainty regarding the respective sides to which the different kinds of mental experience belong. [n. To make matters worse they became sadly mixed up as to right and left hand.] But the majority favour the allocation of good emotions to the right and the bad ones to the left. They have noted the frequent disparity in size and shape between the two lobes of the pig's liver, one being well developed, while the other is small and 'crooked'; and the predominance of one or the other kind of temper is described accordingly. Whether it is bigness or smallness or crookedness that makes for the predominance of the relevant passions is just the point on which informants are most uncertain; but in the midst of this uncertainty it is agreed that the good side, right or left, large or small, is *iki amua*; and the man whose liver so to speak secretes the corresponding thoughts, emotions, or desires, is an *iki amua haera*. (Williams 1940: 90–1)

Johnson (1964) also discusses in detail a similar 'physiological psychology' of the heart, bowels, and kidneys of the ancient Israelites, as mentioned above, p. 404.

The Mbowamb and the Mae Enga apparently locate the soul in the heart, in one part of which are located the passions, and in the other the processes of deliberate thought and calculation, which are seen as in conflict with one another, but capable of being brought into balance. Kenny, who draws attention to this representation of the different 'forces' at work in the person (Kenny, n.d.), also states correctly that this conception of balance is of central importance in New Guinea society generally:

The concept of balance is found in the attempts to maintain equilibrium between the debts and credits of individuals and social groups; concepts of 'psychological' balance are closely related to the degree of success in attaining this. Exchange produces balance and much of New Guinea society is dependent on it; it is that which creates social life and breaks down the parochialism of lineage and locality. (Kenny: 8)

It is undoubtedly the case that indigenous models of the person will be affected by such basic social processes as reciprocity and balance of forces. Thus we may expect to find that in different societies the model of the organization of the person will vary in accordance with their basic social principles and world-view generally. It is also possible that many African societies regard certain emotional experiences as objectively generated, which in New Guinea would be regarded as coming from inside a person.

But these variations are secondary elaborations on the common and basic theme of conceptual realism which regards mental and affective states as physically real, and the treatment of processes as things. In so far as emotions are conceived as things, localized within the body, some cultures suppose that one may rid oneself of them almost like physical encumbrances:

In Cabras and in other areas of Sardinia, when somebody is tired, strained, and unable to work, he submits himself to the diagnosis of relatives and friends. Soon they will conclude they are dealing with fright or, as they say, *assustu*. This is a particular kind of fright which can have a mechanistic cause but the true origin of which we must find in a logic scheme far away from the mechanistic one. In fact when they think they have found the incidental cause of the fright, they pass to a therapeutic technique called *imbrusciadura*. This ritual consists in making the subject go back to the exact point where he was shocked and there he has to roll on the ground in predetermined movements. After this, the subject will leave the place without looking back in case the fright should return. Some times they say: 'From the earth I took you and to the earth you must return.' (Peluffo 1967: 190)

The various aspects of the person, such as personality and vitality, are thus seen, in primitive thought, as separate entities. A particularly interesting example of this, for the purposes of the present discussion, is the prevalent West African belief in a personalized destiny, proper to each person, which is responsible for the vicissitudes of his career and which we would consider to have some important resemblances to our notion of the subconscious. But here again, we find that these 'destiny souls' are essentially external to the subject and depend also on a notion of the individual person as fragmented into a number of different elements corresponding to activities which have become hypostatized as entities.[4]

At this point we may usefully summarize what seem to be the general characteristics of primitive representations of the person, and the relations between the psychical and the physical. In the first place, inner states, both of cognition and feeling, are assessed on the basis of their behavioural manifestations. Because what we do and say are the expressions of inner states, it is necessarily the case that terms in the lexicon of a primitive language will carry an implicit reference to these, but there is little evidence for the exploration of inner states of the kind accomplished by novelists in our culture, and still less for any psychological or philosophical analysis of cognition.

Corresponding with this, we find that the person is comprehended not as a mind/body duality but rather synthetically, as a fusion of the psychical and the physical, such that organs and members of the body have psychical attributes, and the result is a physiological psychology of which various examples have been cited.

While there seems to be a very general notion among primitives

---

[4] In this connection see Horton's material on the Kalabari (1961).

that the person is a composite of various entities, such as flesh, life, vitality, soul, and so on, these are not understood as processes so much as entities, and we shall consider the primitive propensity for the hypostatization of process in the next chapter. Also, the general absence of an awareness of the cognitive function of the mind as the translator and mediator of experience seems to be the basis for an apparently widespread belief that what we would regard as inner states are of external origin, and, in some cases, that thoughts and feelings have the power to influence the things to which they are directed.

3. NOMINAL REALISM

We noted at the beginning of this chapter that the understanding of the relation of words and names to their referents is one of the basic aspects of conceptual realism. As the Ommura material so clearly illustrates, in primitive society, as among children, names are regarded as inherently related to the things they denote. This is only one facet of the primitive view of language as an integral aspect of action and social relations generally, not as a conceptual tool of analysis. Malinowski expresses this essential point with great clarity:

A word, signifying an important utensil, is used in action, not to comment on its nature or reflect on its properties, but to make it appear, be handed over to the speaker, or to direct another man to its proper use. The meaning of the thing is made up of experiences of its active uses and not of intellectual contemplation. Thus, when a savage learns to understand the meaning of a word, this process is not accomplished by explanations, by a series of acts of apperception, but by learning to handle it. A word *means* to a native the proper use of the thing for which it stands, exactly as an implement *means* something when it can be handled and means nothing when no active experience of it is at hand. Similarly, a verb, a word for an action, receives its meaning through an active participation in this action. A word is used when it can produce an action and not to describe one, still less to translate thoughts. The word therefore has a power of its own, it is a means of bringing things about, it is a handle to acts and objects and not a definition of them. (Malinowski 1923: 321–2)

Since people learn their language as children it is therefore seen as an integral part of growing up and partaking more fully in social relations. Rather than learning language as such, children seem to have their language inside them, and gradually express it, a view of the process of language acquisition which is often apparently supported by the actual behaviour of children. I well remember the little son of a Konso man in whose homestead I was staying who, although about two and a half years old, was extremely silent. I was assured that he could understand what people said, despite this, and when I returned after a few months' absence I found him chattering volubly. Thus the anthropologist, too, is seen not as learning the language of his hosts in some purely cognitive way, distinct from social relations, but as gradually becoming one of them, socially speaking.

It might be suggested that the phenomenon of bilingualism or trilingualism, found in most, if not all, primitive societies, must bring an awareness of the conventional aspect of language and produce the ability to consider it apart from the context of utterance. But primitives do not think of languages in the manner of philologists' comparative word lists,[5] with sets of equivalent but different terms set out neatly in rows and columns, so making it obvious that all these words are conventional and arbitrary associations between certain sounds and objects. When primitives encounter different languages they are also encountering different groups of people, with different sets of social relations and customs, and so on. So it is highly implausible to suppose that in these circumstances primitives even think in terms of individual words and their different translations in the various languages they know, and so reflect that since the word for 'sky' is X in one language, and Y in another, words are attributed to things purely by social convention. They do not experience language in this disembodied, atomistic way, but rather as an integral part of social relations.

It is also becoming clear from modern research that (as the grammarians of Greece and Rome believed) there are inherent relations between certain sounds and word meanings. Werner refers to the 'physiognomic' properties of language in which rhythm, vowel pitch, vowel quantity, consonant quality, muscle tension, tongue position, etc., have physical properties appropriate to certain meanings of words in which these sounds are employed, an

---

[5] Dr Barnes informs me that the Kédang, who are bi- and trilingual, often comment on, and identify, word equivalences. It would be interesting to know what effect the spread of literacy has had on the Kédang in this respect.

appropriateness which is not be confused with mere on-omatopoeia.[6]

Jespersen points out that 'The vowel [i], especially in its narrow or thin variety, is particularly appropriate to express what is small, weak, insignificant, or, on the other hand, refined or dainty, (1922:402), and also a very short time, and what is near rather than far.

Sapir (1929a) conducted experiments with English- and Chinese-speaking subjects (very few of the latter) and found an overwhelming preference for *a* as symbolizing 'large' and *i, e, ε,* or *ä* as symbolizing 'small':

It is difficult to resist the conclusion that in some way a significant proportion of normal people feel that, other things being equal, a word with the vowel *a* is likely to symbolize something larger than a similar word with the vowel *i,* or *e,* or *ε,* or *ä.* To put it roughly, certain vowels and certain consonants 'sound bigger' than others ... It is possible that the inherent 'volume' of certain vowels is greater than that of others and that this factor alone is sufficient to explain the results of the experiment. On the other hand, it should be noted that many unconsciously feel that the tongue position for one vowel is symbolically 'large' as contrasted with the tongue position for another. In the case of *i* the tongue is high up toward the roof of the mouth and articulates pretty well forward. In other words, the vibrating column of air is passing through a narrow resonance chamber. In the case of *a* the tongue is very considerably lowered in comparison, and also retracted. In other words, the vibrating column of air is now passing through a much wider resonance chamber. This kinesthetic explanation is just as simple as the acoustic one and really means no more than that a spatially extended gesture is symbolic of a larger reference than a spatially restricted gesture. (Ibid. 235)

---

[6] Werner refers to Westermann's researches (Westermann 1927) according to which in some West African languages high pitch can express: something fine, tender, small; something narrow, sharp; something silent, secret; something quick, agile; something energetic, fresh, alert; intensity; loudness of colour; sourness or sharpness of taste. Conversely, low pitch may express: something big; something plump, awkward, slow; something blunt; something loose, not dense; something confused, disordered; something muggy, dim, dark; something dull, silly, stupid; something swollen, sick; something weak, frail, powerless; something colourless, tasteless; something flat sounding, hoarse. The prevalence of the semantic dimensions of Evaluation, Potency, and Activity in this list will be obvious from our previous study of synesthesia in Chapter 4, and there is a remarkable concordance with the findings of Karwoski *et al.* referred to there; we recall that they found the associations of high and low pitch to be as follows:

> treble: light, up, small, thin, distinct, angular
> bass: dark, down, large, thick, blurred, rounded.

Brown, Black, and Horowitz (1955) gave a test consisting of twenty-one English antonym pairs translated into Chinese, Czech, and Hindi to eighty-six American college students who were totally ignorant of these languages. Of the twenty-one pairs, nine pairs in each language were correctly judged in 64 per cent or more cases, and the antonyms blunt/sharp, bright/dark, hard/soft, warm/cool were especially clearly distinguished. Only half as many results were significant in the incorrect direction. (Weiss (1963) used twenty of the same pairs of antonyms, translated into Chinese and Hindi; but the scores of his subjects, while significantly above chance, were often successful with *different* pairs from those with which the subjects of Brown, Black, and Horowitz had succeeded.)

Slobin (1968) used pairs from the three dimensions of the semantic differential discussed in Chapter 4 (Evaluation, Potency, and Activity) for Thai, Kanarese, and Yoruba, in relation to both sensible and non-sensible qualities. He concluded that magnitude, brightness, strength, sharpness, and some concepts of comfort or pleasantness and their opposites are qualities which can be expressed in phonetic symbolism, and he stresses that

... phonetic symbolism in natural languages is not restricted to the sensible category, as Brown and Nuttall (1959) suggested, and it is certainly not restricted to magnitude and its associates. A phonetic symbolism of evaluation is perhaps as strongly evident as that of potency and activity. (Ibid. 304)

Klank, Huang, and Johnson (1971) also tested eight pairs from the three dimensions of the semantic differential, for antonyms in Czech, Hindi, Chinese, Japanese, and Tahitian, and eight pairs which were not significant in terms of the three semantic dimensions. The results showed that with the antonym pairs not from the three semantic dimensions subjects guessed correctly with only a chance level of accuracy, as they did in the case of *non-antonym* pair members from the same end of the same semantic dimension. But when pairs were antonyms from the same semantic dimensions, or not antonyms, but from *different* semantic dimensions, then the successful guesses reached a high level above that of chance ($p < .0001$). Further tests with English-Chinese antonyms showed that

The high vowels and front vowels occur more often, proportionately, in

words denoting smallness; the large vowels and back vowels in words denoting largeness ...

... for both Chinese and English more slow words have initial consonant phonemes which are stops, and more fast words have initial consonants that are affricates and fricatives. (Klank, Huang, and Johnson
1971: 147)

So inasmuch as qualities of potency, activity, and evaluation and
others seem to be phonetically expressed in language, this may well
be a further factor contributing to nominal realism.

It might also be suggested that in the naming of their childrren,
for example, primitives must be aware that the name has an arbitrary, conventional relationship with the person named, and that
this might well lead many of them to realize that words are only
conventionally related to what they denote. But it is evident, in
fact, that primitives do not make any distinction between proper
and class names, and it seems to be the general rule in the languages they speak that the same term is used both for 'word' and
for 'name'; we should thus interpret their word for 'name' as covering our word for 'word', rather than supposing that they have a
word for 'word' which they extend to 'name'. (Piaget notes that
children find the idea of 'name' much easier to grasp than that of
'word'.) For us, of course, a proper name, unlike a class name, has
no intension or connotation, and so we cannot sensibly ask what
characteristics two 'Fred Smiths' have in common to justify their
both being called 'Fred Smith', as we could ask if they had been
called 'engine-drivers'. Nor is a proper name a case of a class with
only one member. 'The Creator' is a class with only one member,
but this is logically quite distinct from 'Yahweh', which was His
personal name among the ancient Israelites.[7]

But while names have no connotation, they do have the same
physiognomic properties as ordinary words. They may have descriptive origins, as many English place names and occupational
surnames demonstrate; and there may be rules or conventions
governing the inheritance or bestowal of names, which prescribe
certain names for different sexes, classes, or families, and so on.
Among the Konso, for example, first names (as opposed to patronymics) are bestowed on children in accordance with the state of

---

[7] I am aware that the distinction between proper and class names is a matter of great
complexity and debate among logicians, but the elementary distinction drawn here
would, I think, be broadly acceptable for the limited purposes of the present discussion.

TABLE XX

Names Male	Female	Meaning
Ꞵo	Ꞵido	Born during planting (Ꞵa = planting season)
Kadano	Kadana	Born during first rains (Kadana = first rains)
Armada	Armana	Born at weeding time (Arma = weeding)
Rōbo	Rōpa	Born during rain (*rōba* = rain)
Ludīdo	Ludīya	Born during bird scaring (*lūdeda* = to scare birds)
Kalabo	Kalle	Born at night (Kalabta = darkness)
Tēgando	Tēgo	Born in morning (*tēganda* = morning)
Urmalle	Urmala	Born on market day (*urmala* = market)
Torīdo	Torīya	Born at time of law suit (*tora* = law suit)
Kapino	Kapina	Born in bush, forest (*kapina* = bush)
Shakido	Shakiya	Puny infant (*ashaka* = small)
Olado	Olato	Born late (*olada* = to delay)
Garo	Garide	Born in house of a member of Togmaleda clan (*gaharta*, ewe, is totem of Togmaleda)
Odīyo	Odīya	Born in house of a member of Argamīda clan. (Odīya is name of a ritual group of clans, of which Argamīda is chief)
Sagaro	Sagara	Born when father has killed dik-dik (*sagarita* = dikdik)
Garmo	Garmōde	Born when father has killed lion (*garma* = lion)
Kudano	Kudana	Born while father hunting (*ĝudeda* = to hunt)
Kergito	Kergēya	Born when father gone to Borana country (Kerge = Borana)

the seasonal/agricultural cycle and other circumstances at the time of birth, including the activities of the father, as Table XX illustrates.

The Konso system of name inheritance also illustrates that personal names are an integral part of social relations. A man has two names, a forename and a patronymic, which together we represent as aX (see Figure 35). If he is an eldest son, his sons will all take X as their patronym, but if he is a younger son all his sons will take the patronymic a.

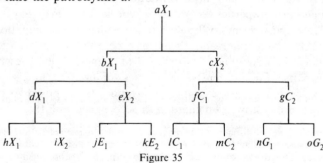

Figure 35

The consequence of this system of name inheritance is that the senior line retains the same patronymic, X, in perpetuity, while junior lines change their patronymics in each successive generation, except for the sons of eldest sons, who retain their fathers' patronymics. Among the Konso, succession from eldest son to eldest son is the basis of the office of the lineage and sacrificer, the *poĝalla*, who appropriately retains the patronymic of the lineage founder.

Thus names among the Konso, as for many societies, are not arbitrarily bestowed, but on the contrary are an integral part of social relations.

4. THE EXPLANATION OF DREAMS

Of all forms of subjectively generated mental phenomena dreams (except for waking hallucinations) are the most striking, and in primitive society the common assumptions about the nature of dreams generally conform to the conceptual-realist model—dreams are experiences of external origin, not sets of images generated within the head of the dreamer, these experiences being undergone by the soul and not by the body or its sense organs. We also find that primitives very commonly give symbolic interpretations to commonly recurring motifs in dreams. In this respect, and in their explanation by the activities of the soul, there is clearly a social elaboration on the facts of individual experience, and on the realist model, which does not seem to occur in European children's explanations of dreams.

Among the Greeks, Dodds says:

... we may notice that the language used by Greeks at all periods in describing dreams of all sorts appears to be suggested by a type of dream in which the dreamer is the passive recipient of an objective vision. The Greeks never spoke as we do of *having* a dream, but always of *seeing* a dream—ὄναρ ἰδεῖν, ἐνύπνιον ἰδεῖν. The phase is appropriate only to dreams of the passive type, but we find it used even when the dreamer is himself the central figure in the dream action. (Dodds 1951: 105)
[and]
In most of their descriptions of dreams, the Homeric poets treat what is seen as if it were 'objective fact'. The dream usually takes the form of a visit paid to a sleeping man or woman by a single dream-figure (the very word *oneiros* in Homer nearly always means dream-figure, not dream-experience). This dream figure can be a god, or a ghost, or a pre-existing

dream-messenger, or an 'image' (*eidōlon*) created specially for the occasion; but whichever it is, it exists objectively in space, and is independent of the dreamer. It effects its entry by the keyhole (Homeric bedrooms have neither window nor chimney); it plants itself at the head of the bed to deliver its message; and when it is done, it withdraws by the same route. The dreamer, meanwhile, is almost completely passive: he sees a figure, he hears a voice and that is practically all. (Ibid. 104–5)

A different notion of dreams is supplied by the Nupe of Nigeria, by whom the dreamer or his soul is seen as participating actively in the dream:

When I dream, my *rayi* [life principle, not a personal soul] wanders about and sees all the things that come to me in the dream. But the *rayi* does not wander alone; it takes something with it that is, though not of the body, yet of bodily shape; for I may appear to others in their dreams, as in turn I dream of other persons. It is not, of course, the real, full person that is met with in dreams (for the real person may be away in other parts, or asleep at home), but only his or her image or shadow—the *fifingi*.

Fifingi means 'shadow' much as we understand the word, that is, the shadow thrown by men and animals, not the shade caused by inanimate things. But the word has a second, mystic meaning, best translated as 'shadow soul'; for when a person dies and his body decomposes the *fifingi* continues to exist and will still be visible (as in our dreams of dead people). (Nadel 1954: 22)

We have seen from Piaget that it is the contradiction between dream content and waking reality that finally convinces the child of the subjective origin of dreams. But the case of the Tikopia shows how easily collective representations may be elaborated by a society to explain away these apparent contradictions:

The Tikopia explanation of the cause of dreams varies according to the precise nature of the experience, but rests at bottom on the general theory of the mobile soul. Every person has a *mauri* or *ora*, an intangible entity normally invisible to the waking eye, which may for convenience be designated the spirit or life principle—the Tikopia terms being generally being used synonymously—and this is capable of leaving the body during sleep and wandering abroad ... The Tikopia have no clear theory as to the relation between spirit and body at this time: they are separate, yet the adventures of the spirit part become the responsible agent, the property of the whole, and a person in narrating a dream uses the pronoun 'I'. Both spirit and body, in fact, are treated as the Ego. Other persons seen in dreams are *prima facie* the *mauri* of such persons, though here an important qualification has to be made as will be seen below.

Dreams of visits to distant places are readily explained by the mobility of the *mauri*, which can flash about at will, annihilating space, while the same power also allows it to journey to Rangi, the Heavens, and have contact with persons long dead. These are represented by their own spirits known as *mauri* in their lifetime, but now as *atua*. The recognition of another person either living or dead in a dream encounter, however, is not necessarily taken to mean that it is his own spirit entity which is present. Many dream experiences are the result of the interposition of *atua* of another kind, spiritual beings who have never belonged to human kind and lived upon earth, but who for their own purposes, generally malicious, counterfeit familiar forms in order to deceive the dreamer. (Firth 1967: 164)

Dreams of the past offer no problems for the Tikopia, since the dreamer is said to be meeting the souls of the dead; dreams of sexual intercourse with known people are said to be the result of a spirit impersonation of the person in question. Since dreams may have a symbolic meaning, they may in a sense be false, when they predict something which does not happen. Such 'false' dreams which incorrectly represent the future are said to be the work of mischievous *atua*.

Some dreams, too, have no significance attached to them. It may be said, indeed, that the weight attached to a dream varies as the emotional intensity of the personal situation at the time, that a dream receives attention and credence largely in so far as it can be related to some question immediately at issue within the social horizon of the dreamer. (Ibid. 163)

Thus it is quite possible for primitives to find many ways of explaining apparent conflicts between dream events and waking reality.

In many primitive societies dreams are given symbolic interpretations, of which the following instances from the Konso are typical examples:

[In dreams] People going to the fields are not going, as in real life, to weed and reap, but to dig a grave; if they are building a wall, it is not a terrace wall, but the circular wall around a grave. Stones in dreams are the stones of these grave walls, and a *'daga 'deeruma* [stone commemorating a victory in battle] portends the death of strong men. A hole is always a grave, and even for a weaver to dream that he is putting his feet into the small pit beneath his loom is to dream of his own grave ... Dreams of fire are always bad, and signify death and destruction; ashes signify poverty. Smoke and mist are alike bad and are signs of sickness. Birds are symbols of famine, high winds mean death . . . Climbing a tree or hill is a good sign associated with food. All dreams to do with food or water are good, and even the dream of a man falling into a well is good. Curiously, to dream of honey is a portent of sickness. Fetching water is an auspicious sign, and so is a snake, which symbolizes water. Soot is a good omen for women, and picking up iron on the path symbolizes money. (Hallpike 1972: 162–3)

It might be supposed that the interpretation of dreams not as the psychic experiences of the soul, but in terms of their symbolic meaning, represented a cognitively more advanced stage in the understanding of their nature, by which they are treated as 'unreal' in their manifest content. Dodds quotes the theory of H. J. Rose that there are three pre-scientific stages in the understanding of dreams, '(1) "to take the dream vision as objective fact"; (2) "to suppose it . . . something seen by the soul, or one of the souls, while temporarily out of the body, a happening whose scene is in the spirit world, or the like"; (3) "to interpret it by a more complicated symbolism"' (Rose, *Primitive Culture in Greece,* p. 151, quoted in Dodds 1951: 104). But Dodds points out that this theoretical sequence does not correspond with the historical development of Greek attitudes to dreams:

If we look at Homer, we shall see that the first and third of Rose's 'stages' coexist in both poems, with no apparent consciousness of incongruity, while Rose's second 'stage' is entirely missing (and continues to be missing from extant Greek literature down to the fifth century, when it makes a sensational first appearance in a well-known fragment of Pindar). (Ibid. 104)

Dodds also draws attention to the persistence of the Homeric notion of the objective dream image (*eidolon*) in intellectual circles of the late fifth century:

. . . Democritus' atomist theory of dreams as *eidola* which continually emanate from persons and objects, and affect the dreamer's consciousness by penetrating the pores of his body, is plainly an attempt to provide a mechanistic basis for the objective dream; it even preserves Homer's word for the objective dream-image. (Ibid. 118)

Just as notions of dreams as experiences of the soul retain the basic assumption of the external origins of dreams, so too this same assumption is not controverted by the symbolic interpretation of dreams. For in waking life it is common in primitive society for a wide variety of events to be given the symbolic status of omens, e.g. 'A certain kind of ribbed cloud structure denotes to the Tikopia not merely a kind of weather but also the approach of a vessel which is as yet invisible below the horizon. Similarly a rainbow or the sound of thunder can be a vessel sign. Even a sneeze can be so interpreted' (Firth 1967: 146). In our own society those who believe when seeing magpies that a single one foretells sorrow, and two joy, do not suppose that the magpies in question are in any way abnormal or spiritual birds. It therefore seems more consistent with the facts to regard the dream symbolism of primitive cultures simply as another example of omens; and given the pronounced assimilatory aspects of both dreams and symbolism noted in Chapter 4, it is not surprising that dreams should be rich in omens of this type.

By the time of the Pre-Socratics, some philosophers were capable of recognizing the subjective basis of dreams, e.g. Heraclitus: 'To those who are awake, there is one ordered universe common (*to all*), whereas in sleep each man turns away (*from this world*) to one of his own' (fr. 89; K. Freeman 1971: 30), although, as we have seen from Dodd's remarks, it was still possible for other philosophers to maintain that dreams were objective in origin.

Turner provides an illuminating example of a highly intelligent informant, Muchona, who could recognize that at least some of his dreams were simply memories:

... Muchona, the homeless, was peculiarly susceptible to nostalgia. He had a recurrent dream which I translate literally to keep the smack of his speech. 'I dream of the country of Nyamwana where I was born and used to live. I am where my mother died. I dream of the village which is surrounded by a palisade, for bad people raided for slaves. Streams which were there I see once more. It is as though I were walking there now. I talk, I chat, I dance. Does my shadow (*mwevulu*—the personal life principle) go there in sleep?' Here the rational side of Muchona came uppermost, for he went on: 'I find that place the same as it was long ago. But if I had really visited it, the trees would have grown big, grass perhaps would have covered it. Would there have been a stockade? No, it is just a memory.' He shook his head lugubriously and said, lingering on each syllable. '*Ākā*' (meaning 'alas', with a flavour of 'Eheu fugaces!'). (Turner 1967: 138–9)

But the late emergence of views such as those of Heraclitus on the subjectivity of dreams, the fact that later thinkers did not agree with him, and the rarity of men like Muchona in primitive society who can recognize the basis of at least some of their dreams in memory, testify to the great difficulty which the understanding of dreams presents, and their tendency to reinforce realist assumptions about mental activity. It is also clear that other culturally elaborated beliefs about reality can play an essential part in maintaining the notion that dreams are of objective origin. For example, with regard to the explanatory function of the soul in primitive theories of dreams, it is evident that the soul is a means by which disparities between dreaming and waking experiences can be reconciled—visiting distant places, seeing people who are dead, meeting living people who have, in waking experience, no recollection of any such encounter, and so on. In addition, as we have seen, dreams are often supposed to be not simply the experiences of the dreamer, but the manifestations of spirits, divinities, and the dead, all of which are collective representations, and not available as explanations for children in the European cultural milieu. One suspects that the symbolic aspect of dreams also helps to prevent the grasp of their subjectivity, since it is possible by this form of interpretation entirely to ignore all disparities between dream content and experience.

5. CONCLUSIONS

Piaget considers that the principal factors in the disappearance of conceptual realism are contact with others in the form of discussion and collaboration, which force the child to recognize the distinction between his own point of view and that of other people. This is evidently the case in so far as the development of an awareness of 'interior states' is concerned, since the child thereby comes to recognize not only that his own emotions and attitudes are not necessarily shared by others, but that he can conceal them from others, and others can do the same with their feelings and attitudes. But equally important in generating the awareness of the critical distinction between seeming and being must be, in the European child, the growth of operational thought, in which the child is obliged more and more to exercise his judgement on the phenomenal appearance of things and to correct those appearances which he learns to distinguish from reality with increasing accuracy and assurance.

It is evident that conceptual realism is a pervasive aspect of the thought of primitive peoples, and the reasons for its persistence seem to be these:

1. There is, in primitive society, very little opportunity for the operational correction of perception, of the kind which our environment constantly requires of us. Dealing as we do in a man-made environment with a vast array of unfamiliar objects and perceptual situations, we have constantly to distinguish between 'being' and 'seeming': the large block of unexpectedly light wood which weighs less than a smaller block; the correlation of subjectively experienced duration with duration as measured by a clock; being surprised by the number of gallons of paint needed to cover an area of wall or by the number of cups of tea to be poured from a particular pot, and so on. The result is that we are always being made aware of the necessity to correct our sensory impressions of things by operational procedures, and hence of the distinction between the sensory *appearance* of the world and the world as corrected by cognitive constructions.

2. In primitive society there is very little evidence for the awareness of the notion of 'argument'—the possibility of skill in deductive inference—as opposed to oratory and the ability to score debating points. While disputes occur among all human beings, it is clear that in primitive society they are conducted in terms of factual contradiction or of appeals to custom, and not of assertions that an opponent is begging the question, or of choosing unrepresentative evidence, and so on. In particular, we have noted the resistance of primitive thought to arguments based on counterfactual hypotheses (see §6 below).

3. In primitive society the expression of individual experience is very limited. While 'interior states' such as motives, feelings, and knowledge are recognized their manifestations are assessed on the basis of behaviour; and while this behavioural assessment is often highly sophisticated, we find no elaborate terminology for the development of this awareness into the ability to express any of the finer shades of private experience such as the educated in our society take for granted (in the work of novelists, for example). It seems, therefore, that in primitive society there is very much less awareness of the distinctions between private and public awareness than we have. The individual feels, suffers, plots, and thinks, as we do, but the relative lack of representations of private experience

means that while primitive man is aware that his neighbour is feeling, suffering, plotting, and thinking, these private states are not elaborated by those who experience them. So it is that the private experience of others is commonly regarded in primitive society as mysterious and unknowable. But in our society it is the capacity to express this experience that is crucial to the development of what Piaget terms 'socialized thought', by the adjustment of our points of view to that of other individuals. In primitive society there is only one point of view—that of the group—and for this reason a very important foundation for the development of a notion of 'mind' is lacking.

4. Again, in primitive society, because collective representations are intimately bound up in social institutions and customary behaviour, there is no clear distinction between beliefs on the one hand and practice on the other. Only in a society whose world-view can be explicitly generalized is it possible to make this distinction and to separate belief from action. While of course there are sceptics in primitive societies who regard conventional explanations of magic or witchcraft as false, their scepticism is as unformalized as is the acceptance of the conventionally minded. To be able to distinguish systematically between states of belief is an important foundation for an awareness of the operation of mind.

5. We also become aware of mental activity through school experience and acquisition of literacy in particular. As we have seen, problem solving divorced from the context of 'real life' situations is of great importance in producing awareness of *cognitive* problems to which there are solutions, as opposed to the customary difficulties of ordinary work which are surmounted in non-verbal ways. Literacy produces an awareness of language as opposed simply to speech, and of the fact that language is a code which translates public and private experience and which can be considered as a phenomenon separate from the context of utterance and from the ordinary restrictions attendant on real dialogue.

6. Schooling and literacy in particular are obviously crucial to the ability to think hypothetically—that is, to make suppositions which are not based on, and may even contradict, actual experience. Probably all primitive languages have the syntactical means of expressing conditional sentences of the form 'If your pig eats my sweet potatoes, I will kill it.' But conditional sentences refer merely to possible future events, and are in this respect not the same as

truly hypothetical statements. Hypothetical thought is, of course, the basis of formal, deductive thinking, which occurs only at the age of about eleven to twelve in European children; only at this stage do children become capable of understanding what adults mean by such words as 'mind', 'thought', 'idea', and so on.

7. It is also of the greatest importance to recollect that symbolic thought is inherently harder to discriminate into its subjective and objective aspects than is language, since symbols are motivated in a way that language is not, for the most part. Thus the qualities and properties associated with symbols both inhere in the symbols and create an affective reaction in the mind which is easily attributed to the symbols themselves.

The conceptual realism of primitives must inevitably have profound implications for their notion of causality. The themes of nominal realism, the objective reality of symbolic relations, as well as the general subjectification of sensory experience, are perhaps the most obvious examples of this—and it will become apparent in the next chapter that conceptual realism is an inseparable aspect of causality.

10

Causality

In the analysis of primitive causality, the notions of magic and animism have long occupied an important position, although animism has now fallen into disuse. Mauss believed that a single idea, *mana*, mystical power or force, underlies all manifestations of magic, and in his *General Theory of Magic* he attempts to show

... how the magical value of persons or things results from the relative position they occuupy within society or in relation to society. The two separate notions of magical virtue and social position coincide in so far as one depends on the other. Basically in magic it is always a matter of the respective values recognized by society. These values do not depend, in fact, on the intrinsic qualities of a thing or a person, but on the status or rank attributed to them by all-powerful public opinion, by its prejudices. They are social facts not experimental facts. And this is excellently demonstrated by the magical power of words and the fact that very often the magical power of an object derives from its name. Consequently, since they depend on dialects and languages, the values in question are tribal or national ones. In the same way, things and beings and actions are organized hierarchically, controlling one another, and magical actions are produced according to this ordering: they go from the magician to a class of spirits, from this class to another, and so on, until they achieve their effect. The reason why we like Hewitt's phrase 'magic potence', which he uses to describe *mana* and *orenda* is because it brings out precisely the presence of a kind of magical potential, and it is, in fact, exactly the idea we have been describing. What we call the relative position or respective value of things could also be called a difference in potential, since it is due to such differences that they are able to affect one another. It is not enough to say that the quality of *mana* is attributed to certain things because of the relative position they hold in society. We must add that the idea of *mana* is none other than the idea of these relative values and the idea of these differences in potential. Here we come face to face with the whole idea on which magic is founded, in fact with magic itself. It goes without saying that ideas like this have no *raison d'être* outside society, that they are absurd as far as pure reason is concerned and that they derive purely and simply from the functioning of collective life. (Mauss 1972: 120–1)

I have quoted this passage at length because it illustrates very well the inadequacy of sociological attempts to derive modes of thought entirely from social institutions and relations, without regard to the thought processes of individuals and the nature of the problems that are to be solved. Apart from the vagueness and inadequacy of 'magic' as an analytical category, Mauss's attempts to explain such notions as *mana* and *orenda* by reference to differences in role and status (as it might be of the ancestors in relation to the king, or women in relation to men) confounds the social milieu in which certain fundamental ideas are expressed, and those ideas themselves. Of course, sacrifice, spells, witchcraft, cursing and blessing, divination, priests and magicians, are social categories, forming an integral part of each society, and must be analysed as such. But to assert that 'the idea of *mana* is *none other* than the idea of these relative values and the idea of these differences in potential' does not do justice to the complexities of primitive notions of causality or to the relations of these notions to other aspects of primitive thought.

To understand primitive causality it is essential to discard sociological categories and vague terms such as magic and *mana*, and to focus instead on the basic cognitive processes which we have been considering in this book. Three of these in particular claim our attention—conceptual realism; the inability to construct operatory systems based on dimensional analysis and the relations between objects; and the general lack of taxonomic classification and generalization based on logical class, as opposed to prototypes and complexes.

In our discussion of conceptual realism we had occasion to consider the roots of nominal realism and the assumption that words had an inherent association with their referents, such that knowing the name of something or someone is the essential means to power over it or him. This theme, that speech is power, is so prevalent in magic that it seems unnecessary to provide further ethnographic illustrations of it here.

In the same way, we have already noted that conceptual realism also prevents primitives from treating symbolic associations simply as subjective mental associations. We therefore commonly find that symbolic properties are also regarded as empirically real properties which may be utilized to bring about changes in the physical world. This is clearly the origin of many of the 'participations' noted by Lévy-Bruhl and others. Thus in portraits or photographs of a person, while we regard the representation simply as creating a subjective association in the mind of the beholder, the primitive, with no awareness of the mind, must perforce regard the sensations of familiarity produced by the representation as inhering in the representation, and not as in his own mind. The representation is thus conceived as having captured part of the essence of the original.[1]

The lack of operatory analysis and co-ordination leads, as does conceptual realism, to explanations in terms of essences, the reification of properties, and the treatment of processes as substances, a world of forces which are awakened in things rather than being transmitted. Operatory causality is a universe of relations in which attributes are relative, as opposed to a world of absolute substances and essences such as heat and coldness, heaviness and lightness, whose associations are static and irreversible.

[1] The possible origins of the reported belief that primitives often imagine that the camera captures their souls was the subject of a letter by Needham to the *Times Literary Supplement* (Needham 1976), which stimulated a number of letters in reply. Professor Needham has kindly made his file of correspondence on this matter available to me. It is clear from the evidence provided by these various sources that the question of cameras capturing souls is not simply a matter of conceptual realism, but also involves (a) the camera lens interpreted as an eye and the very common notion among primitives that the eye can penetrate and/or emit some kind of force, be it light, feelings, or some other emanation (such an interpretation would be strengthened by the use of those cameras which are held at eye level, as opposed to plate cameras or twin-lens reflexes); (b) the camera as box, into which things can be put—this aspect of cameras is of particular relevance in the case of early plate cameras equipped with opaque screens onto which the view (inverted, incidentally) is projected by the lens; (c) the negative itself; again, in the early days of photography processing was often carried out on the spot, and subjects had the opportunity of seeing themselves and their surroundings reproduced in concrete and miniature form, and with black and white reversed, with obvious symbolic implications; (d) the very common belief that the soul is manifested in the shadow or the reflection, both of which beliefs having obvious associations with the negative and the print; (e) the frequent occurrences of graphic representations in magic which have obvious implications for photography. Not only are there many reports from all over the world of cameras being supposed to capture souls, but artists who sketched primitive subjects (such as Bowdich among the Ashanti, and Catlin among the North American Indians) were supposed to be capturing the soul or vital essence of their subjects. In view of these many different aspects of the camera, it would be unwise to suppose that any single interpretation of its alleged efficacy in capturing souls would apply to all cases.

In Chapter 3 we referred to the subjectification of experience which necessarily occurs when the properties and qualities of things are assessed primarily in terms of how they affect men's bodies and senses rather than in terms of their effects on other objects. In a world of absolute qualities, of essences, and of hypostatized processes, and in which the sensations of man are not clearly differentiated from objective physical properties, it is easy to see how psychic states, such as purpose, vitality, and responsiveness to the wishes or behaviour of men, may be attributed to material objects and events. This propensity is greatly augmented by the primitive apprehension of speech as having power in itself, through the adherence of names to the thing named, to control the real world, and by the parallel inability of primitives to regard symbolic associations as purely subjective.

As we saw in our earlier study of classification, complexive groupings and prototypical images are based on the functional, perceptual, and contextual associations which things have with one another in everyday life, not on taxonomic properties which are the basis of logical class. This inhibits the abstraction of those properties and qualities that are the basis of operatory co-ordination, and the kinds of generalization about the material world that are the basis of scientific laws.

Thus conceptual realism, lack of operatory co-ordination, and complexive classification and prototypical imagery are closely interrelated factors in the construction of primitive causality. It is these cognitive factors, rather that any simple projection of personal relations into the realm of nature, that are responsible for the frequently noted anthropomorphism of primitive notions of causality. We may now discuss these primary factors in more detail.

1. ABSOLUTISM, ESSENTIALISM, AND THE HYPOSTATIZATION OF PROCESS

At the level of pre-operatory thought the failure clearly to distinguish between the objective properties of things and the subject's own sensory reactions to these goes hand in hand with the propensity to think of the properties of things as absolute and inherent in those things, rather than as the product of relations between things. Thus the pre-operatory subject supposes that movement is a manifestation of a force or vitality that is inherent in the moving object, and also easily assumes that this vitality is purposive, goal-directed. In particular, the subject's own muscular reactions with his physical environment are the basis for his notions of force, which he uses to explain all movement. Since he treats the resistance offered by an object when he tries to move or lift it as a manifestation of the active power of that object, he therefore regards heaviness, not as we do as passive and inert ('a dead weight', 'stone dead', etc.) but as an active property closely allied to that of strength.

Thus force is seen as a manifestation of life and purpose; and it is also seen as a substance. It is closely identified with life; and the child does not think, as we do, of energy being transmitted from body to body, but as being a *sui generis* constituent of every body, unacquired and intransmissible. Force is not transmitted but awakened.

Being unfamiliar with explicit comparison and the relativity of relations, the child does not think of the same object *A* as heavy in relation to another object *B*, and as simultaneously lighter than a third object *C*; *A* is conceived as heavy in an absolute sense. Thus instead of comparing the weight of an object with its volume or with the weight of the medium which supports it, he simply assumes that boats, for example, float because of their intrinsic capacity to do so. As Piaget says:

During the early stages, every movement is regarded as singular, as the manifestation, that is, of a substantial and living activity. In other words, there is in every moving substance a motor substance: the clouds, the heavenly bodies, water, and machines, etc, move by themselves. Even when the child succeeds in conceiving an external motor, which already takes away from the substantiality of movement, the internal motor continues to be regarded as necessary. Thus a leaf is alive, even though it moves with the wind, *i.e.* it retains its spontaneity even though the wind is needed to set it in motion. Similarly, a cloud or one of the heavenly bodies remains master of its movements, even though the wind is necessary to start it on its path. But later on, the movement of every body becomes the function of external movements, which are regarded no longer as necessary collaborators but as sufficient conditions. Thus the movement of clouds comes to be entirely explained by that of the wind. Then these external motors are conceived as themselves dependent upon other external motors, and so on. In this way there comes into being a universe of relations which takes the place of a universe of independent and spontaneous substances. (Piaget 1930: 249–50)

These contentions are well illustrated by the pre-operatory concept of weight:

The idea of weight supplies us with an excellent example of this advance towards relativity, and the evolution in this particular case is closely bound up with the advance towards reciprocity ... During the earliest stages, weight is synonymous with strength and activity. A pebble sunk in water weighs on the water, even when the latter is motionless, and produces a current towards the surface. An object floats because, being heavy, it has the strength to keep itself up. Weight is an absolute thing: it is a quality possessed by certain bodies, a variant of that life, or substantial force which we have described. Later on, weight is regarded as relative to the surrounding medium: bodies float because they are lighter than water, the clouds because they are lighter than air, etc. But the relation is still vague: the child simply means that for the water in the lake, such and such a boat is light, but no comparison has been made which introduces proportional volumes. The wood of the boat is regarded as heavier than an equal volume of water. Finally, between the years of 9 and 10, 'lighter than the water' begins to mean that the body in question is, taken at equal volume, lighter than water. Thus do the ideas of density and specific weight make their appearance: absolute weight is succeeded, in part at any rate, by relative weight. (Ibid. 250)

Ethnographic literature is replete with examples of the way in which primitives treat mental and bodily conditions and processes, properties and qualities of physical objects, and physical processes, as well as conditions of society such as ill luck, sin, and general ill health, as entities which can be transmitted from man to nature, from one natural object to another, and from natural objects to man, in an enormous variety of ways. The true significance of this cognitive phenomenon is not so much that it is a case of Frazer's homeopathic magic, of 'like producing like', as of the pre-operatory propensity to isolate particular phenomena and treat them as bounded entities which can be detached from their physical context with absolute properties and an inner dynamism of their own. The reification of process in particular is a notable example of this proclivity of mind, which we shall consider in more detail shortly. The following examples are taken from Frazer's *Golden Bough*:

In the western district of the island of Timor, when men or women are making long and tiring journeys, they fan themselves with leafy branches, which they afterwards throw away on particular spots where their forefathers did the same before them. The fatigue which they felt is thus supposed to have passed into the leaves and to be left behind. (Frazer 1900, iii.3–4)

An ancient cure for the gripes, recorded both by Pliny and Marcellus, was
to put a live duck to the belly of the sufferer; the pain then passed from the
man to the bird, to which they proved fatal. (Ibid. iii.23)

A Northamptonshire and Devonshire cure for a cough is to put a hair of
the patient's head between two slices of buttered bread and give the sand-
wich to a dog. The animal will thereupon catch the cough and the patient
will lose it. (Ibid. iii.24)

. . . every year, generally in March, the people of Leti, Moa, and Lakor
send away all their diseases to sea. They make a proa about six feet long,
rig it with sails, oars, rudder, etc., and every family deposits in it some rice,
fruit, a fowl, two eggs, insects that ravage the fields, and so on. Then they
let it drift away to sea, saying, 'Take away from here all kinds of sickness,
take them to other islands, to other lands, distribute them in places that lie
eastward, where the sun rises.' (Ibid. iii.105-6)

At Tabor in Bohemia the figure of Death is carried out of the town and
flung from a high rock into the water, while they sing—

> Death swims on the water,
> Summer will soon be here,
> We carried Death away for you,
> We brought the Summer.
> And do thou, O holy Marketa,
> Give us a good year
> For wheat and for rye.

In other parts of Bohemia they carry Death to the end of the village,
singing—

> We carry Death out of the village,
> And the New Year into the village.
> Dear Spring, we bid you welcome,
> Green grass, we bid you welcome. (Ibid. ii.84)

Dyak priestesses expel ill-luck from a house by hewing and slashing the air
in every corner of it with wooden swords, which they afterwards wash in
the river, to let the ill-luck float away down stream. Sometimes they sweep
misfortune out of the house with brooms made of the leaves of certain
plants and sprinkled with rice water and blood. Having swept it clean out
of every room and into a toy-house made of bamboo, they set the little
house with its load of bad luck adrift on the river. (Ibid. iii.2-3)

To explain the universal custom of throwing sticks or stones onto
cairns at graves and other places where evil or hostile forces are
supposed to reside, Frazer suggests what is the most likely explanation:

To rid himself of that pollution which, as usual he conceives in a concrete form, the savage seeks to gather it up in a material vehicle and leave it behind him on the hazardous spot, while, having thus cast care away, he hastens forward with a lighter heart. (Ibid. iii.10)

... in Syria when a fruit tree does not bear, the gardener gets a pregnant woman to fasten a stone to one of its branches; then the tree will be sure to bear fruit, but the woman will run a risk of miscarriage, having transferred her fertility, or part of it, to the tree. The practice of loading with stones a tree which casts its fruit is mentioned by Maimonides, though the Rabbis apparently did not understand it. The proceeding was probably an imitative charm designed to load the tree with fruit. In Swabia they say that if a fruit-tree does not bear, you should keep it loaded with a heavy stone all summer, and next year it will be sure to bear. (Ibid. i.38)

... the Galelareese think that when your teeth are being filed you should keep spitting on a pebble, for this establishes a sympathetic connection between you and the pebble, by virtue of which your teeth will henceforth be as hard and durable as a stone. On the other hand, you ought not to comb a child before it has teethed, for if you do, its teeth will afterwards be separated from each other like the teeth of a comb. (Ibid. i.43–4)

And the Tauade say that if a man repeats the name of a particular wind, he will become as swift of foot in battle as that wind.

The Breton peasant fancies that clover sown when the tide is coming in will grow well, but that if the plant be sown at low water or when the tide is going out, it will never reach maturity, and that the cows which feed on it will burst. His wife believes that the best butter is made when the tide has just turned and is beginning to flow, that milk which foams in the churn will go on foaming till the hour of high water is past, and that water drawn from the well or milk extracted from the cow while the tide is rising will boil up in the pot or saucepan and overflow into the fire. (Ibid. i.46)

Examples of similar beliefs that processes carried out under a waxing or a waning moon will concordantly prosper or wither away are numerous in ethnographic literature.

In Thüringen the man who sows flax carries the seed in a long bag which reaches from his shoulders to his knees, and he walks with long strides, so that the bag sways to and fro on his back. It is believed that this will cause the flax to wave in the wind. In the interior of Sumatra rice is sown by women who, in sowing, let their hair hang loose down their back, in order that the rice may grow luxuriantly and have long stalks. (Ibid. i.35)

... some Bechuanas wear a ferret as a charm, because, being very tenacious of life, it will make them very difficult to kill. Others wear a certain insect, mutilated, but living, for a similar purpose. Yet other Bechuana warriors wear the hair of a hornless ox among their own hair, and the skin of a frog on their mantle, because a frog is slippery, and the ox, having no horns, is hard to catch; so the man who is provided with these charms believes that he will be as hard to hold as the ox and the frog. (Ibid. i.41–2)

The chief product of some parts of Laos, a province of Siam, is lac. This is a resinous gum exuded by a red insect on the young branches of trees, to which the little creatures have to be attached by hand. All who engage in the business of gathering the gum abstain from washing themselves and especially from cleansing their heads, lest by removing the parasites from their hair they should detach the other insects from the boughs. (Frazer 1922: 21)

The Melanesians believe that certain sacred stones are endowed with miraculous powers which correspond in their nature to the shape of the stone. Thus a piece of water-worn coral on the beach often bears a surprising resemblance to a bread-fruit. Hence a man who finds such a coral will lay it at the root of one of his bread-fruit trees in the expectation that it will make the tree bear well ... Similarly, a stone with little discs upon it is good to bring in money; and if a man found a large stone with a number of small ones under it, like a sow among her litter, he was sure that to offer money upon it would bring him pigs. (Frazer 1900: i.45)

Amongst the Omaha Indians of North America, when the corn is withering for want of rain, the members of the sacred Buffalo Society fill a large vessel with water and dance four times round it. One of them drinks some of the water and spirts it into the air, making a fine spray in imitation of a mist or drizzling rain. Then he upsets the vessel, spilling the water on the ground; whereupon the dancers fall down and drink up the water, getting mud all over their faces. Lastly, they spirt the water into the air, making a fine mist. This saves the corn. (Ibid. i.82)

In addition, the infinite variety of symbolic resemblances, based on colour, form, texture, number, and other characteristics of physical objects possess, as we have seen, the power to encapsulate properties and to transmit them between things.

The pre-operatory failure to take account of the relations between things, and the consequent treatment of phenomena as 'things' or essences, is well illustrated by the case of shadows. Our examination of pre-operatory representations of space showed that the understanding of projective relationships, which is essential to a proper understanding of the nature of shadows, matures only at the level of concrete operations, since it involves the notion of the geometrical straight line, projective relations, and the ability to objectify one's point of view so that one can visualize the projection of a shadow from the point of view of the light source. Piaget's work on the child's understanding of shadows demonstrates that the primitive understanding of them conforms closely to the cognitive level of pre-operatory thought.

In the first stage (average age five years), shadows are conceived as due to the collaboration or participation of two sources, the one internal (the shadow emanates from the object), the other external (shadows come from trees, from night, from the corner of the room, etc.). During the second stage (average age six to seven) shadows are believed to be produced by the object alone. They are a substance emanating from the object, but in no particular direction. At this stage the child is not yet able to say on which side the shadow will fall when the screen is placed in front of the source of light. In the second stage, the element of participation disappears, but the child still believes that the shadow is a substance and that it is produced at night, only it is impossible for us to see it:

(Leo, 7 years of age)
Q. When it is night, does [a person] make [a shadow] too?
A. He makes one then (but) you don't see it because it's night.
Q. How do we make one?
A. You make it when you walk, because every step you make, it follows us behind.
Q. Why does it follow us?
A. Because it is the person who makes it on the ground.
Q. But how can the person do that?
A. He walks.
Q. Where does the shadow come from?
A. It comes out of the person, we have a shadow inside us. (Piaget 1930: 187)

At the third stage (about eight years) the child is able to predict the orientation of shadows, but still believes that the shadow is an emanation of the object that drives away the light, and that it will therefore always be on the side of an object opposite to the source of light. At the fourth stage (about nine years) the correct explanation is found.

The child grasps the correct explanation only when he applies the judgements of geometrical relations of perspective to his own predictions of the behaviour of shadows; and when he does this he ceases to think of shadows as substances:

For to explain the phenomenon of shadows is, at bottom, to rely upon judgments of geometrical relations; it is to place oneself in imagination behind the object which acts as a screen and to grasp the fact that from that position the light is hidden. As soon as you have succeeded in handling these relations of perspective, you will understand why shadows vary in shape and orientation according to the position of the source of light, and in this way alone the substantialist explanation will be rendered useless. To explain a shadow is therefore to ascertain by means of the logic of spatial relations to what extent you can or cannot see the light if you walk round the object which acts as a screen. The explanation of shadows is purely geometrical. (Piaget 1930: 191–2)

We cannot therefore expect an understanding of the nature of shadows in cultures whose members have no grasp of the laws of perspective, or even of the geometrical straight line. We find that, instead of being able to explain shadows by an analysis of relations, primitives generally regard shadows as substances or emanations from the person, and have little interest in the shadows cast by objects.

An example from the Dobu shows that the shadow and the reflection are both regarded as manifestations of the soul. The test of this is that the Dobuans take a number of precautions to protect their shadows from dangerous associations:

Every person is believed to have a bodily and a ghostly self. This ghostly self survives after the body is rotted in the grave and the skull alone retained of it in the house of the next-of-kin. It is the reflection seen in a pool—the only mirror before the white man came—and in a mirror. It is related to the shadow in a way that the native refuses to define clearly. Sometimes he says that the shadow goes to Bwebweso, the Mountain of the Spirits in Normanby Island, sometimes he says not, thinking of the shadow's difference from the spirit. On the whole, however, the shadow is a form the spirit may take; and a native would sometimes comment in a tone that left no doubt as to its spiritual quality on my great shadow cast on my mosquito net by my Tilley lamp as I sat at night at my table writing. Again, a native takes great care to keep his shadow clear of an object upon which he is placing an evil incantation. The spirit is reflection and shadow; but more importantly and more decisively it is the shapes that are seen in dreams. (Fortune 1932: 180–1)

Among the Gnau, 'the living person has a shadow (*malauda*) which the sun casts upon the ground. *Malauda* is also his tiny image in another's eye, his reflection in a pool. In dreams if you see other living men, you as a *malauda* meet their similar reflections' (G. Lewis 1975: 156). (In other cases, however, one finds that the shadow or reflection, while perhaps etymologically associated with the soul, and even said to 'be' the soul, is not the object of any special precautions, and, as among the Orokaiva (Williams 1930: 261) or the Konso (Hallpike 1972: 160) the use of the same word for shadow or reflection, and for 'soul', seems to be essentially metaphorical.)

The lack of operatory co-ordination of spatio-temporal representations is closely linked with the inability to understand process except as a sequence of static stages, or as initial and final states, as in the case of 'Just So' myths of origin. Thus what we regard as the *processes* of life and death, sickness and health, conflict generation and resolution, become hypostatized into *entities*, such as 'Life', 'Death', 'War', 'Peace', 'Health', and so on, which have volition and an inner cohesion and dynamic which may be controlled.

Thus, commonly recurring types of events, which have affective significance in daily life, tend to become hypostatized and seen as entities, with a will and intention of their own.

We would explain, for instance, that certain atmospheric changes broke a drought and brought about rain. The Babylonians observed the same facts but experienced them as the intervention of the gigantic bird Imdugud which came to their rescue. It covered the sky with the black storm clouds of its wings and devoured the Bull of Heaven, whose hot breath had scorched the crops.

In telling such a myth, the ancients did not intend to provide entertainment. Neither did they seek, in a detached way and without ulterior motives, for intelligible explanations of the natural phenomena. They were recounting events in which they were involved to the extent of their very existence. They experienced, directly, a conflict of powers, one hostile to the harvest upon which they depended, the other frightening but beneficial: the thunderstorm reprieved them in the nick of time by defeating and utterly destroying the drought. (H. and H. A. Frankfort 1949: 15)

An excellent example of this tendency toward concreteness is the primitive conception of death. Death is not, as for us, an event—the act or fact of dying, Webster has it. It is somehow a substantial reality . . .
[Thus] . . . the cupbearer Siduri pities Gilgamesh in the Epic:
> Gilgamesh, whither are you wandering?
> Life, which you look for, you will never find.

> For when the gods created man, they let
> death be his share, and life
> withheld in their own hands.

Note, in the first place, that life is opposed to death, thus accentuating the fact that life in itself is considered endless. Only the intervention of another phenomenon, death, makes an end to it. In the second place, we should note the concrete character attributed to life in the statement that the gods withheld life in their hands. In case one is inclined to see in this phrase a figure of speech, it is well to remember that Gilgamesh and, in another myth, Adapa are given a chance to gain eternal life simply by eating life as a substance. Gilgamesh is shown the 'plant of life', but a serpent robs him of it. Adapa is offered bread and water of life when he enters heaven, but he refuses it on the instruction of the wily god Enki. In both cases the assimilation of a concrete substance would have made the difference between death and immortality. (Ibid. 23)

Primitive man finds great difficulty in the analysis of natural and social process. While he perceives an initial and an end state, how the latter is attained is often obscure to him. As the Frankforts say of the Egyptians and Babylonians:

We must remember that mythopoeic thought does not require its explanation to represent a continuous process. It accepts an initial situation and a final situation connected by no more than the conviction that the one came forth from the other.

Changes can be explained very simply as two different states, one of which is said to come forth from the other without any insistence on an intelligible process—in other words, as a transformation, a metamorphosis. We find that, time and again, this device is used to account for changes and that no further explanation is then required. One myth explains why the sun, which counted as the first king of Egypt, should now be in the sky. It recounts that the sun-god Rē became tired of humanity, so he seated himself upon the sky-goddess Nut, who changed herself into a huge cow standing four square over the earth. Since then the sun has been in the sky. (H. and H. A. Frankfort 1949: 27)

It is the gap between action and result that leads the Azande to posit the action of a soul as a causal explanation in many processes:

Although, for descriptive purposes, I have defined ritual and empirical actions by reference to their objective results and the notions associated with them, a differentiation on such lines is open to objection on theoretical grounds, for it is the number of steps in an activity which are, or are not, subject to observation and control that is the important differentiating factor in human activities. Once we accept a quantitative difference it is no longer possible to make a clear qualitative division into ritual and empirical categories ... Azande offer the same explanation of a 'soul' acting to produce certain results in those technological activities in which there is a similar gap between action and result to the gap in magical techniques, a gap where nothing can be seen of what is happening—e.g. it is the 'soul' of the eleusine which accounts for the gap between planting of the seed and its germination and appearance above the ground. (Evans-Pritchard 1937: 463–4)

As noted in Chapter 3, primitive understanding of causation is also greatly inhibited by the absence of machines, by which reversible systemic processes can be analysed. In the pre-mechanistic stage, the child cannot construct a series of events proceeding from cause to effect; he always proceeds immediately from the one to the other. So, for example, he imagines that the fire in a stationary steam engine turns the wheel by direct influence without regard to the intervening mechanism, and we saw earlier that children are initially incapable of drawing the intermediate stages in the bending of a piece of wire, for example. The ability of children to break down a cause/effect relationship into a series is closely associated with the understanding of reversibility. For in the early years, when the world is seen as governed by relations of will, force, and obedience, these relations are also irreversible. In a state of conceptual realism

... the flow of consciousness, psychological time, the whims of desires and actions which follow one another without order or repetition—all these things are projected in their entirety into the external world. Similarly, in as much as it is near to immediate perception, the child's universe is irreversible, for perception never shows us the same sun nor the same trajectory, nor the same movements twice. Events cannot happen over again in the same way. It is the mind that builds up reversible sequences underneath perception. To the extent that the child's universe is removed from these constructions and close to the immediately given, it is irreversible. (Piaget 1930: 271)

It is the experience of machines and of technological processes in general, that is essential in the development of the understanding of reversibility and of mechanical causality as a whole. Piaget has found that the interest in machines and the ability to apply correct mechanistic explanations of their operation precede the mechanistic explanation of natural phenomena, in which children are initially largely devoid of interest, at least in our culture:

If we examine a mechanism of any complexity that has been correctly
understood by a child of 8–10 we shall always find that it is a reversible
mechanism ... When a child has understood how the pedal of a bicycle
makes the wheel move round, he sees that by turning the wheel the pedals
can be made to turn ... This reversibility does not exclude the existence of
a series in time. Only, the series in question is one that can happen in two
different directions. (Piaget 1930: 269–70)

[and]

Thus, although in their views about the origin of things these children are
still entirely mythological, although they are still animistic, and explain the
movement of bodies by means of conscious and internal forces, on the
subject of a bicycle, they can attain to the conscious grasp of a purely
mechanical explanation. (Ibid. 233)

Children are thus capable of applying mechanistic explanations
to machines before they apply them to nature—'it would seem that
progress made in the sphere of machines preceded progress in the
explanations of natural events'. Piaget points out the

obvious disproportion between the interest which boys take in nature and
that which they take in machines. The latter ... is quite remarkable.
Interest in nature certainly exists, but it is far less active. In their conversa-
tions, children are almost silent about nature, but they are full of remarks
about machines ... [and in any case].

Mere observation of nature is far too strongly coloured with pre[mech-
anistic] relations to account for the decline in artificialism. It is in making
things and in seeing them made that the child will learn the resistance of
external objects and the necessity of mechanical processes. Thus the
understanding of machines would seem to be the factor which brought
about the mechanisation of natural causality and the decline of artificialism in the child. (Ibid. 233–4)

Lloyd (1966) draws attention to the importance of technological processes in the formulation of causal analysis by Plato and
Aristotle:

... the *Timaeus* is the first Greek document in which the fashioning of the
world *as a whole* is attributed to a craftsman-deity. The variety of the
technological imagery which Plato uses in this work is extraordinary ...
Carpentry, modelling and weaving provide some of the most vivid examples. The gods are imagined as working on lathes (τορνεύεσθαι, 33b 5;
περιτορνεύειν, 69c 6, 73e 7), boring or piercing holes (συντετραίνειν, 91a
6; κατακεντεῖν, 76b 1), and gluing or fastening things together with
bolts (κολλᾶν, 75d 2; συγκολλᾶν, 43a 2; γόμφοι, 43a 3). The Craftsman
himself is called the 'wax-modeller' (κηροπλάστης, 74c 6), and πλάττειν

(mould) is used to describe the construction of vertebrae from bone, for example. πλέκειν (plait and ὑφαίνειν-(weave) and their compounds are used to describe the joining together of soul and body (36e 2), the interlacing of the veins (77e 1) and so on. Plato also draws on the techniques of agriculture for some of his images. The gods sow (σπείρειν, e.g. 41c 8), and engraft (ἐμφυτεύειν, 42a 3) different things, and the structure of the veins is compared with a system of irrigation channels (77c ff.). And sometimes he combines images from different skills to describe the creation of a compound substance, as, most notably, in the account of the formation of bone. At 73e f. the Crafts man first sifts earth until it is smooth and pure, and then kneads (φυρᾶν) and moistens (δεύειν) it with marrow: so far the image is one of a baker sifting flour and kneading dough (cf. Empedocles Frr. 34 and 73). But then he is described as placing this stuff in fire, dipping it in water and repeating this process until it cannot be melted either by fire or by water. Here Plato seems to be thinking chiefly of some such process as the hardening of iron by submitting it to heat and cold alternately: iron, of course, remains fusible however often this process is repeated, but Plato imagines that the bone-stuff treated in this way acquires the new property of being insoluble by fire or water—as clay, for example, becomes when it is fired. (Lloyd 1966: 277–8)

And in the case of Aristotle,

... it is the sphere of artificial production which provides Aristotle with the majority of his illustrations when he expounds the theory of the four causes. Thus when the four causes are distinguished, perhaps for the first time in the extant treatises, in *Ph.* B3, most of the examples to which he refers are drawn from the arts, particularly from sculpture, architecture and medicine. Again in *Metaph.* Z 7–9 artificial productions—the house, the bronze sphere, health (the product of the medical art)—are considered at length, and when he comes to deal with natural causation ... he says that 'the case is the same with the things that arise naturally as with these [i.e. the products of art]: for the seed produces things in the same way as things are produced by art' (1034a 33f.). (Ibid. 287–8)

In the analysis of process experiment is naturally crucial, but it is clear that in the elementary technologies of the primitive milieu there is little place for experiments designed to examine processes and relations. In a trivial sense, of course, all life is experiment, from the sensori-motor stage onwards. If we poke a hedgehog with a stick to see if it is alive, we can in a loose sense be said to be experimenting. To this extent, primitives constantly experiment, and may in this way make important discoveries, such as how to construct effective trigger mechanisms for traps, how to leach poisonous substances from manioc, or how to extract salt from grasses, and so on.

But we have seen from Piaget's material that experimental design, holding certain factors constant and systematically eliminating others as potential causes, begins to develop only at the stage of concrete operations and has to wait for its full development until the stage of formal operations. At the pre-operatory stage, and during the early part of the concrete operatory stage, children can indeed suggest causal associations, but these are unsystematically arrived at and tested. While this is clearly a serious oversimplification in the case of the causal reasoning of members of primitive societies, we nevertheless find that while some causal conclusions relating to natural phenomena are correct, they are based on relatively elementary associations of factors, and are not tested in any systematic way—often for reasons of sound common sense, no doubt. Cases of controlled experiment even at the simple level of the following example are rarely recorded in primitive society.

In the case of Handsome Lake, in the late eighteenth century a Seneca Indian prophet conducted an experiment to prove the evil effects of alcohol:

... good food is turned into evil drink. Now some have said that there is no harm in partaking of fermented liquids.

Then let this plan be followed: let men gather in two parties, one having a feast of food, apples, and corn, and the other cider and whiskey. Let the parties be equally divided and matched and let them commence their feasting at the same time. When the feast is finished you will see those who drank the fermented juices murder one of their own party but not so with those who ate food only. (Wallace 1962: 356)[2]

Evans-Pritchard also emphasizes that the Azande act experimentally within the limits of their beliefs. They are, for example, aware that the poison used in the chicken oracle may be defective, and it is important that it should not kill or spare all the chickens, and not give contradictory answers. At the end of a satisfactory seance, Evans-Pritchard comments on the reasons for their approval of the results:

[2] Wallace quotes as his authority for this anecdote A. C. Parker, *New York State Museum Bulletin* no. 163, 1913, but I have been unable to locate the quoted passage there, although it is an account of the life of Handsome Lake. Despite the erroneous reference the incident is of sufficient interest to merit inclusion here.

The poison used at this seance was at once seen to be discriminating. It killed the first fowl and showed that it was not impotent because when *benge* [oracle poison] is impotent all the fowls survive. It spared the second fowl, showing that it was not stupid, over-potent poison, for when it is such all the fowls die. It spared several other fowls, but at the finish killed the last fowl, showing that it maintained its potency. Azande look to these evidences in every test to establish that the poison is good. (Ibid. 306)

More generally, he says:

It will have been noted that Azande act experimentally within the cadre of their mystical notions. They act as we would have to act if we had no means of making chemical and physiological analysis and we wanted to obtain the same results as they want to obtain. As soon as the poison is brought back from its forest home it is tested to discover whether some fowls will live and others die under its influence. It would be unreasonable to use poison without first having ascertained that all fowls to which it is administered do not die or do not live. The oracle would then be a farce. Each seance must be in itself experimentally consistent. Thus if the first three fowls survive Azande will always be apprehensive. They at once suspect that the oracle is not working properly. But if then, afterwards, the fourth fowls dies, they are content. They will say to you, 'You see the poison is good, it has spared the first three fowls but it has killed this one.' Zande behaviour, though ritual, is consistent, and the reasons they give for their behaviour, though mystical, are intellectually coherent. (Ibid. 336)

While primitive induction may associate events in terms of co-presence, co-absence, and co-variation, these inductive principles are by themselves insufficient to prove a causal relationship unless all possible factors are accounted for systematically. For example, the Konso believe that mosquitoes are the cause of malaria. In the dry highlands above 5,000 feet, which are their traditional habitat, both mosquitoes and malaria are absent. Those who remain there permanently never contract malaria; Europeans find it possible to sleep in safety without mosquito nets. But in the lowlands, especially in the vicinity of the Sagan River, mosquitoes abound and anyone who goes there from the highland plateau can expect to catch it.

It should be noted, however, that while this explanation satisfies the base criteria of inductive logic, it is not a fully scientific explanation. In the first place, alternative explanations are not effectively ruled out—such as the 'bad air' hypothesis which gave malaria its name in Europe. Nor can their theory, by itself, explain the periodic recurrence of the disease even though the patient has not returned to the lowlands since its last appearance. Nor can the Konso explain the precise aetiology by which the disease is transmitted to humans by mosquitoes—their own explanation is that the mosquitoes have evil spirits which cause the symptoms to appear in man.

But the Konso also use this reasoning, which is basically transductive, to explain the transmission of Rift Valley encephalitis from buzzards to humans, a theory which they hold as confidently as their mosquito theory of malaria, but which has no foundation at all in fact. Finally, they have not, as far as I know, carried out any experiments to test their theory of the cause of malaria, such as taking a control group to the lowlands and making sure they are not bitten, or, contrarily, bringing back some mosquitoes from the lowlands and testing their effects on those who have never been to the lowlands. No doubt obvious practical and ethical considerations would make them reluctant to embark on such experiments, but notwithstanding it can still be claimed that their theory of the cause of malaria is right, if not for the wrong reasons, then on the basis of very inadequate reasons.

Indeed, the basic principles of inductive logic, when not used in association with the other principles of scientific investigation, may be little different in operation from a simple, transductive, association of ideas. The Konso are just lucky that the aetiology of malaria is, in their case, a simple two-variable problem. I say 'in their case', because in principle the malarial situation is a good deal more complicated; it requires moisture for the mosquitoes to breed, and a human population already infected to supply the mosquitoes with a further supply of parasites to begin the cycle of infection again; a different ecology could have masked the malarial problem entirely. As we saw, the Konso give an explanation of Rift Valley encephalitis which derives from another association of two events—the shadow of the buzzard when it falls upon someone, and the incidence of the disease—and which is quite invalid. The same applies to their explanation of *dodita*, characterized by a sudden attack of stabbing pains in the side and a bloody flux from the nose and mouth, which is said to occur chiefly on the plain between Konso and Gidole, about 15 miles to the north. These plains are the haunt of evil spirits and the angry ghosts of strangers who have died in Konso far from their own people, and who in consequence are enemies of living men. These spirits are supposed to be the cause of the disease, which is probably pneumonia. Here, as in the case of the encephalitis, a quite spurious association between two factors—disease and locality—is the basis of the explanation. Similar instances of transduction, based on *post hoc* reasoning, are legion in primitive society, one of the best examples being the very widespread belief that the stars that rise at a particular time of the year *cause*, as well as merely accompany, the seasonal events with which they are synchronized.

2. CLASSIFICATION AND CAUSALITY

As we saw in the chapter on classification, primitives classify by concrete and contextual association and function, rather than taxonomically, and thus their world is principally composed not only of categories but of natural realms of things, such as jungle, sea, sky, earth, the world of men, and so on, which have an integrated reality transcending that of mere classification.

Because primitive classification is heavily context-dependent, it tends to treat the same entity as differing in its inherent nature when it occurs in different contexts—thus rain water may be symbolically distinguished from well water, and both may be differentiated from river and stream water, even though the word for 'water' may be used for all of them. Moonlight, sunlight, and firelight may all be regarded as distinct, so that it may be incorrect to use the word for 'light' for all three of them. Clearly, such a context-dependent and symbolically loaded type of classification will effectively prevent the formation of a generalized system of representations which focuses taxonomically on the physical attributes of things to the exclusion of context or particular phenomenal attributes.

Mobile, reversible transformational relationships depend on the use of explicit conceptual analysis for the understanding of natural and social causal phenomena, and this depends on the ability to ignore particular contextual associations and to analyse common configurations of phenomena into their component elements. Our educated conception of 'light' is an example of this. Talking of the principle of the rectilinear propagation of light, Toulmin says:

Before the discovery is made, the word 'light' means to us such things as lamps—the 'light' of "Put out that light"; and illuminated areas—the 'light' of "the sunlight on the garden". Until the discovery, changes in light and shade, as we ordinarily use the words (i.e. illuminated regions which move as the sun moves), remain things primitive, unexplained, to be accepted for what they are. After the discovery, we see them all as the effects of something, which we also speak of in a new sense as 'light', travelling from the sun or lamp to the illuminated objects. A crucial part of the step we are examining is, then, simply this: coming to think about shadows and light patches in a new way, and in consequence coming to ask new questions about them, questions like "Where from?", "Where to?", and "How fast?", which are intelligible only if one thinks of the phenomena in this new way. (Toulmin 1953: 21)

And, just as the inability of the primitive to think of 'light' in this way prevents him from conceiving a shadow simply as the absence of 'light', so, not thinking of light as propagated from a source of energy, he is incapable of thinking of the eyes as essentially *receivers* of light. He regards 'the eye not as a kind of sensitive plate, but as the source of antennae or tentacles which stretch out and seize on the properties of the objects it surveys', as Toulmin puts it (ibid. 23).

Consider the following protocol from one of Piaget's experiments:

(Pat. 10; 0)
Q. Tell me the things which give light.
A. The sun, the moon, the stars, the clouds and God.
Q. Can you give light?
A. No . . . yes.
Q. How?
A. With the eyes.
Q. Why?
A. Because if you hadn't eyes you wouldn't see properly. (Piaget 1929: 48)

And one of Piaget's collaborators stated:

When I was a little girl I used to wonder how it was that when two looks met they did not somewhere hit one another. I used to imagine the point to be half-way between the two people. I used also to wonder why it was one did not feel someone else's look, on the cheek for instance if they were looking at one's cheek. (Ibid. 48)

Primitive classification based on the contexts and associations of things therefore lends itself to a hypostatization of 'realms' of experience, such as 'the bush', 'the forest', 'the village', 'the lowlands', and so on, which may come to be regarded as possessing some kind of inner animated vitality of their own.

The Dinka's understanding of their spiritual beings—Divinities and Powers—illustrates very well the combination of conceptual realism and complexive classification, the inability of pre-operatory thought to analyse ordered systems and processes, and the *naïveté* of supposing that they are simply projecting human relationships into their experience of nature.

As we have seen, the Dinka have no conception of 'mind' as mediating and storing up experiences of the self. They thus attribute an external reality to what we should call 'experience':

> It is perhaps significant that in ordinary English usage we have no word to indicate an opposite of 'action' in relation to the human self. If the word 'passions', *passiones*, were still normally current as the opposite of 'actions', it would be possible to say that the Dinka Powers were the images of human *passiones* seen as the active sources of those *passiones*. (Lienhardt 1961: 151)

So the awareness of the ordered quality of the various types of experience and the affective impact of that experience are implicitly ascribed an 'objective' quality, whereas we would say that Dinka ordering of experience and reactions to it were purely subjective. Thus Divinity itself, the most all-embracing spiritual 'being', is an image of 'the lived experience of community and concord, and as imaging the widest community the Dinka can conceive, also represents truth, justice, honesty, uprightness, and such like conditions of order and peace in human relations' (ibid. 158). The image of Divinity thus arises from a wide variety of concrete experience, associated in a complex manner, such as order in relation to disorder, life in relation to death, creativity, and human fatherhood, as when Divinity is represented as the head of a homestead, barring the door of his huts against the dangers of the night.

There are a number of 'free divinities' which are the images of more specific aspects of experience. While these divinities or Powers are seen as distinct from Divinity, the Dinka will still say that they 'are' Divinity, even in the case of Macardit, which is the image of barrenness and sterility, pointless death, darkness, and the forces of the wild.

Since Divinity ultimately is the grounds of everything that is in man and nature, Divinity is the grounds of sterility, barrenness and pointless or apparently pointless death as he is the grounds of creativity, fertility, and prosperity. (Ibid. 159)

[The Powers] . . . are not conceived as 'beings' actively pitted against each other, as experiences in themselves cannot actively oppose each other. The difference between them is not intrinsically in them, but in the human experiences they image. (Ibid. 159)

. . . The Powers may be understood as images corresponding to complex and various combinations of Dinka experience which are contingent upon their particular social and physical environment. (Ibid. 170)

Thus we find that Deng, Abuk, and Garang are conceived as related in a manner analogous to a family. Deng represents the phenomena of the sky associated with rain, and hence also rain-clouds, thunder lightning, and sudden death; and also, by association, coolness, pastures, cattle, milk, procreation, abundance, life and light—a typical complexive association of phenomena. Abuk is a female divinity, presiding over women's affairs, gardens, crops and food, and the earth generally, while Garang represents the heat of the sun and certain heated conditions of the human body.

These three divinities form a family: Garang the father, Abuk the wife, and Deng as son or husband of Abuk:

. . . taking only one of the elements of the experience imaged by DENG and ABUK in relationship, the rain-associations of DENG suggest equally the lush pastures which the Dinka want for their cattle, and the rich harvests from which their women will prepare porridge and beer. The cattle are the affair of men—of husbands and sons—and DENG is a male divinity, and a husband and son. The gardens, though partly worked by men, belong primarily to the women, who in any case do the work of turning their produce into food. ABUK similarly is a female divinity and presides over women's affairs, and she and DENG are called upon together, often as mother and son, to bring the Dinka the fertility and prosperity—the 'life'—which the joint labours of men and women among the cattle and the crops in suitable conditions of rain and sun will bring. GARANG, associated with the sun among other things, is part of this family of three. By the association often made between GARANG the Power and Garang the first man, between ABUK and Abuk the first woman, and between DENG and Deng, their son or ABUK's husband, the whole configuration of experiences they image together is further enriched by the inclusion in it of an original fatherhood, motherhood, and sonship . . . it is in the representation of extremely complex configurations of moral and physical experience, the elements in which are not distinct from one another, but are embedded, as it were, in extensive metaphors, that the Powers have their force. (Lienhardt 1961: 160–1)

It is important to note that these Powers are not simple projections of human behaviour into natural phenomena:

DENG, for example, is not merely a 'personification' of rain, lightning etc.— rain and lightning endowed fancifully or through ignorance with human personal qualities. The name DENG re-creates for the Dinka the whole syndrome of experience of these natural phenomena as they touch directly upon human life. Rain and its associated phenomena, for people like the Dinka whose subsistence economy makes them directly dependent upon the grass and the crops, do in fact mean life and abundance, just as their absence, or their presence at the wrong time or place, can mean death and misery. (Ibid. 161)

There are also Powers that are not general but are images of more particular experiences, those of one's own social group—the clan divinities:

The clan divinities are easily seen as representative of a particular limited field of Dinka experience, that of agnatic kinship ... They reflect experience of the abiding descent-group structure of Dinka society. If Divinity represents among other things the situation of human beings as the children of a common father, the clan-divinities are the counter-parts of the particular and distinct patrilineal descent-groups and reflect experience and knowledge of them and the value attached to them. (Ibid. 169)

They are not emblems to distinguish one descent group from another, or to act as a focus of loyalty:

The clan divinities have their meaning in relations to the nature of clanship as members of their clan know it, as membership of agnatic descent groups which transcend their individual members, and yet of which each individual membership is representative. They provide the clearest example of the structure of experience represented by the Powers. (Ibid. 166)

A similar pattern of hypostatization of experience can be found among the Malays, according to Endicott's analysis. In the Malay scheme of things there seem to be two modes of existence—things apparent to the senses, and essences, composed of the ubiquitous vital principle, sĕmangat. While Endicott does not refer to Lienhardt's analysis of Dinka thought, it is evident that Malay notions of essence or sĕmangat are basically the same as Dinka notions of Spirit since sĕmangat, too, is ubiquitous, Many–One, and 'the image of human passiones seen as the active sources of those passiones'.

In its most general form, sĕmangat is that which is present in all *organized* things, maintaining their existence as co-ordinated wholes and, when appropriate, guiding and controlling their actions. Houses and boats, for example, although they do not move, nevertheless have *sĕmangat*, which seems to correspond to the experience of their organized interrelation of parts, and which preserves those parts from dissolution. What is organized can become dis-organized:

> The control of the actions of things is only one aspect of the close interaction between the *sĕmangat* and the body it occupies. Any strength or weakness of the *sĕmangat* is transmitted to the body and vice versa. They are both weakened by illness, care, or worry, and, above all, by fear. Only when the *sĕmangat* is in a weakened condition can a spirit enter the body and cause some disruption. (Endicott 1970: 50)

The presence of *sĕmangat* in anything is closely related to the clarity of the boundaries between that thing and the physical environment, and to the extent to which anything can be seen as simply a member of a larger group. Thus in the case of rice, the Malays do not conceive each grain of rice as having *sĕmangat*, which is seen as common to the whole field. Plants generally share a single *sĕmangat* within a limited area, and only the largest forest trees have one *sĕmangat* each. Correspondingly, the members of classes of things that are very distinctive have the most *sĕmangat*, and for this reason Malays attribute unusual powers to unusual objects.

Thus the presence of *sĕmangat* in things depends on their distinctiveness, both in type and number, and is a variable property. *Sĕmangat* may also exist in the form of free spirits, *hantu*, which are bodiless, and can vary their size and form of manifestation at will. But there is a basic similarity between *sĕmangat* and *hantu*—

> It seems that when one *sĕmangat* is shared by members of a class in which the members are regarded in some contexts as discrete, the *sĕmangat*, by appearing in all of these members, gives the appearance of flitting from one to the other. In other words, a simple shift in perspective transforms a *sĕmangat* into a free spirit. (Ibid. 52–3)

It is the clarity of definition of things, and the boundaries between them and their environment, which is of basic importance in the power of their essences.

> The most powerful essences are only vaguely defined, while the more clearly defined essences are more vulnerable to the constraint of material

boundaries. Free spirits, corresponding to vague anxieties, are much more powerful than *sěmangat*, which are bound to the physical bodies from which their clear definition is largely derived. If permanent differences in the power of essences depend on the degree of definition of the concepts, it follows that to change the degree of differentiation of the vital principle composing an essence would affect the power of the essence ... I would interpret the recitation of information about the essence addressed in a spell, then, as being a tactic by which the freedom and power of conceptual obscurity are stripped from the essence, making it more susceptible to constraint by boundaries and more predictable in its behaviour. (Ibid. 132)

Sěmangat is not only 'vital principle', but the image of the experience of order and organization. Spirits are derived from this principle, and their close relation to *sěmangat*, as opposed to certain other aspects of the *human* soul, suggests that spirits may be differentiated on similar principles to those of *sěmangat*. Endicott suggests that the 'bodies' of spirits are the realms or categories into which the Malay divides his environment:

I think that the categories earth, water, and jungle are the 'bodies' of free spirits. A natural realm is vaguely constraining to its spirits, and they, as a group, serve their domain as a *sěmangat* serves its more condensed body. They control the body's parts, the ore and fish and animals, and protect it from outside invasion, in this case not by spirits, but by men. There is also some suggestion that the natural spheres are seen as analogous to the domain of man, but with other creatures playing the dominant role. The cities deep in the jungle where tiger or elephant spirits go about in human form, can be understood in this light. (Ibid. 119)

The basic realms of the Malay world, water, earth, jungle, and the habitations of men, are further divided, where they concern man, into roughly bounded classes of things, such as mines, fishing grounds, and fields. More specific classes of things are distinguished within the various realms. The differentiation of *sěmangat* corresponds to this categorization of experience. Vague free spirits, identified only with the division of the world that is their habitat, roam widely. Some spirits are associated with more specific classes of matter and are sometimes called their souls. Some, such as the souls of animals, are quite distinct and are attached to particular classes of body. Finally, individualized particles of the vital principle exist in conjunction with particular human beings and higher animals. Each member of an associated pair of such divisions contributes fundamentally to the definition of the other, to setting it off from similar divisions on its own plane and, thereby, to its existence as a discrete entity. Essences are partially defined by the categories of matter they inhabit and in turn help to define these categories. So well-defined bodies appear to constrain well-defined essences much more than vaguely defined categories of matter constrain their poorly defined inhabitants. Thus spirits are more powerful in relation to boundaries than *sĕmangat*, and clearly defined bodies are more powerful in relation to essences than bodies with vaguely defined boundaries. The most powerful spirits are those associated with broad categories of matter, while weak essences are attached to constricted, localized bodies.

The differentiation of spirits and *sĕmangat* varies according to the kinds of category to which the vital principle is adapted. Material bodies are the most constraining, but it is the low level of definition of the categories represented by spirits that gives the spirits power to break through the boundaries of more highly developed categories, such as bodies. Spirits, being only slightly differentiated from the mass of the vital principle, retain much of the power they derive from its infinite flexibility.

Endicott sums up the role of the vital principle, which includes the definition and differentiation of categories and the persistence of organized wholes:

The power in the Malay system of ideas seems to lie ultimately with the ubiquitous vital principle. It is the force that, differentiated into *sĕmangat* in the narrow sense, maintains the existence of material 'things', and it is also the force, in the form of spirits, that threatens their existence. The power is manifest, in other words, as both the ability to maintain boundaries in the material world and the ability to violate them. Although the power of essences inside bodies is similar to that of ones outside, the two kinds of power are not used in the same way. Because a *sĕmangat* uses all of its power to control and maintain the thing with which it is conjoined, it has no power in its own right, no freedom or independence like that of a *hantu*. The power of *sĕmangat* in the narrow sense can be seen simply as the capacity of things to exist, specifically, the ability of a category of matter to resist the invasion of free spirits and to retain the aspects of the soul that are partially independent of the body. At this level of analysis, the opposed forces are the power of essences and the power of categories that the culture imposes on the world. (Ibid. 125)

3. PROBABILITY AND THE NOTION OF ACCIDENT IN PRIMITIVE THOUGHT

We have seen that primitive notions of causation are absolutist, phenomenonalist, psychologistic, irreversible, and static, lacking a real grasp of process. Moreover primitives do not analyse natural phenomena such as 'light', 'fluid', 'lever', and so on into general and discrete categories with clearly defined properties. The world is perceived globally, such that each phenomenon is considered in its context: rain water, well water, and stream water, or sunlight, fire-light, shadows, and reflections, are all treated as separate entities, knowable only in relation to their other physical associations in particular circumstances, while categories are seen as entities having essential potency proportional to their generality.

It does not follow from this, of course, that primitives are incapable of reaching perfectly sound conclusions about the actual regularities of nature, experienced in everyday life. But the special characteristics of primitive causality do raise the issue of the extent to which such concepts as randomness, luck, coincidence, chance, and probability, possibility, and impossibility are likely to be found in non-literate societies. These ideas are extremely subtle and complex and have also undergone considerable modifications among the learned in the last three centuries, as Hacking (1975) has shown in detail. This suggests not only that we are most unlikely to find any notions comparable to scientific theories of probability among primitives, but that we must in addition take special care to define exactly what *we* mean by the interrelated notions of chance and probability, randomness, and accident.

To be fully and most easily comprehensible, these ideas require us to posit a set of objects with a given permutation and combination of elements or states of an object (such as a die), from which samples are taken in a series of selections, or the object successively manipulated in a non-deliberate way. What we call 'randomness' reflects the absence of constant causal relationships, such that all possible relationships between the objects or states will tend to occur in closer proportion to their distribution in the set the longer the series of trials. This conception of randomness is based on the assumption that where there is no factor constantly predisposing something to happen in one way rather than another, all possible ways for it to happen will in fact occur, in proportion to the frequency of their distribution.

In this model, each throw or draw is an accident, the outcome of an unstructured or unco-ordinated interaction of forces, and while the outcome of any one trial is unpredictable, the probability of the occurrence of any combination of outcomes can be calculated mathematically by relating this to the distributional frequencies as a whole.

Finally, the model assumes that the outcome of each trial has no effect on subsequent trials.

Such a model when applied to nature involves a number of crucial consequences:

1. That regular frequencies can be produced by chance alone (e.g. six consecutive sixes in dice etc.).

2. That one can only estimate the mathematical probabilities of an occurrence by calculating *all* the possible combinations of possibilities. (Thus an apparently significant event may not have a high degree of mathematical improbability.)

3. The longer the number of trials, the greater the expectation of a predictable frequency of outcomes, the law of large numbers.

This model is, of course, derived from games of chance (the word itself deriving from the Latin *cadentia*, 'falling', of dice), and we know that such games are not common in primitive societies. Even if they were, the model is not easily applied to many aspects of ordinary life. This is because, unlike the situation with dice, or card games, or actuarial statistics, which have all been crucial in the development of probability theory, there is no ready means of quantifying the total distributional frequencies in an ordinary situation of everyday life. As Keynes has expressed it,

> ... consider the ordinary circumstances of life. We are out for a walk— what is the probability that we shall reach home alive? Has this always a numerical measure? If a thunderstorm bursts upon us, the probability is less than it was before; but is it changed by some definite numerical amount? ...
>
> In these instances we can, perhaps, arrange the probabilities in an order of magnitude and assert that the new datum strengthens or weakens the argument, although there is no basis for an estimate *how much* stronger or weaker the new argument is than the old. (Keynes 1921: 29)

Keynes here, then, introduces a wider sense of 'probability'— that of 'the reliability of a prediction'. As Hacking says of our notion of probability, 'It is notable that the probability that emerged so suddenly is Janus-faced. On the one side it is statistical, concerning itself with stochastic laws of chance processes. On the other it is epistemological, dedicated to assessing reasonable degrees of belief in proportions quite devoid of statistical background' (Hacking 1975: 12).

The question before us then is, to what extent do primitives possess notions of 'accident', 'differing degrees of probability', and 'differing degrees of reliability of evidence or predictive argument'? A suitable preliminary to answering this will be an examination of the results of Piaget's investigation of the growth of the ideas of chance and probability in children.

In his book (1975) Piaget used four basic experiments to investigate children's cognitive development in the understanding of chance and probability. In the first, a rectangular tray which could be tilted from side to side contained two equal sets of white and red balls, separated by a small partition. The problem is to predict their interactions when the tray is successively tilted from side to side, allowing the balls to collide and intermingle. The second experiment consists of a set of boxes inclined from the vertical with a funnel at the top, down which a collection of equal-sized steel balls can be passed so that they roll into a variable set of partitioned spaces at the bottom, in one experiment being interrupted by a regular pattern of nails. The problem is to predict the frequency with which the different partitioned spaces will be filled and to explain the reasons for these differences. In a third experiment a balanced iron bar is rotated, being allowed to come to rest like a roulette wheel opposite any of eight coloured divisions on a circular cloth. The performance of the bar is altered by the placing of matchboxes on the coloured divisions, two of the eight boxes containing magnets, though they are not the heaviest, since two of the other boxes contain lead weights. The point of the experiment is for the child to explain the regularities of the bar's performance after the boxes with the magnets have been introduced. The fourth experiment consists of bags of different-coloured beads, of a frequency given in a model displayed near the bag, and the child has to predict what colour bead he will draw from the bag. A similar experiment is conducted with counters having crosses on one side and circles on the other.

Piaget's results can be summarized as follows. In the first stage, corresponding to the pre-operatory level of thought, we find that children regard any initial order (such as the separation of white from red balls in the first experiment or the different-coloured beads in the bag in the last experiment) as privileged, in the sense that it will tend to persist or, if disturbed, be returned to after an interlude of mixture. There is no grasp of the paths of the different balls, nor of the way in which these are affected by collisions, nor is there any idea of causal chains independently interacting. While the mixture of, for example, the different-coloured beads in a bag can be grasped as an empirical fact, it is not conceived as a set of combinations of different sorts of elements. Piaget comments, however, on the precocity of intuitions of frequency and rarity which emerge in very young children and clearly have nothing to do with true estimation of probability or the understanding of combinations.

There is no understanding of the possibility that while elements may behave or be distributed irregularly, the group or sequence of events as a whole may display regularity. The compensatory tendency of the rotating bar, for example, to stop at different colour segments at every rotation is seen as the manifestation of a hidden cause which produces compensations. Thus the child thinks that each trial in the experiment is causally related to its predecessor and successor—that the roulette wheel has a memory and a purpose—and for this reason is incapable of seeing anything strange in the fact that when the magnets are surreptitiously introduced into the experiment the bar should stop at the same colour each time. Since the child's conception of causality is irreversible at this stage, he has no criteria for distinguishing the genuinely irreversible relations of chance from those produced by a specific causal factor. Thus for him the fortuitous regularities of the rotating bar without the magnets are not different in kind from the regularities produced by the introduction of the magnets.

At this stage also, we find the general characteristics of phenomenalism, when appearance is accepted as easily as reality, so that for example in a game of 'heads or tails' with counters, in which false counters with a cross on both sides are introduced in place of counters with a cross on one side and a circle on the other, the skewed results are accepted without question. Again, while children at this stage can draw conclusions and make predictions incorporating intuitions of frequency and rarity, their mode of induction is essentially passive, as opposed to that of children in stage II, which begins to be active and experimental.

In stage II, the initial state of a set or arrangement loses its privileged, 'natural' status and successive states of a mixture are regarded as having the same status as the original. There is no longer any expectation that a mixture will have any propensity to return to its original state, and since each trial is now seen as separate from its successor and compensations are now increasingly regarded as fortuitous and not the manifestation of hidden causes, the child begins to understand that the whole can be regular and predictable even if the individual case is not. In the second experiment in which the balls are allowed to roll down the board into different boxes, children can grasp individualized trajectories rather than just picturing group movements, and it is recognized that the balls have equal chances of going in either direction on a collision and that the greater the number of collisions the more regular the final distribution will be, up to a point. For children at this stage can still only grasp the law of 'small' large numbers; that is to say, because they can still only think in terms of concrete instances, up to twenty or thirty trials for example, they suppose that if there were very many trials observed, irregularities in the results might *increase*.

There is also a persistence of static imagery. The children tend to focus their thought on the movement of each ball (in experiments 1 and 2) and not to consider the simultaneous movements of the other balls. Only children at IIb can grasp the fortuitous nature of collisions, while no child at stage II can make his drawings of the trajectories of the balls correspond with his drawings of their position. There is thus great difficulty in conceiving a play of simultaneous and fortuitous combinations in a series of transformations, as opposed to the simple task of forming a static representation of a finished mixture of elements.

But we find that children display an increasingly active induction at this stage, in contrast to their passive acceptance of the order of events in stage I. In their explanations they begin to exclude certain possible causal factors and others are held constant so as to permit the reconciliation of data in a way that takes apparent consistencies into account and allows a general and constant relationship between factors to be deduced. Thus chance regularities can be separated from those produced by genuine causal factors.

The child also achieves a global sense of the probabilities of a distribution in a set of objects—e.g. the probability of drawing a certain coloured bead from the bag, or of a ball falling into a particular slot in experiment 2; but he is still incapable of quantifying this accurately, and does not understand that there are different degrees of probability. In relation to this problem he does not appreciate the nature of proportional differences, and evaluates differences between ratios solely in terms of absolute rather than relative differences.

By stage III true understanding of proportionality and the grasp of relative, as opposed to mere absolute, differences is achieved. Probabilities are quantified, since there is a clearer grasp of the combinations and permutations in an experimental design, allowing the child to separate the factors at work more clearly. Thought is used to generalize and to exclude as a function of a set of implications, setting aside the limitations of concrete instances, so that the law of large numbers is finally completely understood. At this stage the child can also reconcile and co-ordinate the permutations of the final states with the collisions of actual paths, which in turn can be more precisely imagined in a way that synchronizes the sequence of collisions with the final positions of the balls.

To what extent are these findings relevant to our ethnographic material? Piaget, thinking of the difficulty experienced by pre-operatory children in distinguishing between a chance regularity and a regularity produced by a definite cause, and of the child's belief in an underlying order and the prevalence of hidden causes, says: 'Since the primitive saw every event as the result of hidden as well as visible causes, and since he lacked the rational or experimental criteria to rule out even the strangest and most unforeseen connections, the prescientific mind could not have an intuition of probability as we have' (Piaget 1975: xiv).

In view of the very recent development of notions of probability and chance in our civilization, it may readily be conceded, as we have already noted, that we need not expect our notions of these concepts to appear in primitive society. But it is still possible for primitives to distinguish between statistical abnormalities and categorical abnormalities, and to have some conception of 'accident' in the sense of events that 'just happen', without any special explanation being required or even available.

Referring back to the emergence of intuitions of frequency and rarity at an early stage of cognitive development, it is clear that animals, as well as men, direct their strategies for survival on the basis of actually experienced frequencies in the natural world. We therefore find a full awareness among primitives that some events are commoner than others, that in certain circumstances one outcome is more likely than another, and that some things never happen and others always do. There is also a universal awareness that some things happen in a certain sequence, and/or take place in a certain location or type of location. The use of a word roughly translatable as 'likely' or 'probably', as in the case of 'Are there crocodiles in this river?'—'Probably', does not mean that the savage in question has a clear grasp of the total combinatorial possibilities of a situation, and has quantified his probability estimate accordingly, but simply that, on the basis of his experience he and others have often seen crocodiles in this river at this time of day— an unquantified use of 'probable' which is of course familiar to us in our everyday thought as well, and is adverted to by Keynes in the passage already quoted. The 'probability' of the savage is therefore based simply on his own and other people's past experience, and has no relation to the combinatorial possibilities of a situation.

Moreover, at least in principle, the primitive can distinguish between a statistical abnormality and a categorical one. For example, he may notice that in a particular rainy season there has been an unusual absence of thunderstorms, but this will be an oddity of a quite different sort from the ability of someone possessed by a spirit, according to native beliefs, to place his foot on glowing coals without suffering any harm.

The root of the distinction between apparently meaningless anomalies like the absence of thunderstorms and the categorical anomalies like fire-walking lies, it seems, in the way in which people structure the world for explanatory purposes. Every society has a belief system which accentuates certain categories and ignores others, which gives great emphasis to some types of relationships and explanations and ignores others, and it is in relation to these official categories, beings, relationships, and explanations that some events are deemed relevant and others irrelevant. When primitives say of some event that it 'just happened' what they frequently mean is that, in terms of the way they see the world, whatever may have caused such an event has no relevance to the factors they consider really important. An example will clarify this. The Konso regard God as the source of morality and justice, and believe that He punishes towns in which there is too much quarrelling or other sin, by withholding the rain from them and their fields. Again, certain cerebral disorders, such as encephalitis and meningitis, or states of possession, are regarded as the work of evil spirits, while witchcraft and magic can produce yet other fairly specific afflictions to people, beasts, food, crops, and land. Some illnesses such as colds and bronchial conditions are associated, if somewhat vaguely, with the mountain range of Gidole, often blanketed in mist, and cold and wet for much of the year. But when I asked Sagara Giya, one of my most intelligent informants, who was in the throes of dysentery, where the disease had come from, he replied that it just came and that there was no agency responsible for it. I would interpret this type of response, which is in fact extremely common for a whole variety of events in primitive society, as signifying that there was not, for the Konso, anything about dysentery that made it appropriate to attribute it to any of the conventional agencies in their belief system. If one had been able to show them, by the use of the microscope and so on, the amoeba or bacteria responsible for their condition, they could have accepted this quite readily without needing to adjust their attitude to the explanation of the disease or the categories of their belief system.

Thus the notion of 'accident' means for the primitive some event that has no wider significance in terms of their belief system and world-view, and in so far as some peoples are more paranoid than others, such as the Azande, we can expect to find them trying to explain the significance of events that other cultures would simply ignore. It does seem, however, that certain categories of unpleasant events are more readily dismissed as 'meaningless', 'accidental', than others. Simple physical injuries, such as burning oneself when taking a coal from a fire to light one's pipe, or getting a thorn in one's foot, where the events are commonplace and the causes are obvious and immediate, seem often to be disregarded. Lewis cites cases of the reaction to abnormal breast abscesses among the Gnau of New Guinea as follows:

On a few occasions, women came to me for treatment with large discharging breast abscesses; these, it was said, sometimes happened if a child had died in early infancy; the milk swelled the breast, it was blocked and changed to pus. They did not suggest it was caused by something. It happened; they gave examples of other women to whom it had happened ...

I happened to try and treat a young woman whose breast abscess was large, painful and long-lasting, and I was much surprised that no one, even when prompted by my questions about spirits, sorcery and the death of her child, ventured beyond the quite detailed natural explanation I have given for her abscess.

The abscess appeared to me sufficiently abnormal for me to expect from them some particular explanation, which I did not obtain. They regarded it as ordinary in the way that most infected sores are ordinary. (G. Lewis 1975: 197–8)

In Lewis's experience among the Gnau, diseases were felt to call for more than an 'it just happened' explanation if they affected the whole body, or were subjectively felt to do so, and not just a part of it; and also if they were severe, long lasting, totally out of keeping with the patient's previous life history, or noticeably more severe than circumstances seemed to warrant.

Mechanical causes of affliction, then, are to be expected as one type of event that will not call for further explanations in terms of the belief system. The same may also be true of afflictions that are very common in certain age groups, such as conjunctivitis and head lice in children, or arthritis in the elderly. Societies with no conception of a Supreme Being but only of sorcery may regard epidemics as things that 'just happen', while theists will have greater conceptual opportunities for seeing them as punishments visited on the whole society. To the extent that certain events seem to have very localized and/or automatic explanations, or are very general or regular in occurrence, then explanation in terms of the volitional causative idiom that pervades primitive thought would seem clearly inappropriate.

We can see that while most primitives may perhaps not reach stage II of the understanding of chance and probability, this need not prevent them from having clear ideas of frequencies and actual probabilities, based on past experience and of a non-quantifiable sort, and from having notions of 'accident' based on the absence of significance of an event or the very localized nature of that significance. To this extent Piaget was mistaken in supposing that primitives regard anything as possible and are incapable of distinguishing between statistical and categorical abnormality.

There is, however, a further set of questions arising from Piaget's work:

    1. Can primitives conceive a random mixture or set of events?

2. Can they recognize the possibility of an apparently significant event being produced by chance, i.e. mere coincidence or
luck?

3. Can they understand the idea of orderly relations being produced by stochastic processes?

4. Can they treat lotteries or other randomizations as having
no significance?

On the assumption that the types of causal explanation employed by primitives are highly structured and lead them to dismiss
large areas of experience as of no concern, or else as so regular that
no explanations are needed, we can understand why randomness in
the statistical sense will pass quite unnoticed, since it requires that
awareness of the frequency distribution of the combinative possibilities of a given set of elements that we saw was only developed in
Piaget's stage III, at the level of formal operations. When primitives attempt to conceptualize disorder we frequently find that
they achieve this by inverting the existing order of things—quite
literally among the Lugbara, who imagine that those people who
are very different from them socially walk about upside down; a
similar association is made by the Kédang, who associate upside-
downness with incest. Primitives often conceive disorder as a state
of affairs in which nothing has a name. Conceptualizations of
'states of nature', when men were not socialized and had not yet
acquired the civilized arts are portrayed by similar inversions, as
when men are represented living alone in the forest eating their
firewood and burning their meat for fuel. Thus the de-structuring
of human behaviour leads to notions of inversion and reversal, not
of statistical randomness, while in the physical world the attention
of primitives is simply not apt to be caught by the distribution of
rain-drops on a patch of ground or the motions of dust particles in
a sunbeam, since these activities will be perceived as wholes, rather
than in terms of the individual rain-drops or dust particles with
their several paths, collisions, and distribution.

The inability of primitives to form any conception of randomness is of particular importance when we pass on to consider
the interpretation of such widespread randomizing devices as lots,
dice, and divinatory techniques, such as those based on the pattern
of falling objects like beans, sticks, and stones, in particular. Re-
calling the general indifference of primitives to events that fall out-

side the conventional explanatory framework of their culture, there is no reason why they may not regard some instances of a randomized distribution or drawing of lots as 'accident', and other instances of the same technique but in a different context as a significant manifestation of hidden causes.

For example, among the Konso, diviners haruspicate the stomach and intestines of beasts that are ritually sacrificed, believing that the distribution of dark spots on the membranes of these organs are of particular significance, but they do not regard the stomachs and intestines of beasts killed at markets as capable of revealing anything of significance. We may expect to find, in line with what we have already determined about the structure of primitive notions of causation, that it is, above all, context that will be decisive in determining whether randomized events will be regarded as potentially the manifestation of hidden causes or as of no interest. A further example, again from my field-work among the Konso, is provided by an instance of the drawing of lots which I observed.

Some boys and an adult man were sitting in the doorway of my hut one evening, and several of those present were breaking wind—a consequence of their grain diet. After a particularly vile effusion, at which we all held our noses with more than the usual cries of disgust, the man present decided to draw lots to discover 'Who's the farter?'! He pulled a number of straws from the thatch of my house, equivalent in number to those present, including myself, broke one of them short, and then, holding them between his clenched knuckles, handed them round to all in turn, including me. When one of the boys picked the broken straw there were cries of delight and all the boys set on him and gave him a good-natured pummelling. There was no suggestion that they had discovered the true culprit, and the whole affair was treated as a joke, farting being a subject of much ribald amusement among the Konso.

On the other hand, in a divinatory context, the fall of coffee beans, an equally random process objectively speaking, is regarded as a manifestation of hidden causes. In the same way we ourselves may use the same pack of playing cards for a game of bridge and then for telling fortunes. In a game of bridge we regard a succession of unusual hands as the result of bad shuffling or of chance, but if the future foretold by the cards was peculiarly or strikingly appropriate to the circumstances of the inquirer, we should perhaps be rather less ready to think in terms of shuffling and random distributions.

But while Piaget is mistaken in supposing that such a distinction between causal significance and insignificance in a random situation would not be made by primitives, his basic contention that primitives could not understand the possibility of an accidental confluence of forces producing apparently significant responses or effects, seems to be correct. For if, whether in a randomized or in a causally structured situation, significance is bestowed on events, then our objection that it may be due to chance will not be meaningful to the primitive. There is, in other words, a notion of 'insignificant accident', but not of 'significant accident'. An example is provided by the divinatory techniques of the Azande, in their administration of the poison oracle to chickens. Here the oracle is checked for validity, but in terms of the *consistency* of its replies, not in relation to the probability of these replies in relation to chance expectations, of which the Azande may be expected to have no idea.

There are two tests, the *bambata sima*, or first test, and the *gingo*, or second test. If a fowl dies in the first test then another fowl must survive the second test, and if a fowl survives the first test another fowl must die in the second test for the judgement to be accepted as valid. Generally the question is so framed that the oracle will have to kill a fowl in the first test and spare another fowl in the corroborative test to give an affirmative reply, and to spare a fowl in the first test and kill another fowl in the corroborative test to give a negative reply; but this is not invariably the case, and questions are sometimes framed in an opposite manner. The killing of a fowl does not give in itself a positive or negative answer. That depends on the form of the question. I will illustrate the usual procedure by an example.

A

First Test 'If X has committed adultery poison oracle kill the fowl. If X is innocent poison oracle spare the fowl.' The fowl dies.
Second Test 'The poison oracle has declared X guilty of adultery by slaying the fowl. If its declaration is true let it spare this second fowl.' The fowl survives.
Result A valid verdict. X is guilty.

An example of an invalid verdict is the following:

C

First Test 'If X has committed adultery poison oracle kill the fowl. If X is innocent poison oracle spare the fowl.' The fowl dies.

Second Test 'The poison oracle has declared X guilty of adultery by slaying the fowl. If its declaration is true let it spare the second fowl.' The fowl dies.
Result The verdict is contradictory and therefore invalid. (Evans-Pritchard 1937: 299–300)

It should be noted that the two tests are not necessarily made at the same seance, unless the matter is urgent and there is sufficient oracle poison. 'Often Azande consider a single test sufficient, especially if the oracle gives its answer decisively by killing the fowl without hesitation.' The object of these tests is to discover if the poison is acting indiscriminately, killing all the fowls, or letting them all live; it is not a test designed to raise the probability of the answer. Clearly, if the chance of a particular answer to any question asked of the poison oracle in any test is 1/2, the probability of the same answer being given by a reversal of the instructions in the second test is 1/4. But the consistency of the oracle's reply is also at the same level of probability—1/4. On the hypothesis that a real response is being made by the oracle, the Azande procedure makes sense, but being ignorant of the laws of probability they do not stop to consider that the same results could be obtained by any pseudo-random procedure.

It is instructive to examine further their pursuit of the hypothesis that the oracle can give meaningful responses, but may in some cases give absurd answers because the poison is ineffective.

They say that they sometimes test new poison or old poison which they fear has been corrupted by asking it silly questions. At full moon they administer the poison to a fowl and address it thus:
'Poison oracle, tell the chicken about those two spears over there. As I am about to go up to the sky, if I will spear the moon to-day with my spears, kill the fowl. If I will not spear the moon to-day, poison oracle spare the fowl.'
If the oracle kills the fowl they know that it is corrupt. (Ibid. 336–7)

A man also makes fun—for the Azande see the humour of these tests—of the termites. He thrusts two branches into their runs, but instead of addressing the termites and asking them to foretell the future by eating either branch and leaving the other uneaten he remains silent. If he discovers on the following morning that the termites have gnawed either or both the branches he says that they eat because they are hungry and not in answer to questions put to them as oracular agents, and he will not consult the termites of that mound again. (Ibid. 337)

Yet the Azande fail to see that the mere fact of an oracle giving a coherent answer to their questions does not of itself guarantee that it is giving a genuine response differing in kind from that of random behaviour.

Estimations of causal efficacy must be made on the basis, among other factors, of the *proportion* of success to failure, as opposed to *absolute* success and failure rates, as well as the severity of the conditions obtaining during the different trials, the possible biases in the samples, and so on. It seems likely that primitives will, except in the most obvious cases, ignore proportional in favour of absolute success rates, and will ignore also the possibilities of bias in samples unless this too is obvious. By 'obvious' I mean something like this: among the Tauade adultery is extremely common, and they have a joke which consists of taking a certain type of beetle which, when held between the fingers, nods its head. The beetle is asked, 'Are people copulating?', to which, of course, it nods its head—nodding is taken, among the Tauade as among ourselves but not universally, as a sign of assent. The joke, if I understand it correctly, is that public reference is made to one's neighbours' sexual activities and that even an insect should apparently know of these, so frequent are they in Tauade society. But in addition it is clear from the manner in which this piece of 'divination' is carried out that it is merely a joke, and we may perhaps infer that in Tauade eyes, if something is very common, any prediction about its occurrences has correspondingly little value. Here the sample of 'predictable instances' is deemed to be so biased in favour of 'copulating' as opposed to 'not copulating' that the test is obviously as valueless for the Tauade as it would be for us.

An example of failure to take sample bias into account, and of thought in terms of absolute as opposed to relative success and failure rates, is the following instance of the Konso's estimation of the success of my medical treatment when compared with that of the Lutheran Mission.

I used to treat them for conjunctivitis, dysentery, headaches and malaria, and the usual cuts and burns, in which I am glad to say I was usually successful. This was because the injuries and diseases in question were themselves simple to treat, and the people had mostly never previously been given modern antibiotics, and reacted very favourably to them. But Sagara Giya (a celebrated diviner and lineage priest in whose home I lived), for example, like a number of other people, would never go to the clinic, and relied on me for treatment. He had never known me to fail, whereas many people who had been taken to the clinic never came back alive. There were many people who feared the clinic for this reason, saying that it was a bad place because people died there. (adapted from Hallpike 1972: 308–9)

It should be noted, however, that on one occasion I was called to treat a girl suffering from what was probably a form of encephalitis, and that while she appeared to recover initially, a few weeks later she died. This was not held to my discredit, however, as her father believed that an evil spirit was responsible and that in such case no one could have cured her. On another occasion I was unable to do anything for a man in the extremities of a wasting disease and suffering from a high fever. But the Konso seem to have reasoned that since I had fewer failures, in absolute terms, than the mission clinic, I was therefore the better bet. It might be argued that they preferred coming to me because I provided medical attention without charge, but this does not explain why some of them simply refused to go to the mission clinic at all, whether or not they came to me. Clearly this refusal was based on the absolute incidence of failures, i.e. deaths at the mission, without any attempt to take into account either (a) the proportion of these deaths to instances of cures or (b) the possibility that those who died at the mission would have died in any case. In fact the reasons for my 'greater' success were (a) because the clinic had many more patients than I did, and (b) because many of its patients were far more dangerously ill than any I saw, and some of them were bound to die in any case. These, however, are reasons of a statistical nature—(1) out of any number of instances, given a certain risk rate, the greater the number in the sample, the higher will be the number at risk, and (2) this number at risk will obviously be much greater if the members of each sample are not evenly matched with respect to risk. In so far as primitives reason in terms of absolute rather than proportional frequencies, they can have no grasp at all of the law of large numbers, since if they treat absolute frequencies as self-evident manifestations of causal efficacy, the notion that such frequencies are the result of a sampling error would be meaningless to them.

Thus the notions of chance and probability, which are basic to our educated notions of causality, are lacking in primitive thought because these ideas are derived from operatory co-ordinations and combinations of all *possible* events, as opposed to those that have actually occurred in reality. It is this lack of co-ordinated reasoning that is typical of pre-operatory thought.

4. INCONSISTENCY AND THE EVASION OF CONFLICT BETWEEN BELIEF AND EXPERIENCE

. . . to suggest that there is, to the primitive, as much conflict between his beliefs and experience as there seems to us to be is to fail to realise that 'experience' itself is not the same for people of different cultures. While conflicts between beliefs and facts can theoretically occur for the savage when the predictions of oracles are proved false, or when rain-makers fail to produce rain, there are always let-outs in their system of thought, . . . so when particular persons in the realm of magic and divination are seen to fail, the system of beliefs which they and their audiences believe in is not questioned, but their success or failure in terms of those beliefs. (Hallpike 1964: 243–4)

Polanyi (1958: 286–92) makes the following points in discussing the power of the Azande system of witchcraft beliefs to withstand the commonsense assaults of Europeans. There are at least three prime sources of stability for a system of implicit belief:

1. Circularity—the capacity of a system of implicit beliefs to meet objections one by one. 'So long as each doubt is defeated in its turn, its effect is to strengthen the fundamental convictions against which it is raised.'

2. The second source of stability arises from the automatic expansion of the circle in which the interpretative system operates. That is, there will be a tendency for the elaboration and proliferation of secondary theories to explain why first-order predictions fail.

3. The third source of the stability of such systems

is manifested . . . in the way it denies to any rival conception the ground in which it might take root. Experiences which support it could be adduced only one by one. But a new conception e.g. that of natural causation, which would take the place of Zande superstition, could be established only by a series of relevant instances, and such evidence cannot accumulate in the minds of people if each of them is disregarded in its turn for lack of the concept which would lend significance to it. (Polanyi 1958: 291)

The force of Polanyi's contentions can be better appreciated by a closer examination of the way in which the Azande manage to evade apparent inconsistencies in their beliefs about witchcraft substance and the nature of oracle poison, which Evans-Pritchard has analysed in great detail.

Among the Azande the capacity to bewitch is believed to be inherited by men from their fathers, and by women from their mothers, the actual witchcraft substance which is the focus of these powers being discoverable in the viscera by autopsy.

To our minds it appears evident that if a man is proven a witch the whole of his clan are *ipso facto* witches, since the Zande clan is a group of persons related biologically to one another through the male line. Azande see the sense of this argument but they do not accept its conclusions, and it would involve the whole notion of witchcraft in contradiction were they to do so. In practice they regard only close paternal kinsmen of a known witch as witches. It is only in theory that they extend the imputation to all a witch's clansmen . . .

If a man is proven a witch beyond all doubt his kin, to establish their innocence, may use the very biological principle which would seem to involve them in disrepute. They admit that the man is a witch but deny that he is a member of their clan. They say he was a bastard, for among Azande a man is always of the clan of his *genitor* and not of his *pater*, and I was told that they may compel his mother if she is still alive to say who was her lover, beating her and asking her, 'What do you mean by going to the bush to get witchcraft in adultery?' More often they simply make the declaration that the witch must have been a bastard since they have no witchcraft in their bodies and that he could not therefore be one of their kinsmen, and they may support this contention by quoting cases where members of their kin have been shown by autopsy to have been free from witchcraft. It is unlikely that other people will accept this plea, but they are not asked either to accept it or reject it.

Also Zande doctrine includes the notion that even if a man is the son of a witch and has witchcraft-substance in his body he may not use it. It may remain inoperative, 'cool' as the Azande say, throughout his lifetime, and a man can hardly be classed as a witch if his witchcraft never functions . . .

Azande do not perceive the contradiction as we perceive it because they have no theoretical interest in the subject, and those situations in which they express their beliefs in witchcraft do not force the problem upon them. A man never asks the oracles, which alone are capable of disclosing the location of witchcraft-substance in the living, whether a certain man is a witch. He asks whether at the moment this man is bewitching him. One attempts to discover whether a man is bewitching some one in particular circumstances and not whether he is born a witch. If the oracles say that a certain man is injuring you at the moment you then know that he is a witch, whereas if they say that at the moment he is not injuring you you do not know if he is a witch or not and have no interest to inquire into the matter. If he is a witch it is of no significance to you so long as you are not his victim. A Zande is interested in witchcraft only as an agent on definite occasions and in relation to his own interests, and not as a permanent condition of individuals . . . Azande are interested solely in the dynamics of witchcraft in particular situations . . .

Lesser misfortunes are soon forgotten and those who caused them are looked upon by the sufferer and his kin as having bewitched some one on this occasion rather than as confirmed witches, for only persons who are constantly exposed by the oracles as responsible for sickness or loss are regarded as confirmed witches, and in the old days it was only when a witch had killed some one that he became a marked man in the community. (Evans-Pritchard 1937: 24–6)

Again, Azande say that men bewitch deliberately, because they always suspect their enemies when they suffer misfortune, and so they think primarily in terms of other men's malice being directed against themselves and are thus amazed when they themselves are picked out as witches by an oracle. In such cases they try to find reasons why the oracle is mistaken, or claim that their witchcraft is operating unconsciously. When a man is accused himself, it becomes a special case in which he has only his own experience to rely on, whereas when others are accused he accepts the official doctrine that all witchcraft is deliberate. In the same way, witchdoctors know that their own 'removals' of objects from patients' bodies are fraudulent, but believe that other witchdoctors are genuine.

We must bear in mind that a formal doctrine need not be evoked in all situations. It may be excluded by a man in certain circumstances and enunciated in other circumstances, or its meaning may be twisted to suit the requirements of the same person at different times. (Ibid. 120).

Zande doctrines are so numerous, varied, and plastic that a man can always find in them an element to serve his interests in any given situation. He does not deny the doctrines, but he selects from them what is most to his advantage in each situation and excludes the rest. (Ibid. 133).

. . . each situation demands the particular pattern of thought appropriate to it. Hence an individual in one situation will employ a notion he excludes in a different situation. The many beliefs I have recorded are so many different tools of thought, and he selects the ones that are chiefly to his advantage. Thus A consults the oracle, and it declares that B has committed adultery with his wife and B knows that he is innocent or wishes to convince others that he is. A declares that the poison oracle cannot err and that in its revelations he has absolute proof of B's guilt. B can make one of the following pleas: (*a*) that the oracle has never been consulted at all, (*b*) that a witch put up his name to the oracle to spite him or protect himself, (*c*) that the verdict is due to sorcery. (Ibid. 349–50).

Nor do the Azande compare notes on the success of their vengeance magic against witches, so that it is generally known that a man *X* is nominated as a killer by witchcraft, and a target for vengeance by his victim's kin. On the contrary, the identity of witchcraft 'killers', as revealed by the oracle of the victim's kin, is kept secret, although before vengeance is taken the prince's oracle must confirm the verdict of the kin's oracle. Secrecy as to the target of magical vengeance is essential:

If it were known that the death of a man *X* had been avenged upon a witch *Y* then the whole procedure would be reduced to an absurdity because the death of *Y* is also avenged by his kinsmen upon a witch *Z*. (Ibid. 27).

Princes must be aware of the contradiction because they know the outcome of every death in their provinces. When I asked Prince Gangura how he accepted the death of a man both as the action of vengeance-magic and of witchcraft he smiled and admitted that all was not well with the present-day system. Some princes said that they did not allow a man to be avenged if they knew he had died from vengeance-magic, but I think they were lying. One cannot know for certain, for even if a prince were to tell the kin of a dead man that he had died from vengeance-magic and might not be avenged he would tell them in secret and they would keep his words a secret. They would pretend to their neighbours that they were avenging their kinsman and after some months would hang up the barkcloth of mourning as a sign that vengeance was accomplished, for they would not wish people to know that their kinsman was a witch. (Ibid. 28–9)

There is, in fact, no certain way of detecting failure of oracles by empirical means, since the forces whose actions they purport to reveal are mystical, the predictions are vague, and there are many possible secondary reasons for its failure. Referring to the generality of oracular predictions, Evans-Pritchard says of his own experiments with the rubbing-board oracle:

I tried on other occasions to trap the oracle by asking questions concerning my own affairs in such a way that I could shortly afterwards test the accuracy of its replies, e.g. 'Will it rain tomorrow?' 'This afternoon I am going to visit Prince Gangura, will I find him at home?' 'I am going hunting tomorrow, will I kill meat?' The oracle would answer 'I do not know'. When I asked it questions in more general terms, as the Zande does, it gave me straight affirmative or negative replies, and usually correct ones. (Ibid. 367).

When an oracle contradicts itself, it may be for a number of reasons:

1. The wrong variety of poison was used.
2. There was a breach of taboo by the operator.
3. Witchcraft prevented the oracle from working properly.
4. The anger of the owner of the forest where the oracle-poison creeper grows affected the quality of the poison.
5. The poison was too new or too old, or had been used too many times.
6. The anger of the ghosts spoilt the oracle.
7. Sorcery spoilt the oracle.

Moreover, various supernatural beliefs, in oracles, sorcery, witchcraft, and in the efficacy of witchdoctors form a mutually supporting set of ideas:

Since there is witchcraft there are naturally witch-doctors. There is no incentive to agnosticism. All their beliefs hang together, and were a Zande to give up faith in witch-doctorhood he would have to surrender equally his belief in witchcraft and oracles. A seance of witch-doctors is a public affirmation of the existence of witchcraft. It is one of the ways in which belief in witchcraft is inculcated and expressed. Also, witch-doctors are part of the oracle-system. Together with the rubbing-board oracle they provide questions for the poison oracle which corroborates their revelations. In this web of belief every strand depends on every other strand, and a Zande cannot get out of its meshes because this is the only world he knows. The web is not an external structure in which he is enclosed. It is the texture of his thought and he cannot think that his thought is wrong. Nevertheless, his beliefs are not absolutely set but are variable and fluctuating to allow for different situations and to permit empirical observation and even doubts. (Ibid. 194–5).

Azande beliefs about the nature of the oracle poison are similarly inconsistent, but the average man can escape these implications:

It is true that *benge* is derived from a wild forest creeper and that its properties might be supposed to reside in that creeper, i.e. to be natural properties, but in Zande eyes it only becomes the *benge* of oracle consultations (and they have no interest in it outside this situation) when it has been prepared subject to taboos and is employed in the traditional manner. Properly speaking, it is only this manufactured *benge* which is *benge* at all in Zande opinion. (Ibid. 314).

If there is one product possessed by Azande that is certainly poisonous, it is *benge*, and daily its lethal properties are demonstrated on fowls, and sometimes have been demonstrated on men, yet they have no idea that it might be possible to kill people by adding it to their food. (Ibid. 316).

The suggestion that *benge* might be so used is dismissed by saying that it would be useless for such a purpose, since its efficacy is seen as deriving from its mystical properties, which require it to be properly addressed, and used in the name of an oracle. The notion of mystical power is inherent in Azande ideas of medicines as a whole:

Some Zande medicines actually do produce the effect aimed at, but so far as I have been able to observe the Zande does not make any qualitative distinction between these medicines and those that have no objective consequences. To him they are all alike *ngua*, medicine, and all are operated in magical rites in much the same manner. A Zande observes taboos and addresses fish-poisons before throwing them into the water just as he addresses a crocodile's tooth while he rubs the stems of his bananas with it to make them grow. And the fish-poison really does paralyse the fish while, truth to tell, the crocodile's tooth has no influence over bananas. Likewise the milky sap of the *Euphorbia candelabra* is used as an arrow poison. But Azande do not merely tap the succulent. It must be given offerings, and the hunter addresses the sap in the same manner as he addresses some magic unguent which he is rubbing into his wrist to ensure swiftness and sureness in throwing his spear. Therefore, since Azande speak of, and use, medicines which really are poisonous in the same way as medicines which are harmless, I conclude that they do not distinguish between them. (Ibid. 316).

It is not always easy to reconcile Zande doctrines with their behaviour and with one another. They say that men will sometimes eat fowls after having cleansed them of poison, and this action would imply a knowledge of the natural properties of *benge* that they refuse to allow in other situations. The owner of a dead fowl may have its stomach and neck removed and the fowl prepared for food. My informants said that they try to remove all the poison from the carcase. I do not know whether many men eat these fowls, but certainly some do . . .

Nevertheless, the very fact of cleansing fowls of poison suggests that Azande are to extent aware of its natural properties. In fact they have ample knowledge to show them that *benge* is a natural poison that works regardless of taboos and spells—that is to say, if an educated European uninfluenced by Zande culture possessed their knowledge he would at once draw this conclusion. According to Mgr. Lagae, the *andegi* variety of the poison creeper is so called because *andegi* birds die when they eat of its flowers . . . some Azande hold that the poison will deteriorate with age, and that it becomes more potent when exposed to the sun and less potent when diluted in water . . .

Without laboratory experiments it is impossible to see any uniformities in the working of the oracle. Bare observation by itself is insufficient to explain why some fowls die and others survive. As a matter of fact, Azande act very much as we would act in like circumstances and they make the same kind of observations as we would make. They recognize that some poison is strong and other poison is weak and give more or fewer doses according to the kind they are using. One often hears it said during a seance, 'It is not strong enough,' 'You have given the fowl enough,' and like expressions. But Azande are dominated by an over-whelming faith which prevents them from making experiments, from gener-alizing contradictions between tests, between verdicts of different oracles, and between all the oracles and experience. To understand why it is that Azande do not draw from their observations the conclusions we would draw from the same evidence, we must realize that their attention is fixed on the mystical properties of the poison oracle and that its natural proper-ties are of so little interest to them that they simply do not bother to consider them. To them the creeper is something other than the final pro-duct of manufacture used in ritual conditions, and the creeper scarcely enters into their notions about the oracle. If a Zande's mind were not fixed on the mystical qualities of *benge* and entirely absorbed by them he would perceive the significance of the knowledge he already possesses. As it is the contradiction between his beliefs and his observations only becomes a generalized and glaring contradiction when they are recorded side by side in the pages of an ethnographic treatise.

I have collected every fact I could discover about the poison oracle over many months of observation and inquiry and have built all these jottings into a chapter on Zande oracles. The contradictions in Zande thought are then readily seen. But in real life these bits of knowledge do not form part of an indivisible concept, so that when a man thinks of *benge* he must think of all the details I have recorded here. They are functions of different systems and are uncoordinated. Hence the contradictions so apparent to us do not strike a Zande. If he is conscious of a contradiction it is a particular one which he can easily explain in terms of his own beliefs. (Ibid. 317–19).

The force of Evans-Pritchard's argument will be apparent to every ethnographer. When one works in primitive societies, context-dominated, conventional, and idiosyncratic, it is extraordinarily difficult to maintain a generalizing and comparative frame of mind. Customary behaviour and speech fit so easily into the background and associations that it is only by a determined mental effort that one is able to stand outside the context of events and discern underlying patterns and inconsistencies.

It is also necessary to remember that the Azande system of beliefs can tolerate scepticism:

It is important to note that scepticism about witch-doctors is not socially repressed. Absence of formal and coercive doctrines permit Azande to state that many, even most, witch-doctors are frauds. No opposition being offered to such statements they leave the main belief in the prophetic and therapeutic powers of witch-doctors unimpaired. Indeed, scepticism is included in the pattern of belief in witch-doctors. Faith and scepticism are alike traditional. Scepticism explains failures of witch-doctors and being directed towards particular witch-doctors even tends to support faith in others. (Ibid. 193).

On the basis of Evans-Pritchard's analysis of Azande beliefs we can therefore suggest the following specific factors as being of particular importance in preventing accommodation to reality:

1. No true understanding of probability.

2. The interpretation of events in terms of their motivation in relation to oneself.

3. A consequent indifference to theoretical generalization based on the objective comparison of oracle predictions.

4. Differing interpretations of mystical events according to one's own social situation and interests.

5. Various social obstacles to the analysis of the working of oracles and witchcraft, the principal one being secrecy.

6. The domination of experience by contextual associations.

7. The mutual interdependence of supernatural beliefs.

8. The proliferation of secondary explanations to explain the failure of basic predictions.

9. Mystical action and process, such as witchcraft and sorcery, inherently unverifiable.

10. Oracular predictions too vague and general to be liable to conclusive refutation by subsequent facts.

11. Individual experience devalued in relation to orthodox opinion.

5. THE PARANORMAL AND PRIMITIVE NOTIONS OF CAUSALITY

It might be supposed from what we have discovered about the characteristics of primitive notions of causality—essentialism, the hypostatization of process, conceptual realism, and the lack of an operatory grasp of probability, for example—that primitive beliefs in 'paranormal' influences and phenomena could be explained as the product of pre-operatory thought. There is, moreover, a wide variety of psychological phenomena which are universal, such as (besides dreams) hallucinations, auto-suggestion, dissociation and alienation, and trance states, all of which must appear to the primitive as evidence for the operation of unseen forces or beings on the person who experiences them, especially where such a person displays unusual strength, altered voice, unexpected or inexplicable knowledge, or resistance to fire or injury. These phenomena combine easily with the world-view engendered by pre-operatory thought, especially in the primitive milieu, to reinforce the notions of primitive causality which we have been considering in this chapter. But I believe that this would be almost as simplistic a solution to the universal belief in paranormal phenomena as the attempts to explain such beliefs in purely sociological terms.

The prevailing orthodoxy on the social origins of spiritual beliefs is probably well represented by Leach:

From all this it becomes clear that the various *nats* [spirits] of Kachin religious ideology are, in the last analysis, *nothing more* [my emphasis] than ways of describing the formal relationships that exist between real persons and real groups in ordinary human Kachin society.

The gods denote the good relationships which carry honour and respect, the spooks and witches denote the bad relationships of jealousy, malice and suspicion. Witchcraft becomes manifest when the normal constraints of the ideally correct social order lose their force. (Leach 1954: 182).

That spiritual beings and forces are in each society endowed with characteristics relevant to the dominant themes of social relations in that culture has been demonstrated time and again by ethnographers, but to argue that spiritual beings are *nothing more* than statements about social relations is an unjustifiable inference, since there is a striking resemblance between 'supernatural' phenomena which transcends the limitations of time and culture and which would be inexplicable on the supposition that supernatural beliefs were merely expressions of social relations.

As Andrew Lang, the first, and until very recently the last, anthropologist to take paranormal phenomena seriously, observed:

.. the extraordinary similarity of savage and classical spiritualistic rites, with the corresponding similarity of alleged modern phenomena, raises problems which it is more easy to state than to solve. For example, such occurrences as 'rappings', as the movement of untouched objects, as the lights of the *séance* room, are all easily feigned. But that ignorant modern knaves should feign precisely the same raps, lights, and movements as the most remote and unsophisticated barbarians, and as the educated Platonists of the fourth century after Christ, and that many of the other phenomena should be identical in each case, is certainly noteworthy. (Lang 1896: 35).

Lang suggested that the widespread occurrence in different epochs and societies of such phenomena as clairvoyance, crystal gazing, hallucinations and apparitions, demoniacal possession and spirit mediumship, and divining sticks, were not mere illusions but evidence of genuine human faculties unrecognized by science:

In my opinion the issue is: 'Have the Red Indian, the Tatar, the Highland seer, and the Boston medium (the least reputable of the menagerie) observed and reasoned wildly from, and counterfeited, and darkened with imposture, certain genuine by-products of human faculty, which do not *prima facie* deserve to be thrown aside?' (Lang 1900: 5–6).

This open-minded attitude has, unfortunately, remained almost unique in the subsequent history of the discipline. Anthropologists have simply assumed, without, as far as one can tell, having made an impartial attempt to assess the evidence (especially that provided by researchers in our own society), that the notion of paranormal phenomena is superstitious nonsense which has been conclusively refuted by 'science'. In any case, we are not here concerned with the *nature* of the paranormal, so much as with the fact that there are many types of phenomena—whatever their true nature may prove to be—which are capable of suggesting the reality of powers transcending the purely material, not only to primitives but to educated members of our own society. This strongly suggests that explanations of such beliefs in the paranormal cannot be derived from the characteristics of pre-operatory thought or from cultural factors, though the form and extent of such beliefs will doubtless be strongly influenced by such factors.

Durkheim, however, did not so much dismiss the possibility of the paranormal, in his discussion of Lang's theory, as maintain that 'spiritualistic' experiences are not sufficiently frequent or striking to act as the basis of all the religious beliefs and practices connected with souls and spirits, but one does not need to propose so radical and universal an influence for paranormal phenomena. It is sufficient to suggest for them a significant place in the aetiology of primitive belief in non-material causality.

In 1894, for example, the Society for Psychical Research issued a celebrated report on a census of cases of hallucinations of the living (*Phantasms of the Living*, by Gurney, Myers, and Podmore). From a sample of about 17,000 persons over the age of ten, the committee found that 9·9 per cent gave affirmative answers to the question 'Have you ever, when believing yourself to be completely awake, had a vivid impression of seeing or being touched by a living being or an inanimate object or of hearing a voice; which impression, so far as you could discover, was not due to any external cause?' After further calculations, taking into account the tendency to forget, and the fact that some of those giving an affirmative answer had experienced more than one hallucination, out of the 17,000 members of the sample, it appeared that 140 unmistakable waking visual hallucinations had occurred every year—quite a sufficient frequency in a primitive society to supply fresh and lively anecdotes of spirits and apparitions.

The question becomes even more interesting, however, when the matter of veridical hallucinations of the death of the person appearing in the hallucination was examined. The committee confined itself to deaths, since death is a clear, well-recorded event which is unique in every life-span. A 'death-coincidence', then, fulfils the following conditions, as Broad defines them:

(i) A certain person, A, had a waking hallucination which he *recognized at the time* as an appearance as of a certain other person B.

(ii) Within a period between 12 hours before and 12 hours after this experience of A's, B did *in fact die*.

(iii) At the time, A did not know of B's death by normal means, and had no normal reason to expect it. (Broad 1962: 105).

The census showed that there were reliable accounts of thirty-two out of 2,093 reports of hallucinations that were death coincidences, that is 1/65. Broad calculates on the basis of death rates of the English population:

Since the chance of a person, chosen at random from the population, who was alive at a given date in the period under consideration, being dead within 365 days was 19/1000, it is plain that the chance of his being dead within 24 hours is 19 in 365,000. That is roughly 1 in 19,000. So, if death-coincidences be purely fortuitous concurrences of two events, it is reasonable to conjecture that about 1 in 19,000 of such hallucinations as we have been considering would be associated within 24 hours with the death of the person to whom the hallucination refers. But, as we have seen, the actual ratio was about 1 in 63. (Broad 1962: 109).

(The census was repeated in 1948 by Dr D. J. West, the results showing a comparable or higher incidence of hallucinations than in 1890, but it was not possible to make a study of veridical hallucinations.)

The evidence of these surveys suggests that, far from being too rare to have any significant effect on beliefs, as Durkheim supposed, paranormal experience is by no means uncommon, and in a society which does not repress its existence, such as ours, it can be expected that when such events occur, information about them will be widely disseminated through the population.

Anthropologists have frequently encountered phenomena which are extremely difficult to explain in terms of conventional material science, and which provide prima-facie support for primitive beliefs in supernatural agencies. I quote three examples by way of illustration.

The Azande believe that what they call *mbisimo mangu*, the soul of witchcraft, leaves the body of the witch to attack his victim:

It sails through the air emitting a bright light. During the daytime this light can only be seen by witches, and by witch-doctors when they are primed with medicines, but any one may have the rare misfortune to observe it at night. Azande say that the light of witchcraft is like the gleam of fire-fly beetles, only it is ever so much larger and brighter than they are. (Evans-Pritchard 1937: 33–4).

I have only once seen witchcraft on its path. I had been sitting late in my hut writing notes. About midnight, before retiring, I took a spear and went for my usual nocturnal strole. I was walking in the garden at the back of my hut, amongst banana trees, when I noticed a bright light passing at the back of my servants' huts towards the homestead of a man called Tupoi. As this seemed worth investigation I followed its passage until a grass screen obscured the view. I ran quickly through my hut to the other side in order to see where the light was going to, but did not regain sight of it. I knew that only one man, a member of my household, had a lamp that might have given off so bright a light, but next morning he told me that he had neither been out late at night nor had he used his lamp. There did not lack ready informants to tell me that what I had seen was witchcraft. Shortly afterwards, on the same morning, an old relative of Tupoi and an inmate of his homestead died. This event fully explained the light that I had seen. I never discovered its real origin, which was possibly a handful of grass lit by someone on his way to defecate, but the coincidence of the direction along which the light moved and the subsequent death accorded well with Zande ideas. (Ibid. 34).

The suggestion that the light was produced by a burning handful of grass carried by someone on his way to defecate seems implausible, since if this had been the case there would surely have been so many such occasions when moving lights were seen at night that the Azande would not have been as ready as they were to identify moving lights at night as witchcraft. In addition, Evans-Pritchard compares the light to a lamp, presumably a pressure-lantern, which has little resemblance to burning grass.

The second case is reported of a witch-doctor by a South African anthropologist:

Ndlaleni first came to the Museum some sixteen months ago in the company of another witchdoctor, and immediately agreed to my testing her spirit. Leaving her in my office with the other witchdoctor and Miss Costello I went to a neighbouring building and took out the skin of a gemsbok. This I hid beneath the canvas sail on the back of my Land Rover. I then called her outside and told her I had hidden something which she must find. With the aid of the other witchdoctor she knelt down and began to sing softly. Then in trance state, she informed me that I had hidden something on the other side of the building, over there. She told me that it had more than one colour, that it came from an animal, that it was raised up off the ground. Suddenly she got up, ran round the building, out into the front where the Land Rover stood and knelt down beside the Land Rover. Again she began singing softly and within five minutes of this she tore off one of her necklaces and holding it in front of her like a divining rod, she walked around the Land Rover, climbed onto the back, and took out the skin. (Boshier 1974: 282–83).

The third case was one which I experienced myself among the Konso, and while it would be classified by us as psychosomatic, there is to the best of my knowledge no medical theory to account for it, and it certainly reinforces Konso beliefs in spirit possession.

I used to visit a female diviner called 'Gon'dina, who danced herself into a trance state on Saturday evenings, preparatory to giving consultations the following day. These seances took place in her hut, on the floor of which was a brightly glowing charcoal fire, between the usual three stones. On the evening in question she became angry during her trance, and said that her spirit was angry because it had been called down at a time when someone had died, and this was forbidden. She continued dancing, and suddenly flung a spear with great force into the door-post. Then, as she continued to dance, she placed her right foot on the glowing coals of the fire on the floor, and kept it there for about eight seconds. She was about five or six feet from me. As the dance continued she returned to the hearth and placed the same foot on the coals again, for a similar length of time, without showing any signs of what she was doing. She later evinced no signs of pain in her foot, and no injury either, and was quite unaware of what she had done. Some days after this I asked a companion who had just lit his pipe with a glowing ember to stamp it out with his bare foot, but although the sole of his foot was extremely hard and calloused he refused very emphatically, saying that he would be burnt, and that only diviners could do that when the spirit possessed them.

(For other accounts of remarkable experiences of this nature in primitive societies, see, for example, Smythies 1951, and Bekker 1947.)

Psychical research in primitive society is an almost entirely neglected area of anthropology, but only when we have fully investigated the possibilities of paranormal phenomena shall we be able to claim that our theories of primitive causality and spiritual beliefs are entirely objective and not distorted by the contemporary orthodoxies of our own culture.

11

Action and Thought

When I began this book it was my intention to investigate the utility of Piaget's developmental paradigm when applied to the collective representations of primitive society—and the thinking of individuals, where possible. Looking back over the ground we have covered it may, I think, reasonably be claimed that the concepts of developmental psychology, of 'accommodation', 'assimilation', and 'equilibration', of centration, reversibility, conservation, and operation, and the basic stages of the sensori-motor and the pre-operatory, and those of concrete and formal operations, are of far greater analytical utility in distinguishing between 'modes of thought' than the concepts hitherto employed by anthropologists and philosophers. In particular, there is a striking consistency between the later stages of pre-operatory thought and the characteristics of a wide range of primitive thought.

At the same time, we have been obliged to modify Piaget's theory of symbolism as basically private, as opposed to language which he sees as the principal vehicle of social interaction. It is not the case that concrete operations must be developed in every milieu, since the more elementary demands of primitive society allow pre-operatory thinking to provide stable representations of reality, while if co-operation is based on participation in tasks and on shared experience rather than on verbal analysis and explication, it will be possible to have co-operation without accommodation to the private points of view of individuals.

But as the book grew I became increasingly aware that one of the central premises of developmental psychology, that action is a form of knowing, and that how we interact with the physical environment and our fellows is crucial to the kinds of representation of nature and society that we construct, was forcing me totally to reappraise the significance of the body in the construction of representations of reality; the relations between individual thought and collective representations, the relations between language and thought; environmental determinism; and cultural relativism. These implications take us far beyond the location of primitive thought at some point on the developmental scale.

Taking the issue of cultural relativism first, it is obvious, once the significance of our interaction with our natural and social environment is recognized, that any extreme form of cultural relativism becomes untenable, since we all inhabit the same physical world and all live in a society of some type: the basic similarities of primitive thought, and its resemblances to the pre-operatory, are the best demonstration of this. As Bruner says:

Cultures, so goes the classic line of relativism, are all different. Yet to take this position in analyzing the impact of culture on growth dooms one to a study of what is different about growing up in different places, and that is surely a trivial pursuit in comparison with the study of the few powerful shaping forces in culture that produce enormous uniformities in growth, and a few crucial differences. (Bruner 1966b: 58–9)

When we cease to think of modes of thought relativistically, as basically determined by social institutions which vary from culture to culture, but rather as constructed in interaction with the total environment, we are able to recognize the significance of a developmental perspective, the real importance of which is not that we are able to say that the members of a particular society have topological representations of space, or spatialized conceptions of time, but that we can relate the cognitive aspects of these representations to the circumstances of the people's lives. Thus stages of cognitive growth are not so much important in themselves, as manifestations of the way in which organized knowledge (like other forms of organization) develops in an adaptive relationship with its environment. The concept of evolution[1] has acquired a poor reputation in British anthropology, mainly because of its early overemphasis on rigidly defined stages of society; but it is quite obvious that societies, like other systems, pass through a developmental sequence, and if we concentrate on the 'how' of this process rather than on a premature definition of social stages, we shall succeed in

---

[1] My reference to evolution here should be construed in a purely developmental sense, and not as implying that the biological theory of natural selection on random mutation has any relevance to social evolution, as some anthropologists suppose.

transcending the essentially futile and anti-scientific relativism which has been fashionable for so long.

I referred just now to human beings inhabiting 'the same physical world', but this statement is liable to a severe qualification. In one sense obviously the world is the same for all men, in all those measurable physical properties and relations that we have been considering in this book, and if there were no objective, stable world of things and relationships 'out there' it would be pointless to debate the extent to which people did or did not accommodate to it.

But the qualification is this: when that world is considered in respect of its *interactive* properties, of its capacities for being transformed by human action, or its possibilities for limiting the range of those actions or of expanding them, it ceases to be the same world for all men. Imagine for a few moments two castaways on a desert island, one an effete intellectual and the other a man of robust common sense, skilled with his hands and in the techniques of survival. Evidently, in the sense of measurable physical properties, it is the same island for both of them, but in the second sense, of its interactive properties, it is quite different for the intellectual, hard put to gather a few leaves to shelter himself from rain and sun, to grub up some wild yams, and to collect fallen coconuts, and for the practical man, with his knives, gouges, and augers of shell and stone, his palm-leaf matting and cord of coconut fibre, his cunningly placed fish-traps of basket-work, his earth ovens, his canoe, and so on. The *interactive* environment, in short, is not a stable, unchanging reality 'out there', but is itself dependent on the way in which men understand it, and this understanding is an integral aspect of action. In so far then as the model of an environment with fixed, static potentialities must be replaced by the model of an environment which is dependent in many respects on the actions and understanding of men, it is senseless to regard the environment as *determining* men's representations, since these depend as much on assimilation as on accommodation, and a deterministic model derives its whole force from the supposition that what determines shall be unaffected by that which it determines. The determinist model derives its plausibility in fact from the assumption that the world of sense-data is the only world and that in so far as we interact with it, we do so in a manner dictated solely by our sensations. We have seen that it is possible to accommodate to the physical environment by pre-operatory thought, which is perfectly adequate to ensure survival, and that concrete and formal operations need not develop. While cognitive skills are developed in relation to problems, and problems, especially for primitives, are closely bound up with environmental tasks, the needs by which problems are defined, those environmental tasks themselves, are not just reflections of the immutable environment, but are established and changed by social processes as well, and in these processes conceptual representations play an essential part. We saw, for example, that the stone circles of the megalith builders involved and led to the development of a high degree of geometrical and astronomical knowledge, but the need for those stone circles was not a product of objective necessity, in the sense that they were a *sine qua non* of survival. Thus not only is the nature of the interactive environment itself dependent on the skill and understanding of men, but the very problems whose solution is considered essential are themselves decided by what are, in a particular culture, defined as needs.

Again, we have seen that it is perfectly possible to have, as in the case of myth and symbolism, representations of the world which are not accommodated to the reality of objectively measurable properties and relations. Thus reality as it is experienced by the Kukukuku allows them to suppose that the sun is a man, that the moon is a women, that the morning dew is the moon's urine, and that the sun is red in the morning because he is embarrassed by what his wife has done. There is evidently an almost limitless potential for imaginative elaboration of symbolism, myth, cosmology, and systems of classification, such that we can never predict from a knowledge of the form of social institutions and the ecology just how this experience will be organized in the collective representations of the culture.

Thus, while it is true that we can say with some precision what the *basic* characteristics of thought will be in a primitive society, it does not follow from this that we shall be able to go on from this to a more precise prediction of the details and elaboration of that thought. For, as I have frequently stressed, while developmental psychology can explain the fundamental features of thought, it is powerless to predict anything about the content of those basic thought processes, which is the product of social processes specific to each culture, and which will also reflect the creative imagination and the experience of its members.

With regard to the relation between language and thought, it is clear that the range and nature of non-verbal interaction in communities where all share a common experience and common tasks, where everyone knows everyone else, and where written communication is non-existent, makes the traditional conception of language as *the* basis of thought untenable, when considered in relation to the findings of developmental psychology. I have been at pains to refute the notion that language is the encapsulation of thought, such that people learn the categories of their culture simply by acquiring its language. Some categories have no linguistic formulation at all, while others, even if named, are diffused among a wide variety of customs and institutions. More importantly, language does not of itself determine classification, which, as we saw, at the level of pre-operatory thought is based on prototypes and complexes. Because there is an indefinitely large number of ways of expressing an idea in any language, and because thought also occurs at the level of action and imagery, it is an evident fallacy to suppose that categories and representation are learned merely by acquiring language, in the way that Durkheim, Lévy-Bruhl, Whorf, Leach, and others suppose. Language is *an* essential means for learning the categories and representations of a culture, whether for the child or the ethnographer, but in the case of primitive society especially, where so much thought is embodied in action, symbolism, and ritual, language is not enough—the evaluation of the people's experience of their total environment is also essential; without this motor, affective, and perceptual awareness, and general understanding of the way in which people interact with the objects employed in symbolism, for example, the verbal propositions of a people that bear on categories and beliefs cannot be adequately explained.

Because language is so flexible an instrument, its structure cannot impose any fundamental constraints on thought. Missionaries can use the languages of primitive societies to express ideas never before imagined by the traditional speakers of those languages, even if their attempts to translate Christianity are only partially successful. And despite the enormous variety in the structure of human languages we have found numerous basic similarities between the fundamental thought processes of primitives from all over the globe, and with the pre-operatory thought of Europeans. This could scarcely be the case if Whorf's basic theory were correct.

The real difficulty encountered in the understanding of primitive thought is not as some philosophers suppose, that its 'supernatural' beliefs are refractory to rational understanding, but that symbolism is linguistically untranslatable and its ideas encapsulated in action, ritual, and social institutions; that is, they exist at a sub-verbal level. As Bruner in particular has pointed out, the translation of experience from the enactive and symbolic modes into verbal form is a major cognitive problem, and it is a skill fostered above all by schooling and literacy and intimately bound up in the analysis, generalization, and co-ordination of experience. It is a fact of human psychology that while linguistic structures embody logical relations, these cannot be extended beyond language without many years of intellectual effort and schooling. In so far as the grammatical structures of language are self-contained and isolated from other aspects of human thought, there is no justification for seeing them as providing some sort of prototype for all thought, which can proceed to a high level, as in the case of mathematical, diagrammatic, and mechanical skills, without the need to verbalize problems as a prerequisite of solving them.

There is thus no reason to suppose that a concentration on linguistically formulated categories of a culture or on what the natives say about their customs and institutions will *of itself* be sufficient to illuminate the full significance of those categories and institutions in the culture, without an awareness of the characteristics of non-verbal thought.

Philosophers who have interested themselves in the questions of primitive thought have laboured under the double disadvantage of knowing nothing of developmental psychology, and knowing no ethnographic facts either. Their discussions of primitive thought have therefore ignored the fact that thought exists at the levels of action and imagery, and treated it on the purely verbal level, as though thought could be broken up into a series of atomistic propositions. Wolfram, for example, in trying to establish what might count as basic differences of thought, says: '[Thoughts] can be divided up in a variety of ways: into affirmative and negative, for instance, or into those which concern definite particulars and those which do not, into thoughts about how things are, thoughts about how they might be, ones about how they ought to be, or, again, into correct, incorrect and untestable ones' (1973: 362). When Wolfram refers to 'thoughts' she clearly has in mind 'propositions', which she is classifying according to conventional logical and grammatical criteria; not surprisingly, it is easy to show that propositions of these types are to be found in all societies.

Philosophers are experts in the analysis of explicit, propositional statements made by isolated individuals. They have little experience in the analysis of the social functions of speech in living societies, of the analysis of thought expressed in action and imagery, or of the analysis of collective representations of a non-verbal type. The 'facts' which philosophers habitually employ in discussing primitive thought seem primarily designed as ammunition in advancing some philosophical theory, rather than derived from any real understanding of the ethnography.

The recognition that action is a form of knowing[2] has truly seminal and revolutionary consequences for our understanding of thought in general, and of primitive thought in particular. Associated with this, the fact that the primitive lives in a *man*-centred world, whereas we live in a *thing*-centred world takes on new meaning. For when reality is interpreted on the basis of how it affects the bodies of men there results a subjectification of experience which we have followed through symbolism and classification, measurement, dimensional analysis, and representations of space, time, and causality, and conceptual realism. For us, forced to interpret reality in terms of the way that things affect, not so much ourselves, as other things, the consequences are the objectification of experience and the construction, through the analysis of operatory systems, of invariant relations that transcend the phenomenal appearances of things and render the thoroughgoing symbolic representation of reality as practised by primitive man an impossibility.

Looking back, then, at the ground we have covered, we can sum up the basic characteristics of primitive thought in the following way:

(*a*) It is bound up in rigid, irreversible associations between the phenomenal attributes of things.

(*b*) While it constructs systems of relationships, these are of a concrete and affective type, and are not the systems of invariant relationships of operatory thought, which are the basis of conservation, logical class, and mechanistic causality.

---

[2] And, of course, that knowing is a form of action, as internalized *operations*.

(c) It is not analytic—that is, it does not abstract taxonomic properties and use them as the basis for generalization, based on logical classes, so that its main type of classification is complexive.

(d) Language is used as a means of social interaction rather than as a conceptual tool, and there is little or no awareness of language as a phenomenon distinct from speech.

(e) Consequently, we find no awareness of the possibilities of purely logical inference and deduction; words are often thought of as having power in themselves and names as having an inherent relation with the thing named.

(f) Primitive thought is unable to grasp the notion of mind as the mediating factor between the external world and the experiencing subject; correspondingly there seems to be no awareness of the body as an organized system distinct from the mind. It is this conceptual realism that is the basis of the projection of mental states into the external world, and of the parallel assumption that some mental states originate in the external world, with all that this implies for notions of causality.

(g) Primitive causality is also incapable of analysing process into a series of stages and reversible relations: primitive causal thought is concerned with metamorphosis, essences, absolute properties and the hypostatization of qualities, vitalism and volitional behaviour, while notions of probability are confined to intuitions of frequency and rarity, and take no account of the total, hypothetical possibilities of situations so that there is no idea of significant accidents.

It appears to be a general law that the higher the level of thought, the more dependent it becomes on verbal representation (or its equivalents such as mathematics and diagrams), and on the accumulation of cultural aids such as literacy, mathematical notation, mechanical devices, and intensive and specialist education, among many others. Thus sensori-motor development seems, on the very limited evidence available, not to be affected at all by the primitive milieu. The stages of pre-operatory thought take longer to complete in primitive societies than in industrial societies, while concrete operations are attained in very fragmentary form by primitive populations such that the more advanced operations may not appear at all. The development of formal operations seems largely dependent on the availability of literacy and specialist full-time educational facilities during adolescence.

I remarked in Chapter 1 that the concepts of 'logic', 'rationality', and 'science' were too complex to be used as convenient analytical terms in the comparison of primitive thought with that of literate, industrial society. It would be appropriate to conclude by examining them in more detail here.

Our study of primitive thought has shown that there is no evidence that primitives employ a *different* logic from that recognized by Western philosophers. Lévy-Bruhl initially (1912, 1926) supposed that 'participation' involved a 'pre-logical' confusion of species, as when the Trumai of Northern Brazil refer to themselves as aquatic animals, and the Bororo claim to be parakeets, which Lévy-Bruhl saw as an indifference to the law of identity (1926: 28). But there is nothing *logically* contradictory in men's claim to be *really* parakeets as well as men: a logical contradiction is of the form that something is both A and not-A, which is quite different from an assertion that something is both A and B, even if it happens to be physically impossible for anything to be both A and B simultaneously. (In his *Notebooks* (1975) Lévy-Bruhl came to recognize this, and conceded that he was wrong to refer to what should properly be described as physical incompatibility of class membership as a logical contradiction.) Additionally, it has been shown that in many cases where primitives appear to be asserting that 'men are parakeets', the identity is symbolic rather than natural, as Evans-Pritchard demonstrated in a famous passage discussing the Nuer belief that twins are birds (Evans-Pritchard 1956: 128–33).

A willingness to tolerate inconsistency has also been adduced as evidence that primitives are unaware of logical contradiction. Cooper (1975) proposed, as an alternative, that they employed a multi-valued logic instead of the traditional two-valued, true/false, logic with which we are chiefly familiar. But we saw in our discussion of this that the simplest explanation of the toleration of inconsistency is that in societies where thought is embedded in a context of action and concrete symbolism, and where there is little concern with the explicit co-ordination and generalization of experience, people are simply unaware of inconsistency until someone like an anthropologist draws their attention to it. Symbolism is inherently incapable of assigning truth values to symbolic statements and hence is incapable of being convicted of logical contradiction; symbolism, indeed, is not concerned with logical class and inference at all but with affective and concrete associations and is thus non-logical rather than illogical.

It is far more fruitful to regard primitive thought as based on an incomplete logic rather than on a different logic from that which we know and, indeed, as far as I am aware the possibility of a wholly different logic has never even been demonstrated. There are of course different types of logic, just as there are different types of geometry, but these all depend on the same principles of inference even if some of their basic axioms differ, and there is no question of specialists in one type of logic being unable to understand other types.

There is no evidence that formal logical inference is attained in primitive society, either collectively or individually. The reasons seem to be that primitives are highly resistant to counter-factual hypotheses; that they are unfamiliar with the use of language in a purely formal sense independent of some specific context of utterance; that the grasp of logical class, class inclusion, logical quantifiers such as 'some' and 'all', and the comparison and relation of classes, is very poorly developed; and that many aspects of formal, hypothetico-deductive thought consist of second-order operations —that is, operations on operations—and since we have seen that in many primitive societies their members do not attain the more advanced concrete operations, it could scarcely be expected that the average members of such societies would be capable of second-order operations.

It has been shown in detail that primitive thought generally conforms to Piaget's criteria of the advanced stages of pre-operatory thought at the level of collective representations. But it has been a consistent theme of this study that pre-operatory thought is not 'absurd' or 'mistaken', but rather of limited generality and much more restricted to the phenomenal appearance of things than our own. Within these limits it is quite capable of solving the practical problems that are encountered in the circumstances of daily life, since dimensional analysis and the conservation of invariant relations in co-ordinated systems of thought is not required. In particular, it is well adapted to the characteristics of *social* relations in small, face-to-face communities where experience is largely homogeneous and unchanging, where values, affect, and participation in action are all-important, and where explicit verbal analysis and generalization have little relevance, but it is, of course, thoroughly inadequate for the analysis of the relations between objects and the dynamic representation of natural systems, for which operatory thought at least is required.

There have been many attempts to analyse the 'otherness' of primitive thought in terms of its lack of 'rationality' or its divergence from 'science'. The most generally accepted criteria of rational beliefs would probably be that they were mutually consistent; based on relevant evidence; held reflectively and not merely dogmatic convictions; uninfluenced by the passions or self-interest of those who hold them; and capable of articulation and generalization to a variety of circumstances, while rational action is goal-directed and adopts appropriate means for the attainment of those goals. 'Science', which is clearly a specialized type of rational thought and action, might further be characterized as experimental, theory testing, and exhaustive, and inherently involved in the discovery of new facts relevant to existing theory. To the extent that primitive thought is bound up in imagery and the concrete, phenomenal properties and associations of the physical world, permeated by moral values and affective qualities, unco-ordinated, dogmatic and unsubstantiated by argument, static, relying on perceptual configurations and prototypes and the reification of process and realms of experience, it is not 'rational' according to these criteria. It is mere humbug to claim that, *within its context,* primitive thought is as effective as formal hypothetico-deductive thinking, since it is a fact that the latter type of thought is more powerful, just as a caterpillar tractor is more powerful than a horse; a horse may be able to do all the work we need, and be more beautiful than the tractor into the bargain, but it would be absurd to maintain that it was stronger.

But these criteria do not exhaust the connotation of 'rationality': for reason can be opposed, in terms of other aspects of its meaning, to some perfectly respectable forms of thought, or excludes some aspects of thought, such as values and feelings, which would not be considered in themselves 'irrational', even if they are non-rational. We can best appreciate this wider range of meanings by a series of oppositions (Table XXI).

Considerations of this list will reveal that there are many elements of List B that would be considered quite compatible with being

TABLE XXI

	A Rational	B Non-rational
1	science	art, and imagination in general
2	sanity	insanity, absurdity
3	wisdom	folly
4	demonstration	faith
5	calculation	emotion
6	objectivity	subjectivity
7	system	uncoordinated facts
8	theory	practical knowledge (inarticulate 'knowing how' as opposed to articulate 'knowing that')
9	articulate	inarticulate
10	discussion	violence
and the ideologically biased might add		
11	materialism	supernaturalism

an educated and intelligent member of our society, e.g. B 1, 4, 5, 7, 8, 11, and even as adornments. Rationality and science are thus narrow aspects of mental functioning, and even if we say that in this narrow sense primitive thought is not rational, and that it is more aptly described by the criteria in list B, it is still possible to say that primitive thought can be true, practical, creative, and wise. So even if it lacks many of the strictest criteria of rationality, to claim that primitive thought was irrational would also involve condemning art, imagination, practical knowledge, feelings, values, and religious faith, which have shown themselves to be essential aspects of the most civilized societies, but which certainly have no direct dependence on rationality in the narrow sense.

Primitive cosmologies are capable of expressing important truths about the status of man and society in relation to nature. These involve not only the culture/nature relation, but the complementary roles of men and women in relation to social order, power versus right, destruction and creativity, and many more in the form of proverbs, riddles, and myths. This is not to say that we cannot formulate these truths in abstract and general terms, but rather, that we should not suppose that simply because primitives think with relatively simple cognitive processes, that their ideas are inherently mistaken or incapable of profundity.

Our own attitudes to the sanctity of human life, to the differences between the sexes, to the respect for the aged and the weak, to drug taking, cannibalism, buggery, and bestiality, cannot be justified on purely scientific grounds, or even by the timid claims of utility. Science itself is just a tool, for good or ill, and as the basis of a world view it is a moral waste land. It has to be comprehended in a wider system of wisdom, which recognizes the limitations of formal thought, and that each level of thought has its proper place in the scheme of things. Because human beings have affective natures and needs, and because a system of values and a set of beliefs about the nature of man is basic to all societies, a *purely* rational philosophy and culture is doomed to sterility or madness. Science is a vast creative achievement, and to deny this and exaggerate the claims of primitive thought is a romantic illusion. At the same time we must recognize the limits of rational thought. Wisdom consists in placing rational thought in its proper perspective, in the world as it is, and not as we might wish it to be.

Indeed, the very strengths of formal thought are also the source of its principal weakness—its capacity to cut itself off from concrete experience and operate in a propositional world of abstract generalities which may degenerate into autistic idiocy, e.g.:

The radical alternative we seek to the University's present commitment must be a non-absorbable, unifying conceptualisation which will provide political cohesion, both in the short and in the long range, for our programme and our activities; it must concretise our revolutionary socialist roles without limiting on any levels of specificity our explorations and articulations of concrete mediations of oppression and injustice. (Quoted in Ingrams 1973: 12)

Ideally, formal thinking should be able to elucidate more elementary modes of thought and translate them into its own forms, in the way that Piaget and others have revealed the structure of children's thought, but in practice the ability to think at the formal level often cuts off the educated from the simple and the rational scholar from the attitudes and beliefs of primitive men, to produce a new kind of ethnocentrism:

[Sydney Webb] used to relate how during the First World War his housemaid had been afraid of falling bombs. So to set her mind at rest he one day took paper and pencil, noted down the population of London and the average number of bombs dropped in a week; then performed a quick calculation which proved that the housemaid's chances of survival were statistically so high that she could regard herself as virtually immune. But she continued obstinately to be afraid of bombs! Sydney used to tell Labour Party colleagues this story to demonstrate what a rational man had to contend with in his efforts to overcome popular superstitions. (Caute 1973: 80)

In the same way, anthropological literature is full of attempts to 'explain' primitive beliefs in supernatural beings as projections of social relations, warfare as a device for the redistribution of population in relation to resources, magic as a means of reducing tension in individuals, or ritual as a device for creating social solidarity. That primitives could have genuine, even if sometimes mistaken or inadequate, reasons for these beliefs and behaviour is dismissed as the fallacy of taking native explanations at face value. Because such beliefs and practices are considered absurd, there must be a pragmatic, utilitarian reason for their existence which will satisfy the rational Anglo-Saxon, but which the people themselves are incapable of appreciating. Much functionalist explanation derives from a failure to understand the special characteristics of pre-operatory thought, and indeed, the motivations and attitudes of uneducated people in general, and so supports the attempt to supplant indigenous ignorance by an appeal to ecological and social determinants which are supposed to obviate the need to understand the actual thought processes of the members of these societies by going beneath them to the 'true' determinants of behaviour.

In so far as formal thought concerns itself with human behaviour and social facts, as opposed to technology, physical science, mathematics, and logic, it is as liable to the distortions of emotion and dogmatic absolutism as more elementary forms of thought, and the diminished ability to appreciate concrete experience and feeling which often accompanies an over-valuation of purely verbal analytical skills leads not merely to academic ethnocentrism, but to fantasies about the nature of reality.

Rationalism,[3] which is a disease peculiar to formal, hypothetico-deductive thought, rejects the idea of non-propositional knowledge and regards practical skills and customs as inherently irrational because they cannot be formulated in words and justified by argument and have not been developed in accordance with explicit principles or designed with certain ends in view.

The rationalist rejects the collective experience of his society: for him the true source of knowledge is the independent, open, self-moved mind, accepting only the authority of reason. No one can in fact reason about human affairs in the absence of experience, and the rationalist in practice makes his own experience the basis of

---

[3] My discussion of rationalism owes much to M. Oakeshott's (1962) treatment of this subject.

his theories. But detachment, as well as experience, is a necessary condition for formulating ideal goals for society. These goals are governed by a craving for certainty and conclusiveness and the assumption that social affairs are a set of problems, that each has a single logically optimum solution, which can be attained by the application of the correct techniques of inference and procedure. The rationalist society is thus based on certain axioms about the proper ends of life (the American Constitution being an excellent example), and inevitably regards the creation of coherent structures and the uniformity of norms as the ideal of human society. It is thus rigid and has great difficulty in accommodating to reality because of its inherent search for simplicity and coherence.

The interplay of events and motives, which cannot be reduced to the rationalist scheme of things, is thus seen as 'irrational' or even 'wicked', because the rationalist is unable to grasp that doing is itself a skill quite entitled to be called rational, in the broad sense of that word. But the rigidity of the rationalists' philosophy generates an equally absurd reaction, that of 'irrationalism', the glorification of feeling, impulse, fantasy, and irresponsibility for their own sakes. The only solution is a proper respect for practical skill, and a recognition that intelligent life is an open-ended process of growth and discovery, or it is nothing, since practice is always in advance of theory.

Wisdom transcends this; its hall-marks are a recognition of human nature as it is, and not as we might wish it to be—a respect for practical knowledge and a sense of proportion, so that we use each type of thought—action, symbolic representation, and formal thought—in its proper context, and do not try to govern our lives by one of these alone to the neglect of the others.

In so far as primitive thought is concerned with men and their affairs, it is possible for it to use the resources of pre-operatory thought to express important truths about life and sciety, since the essence of these can be conveyed without the need for concrete or formal operations. As we have seen, experience and judgement are essential aspects of wisdom, and differentiate the adult from the child in primitive society as much as in ours. The limitations on this wisdom are those of its generalizability, its lack of system at the explicit level, and the limited experience on which it is based. Evidently, a people who have no other experience than that of an isolated valley in New Guinea will have relatively little to say on a

wide variety of human themes, and primitive thought in general
will suffer from parochial narrowness, which does not so restrict
the thought of larger-scale societies which have experience of different modes of belief and social organization.

But because we live in societies of real people, co-ordinated by
living relations of custom, inherited values, and practical skills, it
follows that the rationalist virtues of eclecticism and 'objectivity'—
the readiness to see alternative points of view and discount one's
own—when taken beyond a certain degree, become ridiculous and
can only lead to personal disorientation and to the disintegration
of society. It is thoroughly sensible to love one's own society and
to dedicate oneself to its interests in preference to those of other
societies, to prefer the company of those of one's own kind to that
of strangers, to adhere to some values rather than to others, and to
believe in one religion rather than another, even while respecting
some common inter-cultural standards of behaviour. The attempt
to produce a world of homogeneous people, or 'human units of
administration', undifferentiated by the customary criteria of
nationality, class, religion, race, sex, age, or even sanity, is an
absurdity. Equally absurd is the notion that because people are
different from us they cease to be human. But to be fully human
is to participate in *this* society and not in *that*, to follow *this*
career, not *that,* to believe *this* religion and not *that,* because these
different ways of life and thought are not in books, but lived, and
living communities develop their own rules and world view which
must differentiate them from other communities. A wise ordering
of human affairs recognizes that differentiation is not 'divisive', as
modern cant would have it, but provides the basis by which people
can be truly human.

Glossary of Psychological Terms

(All quotations are from the writings of Piaget cited in A. M. Battro *Piaget: Dictionary of Terms*, Pergamon Press, 1973, which should be consulted for the original references.)

accommodation Together with *assimilation* comprises the process of *equilibration*. An activity of the subject in reaction to the characteristics of objects, and not imposed as such by those objects: 'The pressure of things always results, not in passive submission, but in a simple modification of the action directed toward them.'

assimilation Together with *accommodation* comprises the process of *equilibration*. The incorporation of objects into the schemata of behaviour or systems of operations by the activity of the subject and the construction of relations as a function of that assimilation.

centration Concentration upon a single dimensional attribute of a thing or process; a perceptually dominated, irreversible, unco-ordinated, and hence rigid but unstable schema typical of pre-operatory thought.

compensation The inherent relation between the different dimensions of objects or systems of relations such that the increase or decrease of one dimension necessarily involves a commensurate decrease or increase in another dimension. The understanding of compensation is one of the foundations of conservation.

concept A classification based upon explicit criteria and an understanding of logical class and class inclusion.

conservation The ability to recognize the constancy of a property in spite of the transformations of other related properties in a thing or system of relations. This requires reversibility, decentration, and mobility of thought, and the grasp of compensation, and is one of the distinctive characteristics of the stage of concrete operations.

décalage Developmental lag in the mastery of cognitive skills. The 'horizontal *décalage*' occurs within the same developmental level, such that e.g. the conservation of quantity is typically attained later than that of number. The 'vertical *décalage*' occurs between different developmental levels, such that the child may not be able to reflect in words and concepts upon a task which he can perform at the sensori-motor level, in action.

egocentrism — A state of indissociation between the conscious self and the external world, between 'subjective' and 'objective', and between one's own point of view and that of others; it also implies the inability to reflect on one's own mental processes in so far as these are involved in the analysis of the external world. Should be clearly distinguished from the use of 'egocentrism' in the moral sense of 'selfishness'. (See also 'realism'.)

equilibration — A dynamic process of interaction between the subject and the external world at all developmental levels whereby stable structures of thought and action are generated through a combination of accommodation and assimilation. But it should be noted that 'a state of equilibrium is not a state of final rest, but constitutes a new point of departure.'

image — 'The mental image is a product of interiorization of intellectual acts', it is 'a copy, not of the object itself, but of the accommodations appropriate to the actions which bear upon the object.' It is thus an interiorized imitation, a symbolic signifier for the actions which bear upon objects; '. . . it is not a first fact . . . it is, like imitation itself, an accommodation of the sensori-motor schemata, that is to say, an active copy, and not a trace or sensory residue of the perceived objects.'

intuition — The apprehension of things and relations at the phenomenal level, in terms of concrete, static imagery and global configurations, without reversibility, compensation, and the other characteristics of operatory thought.

mobility — Characteristic of operatory thought, and distinguished by decentration and reversibility, anticipatory planning without the need for actual trial-and-error manipulations, and the retroactive shifting of criteria in classification.

operations — 'Interiorized actions or interiorizable actions, reversible and co-ordinated in total structures.' An operation involves the mobility, reversibility, and decentration of thought, and the grasp of the compensation of dimensional change, and is therefore characteristic of conservation.

concrete operations, stage of
: The stage at which operational thought is possible but still restricted to the concrete manipulation of objects.

formal operations, stage of
: Also known as 'hypothetico-deductive operations', based on concrete operations, 'but transposed into terms of propositions, i.e., integrating concrete classes and relations into a system of implications and of incompatibilities expressed by propositions.'

pre-operatory thought
: The stage of development succeeding the sensori-motor. and prior to concrete operations. Characterized by intuitive thought, egocentrism, lack of reversibility, mobility, the understanding of compensation, and of conservation in general.

pseudo-conservation
: An intuitive apprehension of identity, but one not based on a grasp of compensation and reversibility. Pseudo-conservation is replaced by non-conservation when subjects are obliged to take dimensional transformations into account.

realism
: The implicit assumption that the contents of consciousness have the same kind of real existence as objects in the external world, the attribution to external reality of characteristics which are really subjective; hence initially an unawareness of mental processes, and later the location of these in the external world. (See also 'egocentrism'.)

reversibility
: 'We shall call reversibility the capacity to execute the same action in both directions but being conscious that we are dealing with the same action.' 'Operational reversibility is . . . only the final state of mobile equilibrium which has been attained by perceptual and then intuitive regulations . . .' Thus reversibility is found in an incomplete form at the perceptual level as the addition and subtraction of elements, and achieves its final form at the stage of concrete operations.

sensori-motor stage
: The first stage of cognitive development, prior to the emergence of imagery and language.

References

ALLEN, A. L., THOMAS, N. D., PATU, P. (1975) 'Abilities of newly trained indigenous secondary mathematics teachers in Papua New Guinea', *Papua New Guinea Journal of Education* 11(1), 1–7.

D'ALVIELLA, G. (1911) 'Cross', in *Encyclopaedia of Religion and Ethics*, 4, ed. Hastings, Edinburgh, T. and T. Clark, 324–9.

ASCH, S. E. (1958) 'The Metaphor: A Psychological Inquiry', *Person Perception and Interpersonal Behavior*, R. Tagiuri and L. Petrullo, eds. 88–93, Stanford University Press.

BARNES, J. A. (1971) 'Time flies like an arrow', *Man* (n.s.), 6, 537–52.

BARNES, R. H. (1974) *Kédang. A Study of the Collective Thought of an Eastern Indonesian People*, Oxford Monographs on Social Anthropology, Oxford, Clarendon Press.

BASOV, M. (1929) 'Structural analysis in psychology from the standpoint of behaviour', *Journ. Genet. Psychol.* 36, 267–90.

BATESON, G. (1958) *Naven*, 2nd edition, California, Stanford University Press.

BEATTIE, J. H. M. (1964) *Other Cultures. Aims, Methods and Achievements in Social Anthropology*, London, Cohen & West.

BEIDELMAN, T. O. (1963) 'Kaguru time reckoning: an aspect of the cosmology of an East African people', *S.W.J.A.* 19, 9–20.

BEKKER, J. H. (1947) Communication to Society for Psychical Research, *Journ. Soc. Psych. Res.*, 32, 80–5.

BERLIN, B. and KAY, P. (1969) *Basic Color Terms: Their Universality and Evolution*, Berkeley, University of California Press.

BERNSTEIN, B. (1971) *Class, Codes, and Control*, London, Routledge & Kegan Paul.

BLACK, M. (1968) 'Linguistic relativity: the views of Benjamin Lee Whorf', in *Theory in Anthropology. A Source Book*, eds. R. A. Manners and D. Kaplan, London, Routledge & Kegan Paul.

BLACKWOOD, B. (1978) *The Kukukuku of the Upper Watut*, ed. with Introduction by C. R. Hallpike, Oxford, Pitt Rivers Museum.

BLAUT, J. M., McCLEARY, G. S., and BLAUT, A. S. (1970) 'Environmental mapping in young children', *Environment and Behaviour*, 2(3), 335–49.

BOAS, F. (1888) 'The Central Eskimo', *Sixth Annual Report of the Bureau of Ethnology*, Washington, D.C., 1–261.

BOHANNAN, P. (1967) 'Concepts of time among the Tiv of Nigeria', in *Myth and Cosmos. Readings in Mythology and Symbolism*, ed. J. Middleton, American Museum Sourcebooks in Anthropology, New York, Natural History Press.

BOSHIER, A. K. (1974) 'African apprenticeship', in *Parapsychology and Anthropology*, Proceedings of International Conference in London, 1973, eds. A. Angoff and D. Barth. New York, Parapsychology Foundation.

BOVET, M. C. (1974) 'Cognitive processes among illiterate children and adults', in *Culture and Cognition: Readings in Cross-Cultural Psychology*, eds. J. W. Berry and P. R. Dasen, London, Methuen, 311–34.

—— (1975) 'Étude interculturelle de processus de raisonnement. Notions de quantité et relations spatio-temporelles', Ph.D. Thesis, University of Geneva.

BRIGHT, J. O., and BRIGHT, W. (1970) 'Semantic structures in North-western California and the Sapir–Whorf hypothesis', in *Cognitive Anthropology*, ed. S. A. Tyler, New York, Holt, Rinehart Winston, 66–78.

BROAD, C. D. (1962) *Lectures on Psychical Research*, International Library of Psychology, Philosophy, and Scientific Method, London, Routledge & Kegan Paul.

BROWN, R. W., BLACK, A. H., and HOROWITZ, A. E. (1955) 'Phonetic symbolism in natural languages', *Journ. Abnorm. and Soc. Psychol.* 50, 388–93.

BROWN, R. W. and LENNEBERG, E. H. (1954) 'A study in language and cognition', *Journ. Abnorm. and Soc. Psychol.* 49, 454–62.

BRUNER, J. S. (1965) 'The growth of mind', *American Psychologist*, 20(12), 1007–17.

—— (1966a) 'On cognitive growth (I)', in *Studies in Cognitive Growth*, eds. J. S. Bruner, R. R. Olver, P. M. Greenfield, New York, Wiley, 1–29.

—— (1966b) 'On cognitive growth (II)', in *Studies in Cognitive Growth*, eds. J. S. Bruner, R. R. Olver, and P. M. Greenfield, New York, Wiley, 30–67.

—— (1966c) 'On the conservation of liquids', in *Studies on Cognitive Growth*, eds. J. S. Bruner, R. R. Olver, and P. M. Greenfield, New York, Wiley, 183–207.

—— (1966d) 'An overview', in *Studies in Cognitive Growth*, eds. J. S. Bruner, R. R. Olver, and P. M. Greenfield, New York, Wiley, 319–26.

—— and GOODMAN, C. C. (1947) 'Value and need as organising factors in perception', *Journ. Abnorm. and Soc. Psychol.* 42, 33–44.

—— and POSTMAN, L. (1949) 'On the perception of incongruity: a paradigm', *Journ. Personality*, 18.

BULMER, R. N. H. (1967) 'Why is the cassowary not a bird? A problem of zoological taxonomy among the Karam of the New Guinea Highlands', *Man* (n.s.), 12(1), 5–25.

—— (1970) 'Which came first, the chicken or the egg-head?', in *Échanges et communications. Mélanges offerts à Claude Lévi-Strauss à l'occasion de son 60ème anniversaire,* eds. J. Puillon and P. Maranda, 2 vols., The Hague, Mouton, ii.1069–91.

BUNZEL, R. (1929) *The Pueblo Potter,* New York, Columbia University Press.

BURRIDGE, K. O. L. (1969) *Tangu Traditions. A Study of the Way of Life, Mythology, and Developing Experience of a New Guinea People,* Oxford, Clarendon Press.

CAROTHERS, J. C. (1953) *The African Mind in Health and Disease. A Study in Ethnopsychiatry,* Geneva, World Health Organisation Monograph Series no. 17.

CARPENTER, E., VARLEY, F., and FLAHERTY, R. (1959) *Eskimo* (no pagination), University of Toronto Press.

CAUTE, D. (1973) *The Fellow Travellers, a Postscript to the Enlightenment,* London.

CHOMSKY, N. (1972) *Language and Mind,* 2nd edition, New York, Harcourt Brace Jovanovich.

COHEN, L. J. (1966) *The Diversity of Meaning,* London, Methuen.

COLBY, B. and COLE, M. (1973) 'Culture, memory and narrative', in *Modes of Thought. Essays on Thinking in Western and Non-Western Societies,* eds. R. Horton, and R. Finnegan, London, Faber & Faber, 63–91.

COLE, M. (1976) 'Introduction' to A. R. Luria *Cognitive Development. Its Cultural and Social Foundations,* Cambridge, Mass., Harvard University Press, xi–xvi.

—— GAY, J., & GLICK, J. (1974) 'Some experimental studies of Kpelle quantitative behaviour', in J. Berry & P. R. Dasen, eds. *Culture and Cognition: Readings in Cross-Cultural Psychology,* London, Methuen 159–96.

—— GAY, J., GLICK, J., SHARP, D. (1971) *The Cultural Context of Learning and Thinking. An Exploration in Experimental Anthropology,* London, Methuen.

—— and SCRIBNER, S. (1974) *Culture and Thought: a Psychological Introduction,* New York, Wiley.

COLLINGWOOD, R. (1939) *An Autobiography,* Oxford University Press.

CONANT, L. L. (1896) *The Number Concept. Its Origin and Development,* New York, Macmillan.

COOPER, D. E. (1975) 'Alternative logic in "primitive thought"', *Man* (n.s.), 10, 238–56.

CUNNINGHAM, C. (1964) 'Order in the Atoni house', *Bijdragen tot de Taal-. Land- en Volkenkunde,* 120, 34–68.

DASEN, P. R. (1973) 'Piagetian research in Central Australia', in *The Psychology of Aboriginal Australians,* Sydney, Wiley & Sons, 89–96.

—— (1974) 'The influence of ecology, culture and European contact on cognitive development in Australian aborigines', in *Culture and Cogni-*

502

tion: Readings in Cross-Cultural Psychology, eds., J. W. Berry and P. R. Dasen, London, Methuen, 381–408.

—— (1977) 'Are cognitive processes universal? A contribution to cross-cultural Piagetian psychology', in *Studies in Cross-Cultural Psychology*, vol. 1, ed. N. Warren, London, Academic Press, 155–201.

DENNES, W. R. (1924) *The Method and Presuppositions of Group Psychology*, Berkeley, University of California Publications in Philosophy, 6(1).

DODDS, E. R. (1951) *The Greeks and the Irrational*, Berkeley, University of California Press.

DOUGALL, J. W. C. (1932) 'Characteristics of African thought', *Africa* 5(3), 249–65.

DOUGLAS, M. (1966) *Purity and Danger. An Analysis of Concepts of Pollution and Taboo*, London, Routledge & Kegan Paul.

—— (1973) *Natural Symbols. Explorations in Cosmology*, 2nd edition, London, Barrie & Jenkins.

DURKHEIM, E. (1913) Review of L. Lévy-Bruhl's *Les Fonctions mentales dans les sociétés inférieures, Année sociologique*, 12, 33–7.

—— (1947) *The Elementary Forms of the Religious Life*, tr. J. W. Swain, New York, Collier Books.

—— (1953) *Sociology and Philosophy*, tr. D. F. Pocock, London, Cohen & West.

—— and MAUSS, M. (1963) *Primitive Classification*, tr. R. Needham, London, Cohen & West.

EKMAN, P. (1972) in *Cognitive Development and the Acquisition of Language*, ed. T. E. Moore, Nebraska, University of Nebraska Press, 207–83.

ENDICOTT, K. (1970) *Malay Magic*, Oxford Monographs on Social Anthropology, Oxford, Clarendon Press.

EVANS-PRITCHARD, E. E. (1937) *Witchcraft, Oracles and Magic among the Azande*, Oxford, Clarendon Press.

—— (1940) *The Nuer*, Oxford, Clarendon Press.

—— (1951) *Social Anthropology*, London, Cohen & West.

—— (1956) *Nuer Religion*, Oxford, Clarendon Press.

—— (1962) '*Sanza*, a characteristic feature of Zande language and thought', in *Essays in Social Anthropology*, London, Faber, 204–28.

—— (1965) *Theories of Primitive Religion*, Oxford, Clarendon Press.

FEUER, L. S. (1968) 'Sociological aspects of the relation between language and culture', in *Theory in Anthropology. A Source Book*, eds. R. A. Manners and D. Kaplan, London, Routledge & Kegan Paul, 411–20.

FIRTH, R. (1967) 'The meaning of dreams', in *Tikopia Ritual and Belief*, Boston, Beacon Press, 162–73.

FISCHER, N. (1968) *Negwa. Eine Papua-Gruppe im Wandel*, Munich, Klaus Renner.

FISHMAN, J. A. (1974) 'A systematization of the Whorfian hypothesis' in *Culture and Cognition: Readings in Cross-Cultural Psychology*, eds. J. W. Berry and P. R. Dasen, London, Methuen, 61–86.

FLAVELL, J. H. *The Developmental Psychology of Jean Piaget*, New York, Van Nostrand Reinhold.

—— and WOHLWILL, J. F. (1969) 'Formal and functional aspects of cognitive development', in *Studies in Cognitive Development*, eds. D. Elkind and J. H. Flavell, Oxford University Press.

FORTES, M. (1938) 'Social and psychological aspects of education in Taleland', Supplement to *Africa*, 11(4), also Memorandum xvii of *Int. Inst. African Languages and Cultures*, London, Oxford University Press.

FORTUNE, R. (1932) *Sorcerers of Dobu*, London, George Routledge.

FRANKFORT, H. and FRANKFORT, H. A. (1949) 'Myth and reality', in *Before Philosophy. The Intellectual Adventure of Ancient Man*, by H. Frankfort, H. A. Frankfort, J. A. Wilson, and T. Jacobson, London, Penguin Books.

FRAZER, J. G. (1900) *The Golden Bough. A Study in Magic and Religion*, 2nd edition, 3 vols., London, Macmillan.

—— (1922) *The Golden Bough*, abridged edition, London, Macmillan.

FREEMAN, K. (1971) *Ancilla to the Pre-Socratic Philosophers*, Oxford, Blackwell.

FURTH, H. (1961) 'The influence of language on the development of concept formation in deaf children', *Journ. Abnorm. and Soc. Psychol.* 63, 386–89.

GAY, J., and COLE, M. (1967) *The New Mathematics and an Old Culture*, New York, Holt, Rinehart Winston.

GEHLKE, C. E. (1915) *Emile Durkheim's Contribution to Sociological Theory*, New York, Columbia University Studies in History, Economics, and Public Law, 63(1).

GELL, A. F. (1975) *Metamorphosis of the Cassowaries: Umeda Society, Language and Ritual*, Lond. Sch. Econ. Monogrs. Soc. Anthrop. 51, London, Athlone Press.

VAN GENNEP, A. (1960) *The Rites of Passage*, tr. M. B. Vizedom and G. L. Caffee, London, Routledge & Kegan Paul.

GIBBON, E. (1960) *The Decline and Fall of the Roman Empire*, (abridged D. M. Low), London, Chatto & Windus.

GIRARD, F. (1968–9) 'Les notions de nombre et de temps chez les Buang de Nouvelle Guinee (District du Morobe)' *Société d'Ethnographie de Paris*.

GITIN, S. R. (1970) 'A dimensional analysis of manual expression', *Journ. Pers. and Soc. Psychol.* 15, 271–7.

GLADWIN, H. (1970) 'Decision Making in the Cape Coast (Fante) Fishing and Fish Marketing System', Ph.D. Thesis, Stanford University.

504   REFERENCES

GLADWIN, T. (1970) *East is a Big Bird. Navigation and Logic on Puluwat Atoll*, Cambridge, Mass., Harvard University Press.

GLUCKMAN, M. (1949–50) 'Social beliefs and individual thinking in primitive society', *Memoirs and Proceedings of the Manchester Literary and Philosophical Society*, 91, 73–98.

GOODENOUGH, W. (1951) 'Native astronomy in Micronesia: a rudimentary science', *Scientific Monthly*, 73, 105–10.

GOODNOW, J. J. (1962) 'A test of milieu differences with some of Piaget's tasks', *Psychol. Monogr.* 76, no. 36, (whole of no. 555).

GOODY, J.(1973) 'Evolution and communication', *Brit.Journ.Sociol.*24, 1–12.

—— (1977) *The Domestication of the Savage Mind*, Cambridge University Press.

—— COLE, M., and SCRIBNER, S. (1977) 'Writing and formal operations: a case study among the Vai', *Africa*, 47(5), 289–304.

GREENBERG, J. H. (1954) 'Concerning inferences from linguistic to non-linguistic data', in *Language and Culture. Conference in the Inter-relations of Language and Other Aspects of Culture*, ed. H. Hoijer, University of Chicago Press, 3–19.

GREENFIELD, P. M. (1966) 'On culture and conservation', in *Studies in Cognitive Growth*, eds. J. S. Bruner, R. R. Olver, P. M. Greenfield, New York, Wiley, 225–56.

—— and BRUNER, J. S. (1966) 'Culture and cognitive growth', *Intl. Journ. of Psychol.* 1(2), 89–107.

—— REICH, L. C., and OLVER, R. R. (1966) 'On culture and equivalence (II)', in *Studies in Cognitive Growth*, eds. J. S. Bruner, R. R. Olver, and P. M. Greenfield, New York, Wiley, 270–318.

GRIAULE, M., and DIETERLEN, G. (1954) 'The Dogon of the French Sudan', in *African Worlds*, ed. D. Forde, Intl. African Inst., London, Oxford University Press, 83–110.

HACKING, I. (1975) *The Emergence of Probability. A Philosophical Study of Early Ideas about Probability, Induction, and Statistical Inference*, Cambridge University Press.

HALLOWELL, A. I. (1937) 'Temporal orientation in Western civilization and in a preliterate society', *American Anthropologist*, 39, 646–70.

—— (1942) 'Some psychological aspects of measurements among the Saulteaux', *American Anthropologist* 44, 62–77.

HALLPIKE, C. R. (1964) 'The Notion of Causation among Selected African Peoples, as Found Especially in their Beliefs in Divinities, Witches, Ancestor-Spirits, and Destiny', B.Litt. Thesis, Bodleian MS B.Litt. d.1036.

—— (1969) 'Social hair', *Man* (n.s.) 4(2), 256–64.

—— (1972) *The Konso of Ethiopia. A Study of the Values of a Cushitic People*, Oxford, Clarendon Press.

—— (1976) 'Is there a primitive mentality?', *Man* (n.s.) 11, 253–70.

REFERENCES 505

—— (1977) *Bloodshed and Vengeance in the Papuan Mountains. The Generation of Conflict in Tauade Society,* Oxford, Clarendon Press.

HEIDER, E. R. (see ROSCH, E.) (1972) 'Universals in color naming and memory', *Journ. Exper. Psychol.* 93(1), 10–20.

HERSHMAN, P. (1974) 'Hair, sex and dirt', *Man* (n.s.) 9(2), 274–98.

HERTZ, R. (1960) *Death and The Right Hand,* tr. R. Needham, London, Cohen & West.

HOLLIS, A. C. (1905) *The Masai,* Oxford, Clarendon Press.

HORTON, R. (1961) 'Destiny and the unconscious in West Africa', *Africa,* 31(2), 110–16.

—— (1967) 'African traditional thought and Western science', *Africa,* 37, 50–71, 155–87.

INGRAMS, R. (1973) *Private Eye's Book of Pseuds. A Mood Statement* ed. R. Ingrams, London, Private Eye Publications.

INHELDER, B. (1969) Discussion following 'The gaps in empiricism', in *Beyond Reductionism. The Alpbach Symposium,* eds. A. Koestler and J. R. Smythies, London, Hutchinson [J. Piaget and B. Inhelder].

—— and PIAGET, J. (1958) *The Growth of Logical Thinking from Childhood to Adolescence,*London, Routledge & Kegan Paul.

—— and PIAGET, J. (1964) *The Early Growth of Logic in the Child. Classification and Seriation,* tr. E. A. Lunzer and D. Papert, London, Routledge & Kegan Paul.

IRWIN, M. H. and MCLAUGHLIN, D. H. (1970) 'Ability and preference in category sorting by Mano schoolchildren and adults', *Journ. of Soc. Psychol.* 82, 15–24.

ISAACS, N. (1957) 'The wider significance of Piaget's work', in *Some Aspects of Piaget's Work,* London, National Froebel Foundation 2nd edition.

ISAACS, S. (1930) *Intellectual Growth in Young Children,* London, George Routledge.

JESPERSEN, J. O. H. (1922) *Language: Its Nature, Development, and Origin,* London, Allen & Unwin.

JOHNSON, A. R. (1964) *The Vitality of the Individual in the Thought of Ancient Israel,* Cardiff, University of Wales Press.

KARWOSKI, T. F., ODBERT, H. S., and OSGOOD, C. E. (1942) 'Studies in synesthetic thinking: II. The role of form in visual responses to music', *Journ. of General Psychol.* 26, 199–222.

KELLY, M. R. (1971) 'Some aspects of conservation of quantity and length in relation to language, sex, and years in school', *Papua New Guinea Journ. of Educ.* 7, 55–60.

KENNY, M. G. (n.d.) 'The concept of the self in New Guinea', mimeograph, 15 pp. and bibliography.

KEYNES, J. M. (1921) *A Treatise on Probability,* London, Macmillan.

KLANK, L. J. K., HUANG, Y-H., and JOHNSON, R. C. (1971) 'Determinants

506

of success in matching word pairs in tests of phonetic symbolism', *Journ. of Verbal Learning and Behaviour,* 10, 140–48.

KROEBER, A. L. (1925) *Handbook of the Indians of California,* Bulletin 78, Bureau of American Ethnology.

DE LACEY, P. R. (1974) 'A Cross-cultural study of classificatory ability in Australia', in *Culture and Cognition: Readings in Cross-Cultural Psychology,* eds. J. W. Berry and P. R. Dasen, London, Methuen, 353–66.

LANG, A. (1896) *Cock Lane and Common Sense,* London, Longmans, Green & Co., 2nd edition.

—— (1900) *The Making of Religion,* London, Longmans, Green & Co., 2nd edition.

LAWRENCE, P. (1964) *Road Belong Cargo,* Melbourne University Press.

LEACH, E. R. (1954) *Political Systems of Highland Burma: a Study of Kachin Social Structure,* London, Bell.

—— (1961) 'Two essays concerning the symbolic representation of time', in *Rethinking Anthropology,* Lond. Sch. Econ. Monogrs. in Soc. Anth. 22, London, Athlone Press.

—— (1964) 'Anthropological aspects of language: animal categories and verbal abuse', in *New Directions in the Study of Language,* ed. E. H. Lenneberg, Cambridge, Mass., MIT Press.

—— (1976) *Culture and Communication. The Logic by which Symbols are Communicated. An Introduction to the use of Structuralist Analysis in Social Anthropology,* Cambridge University Press.

DE LEMOS, M. M. (1973) 'The development of conservation in aboriginal children', in *The Psychology of Aboriginal Australians,* eds. G. E. Kearney, P. R. de Lacey, and G. R. Davidson, Sydney, Wiley, 71–88.

—— (1974) 'The development of spatial concepts in Zulu children', in *Culture and Cognition: Readings in Cross-Cultural Psychology,* eds. J. W. Berry, P. R. Dasen, London, Methuen, 367–80.

LENNEBERG, E. H. (1964) 'A biological perspective of language', in *New Directions in the Study of Language,* ed. F. H. Lenneberg, Cambridge, Mass., MIT press.

LEVINE, B. B. (1963) 'Nyasongo', in *Six Cultures: Studies of Child Rearing,* ed. B. B. Whiting, New York, Wiley.

LEVINE, R. A. and PRICE-WILLIAMS, D. R. (1974) Children's kinship concepts: cognitive development and early experience among the Hausa, *Ethnology,* 13, 25–44.

LÉVI-STRAUSS, C. (1963) 'Linguistics & anthropology', in *Structural Anthropology,* tr. C. Jacobson and B. G. Schoepf, New York, Basic Books, 67–80.

—— (1966) *The Savage Mind,* Nature of Human Society Series, London, Weidenfeld & Nicholson.

—— (1969) *The Elementary Structures of Kinship,* tr. J. H. Bell and J. R. von Sturmer, ed. R. Needham, Boston, Beacon Press.

—— (1971) *Mythologiques IV: L'Homme nu*, Paris, Plon.

LÉVY-BRUHL, L. (1926) *How Natives Think*, tr. L. A. Clare (from *Les Fonctions mentales dans les sociétés inferieures*, 1912) London, Allen & Unwin.

—— (1975) *The Notebooks of Lévy-Bruhl*, tr. P. Rivière, Oxford, Blackwell.

LEWIS, D. (1976) 'Observations on route finding and spatial orientation among the Aboriginal peoples of the Western Desert region of Central Australia', *Oceania* 46(4), 249–82.

LEWIS, G. (1975) *Knowledge of Illness in a Sepik Society. A Study of the Gnau, New Guinea*, Lond. Sch. Econ. Monogrs. Soc. Anth. no. 52, London, Athlone Press.

LIENHARDT, G. (1961) *Divinity and Experience. The Religion of the Dinka*, Oxford, Clarendon Press.

LITTLEJOHN, J. (1963) 'Temne space', *Anthrop. Quarterly*, 36, 1–17.

—— (1967) 'The Temne house', in *Myth and Cosmos. Readings in Mythology and Symbolism*, ed. J. Middleton, American Museum Sourcebooks in Anthropology, New York, Natural History Press, 331–48.

LLOYD, G. E. R. (1966) *Polarity and Analogy. Two Types of Argumentation in Early Greek Thought*. Cambridge University Press.

LUNZER, E. A. (1960) 'Some points of Piagetian theory in the light of experimental criticism', *J. Child. Psychol. and Psychiat.* 1(3), 191–202.

LURIA, A. R. (1971) 'Towards the problem of the historical nature of psychological processes', *Int. Journ. Psychol.* 6(4), 259–72.

—— (1976) *Cognitive Development. Its Cultural and Social Foundations*, tr. M. Lopez-Morillas and L. Solotarof, ed. M. Cole, Cambridge, Mass., Harvard University Press.

LYONS, J. (1977) *Semantics* (2 vols.), Cambridge University Press.

MAEGRAITH, B. G. (1932) 'The astronomy of the Aranda and Loritja tribes', Adelaide University Field Anthropology no. 10, *Transactions of the Royal Society of Australia*, 56.

MALINOWSKI, B. (1922) *Argonauts of the Western Pacific. An Account of Native Enterprise and Adventure in the Archipelagoes of Melanesian New Guinea*, London, Routledge & Kegan Paul.

—— (1923) 'The problem of meaning in primitive languages' in *The Meaning of Meaning. A Study of the Influence of Language upon Thought and of the Science of Symbolism*, C. K. Ogden and I. A. Richards, London, Routledge & Kegan Paul, 296–336.

MALLERY, G. (1893) 'Picture-writing of the American Indians', *Smithsonian Institution Bureau of American Ethnology*, 10, 724–25.

MANLEY, B. F. J., ALLEN, A. L., and SHANNON, A. G. (1974) 'A analogical replication of a Piagetian experiment on New Guineans', *Malaysian Journ. of Educ.* 11, 77–82.

MATHIASSEN, T. (1928) 'Material culture of the Iglulik Eskimos', in *Report*

508   REFERENCES

of 5th Thule Expedition 1921–4 vol. VI, Gyldendalske Boghandel
Nordisk Forlag, Copenhagen.

MAUSS, M. (1972) A General Theory of Magic, tr. R. Brain, London,
Routledge & Kegan Paul.

MAYS, W. (1972) 'Introduction' to The Principles of Genetic Epistemology,
J. Piaget, London, Routledge & Kegan Paul, 1–9.

MEAD, M. (1930) Growing Up in New Guinea, New York, New American
Library.

—— (1932) 'An investigation of the thought of primitive children, with
special reference to animism', Journ. Roy. Anthrop. Inst. 62, 173–90.

—— (1960) Discussion in Discussions on Child Development, eds. J. M.
Tanner and B. Inhelder, Geneva, Tavistock Publications, 1956–60, p.
114.

MEHRABIAN, A. (1972) Nonverbal Communication, Chicago, Aldine–Ather-
ton.

MEIGS, A. S. (1978) 'A Papuan perspective on pollution', Man (n.s.) 13(2),
304–18.

MIDDLETON, J. (1960) Lugbara Religion, Oxford University Press.

MOORE, O. K. and OLMSTED, D. R. (1952) 'Language and Professor Lévi-
Strauss', American Anthropologist, 54, 116–19.

MORRIS, B. (1976) 'Whither the savage mind? Notes on the natural taxonomies of a hunting and gathering people', Man (n.s.) 11, 542–57.

NADEL, S. F. (1954) Nupe Religion, London, Routledge & Kegan Paul.

NEEDHAM, J. (1965) Time and Eastern Man, Henry Myers Lecture 1964,
London, Royal Anthropological Institute.

NEEDHAM, R. (1960) 'The left hand of the Mugwe: an analytical note on
the structure of Meru symbolism', Africa 30, 20–33.

—— (1963) 'Introduction' to translation of Primitive Classification by E.
Durkheim and M. Mauss, tr. R. Needham, London, Cohen & West,
vii–xlviii.

—— (1967) 'Right and left in Nyoro symbolic classification', Africa 37(4),
423–51.

—— (1972) Belief, Language, and Experience, Oxford, Blackwell.

—— (1973) 'Introduction' to Right and Left. Essays on Dual Symbolic
Classification, ed. R. Needham, Chicago, University of Chicago Press,
xi–xxxix.

—— (1975) 'Polythetic classification: convergence and consequences', Man
(n.s.) 10(3), 349–69.

—— (1976a) 'Little black boxes', letter to Times Literary Supplement, May
28, 647.

—— (1976b) 'Nyoro symbolism: the ethnographic record', Africa, 46, 236–
46.

—— (1976c) 'Skulls and causality' Man (n.s.) 11, 71–88.

NILSSON, M. P. (1920) Primitive Time-Reckoning. A Study in the Origins and First Development of the Art of Counting Time among the Primitive and Early Culture Peoples, Skrifter Utgivna av Humanistika Vetenskapssamfundet i Lund I, Lund, C. W. K. Gleerup.

OAKESHOTT, M. (1962) Rationalism in Politics and Other Essays, London, Methuen.

ODBERT, H. S., KARWOSKI, T. F., and ECKERSON, A. B. (1942) 'Studies in synesthetic thinking: I musical and verbal associations of color and mood', Journ. of General Psychology, 26, 153–73.

OGDEN, C. K. (1967) Opposition, Bloomington, Indiana University Press.

OLERON, P. (1957) Recherches sur le développement mental des sourdes-muets, Paris, Centre National de la Recherche Scientifique.

ONIANS, R. B. (1954) The Origins of Modern European Thought about the Body, the Mind, the Soul, the World, Time, and Fate: New Interpretations of Greek, Roman and Kindred Evidence, also of Some Basic Jewish and Christian Beliefs, 2nd edition, Cambridge University Press.

OSGOOD, C. E. (1960) 'The cross-cultural generality of visual-verbal synesthetic tendencies', Behavioral Science, 5, 146–69.

—— (1963) 'Language universals and psycholinguistics', in Universals of Language, ed. J. H. Greenberg, Cambridge, Mass., MIT Press, 299–322.

—— (1964) 'Semantic differential technique in the comparative study of cultures', American Anthropologist, 66, 171–200.

—— MAY, W. H., and MIRON, M. S. (1975) Cross-Cultural Universals of Affective Meaning, Urbana, Illinois, University of Illinois Press.

PANOFF, M. (1969) 'The notion of time among the Maenge people of New Britain', Ethnology, 8, 153–66.

—— 'Father arithmetic: numeration and counting in New Britain', Ethnology, 9, 358–65.

PELUFFO, N. (1967) 'Culture and cognitive problems', Int. Journ. Psychol. 2(3), 187–98.

PIAGET, J. (1928) Judgement and Reasoning in the Child, tr. M. Warden, London, Routledge & Kegan Paul.

—— The Child's Conception of the World, tr. J. and A. Tomlinson, London, Routledge & Kegan Paul.

—— (1930) The Child's Conception of Physical Causality, tr. M. Gabain, London, Routledge & Kegan Paul

—— (1932) The Moral Judgement of the Child, London, Routledge & Kegan Paul.

—— (1952a) The Child's Conception of Number, tr. C. Gattegno and F. Hodgson, London, Routledge & Kegan Paul.

—— (1952b) The Origins of Intelligence in Children, New York Int. Univ. Press.

—— (1959) The Language and Thought of the Child, 3rd edition, tr. M. and R. Gabain, London, Routledge & Keegan Paul.

—— (1962) *Play, Dreams, and Imitation in Childhood*, tr. C. Cattegno and F. M. Hodgson, London, Routledge & Kegan Paul.

—— (1967) Review of J. S. Bruner *et al*. Studies in Cognitive Growth, 1966, in *Contemporary Psychology* 12(11), 532–3.

—— (1970) *The Child's Conception of Time*, tr. A. J. Pomerans, London, Routledge & Kegan Paul.

—— (1971) *Structuralism*, tr. and ed. C. Maschler, London, Routledge & Kegan Paul.

—— (1972) *The Principles of Genetic Epistemology*, tr. W. Mays, London, Routledge & Kegan Paul.

—— (1974) 'Need and significance of cross-cultural studies in genetic psychology', in *Culture and Cognition: Readings in Cross-Cultural Psychology*, eds. J. W. Berry and P. R. Dasen, London, Methuen, 299–310.

—— (1975) *The Origin of the Idea of Chance in Children*, tr. L. Leake, P. Burrell, H. D. Fishbein, London, Routledge & Kegan Paul.

—— and INHELDER, B. (1956) *The Child's Conception of Space*, tr. F. J. Langdon and J. L. Lunzer, London, Routledge & Kegan Paul.

—— and INHELDER, B. (1969a) *The Psychology of the Child*, tr. H. Weaver, London, Routledge & Kegan Paul.

—— and INHELDER, B. (1969b) 'The gaps in empiricism', in *Beyond Reductionism. The Alpbach Symposium*, eds. A. Koestler and J. R. Smythies, London, Hutchinson, 118–60.

POCOCK, D. (1967) 'The anthropology of time-reckoning', in *Myth and Cosmos. Readings in Mythology and Symbolism*, ed J. Middleton, American Museum Sourcebooks in Anthropology, New York, Natural History Press, 303–14.

POLANYI, M. (1958) *Personal Knowledge, Towards a Post-Critical Philosophy*, London, Routledge & Kegan Paul.

POSTMAN, L., BRUNER, J. S., and MCGINNIES, E. (1948) 'Personal values as selective factors in perception', *Journ. Abnorm. and Soc. Psychol.* 43, 142–54.

PRICE-WILLIAMS, D. R. (1961) 'A study concerning concepts of conservation of quantities among primitive children', *Acta Psychologica*, 18(4), 297–305.

—— (1962) 'Abstract and concrete modes of classification in a primitive society', *Brit. Journ. Educ. Psychol.* 32, 50–61.

PRINCE, J. R. (1969) *Science Concepts in a Pacific Culture*, Sydney, Angus & Robertson.

RADCLIFFE-BROWN, A. R. (1952) *Structure and Function in Primitive Society*, London, Cohen & West.

RADIN, P. (1957) *Primitive Man as Philosopher*, New York, Dover Publications.

RASMUSSEN, K. (1932) 'Intellectual culture of the Copper Eskimos', in

Report of 5th Thule Expedition 1921–4, Gyldendalske Boghandel Nordisk Forlag, Copenhagen.

READ, K. E. (1955) 'Morality and the concept of the person among the Gahuku-Gama', *Oceania*, 25(4), 233–82.

READ, M. (1959) *Children of their Fathers*, London, Methuen.

ROSCH, E. (see HEIDER, E. R.) (1977) 'Human categorization', in *Studies in Cross-Cultural Psychology*, vol. i, ed. N. Warren, London, Academic Press, 1–49.

ROSENSTEIN, J. (1960) 'Cognitive abilities of deaf children', *Journ. Speech Hearing Res.* 3, 108–19.

SAPIR, E. (1929a) 'The status of Linguistics as a science', *Language*, 5, 207–14.

—— (1929b) 'A study in phonetic symbolism', *Journ. Exper. Psychol.* 12, 225–39.

SEGALL, M. H., CAMPBELL, D. T., and HERSKOVITZ, M. J. (1966) *The Influence of Culture on Visual Perception*, Chicago, Bobbs-Merrill.

SERPELL, R. (1969) 'The influence of language, education and culture on attentional preference between colour and form', *Int. Journ. Psychol.* 4(3), 183–94.

SINCLAIR, H. (1967) *Acquisition de langage et développement de la pensée*, Paris, Dunod.

SLOBIN, D. I. (1968) 'Antonymic phonetic symbolism in three natural languages', *Journ. of Personality and Soc. Psychol.* 10, 301–5.

SMITH, W. ROBERTSON (1907) *Lectures on the Religion of the Semites*, 2nd edition, London, Adam and Charles Black.

SMYTHIES, E. A. (1951) 'A case of levitation in Nepal', *Journ. Soc. Psychical Res.* 36, no. 664, 415–26.

SNELL, B. (1960) *The Discovery of the Mind. The Greek Origins of European Thought*, New York, Harper Torchbooks.

SPERBER, D. (1975) *Rethinking Symbolism*, tr. A. Morton, Cambridge Studies in Social Anthropology, Cambridge University Press.

SUCHMAN, R. G. (1966) 'Color–form preference, discriminative accuracy and learning of deaf and hearing children', *Child Development*, 37, 439–51.

THOM, A. (1967) *Megalithic Sites in Britain*, Oxford, Clarendon Press.

THOMPSON, F. (1948) *Lark Rise to Candleford*, London, The Reprint Society.

TOULMIN, S. (1953) *The Philosophy of Science: an Introduction*, London, Hutchinson University Library.

TURNER, T. (1973) 'Piaget's structuralism', *American Anthropologist*, 75, 351–73.

TURNER, V. W. 1962 *Chihamba. The White Spirit. A Ritual Drama of the Ndembu*, Rhodes–Livingston Papers 33, Manchester University Press.

—— (1967) *The Forest of Symbols. Aspects of Ndembu Ritual*, New York, Cornell University Press.

TYLOR, E. B. (1871) *Primitive Culture: Researches into the Development of Mythology, Philosophy, Religion, Art, and Custom*, 2 vols., London, John Murray.

VANSINA, J. (1973) *Oral Tradition. A Study in Historical Methodology*, tr. H. M. Wright, London, Penguin Books.

VERNON, P. E. (1970) *Creativity*. Penguin Modern Psychology Readings, ed. P. E. Vernon, Penguin Books, Harmondsworth, England.

VYGOTSKY, L. S. (1962) *Thought and Language*, Cambridge, Mass., MIT Press.

WALLACE, A. F. C. (1962) 'Culture and cognition', *Science*, 132, 351–57.

WEISS, J. H. (1963) 'Role of "meaningfulness" versus meaning dimensions in guessing the meanings of foreign words', *Journ. of Abnorm. and Soc. Psychol.* 66, 541–46.

WERNER, H. (1948) *Comparative Psychology of Mental Development*, revised edition, New York, International Press.

—— and KAPLAN, B. (1948) 'The developmental approach to cognition: its relevance to the psychological interpretation of anthropological and ethnolinguistic data', *American Anthropologist*, 58, 866–80.

WESTERMANN, D. (1927) 'Laut, Ton und Sinn in Westafrikanischen Sprachen', *Festschrift Meinhof*.

WEXNER, L. B. (1954) 'The degree to which colors (hues) are associated with mood-tones', *Journ. Appl. Psychol.*, 38, 432–35.

WHORF, B. L. (1956) *Language, Thought, and Reality: Selected Writings of Benjamin Lee Whorf*, ed, J. B. Carroll, New York, MIT.

WILHELM, R. (1968) Preface to *The I Ching or Book of Changes*, Bollingen Foundation, Princeton University Press.

WILLIAMS, F. E. (1930) *Orokaiva Society*, Oxford, Clarendon Press.

—— (1940) *Drama of Orokolo. The Social and Ceremonial Life of the Elema*, Oxford, Clarendon Press.

WOBER, M. (1974) 'Towards an understanding of the Kiganda concept of intelligence', in *Culture and Cognition: Readings in Cross-Cultural Psychology*, eds. J. W. Berry and P. R. Dasen, London, Methuen, 261–80.

WOLFERS, E. P. (1972) 'Counting and numbers', in *Encyclopaedia of Papua and New Guinea*, Melbourne University Press and University of Papua New Guinea, 216–20.

WOLFRAM, S. (1973) 'Basic differences of thought', in *Modes of Thought. Essays on Thinking in Western and Non-Western Societies*, eds. R. Horton and R. Finnegan, London, Faber.

Index